Rethinking Nationalism

Rethinking Nationalism

**EDITED BY
JOCELYNE COUTURE,
KAI NIELSEN,
AND
MICHEL SEYMOUR**

University of Calgary Press
Calgary, Alberta, Canada

ISSN 0229-7051   ISBN 0-919491-22-7

© 1998 The Canadian Journal of Philosophy
ISBN 0-919491-22-7
ISSN 0229-7051
CJP Supplementary Volume 22 (1996)

University of Calgary Press
2500 University Drive NW
Calgary, Alberta
Canada T2N 1N4

Canadian Cataloguing in Publication Data

Main entry under title:
    Rethinking nationalism

    (Canadian Journal of Philosophy. Supplementary
volume, ISSN 0229-7051 ; 22)
        Includes bibliographical references and index.
        ISBN 1-919491-22-7

    1. Nationalism. I. Couture, Jocelyne. II. Nielsen, Kai. III.
    Seymour, Michel, 1954– IV. Series.
JC311.R47 1998   320.54   C98-910262-9

COMMITTED TO THE DEVELOPMENT OF CULTURE AND THE ARTS

Financial support provided in part by the Alberta Foundation for the Arts.

Printed and bound in Canada.
∞ This book is printed on acid-free paper.

Table of Contents

Preface

When we asked the authors of the essays which appear in this volume to write on nationalism, we gave them *carte blanche*. They were to write whatever they fancied as long as the subject was nationalism. Since their disciplines and intellectual formations varied, and since the subject is vast and many faceted, we, predictably enough, ended up with some very different essays – sometimes varying along many dimensions. One of our jobs as editors was to introduce some order into this jumble of fascinating contributions, so that the resulting volume could be read as a coherent whole. Our ordering is not, of course, the only possible ordering, but it is, we believe, one that groups together certain themes and issues and facilitates a certain amount of point-counterpoint between some of the essays, something which is carried further in the Afterword.

Any such ordering will reflect the preconceptions and preoccupations of its editors, as well as their beliefs about both what are the key issues and where the sticking points are. We have not wanted to escape that, nor would we have been able to even had we tried. It is our hope, as well as our belief, that we have avoided partisanship and arbitrariness in so structuring the contributions to this bewildering, complex, challenging, and often politically divisive topic. It will be for our authors, as well as our readers, to decide how far we have succeeded.

With respect to our five subheadings, two essays in Part I ('Methodological Turnings') may cause raised eyebrows. We refer to the essays by Liah Greenfeld and Barrington Moore Jr. Unlike the other essays in Part I, by Yael Tamir and Robert X. Ware, these two appear to be substantive rather than methodological contributions to issues concerning nationalism. And they are indeed substantive, but they also have very interesting methodological interludes that contrast in revealing ways with Tamir's methodological perspective. That is why they are placed where they are. But, as we try to show in the first section of our Afterword, their substantive contributions should not be neglected.

In the Introduction and Afterword we mention and often discuss many, but understandably not all, of the essays. We want to insist, although this will become evident to the readers, that the attention paid to individual essays can in no way sustain a judgment on our part of their worth relative to essays we do not discuss. Our choice here only reflects, beside the programmatic intent of the Introduction and of the Afterword, the ways particular essays, in our view, mesh with our overall themes.

We, especially in the Afterword, frequently quote from the contributors. However, since we were working from their manuscripts, no page references could be given.

A note on our bibliography is also in order. It is a severely stripped down bibliography rather ruthlessly selected from an enormous and burgeoning literature, contributed to by many disciplines. Our intention was not to be exhaustive, but rather to put together a set of basic references to the study of nationalism, including some of the most recent and sometimes not easily accessible references. In that spirit, we have made no effort to include or exclude the bibliographical items cited in the individual essays in *Rethinking Nationalism*. Some of their references reveal, and quite appropriately, specialist's interests that in themselves are not, nor do they purport to be, contributions to nationalism, but are referred to by our contributors relevantly to their own contributions to a discussion of nationalism.

We would, finally, like to thank Merlette Schnell for her speedy and accurate typing of the first, crude, handwritten version of the Afterword. We would also like to thank both the contributors to this volume and the editors of *The Canadian Journal of Philosophy* as well as The University of Calgary Press for their patience – indeed, their long-suffering patience – in the face of the much-delayed appearance of this book. It is something we have again and again anguished over.

CANADIAN JOURNAL OF PHILOSOPHY
Supplementary Volume 22

Introduction:
Questioning the Ethnic/Civic Dichotomy

MICHEL SEYMOUR
Université de Montréal

with the collaboration of

JOCELYNE COUTURE
Université du Québec à Montréal
and
KAI NIELSEN
University of Calgary and Concordia University

1 A Daunting Task

Students of nationalism now face the daunting task of renewing their subject matter. In the last two decades, nationalism has become a multiform and complex phenomenon which no longer seems to correspond to the accounts given just a few years ago by sociologists, political scientists, and anthropologists. Whether they merely want to understand this phenomenon or whether they want in addition to assess it from legal, moral, or political standpoints, students of nationalism face the challenge of re-examining in a different world the very categories through which nationalism has been understood in the past decades.

Such is our contention – a contention that in the first place motivates the very existence of the present volume, which contains, we believe, some of the most innovative samples of present reflection on nationalism. It includes, moreover, contributions from a variety of disciplines, from different parts of the world, often reflecting very different ways of thinking about nationalism and sometimes reflecting very different methodologies, substantive beliefs, and underlying interests.

We seek here to set the stage for these discussions. We want to show how most accounts of nationalism have been explicitly or implicitly

1

based on the dichotomy between ethnic and civic nationalism. In our view, these accounts trace a truncated picture, and yield in important ways a distorted understanding, of the complex phenomenon that nationalism has become. Yet despite the vast number of books and articles that have recently appeared on the subject, that dichotomy – and the understanding of nationalism that it reflects – is still a, if not the, prevalent one.[1] Moreover, such an understanding of nationalism provides the basis for normative assessments, which in some cases can be no more than tragic mistakes, and for policies that can have disastrous practical consequences.

Although a growing number of philosophers and social scientists feel that any acceptable conception of nationalism should attempt to steer a course between the two opposite views which form that dichotomy, this is not, as we shall see, easily done. In the last sections of this introduction, we attempt to argue for our own characterization of nationalism, a characterization which breaks free from what has become a hallowed dichotomy, as revered in circles discussing nationalism as the analytic/synthetic dichotomy once was in analytic philosophy. But let us for the moment consider the two traditional accounts.

II Two traditional conceptions

The *civic* conception of nationalism is often associated with the name of Ernest Renan.[2] It is exemplified in the events of the French Revolution; it is based on the idea that a nation is a voluntary association of individuals. As Renan puts it, it is a 'daily plebiscite.' According to this view, individuals give themselves a state, and the state is what binds

---

1 For recent surveys of the literature, see John Hutchinson and Anthony D. Smith, eds., *Nationalism* (Oxford: Oxford University Press 1994), Gopal Balakrishnan, ed., *Mapping the Nation* (New York: Verso 1996), Omar Dahbour and Micheline R. Ishay, eds., *The Nationalism Reader* (Atlantic Highlands, NJ: Humanities Press 1995), and Gil Delannoi and Pierre-André Taguieff, eds., *Théories du nationalisme* (Paris: Éditions Kimé 1991).

2 Ernest Renan, *Qu'est-ce qu'une nation?* (Paris: Calmann-Levy 1882)

together the nation. It is usually said, by people taking such a general orientation, that that concept of nation is subjective since it emphasizes the *will* of individuals. And it is individualistic since the nation is nothing over and above willing *individuals*.

The *ethnic* conception of nationalism is often traced back to Johann Gottfried Herder,[3] and is exemplified by the German nationalism that arose during the period of German Romanticism. It is largely based upon language, culture, and tradition, and thus appeals to more or less objective features of our social lives. According to this view the nation precedes the state, and is a collective body which transcends each individual. It has been interpreted as an ethnic conception because, at the time when Herder wrote, if people shared the same language, culture, and history they usually also shared, up to a certain point, the same ancestry, the same lineage, the same blood. Or at least so legend has it.

A careful reader of Renan and Herder will protest that this is an oversimplification of their views, for both authors integrate objective and subjective features in their characterization of the nation. For instance, Renan describes the nation as 'a soul, a spiritual principle.' On his conception, the nation also involves the past, not only the present. It is a 'legacy of remembrances,' and not only a will to live together. As far as Herder is concerned, we must acknowledge that he does not altogether reject the civic aspects of a nation. Moreover, he cannot justifiably be accused of irrationalism, as we often do accuse when we say that someone is an ethnic nationalist, though, as André Van de Putte aptly shows in this volume, the same cannot be said for all German Romantics who took a generally similar line to Herder on nationalism. Finally, it should be said that, when taken literally, Herder's views are much closer to what could be described today as a 'cultural nationalism,' and this conception is much less problematic than a purely ethnic conception.

Why should we want to transcend such an opposition? It is not our purpose to provide, immediately, a complete answer to this question; this introduction as a whole can be regarded as an attempt to explain

---

3 Johann Gottfried Herder, *Outlines of a Philosophy of the History of Man* (London: 1800)

why the dichotomy should be rejected. But we can perhaps at this point explain some of the general motivations behind this attempt. It could be argued, first, that there are conceptual difficulties involved in having to choose between the two accounts. There are a large variety of nationalist movements in the contemporary international arena. As it is sometimes said, there are nationalisms and nationalisms, and a simple dichotomy such as the one under consideration may prove to be conceptually too weak to account for such a wide spectrum of phenomena. We most probably need to enrich our conceptual tools and make our notions more complex if we want to grasp such a complex reality.

It could also be argued that there are conceptual and empirical difficulties involved in theories that fail to account for the pluricultural nature of contemporary liberal societies. We need to reflect on the changes that these new sociological facts entail for our understanding of the nation. It could be argued that the traditional dichotomy fails in this respect, for neither the ethnic nor the civic conception can easily incorporate a recognition of the multicultural diversity within modern societies.

There are also what, arguably, are moral failings involved in both accounts of the nation. In order to see clearly what is at issue here, we must first notice that the adoption of a certain conception of the nation can, wittingly or unwittingly, play a role in our normative discourse, and can in effect serve as a rule of conduct. It is by relying upon a certain conception of the nation that we adopt a certain behaviour or a set of attitudes toward nationalism. There are thus important moral consequences that follow from endorsing a particular account, and it could be argued in particular that both ethnic and civic nationalisms lead to some form of exclusion. The demonstration has often been made in the case of ethnic nationalism, so we need not belabour that point. But it is now being argued in some quarters that similar kinds of remarks apply to an exclusively civic nationalism. Since they see only one alternative to the civic conception of the nation, civic nationalists are tempted to describe all forms of nationalism coming from a subgroup within a sovereign state as ethnic in character. And since they are unable to conceptualize the cultural diversity that we now frequently encounter within sovereign states, they also tend to minimize the importance of pre-civic national ties, i.e., ones that can take place independently of citizenship in a sovereign state. Another problem is that they very often, wittingly or unwittingly, conceal the way that nations that form majorities dominate other nations and groups within such multination states. This domination is, in effect, supported by civic nationalism and, where civic nationalism is institutionalized, it tends to induce frustration on the part of the minority nations within those states.

There are those who think that the above remarks give us good reasons for rejecting nationalism altogether. They tend to agree that the dichotomy provides the only available alternatives, and conclude that the root of the problem is with nationalism as such. They are for that reason inclined to seek to ban nationalism itself, no matter what form it takes. This attitude is very different in intention from civic nationalism, but it has the same moral consequence: it also leads to exclusion. Whether we like it or not, we live in a world where the politics of recognition is becoming increasingly important, and it is thus naive to expect that the problems are going to disappear simply by arguing that nationalism should be banned. In our day and age, adopting such an attitude is also adopting an extreme position. What is morally and conceptually problematic is thus not only to adopt one of the two options imposed by the dichotomy, but also to adopt the dichotomy itself.

These moral and conceptual failings thus provide motivation for trying to formulate a new conception of the nation and of nationalism. It appears that if we don't, then we fall prey to a logic of exclusion, and we, as well, will fail to grasp one important cause of nationalist tensions.

There are many reasons why the ethnic and civic conceptions remain the prevalent ones, and why it is so difficult to come up with a new characterization of the nation. We might at first sight be inclined to think that the new and correct account must simply incorporate both subjective and objective features, and, by uncritically acquiescing in that, we might mistakenly be led to believe that we already have at our disposal a conception that overcomes the traditional dichotomy. Indeed, according to what many think, a nation involves sharing a common language, culture, history, and ancestry, but it also involves subjective elements such as a national consciousness and the will to remain together. This is the most common characterization, and it is in a way partly 'ethnic' and partly 'civic.' But it is not enough to transcend the ethnic/civic dichotomy, since both civic and ethnic conceptions must themselves be understood as a compound of subjective and objective features. The difference between ethnic and civic nationalism rests, not on one being purely objective and the other purely subjective, but in the insistence with which authors characterize certain relatively objective features rather than others as being constitutive of nationalism, or at least take one rather than another cluster of features as being the most salient for nationalism. For example, the ethnic characterization of nationalism may include some of the civic properties of the nation, but these are very often considered secondary. In the same way, the proponent of a civic characterization of nationalism may acknowledge the fact that there are other features apart from those that are civic, but she will very often ignore them or treat them as 'private matters.' They are not, on the civic conception, what is salient for our understanding of nationalism.

So one of the reasons why the ethnic/civic dichotomy appeals so much to so many people might be that it is implicitly involved in the hybrid characterization we arrive at when we give what appears to be the most adequate conception. Our dichotomy is not an easy one to overcome even if we are apparently able to articulate a characterization that seems to supersede it in a way.[4] By coming up with a new characterization that would incorporate some elements belonging to the two conceptions, we tend to enhance the importance of the dichotomy itself. When a conception of the nation integrates objective and subjective features (as indeed most of the conceptions of nationalism do), it usually still remains under the spell of the ethnic/civic dichotomy, and the reason is that any new account will almost invariably lead to a hybrid account that exploits ethnic and civic features, and so exploits the dichotomy itself instead of truly transcending it. This is the first difficulty that we encounter in trying to go beyond the dichotomy.

A second reason why the dichotomy is so hard to overcome is that both ethnic and civic nationalism, however they are construed, seem adequately to fit a predominant – but increasingly outdated – model of political community. Many theoreticians belonging to either of these groups are willing to consider the nation-state as the only available model of a state. They favour an international arena in which the partners are all

---

4 For a clear case of such an hybrid characterization, see Frans De Wachter's contribution to the present volume.

sovereign nation-states. But this, in our view, is more of a reason to be suspicious of these accounts of nationalism than a reason to rely on them.

To illustrate the point, those who subscribe to an ethnic characterization of nationalism must endorse the *nationalist principle*, i.e., the principle according to which each nation should have its own sovereign state. Some even *define* nationalism as the view according to which each nation should have its own sovereign state. So it is clear that ethnic nationalists tend to promote the nation-state model of a political community. It is generally agreed that a systematic application of the nationalist principle would lead to chaos. No wonder those who fall prey to that account of nationalism see nationalism *per se* as automatically generating incessant conflicts and wars between nations. Such a conception of nationalism – many of whose exemplifications in the political arena Carol Prager has aptly called 'barbarous nationalisms' – has prompted many others to the view that only civic nationalism could be politically and morally acceptable.

The situation seems less clear, however, in the case of civic nationalists. They do not accept the nationalist principle as such; they only accept a principle which asserts the 'sovereignty of the people.' A nation is viewed principally as a purely legal and political reality. This is quite different from ethnic nationalism, since it means that power should ultimately be in the hands of all citizens, and these need not be part of the same ethnic group. But as it turns out, behind most if not all existing nation-states, there is a majority of people sharing a certain comprehensive culture, mother-tongue, history, and set of traditions, and these cultural features, as Ross Poole has well argued in this volume, strongly constrain the hand of the nation-state. Civic nationalists are almost forced to conceal the fact that very often 'the people' is composed of a majority which, through an elite or dominant class, is in control of the state. If an exclusively civic nationalism were to exist (or even could exist) somewhere, it would have to conceal these indisputable facts. As we said before, civic nationalism tends to ignore cultural factors and relatedly to ignore, or at least to minimize, the existence of minority groups. By ignoring or concealing these facts, it tends to exclude these minority groups, and this creates favourable conditions for their assimilation. When assimilation succeeds, 'the people' becomes linguistically and culturally homogeneous. As Barrington Moore, Jr., remarks, "peasants were turned into Frenchmen." Eventually, we might even come to a point where the vast majority of the population represents itself – though in an illusory way – as sharing the same ancestry. So even if it cannot be admitted, the civic nation-state that offers the best prospects for survival is the one in which 'the people' coincides with a fairly homogeneous national group. Therefore, civic nationalists themselves have tended to reinforce the credibility of something that looks very much like the nationalist principle. Very often, the viability and political stability of the civic nation-state itself lead to an indirect defense of the nationalist principle.

Whether someone is an ethnic or a civic nationalist, then, it seems that she is forced to accept the idea that to each and every ethnic nation should correspond a sovereign nation-state. The common idea exemplified in the ethnic and civic accounts is that of the nation-state, understood as an ethnic nation in a sovereign state. Both views tend to promote, though for different reasons, the nation-state as the most important model of political community. If this picture is accurate, then transcending the opposition between the two approaches is tantamount to transcending a theoretical fixation on the nation-state itself, as the sole state form and only possible model of the modern political community. But as we all know, this is a very difficult task indeed. The multiplication of nation-states in the twentieth century shows how well entrenched that conception of the state is. The difficulty is not just theoretical. It is not enough to announce, as in some kind of mantra, that national sovereignty is becoming an illusion or that we are about to witness the end of the nation-state. The facts stubbornly persist against these pronouncements. And if anything, globalization serves to reactivate nationalist inclinations. So the tenacious persistence of the nation-state model, a model which is shared by the two views, is perhaps a second reason why it is so hard to overcome the opposition between them.

That the sovereign nation-state is the only form of political community that fits the ambitions of any sort of contemporary nationalism – or even of any plausible sort of such nationalism – is the improbable picture given by these accounts based on accepting the civic/ethnic dichotomy. And that nationalism of any sort is a detestable phenomenon is what we should apparently conclude from both ethnic and civic 'descriptions' of nationalism. But this message has introduced more confusion and more disputes in the public forum than it has shed light on the nationalisms now emerging in the contemporary world.

Perhaps nationalism is altogether a despicable phenomenon that should clearly, once and for all, be seen as and assessed as such. But before we can justifiably come to such a conclusion we have to make sure that we have discovered all the various forms that nationalism can plausibly take and in various circumstances have taken. A number of contributions to this volume show that at least some forms of nationalism can, and indeed should, be argued for from the point of view of justice, democracy, and equity between peoples or, alternatively, as a matter (*pace* Liah Greenfeld) of genuine *de jure* political legitimacy. While some, Harry Brighouse for example, argue that nationalism in even its most benign forms diminishes autonomy and equality, others, such as Ross Poole, argue just the opposite.

We have already mentioned two reasons why the ethnic/civic dichotomy is a hard one to abandon, but we are inclined to believe that the main reason why it is so difficult to get rid of the distinction lies elsewhere. The debate over the two views is in a way over, and it has been won by the partisans of the civic conception. Since the Second World War, nobody can seriously put forward an ethnic conception of the nation. More precisely, in the ambience of liberal democracies, no one can seriously *promote* ethnic nationalism. In such societies, the German conception of the nation has been thoroughly defeated and discredited once and for all. Since then, for almost everybody in the literature, the only acceptable conception is the civic one. The ethnic conception is the view held by the bad guys. The opposition remains, but it is now between ethnic nationalist *movements* on the one hand and intellectuals or academics defending the civic conception on the other. The ethnic conception is still very widely discussed as a prevailing phenomenon, but it is theoretically supported by virtually no one in liberal societies. Since the civic conception has definitely won, there does not seem to be a need to revise it. To criticize it, some think, is in effect to betray an implicit inclination towards its opposite, the ethnic conception. So even if there is a growing resistance to an exclusively civic conception, it has up to now been a fairly unsuccessful attempt, at least in the political arena. Civic nationalists have been able to counterattack by characterizing any defense of nations within multination states as an instance of ethnic nationalism. It will be the burden of our argument to show that there is here more ideology than social reality and intellectual cogency.

In the next two sections we want to show how the dichotomy between ethnic and civic nationalism has been enhanced and indeed reinforced in some of the most influential studies on nationalism. A main source of such reinforcement has been, in our view, theories purporting to give an historical account concerning the origin of the nation, and it is to a brief examination of that literature that we shall now turn.

III   The Origins of the Nation

As we shall now see, there is another reason why the ethnic/civic distinction remains the prevalent option. An important literature was developed on nationalism after the contributions of Renan and Herder, but the focus of the discussion has moved away from the problem of the definition of the nation to the question concerning its origin. How does the nation come to existence? There are two important groups of writers that give opposite explanations depending on whether they see nationalism as a modern phenomenon or not. The most well known authors defending the modernist explanation are Benedict Anderson, John Breuilly, Karl Deutsch, Ernest Gellner, Liah Greenfeld, E.J. Hobsbawm, and Elie Kedourie. Amongst those who defend one version or another of the premodern origin of the nation, we should mention John Armstrong, Clifford Geertz, Susan Reynolds, Hugh Seton-Watson, Anthony D. Smith, and Pierre Van den Berghe. These two groups do not necessarily reinstate the opposition between the civic and ethnic views at the level of historical explanation, but do not try to transcend it either. These contributions are the works of historians, sociologists, anthropologists, and political scientists. They provide very deep and insightful contributions, but they almost never try to develop a new conception that would go beyond those of Renan and Herder. They offer a clinical observation of the phenomenon, attempt to interpret it, offer an explanation of its origin, and very often do not *intend* to be normative or prescriptive about how we should assess the legitimacy of the nation. Indeed some but certainly not all of them may, as Greenfeld does in this volume, regard the very idea of *de jure* legitimacy as a mirage and *de facto* legitimacy as the only intelligible form of legitimacy, thus leaving no conceptual space for normative arguments or normative issues.

Some of the authors who favor a modernist explanation believe that national sentiments depend on the intensity of personal exchanges on a given territory. According to Karl Deutsch,[5] national sentiments manifest themselves for a variety of reasons which are all related to the various features that make communication possible between the members of the community. These features could be urbanization, mail, road systems, or commerce. Nationalism goes hand in hand with the development of a communication network, which in many respects is a function of easy access to available resources of the modern era. It could thus not have been a powerful force in premodern times.

The same sort of remarks can be found in Benedict Anderson's[6] influential contribution to this debate. Anderson goes so far as to link the occurrence of national sentiments with the beginnings of the printing industry, which, alongside an emerging capitalism, allowed individuals to become aware of the presence of other individuals whom they had never met. For that reason, national sentiments are, according to Anderson, to a large extent a product of the imagination.

E. J. Hobsbawm[7] is a Marxist historian who sees the nation as an invented tradition, an ideological product of modern states. He sees it as the result of a process of *state-nation* building, i.e., of a process in which the nation is created by the state. This process took place in Europe in the nineteenth century. The French state of the Third Republic, for instance, used *instituteurs*, invented public ceremonies, and produced public monuments in order to enhance in the population a sense of belonging to a single nation. It is clear that in the case of France, the state created the nation. Of course, it is often thought that, contrary to France and England, nations sometimes precede states. It is then suggested that the process must instead be characterized as one of *nation-state* building. According to that view, it is this kind of process that took place for Germany and Italy. But Hobsbawm argues that the so-

---

5 Karl Deutsch, *Nationalism and Social Communication*, 2d ed. (Cambridge, MA: MIT Press 1966)

6 Benedict Anderson, *Imagined Communities*, rev. ed. (New York: Verso 1991)

7 E.J. Hobsbawm, *Nations and Nationalism since 1780*, 2d ed. (Cambridge: Cambridge University Press 1992)

called 'preexistence' of the nation is itself an invention of the state. William II, for instance, tried to establish a view according to which the Empire of 1871 was the realization of the national aspirations of the German people. And in order to do that, he constantly referred to so-called common past experiences of Prussia and of the rest of Germany. According to Hobsbawm, the exploitation of an already existing national consciousness was itself an ideology forced on the population in the course of a state-nation building process.[8]

Ernest Gellner[9] thinks that nationalism can only take root in societies in which education is a universal virtue. And if the masses are to be educated by the elites, a certain amount of homogeneity must exist between them. In particular, it must be possible for them to communicate in the same language. But it is much easier to adopt the vernacular language spoken by the ordinary people than to try to introduce into very large populations the use of Latin, for instance. This is why nationalism coincides with the emergence of vernacular languages. Another constraint is that the community must be large enough to sustain an educational system. All these factors – the intelligentsia, the proletariat, a common language, and the educational system – are the basic ingredients involved in the nation, and they determine the minimal size of the political community. But how are we to gauge how large it can be? What are its upper limits? Why is it impossible for the nation to be a very large political unit? In order to provide an appropriate answer, we have to understand modernization and industrialization. For Gellner, nationalism is a result of their uneven diffusion. It is the existence of social conflicts that causes the members of a given community to form a national community. Gellner endorses the proposed connection between the occurrence of less-favoured industrial societies and the emergence of nations. The mobilization of the work force,

---

8 For an alternative approach in the Marxist tradition, see Tom Nairn, *The Break-up of Britain: Crisis and Neo-Nationalism*, 2d ed. (London: New Left Books 1977). See also Kai Nielsen, 'Cultural Nationalism, Neither Ethnic nor Civic,' *Philosophical Forum* **28:1-2** (1996-97) 1-11; 'Secession: The Case of Quebec,' *Journal of Applied Philosophy* **10:1** (1991) 29-43.

9 Ernest Gellner, *Nations and Nationalism* (Oxford: Blackwell 1983)

which is an inevitable consequence of an uneven industrialization, creates national sentiments if the population in question feels as though it must fight against the hegemony of another community. So it is nationalism which engenders nations, and not the other way around. And so we must not see nationalism as a source of economic development; it is, rather, the economic development which generates nationalism. In conclusion, for Gellner, the occurrence of nations and of nationalism is to be explained causally by the emergence of modern states and capitalism.

Elie Kedourie,[10] by contrast, conceives the nation as a product of an ideology. It is the result of an elite diffusing a certain number of key ideas in response to the needs of a large population, ideas which enable them to identify with a stable organization. This ideology, he believes, would never have come to exist without the contributions of modern thinkers such as Kant, who established the autonomy of the human agent, and of all those who contributed to the separation of politics from religion. And it would never have been possible without the influence of thinkers such as Fichte and Herder, who insisted upon natural language differences between the communities.

John Breuilly[11] sees nationalism as a political ideology of the nineteenth century which has its origin in the historicist arguments of intellectuals such as Herder and Frantisek Palacky, arguments which were designed to provide an answer to the conflict that occurred in the seventeenth century between the state and the civil society. Breuilly is willing to concede that there might have been a certain amount of national consciousness before the modern era, but nationalism as such is also for him a modern creation. He defines it as essentially aggressive and expansionist. When it is described in this way, nationalism indeed appears to be intimately related to the large-scale nationalist movements that began to occur after the French Revolution in Europe. As the Ottoman, Habsburg, and Tzarist empires began to decline, Napoleon III, Bismarck, Cavour, and many other political leaders entered into a complex

---

10 Elie Kedourie, *Nationalism*, 4th ed. (Oxford: Blackwell 1994)

11 John Breuilly, *Nationalism and the State*, 2d ed. (Chicago: University of Chicago Press 1994)

interplay of territorial advances, colonial ambitions, and aggressive be-haviours that are characteristic traits of nationalism. Breuilly thus situ-ates the birth of nations and nationalism in the middle of the nineteenth century.[12]

Liah Greenfeld[13] has offered the most recent systematic historical survey on the origin of nationalism. In her *Nationalism: Five Roads to Modernity*, she describes how nationalism occurred in the case of five distinct countries: Great Britain, France, Russia, Germany, and the United States. She sees it as essentially occurring for the first time in Britain in the seventeenth century. According to Greenfeld, it was in Britain both an individualist and a universalist phenomenon. That is to say, nationalism served in Britain to promote, above all, the autonomy of each and every individual member within society, and to treat these values as universal. It was, she suggests, only after this first inception in Britain that nationalism became ethnic, collectivist, authoritarian, and rooted in resentment. It was especially so in the case of Russia and Germany, and less so for France, which tried to be at once both civic and collectivist. But for Greenfeld this is an unstable position, and the choice is most of the time between the two following models : the indi-vidualist, universalist, and civic, on the one hand, the collectivist, particularistic, and authoritarian, on the other.

The contributions of Deutsch, Anderson, Hobsbawn, Gellner, Kedourie, Breuilly, and Greenfeld have many important points in com-mon. The nation, according to them, is more like a deliberate construc-tion than a spontaneous occurrence, and it is the result of modernization. Without always reducing it to a mere collection of individual wills, all of them (except perhaps for Greenfeld) underline the subjective aspect

---

12 For recent comprehensive historical surveys, see Yves Santamaria and Brigitte Waché, *Du Printemps des peuples à la Société des nations. Nations, nationalités et nationalismes en Europe 1850-1920* (Paris: La Découverte 1996), Patrick Cabanel, ed., *Nations, nationalités et nationalismes en Europe, 1850-1920* (Paris: Éditions Ophrys 1995), Pierre Saly *et al.*, eds., *Nations et nationalismes en Europe 1848-1914* (Paris: Armand Colin 1996), and Hagen Schulze, *States, Nations and Nationalism, from the Middle Ages to the Present* (Oxford: Blackwell 1996).

13 Liah Greenfeld, *Nationalism: Five Roads to Modernity* (Cambridge, MA: Harvard University Press 1992)

of nationalist sentiments, and these are themselves to be explained in relation to circumstances which came into existence with the modern era. Thus while the nation is not merely a legal entity, as in the traditional civic approach, still the phenomena to which the ethnic nationalist alludes in support of her views is not something inherent to human societies. The so-called objective features (common language, common culture, same tradition, same history, same ancestry) are to a large extent mythical, since they are the result of projecting onto reality our nationalist sentiments. Of course, the presence of such nationalist sentiments cannot be denied, but it is a phenomenon that has to be explained. The subjective dimension of the nation may perhaps not entirely be reduced to Renan's 'daily plebiscite.' It is found far deeper within the personality of the individual, since it takes the form of nationalist sentiments. But these are not primitive feelings common to all humankind at all times and places, and they can be explained as projections, since they arose and were maintained because of the circulation of books and newspapers, the development of an educational system, the expansion of trade, the power of the state, or the influence of an educated elite. They are very often seen by the modernists as functional requirements of industrial societies.

In a way, the modernist account of the origin of nationalism leaves the distinction between ethnic and civic nationalism intact, since what it does essentially is to consider certain aspects generally associated with the ethnic view, and explain them away as not being founded upon an objective reality. This is something that Andrew Levine repeats in a sophisticated way in this volume. According to these authors, Levine included, we really cannot appeal to a common tradition, history, ancestry, or culture without simultaneously falling prey to a mythical illusion. These features of the ethnic nation no longer appear as objective realities. Yet the opposition between ethnic and civic nationalism remains. The only difference is that we are now demystifying the objective reality on which the ethnic conception was supposedly founded. However, it may also be added that the account is not so innocent and neutral, since it says something about the validity and legitimacy of nationalist movements.

Perhaps the clearest example of this is given by the work of Benedict Anderson. He is, moreover, one of the most influential of the modernist authors. As already suggested, he develops a view of the nation as an imagined community, and offers an account which enables him to explain its deeply subjective nature. What looks like a primitive phenomenon happens to be something that was possible only because of a certain development in the circulation of the printed word at the beginning of capitalism. The sense of belonging that was generated should then partly be explained by the influence of the elites, who were confronted on a regular basis with the printed word. But how does this affect the ethnic/civic distinction? It does not seem to affect it very much, except perhaps in the sense that it proves useful in trying to underline the subjective origins of ethnic nationalism and to explain them away. If Anderson is right, there are no such things as nations, there since the dawn of history, and no historically invariant nationalist sentiments. What looks like an objective reality turns out to have its roots in our imagination, though there are social, political, and economic facts which constrain the emergence of such a subjective phenomenon.

Most of the modernist accounts emphasize material conditions which explain the emergence of nationhood. The sense of cultural belonging is to be explained by the creation of a uniform educational system, by the circumstantial solidarity of an economically disadvantaged group of people, or by a strategic ideological program aimed at mobilizing the masses. There are, of course, important differences between these accounts. For instance, if most of them stress the social and economic forces behind the creation of nationalism, some, like Kedourie, give much more importance to the influence of ideas. Another important difference is that some authors see nationalism as a phenomenon that will continue to prevail, while others believe it is bound to disappear. But two things are certain: it has deeply subjective roots, and it is the result of modernity. In sum, the modernists have shown that the roots of nationalism are historically conditioned, and that nationalist sentiments are functional for these material conditions, i.e., help develop the forces of production.

Contrary to this approach, there are those who formulate a premodern explanation of the origin of the nation and who see nationalism in the nineteenth century as something that followed it. The nation, that is, had this premodern origin, and the later formations of nationalism were something that arose from it and in important respects were rooted in it. But whether or not they see the nation as a social construct, they do more than simply disagree on the time when it came into existence. They also disagree about the essential components of the nation. The premodernists maintain that ethnicity is the core of nationality. Hugh Seton-Watson,[14] for example, distinguishes between old and new nations. Among the old European nations, he mentions the English, Scots, French, Dutch, Castilians, Portuguese, Danes, Swedes, Hungarians, Poles, and Russians. In particular, the existence of French and English nations was a reality by the year 1600.

Susan Reynolds[15] argues that the reason why historians explain the origin of the nation as a modern phenomenon is that they wrongly associate nationalism with aggressive, xenophobic, and deplorable political movements. In her view, if we don't make this wrong association, then we can uncover the existence of nations in many medieval societies. This premodern account need not be interpreted as suggesting that nations exist as an entirely objective phenomenon. Nations can exist only because individuals believe that they exist. Reynolds also rejects the suggestion according to which the Latin word *natio* was used only to refer to different groups of students in the universities. In addition to that use, she insists, the word also meant 'a people.'

John Armstrong[16] underlines another mistake made by the modernists. Since European nationalism was preceded by absolutism, it is thought that it is essentially a recent phenomenon. But as a matter of fact, he claims, there was a form of national consciousness long before that. Another related problem is that nineteenth-century nationalists have tried to specify the essential characteristics of national identity, and this has influenced our understanding of nationalism. We have been led to ignore the fact that ethnic identity is strictly oppositional. Members of a national community are individuals who share the same 'perceived boundaries' and who define themselves by excluding other communities. When the group is understood this way, many of its im-

---

14 Hugh Seton-Watson, *Nations and States* (London: Methuen 1977)

15 Susan Reynolds, *Kingdoms and Communities in Western Europe (900-1300)* (Oxford: Clarendon Press 1984)

16 John Armstrong, *Nations before Nationalism* (Chapel Hill: University of North Carolina Press 1982)

portant characteristics may disappear without affecting its identity. The reason is that the group maintains its identity by opposition to the other communities. We can thus explain why a single national community may undergo important modifications in its national character. Moreover, different types of characteristics may be relevant for the national identity of different groups. Some types of characteristics may be important for one community and not important for someother. Some will insist on language and culture, while others will find more importance in their historical heritage. Once again, the main reason is that all these people share the same opposition to other communities. When things are seen from this perspective, we are in a position to recognize the existence of nations in premodern times.

Clifford Geertz[17] adopts an explanation which stresses certain permanent and 'primordial' features such as religion, culture, race, and language. These features are perennial, and they very often clash with the need to maintain civic ties. The debates surrounding nationalism come from a confrontation between these two fundamental sorts of allegiances. As a primordialist and perennialist, Geertz finds himself clearly siding with the premoderns.

Anthony D. Smith[18] rejects Geertz's account, which involves reference to primordial features, but he nevertheless shares with him a concern for the ethnic origin of the nation. Smith underlines the ethnic origins of nations, and also tries to understand the process by which ethnic groups became nations with the dawning of the modern age. He is willing to grant that nations as such came into existence in the modern era, but he insists that an important aspect of the nation, the *ethnie*, was there long before it. Nations were forged on the basis of ethnic groups through diverse influences of traditionalist, assimilationist, and reformist groups, each of which reacted differently to modernity. Ideology also played an important role according to Smith,

---

17 Clifford Geertz, 'The Integrative Revolution: Primordial Sentiments and Civil Politics in the New States' in Clifford Geertz, ed., *Old Societies and New States: The Quest for Modernity in Asia and Africa* (New York: Free Press 1963)

18 Anthony D. Smith, *The Ethnic Origins of Nations* (Oxford: Blackwell 1986) and *National Identity* (London: Penguin 1991)

but nationalism is not just an ideological construct. Nations would never have come to existence were it not for ethnicity. The nation is thus for Smith considered partly as a premodern phenomenon.

Pierre Van den Berghe[19] describes ethnicity and race as extensions of kinship relations; they have a partially biological basis. This must not be understood as meaning that there is a gene for ethnocentrism. It is rather that groups that had institutionalized norms of nepotism and ethnocentrism had a strong selective advantage over those that did not. He is willing to agree that race is essentially a social construct and that it must not be understood as referring to subspecies of *Homo sapiens*. He recognizes that the trivial phenotypes used in distinguishing races are social constructs, and do not count as objective means of dividing human beings into different groups. Moreover, cultural traits, and not biological traits, are what most of the time differentiate one ethnic group from another. However, he sees these cultural traits as having been historically instrumental for maintaining kinship relations intact. Phenotypical traits vary only by degree from one region to another, and there can very often be more differences within the group than there are with members of other groups, so they are an unreliable means of discriminating between members and non-members of the group. This is why humans have relied upon cultural traits such as language, customs, and traditions. But the key point is that cultural traits have historically been instrumental in the maintenance of kinship relations. It is in this sense (arguably a rather strained sense) that Van den Berghe's concepts of ethnicity and race are partly biological notions. They are to be understood in evolutionary theory as extensions of kinship relations. His account is compatible with the fact that kinship relations may have become putative and not real. He is also willing to agree that intergroup relations, understood in this way, are typically antagonistic. Nevertheless, he is still inclined to say that there is a continuum between kinship relations and ethnic groups.

Here again, we are confronted with authors who have many diverging points of view but agree on a central premise. Contrary to the mod-

---

19 Pierre Van den Berghe, 'Race and Ethnicity: A Sociobiological Perspective,' *Ethnic and Racial Studies*, **1:4** (1978) . See also *The Ethnic Phenomenon* (New York: Elsevier 1979).

ernist authors mentioned above, there are, these authors all agree, fundamental ethnic components in the basic characteristics of a nation. It has, that is, an ethnic core. This is so for Armstrong and Geertz as well as for Smith and Van den Berghe. And since nations are at their core ethnic in character, nationalism must in part be ethnic. This ethnic component is explained by the fact that a whole community represents itself as sharing the same ancestry. Most of these authors agree that such an 'ethnic core' existed long before nations were created, and that it is still an important feature of contemporary nations. It does not, they believe, matter whether this self-representation of the community is mythical or not. Talking about such an ethnic core does not necessarily mean that there really exists a common ancestry. There are nowadays very few, if any, examples of nations in which all the individuals have the same ancestors. The claim is rather that the mythical sense of sharing the same ancestry was important even before modernity, and cannot therefore be explained by features of modernity. Some of these authors may be willing to admit that this aspect of nationalism is up to a certain point mythical and invented, but they emphasize the importance of these myths and show that they existed long before the modern era.

Smith challenges all primordialist approaches, and puts forward a subjectivist explanation. But he insists along with Geertz on the tight connection between nationalism and ethnicity. And in any case, Geertz himself often speaks of primordial *sentiments* that are not entirely objective. Indeed, Geertz sometimes gives to some of his so-called primordial features a subjective twist that should not pass unnoticed. So almost all these authors are willing to agree that nationalism has a partly subjective source. The differences between Geertz and Smith are thus actually smaller than would at first blush be thought. What is generally agreed upon by those who take this premodernist turn is the idea that nationalist sentiments prevailed in some form or another as ethnicity long before the birth of the modern era. What is important, whether or not they agree on the partly subjective nature of the nation, is that national sentiments should not be explained exclusively by recourse to features of the modern era.

We are not happy with this notion of an ethnic core, because we are skeptical about its adequacy as a device of representation for our present social world. Nowadays, the cultural, linguistic, and historic cores of national communities no longer coincide with ethnicity, whether it is founded upon objective or subjective facts. And the myth of a common ancestry surely seems to be less and less important to Western cultures. But there is nevertheless considerable merit in these accounts. The authors that we are now considering are perfectly right in emphasizing the point that national sentiments rest upon an attachment that cannot entirely be explained as an instrument of modern ideology. Nationalism is not just an ideological construct, nor is it simply an instrument to mobilize the masses. It is, in part, rooted in ancient group identities of people with distinct cultural patterns.

However, since the additional ingredients involved are very often described as 'ethnic,' we are perhaps justified in concluding that the premodernist authors do not wish to transcend the opposition between the ethnic and civic conceptions. It is not only the word 'ethnicity' that is at stake here, but also the suggestion that a nation is made out of people who represent themselves as sharing the same ancestors. Most liberal societies are composed of individuals having different origins. So even if premodernist authors are getting closer to a description of the modern nation as an hybrid entity, it is very often understood as a compound of ethnic and civic features. Their view on the origin of the nation, then, only deepens the importance of the opposition between the civic and ethnic characters of the nation.

There is another peculiar feature of the premodernist account that we wish to underline. When Smith speaks of ethnicity, one would be wrong to interpret his position as entirely critical of nationalism. Nationalism, on his view, must not entirely be rejected even if it is partly ethnic. In his most recent book, for instance, Smith argues that the nation-state is probably still the best model of political community.[20] For most authors, the words 'ethnic nationalism' are pejorative, but not for all the premodernist authors under consideration. Is there anything wrong with that? Well, the problem is perhaps not to be located in their appraisal of nationalism; it has more to do with the conceptual resources with which they appreciate it. By appealing to ethnicity, they

---

20 Anthony D. Smith, *Nations and Nationalism in a Global Era* (Oxford: Polity Press, Blackwell 1995)

present a weak case for their own view. Indeed, by describing the missing element in the modernist account as 'ethnic,' the premodernist explanation indirectly serves to confirm civic nationalists in their position.[21] It is true that their historical insights involve an implicit criticism of the exclusively civic approach, and that by insisting on the ethnic core of the nation they draw attention to something that is concealed by the civic nationalist. But when they describe this missing element as being in essence 'ethnic,' they at the very least encourage the civic nationalist to emphasize civic traits at the expense of all others. The reason is that appealing to ethnicity in a justificatory context is nowadays correctly seen as morally problematic, to put it in mild terms. So in spite of the deep divide that sets them apart from the modernist explanation, this second group of authors have also unintentionally contributed, albeit indirectly, to a rejection at the normative level of all the non-exclusively civic forms of nationalism. This is at least the conclusion that can be drawn by those who condemn ethnic nationalism, and, as we have seen, they comprise today the vast majority of intellectuals and academics in modern liberal societies. We submit that this appreciation is not totally unfounded, given the extremes to which ethnic nationalism can lead. If all nationalist movements are in essence ethnic, then so much the worse for nationalism, and this reinforces the point of view according to which the nation *should* be exclusively civic.[22]

Be that as it may, it remains clear that both groups of authors have not been concerned to question the legitimacy of the ethnic/civic

---

21 An important exception is perhaps Susan Reynolds, who tries to avoid as much as possible using words like 'race' and 'ethnicity.' See Reynolds, *Kingdoms and Communities*, 251-6.

22 Of course, the situation is not as simple as the one that we have just described. Almost all of the modernist authors mentioned above (except perhaps for Kedourie) tend to recognize the importance of *national sentiments*. When Benedict Anderson, for example, speaks of the nation as an imagined community, he is not entirely denouncing the phenomenon. He is not suggesting that all manifestations of nationalism are bad and that they must be overcome. The division between moderns and premoderns is not always sharp. In their anthology, *Nationalism*, Hutchinson and Smith classify Seton-Watson as a premodernist, while in the present volume, Allen Buchanan describes him as a modernist.

dichotomy. On the contrary, if we are right, they have indirectly contributed to its continued acceptance and currency.

IV   The Prevalence of the Ethnic/Civic Dichotomy

The ethnic/civic dichotomy has not really been challenged in the literature on nationalism. On the contrary, it has often been reinstated in different terms via other distinctions. First, it more or less coincides with the traditional German distinction between *Kulturnation* and *Staatnation*. Another old view, which used to be applied to Europe, distinguishes between historical nations and those that do not have a history. The historical nations are those that existed as political communities whether or not they were part of a larger empire, and whether or not they were sovereign nation-states. Non-historical nations were characterized merely in terms of language, culture, and ethnicity.[23] So this distinction clearly seems to be an instance of our initial dichotomy. Finally, Hans Kohn[24] suggested a distinction between Eastern and Western views of the nation, but this once again is an instance of the ethnic/civic dichotomy.

Even when new conceptions are introduced, they are often compatible with the initial distinction we made between the ethnic and the civic. For instance, some have proposed to distinguish between instrumentalists and primordialists.[25] The first insist on the idea that nations were created for a specific mediated purpose, whether it is political stability, ideology, social solidarity, or control of the masses. It is a view

---

23 The distinction between historical and non-historical nations was designed for the case of Europe, and was especially in vogue among thinkers like Marx and Engels in the last century. Germany, Poland, and Hungary, for instance, were described as historical nations. They were nations which were thought to have been from the very beginning in the process of becoming states. The non-historical nations included Ukraine, Slovakia, and Slovenia, and were perceived as never being able to become states. For a discussion, see Stéphane Pierré-Caps, *La multination* (Paris: Odile Jacob 1995), 37-45.

24 Hans Kohn, *The Idea of Nationalism* (New York: Macmillan 1945)

25 Anthony D. Smith, *Nations and Nationalism in a Global Era*, 30-35

held by most modernists. Primordialists, on the other hand, underline the pervasive traits of the nation that have followed humans through their evolution, whether it is race, religion, language, culture, or tradition. The champion of primordialism is Clifford Geertz. According to that view, the fundamental aspects of the nation cannot be explained away: they are fundamental characteristics of humankind. Notice that this account can be formulated in subjective as well as objective terms. It is true that Geertz's approach suggests an objective reading, but one could reformulate it in a way that turns all these features into subjective ones. At the core of nationalist sentiments, there may be primordial *subjective* features such as religious feelings, a sense of cultural belonging, mythical attachments to a race, or some groundless belief in a shared tradition.

This subcategorization into instrumentalists and primordialists perhaps does not simply reproduce our dichotomy in a new vocabulary, but it does nothing to break it either. It only captures some of the aspects involved in the two opposing views. Ethnic and civic nationalists may be grouped in many different ways, but a mere reshuffling of the cards will not help to go beyond the traditional views.

The same thing can be said about the debate over the fate of the nation. Some think that nations are here to stay and that they will survive the end of the modern era. They were there before, and they will remain after the demise of the modern world, if some 'postmodernist world' of some sort is to take its place. People who so construe things are known as perennialists. The most well known example of these thinkers is once again Clifford Geertz. Others think that since the nation is essentially tied to modernity, nationalism is a phenomenon that will disappear when the modern world disappears, if it ever does. Most civic nationalists fall into this category. Finally, there are those who think that even if the nation is a product of modernity, it has only a contingent existence and, as the modern world continues to develop, nationalism will slowly disappear. This is, for instance, the view held by E.J. Hobsbawm.

The debate concerning the fate of the nation is in a way the reverse of the one concerning its origin. It is only remotely related to our problem of trying to overcome the distinction between the ethnic and the civic conceptions of the nation. Still it is useful to mention these different approaches because they indirectly serve to show how pervasive the distinction is and how much it imposes itself upon our mentalities.

The traditional civic conception is also still very much present in the writings of contemporary 'continental' philosophers and social scientists. To mention just a few, Dominique Schnapper,[26] Pierre-André Taguieff,[27] and at one time Alain Finkielkraut[28] all have proposed a civic account. It is true that in her *La communauté des citoyens* as well as in her contribution to this volume, Schnapper also tries to overcome the traditional dichotomy. But she does so by suggesting that ethnic nationalists were themselves always motivated by a political agenda, as illustrated by the classical example of Alsace-Lorraine in the wars that set France and Germany against each other. She argues, in a manner similar to Hobsbawn, that the reunification of 'cultures' or of a population with a 'same ancestry' was in that case instrumental for expansionist political goals, and that in general it is an expression of a political nation building (of the state-nation variety). She is willing to admit that civic ties are not enough for social bonding and that political authorities use language, culture, and tradition in order to consolidate the sense of national identification, but these additional features do not belong to the 'analytical' concept of the nation. According to Schnapper, one must not confuse what goes into the characterization of the nation with what has historically been done by the nationalists. And if we make this distinction, we shall, she argues, come to see that all nations are the creation of the state.

She is also willing to admit that many civic nations tend to favour a certain homogeneity, and she describes this homogeneity in cultural terms. But she does not entirely remove herself from the traditional dichotomy. Even if she is ultimately led to a sort of synthetic approach that in a way transcends the traditional distinction, still, in the end, Schnapper is in effect proposing a civic account. She discards the *ideological* distinction between the two views because, as a matter of fact,

---

26 Dominique Schnapper, *La communauté des citoyens* (Paris: Gallimard 1994)

27 Pierre-André Taguieff, 'Nationalisme et anti-nationalisme. Le débat sur l'identité française,' in Coll., *Nations et nationalismes*, Les dossiers de l'état du monde (Paris: La découverte 1995), 127-35

28 Alain Finkielkraut, *The Defeat of the Mind* (New York: Columbia University Press 1995)

the only sort of nation that actually exists is the civic nation, and the only sort of nation building is the state-nation building. The ideological dichotomy has to be suppressed, because there is really no such thing as an ethnic nation. The struggles between different populations are always of a political nature, and when they are nationalist in character, they are specifically related to a policy of state-nation building.

A civic conception of nationalism is also implicit in the works of Jürgen Habermas where he defends a post-traditional form of nationalism which he calls 'constitutional patriotism.'[29] Unlike Schnapper, Habermas is more normative and less preoccupied with a sociological description. In taking this normative view, he is very critical of the continued maintenance of the traditional nation-state. His constitutional patriotism is something that could also be implemented in supranational states such as Europe.[30] And he speaks, in considering Europe, of a post-national identity coming into being.

All the accounts that we have described so far in this section share a certain feature. Whether or not they propose a defense of the traditional nation-state, they more or less endorse, where they make any endorsement at all, an exclusively civic form of nationalism. Now one cannot deny, at least initially, the plausibility of this conception. All the above civic nationalists argue that the only way to neutralize ethnic nationalism is to set it aside and replace it with a radically different conception. They confront their opponents with an enormous challenge. They predict that any attempt to replace the exclusively civic conception by some other form of account will lead to a vindication of ethnicism or ethnocentrism. They argue that their opponents are not entirely conscious of the enormous forces behind ethnicism. If they were, so the argument goes, they would realize that its replacement by an exclusively civic account is required and that civic nationalism is the only reasonable and morally or politically acceptable option left.

In our opinion, these arguments reveal the force of the exclusively

---

29 Jürgen Habermas, 'Historical consciousness and post-traditional identity: The Federal Republic's orientation to the West,' in *The New Conservatism: Cultural Criticism and the Historian's Debate* (Cambridge, MA: MIT Press 1989), 249-67

30 For the distinction between nationalism and patriotism, see also the contribution of Andrew Levine to the present volume.

civic account. Many would argue that the events that took place around the world since the breakup of the Berlin wall confirm this diagnosis. There have been wars fought all over the world in which ethnicity seemed once again to be playing a major role. The worst recent cases are offered by the Serbs in Bosnia or by the Tutsis and the Hutus in Rwanda, but many other examples could be given to show that ethnicism is more than ever present. We have had a plethora of what Carol Prager aptly calls barbarous nationalisms. And paradoxically, their reemergence gives a renewed credibility to the exclusively civic conception.

There are, of course, new approaches which criticize the primacy of the exclusively civic nation-state, and some even challenge the coherence of such a conception, but many who make such criticisms are against all forms of nationalism, whether it is civic or ethnic. Many defenders of the Maastricht Treaty and some Canadian federalists find themselves endorsing this ultra-civic approach which turns individuals into citizens of a 'supranational entity.' Some, like Martha Nussbaum,[31] even think in terms of an ideal conception in which individuals are thought of as citizens of the world. We suggested above that civic nationalists were in favour of the nation-state and it might look as though a supranational approach runs against such a conception. But this is not entirely accurate. Those who announce the end of the nation-state and who favour its replacement by an exclusively supranational organization might be characterized as simply wanting to reproduce a certain form of civic state at a higher level. So even if they are not just proposing a variant of civic nationalism, there is not much conceptual difference involved between this 'post-national' or 'supranational' model and the more traditional forms of civic nationalism. As suggested by Greenfeld, it is perfectly coherent for a civic nationalist to favour its implementation on a world scale. It is probably wrong, however, *pace* Greenfeld, to describe someone who subscribes to such a view as an ultra-civic nationalist in disguise, for we

---

31 Martha Nussbaum, 'Patriotism and Cosmopolitanism,' in Joshua Cohen, ed., *For Love of Country: Debating the Limits of Patriotism* (Boston: Beacon Press 1996). In the same volume, Michael Walzer's trenchant criticism of these views should be noted.

must acknowledge an important difference between this approach and the traditional civic one. It is that those who defend such a supranational model often go as far as equating all nationalism with ethnic nationalism, or at least characterizing it in pejorative terms. They will condemn nationalism as such because, as François Mitterand used to say, "it can only lead to violence." Still this approach does not run counter to most of the essential aspects of the traditional civic conception.

At the other end of the spectrum, Walker Connor[32] makes a correlation between all nationalisms and ethnicisms (he even coined the word 'ethnonationalism'), but he also argues that it has become a fundamental feature of our contemporary world. Without doubt the ethnically 'pure' nation does not exist anymore (if it ever did), but the fact that ethnonationalism has no objective import does not make it less important as a political phenomenon. Like Smith, he rejects Clifford Geertz's insistence on allegedly primordial traits, but he agrees that ethnonationalism is a fundamental driving force in contemporary politics. There are also, according to Connor, many 'non-rational' positive qualities within nationalist movements that must properly be recognized as such, and these must not be taken to be irrational. After all, what is non-rational need not be irrational. He rejects the premodernist account of the nation, but he also criticizes the modernist approach. In many of his papers, Connor effectively shows how intellectuals, both in North America and Europe, have failed to understand the reality of nationalism. Against those who think that it has been around for a long time, he argues that it reached the masses only at the beginning of the twentieth century. At the same time Connor thinks that intellectuals wrongly underestimate its actual force. So Connor thinks that both premodern and modern historians are wrong in this respect. They tend to concentrate only on the élites and fail to appreciate that the lower classes were until very recently indifferent towards the nation.

In any case, whether one defends a certain form of supranationalism or asserts the inescapable presence of ethnonationalism, we are still not able to go beyond our initial opposition. This is also true in the

---

32 Walker Connor, *Ethnonationalism: The Quest for Understanding* (Princeton: Princeton University Press 1994)

context of Canadian politics.[33] We are still under the spell of the views held by Pierre Elliott Trudeau[34] and Ramsay Cook.[35] Trudeau has always seen Quebec nationalism as a tribal phenomenon, and Cook has for the same reason criticized the view that Canada is a pact between two founding nations. Quebec nationalism is still perceived by a majority of Canadians as ethnic in essence, and the only alternative seems to be civic nationalism.[36] There are indeed conceptual mistakes here, but there is much more involved.[37] Such remarks plainly have consequences in the political forum. But unfortunately, this is where things stand in Canadian politics at the moment. That is not to say that no other voices are being heard, but the main political orientations in Canada operate, whether wittingly or unwittingly, within the limits of an exclusively civic interpretation.

---

33 For recent philosophical contributions that are sensitive to the Quebec situation, see Michel Seymour, ed., *Une nation peut-elle se donner la constitution de son choix?* (Montréal: Bellarmin 1995).

34 Pierre Elliott Trudeau, *Le fédéralisme et la société canadienne-française* (Montréal: HMH 1967)

35 Ramsay Cook, *Canada and the French Canadian Question* (Toronto: Macmillan 1966)

36 The reaction of Canadians towards the remarks of the former Premier of Quebec, Jacques Parizeau, on the referendum night of 30 October 1995, are quite revealing in this respect. The *Calgary Herald* spoke about Quebec nationalism as involving a 'tendency toward ethnic cleansing.' The *Vancouver Sun* talked about 'xenophobia,' 'ethnic superiority' and 'tribalism.' The *Hill Times* of Ottawa accused Parizeau of 'unleashed racism.' The *Edmonton Sun* said that Parizeau has admirers among members of the Heritage Front and Jean-Marie Le Pen's National Front. The *Winnipeg Sun* suggested that Parizeau should go to Bosnia and ask the Serbs for a job. The *Vancouver Province* spoke of racism and suggested that Quebec nationalism is an instance of an ethnic nationalism that leads to gas chambers and apartheid, to Bosnia and Rwanda. The *Toronto Sun* spoke of 'ethnic cleansing.' The *Financial Post* spoke of hatred, and the *Ottawa Sun* denounced the sickness of the minister of finance Bernard Landry. These extreme statements go far beyond anything that Parizeau said or wanted to say. Those who make them paradoxically create the violence that they are purportedly denouncing. These reactions are so outrageously exaggerated that they cannot be explained solely by what Parizeau said, but must rather be explained by invoking a general misperception of Quebec sovereignists as ethnic nationalists.

37 See Nielsen, 'Secession: The Case of Quebec.'

V   Cultural Nationalism

The debate over the origin of nationalism should not be of primary concern to philosophers, for the questions raised by nationalism exceed such supposedly 'merely factual' concerns. Perhaps when we adopt a normative and political perspective it does not matter whether nationalism was at the beginning essentially an ethnic or a civic phenomenon. What matters is whether we *should* now adopt either of those conceptions in describing and interpreting social and political realities, and in our normative appraisals of nationalism. The question is to a very large extent a normative and critical one and not (if there is such a thing) a purely descriptive or explanatory one. Moreover it can be argued that in polyethnic, pluricultural or multinational societies, no conceptions that are founded upon exclusion can be justified. Cultural diversity has turned our contemporary societies into culturally diverse sociopolitical realities, and we need to develop complex notions in order to grasp this complex reality.

There are some authors who are now moving away from the ethnic/civic dichotomy and who defend a certain form of cultural nationalism. We could mention, for instance, the names of Yael Tamir[38] and David Miller.[39] These two authors are among the very few who have developed an account of the nation which is neither ethnic nor exclusively civic.[40] Because of them, we are beginning to understand why some non-exclusively civic forms of nationalism can be legitimate. Tamir and Miller emphasize the cultural aspects of the nation as well as its civic aspects. Both stress the importance of cultural belonging and underline its legitimacy in order to rehabilitate the concept of the

---

38   Yael Tamir, *Liberal Nationalism* (Princeton: Princeton University Press 1993)

39   David Miller, *On Nationality* (Oxford: Oxford University Press 1995)

40   There are many defenders of the cultural definition of the nation in Canada. We could mention, for instance, Charles Taylor in *Reconciling the Solitudes: Essays on Canadian Federalism and Nationalism* (Montréal: McGill-Queen's University Press 1993). Fernand Dumont develops similar views in *Raisons communes* (Montréal: Boréal 1995). Finally, we should also mention Will Kymlicka in *Multicultural Citizenship* (Oxford: Clarendon Press 1995).

nation. Of course, there are many other authors who have discussed the cultural features of the nation, but these two authors are distinctive, in the sense that they are among the very few who systematically argue for a certain kind of *cultural nationalism*.[41] They are among those who do not condemn out of hand a nationalism that is more than 'a purely civic nationalism.' Both of them are philosophers whose books were published almost simultaneously, and they also make contributions to the present volume. In this section, we will briefly discuss their books.

It should first be noted that Tamir and Miller do not entirely reject the traditional civic model, though their reasons for holding on to certain aspects of it are not the same. For instance, Tamir does not wish to distance herself from some crucial features of the traditional civic conception. Even when she emphasizes the cultural aspects of the nation, and stresses the importance of cultural belonging, she puts forward an ethical individualism which remains essentially tied to the traditional civic conception. Recall that this conception, as we characterized it, is essentially individualistic since nations are, to the civic nationalist, nothing more than compounds of individual citizens.

Tamir is willing to recognize the importance of cultural belonging, but she does not draw any anti-individualistic conclusions from these facts. It is for that reason that she devotes considerable space to criticizing collective rights and emphasizing the primacy of individual rights and liberties over any kind of collective interests. She puts all her efforts into showing the compatibility between nationalism and liberalism, but she seems to ignore the fact that some of the traditional liberal thinkers such as T.H. Green and John Dewey were not individualists. The liberal philosopher can, according to Tamir, acknowledge the value of cultural belonging while remaining an ethical individualist. And since a sense of cultural belonging is at the core of nationalist sentiments, nationalism can be accommodated within a liberal theory.

There are those who will feel some dissatisfaction with such an account. After all, some will think, there does seem to be a way to show that liberalism is compatible with the admission of an adequate balance between individual and collective rights. These two kinds of rights

---

41 See also John Hutchinson, *The Dynamics of Cultural Nationalism* (London: Allen and Unwin 1987).

may compete with each other without leading to a rejection of basic liberties. Some collective rights may impose reasonable limits upon individual liberties, just as individual liberties may impose reasonable limits upon collective rights. It could be argued that a liberal should be willing – and indeed some are willing – to accept these mutual constraints imposed by both kinds of rights. It is essential for a liberal philosopher to promote individual liberties, but she need not give to them an absolute priority over collective rights. In short, a liberal philosopher need not be an ethical individualist.

Of course, Tamir does break away from some aspects of the traditional civic model. For instance, and we believe importantly, she does not see the nation-state as necessarily the best form of political community. She believes that liberal nationalism may be realized in multicultural political associations. However, since she rejects collective rights that are not reducible to or justified by individual rights, this could weaken the force of her claims. As we shall see in the next section, ethical individualism makes it hard to accommodate the rights of nations in multicultural political associations.

Tamir thinks that collective rights can be reduced to or justified by individual rights. But it could be argued in response that the rights of national communities to create, control, and develop their own basic cultural, political, and economical institutions can neither be reduced to nor justified by any appeal to individual rights. For instance, these national communities have a right to survive through time independently of the individuals who presently happen to be members of such communities, and this right goes beyond the rights of individuals to maintain their cultural belonging.[42] The same kind of remarks apply to the rights to create, develop, and control their institutions. It seems that individuals are entitled to do these things only because they live in communities which have that right. This order of explanation (but more on that later when we discuss Will Kymlicka) is perhaps also needed if we are to justify the integration of immigrants in a welcoming community.

---

42 A similar point is made by Charles Taylor in 'The Politics of Recognition,' in Amy Gutman, ed., *Multiculturalism and 'the Politics of Recognition'* (Princeton: Princeton University Press 1992), 40-1, footnote 16.

Moreover, there seems to be another problem with the suggestion that the collective rights of nations must be reduced to or justified by individual rights. According to this view, the self-determination of a nation should either be reduced to or justified by the self-determination of the individuals that compose the nation. But if that is so, it is going to be difficult to oppose partitionism and irredentism. Most of these movements presuppose an individualistic interpretation of self-determination and give an absolute priority to it over the self-determination of nations conceived as competing claimants of rights.

There is yet another crucial problem that confronts many individualistic accounts which allow for the multinational model of political community. One wonders how it is possible to expect nations to enter into such a community if we also ask them to renounce political recognition as such. If we adopt the multinational model we should, in order to yield a perspicuous representation of the phenomenon, at the same time allow for the political expression, recognition, and emancipation of the nations that compose this political community. But how shall we do that if we are reluctant to recognize the collective rights of the component nations? This may not be a problem for all cultural nationalists, but it could confront those who are willing to envisage multinational political arrangements while remaining at the same time ethical individualists. Of course, Tamir does not want to reject collective rights as such. She simply believes that those which are compatible with liberalism (and thus on her reading those which are legitimate) are either reducible to or justified by individual rights to cultural protection; it remains to be seen whether this kind of ethical individualism creates difficulties for the cultural nationalist. We wish at this point, however, to postpone the discussion of this particular question, for we shall return to it in the next section when we discuss Kymlicka's contribution to the issue.

Miller does not have any kind of commitment to ethical individualism, since he is willing to accept a 'communitarian foundation to liberalism.'[43] He argues for a view of nationality based upon five different features. A nation is a community (1) constituted by shared belief and

---

43 Miller, *On Nationality*, 193

mutual commitment, (2) extended in history, (3) active in character, (4) connected to a particular territory, and (5) marked off from other communities by its distinct public culture.[44] He thus also endorses a cultural account of the nation. However, Miller concentrates most of his attention on a defense of the nation-state as the best model of political community in modern societies. For him, the nation is inherently political in the sense that it aspires to a certain autonomy. It is not identical to a political community, but it aspires to be one, whether in the form of a nation-state, as it should most of the time be, or some weaker form of self-government, as it is sometimes (exceptionally) compelled to be. This aspiration is built into the very nature of the cultural nation. As a social construct, it is essentially a cultural community, but we also have to acknowledge its aspiration to political expression, recognition, and emancipation.

Miller expresses his conviction that the nation-state is of central importance in our political lives.[45] He clearly favours nation-states over multination states. So even if he does not endorse the premise according to which nationalism is nothing over and above the promotion of the nation-state, he puts a lot of emphasis on this particular form of political arrangement. We are most of the time presented with arguments that explain why the nation-state is probably the best regime that there is. It is here that Miller appears to be still entangled in the traditional mold. We have seen that both ethnic and civic nationalists agree on the appropriateness of the choice of the nation-state as the basic political unit in modern societies, and it appears that Miller does not wish to break away from this idea. It is true that he thinks there are important exceptions to the principle of national self-determination, and in his contribution to the present volume, he gives us a good indication of his rationale for that, but he does seem to treat the multination state only as an alternative to the nation-state, and not as an equally interesting and equally basic form of political organization. It is only for pragmatic reasons that the multination state model should on some occasions be adopted.

---

44 Miller, *On Nationality*, 27

45 Miller, *On Nationality*, 98

There are two problems that we want to mention concerning Miller's account. First, there seems to be a tension between the simultaneous promotion of cultural nationalism and nation-states. We must first note that the cultural nation is in most accounts defined in terms of a common language and culture. Of course, when it is a liberal nation, it must also be inclusive, that is to say it must integrate incoming immigrants and, more generally, individuals with different national origins. But in most accounts, it does not include national minorities, i.e., extensions of other nations which happen to be on closely situated territories. For instance, according to cultural nationalists such as Miller, Taylor, and Dumont, there is a French Canadian nation that is situated mostly but not exclusively on Quebec's territory, and there is an English Canadian nation mostly but not exclusively situated in the rest of Canada. Now since cultural nations very often overlap in such a manner on different legal jurisdictions, it is unclear why we should in general favour nation-states if the nation is conceived as a cultural nation. And indeed, Miller is perfectly aware of the difficulty in the case of so-called 'French Canadian' nationalism. But more generally, how can we accommodate the cultural nation with a defense of the nationalist principle? How can these two conceptions be reconciled? There are many pluricultural societies in the world resembling Canadian society, i.e., societies containing one 'cultural' majority nation but many national minorities. By 'national minority,' we are not merely talking about individuals with a different ethnic origin, but rather about an extension on a certain territory of a nation closely situated on a different territory. What about these national minorities? Are they not a part of a political community along with a cultural majority? And is this complex reality not a more adequate conception of the nation? Miller will perhaps want to say that they might share the same citizenship, even if they are not part of the same nation, and this answer is perhaps a way out which shows the relative strength of the cultural account of the nation. And, indeed, when we consider states in which political sovereignty has already been achieved, that view does not appear to be problematic. But the problems with the cultural view of the nation become apparent as soon as we begin to reflect upon the conditions under which a cultural nation can become sovereign. This is the second difficulty of his account to which we shall now turn and it is one which perhaps cannot so easily be answered. It may be the central difficulty that awaits any cultural account, including the one proposed by Tamir.

Miller's cultural nationalism leads him to say that when the membership in the 'nation' is numerous enough, has a national consciousness, and is determined to persist as a nation, then it should become sovereign if this is what its members democratically decide. Since nations are partly defined in cultural terms, it seems that it is the group formed by the conjunction of all the individuals sharing the same language and culture that should become sovereign. But what happens if the group in question is not all concentrated on the same territory? Very often, some of the members of the same 'cultural nation' form a minority on the territory of another 'cultural nation.' Does it then mean that, in the case of secession, this other nation should abandon some of its territory in order to accommodate the needs of the seceding nation? How does this differ from irredentism?

Another related problem concerns the fate of the national minorities that happen to live on the territory of the seceding nation. As we pointed out, in many if not most of our contemporary societies there are no culturally homogeneous groups of people occupying a single territory. And so it is hard to find a case where a single group of individuals sharing the same language and culture could aspire to self-determination on an already existing legally recognized territory without in effect, if not in intention, forcing some members with a different cultural background to follow them in the same adventure.

If cultural nations achieve political sovereignty, this could affect the existing territorial delimitations and the self-determination of other cultural nations. If nations are exclusively cultural, then subgroups belonging to the same culture as the seceding nation, but living on the territory of other cultural nations, will be part of the seceding nation and so will have to secede. The same holds for the national minorities that live on the territory of the seceding nation itself. If the cultural nation is the subject of the right to self-determination, the territory of the seceding nation should thus include all and only the territories on which the cultural nation is based, and hence, it should not include the territory held by the national minorities. This means, among other things, that most of the time the new territorial delimitations of the seceding nation cannot be those that it had, whether these are of a county, a state, a province, or some other kind of boundaries recognized within the encompassing state. Secession will affect the territories of the other cultural nations, and it will also affect the territorial delimitations of the seceding nation itself. What could be the moral justification for such a seceding movement? This appears to us to be a *reductio* of such a purely cultural conception of nations.

These are some of the difficulties involved with the cultural account. There are many examples all over the world of sovereign states in which purely cultural nations cohabit with national minorities on the same territory. If one promotes the view according to which sovereign states should be composed of all and only the members belonging to the same cultural nation, this would entail a large-scale reform of international borders, and perhaps very extensive partitions. Why should we engage in such dramatic changes? Is it just to fit an *a priori* view of the nation as purely cultural? Let us suppose that we do not choose this course of action, and that most cultural nationalists would want to resist such a reform. Even if an extension of the seceding nation happens to be on the territory of another nation, let us suppose that we do not wish to include the territory of these minorities in the territory of the seceding nation. Let us suppose also that the minorities that are on the territory of the seceding nation should be involved in the seceding process. If we make these choices, choices that certainly seem reasonable, the question can now be asked: what is the use of adopting a purely cultural definition of the nation? If not all the members of the cultural nation are part of the process leading to sovereignty, and if members of another cultural nation are included, there does not seem to be any normative usefulness in the cultural conception of the nation. To put things differently, if the cultural nation is not the subject of the right to self-determination, why do we need to use such a concept? Perhaps we should instead conceive of the nation as a political community very often composed of a national majority and, if there are any on the territory, of national minorities and individuals with other national origins.[46]

---

46 For such a conception, see Michel Seymour's 'Une conception sociopolitique de la nation,' *Dialogue*, **37**:3 (1998). As conceptualized by Seymour, a nation or a people can be a political community which, on a (legally or conventionally) recognized territory, consists most of the time of a national majority (i.e., a majority on a given territory, which also happens to be in the world

The above difficulties of the purely cultural account concern the conditions under which nations become sovereign. It affects the cultural view of the nation whether or not we follow Miller in advocating the primacy of the nation-state over the multination state. Even if, as Yael Tamir does, we allow for an alternative model such as the multination state, the cultural account of the nation is still faced with difficulties related to the process by which sovereignty is achieved. Of

---

the majority of a group of people with a specific language and culture), along with national minorities (i.e., minority extensions of neighbouring nations) and citizens of other origins, if there are any such minorities and individuals on the same territory. (Of course, a majority within the political community must also share a certain national consciousness and a will to live together.) National majorities can be 'majorities' in two different senses of the word. They very often form a majority on a given territory, although this need not always be the case (e.g., the Catalans in Catalonia). But even when it is the case, it certainly is not sufficient, for if we were to include cities or districts among recognized territories, it would be possible to find an indefinite number of such majorities. More importantly, a national majority is a compound that forms a majority of the people having a certain language and culture when compared to all those who have the same language and culture but who live on other territories throughout the world. Of course, there can also be counterexamples to this. Indeed the 'national majority' could in principle be larger only in the sense that it is the largest sample of a group of people with a given language and culture, and thus not an *absolute* majority of such people. There could be more people outside the territory sharing the same language and culture. It could in some special circumstances even fail to be the largest sample, as long as it is the only one that forms a majority on its own territory. Even if there are larger compounds of people with the same language and culture on some other territories, these compounds will not become nations if they form minorities on their respective territories. In sum, in order to be a national majority, a group of people must either be the largest compound in the world of people with a specific language and culture or, alternatively, if it is not the largest, be the only compound of such a people that forms a majority on its territory.

There is another (trivial) case of a 'national majority' that fails to be a majority. It is when there are no national minorities and no individuals of different origins on its territory (e.g., Iceland). But most of the time, if not always, there are at least some individuals with a different national origin. It must also be noted that the national majority is composed of individuals who share the same language *and* culture, and the cultural component is perhaps more important. So even if there are more English-speaking Americans than there are English-speaking Canadians, English Canada could still form a national majority since

course, we have described these difficulties as though Miller and Tamir were not aware of them, and this is certainly not the case. For instance, Miller responds to those difficulties by arguing that when nations are spread on many different legal territories, they should not secede from the encompassing state. These are, for instance, the reasons that he gives for rejecting secession in the case of Quebec.[47]

But why should we introduce such a conception, if the nation, so characterized, cannot consistently exercise her right to self-determination under any conditions? The purpose of introducing a new conception of nation should be at least in part normative, and not only descriptive. If cultural nationalists propose a new characterization, it must be in part for normative reasons, which in the present case amount to political and ethical reasons. It means among other things that it should play a role in a discourse reflecting upon the moral reasons for exercising self-determination, and upon the moral conditions under

---

it has a different culture. If such a conception were accepted, then Belgium, Spain, Switzerland, and Canada would offer clear cases of multination states. According to that conception, there is within Quebec's territory a Quebec nation which includes a national French-speaking majority, a national English-speaking minority, and Quebeckers of other national origins. Eleven Native nations also live within that same territory. Of course, this conception is just one among many. It could and should be introduced simultaneously with the conception of the nation as a diaspora. This last conception is as important as the first one, and it does not fit the model according to which the nation is identical with a certain kind of political community. We could roughly define a diaspora nation as a group of people sharing the same language and culture which does not have a national majority in any sense of the word 'majority' (e.g., the Kurds). For an even wider conception, indeed a deliberately extended conception of a nation, distinct from the ones articulated here, see Brian Walker's contribution to this volume.

47 Miller, *On Nationality*, 114. We agree with Miller that in such a case, our first choice should be to try resolutely to adopt reforms within the confines of the multination state. And, as a matter of fact, Quebeckers have precisely sought to do just that for more than 130 years. From the very beginning of the Canadian confederation, they thought they could maintain multiple identities by preserving their national identity within a multination state. But the question to be asked now is the following: what should be done if, after all that time, most Canadians still reject any kind of constitutional, political, and administrative reform that would entail a recognition of the Quebec nation within Canada?

which this process can rightly be achieved. But if there is almost never a case of a purely cultural nation that can morally be justified in exercising its right to self-determination on a given territory, then there are reasons to doubt the adequacy of such a conception. Indeed, given some reasonably deeply embedded considered moral judgments of most people in liberal democracies, it is a kind of moral *reductio*.

The cultural nationalist seems to be confronted with a dilemma. If the cultural nation is allowed to achieve sovereignty, it will almost always affect, in the present world anyway, the self-determination of another cultural nation and always affect its territory. But if, given the situation in the modern world, e.g., the pervasiveness of multicultural societies, secession is almost never justified, then it throws into very considerable question whether the use of such a purely cultural conception of the nation, running against our considered moral judgments as it does, can play a useful normative role. Furthermore, if we consistently stick with that conception, it seems that we encourage the project of a Great Serbia as envisaged by the Serb leaders. It is not only their systematic violation of human rights which is morally unacceptable, but also the expansionist notion of *la Grande Serbie*. Moreover, cultural nationalism seems at least to encourage those with partitionist and irredentist ambitions. All this serves to show that cultural nationalism is perhaps too closely related to ethnic nationalism. As things stand, it creates enormous tensions. And if we choose instead not to follow that line and come to reject the aspirations of 'cultural nations' for sovereignty, then it appears that cultural nations which do not already have a sovereign state cannot hope to find moral reasons justifying the exercise of their right to self-determination. So it is hard to see how the concept of a purely cultural nation could play any fruitful role in a normative evaluation of contemporary nationalist movements.

However, we should not prejudge the issue here. It is in large part an empirical one. Miller can challenge the claim that, some very exceptional cases apart (e.g., Iceland), there are no homogeneous cultural nations on legally recognized territories. For instance, if we leave aside the Brussels region, the Flemish and Walloons each occupy five distinct provinces in Belgium. There is almost no overlap between the two communities, except for a very few regions. Some, like the Fourron community which occupies a part of the Flemish territory, are the exceptions and not the rule in Belgium. The same remarks apply to the different nations in Switzerland. With more than two-thirds of the population, the German part of Switzerland, for instance, occupies 19 cantons out of 26. Similar arguments could be made regarding Scotland and Wales in Great Britain. However, the situation as described only appears to favour Miller's account, for it is also implicitly suggested that if nations like the Welsh, the Scottish, the Flemish and the Walloons were to become separate political entities, they would occupy territories that roughly coincide with their actual borders.[48] We might agree with the above description in most cases, but for very different reasons. The question that must be asked, supposing that secession is justified for a given nation, is whether, in the process of achieving sovereignty, we should preserve the *territorial* integrity or the *cultural* integrity of the seceding nation. It is clear that in international law, the successor state exercises its sovereignty over the territory that the nation had as a political community before it became sovereign. This suggests that we should in general use actual territorial delimitations and not cultural identity as a criterion for determining the territory of the seceding nation. If there are apparent examples of fairly homogeneous cultural nations which could become sovereign on specific territories, it is perhaps not because they are culturally homogeneous, but rather because the territorial delimitations of the nations are rather clear.[49] These territorial boundaries, by the way, need not be legally recognized as is the

---

48 Actually, we should be careful not to draw any such conclusions in the case of Belgium. In addition to the Fourron community, we should take into consideration the fact that Brussels is part of the Flemish Brabant, and that more than 80% of its population speaks French. There are also more than sixty thousand German-speaking individuals living in the Walloon region.

49 This is not to say that we endorse a territorial conception of the nation, for there could be many nations partly occupying the same territory. This is, for example, the case of Quebec in which there are eleven aboriginal nations in addition to the Quebec nation. Even if they constitute only a small proportion of the Quebec population (74 000 out of seven million), each of the eleven aboriginal nations have a right to self-determination. This could in principle create a problem in the context of Quebec's secession from Canada, but it is generally agreed from a political point of view, as well as from the point of view of international law, that aboriginal nations should have a somewhat limited moral right to self-determination which includes self-government, but does not include a (moral

case for federated states within federations. If nations are conceptualized as certain sorts of political communities, there will very often be an internal or international recognition of its territory, whether this recognition is legal or a mere convention, since a political community, by definition, exercises a certain authority on a determinate territory.

But, of course, Miller could challenge the suggestion that the conception of the nation has to be introduced essentially for normative reasons. He could argue that even if we were left with almost no normative uses, the descriptive cultural concept of the nation would be the only reasonable one to hold. He could also claim that his conception does have practical implications, but suggest that these are not confined to the process of secession. In his *On Nationality*, for instance, he discusses the relationship between national solidarity and social solidarity which could be invoked as having important ethical consequences. Miller can claim in addition that his own conception has a dual aspect. It is both descriptive and normative, for he is after all able to distinguish questions about the nature of national identity from the politics of national identity. True, perhaps there are now very few purely cultural nations that can claim justification for sovereignty. But this does not show that his own notion has no normative or prescriptive import. The apparent lack of normative import may be explained by the fact that prior secessions of actually sovereign cultural nations were less problematic than the cases of cultural nations which now share the same aspirations. In other words, the previous cases of seceding cultural nations were the result of a difficult but viable equilibrium between a cultural nation and their minorities. Most of the remaining cultural nations that are not politically sovereign are perhaps in a more delicate situation, and sovereignty might not be the solution to their problems. The idea of a cultural nation cannot easily be useful in such cases, but generally it is not useless. Quite the contrary. It is just that, as it stands, it is becoming more and more normatively useless, since there are almost no cases left of cultural nations that could have a reasonable moral

---

or legal) right to secede or any right to violate the territorial integrity of the encompassing state. There could, of course, be important exceptions to this rule, but it is generally agreed that the self-determination of aboriginal nations is compatible with the territorial integrity of the state.

justification for exercising a full right of self-determination. We mentioned earlier Miller's view concerning the case of Quebec, but he also has reasons for resisting the independence of Wales, Scotland, and Catalonia. Miller could argue that the norms introduced show that these nations do not have a right to secede. The cultural view of the nation is useful since it helps us in showing why these nations should not secede.

Miller can also argue that a certain normative use of the cultural nation could still be made even if there are now very few examples of cultural nations which can legitimately aspire to sovereignty. For they can, alternatively, at least aspire to a certain political autonomy. Even if, in general, the nation-state remains the best model of political community, there might be exceptions to this general rule. And for these remaining cases, the cultural conception of the nation could still play a role in normative discourse because it could lead one to formulate conditions under which a given nation may achieve a certain form of self-determination, even if it is less than full sovereignty. If Miller were to pursue this line of argument, and there are many places in his book where he does follow that line, there would be less difference between the position that he holds and the one held by Tamir or most of the other proponents of the cultural conception. Most of them tend to develop simultaneously the idea of a multicultural citizenship, and thus of cultural nations in multination states. It is, for instance, a line pursued by Will Kymlicka and Charles Taylor.

However, such a vindication of the cultural account of the nation has little force, because it leaves out an important aspect of contemporary liberal societies. Nations are becoming more and more pluricultural political communities. And for that reason it may be thought that the diagnosis offered by Miller against the secession of those 'cultural nations' that are not yet sovereign could in certain cases at least reveal, more than anything else, the outdated character of the purely cultural conception of the nation. If nations were conceived instead as pluricultural political communities, then the presence of national minorities on different territories would no longer be seen as a moral obstacle to secession.[50] And among those nations, some could in very special

---

50 However, it might be seen as a moral obstacle against a complete separation. When two sovereign nations have national minorities that are present on each

circumstances be justified in seceding. The most appropriate political regime for such nations might be the multination state, but it is not the only available option. If this is a correct diagnosis, then we may have to think of another normative conception in order to deal with all the political communities, sovereign or not, in which a national majority cohabits with different national minorities. In other words, we are perhaps compelled to provide a new account of the nation that can accommodate the cultural diversity of our contemporary societies. It can also be replied that the suggestion concerning the previous cases of secession is empirically false. It simply is not true that most previous secessions were the result of a process in which a purely cultural nation became independent. A very large number of sovereign states contain national majorities, national minorities, and individuals of different origins.

Given the above criticisms made against the cultural account of the nation, it is not surprising to note that, among those who defend that view, most authors clearly favour the multination state model of political community. As we pointed out, in contemporary liberal societies the cultural conception enters into tension with the promotion of the nation-state. Those who, like Miller, still express a preference for the nation-state tend to be conservative concerning those 'cultural nations' which have not yet achieved independence. But, as we shall see in the next section, we have to ask whether it is the nation-state model as such, not the purely cultural view of the nation, which is responsible for the problem. If the nation-state appears to be a bad way to accommodate cultural diversity, it is perhaps not because there is something inherently wrong with the nation-state: it might rather be because there is a problem with our purely cultural account of the nation.

Our purpose here is not to settle the issue, but rather to raise it, and it is with that in mind that we shall now turn to an examination of multination states.

---

other's territory, they should perhaps engage in some kind of political partnership with each other.

VI   Multination States

In discussing recent accounts of the multination state, we shall once again restrict our attention to two important recent works: *La multination* by Stéphane Pierré-Caps[51] and *Multicultural Citizenship* by Will Kymlicka.[52] These two authors make a very considerable effort to think about the accommodation of cultural pluralism within actual sovereign states, and attempt to reflect upon the conditions under which multination states could be acceptable. It is important to note that there is a deliberately prescriptive dimension involved in their writings. These authors argue that, in already existing multination states, an explicit recognition of national communities can and must be made. Thanks to these writers, we are getting close to an explanation of the causes behind nationalist movements. We are forced to recognize that, very often, sovereign states do not recognize their own multinational character. We thus also begin to understand that nations must be recognized within the encompassing states, and that their exclusion is not a morally or perhaps even a politically viable solution. We begin to understand that, if nations are not granted such recognition, they could have a moral justification for secession. If Pierré-Caps and Kymlicka are right, the *status quo* in already existing multination states that do not recognize themselves as such is unacceptable.

These two works present many advantages over the works we have previously examined. Pierré-Caps and Kymlicka reflect upon the moral problems raised by the cohabitation of many different nations within a single sovereign state. And in so doing, they indirectly help us to reflect upon the moral justifications for secession. Moreover, these two works offer a criticism of already existing nation-states, especially the work by Pierré-Caps, who vehemently denounces the unwillingness of many different countries which have invoked self-determination in order to achieve their own sovereignty, but which refuse to grant even a minimum of self-determination to national groups living on their own territory. Pierré-Caps also offers a radical criticism of the exclu-

---

51   Pierré-Caps, *La multination*.

52   Kymlicka, *Multicultural Citizenship*.

sively civic nation-state, one that we seldom find in the literature on the subject. To be sure, these are not trifling qualities but, while we acknowledge them, we shall concentrate on a major difficulty which we feel both authors have not adequately faced.

This is not the place for a detailed discussion, so let us state very bluntly and succinctly some central plausible arguments against these two works. Both fail to draw an appropriate distinction between national minorities and nations and, for this reason, both are unable to account for the possibility of nations which would include national minorities. Recall that by a 'national minority,' we mean a partial extension of a closely situated nation on the territory of another nation.[53] It is a minority group that lives on a territory where there is a national majority, but not just any kind of minority, for there has to be a closely situated nation with which it shares a certain language and culture.

Pierré-Caps uses the word 'national minority' to describe both a nation that happens to be outnumbered within a larger encompassing state and a minority of people which is the extension on a given territory of a close neighbour nation living on another territory. Consequently, for him, there is no distinction to be made between nations that happen to be outnumbered and national minorities. So what we classify as national minorities can, on his conception, be treated as nations, and appear to have self-determination, just like all nations do. He is thus unable, theoretically, to distinguish between secession (an act performed by a nation) and partition (an act performed by a subgroup within a nation). Of course, he is opposed to partition, but it is for no other reasons than the ones invoked in the case of secession. Secessionist movements and partitionist movements are all to be explained, according to Pierré-Caps, by the unfortunate prevalence of the ideology of the nation-state. These movements are in certain circumstances illegitimate, if the actors fall prey to the ideology of the

---

53 For a discussion of the distinction between nations and national minorities, see Seymour, 'Une conception sociopolitique de la nation.' According to that view, the Russian populations in the Baltic states, the Hungarians in Romania or Slovakia, the Croats and Serbs in Bosnia, the Arabs in Israel, the French Belgians in Flemish Belgium, the Anglo-Quebeckers in Quebec, and the French Canadians in English Canada are all national minorities.

nation-state, and they may be legitimate in others, if the actors are *victims* of the ideology of the nation-state. In both cases, the guilt is to be found on the side of those who defend the nation-state.

It could be argued, on the contrary, that the appropriate criticism of an exclusively civic form of nationalism should invite us to redefine the complex reality of the nation outside of the civic/ethnic dichotomy, and not necessarily to condemn nation-states altogether. Of course, if nations are not exclusively civic, we must therefore think of them independently of their existence in a sovereign political community, and this should force us to acknowledge the possibility of multination states. But the problem with the purely civic account also concerns the concept of the *nation*, and there might be no problem as such in the very idea of a *nation*-state, once nations are conceptualized in a new way. Going beyond the civic/ethnic dichotomy certainly requires, as we have seen, entertaining at least the possibility of alternative models to the traditional nation-state, but it does not necessarily mean that we must reject the legitimacy of the nation-state as such. What is wrong in the traditional model is to restrict the notion of a nation-state only to a homogeneous ethnic (or purely cultural) group in a sovereign state, but nation-states can perfectly be acceptable if they allow also for the possibility of nations which are culturally plural. If we distinguish between nations and national minorities, as we can do if the nation is seen as a particular sort of political community, then it becomes coherent to allow for a single 'nation' to contain 'national minorities.' In other words, there are many ways to accommodate the pluricultural character of contemporary liberal societies. We can allow for multination states, but we can also have an open mind toward the nation-state in which the nation is seen as a pluricultural political community.

Pierré-Caps has what is arguably a bias against nation-states, and this influences his understanding of the political problems he is trying to explain. We should perhaps focus our criticisms on the exclusively civic, ethnic, or cultural conceptions of the nation, and remain in this context as neutral as possible concerning the different possible models of political authority. We should adopt a pragmatic approach to the problem, and Pierré-Caps is perhaps not sufficiently pragmatic. In his *La multination*, he systematically attacks the legitimacy of the nation-state and promotes the multination as the best model of political community. But this could be seen as a misconceived diagnosis of the problem. He clearly discerns that both the civic and ethnic conceptions assume the primacy of the nation-state. But if a critical approach should rule out such a primacy, it should not also denounce the very legitimacy of the nation-state as such, for it is not clear that the best model is always the multination. The difficulties with the ethnic and civic conceptions are in their supposition of what it is to be a nation, and this is what should change.

If Pierré-Caps would argue for a conception of the nation as a political community involving a national majority and – if there are any on the territory – national minorities and individuals of other national origins, he would then be in a position to distinguish nations from national minorities. By so doing, he would be able to distinguish between genuine multination states and the case where a nation happens to contain national minorities. The two cases are quite different and both should not be categorized as multination states.

Actually, there are many different sorts of cultural diversity to be accounted for. We must first take into consideration the phenomenon of immigration and reflect upon policies of multiculturalism that provide ways to accommodate these groups within the larger community. We must also try to reformulate a view of the nation that can allow for the existence of national minorities. We must then think of the different ways to accommodate nations within multination states. These states contain many different nations forming political communities which are not sovereign. We must also find a way to accommodate aboriginal nations within those states. And we must finally reflect upon the possibility of supranational states, where sovereign states enter into larger political organizations. All these different levels must carefully be distinguished from one another. They present different challenges to the political recognition of cultural diversity. Allowing for cultural diversity at all levels does not lead to a rejection of the nation-state as such. It certainly leaves room for multination states and for supranational forms of political organization, but it should not rule out a redefined nation-state, now recognized to be in almost all cases pluricultural and multiethnic. A nation may be pluricultural if it contains one or more national minorities on its territory, and it may be polyethnic if it contains individuals of different national backgrounds who still in some way identify themselves in terms of the language, culture, and tradition of their country of origin.

The reasons why Kymlicka fails to make the distinction between nations and national minorities are quite different. Let us take an example that may help to simplify things a little. For Kymlicka, the Quebec nation is composed of the francophones living in Quebec; it does not include Anglo-Quebeckers. This exclusively francophone community is not to be described as ethnic because, as Kymlicka correctly stresses, many different ethnic communities have integrated into the French population of Quebec. Language is itself ethnically neutral. The second reason why the Quebec nation should not be described as ethnic is that it is also territorially based, since it does not include francophones living elsewhere in Canada. Like Tamir, Miller, Dumont, and Taylor, Kymlicka endorses a cultural view of the nation. But he differs slightly from them in the case of Quebec by restricting the cultural nation to francophones living inside Quebec.

For Kymlicka, the Quebec people, or the *Québécois* as he calls them, may simultaneously be described as a cultural nation and as a national minority within Canada, and this is simply because they are outnumbered by a majority of English-speaking Canadians. The Quebec nation is, in the context of Canada, a culturally defined minority. For Kymlicka, a national community is a national minority if it is outnumbered by a larger group on a given territory. It seems that nothing more is involved in his conception of a national minority. So he does not feel the need to make any distinction between nations and national minorities.

There are many difficulties involved in putting national minorities and nations into the same bin. For instance, we doubt whether Kymlicka would be theoretically able not to treat the anglophones living in a sovereign Quebec as a distinct nation entitled to secession. As things stand, the anglophones living in Quebec must, for Kymlicka, be part of the English Canadian majority. But wouldn't they be a national minority in a sovereign Quebec? And, since there seems to be no difference in his account between nations and national minorities, there seems to be no reason not to treat Anglo-Quebeckers in a sovereign Quebec as a distinct nation. But this is surely counterintuitive. Anglo-Quebeckers have never described themselves as a nation, and they have never behaved in this way. In addition, there is a problem related with this account similar to the one that was raised against Pierré-Caps. Since Kymlicka draws no clear distinction between nations and national minorities, he also runs the risk of being theoretically unable to distinguish between irredentist movements and seceding movements. Both groups aim at full self-determination and both groups seem to be able to exercise this right under special circumstances.

However, this criticism is to a certain extent beside the point. Even if Kymlicka does not actually draw any distinction between nations and national minorities, there is nothing that prevents him from doing so, as long as the two sorts of national communities are treated as minorities. Nothing in his theory prevents him from introducing two sorts of national minorities, those that are nations and those that are extensions of a nation on another territory. It is only the first ones which could, under special circumstances, be entitled to exercise a full right of self-determination. If he is able to do so, then he is at least in principle able to distinguish between groups of people that may be the subject of secession and those that would perform a partition. But even if we avoid the difficulty by introducing a new distinction within his theory, we would only be able to locate more precisely where Kymlicka still partly remains, his intentions to the contrary notwithstanding, in the traditional mold of the purely civic model. As we shall see, Kymlicka is an ethical individualist and it is in that sense that he remains tied to the traditional civic account. He can only allow groups to have collective rights if they are a *minority* within a larger group. And since he wants at least certain nations to have collective rights within the encompassing multination state, he must treat them as minorities. Presumably, the majority nation within the state also has some collective rights, but only relative to the larger international community. We have now arrived at the point where we are in a position to uncover the deep motivations behind Kymlicka's temptation to conflate nations and national minorities. *It is because the only acceptable candidates for collective rights are minorities.* But why does he find it necessary to restrict collective rights to minority groups? The reason is that these are the only collective rights that are reducible to, or justified by, individual rights to participatory goods. Kymlicka rejects collective rights that would impose restrictions on the individual liberties of the individual members of society. He rejects collective rights if they involve internal restrictions imposed upon the members of the group and accepts them only if they involve external protections for a minority against a majority. It is, according to Kymlicka, only by proceeding in this fashion that we can develop an account of collective rights which is compatible with political liberalism. Collective rights can be accommodated by liberal theories only if they involve external measures to protect a minority from a majority. They are – indeed on this conception *must* be – illiberal if they impose restrictions on individual liberties.

But why does he think that the only acceptable conception of collective rights for the liberal is the one that involves only external protections and never internal restrictions? The reason is that Kymlicka mistakenly thinks that political liberalism is intimately linked to ethical (or political) individualism, the view according to which individual rights have an absolute priority over collective rights and interests. As mentioned above in the case of Tamir, Kymlicka's individualism thus ultimately explains why he treats nations as national minorities. He wants to accommodate collective rights for nations within the framework of liberalism. But, according to him, it is illiberal to impose internal restrictions on the liberties of citizens. So he must only accept rights that offer external protections for minority groups. Since the rights of cultural minorities are reducible to or justified by special rights given to individuals, this account is indeed compatible with ethical individualism. So ethical individualism requires that nations be equated with national minorities.

Kymlicka can consistently claim that all collective rights may be accepted within his model, including the right to self-determination. It is just that, contrary to the 'collectivist,' he believes that they are all reducible to (or justified by) individual rights. He also argues that there should not be too much emphasis placed on the subject of rights. What is important, according to Kymlicka, is the object and not the subject of rights. It does not matter whether the subject of rights is an irreducible collectivity, or whether it is just individuals. According to Kymlicka, these are ontologically vexing questions that should be put aside and not allowed to intrude in the political debate. If nationalism is to be accommodated within a liberalism which is political and not metaphysical, it must itself be political and not metaphysical. But as a matter of fact, there is nothing wrong, still according to Kymlicka, with the so-called liberal conception according to which individuals must be the sole bearers of rights. For in one sense of 'collective rights,' they are rights belonging to individuals, and it is in this way that we can accommodate them within a liberal framework. A right is treated as 'collective' not because the owner of the right is a group, but rather because the object of the right is a participatory good. When collective rights are understood in this way, they are compatible with a liberal approach. The conclusion is that a liberal state can (and perhaps should) promote and protect the rights of 'cultural groups,' as long as they are reducible to, or justified by, the rights of individuals to cultural protection.

Kymlicka is certainly right to separate political liberalism from metaphysics and (if there is any difference) ontology. This is the essential feature of John Rawls' political philosophy.[54] Liberalism should not, according to Rawls, be founded upon a theory of human nature or on any contestable metaphysics. It involves only a certain political conception of the person. By 'political conception of the person,' Rawls means a certain political self-representation of the person. The adequate conception is that of the 'moral person' who is both rational, in the sense that she behaves in accordance with her own conception of the good, and reasonable in the sense that she is endowed with, and is able to act on, a certain political conception of justice. So there is nothing metaphysical about such a liberal account. But does it mean that we should not for that reason discuss matters related to the subject of collective rights? Must we avoid altogether all references to collectivities at the level of normative political theory? Here, we are afraid, Kymlicka goes way beyond all the restrictions that Rawls would want to impose on political liberalism. In order to recognize collectivities as the subject of collective rights, one (*pace* Ware) need not enter into an ontological discussion concerning the status of collectivities. We can simply register the fact that some groups *represent themselves* as nations. The approach adopted by Rawls concerning the person may also be deployed for the group. An ontological account of nations is not needed. The only thing required is a certain conception of the nation.[55]

---

54 John Rawls, *Political Liberalism* (New York: Columbia University Press 1993)

55 Indeed, Rawls does not seem to have Kymlicka's qualms about collective rights applied to peoples or nations. See 'The Law of Peoples,' in Stephen Shute and Susan Hurley, eds., *On Human Rights, The Oxford Amnesty Lectures 1993* (New York: Basic Books 1993).

Since he is not able to allow for collective rights that impose restrictions on individual liberties, Kymlicka is unable to give a perspicuous expression, a perspicuous realization, and a perspicuous recognition of nations within multination states. It could as well be claimed – though this is a distinct kind of claim – that there is a paternalistic attitude involved in treating the rights of nations as 'minority' rights, and in treating the objects of those rights as external 'protections.' It seems, to understate it, problematic to treat the right to self-determination as a 'protective' measure. Peoples should be treated as equals, and the principle of equality between nations should not involve treating them as minorities that require external protections.

It is also doubtful whether one can *reduce* collective rights to individual rights to participatory goods, or *justify* the former by the latter. If individuals have the right on a given territory to have access to a certain number of participatory goods, it is because there is on that territory a collectivity who is the primary bearer of the right. It is the collectivity who has a right to self-determination, a right to the creation, maintenance, and development of specific cultural institutions, a right to have a distinct political community, a right to control its own specific economic development, etc. Without the existence of such a group, individuals cannot claim a right to these specific participatory goods. Moreover it appears – or so some are inclined to believe – that if these rights were reducible to or justified by individual rights, we would then be unable to justify the linguistic integration of immigrants into their new community and their insertion into a public common culture. The immigrant comes equipped with a particular language and a particular cultural background, and so, if we ignore the collective level, she is in the same situation as the welcoming individuals who are also equipped with a particular language and cultural background. Presumably, both take their language and culture as a primary good. Why should we want to say that the welcoming individual has a right to force the immigrant to integrate into his own linguistic institution and his own culture? Kymlicka has no answer to give as to why there is such a right except to say – it seems to us weakly – that the immigrant who decides to adopt a new community chooses to abandon her own individual right to cultural protection. This is certainly what happens in the vast majority of cases, but why do immigrants feel this way? Isn't it because in order to acquire citizenship, they are willing to integrate into the culture of the welcoming *commu-nity*? And by doing this are they not implicitly recognizing the collective rights of the welcoming community? Why should they simply abandon their own individual right to cultural protection in favour of those held by the welcoming *individuals*? Why should our rights as welcoming individuals be superior to the individual rights of incoming immigrants? Without an appeal to the collective rights of the welcoming community, Kymlicka has no justification to offer in order to explain why the immigrants must integrate into the welcoming community. This problem is by no means just a theoretical one. Kymlicka is certainly right to suggest that in practice the vast majority of immigrants do integrate. But it is most probably because they recognize the rights of the welcoming community. Kymlicka's individualistic account leaves the welcoming community without any justifiable recourse to impose any internal constraints whatsoever on its individual members, and thus on its immigrants. The individualist justification for collective rights is therefore a dangerous idea from a practical point of view. Of course, we do not have any such difficulty if we think that the welcoming community, and not the individuals within it, is the primary bearer of the right.

It may, however, look as though Kymlicka can after all provide a justification for the integration of immigrants within the welcoming community. Recall that, as a minority, the nation may implement measures in order to protect itself from the majority within the encompassing state. Among these measures, there could be different integrative measures regarding incoming immigrants. Kymlicka allows external protections, and it is on that basis that he can, for instance, justify the specific measures introduced by the Quebec government. But this way out is not entirely successful. Because these measures restrict some of the liberties of the immigrants, namely their freedom to speak their own language at work, the freedom to choose the language of school education for their children, and the freedom to use their own language on public signs, it appears that these restrictions should become morally problematic from Kymlicka's own point of view.

Of course, Kymlicka can answer that an immigrant is, by definition, someone who chooses to abandon these rights, or to subordinate these rights to other rights. By choosing to live in a new country, she expresses her will to integrate within a new political community. She must therefore agree to behave in accordance with the prevailing laws, and agree to integrate into a common public culture. If she does not, then she does not know what it is to be an immigrant. But this answer won't do because we have to ask why it is clear that an immigrant is 'by definition' someone who accepts integration into a common public culture. There would not be such restrictions if *most* of the people within the welcoming community spoke the language and shared the culture of the incoming immigrants. Integration is, so to speak, a matter in which numbers count. The individual rights of the members belonging to the welcoming community don't by themselves overrule those of the immigrants. It is rather because they belong to a community which forms a majority of people with a certain language and culture on the welcoming territory. This is why, in matters of integration, it is impossible not to refer to the collective rights of the welcoming community.

This last point reveals a further general difficulty with Kymlicka's account. It is not easy to separate generally measures that would count as external protections from those that involve internal restrictions. Specifically, it looks as though all the measures that count as external protections are simultaneously measures that impose restrictions upon individual liberties. Think for instance about the linguistic laws of Quebec which restrict the use of English on commercial signs, or about the obligation on the part of immigrants to send their children into French-language schools, or about the measures implemented in order to favour the use of French in the work place. These are all measures that, from one perspective, can count as external protections, but they simultaneously count as reasonable internal restrictions on the civil liberties of Quebec citizens and landed immigrants. If internal restrictions cannot be accepted, then these measures cannot be accepted. But since all the external protections simultaneously involve internal restrictions, then Kymlicka's individualism should force him to be 'extremely skeptical' about any kind of collective rights.

All the above difficulties have a common source. Kymlicka endorses ethical individualism, and this is the reason why he is unable to extract himself entirely from the traditional civic model. He is thus unable to provide an adequate moral justification for the recognition of a deep diversity within multination states.

VII   Three Constraints

We shall end by formulating some different constraints on any acceptable conception of the nation. We shall only describe three of these
constraints. The previous discussion should have brought to the surface some of the most important ones that should be accepted. We
should try to avoid as much as possible the traditional dichotomy between the exclusively civic and the ethnic account. These two opposing views describe two extreme positions: abstract universalism and
extreme particularism. A balance should be reached between the two.
On the one hand, as Rawls has powerfully argued, contemporary pluralist societies require a government and a constitutional law that can
transcend particular views about the good life and that will not take
sides on these matters. On the other hand, there is, especially within
actual multination states, a need for cultural protection. So a constitution cannot simply refer to universal principles, and governments must
do more than promote mere constitutional patriotism.

In a way, this moderate intermediary approach is already present in
what was earlier described as 'cultural nationalism.' However, there is
an ambiguity between two different uses of the word 'culture.' As
emphasized by Kymlicka, we must distinguish between the structure
of the culture and the character of the culture. By the 'structure of culture,' we mean a particular set of institutions (a language, a constitution, a judicial system, an educational system, and specific cultural
institutions like museums, newspapers, libraries, etc.). All these institutions are involved in what can be called, to borrow another happy
phrase from Kymlicka, a particular 'context of choice,' i.e., a particular
set of political, cultural, and moral options that offer themselves to the
national community. These options are often the result of influences
exercised by foreign countries who share the same language, or the
same history, or which are in a certain geographical proximity. The
character of the culture, by contrast, is the particular colouration that a
structure of culture may acquire during a certain period. A majority within
the national community may at a given time endorse a particular set of
values, and this is what gives a character to the culture. From time to
time, the character of the culture may change, but these changes may
take place within the same structure of culture. Once that distinction is
made, there does not seem to be anything illiberal about a state which

would provide protection for different structures of cultures. It would certainly be illiberal to impose upon the state an obligation to promote and protect a specific character, but nothing can be said against protecting the different structures of culture with their specific contexts of choice.

The more we think of the nation in terms of a structure of culture and context of choice, the more we are inclined to move away from a purely cultural account of the nation in favour of one in which the nation is seen as a political community containing very often a national majority and different minorities, whether these are national minorities or individuals with different national origins. We arrive at this conclusion if we first acknowledge the fact that the cultural component involved in the so-called 'cultural nation' has to be an encompassing one. It must be able to accommodate individuals of different origins and among them new incoming immigrants. It must be granted that all cultural nationalists admit that point. But there is no reason not to also include in the nation those who belong to national minorities, if there are any on the territory, for they too can integrate and share a common public culture with the majority, up to a certain point. So it appears that even if there must be a common public culture, the nation is or can be (again if there are any national minorities on the territory) pluricultural from a sociological point of view. Finally, the common public culture must be understood in structural terms and not in terms of character, and a structure of culture is nothing but a set of institutions (a language, a constitution, a parliamentary system, an educational system, courts of justice, and specific cultural institutions such as museums, theatres, newspapers, etc.). In other words, it is a political community.

Now since the common element involved in the nation so conceived is a political community, and, as the nation may be pluricultural, it is at best misleading to call this view a 'cultural' conception. If a label must be used, it is perhaps more like a 'pluricultural' conception. It is plain that there would not be a nation if there were not a national majority, i.e., a group which forms a majority on a given territory and which represents on the surface of the globe the largest sample of a community with a certain language and culture.[56] And it is clear that

---

56 For a discussion of the notion of a national majority, see Seymour, 'Une conception sociopolitique de la nation.' See also footnote 46 above.

the common public institutions reflect to a large extent those of the national majority. This is certainly a fundamental aspect that was captured by the cultural account, but it must not blur the (possibly) pluricultural character of the society as a whole and the political character of the community. In any case, it is clear that this conception of the nation would perhaps enable us to properly meet the first constraint, namely the one which suggests that we should transcend the dichotomy between the ethnic and the civic definition.

There is a second constraint that must be satisfied by any acceptable conception of the nation. We should not have any bias in favour of either the nation-state or the multination state. We should adopt instead a pragmatic and contextual approach to that problem. There are some cases where the only option is to remain within an encompassing multination state, but there may be other cases where nations should secede from encompassing states. And there are nations which could, and perhaps should, remain within a multinational state if their collective rights are recognized. Without such a recognition, however, the reasonable option would be for them to secede. Of course, one must not think only in terms of sovereign nation-states and multination states. Sovereign states may enter into an economic and political union with others, as for example the European community. There are also different sorts of multination states, depending on the sort of political autonomy which can be reached. It could involve a massive decentralization, a special status, or an asymmetry in the distribution of powers. Too often, those who discuss nationalism have already made up their mind about a particular model of a political community, but we should be as flexible as possible in this regard. We have to reach a delicate balance between theory and practice. In many multination states, there is no *a priori* answer whether the component nation should secede or not. It all depends on the capacity of the encompassing state to recognize its multinational character.

The third constraint comes from our previous distinction between national minorities and nations. For reasons that we have seen, any adequate definition should allow us to make such a distinction. Here the suggestion is that there are different forms of cultural diversity. Quite independently from the choice of a particular political organization for different groups, we must also distinguish between different kinds of cultural groups, identify their needs, and spell out the particular obligations towards them. Specifically, there are, first, communities involving individuals of different national origins. These are often called 'ethnic communities.' The states that contain them are polyethnic. Second, there are national minorities, and the states that contain such communities are pluricultural. It means that in addition to the structure of culture of the cultural majority, which happens to be the common public culture (which is also sometimes called the 'encompassing' or 'comprehensive' culture), there may be national minorities that have their own particular cultures, and they must somehow also be promoted and protected. Or so it should be argued from a moral point of view. Then there are states which contain many nations, i.e., many political communities often composed of a cultural majority and minorities. These are multination states.[57] Then there are sovereign states which may all at once be polyethnic, pluricultural, and multinational. Finally, there are supranational states which contain many different sovereign states which are to some extent limited by the authority transferred to the supranational state.

These distinctions are crucial for many different reasons. Different sorts of communities with their own sets of problems require specific solutions. It is a superficial understanding of cultural diversity which leads us to confuse them all or run them together. To give a dramatic illustration of the problem, it is important in our evaluation of the nationalist principle to distinguish between multination states and states which contain only national minorities. If we confuse national minorities and nations, then we run the risk of being unable to stop, at least on a theoretical basis, the never-ending applications of the nationalist principle, and this could lead to chaos. The nationalist principle is clearly unacceptable in the absolute, without restriction, but it is especially so if we think that it can be applied to any subgroup within the

---

57 Very often, states are sovereign countries, but in federal systems, the federated entities may also be called 'states.' This is at least something that follows from an understanding of federalism which implies sharing the sovereignty between different levels of government. It may be correct to establish a strong connection between a 'state' and the possession of sovereignty. But, precisely because of that, since the federated entities share sovereignty with the federal state, they can also be understood as 'states.'

state. Too many authors use only one conceptual category to contain all cases of cultural diversity within a sovereign state. But, as we have seen, there are many different sorts of varieties to be accounted for. Different sorts of communities require different sorts of political arrangements. Only nations could be entitled under special circumstances to exercise a full right to self-determination. If we confuse individuals of different national origins, national minorities, and nations, then it will look as though very few sovereign countries are genuine nation-states, since almost all are 'culturally diverse' in some way or other, and it will look as though the nationalist principle could never be applied without engendering chaos. But this is a conclusion that we can draw only if we confuse different sorts of populational variety. If we do not confuse these, then we shall perhaps be able to identify among the different communities within a state those that can count as nations, and specify the nature of their collective rights. We are consequently also going to be in a position to draw the appropriate conclusions if it appears that their collective rights are not respected. In short, the only way to perspicuously accommodate pluralism into our contemporary societies is through a policy that acknowledges its deep diversity. It is only in this way that one reaches a delicate balance between individual and collective rights.[58]

These are then the three main constraints that we wanted to mention in the conclusion of this introduction, since they are in a certain way implied by the discussion of the literature in the previous sec-

---

58 In Canada, the champion defender of deep diversity has certainly been Charles Taylor, and there used to be a time when he was the only one to speak in favour of recognizing the multinational character of Canada. See, for instance, Taylor, *Reconciling the Solitudes.* Nowadays, there are a large number of intellectuals who share this idea. We could mention, for instance, Ken McRoberts, Phil Resnick, Don Lenihan, and Will Kymlicka. These are just a few among a long list of English Canadian authors that now recognize the multinational character of Canada. One could also mention Curtis Cook's collection of essays in which all the contributors acknowledge that Canada is a multination state. See Cook, ed., *Constitutional Predicament. Canada after the Referendum of 1992* (Montreal: McGill-Queen's University Press 1994), 5. Unfortunately, this open-minded attitude is for the most part restricted to an *élite* of philosophers and social scientists, and it is not shared by the vast majority of Canadians.

tions. Of course, there are many other constraints that could have been introduced and discussed. For instance, it is clear that any acceptable conception of the nation must involve an adequate balance between subjective and objective features. It is also clear that it must be compatible with liberalism, and must be the result of a wide reflective equilibrium. Our conception must also somehow jibe with the uses of the word 'nation' made by a critical mass of individuals within the population. Perhaps even more important than anything else, there must be valuable moral consequences that follow from adopting one conception rather than another. It was not our purpose in this introduction to precisely formulate such a conception. We rather sought to show that there was a need for such a formulation. Our argument is precisely that there are important moral as well as conceptual failings with the traditional conceptions that have until now been prevalent in the literature. It is our hope that the reader will find in the following collection of essays the occasion to reflect upon the need to accomplish such a daunting task.

PART I

Methodological Turnings

CANADIAN JOURNAL OF PHILOSOPHY
Supplementary Volume 22

Theoretical Difficulties in the Study of Nationalism

YAEL TAMIR
Tel Aviv University

Philosophical questions are not like empirical problems, which can be answered by observation or experiment or entitlements from them. Nor are they like mathematical problems which can be settled by deductive methods, like problems in chess or any other rule-governed game or procedure. But questions about the ends of life, about good and evil, about freedom and necessity, about objectivity and relativity, cannot be decided by looking into even the most sophisticated dictionary or the use of empirical or mathematical reasoning. Not to know where to look for the answer is the surest symptom of a philosophical problem.

Isaiah Berlin[1]

Critics of recent philosophical analyses of nationalism suggest that nationalism is a unique social phenomenon that cannot, and need not, be theorized. Are there, indeed, some special features constitutive of nationalism that might defy theorization? Those answering this question in the affirmative point to the plurality and specificity of national experiences, as well as to the emotional and eclectic nature of nationalist discourse.

This paper defends attempts to theorize nationalism. The evident diversity of national experiences, it argues, need not stand in the way of constructing a theory of nationalism. Other subject matters of political theory – be they distributive justice, representation and participation, individual rights, or the common good – also exemplify diversity of private and public expressions. Hence, if the plurality of particular experiences hampers the possibility of developing a theory of nationalism, it must be an impediment to the formation of political theories

---

1 R. Jahanbegloo, *Conversations with Isaiah Berlin* (London: Phoenix Paperback 1992), 27

in general. Should we then surrender attempts to write a philosophical exposition of justice, gender relations, or nationalism, and settle for history, sociology, or actual policy recommendations? Certainly not.

Why do claims concerning the uniqueness of particular experiences resonate more in discussions concerning nationalism than in all others? The answer is grounded in both the image of nationalism and the advantages accruing from fostering its non-theoretical image. A closer scrutiny of attempts to de-theorize nationalism will reveal that they could be classified into two different types: the first includes nationalist claims, the second consists of the examination and evaluation of national claims generated by scholars of nationalism.

The next sections are devoted to a more detailed analysis of these two types of claims. One must start, however, by clarifying the meaning of the term 'theory' as used in this context. The diversity and uniqueness of particular national experiences cannot possibly defy the ability to write a history of nationalist ideas or provide a sociological or historical account of nationalist movements, but it may undermine attempts to structure an abstract, normative theory of nationalism prescribing certain norms and modes of political behaviour.

The term 'theory' is used here in this second connotation. The challenge can therefore be formulated as follows: Can one construct a general account of obligations, rights, or prohibitions applying to all cases of nationalism, or are these incidents so diverse and contextualized that they defy all attempts to generalize them? In what follows I argue that theories of nationalism can be constructed and urge more scholars to join the effort to improve them.

The Call of the Wild

One reason the task of constructing a general theory seems implausible is the nature of nationalist rhetoric itself. Nationalistic claims often lend themselves to unfavourable interpretations according to which they are no more than erratic outbursts of emotions from which no set of principles can be deduced. Hence, nationalism is depicted as the most radical antithesis of a theory, as lacking intelligible structure, logical coherence, and inner consistency. The assumption that nationalist thinking is inherently chaotic and unruly is best exemplified by Eli

Kedourie's choice of Yeats's poem '1919' as the motto of his influential book on nationalism:[2]

> We pieced our thoughts into philosophy
> And planned to bring the world under a rule,
> Who are but weasels fighting in a hole.

For Kedourie, nationalism epitomizes the failure of the philosopher's attempt to subject the world to the rule of universal principles. The underlying picture, then, is that of two distinct groups pursuing conflicting ends: philosophers who use reason to explore and refine the structure of the world, and nationalists who evoke human fears and passions to entice their followers to subvert these attempts.

Kedourie is not alone. Nationalism is often portrayed as a chaotic, emotional, irrational force, subverting all rules and rational planning. For post-world wars generations, the first associations evoked by the term 'nationalism' are the rhetoric of blood and soil, fiery exhortations to rally around the flag, demands for total devotion and self-sacrifice, and a collective feeling that sweeps away individual considerations. Nationalism, Ernest Gellner argued, is presented as no more than a cry of passion, a tug of war against reason.[3] Ernest Kriek describes it as the call of "blood which struggles against formal reason; race against purposeful rationality; honour against profit; unity against individualistic disintegration; material virtue against bourgeois security; the folk against the individual and the mass."[4] And in what may be the best known attack on nationalism, Karl Popper claims that nationalism has a strong affinity with the revolt against reason and the open society, as it "appeals to our tribal instincts, to passion and to prejudice, and to our nostalgic desire to be relieved from the strain of individual responsibility which it attempts to replace by a collective or group responsibility."[5]

---

2 E. Kedourie, *Nationalism* (London: Hutchinson 1960)

3 E. Gellner, *Thought and Change* (London: Weidenfeld and Nicolson 1971), 149

4 E. Kriek, in G. H. Sabine and T. L. Thorson, *A History of Political Theory* (Hinsdale: Dryden Press 1973), 816

5 K. Popper, *The Open Society and Its Enemies* (London: Routledge, Kegan Paul 1962), 49

The perception of nationalism as essentially a phenomenon exhibiting "the manifestation of emotions and unreason, of atavistic drives rather than rational deliberation,"[6] is thus pervasive.

The assumption that nationalism is an unruly expression of emotions and therefore cannot be forced into a theoretical framework is common even among sympathetic observers. Daniel M. Weinstock cites Jane Jacobs as an example. Like love, Jacobs argues, nationalism cannot have a rational justification. Trying to argue about national feelings, she concludes, is "as fruitless as trying to argue that people in love ought not to be in love, or that they must be, that they should be cold and hard-headed about choosing their attachments. It doesn't work that way. We feel; our feelings are their own argument."[7]

Nationalism is compared to love in its unruliness, yet love is perceived as grounded in noble feelings while nationalism is seen as no more than a caprice reflecting human desires and fears, "an irrational relic of, or retrogressive return to, a barbarous past."[8] In essence, claims Hugh Seton-Watson, nationalism simply entails the application of the principle of popular sovereignty to the nation – "the rest of nationalist ideology is rhetoric."[9] In the same skeptical spirit, Stanley Benn suggests that, while nationalism "is enormously important for historians and sociologists, it would be absurd to treat it as if inviting serious rational criticism."[10]

A dichotomy thus emerges; on one pole is reason, which is equated with universalizable principles, and on the other passion, which is identified with unstructured emotions and paralleled with nationalism. The clear conclusion is that nationalism is a social force that lies beyond theoretical analysis. One may then gather a collection of nationalist rhetoric and policies and study their social and political impact, but it

---

6 D. M. Weinstock, 'Is There a Case for Nationalism?' *Journal of Applied Philosophy* **13:1** (1996) 87

7 In Weinstock, 'Is There a Case for Nationalism?' 88

8 I. Berlin, 'The Bent Twig: A Note on Nationalism,' *Foreign Affairs* **51** (1972) 19

9 H. Seton-Watson, *Nations and States* (London: Methuen 1977), 445

10 S. Benn, 'Nationalism,' in P. Edwards, ed., *Encyclopedia of Philosophy* (London: Macmillan & The Free Press 1967)

makes no sense to formulate a theory that could explain, structure, and guide the plurality of national expressions. If these claims could be justified then many fine scholars are wasting their time in a vain attempt to tame an incorrigible shrew.

I have no intention to deny the extreme, irrational, erratic forms of some nationalistic expressions, but would argue that these expressions do not exhaust the whole of the nationalistic discourse. Nor do they offer the only kind of justifications for nationalist claims. It follows, then, that if one desires to structure a theory of nationalism one must look beyond these expressions and uncover a structure overshadowed by rhetoric.

Many scholars of nationalism do acknowledge that some forms of nationalism are less erratic than others. Hans Kohn, John Plamenatz, and Anthony D. Smith all distinguish Western from Eastern forms of nationalism.[11] Kohn sees Western nationalism as essentially a rational and liberal way of thinking grounded in the notion of human rights. Eastern nationalism is its opposite: it is mystical, ethnocentric, and grounded in tribal feelings. For Plamenatz, Western nationalism characterizes culturally developed nations that can, from a position of self-confidence, approach each other on an equal footing, seeking cooperation on the basis of mutual respect. Eastern nationalism characterizes primitive nations who, motivated by feelings of inferiority, adopt belligerent polices. Smith speaks of Western nationalism as civic and political, and of Eastern nationalism as ethnic and genealogical.

Whatever the virtues of this dichotomy are, it is often used to disqualify the more structured and temperate forms of nationalism as worthy of that title. Hence, Neil MacCormick feels that his defense of a moderate version of nationalism needs to be prefaced by a somewhat apologetic statement: "Some may think this too weak a version of nationalism to merit the name, others that any version of nationalism is merely a stalking horse for chauvinism and xenophobia. To both I would say that in this, and in other matters, there is much to be said for a

---

11 H. Kohn, *The Idea of Nationalism* (New York: Collier McMillan 1966); J. Plamenatz, *Consent, Freedom and Political Obligation* (Oxford: Oxford University Press 1968); A. Smith, *Theories of Nationalism* (London: Duckworth 1993)

golden mean."[12] MacCormick makes a valid claim. His moderate version of nationalism is still a variant of nationalism. Yet, as he suspected, his attempt to rescue nationalism from its extreme image is met with suspicion. If MacCormick's reasonable political position can be defined as nationalism, Gordon Graham argues, then "a good many people are nationalists unaware." Being horrified by such thought he hastens to reassure his audience that "such a moderate nationalism is not really nationalism at all."[13]

I disagree with Graham and have elsewhere shown both that moderate forms of nationalism exist and that attempts to disqualify them are grounded in an intentional neglect of the more general trends in nationalistic thought and an undue emphasis on its more ethnocentric, irregular forms.[14] In this paper I am less interested in refuting such claims and more in the motivations behind them. Hence, I examine arguments advanced by both nationalists and scholars of nationalism and investigate the nature of the urge to de-theorize nationalism.

The Importance of Being Chosen

Nationalists contribute their share to the non-theoretical perception of nationalist thinking by insisting on the uniqueness of its particular appearances. They thereby deny the option of defining a standard set of nationalist principles, as the very notion of a *standard* suggests a classification based on similarities.

Arguing that nationalist expressions could be standardized to fit into a theory presumes that some general trends cut across the myriad of arguments raised by different national groups. Though such trends exist, nationalists typically attempt to disguise them by grounding nationalist demands in the nation's distinct identity, history, culture, or religion, and by refraining from relying on a general theory that might

---

12 N. MacCormick, *Legal Right and Social Democracy* (Oxford: Oxford University Press 1981), 250

13 G. Graham, *Politics in Its Place: A Study of Six Ideologies* (Oxford: Clarendon Press 1986), 140

14 See Y. Tamir, *Liberal Nationalism* (Princeton, NJ: Princeton University Press 1993).

fit other national groups. In this respect they differ from liberals, socialists, or democrats, who tend to go to out of their way to demonstrate that their values and policies correlate with a general, universalizable theory. The preference for the particular and local is the most evident universal characteristic shared by all nationalist movements.

And yet, despite attempts to mask the resemblances between different nationalist claims the similarities are too obvious to ignore. The most striking example involves a topic which seem the least likely candidate for universalization – that of being chosen. According to Conor Cruise O'Brien virtually every Christian nation adopted the image of a chosen people inhabiting a promised land and applied it to itself. O'Brien provides the following list of nations, which he claims is merely a partial one: England, France, Germany, Poland, Russia, Spain, Sweden, Switzerland, and the United States.[15] The belief that one's nation is chosen is not restricted to the Christian world and is shared by the Jewish people as well as by many Islamic nations such as Egypt, Iran, Iraq, and a host of others. But nationalists would never admit the fact that the claim that their nation is chosen and their land promised follows a general pattern. And for good reason: being chosen is only meaningful if others are not.

As this example shows, nationalist claims can be analyzed using two distinct and incompatible discourses. The first tells a story unique to the national group and refers to arguments meaningful only to fellow nationals. The second encompasses a universal dimension; it places the national narrative within a general framework and associates it with other national narratives, thus generating arguments that are meaningful within a general context.

This duality is evident not only in scholarly analyses of nationalism; as the following example shows, it is part and parcel of the nationalist discourse itself. Zionists couch their support for the establishment of the state of Israel in particularistic terms. They tell the story of the Jews' exile from their land, recall two thousand years of Jewish Diaspora, remember the expulsion of the Jews from Spain, their persecution, the emergence of anti-Semitism, and, of course, the

---

15 C.C. O'Brien, 'Nationalists and Democrats,' *Times Literary Supplement*, 15, August 1991, 29

Holocaust. They tell a very personal and particularistic narrative lead-ing to the conclusion that Jews need a state of their own to secure their existence, where they can freely exercise their national-cultural-reli-gious tradition. And yet one can claim that the right of the Jews to have a state of their own is embedded not in their own, unique and tor-mented history but in more general claims. Suffering and persecutions may be good reasons to grant a group of individuals shelter, to protect them, to entitle them to compensation, but not to grant them national rights. If Jews have a right to national self-determination it is grounded in a universal principle stating that all nations have this right, rather than in their particular history. The best illustration of this approach is the Zionist saying that the Jews ought to become "a nation, among nations, in the law of nations."

According to this approach the right of a nation to self-determina-tion does not derive from the fact that it was chosen by God, or that its members were persecuted or mistreated, but from its equality with other nations, or to be more precise from the equal status of its mem-bers. It is grounded in the right of all individuals to preserve and ex-press their history, their language, their cultural heritage – all those aspects of their identity that bind them to their national group.

Adopting this line does not imply that the special history of a na-tion does not play an important role in the construction and justifica-tion of actual nationalist claims. Whereas the general structure of the justification is independent of the contingent history of each nation, justifications for the particular way in which it should be implemented must depend on each nation's unique history. For example, while a general justification for the right to national self-determination could be adduced without reference to any historical contingencies, the justi-fication of granting that right to a particular nation depends on the development of national consciousness and on the explicit demand of the nation's members to enjoy this right. Thus, in order to know how to implement this right it is important to follow the historical emer-gence of each nation and determine when it has achieved political maturity. Let us reconsider the Zionist example: the special history of Jews does play a role in determining where and when they became a nation deserving self-determination. In modern history, it could be claimed that Jews reached political adulthood in 1897, with the con-vention of the first Zionist congress which was meant to transform the national question of the Jews into a political issue to be settled in the assembly of civilized nations.

The demand that the national homeland is to be established in a particular place is also influenced by the history of a nation. Hence, the demand to establish the Jewish state in the land of Israel rests on the constitutive role of this territory in the history of the Jewish people.

The particular narrative and the universal justifications thus join in explaining the nature of national rights and their implementation, but each carries a different message – the first glorifies the nation's history, language, and culture, while the second bears a message of humbleness and pluralism. The Jewish thinker Ahad Ha'am warns against the consequences of placing exclusive emphasis on the ethnocentric narrative. To be a nationalist, he argues, is to see oneself as different from, rather than as above, other nations. The greatest virtue of the nationalist discourse is that it allows individuals to internalize general humanistic values in a national mould, to recognize themselves as members of a vast human family, but also as members of a specific group of people which has expressed its uniqueness throughout its long history.[16]

The temptation to overlook the universal message embedded in nationalism is nevertheless considerable. The implication of resorting to general justifications is that all nations have the same rights; hence, one's nation is only one among others, obliged by the law of nations. It is no coincidence that nationalists are reluctant to acknowledge this message, as it implies that they ought to see other nations' rights as a source of self-restraint. The moral test of nationalists, argues Michael Walzer, is their attitude toward the nations they are in conflict with.[17] Needless to say, few nations pass this test.

The particularistic nationalist discourse is especially well fitted to reinforce ethnocentric claims which lead to the dehumanization of the enemy and consequently to moral numbness. It is far easier psychologically, and far more beneficial politically, to disregard the fact that one's enemies, like oneself, belong to recognized national groups and

---

16 Ahad Ha'am, *The Collected Essays of Ahad Ha'am* (in Hebrew) (Tel-Aviv: Dvir Publishing House 1954)

17 M. Walzer, 'The National Question Revised,' Tanner Lecture, Oxford, 1989

are entitled to the same rights as oneself. Ethnocentric-nationalist language hardens the heart, and leads individuals to be impervious to others' misery, destruction, and expulsion, blind to injustice, hatred, and death. At the end of the day when national struggles occur, only a few members of each nation actively participate or support hostile activities, but many more are guilty of crimes of omission. They turn inwards and exhibit indifference to their enemies' suffering. This vice is inspired by the particularistic language of nationalism.

By preferring particularistic justifications to general ones, nationalists achieve another advantage: they can endorse an ethnocentric approach to culture and morality affirming that

> all values and standards must necessarily be intrinsic to the national unit, grounded in its history and tradition. This view fosters the belief that nations, and their cultures, are not only unique but also incommensurable with each other. It thus follows that appeals to universality rest on a false view of the nature of man and history.[18]

The implication is that the evaluation of different cultural experiences is impossible, and the encouragement of cultural exchanges makes no sense: each nation must live according to its own norms, fostering its own values and modes of experiences. No external principles can guide its actions. If members of a nation deserve rights or benefits it is because they are French, or Jewish, or German, namely, because they are different from, rather than similar to, members of other nations.

The nationalists' attempt to refrain from any generalization of their experience may indeed be politically beneficial but it is theoretically misleading and morally wrong, and should therefore be rejected.[19] And yet unfortunately this trend is reinforced by arguments offered by some scholars of nationalism. Let me then turn to examine the nature of these arguments.

---

18 I. Berlin, *Against the Current* (Oxford: Oxford University Press 1979), 344

19 If suffering is a necessary qualification of acquiring national rights then the sanctification of suffering is inescapable; if national rights could be supported on more general grounds then the reference to past sufferings might be avoided, and might be replaced with more forward looking, reconciliatory policies.

Siding with the Underdogs

Having clarified why nationalists tend to prefer to couch their claims in particularistic and non-theoretical terms, it is still puzzling to find that scholars of nationalism often prefer to embark on a similar course. One possible explanation is that this approach allows them to align themselves selectively with national demands raised by underdogs – indigenous peoples, discriminated minorities, or occupied nations – whose plight reinforces the moral power of their claims, and dissociate themselves from nationalistic demands that are morally less appealing.

The distinction between more or less defensible national claims is made possible by their duality. We return here to another version of the tension between the general and the particular, yet here particular claims play a different role than in the previous discussion. They make reference to the particular history of the nation not in order to turn inwards, but in order to examine the particular national case in light of a general theory of justice.

Consequently we face, once again, two kinds of justifications. The first is grounded in a theory of nationalism; it assumes that if national rights rest on theoretically and morally sound grounds they ought to apply to all nations, regardless of their power, wealth, past suffering, or even the injustices they may have inflicted upon others. Such a theoretical approach suggests that national rights should not be reduced to measures of remedying past injustices or punishing outlaws, that they are neither a reward for good behaviour nor could they be withheld as punishment from *"enfants mauvais."*

The second kind of justification sees national rights in remedial terms. A demand for national rights, it argues, is only justified if it serves as a means to right a wrong, to compensate those who were victimized by nationalism. The justification of such rights must therefore make reference to the source of the injustice: the heinous events in the former Yugoslavia or in Rwanda, the persecutions suffered by native Indian nations, the Holocaust, the expulsion of Palestinians from their lands, etc.

In her challenging article 'The Moral Significance of Nationalism' Lea Brilmayer explores the relations between the two kinds of justifications. Nationalism, she argues, is itself morally transparent, and this fact accounts for its ability to coexist equally well with good and evil.

> The argument is that the overwhelming relevant normative feature of today's nationalism is the justice (or lack of justice) of the claims nationalists advance on behalf of their nation. The single most important normative feature – indeed, perhaps, the only important normative feature – is the right of the nation to the thing that nationalists assert on its behalf, and this right is not itself a consequence of nationalism but a consequence of other underlying moral claims.[20]

If Brilmayer is right, we need not search for a theory of nationalism which explains what is due to national groups (or to individual members of these groups), by virtue of their nationhood. All that is required is an evaluation of the injustice experienced by particular nations. For example, if annexation is morally wrong, then the Baltic states deserve to be liberated. Such a demand, if framed in terms of the wrongness entailed by annexation, would be justified even if raised by "multicultural, multireligious, and multilinguistic entities,"[21] rather than by distinct national groups.

And yet, the appropriate response to injustice depends on the nature of the group, and if the Baltic nations had not presented their claims in national terms, other types of reparations could have been considered: financial compensation or political measures ensuring their ability to participate in the political system ruling their lives rather than the establishment of their own nation-states.[22] Think of the remedies that might be offered to members of different disadvantaged groups, such as inner-city children, gays, women, or individuals harmed by natural disasters. In each case the compensation granted will have to take into account not only the harm done but also the needs and demands of those who have been harmed. For example, it might indeed make perfect sense to resettle individuals whose houses were demolished in a natural disaster in separate locations if they do not consti-

---

20 L. Brilmayer, 'The Moral Significance of Nationalism,' *Notre Dame Law Review* **71:1** (1995) 7

21 Brilmayer, 'The Moral Significance of Nationalism,' 12

22 See the distinction I draw between the right to national self-determination and the right to self-rule in 'The Right to National Self-Determination,' *Social Research* **58** (1991) 565-90.

tute a national-cultural group, but it will add insult to injury if as a result of such a disaster members of a nation have to disperse, thus losing their ability to retain their national life.

Nationalism therefore does matter, though it does not cover the whole of the moral domain. Consequently demands grounded in a theory of nationalism must be balanced against other moral considerations[23] – when nationalist justifications concur with these considerations there is a stronger reason to pursue them; when they conflict with other rights and obligations there may be reasons to override them; but in neither case are they redundant.

Few theoreticians of nationalism would deny these claims. Most of those who claim that nationalism matters do not argue that it exhausts the moral sphere, that groups (or individuals) who cannot ground their claims in nationalist arguments should be left unprotected, or that national groups must be granted all their demands, disregarding other moral considerations. Such an extreme position would indeed be indefensible. Brilmayer thus seems to be hoisting a nationalist strawman, in order to rebut nationalism altogether.

In fact, she senses that an outright denial of all claims grounded in a theory of nationalism would be misguided, and therefore ends her paper by presenting a more qualified claim. Nationhood, she argues, may generate *prima facie* entitlements to certain basic rights. Thus,

> while philosophers are mistaken if they are assuming that the rights nations have *must be* rights that they hold by virtue of their national status, this does not mean that there *cannot be* rights that they hold on these grounds.... It all depends on the precise nature of the right asserted, and whether it is one on which the question of entity status makes a difference.[24]

Hence, while rightly warning us against the unqualified use of nationalist justifications, Brilmayer accepts their necessity. To develop appro-

---

23 This process demands that the specific features of each case be closely examined: the nature of the groups involved, the history of the conflict, and the possible violation of rights that would follow from the proposed arrangements. Only then will it be possible to determine what kind of national rights are entailed in each specific case.

24 Brilmayer, 'The Moral Significance of Nationalism,' 30-31

priate responses to different national claims we need a theory of nationalism, as without it we will be unable to specify which rights are held on nationalist grounds and which rights are held on other grounds, and to place these claims in a larger, more general, moral framework. Unfortunately scholars of nationalism often misconstrue the grounds of their own justifications, for reasons that are worth examining. In the next section I turn to examine a prominent example of such a confusion.

The Muddy Middle Ground

Individuals embark on the study of nationalism for a variety of personal reasons which influence their theoretical approach. Will Kymlicka's main objective is to protect the needs and rights of the native peoples of Canada as well as of the Quebecois, while sustaining the integrity of the Canadian federation. Brilmayer has in mind the needs and rights of Eritreans, as well as of some other disadvantaged African nations. David Miller views nationalism from a social democratic perspective and deals with its contribution to the development of the welfare state. Neil MacCormick, Joseph Carens, and I each from his/her own national experience attempt to demonstrate that it is possible to reconcile liberal and national values even in circumstances of an ongoing national conflict. And Michael Ignatieff revisits his own past when he travels across lands affected by the most tormented national conflicts, and sees blood and misery wherever he looks. All these approaches are legitimate, but for the purpose of our discussion we need to know which are grounded in a theory of nationalism and draw on national justifications, and which are motivated by considerations of justice.[25] The difference between the two approaches is not, as some may think, between general and particularized arguments, but between two kinds of general abstract theories.

Discussions concerning nationalism, like discussions concerning other political theories, can be held either at an abstract, theoretical

---

25 Note that some approaches will combine both kinds of justifications. Still it will be important to know which kind of justification is grounded in a theory of nationalism and which ones are grounded in other types of theory.

level or at a contextualized one. The former can make use of *a priori* theoretical arguments, aiming to structure general rules, while the latter must be grounded in the contingencies of each case, aiming to offer guidance regarding particular matters. The first level should outline principles, the second should formulate policy recommendations.[26] These two levels ought to nurture each other, but they ought not be dependent on each other, as this might result in unrealistic policies or a misleading theory. This section, then, sends a word of warning against the danger embedded in attempts to structure a theory that would fit the policies one wishes to endorse, thus imposing the contingent limitations of a specific case on a general theoretical structure.

In *Multicultural Citizenship*, Kymlicka attempts to develop a forward-looking theory of minority rights,[27] capable of benefiting those individuals in emerging democracies throughout the world, "looking to the works of Western liberals for guidance regarding the principles of liberal constitutionalism in multinational states."[28] This attempt fails, as Kymlicka tries to structure his theory to fit the unique political needs of the conflict that motivates his search for a theory in the first place.

Guided by a worthy motivation – to secure the rights of native peoples while preserving Canada's federal structure – Kymlicka tends to cluster a variety of justifications reinforcing the right of native peoples to retain their distinct national-cultural identity while dismissing the right of immigrants to do so. In the course of clarifying his terms, Kymlicka unveils the range of political concerns that influenced his decision to distinguish between nations and immigrant groups and, consequently, between a multinational society composed of different national

---

26 The distinction between principles and policies somewhat parallels Max Weber's distinction in 'Politics as a Vocation' between the *ethics of conviction*, which refers to absolute values and need not compromise with reality, and the *ethics of responsibility*, which judges particular situations in a pragmatic fashion, "not leaving absolute moral standards totally out of consideration but at the same time not letting them govern one's political actions." In H.H. Gerth and C. Wright Milles, eds. and trans., *From Max Weber* (London: Routledge, Kegan Paul 1948).

27 W. Kymlicka, *Multicultural Citizenship* (Oxford University Press 1996), 25

28 Kymlicka, *Multicultural Citizenship*, 194

groups and a polyethnic society composed of different ethnic groups. The use of the term 'multiculturalism,' he argues, may lead to confusion, as it might imply that all cultural groups should be treated alike.

But this begs the question: why should different cultural groups, i.e., national minorities and immigrants, be treated differently? Kymlicka's answer, though framed in theoretical terms, is political: granting all cultural groups the same rights may evoke strong political opposition. French Canadians, Kymlicka argues, "have opposed the 'multiculturalism' policy because they think it reduced their claims of nationhood to the level of immigrant ethnicity. Other people had the opposite fear, that the policy was intended to treat immigrant groups as nations, and hence support the development of institutionally complete cultures alongside the French and the English"[29] These fears are certainly legitimate, and prudent politicians will be well advised to take them into account. The question is whether a political theory, especially one aspiring to set general guidelines for groups placed in a variety of political contexts, should be tailored to meet these fears. The answer to this question is obviously no.

Let's take a closer look at Kymlicka's theory in order to illustrate the damages caused by disregarding the distinction between principles and policies. For valuable political reasons Kymlicka embarks on an unsuccessful theoretical attempt to draw a principled distinction between national minorities and immigrant groups. The criteria he offers may fit the Canadian reality, but would not be valid in the Middle East, Asia, or Africa. Are Israeli Jews an immigrant or a national group? The same question could be asked with regard to the Palestinians, and if one looks back a century or two, with regard to most national groups. In fact, even regarding Canadians one may wonder whether French- or English-speaking Canadians are immigrant or national groups.

When does a group change its status? Kymlicka's answer alludes to the notion of *societal culture*. This criterion fails, both as an explanatory tool interpreting and predicting the actual nature of claims put forward by different national groups, and as a justificatory tool defining the kind of rights members of these groups are entitled to. Some national groups,

---

29 Kymlicka, *Multicultural Citizenship*, 17

despite having developed a thick societal culture over generations, may behave like minority groups. Realizing that they are too small, too weak, or territorially divided, they may wish for integration rather than autonomy or secession. The Samaritans are a good example. They are a small, ancient nation – remember the good Samaritan? – with a quite distinctive societal culture, yet with no yearning for independence. Its members acknowledge that, due to their circumstances, the benefits of joining a larger social unit outweigh the costs. The Middle East provides ample illustrations of such groups – Druze, Circassians, Armenians, Bedouins – all fitting this pattern of behaviour. In all these cases, members of small nations develop a set of aspirations similar to that of immigrant groups, not because they lack a structured societal culture but due to other contingencies, mainly size and location.

In contrast, immigrant groups that are large enough, territorially concentrated, and distinct from the majority culture may seek some of the rights traditionally sought by national minorities as was true, for instance, in the case of the Palestinians in Lebanon. Once the Palestinians developed into a sizable group, they endeavoured to change the Lebanese political structure and acquire recognition equal to that of other national groups. This phenomenon has not slipped Kymlicka's attention. He admits that, in theory, immigrants can become national minorities if they settle together and acquire self-governing powers: "After all, this is what happened with English speaking colonists throughout the British Empire, Spanish colonists in Puerto Rico and French colonists in Quebec."[30]

From the point of view of actual claims, we have more of a continuum. On one of its ends stand individuals, who despite their isolation from their communities wish to retain, to the best of their abilities, their communal identity; on the other large national groups, which are territorially concentrated and culturally and politically organized, are to be found. The precise location of each group along this continuum reflects its contingent conditions: its size, territorial position, history, political organization, etc. All of these factors, and many others, must be taken into consideration in the making of actual political demands,

---

30 Kymlicka, *Multicultural Citizenship*, 15

but can they determine the kind of rights to which individuals on different points along the continuum are entitled?

Making entitlements depend on contingencies leads to grave injustice. Let me explain this latter point: Suppose that a given set of circumstances precludes the translation of certain political principles into policy. For instance, let us assume that individuals who are entitled to enjoy certain national rights are unable, due to a wide range of contingencies, to implement these rights. Can we deduce from such a case that the principled justification of their rights is faulty, or that it should be modified? I think not; all that we can learn from an analysis of such a case is that in certain circumstances principles must be compromised. The awareness that circumstances have forced us to compromise our principles is, in itself, significant, as it calls for an attempt to change the limiting circumstances, to offer those who have been harmed some compensating measures, or, if neither option is feasible, at least to acknowledge the injustice done.[31]

Kymlicka's theory is an example of a case in which the weaving of actual political considerations into principles leads to a disquieting inequality of treatment. Kymlicka's theory gives preference to members of minority nations over members of immigrant groups. Such privileging is presented not as a compromise forced by the complexity of the Canadian reality but as a principle. Consequently, not only are members of immigrant groups disadvantaged in comparison to members of national minorities, they also lose their ground for complaint – in the Canadian case as well as in all other cases in which Kymlicka's theory will be adopted.

Let us take a closer look at the implications of Kymlicka's theory. According to this theory, as French Canadians constitute a national

---

31 In her intriguing discussion of the faces of injustice, *The Faces of Injustice* (New Haven: Yale University Press 1990), Judith Shklar reminds us that the definition of injustice is social and political. What usually passes for an injustice "is an act that goes against **some known legal or ethical rule**. Only a victim whose complaints match the rule-governed prohibitions has suffered an injustice. If there is no fit, it is only a matter of the victim's subjective reaction, a misfortune, not **really** unjust." Injustice may sometimes be unavoidable, but we must not ignore it. Our normative rules ought to be structured so as to help us judge what is the best thing to do in each particular case, and to acknowledge injustice even when unable to alleviate it or forced to impose it.

minority in Canada "a group of francophone parents can demand a French school where numbers warrant" while a group of Greeks, who "are not a national minority in Canada,"[32] are not entitled to either individual or collective rights regarding the official recognition of their mother tongue. Why should the state support the rights of francophones and native Indians but not of Greek parents to have classes for their children in their native language? (Assume that in both cases a certain threshold number of interested individual exists.)

One possible answer is that the claims raised by members of national groups are of a stronger moral status than those of immigrants. I would agree that, in the Canadian case, this is indeed true. Nevertheless, this conclusion does not follow from a principled claim suggesting that national minorities ought to have certain national rights immigrants lack, but rather from additional reasons supporting, in the Canadian case, the rights of native peoples. This becomes obvious when one analyzes Kymlicka's justifications for granting special rights to native peoples. In the process of so doing he clusters arguments grounded in four different kinds of justifications:

1. **Granting individuals cultural-national rights**. As cultural-national membership is of immense significance to individuals; they have an essential interest in preserving it and a correlating right to do so.[33]

2. **Remedying injustice**. Individuals placed in a disadvantaged position due to some social action ought to be compensated. If granting them a certain liberty or power is the only way of compensating them for the injustice they suffered, it should be granted.

3. **Keeping promises or respecting contracts**. When individuals have voluntarily joined a political framework and were promised, or it was contracted with them, that they would enjoy a certain political arrangement, the promise or the contract should be respected.

---

32 Kymlicka, *Multicultural Citizenship*, 46

33 The structure of this claim follows J. Raz's definition of a right in *The Morality of Freedom* (Oxford: Oxford University Press 1986), 165–192.

4. **Improving representative democracy**. If electoral policies could be reformed to allow individuals, especially members of disadvantaged groups, better representation and better protection of their legitimate interests, such reforms should be welcome.

Only the first category of justifications is grounded in a theory of nationalism, as it refers to the importance of cultural and national identity to individuals. The other three categories are based on arguments drawn from liberal democratic theory: groups other than national minorities are also entitled to compensation if harmed; contracts should be respected whoever they benefit; and there are good reasons to improve the representation of all sectors of the population. In the case of Canadian native peoples all four kinds of justifications overlap and strengthen each other. Hence, Kymlicka's claim that the Canadian federal state should grant native peoples some preferences over immigrant groups is justified. But the grounds he offers for this distinctive treatment are flawed, and if carried to another context may promote injustice.

Just policies should take all the justifications into account. A theory of minority rights, however, should draw these justifications apart and analyze each component on its own. Two advantages ensue from upholding the distinction between principles and policies. The first concerns the ability to formulate a political theory free of the immediate pressures which are characteristic of conflictual situations. The second concerns the ability to formulate effective policies that might fall short of what is demanded by the relevant principles, without ignoring the gap between what is morally justified and what is presently attainable. When principles and policies are forced to overlap in a non-ideal world, either the policies would be too ideal to implement or the principles would be flawed and too conservative. What we need, then, is both an abstract theory of nationalism and actual policies.

In Defense of an Abstract Theory

A theory of nationalism must structure itself independently of all contingencies. Its basis must be a systematic view of human nature and of the world order, as well as a coherent set of universally applicable values. Some may find the abstract, decontextualized nature of such a theory frustrating, as the guidance it offers appears too vague. But this is true of most political theories which require translation into actual policies via a process of specification. No theory either can, or should, provide a chart including all the necessary modes of action demanded in each particular circumstance. No theory of freedom of speech can provide a final list of all the cases in which free speech should be protected. And no theory of justice can suggest *a priori* who should get what without resorting to socio-economic data. In this respect, then, a theory of nationalism, like all other political theories, must be constructed in the abstract but cannot be implemented outside of a particular context.

It must generate some general principles which allow a critical evaluation of different nationalist claims and of the policies designed to meet them. It may also allow one to distinguish between a theory of nationalism and policies adopted by nationalistic parties (as one distinguishes between democratic, communist, or liberal theory and specific policies pursued by Communist, Democratic, or Liberal parties).

Although the grounds shared by all theories of nationalism may be rather slim, every theory of nationalism must begin with two descriptive assertions:

1. Humanity is divided into nations.

2. There are criteria for identifying a nation and its members.

These descriptive claims, however, need not be followed by a theory of nationalism. In fact, it would be entirely coherent to proceed from the above descriptive claims to a disapproving evaluation of nationalism, claiming that the division of the world into nations is destructive and consequently encouraging attempts to develop individualistic attitudes and a purely cosmopolitan consciousness.

A theory of nationalism must take the opposite route, namely, it must follow the descriptive claims mentioned above by normative claims favouring a national world structure. Depending on the particular theory of nationalism in which they are grounded, such normative claims could draw on a broad spectrum of justifications that support the importance of a national world order. Such justifications may include: metaphysical claims that attribute national diversity to God's will, psychological claims concerning the human need to structure personal identity in relation to others, and economic arguments linking nationalism with economic development. Normative support for the plurality of nations can be grounded in the instrumental value of national membership for individuals, either as a background for strong evaluation and choice, for self-development and self-expression, and most importantly, for self-esteem.[34] Or it can offer a more organic description of society, suggesting that individuals cannot function outside a national cultural context.

From a communitarian point of view, other instrumental justifications for a national world order could be invoked. Reference could be made to the important contribution of a shared national identity for improving social communication and ensuring better understanding and cooperation, or for creating a sense of togetherness that can help sustain mutual responsibilities not only among all living members of a community but also among past and future generations. One could, as John Stuart Mill did, point to the importance of national homogeneity for democracy, or to the importance of nationalism in promoting willingness to transcend egoistic concerns and in extreme circumstances sacrifice oneself for the common good.[35]

Such normative claims must be followed by a set of prescriptive claims concerning the means necessary to ensure the preservation of a national world order, as well as the welfare and prosperity of each particular nation. Among these means, the most important ones are those necessary for expressing and cultivating a shared national identity in the public space. These means justify linking the cultural and political aspects of nationalism, and they support demands for a distinctively national political sphere.[36]

---

34 See mainly the writings of Charles Taylor, on this matter especially *Human Agency and Language* (Cambridge: Cambridge University Press 1985) and 'The Politics of Recognition,' in A. Gutmann, ed., *Multiculturalism: Examining The Politics of Recognition* (Princeton, NJ: Princeton University Press 1994).

35 See J. S. Mill, *Representative Government* (esp. chap. 16) and D. Miller, *On Nationality* (Oxford: Oxford University Press 1995).

36 Defining the desire to preserve and enhance the national or cultural identity as the shared grounds of all theories of nationalism challenges the widely accepted

A theory of nationalism is thus marked by a particular set of descriptive statements, which is followed by normative claims emphasizing the moral, social, and psychological importance of national and cultural membership, and then by a inventory of means necessary to secure it. And yet, theories of nationalism differ quite considerably. Their disagreement can be traced to three substantive issues:

1. The nature of the relations between the nation and its individual members

2. The normative justifications for the existence of nations

3. The political aspirations that nationalism supports

All theories of nationalism advance a normative claim supporting the preservation and development of national frameworks as such, disregarding their particularistic features. Inevitably, such theories embody a general commitment to the existence of all national groups, alongside a particularistic commitment to the survival and flourishing of each nation. In this sense, theories of nationalism are necessarily polycentric and advance a reiterated view of nationalism from which a universal notion of national rights could be derived.[37] No wonder, then, that nationalists committed to advancing their own national case, as well as scholars of nationalism committed to promoting certain specific claims concerning the needs of some nations who suffered severe injustice, are reluctant to turn to such a theory in search of support for their claims.

---

interpretation of nationalism as necessarily prescribing the creation of a nation-state. The statist approach to nationalism is misleading in its endorsement of a specific political solution, which was popular in a particular historical setting as the sole end and the only true interpretation of nationalism.

37 For a discussion of polycentric nationalism see A. Smith, *Theories of Nationalism* (London: Duckworth 1983); for the idea of reiterated nationalism see M. Walzer, 'Two Kinds of Universalism,' Tanner Lecture, Oxford, 1989.

Between Abstraction and Particularities

Those who criticize attempts to construct theories of nationalism find such theories less captivating and moving than journalistic accounts of nationalist struggles, less intriguing and informative than most historical and sociological analyses, and less poetic than nationalist narratives. Criticizing my own attempt to construct a theory of nationalism, Tony Judt claims that it is "disappointingly dry and abstract," and, as it is lacking in detailed examples, "everything hinges on the logic and consistency of the concepts."[38]

I believe Judt's disappointment reflects an interdisciplinary disagreement. The study of nationalism, he argues, cannot proceed in the abstract, it must draw on the plurality of national experiences, rely on actual case studies, and be grounded in ample examples and references to particular national narratives. In short, it should look more like a sociological or anthropological inquiry than a philosophical one.

Is Judt right? Must a theory of nationalism draw on the plurality of national experiences, rely on actual case studies, and support itself with ample examples and references to particular national narratives? In short, must it look more like a sociological or anthropological theory than a philosophical one?

For political theory in general, the role and importance of examples is a sore question. Can examples explain, support, prove, or refute a political theory? What are the theoretical implications of the historical and sociological details of the Canadian case, in which the national struggle did not deteriorate into violence? What can we learn from the fact that in the case of Northern Ireland it did? What are the lessons of the Nazi example, by far the most widely quoted one?

Unfortunately, this question is seldom discussed. A rare exception is an exchange between Ronald Dworkin and Michael Walzer. The occasion is the publication of Walzer's *Spheres of Justice*[39] which offers an innovative way of thinking not only about justice but also about meth-

---

38 T. Judt, 'The New Old Nationalism,' *New York Review of Books*, 26 May 1994, 49–50

39 M. Walzer, *Spheres of Justice* (Oxford: Blackwell 1983)

odological issues. Walzer structures his argument using actual examples, thus hoping to break the grip of the formal style prevalent in Anglo-American political philosophy in recent years. In his review,[40] Dworkin questions the success of Walzer's attempt. Instead of expounding an abstract argument, he complains, Walzer offers anecdotal and historical examples of how in various societies, including our own, different principles of distribution have evolved. The wide range of examples Walzer draws on – from the meritocracies of China under the dynasties, to the Kula practices of gift exchanges among Trobriand islanders, to questions of education among the Aztecs – is captivating, Dworkin admits. It can widen our horizon and enrich our imagination, and yet it cannot substitute for a theory that could serve as an evaluative tool. We cannot leave justice to convention and anecdotes, Dworkin concludes. This conclusion applies to theories of nationalism as well. No amount of nationalist anecdotes can, on its own, offer sound grounds for a theory of nationalism.

The purpose of political theory, Plamenatz claims, "is not to tell us how things happen in the world, inside our minds or outside them; its purpose is to help us decide what to do and how to go about doing it. To achieve that purpose, it must be systematic, self-consistent, and *realistic*."[41] If political theory is to present a realistic utopia, it must be grounded in knowledge of some basic social facts. And yet, when one looks at the most important contributions to political theory in the last two decades, those of Oakeshott, Rawls, Dworkin, and Nozick, "it is noticeable that none of these combines the philosophical analysis of political principles with an empirical understanding of political processes in a wholly successful way. Their work is philosophically sophisticated but poorly-grounded empirically, and highly vulnerable to criticism of social scientists."[42] These political philosophers share the belief that "it would be more promising to focus upon a fundamental

---

40 R. Dworkin, 'To Each His Own,' *New York Review of Books*, 14 April 1983

41 Plamenatz, *Consent, Freedom and Political Obligation*, 29

42 On the problem of abstraction in political theory, see M. Walzer and R. Dworkin, '"Spheres of Justice": An Exchange," *New York Review of Books*, 21 July 1983.

abstract description that would encompass all situations of interests…"[43] And yet none of them suggests that we should ignore social knowledge all together. What must we know and what ought we ignore when constructing a political theory?

Rawls's constructive thought experiment offers one possible answer. The purpose of the experiment is to find the most just and desirable way to govern a society in light of a *given* set of shared values and some basic social facts that are relevant to moral judgments. The process starts with a definition of the epistemological boundaries of the deliberations. These boundaries are determined by the veil of ignorance on the one hand and a set of basic social facts on the other. The veil conceals from the parties those facts that are morally irrelevant. The arbitrariness of the world must be corrected, Rawls argues, "by adjusting the circumstance[s] of the initial contractual situation."[44] Yet some facts concerning the basis of social organization and the laws of human psychology cannot be ignored.

> Indeed, the parties are presumed to know whatever **general facts affect the choice of principles** of justice. There are no limitations on **general** information, that is, on **general laws and theories**, since conceptions of justice must be adjusted to the characteristics of the system of social cooperation which they are to regulate, and *there is no reason* to rule out these facts.[45]

It thus seems that there must be a distinction between general knowledge and contingent matters. The former is necessary for the construction of a theory of justice; the latter is destructive for that same purpose.

How are we to determine which kind of knowledge falls under what description? What is a proper reason to include a certain fact or exclude it? The question of what kind of knowledge is, or isn't, relevant for moral deliberations is bitterly debatable. Does the distribution of personal talents count as a contingent fact that morality should disregard or is it a social fact that a theory cannot ignore? Is the unequal

---

43 R. Nozick, *Anarchy, State and Utopia* (New York: Basic Books 1974), 4

44 J. Rawls, *A Theory of Justice* (Cambridge: Harvard University Press 1971), 141 (my emphasis)

45 Rawls, *A Theory of Justice*, 139.

distribution of resources to be seen as a basic social fact or a contingent one? What about the differences between the genders? And how should the distribution of the world into nations be regarded? How should we treat the reoccurrence of national-ethnic violence? This debate *cannot* be settled on the basis of particular test cases, or actual case studies, but only on the basis of abstract principles.

Like all other political theories, theories of nationalism must start by classifying different facts as general or contingent, relevant or irrelevant. In my own work I have claimed that such a theory must take into account general facts concerning the existence of nations, the role they play in human history, and their importance for their members. It should ignore the status, size, wealth, and power of each particular nation, as this knowledge is morally irrelevant.[46] Like all decisions of this kind, it is a debatable one, but looking at more examples will not save it from being essentially contestable. What is needed are not more examples and more test cases, but more elaborate argumentation that would expose the basic presuppositions each theory relies upon (a task most political philosophers regretfully neglect).

While deliberating on the role of political theories, Ira Katznelson acknowledges that raising the level of abstraction may allow for the desirable philosophical rigour. And yet he worries that these advantages may be achieved at the cost of grave shortcomings: "So much so that this work risks dismissal as being beside the point in our disordered, disarranged world. Yet the historical and sociological temptation promoted as an alternative by Judt threatens to leave our attempts to discover decent ways of living unguided by useful theory or standards."[47] At the end of the day the criterion for accepting a theory or as set of standards as a guide must be that, in view of some set of abstract principles, they seem right, rather than that they have been captured in some conventional practice. As Dworkin states, "Otherwise politi-

---

46 Judt's criticism, according to which a veil which allows members to acknowledge the general division of the world into nations and the fact that they themselves are members of such nations "isn't hiding anything significant," is based on a misunderstanding of the role of the veil.

47 I. Katznelson, *Liberalism's Crooked Circle: Letters to Adam Michnik* (Princeton, NJ: Princeton University Press 1996), 160

cal theory will be only a mirror, uselessly reflecting a community's consensus and divisions back upon itself."[48]

Those who criticize the appeal to the abstract principles often expect these principles to do more than they possibly can. These expectations are grounded in the confusion between policy recommendations and guiding principles discussed earlier. Political theory, Judt argues, must aim at guiding judgments and promoting action; hence, it requires particularity as well as sociologically and politically plausible stories about the world. From this perspective, he asserts, it hardly makes sense to treat national membership as an abstract position. It is rather a "very particular, contingent, partial and variable, historical condition."[49]

The exact distance between a political theory and the social facts it relies upon is hard to define. The decision concerning which facts count for what purpose may be the most difficult decision a political philosopher makes. Hence, I can offer no solution to this debate. All I can say by way of conclusion is that contingent facts and particular narratives are indeed important for some purposes but are irrelevant, and even disruptive, to the construction of a general theory. As the discussion of Kymlicka's latest work revealed, when a set of excellent policy recommendations tailored to fit a particular conflict are presented as a general theory, that theory is likely to be misleading and may, at times, promote actual injustice.

I want to end where I began, and argue that the construction of an abstract theory of nationalism is both a necessary and a feasible task. Some may indeed benefit from sustaining nationalism's non-theoretical reputation, but their gains do not deserve our support. In fact, we need a theory of nationalism in order to undermine these gains, to remind national movements that other national groups enjoy the same rights they do, to encourage scholars of nationalism to evaluate national demands on their own merits while disregarding their own sympathies, and to warn writers of theories of nationalism against letting the national conflict that motivates them be the sole guide to their perception of nationalism.

---

48 R. Dworkin, 'Reply,' *New York Review of Books*, 21 July 1983

49 T. Judt, 'Reply,' *New York Review of Books*, 23 June 1994, 64

CANADIAN JOURNAL OF PHILOSOPHY
Supplementary Volume 22

Is Nationalism Legitimate?
A Sociological Perspective
on a Philosophical Question[1]

LIAH GREENFELD
Boston University

To answer, or even consider, the question 'Is nationalism legitimate?', whether from the sociological or ethical, philosophical point of view, it is first necessary to define what nationalism is or, in other words, to understand its nature and the source of its appeal. As concerns nationalism's definition, there are several points, in regard to which there exists among the students of the phenomenon more or less general agreement, but which, nevertheless, should be emphasized at the outset:

1. Nationalism is a modern phenomenon: for most of its recorded history humanity has not known it; it emerged quite recently and therefore cannot be seen as an automatic response to some universal need; its very historicity presupposes that it is essentially a cultural and not a psychological phenomenon, and that, as any cultural phenomenon, it can develop, take various forms within certain limits, and disappear.

2. Nationalism is a species of identity; whatever else it refers to, it refers first and foremost to the set of ideas and sentiments forming the framework of the identity we call *national*, which is one of the numerous identities human beings and groups can have and, in the course of history, have had, such as religious, class or estate, territorial, occupational, gender identities, or what not. No human group of any duration and no human being, unless severely handicapped or as yet undeveloped mentally (as in early infancy), exists without *an* identity: it appears to be a psychological imperative and thus a sociological con-

---

1 An earlier version of this paper was delivered at the Conference on the Ethics of Nationalism, 22–24 April 1994, University of Illinois at Urbana-Champaign.

stant. But although the development of some identity is inevitable, the emergence of any specific identity – for example, *national* identity – is always, at its roots, a matter of historical contingency; there is nothing in the human nature, and therefore in society in general, which makes any specific identity necessary.

An identity defines a person's – and a group's – position in the social world; it carries within expectations which its bearer, whether an individual or a collectivity, can legitimately have, and defines what can be legitimately expected of the latter, thus orienting the bearer's actions. The least specialized identity that is believed to define the bearer's very essence and, as a result, shapes behaviour in a wide variety of social contexts reflects, and in fact contains in a microcosm, the image of social order or the *social consciousness* of the given society. In the modern world, national identity, rather than any other, has been such a generalized identity. Its framework, nationalism, thus has also been the framework of the modern social consciousness.

Which leads us to the third point.

3. The image of the social order encapsulated in nationalism is a fundamentally secular image; it both is focused on this world and perceives it as autonomous and ultimately meaningful in its own right, thereby sacralizing the mundane. It is in this sense that nationalism, which is comparable to religion because the two are in a very significant measure functionally equivalent (both represent ways to interpret – that is, invest with meaning – the meaningless reality, providing prisms through which it is to be perceived and with those prisms the sense of order), is more usefully conceptualized as a species of political ideology ('political' being defined in the broadest sense of the multiple and heterogeneous facets of human association).

The essence of this ideological species consists in two notions: the notion of the essential equality of the members of the nation (this is the fundamental notion of the social consciousness in the framework of nationalism), and the notion of popular sovereignty (the fundamental notion of the political consciousness in the framework of nationalism).[2] In distinction to other identities, national identity is an identity which

---

2 See extended discussion in Greenfeld, *Nationalism: Five Roads to Modernity* (Cambridge, MA: Harvard University Press 1992), specifically in the Introduction.

derives from the membership in a 'people' which is seen as the bearer of sovereignty, the central object of loyalty, and the basis of collective solidarity. The 'people' is a mass of population whose boundaries and nature are defined in various ways, but which is perceived usually as larger than any concrete community and always as fundamentally homogeneous (essentially as a community of equals) and only super-ficially divided by the lines of status, class, locality, or (in rare cases) even ethnicity. This interpretation of 'people' is implied in its defini-tion as a 'nation.' At the time when the word 'nation' acquired its mod-ern meaning and became the synonym of the 'people' it meant 'an elite,' and specifically 'an elite of representatives of cultural and political authority.'[3] It was in this meaning that it was applied, in the early six-teenth century, to the people of England, making England the birth-place of nationalism and the first nation in the contemporary sense of the word. The word 'people' at that time specifically referred to the lower classes; it meant 'rabble' or 'plebs.' Its equation with the 'na-tion,' therefore, signified nothing less than a conceptual revolution and symbolically elevated the populace to the dignity of an elite. Every member of the 'people' defined as 'nation' partakes in its superior, elite quality, and it is for this reason that a stratified national population is perceived as essentially homogeneous and the people as sovereign, and that nationalism guarantees status.

This remarkable guarantee, as I have argued in *Nationalism* and per-haps more explicitly in the essay 'Transcending the Nation's Worth' in *Daedalus*,[4] which distinguishes national identity from many other iden-tities, has been the source of nationalism's enduring appeal. 'The worth of the nation' – the psychological gratification afforded by national iden-tity and therefore its importance – is inseparably related to the experi-ence of dignity within wide and ever widening sectors of humanity. Quite apart from the fact that the first nations (England, France) were

---

3 Guido Zernatto, 'Nation: The History of the Word,' *Review of Politics* 6 (1944) 351-66

4 Liah Greenfeld, 'Transcending the Nation's Worth,' *Daedalus* (Summer 1993), 47-62. See also my review of Jacob Talmon's *Myth of the Nation and Vision of Revolution* in *History and Theory* 32:3 (October 1993) 339-49.

the dominant Western societies, which made nationalism the political canon, it was this status- and dignity-guaranteeing quality that recommended nationalism as a potent solution to European (and later other) elites whose status was threatened or who were prevented from achieving the status they aspired to, and that ensured the spread of nationalism throughout the world in the last two centuries.

In the following pages (96–99), I shall have to repeat myself and reiterate some arguments I made elsewhere.[5] I would not claim, as does Francis Fukuyama, that the experience of dignity (or social recognition) is essential to human life, since during most of the recorded history most men and women lived without dignity. It is not status attainment, but status maintenance (which applies to low status as much as to high status) which is essential, and during most of human history only high status (that is a very small minority of social positions) was associated with dignity. Yet, dignity is addictive: having known it, one can no longer be happy without it. Who better to quote in support of this claim than the founding father of the discipline of economics and the author of *The Wealth of Nations*, Adam Smith? However disconcerting this may be to those who see in him the advocate of the primacy of economic factors, he considered status to be "the cause of all the tumult and bustle, all the rapine and injustice, which avarice and ambition have introduced into this world." Dignity, said Smith, "when once it has got entire possession of the breast, will admit neither a rival nor a successor. To those who have been accustomed to the possession or even to the hope of public admiration, all other pleasures sicken and decay."[6]

It is safe to assume that in the modern society people will never agree to be deprived of dignity which they acquired with nationality. It is this that explains the staying power of nationalism in the face of the economic interests that ostensibly pull in the other direction and even in the face of the interest of self-preservation, which, many of us believe, should have the same overriding importance for human beings as it does for animals. It is indeed a lesson of recent and ongoing

---

5   Greenfeld, 'Transcending the Nation's Worth'

6   Adam Smith, *The Theory of Moral Sentiments*, D.D. Raphael and L.A. Macfie, eds. (Indianapolis: Liberty Classics 1982), 57

events that people are not animals and that they value survival, whether physical or economic, less than their pride.

In the early days of nationalism, different elite groups which were exposed to nationalist ideas reacted differently to them, in accordance with the relative ability of nationalism to aid them in their status-maintaining and status-aggrandizing pursuits. An interesting example is furnished by the nobility in various German lands who as late as the 1800s remained indifferent to the appeal of nationalism, embracing it rather reluctantly during the wars of liberation. Throughout the eighteenth century, when the French and the Russian nobilities converted to nationalism *en masse*, and until its defeats at the hands of Napoleon, the German nobility enjoyed undisturbed social ascendancy. It was content, its status was as exclusive as ever, and there was no reason why it would welcome anyone else to partake in it. Nationalism had no appeal for this nobility and could offer it nothing. In both France and Russia, in distinction, the status of the nobility was threatened, its exclusivity long gone and its dignity, therefore, devalued; in both countries nobles felt humiliated by the central power and deprived of any power of their own. It was thus worthwhile for them to discard the old – estate – identity, which bred expectations of dignity but no longer provided the means to satisfy them and so condemned one to a life of frustration and fear that whatever remained of one's status would be lost, and adopt a new – national – identity, which redefined the nobility's relations with the central power and guaranteed status and dignity.

In the case of non-noble intellectuals (the second of the two elite groups that were responsible for the initial establishment of nationalism in Europe), the idea of the nation also had to compete with other status-bestowing frameworks. As long as other identities appeared to promise more dignity, it failed to captivate these intellectuals or secure their commitments. French *philosophes* were above particularistic self-content. Voltaire thought that "a philosopher has no *patrie* and belongs to no faction" and that "every man is born with the natural right to choose his *patrie* for himself." Abbe Raynal believed that "the *patrie* of a great man is the universe." Great men, explained Duclos, "men of merit, whatever the nation of their origin, form one nation among themselves. They are free of puerile national vanity. They leave it to the vulgar, to those who, having no personal glory, have to content themselves with the glory of their countrymen."[7] (It was the same consideration, I am certain, that led Samuel Johnson to define 'patriotism' as the last refuge of a scoundrel.) So long as one could reasonably hope to become world-famous (and French *philosophes* in the mid-eighteenth century still had a reasonable chance of that), it was foolish to limit oneself to a small part of the world; and if one was confident in one's superiority and felt assured of recognition, one had no need of the shared dignity of a nation. In fact, one had no need of a nation at all; the *republic of letters* was enough. Ironically, at the very time when French *philosophes* dismissed the nation as too small for their grand designs and exhibited such confidence in their ability to win the hearts of audiences – and therefore prestige – everywhere, audiences everywhere in Europe were, in fact, closing their hearts to them, owing to no small degree to this confidence, making such conquests very difficult and the nation the only place where one could reasonably hope to make them. Another reason why French eighteenth-century intellectuals were hesitant about nationalism was the fact that, as a result of the crisis and the redefinition of the nobility, the latter opened its doors to talent, and noble status was dignified enough for low-born luminaries. It was the nobility's giving up on itself that eventually persuaded many intellectuals to give up their hope of joining the nobility and turn national patriots instead.

German nationalism was a later development than the French, and German intellectuals remained faithful to their cosmopolitan ideals long after their French brethren abandoned theirs. Nicolai considered German nationalism "a political monstrosity"; Schiller claimed to have lost his fatherland "to exchange it for the great world" and wrote "as a citizen of the world." Fichte was a principled cosmopolitan as late as 1799. When, accused of atheism, he lost his professorship at Jena, he hoped for French victory in Germany (for nothing was more certain to him "than the fact that unless the French achieve the most tremendous superiority [there], no German who is known for ever having expressed

---

7 Voltaire, 'Reflexions sur l'histoire,' and 'Annales de l'empire,' in *Oeuvres completes*, v. XXV, 170; v. XIII, 513; Guillaume-Thomas-François de Raynal, *Histoire philosophique et politique des établissements et du commerce des Européens dans les deux Indes* (Geneva: 1775), v. V, 10; Charles-Pinot Duclos, 'Considerations sur les moeurs de ce siècle' in *Oeuvres diverses* (Paris: Dessesartes 1802), 10

a free thought will in a few years find a secure place") and asked to be employed by the French Republic.[8] Nationalism lacked an appeal to German intellectuals before the Napoleonic campaign because they were the only group interested in the redistribution of prestige in society, and, without the support of the nobility and the bureaucracy, they lacked the means to enforce it. To insist on such a redistribution (implied in the idea of the nation) in this situation would only invite ridicule and damage the chances of social advancement some of them had. It was more satisfying to dream that one was an equal member of a community of intellectuals and hope for the recognition of that community (even though in the case of German intellectuals such a hope in the eighteenth century was not reasonable), for this at least would not be laughed at. Nationalism was irrelevant and the nation worthless. The French invasion made it worthwhile. It created a community of interest between the intellectuals and the higher classes, who, so forbidding and inaccessible before in their superiority, now allowed the intellectuals – in fact welcomed them – to take part in their worries and sorrows. What the nobility and the intellectuals shared, and what made the nobles look favorably on intellectuals, was that they were Germans. While cosmopolitanism and the idea of a world intellectual community offered German intellectuals a form of escape, a possibility to dream about social fulfillment and advancement, partnership in a nation offered real possibilities of such advancement.

These examples may be multiplied. Their collective message is that the appeal of nationalism has varied in accordance with the possibilities for dignified status that national identity could offer, whether to all or to a specific group among the presumed members of the nation, and with the availability of (or belief in) other means of status enhancement. So far, attempts to transcend or displace nationalism have been rare and unsuccessful, both because nationalism usually has been able to satisfy people's need for dignity and because for the great majority there were no alternative means to satisfy this need.

---

8 G. P. Gooch, *Germany and the French Revolution* (New York: Russell and Russell 1966), 33-34; Hans Kohn, 'The Paradox of Fichte's Nationalism,' *Journal of the History of Ideas* **10**:3 (June 1949) 321

The question of nationalism's legitimacy is not directly related to its functionality, because numerous highly functional practices (for example, drug dealing or cheating at school) and views (for example, in the United States, the view that some races are superior to others or that women are naturally predisposed to stay at home tending to their children, rather than to develop careers which take them away from domestic duties) are obviously not legitimate. The question of legitimacy, therefore, must be dealt with separately. Is nationalism, which, as it heightens people's sense of dignity and self-respect, also often drives them to degrade, persecute, and kill their fellow-men, legitimate? From the sociological point of view, the answer is: yes, of course.

The sociological definition of 'legitimacy' is very close to its dictionary definition: 'legitimate' means "conforming to accepted rules." The legitimacy of a system is expressed in (to quote Weber) the "probability that [given the rules] to a relevant degree the appropriate attitudes will exist, and the corresponding practical conduct ensue."[9] If nationalism, representing the framework of the image of order or social consciousness in a modern society, thereby dictates the rules, it is legitimate by definition; in fact, it forms the framework of legitimacy in every given case, outside of which questions of legitimacy cannot be even asked.

In sociological discourse, the concept of 'legitimacy' gives a formal expression to the understanding of 'morality' and 'justice' as sociological phenomena. In effect, from the sociological point of view, 'legitimacy,' 'morality,' and 'justice' are equivalent: what is 'legitimate' is also, sociologically speaking, 'moral' and 'just.' All three are empty concepts in the sense that their historical and cultural contents are provisional and changeable, unlike, for example, 'capitalism,' or, for that matter 'nationalism,' which are 'historical individuals,' and, as concepts, are therefore necessarily linked to a specific historical and cultural baggage, which cannot be replaced without changing the concepts themselves. All three refer to systems of socially accepted beliefs and values, assuming as a matter of course that such systems are variable, and thus reflecting the *empirical law* of sociological relativism.

---

9 Max Weber, *Economy and Society* (Berkeley & Los Angeles: University of California Press 1978), v. 1, 214

It was, perhaps, Émile Durkheim who came up with the most forceful statement of this fundamental datum of sociology, which alone justifies its existence as a separate empirical discipline (rather than a branch of biology or psychology). For Durkheim every enduring society was, by definition, a moral community; moral life could only be social life, life in solidarity with fellow members of one's society, and anything social, anything contributing to this solidarity, was moral (and thus, obviously, legitimate). In an exaggerated and striking form this notion was expressed by Durkheim in the statements that God was society and that religion was society worshipping itself.[10] As any proposition on the nature of divinity, these statements cannot be either conclusively proven or refuted, and it is good form to profess agnosticism in their regard. But our respect for the beliefs of others should not prevent us from recognizing that, so far as empirical evidence is concerned (which, admittedly, may be quite irrelevant in this context), Durkheim's sociological theology allows us to account for certain puzzling regularities, which other theologies can only dismiss, specifically, the indisputable fact that notions and interpretations of the divine vary across societies.

The recognition that each society creates its own morals and defines its own legitimacy has very serious implications in regard to the foundations of moral judgment we pass on social systems different from our own and the legitimacy of assessing their legitimacy in terms other than those they themselves provide. In fact, it implies nothing less than the admission that, as self-contained moral universes, different social systems are morally incomparable, and thus should be considered morally equivalent or neutral. There is no moral yardstick external to and thus equally applicable to all of them; based on standards of legitimacy accepted within a certain social system, moral judgment loses its legitimacy the moment it leaves the framework within which it originates; it becomes nonsensical (for it is outside a context where it can make sense) and literally arbitrary. For example, in the case of nationalism, sociological relativism implies that if a society considers ethnic cleansing moral and legitimate (if, to operationalize this proposition, it is probable that a

---

10 See, in particular, E. Durkheim, *The Elementary Forms of Religious Life*, but also *Division of Labor in Society* and *Rules of Sociological Method*.

sufficient number of people would consider ethnic cleansing acceptable to the extent that they would not interfere with it, and a sufficient number would willingly participate in it), then it is moral and legitimate.

Sociological relativism deprives us of the pleasure to feel, by right of our membership in a certain society – or, for the purpose of our discussion, nation – morally superior to other human beings who are members in other societies or nations. From the sociological point of view, it makes no sense, and, therefore, is unjustifiable, to claim that, the United States, for example, is a more moral society than, let's say, Nazi Germany or the Soviet Union, or that the Soviet Union was 'an evil empire,' because, sociologically speaking, evil empires cannot exist.

It is a truism, however, that value-judgments do not derive from and cannot be justified by empirical regularities.[11] This applies to the relationship between sociological relativism and moral relativism as much as to any other. Sociological relativism is a statement of an empirical regularity; as such it does not – and cannot – imply moral relativism, which is an expression of a value-judgment. Sociological relativism by no means precludes moral judgment *within* frameworks in which it can properly be made or the judgment of the agents of moral choice – individuals; in fact, it makes moral choice imperative and fully justifies such judgment. Moral choice has little to do with subscribing to values one believes absolute, which is a matter of conformity; moral conduct, in such circumstances, may be not a question of will, but of pliancy and even cowardice. Subscribing to values one knows to be relative, in contrast, is necessarily a matter of choice. The recognition that our values are relative necessitates an *active* commitment to them, a realization that, *for us*, they must be absolute. I am prepared to make sacrifices for the values I hold dear, not because here I stand and I can do no other, but because I take a stand, I have freely chosen to do so, and by my choice I have bound myself to a certain course of action. And I can judge moral actors in Nazi Germany, the Soviet Union, or Serbia (provided I take into consideration their circumstances), because I assume on the basis of empirical evidence that they too are aware of

---

11 The classical argument behind this proposition is Max Weber, 'Objectivity in Social Sciences,' 50-112 in Max Weber, *The Methodology of the Social Sciences* (New York: The Free Press 1949).

the relativity of their values and multiplicity of alternatives, and, similarly to myself, can, and are in fact required, to make a choice.

This brings me back to the question of the legitimacy of nationalism. The fact that, sociologically speaking, nationalism is legitimate, and murderous nationalism, for instance in the former Yugoslavia, for the simple reason of its being acceptable to a sufficient number of its residents, is as legitimate as a benevolent nationalism (called 'national feeling' so as to sound inoffensive) some place else, does not mean that we are under an obligation to like, or even tolerate, every particular nationalism. So should we, *given our values*, like it? The answer to this question is: this depends on the variety of nationalism.

As I have argued on several occasions, nationalism is not, contrary to the widespread opinion, a uniform phenomenon. There exist several types of nationalism which differ dramatically in their social and political implications and in their possible effects on the quality of people's lives. I believe it is possible to distinguish three types of nationalism, depending on the definition of the nation and the criteria of membership in it: the individualistic and civic type of nationalism, the collectivistic and civic type of nationalism, and the collectivistic and ethnic type of nationalism.

I shall very briefly recapitulate certain parts of the argument I made in *Nationalism: Five Roads to Modernity*. The inventors of nationalism were members of the new – Tudor – aristocracy in England of the sixteenth century. Upwardly mobile commoners who reached the top of the social ladder, they found unacceptable the traditional image of society in which social mobility was an anomaly, and substituted for it a new image, that of a *nation* as it came to be understood in modern times, a sovereign people, with every one of its members partaking in a dignified status and deserving respect.

It is important to recognize that sovereignty of the nation was, in this case, derived from the presumed sovereignties of each member in the national collectivity and that the nation was defined as a composite entity which existed only insofar as its members kept the social compact, and which had neither interests nor will separate from the interests and wills of these members. This original nationalism, therefore, was essentially *individualistic* (which, it should be noted, in no way prevented it from serving as a very firm foundation for social solidarity). It was also *civic* in the sense that national identity – nationality – was, in effect, identical with citizenship and, since the nation existed only insofar as its members kept the social compact, could be in principle acquired or abandoned of one's free will.

It is not coincidental that this original individualistic and civic nationalism is the type of nationalism characteristic of liberal democracies, since its principles – the location of sovereignty within a people defined as a social compact of free and equal individuals – are at the same time the fundamental tenets of liberal democracy. This type of nationalism, though historically first, is the rarest type of all. Much more often a nation is defined not as a composite entity, but as a collective individual, endowed with a will and interests of its own, which are independent of and take priority over the wills and interests of human individuals who compose the nation. Such definition of the nation results in *collectivistic* nationalisms. Collectivistic nationalisms tend to be authoritarian and imply a fundamental inequality between a small group of self-appointed interpreters of the will of the nation (the leaders) and the masses who have to adapt themselves to their interpretations.

Collectivistic nationalisms can be civic. The French nationalism is a nationalism of a collectivistic and civic type, and it was, historically, the second type of nationalism to evolve. The civic criteria of national membership acknowledge the freedom of the individual members, which the collectivistic definition of the nation denies. Collectivistic and civic nationalism is, therefore, an ambivalent, problematic type, necessarily plagued by internal contradictions. The turbulent political history of the French nation is an eloquent testimony to these contradictions.

The third and the latest type of nationalism developed first in Russia and very soon after that in Germany. It also became the most common type of nationalism, today probably characteristic of all Eastern European nations (with the possible exception of the Czech Republic), of numerous nations in Asia and Africa, and, no doubt, of some Western nations as well. This type combines the *collectivistic* definition of the nation with *ethnic* criteria of nationality, according to which the latter is seen as determined genetically, entirely independent of the individual volition but inherent, which can be neither acquired, if one is not born with it, nor lost, if one is. The freedom of the individual in this type of nationalism is denied consistently, or, rather, it is redefined as inner freedom or as recognized necessity, and this denial and redefinition are predicated on the rejection of the individual as a rational being and an autonomous actor. Individuality itself is equated with the 'true' human nature, which expresses itself in self-abnegation and submersion (dissolution) in the collectivity.

In *Nationalism: Five Roads to Modernity*, I analyzed how the three types of nationalism developed and acquired their specific forms in the five countries I studied (England, France, Russia, Germany, and the United States). Here I shall only note some general tendencies.

The initial definition of the nation in every particular case (whether it is defined as a composite entity or in unitary terms) depends on the nature of the groups actively involved in the articulation of the new ideology, and the situations they face. The individualistic type of nationalism is likely to develop if during its formative period nationalism appeals to and serves the interests of wide sectors of the population (i.e., English squires and newly literate urban masses, or the French bourgeoisie), and new, open, upwardly mobile influential groups (such as the sixteenth-century English aristocracy and squirearchy). The collectivistic type is to be expected if originally the social basis of nationalism is limited and it is adopted by and serves the interests of a narrow, traditional elite intent on preserving its status (such as the French nobility) or a new group trying to attain status within the traditional social framework (German *Bildungsbuergertum*, for example), which then transmits it to the masses by indoctrination. A significant change in the situation of the relevant participants may result in the change of the definition. But such changes are extremely rare.

What, above all else, determines whether a particular nationalism will be defined as civic or as ethnic is the *perception* of a nation's status relative to other nations. To a certain extent, such perception is dependent on the traditional, pre-national beliefs in the society in question (which in all cases exert a significant formative influence on the nature of the developing national identity). A very important factor in the development of ethnic nationalisms, however, has been *ressentiment*, a sustained sentiment of existential envy and resentment based on a sense of one's inferiority vis-à-vis the societies from which the ideas of nationalism were imported and which, therefore, were originally seen as models. Societies which imported national ideas from elsewhere (whether they defined themselves as nations early or late), but which at the moment of the adoption of national identity did not believe themselves to be inferior to their models, tended to define themselves in civic terms, because the record of their *achievement* provided them with sufficient reasons for national pride, and they had no need to resort to the claim that their superiority was *inherent* (in their blood, soul, soil, unadulterated language, or what not) rather than apparent. (France and Germany, respectively, exemplify the two possibilities.)

Whenever one attempts to generalize about the relationship between nationalism and other phenomena, or to assess the effects of nationalism and therefore form a judgment about it, one has to take the fundamental distinctions between the types of nationalism into account, because the character of these relationships and effects varies in accordance with the latter. I shall touch only on some of the differences concealed by the indiscriminate use of the terms 'nation' and 'nationalism,' which have particular relevance today and which are of especial importance for our moral judgment of it, namely the differential propensities of different nations to engage in aggressive warfare, and the differential likelihood of brutality in the treatment of adversary populations (in particular non-combatants), while engaging in war.[12]

The above analysis of the nature of the three types of nationalism and the processes of their emergence should lead one to expect from them different behaviour in both respects. These expectations may be summarized in two sets of propositions:

1) Collectivistic nationalisms would be more likely than individualistic nationalisms to engage in aggressive warfare for several reasons. Individualistic nationalisms are not necessarily particularistic; *in principle*, in fact, they are necessarily not particularistic, for they are based on the universalistic principle of the moral primacy of the individual. This goes for any individual, whether or not he or she belongs to the national community, and as a result, the borderline between 'us' and 'them' is frequently blurred. One's nation is not perceived as an animate being which can nurture grievances; neither are other nations regarded as individuals harbouring malicious intentions and capable of inflicting insults. The culprits and the victims in every conflict are specified, and sympathies and antipathies change with the issues and points of view. Moreover, individualistic nationalisms are by definition *pluralisms*,

---

12 These ideas were first developed in Greenfeld and Chirot, 'Nationalism and Aggression,' *Theory and Society* 23 (February 1994) 79-130.

which implies that at any point in time there exists a plurality of opinions in regard to what constitutes the good of the nation. For this reason, it is relatively difficult, in individualistic nations, to achieve the consensus necessary for mobilization of the population for war; it is especially difficult in the case of aggressive war, when no direct threat from the prospective enemy is perceived by the national population.

Collectivistic nationalisms, by contrast, are forms of particularism, whether it is perceived in geopolitical, cultural (in the sense of acquired culture), or in presumably inherent, 'ethnic' terms. The borderline between 'us' and 'them' is relatively clear, and the nation is essentially a consensual, rather than conflictual, pluralistic society. Both of these qualities facilitate mobilization, and both are related to a characteristic of the process of emergence of collectivistic nationalisms. In distinction to individualistic nationalisms which are articulated by upwardly mobile, successful and confident groups, often with a broad social base, collectivistic nationalisms are articulated by small elite groups, which either seek to protect their threatened status (as in France), or are frustrated in their efforts to improve it (as in Germany). Such status-anxious elites define their community – the sphere of their potential influence and membership/leadership, which may be political, linguistic, religious, racial, or what not – as a 'nation,' and tend to present their grievances as the grievances of the nation and themselves as the representatives of the nation. To achieve the solidarity of this larger population, made of diverse strands, they tend (though not invariably) to blame their misfortunes not on agencies within the nation, whom they would as a result alienate, but on those outside it. Thus the nation is, from the start, united in common hatred.

2)   Within collectivistic nationalisms ethnic nationalism is more conducive to brutality in relation to the enemy population during war than is civic nationalism. This is so because civic nationalism, even when particularistic, still treats humanity as one fundamentally homogeneous entity. Foreigners are not fellow-nationals, but they are still fellow-humans, and with a little effort on their part, it is assumed, they may even become fellow-nationals. In ethnic nationalisms, by contrast, the borderline between 'us ' and 'them' is in principle impermeable. Nationality is defined as an inherent trait, and nations are seen, in effect, as separate species. Foreigners are no longer fellow-humans in the same sense, and there is no moral imperative to treat them as one would one's

fellow-nationals (in the same way as there is no imperative to treat our fellow-mammals, or even fellow-great apes, as fellow-humans). The standards of behaviour applied to relationships between species are different from those applied to relationships within the species. The very definitions of ethnic nations presuppose a double-standard of moral (or humane, decent, etc.) conduct. The tendency to 'demonize' the enemy population, considered to be a necessary condition for 'crimes against humanity' is built into ethnic nationalism, for enemy populations within them are not necessarily defined as humanity to begin with.

This tendency of 'demonization' is related to the prominence of *ressentiment* in the formation of ethnic nationalisms; the latter often inspires and always reinforces the former. The object of *ressentiment*, initially perceived as superior (invariably so, for otherwise there would be no sense to insist on equality with it), and therefore a model, is defined as the anti-model, when the degree of the actual inequality between it and the given ethnic nation is realized. This object then becomes, in the minds of the spokesmen and architects of that nation, the incarnation of evil, incorrigible – because it is also defined in terms of inherent traits – and therefore an eternal enemy. According to the characteristic psycho-logic of ethnic nationalisms, the evil other (whoever that may be) is always harbouring malicious intentions, ready to strike against the innocent nation at an opportune moment. For this reason, *ressentiment*-based nations tend to feel threatened and to become aggressive – both to preempt perceived threats of aggression against them and because the evil nature of the adversary justifies aggression, even if no immediate threats are perceived, at the same time as it justifies brutality in relation to the enemy population.

In my own case, and given my values, these considerations alone (and there are, of course, other important differences) provide a perfect justification for my negative judgment of collectivistic and in particular ethnic nationalisms, and the positive assessment of individualistic and civic nationalisms, even though, as a sociologist, I cannot doubt the legitimacy of nationalisms I dislike. Moreover, I recognize that, empirically and for quite obvious psychological reasons, ethnic nationalism serves its function better than individualistic and civic nationalism, and its appeal is, for this reason, stronger. Yet there is not a shadow of a doubt in my mind that my judgment is correct, for, given my absolute commitment to my admittedly relative values, it is the only judgment possible.

CANADIAN JOURNAL OF PHILOSOPHY
Supplementary Volume 22

How Ethnic Enmities End*

BARRINGTON MOORE, JR.
Harvard University

This essay will discuss the feelings and behaviour of presumably oppressed ethnic, national, and religious minorities. I will set aside definitions of 'ethnic' and 'national' for the moment, trusting that their meaning will become clear as the argument proceeds. The literature on this topic is, of course, enormous. I once pressed the button for 'nationalism' on Widener's new computer catalogue and got back the answer that there were some four thousand items on this topic in Widener's holdings.[1] That response brought to mind a remark of Anton Chekhov, who was trained as a doctor. He said that if a disease has many cures, that is a sign that the disease is incurable. Perhaps we should transfer this little gem of wisdom to the social sciences and history. If there are many books about a problem, that is a sign that the problem is insoluble.

Before attempting to tease out some worthwhile generalizations from this mass of facts it may be useful to briefly examine one concrete case. For that purpose I have chosen a set of events from the remote past, the

---

* Revised and expanded version of a lecture delivered at University of Massachusetts, Amherst, November 9, 1995. Stanley Hoffmann's continuing dinner seminar on ethnicity and nationalism crystallized an old inclination to write on this topic. I am especially thankful to Harvard's Russian Research Center under its current director Timothy J. Colton for continuing to make this kind of research possible.

1 Anyone seeking a brief critical selection from this daunting mass should consult the excellent pioneering effort at generalization, E.J. Hobsbawn, *Nations and Nationalism since 1780: Programme, Myth, Reality* (Cambridge University Press 1990), Introduction, pp. 1-13.

suppression and destruction of a religious minority that called itself the Cathars or the Pure Ones in southern France. We first hear of groups like them advocating religious poverty and other 'radical' ideals around the beginning of the twelfth century AD.[2] The last of them were wiped out by 1350.

The story of the Cathars will dispose of two widespread errors in present discussions of militant minorities. The first and less important error lies in holding that militant religious and ethnic minorities are mainly the form that late twentieth-century rebellions have taken against advanced industrialism and especially imperialism. Similarities of a sort there are, to be discussed in a moment. But European elites worried about how to control the Cathars centuries before their contemporary counterparts troubled themselves about the after-effects of colonialism.

The second error is more important. In discussing militant minorities today, it is usually taken for granted that repression never succeeds. The failure of the Roman emperors to stamp out Christianity in its early stages hovers like a ghost in the background of many such discussions. But the claim that repression never succeeds is simply false. As mentioned above, by about 1350, the last traces of Catharism had been wiped out, according to an excellent account.[3] The destruction of the Cathars was the result of new strategy and tactics by the papacy after a long period of failures, or at most bloody but indifferent successes. Therefore the story of the Cathars provides excellent material for distinguishing successful policies of repression and destruction from the failures, and, perhaps most important of all, the political and emotional costs of successful repression.

Before considering such issues, however, it is necessary to uncover, as best we can, the appeal of the Cathars and especially why Catholic authorities – and to a much lesser extent secular leaders – found them so threatening.

---

2 Herbert Grundmann, *Religiöse Bewegungen im Mittelalter* (Hildesheim 1961), 10-11

3 Joseph R. Strayer, *The Albigensian Crusades* (University of Michigan Press 1971; epilogue 1992), 162

As Grundmann points out acutely, the issues that divided Cathari from Catholic officialdom were not matters of dogma.[4] They concerned how churchmen lived. Probably they seemed all the more dangerous for that. By the end of the eleventh century the notions of voluntary Christian poverty and of taking the lives of the original apostles as models were apparently familiar. Priests were to be the poor of Christ and give up all the goods of this world. Around this time, too, dualist notions of God and the devil made their way from the East to Western Europe. Dualism, a doctrine specific to the Cathars, is easier to defend than strict monotheism because the latter faces the difficult problem explaining why an all-powerful God has created suffering and evil. However, since it was hard for Cathars to make a case for dualism out of the New Testament, thereby leaving them open to Catholic criticism, it is by no means certain that dualism was any great help to the Cathari.[5]

The central features of the Cathar way of life recall the romantic egalitarian revolt of a substantial segment of modern middle-class youth in advanced industrial countries. The model for the Cathari was the Apostles' mode of living with its refusal of the good things of life in voluntary poverty. In restless wanderings Cathars preached the Gospel in order to renew Christian life and follow Christian doctrine. At the same time they tried to expose the hierarchical Catholic church as an unjust pretender to the succession of the apostles, insofar as it was not really Christian and apostolic.[6] In brief, the Cathari went back to the foundations of Christianity to expose the existing practice of contemporary Catholicism, a very dangerous move. There was enough truth in Cathar claims to make both ecclesiastical and secular potentates very uneasy.

The attraction of Catharism for the general population has long been the subject of scholarly debate. Modern historians no longer take seriously the notion that Catharism was essentially a movement of the poor against the rich, partly because it did attack segments of the elite.

---

4 Grundmann, *Religiöse Bewegungen,* 39

5 Grundmann, *Religiöse Bewegungen,* 16, 17, 21, 24

6 Grundmann, *Religiöse Bewegungen,* 28

However, the egalitarian element in their doctrine is sufficiently prominent to convince me that this aspect was significant. A different argument points out that, when it was not being actively persecuted, Catharism was a much easier religion to practice than Catholicism. While the *perfecti* or leaders led very rigorous lives, satisfying in this way their oppositionist urges, ordinary believers enjoyed great freedom. The Cathar church, unlike the Catholic, had no social teachings. To attain salvation (the main purpose of life for most people in the Middle Ages) one had to do nothing more than receive the deathbed sacrament. It was not a religion to meddle with daily life. There one could do what one wanted, so far as religion was concerned.[7] Thus the Cathar appeal appears as fundamentally a negative reaction to a wealthy and hierarchical church. This opposition took the form of an archaizing egalitarianism with perhaps a touch of antinomianism. If it could find a firm and broad territorial base, it would be a mortal threat to the papacy and in fact the whole Catholic Church as it had developed by the Middle Ages.

Pope Innocent III (reigned 1198–1216) clearly recognized the danger. His first efforts to ward it off were to call for a series of crusades against the Albigensians, as they were then called. Despite some bloody massacres, the Crusades did not achieve their objectives of wiping out the allegedly heretical Albigenses. For one thing the response to the call to the Crusades was lukewarm and the organization thereof rather ineffectual. To gain the religious and temporal rewards for going on a crusade a knight only had to serve for forty days, ordinarily in the summer. Then he could and often did just go home, no matter what the military situation was.

Another reason for the very limited results of the Crusades is that they became entangled in territorial conflicts among various segments of the French elite. The French king, Philip Augustus (reigned 1180–1223) had his hands full trying to cope with the English King John over his fiefs in Northern France, and had little interest in taking control of southern France, especially Languedoc, where the Cathars were numerous. Oddly enough, French royal authority did take over the region

---

7 Lansing, in Strayer, *Albigensian Crusades*, 211

in the end, though not until after an exhausting struggle. During this time local elites in southern France intermittently promised the Pope to persecute the Cathars while carefully refraining from attacking a peaceable sector of their population and thereby stirring up domestic sedition and disorder. The Albigensian Crusades were at their height from 1208 to 1213 with a final flare-up in 1226. They did not wipe out heresy, though they did ruin many of the protectors of the Cathars. To that extent they prepared the way for the really effective attack on heresy, the Inquisition, about which more in a moment.[8] Meanwhile the French King, Louis VIII, successor to Philip Augustus, managed to take control of southern France in 1226. Relatively settled conditions thereafter enabled the Inquisition to go to work seriously.

The Inquisition gradually perfected its organization for uncovering and punishing alleged heretics. In the twelfth century there was great difficulty catching and convicting a heretic because nobody apparently knew how to identify one.[9] At this early stage too, the organization of the Inquisition was cumbersome, afflicted with competing jurisdictions and local interests, all creating delays. Under the impact of energetic and unscrupulous inquisitors enjoying the nearly continuous support of the papacy, all this was to change. Though Innocent III began the process of creating an energetic and efficient inquisitorial apparatus, the most significant improvements took place well after his death in 1216. In 1233 Pope Gregory IX decided to draw on the help of the Dominicans. Members of this preaching order were trained in theology so they could not be deceived by the quibbles of the heretics. More important, as an order committed to poverty the Dominicans had practical experience of living in towns and cities among the poor and dis-

8 Strayer, *Albigensian Crusades*, 75. Chronology of French events taken from William L. Langer, *An Encyclopaedia of World History*, rev. ed. (Cambridge, MA: 1952), 229-30.

9 Henry Charles Lea, *A History of the Inquisition in the Middle Ages* (New York and London: 1922), I, 305-8. Copyrighted in 1887, Lea's book is a great treasury of nineteenth-century historical writing. It is full of interesting details from primary sources on all the topics discussed in the present essay. The frequent and widespread popular clamor for burning heretics promptly, that Lea reports, reveals the emotional climate of the times.

affected. They knew more about ordinary people than the bishops. Hence Gregory IX informed the French bishops that, because they were so overworked, he was sending in the Dominicans to assist them in exterminating heresy.[10]

By the fourteenth century, if not earlier, the Inquisition had become a power in the land closely comparable to the secret police of Nazi Germany or Stalinist Russia. This was achieved without the technology of a modern industrial state. What made this power possible was the second major change after the death of Innocent III. In addition to drawing on the Dominicans, the Inquisition created an enormous collection of carefully indexed records. With these the Inquisition could pursue a suspect no matter where that suspect fled. If a suspect had made incautious remarks some thirty years before, the Inquisition might use these remarks to destroy him. For that matter, incriminating evidence was not really necessary. Any individual whose personal habits and demeanour were odd by community standards ran a severe risk of becoming a victim of the Inquisition. The whole situation is reminiscent of Kafka and modern faceless bureaucracies. An awareness that all this could happen long before twentieth-century totalitarianism is for us theoretically enlightening – and makes us very queasy.

To do all this the Inquisition needed and obtained a streamlined authority that overrode jurisdictional rivalries and ignored any legal niceties that could impede a conviction for heresy. In fact, the Inquisition was able to focus *both* secular and religious authority on the task of pursing heretics just about whenever it chose to do so. As Lea put it, the Inquisition "... claimed and often exercised [the power] of abrogating all local statutes obnoxious to the Holy Office, and of the duty of every secular official to lend aid whenever called upon. This duty was recognized and enforced so that the organization of the Inquisition may be said to have embraced that of the State, whose whole resources were placed at its disposition."[11]

To return to the basic question with which this discussion began, by what methods did the Inquisition put an end to the Cathars and their

---

10 Strayer, *Albigensian Crusades*, 146-7

11 Lea, *History of the Inquisition*, I, 385

threatening propaganda? The main part of the answer, I suggest, is that the Inquisition managed to penetrate the rather weak walls that surrounded each cell of a few Cathars and then destroy the cell. When the Inquisition caught a Cathari, the first thing they did was extract from the captive a list of other known Cathars. The procedure rapidly multiplied the number of suspects. As the files grew, it became harder and harder to fool the Inquisition with false names. In any case, the Inquisition had no great objection to false arrests. The effect on the Cathars was to sow distrust everywhere, make meetings to profess the faith much harder, undermine morale and weaken what little organization there was. (The leadership of the *perfecti* had already been severely damaged during the Albigensian Crusades.) Once the individual cells of the Cathars had been penetrated, all the Inquisition had to do was to capture the individuals and take them out of circulation. Nothing like this had been tried before, at least not on this scale, and it must have been a big job. But for the inquisitors with their commitment, patience, and ever-growing files, it was just the right kind of a job. (In certain situations do not files become the real basis of political authority?) As we know, the inquisitors finished the job and won.

The accidental survival of complete records of the Inquisition for the little village of Montaillou in the Pyrenees makes it possible to follow the penetration of Catholic orthodoxy in some detail, thanks to the exposition by the distinguished French historian Emmanual Le Roy Ladurie.[12] Around 1200 Catharism had infected large areas of Languedoc. Though Catharism was severely damaged by the Albigensian crusade which coincided with the annexation of Languedoc by France in 1229, it came to life again after 1250 in an area that included Montaillou.[13]

---

12 Emmanual Le Roy Ladurie, *Montaillou: village occitan de 1294 à 1324* (rev. ed.: Paris, 1982). Originally published 1975. English translation by Barbara Bray, *Montaillou: The Promised Land of Error* (Vintage Books 1979). I have used the English version since it is much more accessible. A note on the verso of the title page of the French revised edition reports that the revisions concern references to the Latin text of the major source. I doubt very much that such revisions would affect conclusions I have drawn from the English text.

13 Ladurie, *Montaillou*, ix

The situation in Montaillou for at least a generation before the final intervention of the Inquisition in 1308 was a precarious one of 'live and let live' for both Cathars and Catholics. In this precarious balance the Inquisition, with its headquarters in Carcassonne, held the important cards. Cathar households – religion went by household rather than by individual – were quite numerous. Ladurie gives the impression that most inhabitants knew who the Cathars were, though I cannot locate a specific statement to that effect. On the other hand it is plain that during this period of live and let live there was no open hostility towards Cathars, no petty vexations by villagers on account of religious differences, and certainly no spontaneous persecution of the kind that occurs under anti-Semitism. Nevertheless the Cathars found it advisable to keep very much to themselves. A Cathar house became something of a barricade that limited potentially compromising contacts. To the extent that Catharism made any demands on ordinary adherents, the new faith was practiced in secret. There was much fear of even talking lest it lead to danger.[14]

Thus the Cathar intrusion had damaged the solidarity of the villages and its ability to act as a unit in the face of external threats and interference. To be sure there were still times when local networks in Montaillou could paralyze the forces of the Inquisition.[15] On the other hand, due to the Cathar influx Montaillou apparently lost whatever capacity it may once have had to conduct its own affairs according to its own lights. The village assembly of the heads of families became paralyzed by religious differences.[16] Just how much authority the assembly may have had in the past is not clear. One must not romanticize village democracy. What is clear, and much more important, is that 'big shots' took control of the village. Two powerful and, by local standards, wealthy men ran local affairs in Montaillou up to the time of the final collapse. One, Pierre Cleque, was the dominant priest in Montaillou. His brother Bernard was the bailiff (*bayle*) whose main task was collecting tithes.

The 'functions' of both 'big shots,' as they would be known today,

---

14 Ladurie, *Montaillou*, 13, 27

15 Ladurie, *Montaillou*, 92

16 Ladurie, *Montaillou*, 28

extended far beyond the village and into Carcassonne. Of the two, Pierre had the more complicated job. He was actually the balancing mechanism that, for a time, kept the precarious system of live and let live from tipping over. As the dominant priest in Montaillou he was the respected intermediary between Montaillou and the Inquisition in Carcassonne. He used his connections with Carcassonne to protect his clients in Montaillou. By doing this he was able to consolidate his personal power in both places.[17] Meanwhile his position provided him with abundant opportunities to satisfy his desires as a womanizer, very much in the manner of a 'big shot.'

It took very little – a decision by Carcassonne to tighten up on the collection of tithes on livestock – to smash this charming if precarious equilibrium. The decision to tighten up came from the Inquisition, the main source of oppression from the point of view of Montaillou's inhabitants. The Inquisition was in the habit of using the temporal lord's bailiff, in this case, Bernard, brother of Pierre, against the peasants. Conflicts over tithes are in any case a recurrent theme in the history of heresy. In 1308 Carcassonne ordered the arrest of all adults in Montaillou as a prelude to tightening up the tithes on livestock.[18]

Though details on this crucial episode are sparse, the arrests apparently went off without a hitch. Evidently the forces of authority and orthodoxy were by this time and in this place quite overwhelming. This means that for the investigator there is no point to searching in great detail for vulnerabilities and weaknesses in the situation of the Cathars and Montaillou. I have tried to give enough facts to show why Montaillou collapsed so readily – somewhat odd for even a small mountain village faced with town forces a considerable distance away. Yet one further factor deserves to be mentioned here. Again speaking of the Cathars at this time and place only, theirs was definitely not a religion of martyrdom, of fighting to the last survivor. Except in isolated cases, of which this was not one, Cathar resistance, reports Ladurie, was passive, non-violent, almost non-existent.[19] Ladurie's somewhat

---

17 Ladurie, *Montaillou*, 55-58

18 Ladurie, *Montaillou*, 20-23

19 Ladurie, *Montaillou*, 331

contemptuous judgment of the Cathars' power of resistance differs sharply from an evaluation by Strayer of their behaviour in southern France at a slightly earlier time, that is after 1250. Strayer praises their amazing courage and tenacity in facing the Inquisition. Ordinary members remained steadfast and discreet. Very few *perfecti* were betrayed by the rank and file. Even when after prolonged efforts the Inquisition did succeed in catching a small group of leaders, ordinary believers remained true to their faith.[20] The difference between the two descriptions could be a matter of time and place, a random effect of sampling and hence of no general importance. In contrast to this interpretation I suggest that in Montaillou Catharism had begun to age and lose the doctrinal certainty and appeal of earlier generations. Despite the element of Cathar secrecy we know that there was a great deal of contact between Cathars and Catholics in the course of daily life. Neither Catholic nor Cathari was heavily committed to religious doctrine. Peasants and shepherds have to put too much energy into obtaining subsistence – and getting along with each other – to afford the luxury of religious intolerance. Hence it appears reasonable to hold that continual interaction with Catholics in this situation of precarious toleration had seriously eroded Cathar convictions.

The arrests of 1308, be it noted, were over the issue of tithes, not religious orthodoxy. Their consequence was that Montaillou broke open, so to speak. What solidarity there had been versus Carcassonne and the Inquisition completely disintegrated. As Ladurie expressed it, the village turned into a tragic rat race. Everyone worked to encompass his neighbour's ruin, thereby hoping mistakenly to avert his own.[21] Some of the inhabitants escaped to settle on the Spanish borders. Some were burnt at the stake. Some suffered a long period of imprisonment. The rest were released fairly quickly and allowed to return to the mangled village where they could only group themselves around the leadership of their priest, to grow old in debauchery and denunciation. Pierre Cleque used the system to ruin or otherwise eliminate personal

---

20 Strayer, *Albigensian Crusades*, 159-60

21 Ladurie, *Montaillou*, 30

enemies. For a dozen years he survived, but finally his turn came too. In 1320 he was at last thrown into prison.[22]

By such devices did royal authority and religious orthodoxy triumph in one tiny mountain village in fourteenth-century France. So ended the Cathars as an organized religious movement, defeated by force, files, and treachery.[23]

*****

Instructive though a concrete example such as the fate of the Cathars may be, we cannot hope to understand the nature of ethnic and nationalist enmities simply by accumulating more and more cases. To be sure, that process has to continue. Otherwise, our theories will be empty, sterile, and pretentious. But in this inquiry, as other generally similar ones, it is necessary to begin the search for generalizations early on. Otherwise there is a great risk of drowning amid fragments of meaningless data. We should not be frightened by the hobgoblin of 'premature generalization.' All generalizations are premature when first stated. There is no other way to get started. In time they will get sorted out and qualified. Likewise we should not be disturbed if our generalizations fail to cover all cases. Looking for universal generalizations, in fact, one runs a serious risk of coming up with nothing more than banal platitudes. It is best, of course, if we can specify the conditions under which a general observation holds. That, however, is a counsel of perfection, that may require more facts and time to reflect on them

---

22 Ladurie, *Montaillou*, 63-64, 66

23 For general interpretations of the end of Catharism in southern France and elsewhere see the collection of articles, *Effacement du Catharisme? (XXIe–XIVe S.)*, Cahiers de Fanjeaux: Collection d'Histoire religieuse du Languedoc au XIIIe et au début du XIVe siècle, No. 20 (Toulouse: 1985). The article by Jean-Louis Biget, "L'extinction du catharisme urbain ...", pp. 305-40, argues that repression by the Inquisition was a relatively minor factor. The statistics behind this part of the argument seem dubious to me. He is much more persuasive in holding that what I call later the 'competing attractions' of a modified Catholic orthodoxy – bigger job openings and effective techniques for controlling anxiety and guilt – very seriously undermined the appeal of Catharism. In any case the appeal never extended beyond a very small minority of the population, a discontented segment of the urban *notables*, whose ambitions were temporarily blocked.

than are available to working investigators. The main task, after all, is to find out something that seems worth knowing.

To begin with a very obvious generalization, ethnic enmities are notoriously long-lived social formations. Furthermore they are by no means confined to hostilities between oppressor and oppressed. Conflict between competing minorities over issues neatly expressed by the slang word 'turf' takes up a huge amount of aggressive energy. Obviously it is necessary to gain some understanding of what sustains these enmities before trying to understand how and why they come to an end, which fortunately does happen from time to time.

While not claiming priority for material issues over emotional and intellectual ones we may begin with them. Without as a rule saying so explicitly, the leaders of militant minorities in modern times seek to create within the larger society a protected enclave that eliminates competition from outsiders for jobs, economic resources, language skills, and other cultural attainments such as an indigenous literary tradition. This literary tradition serves the manufacture, distribution, and sale of heroic ancestors in much the same way as the dominant literary tradition with which it competes. Hence it is very useful to persuade distinguished and even undistinguished universities to add courses on the history and society of ethnic minorities to their curricula. In this way such minorities are able to achieve a degree of intellectual respectability.

To win these objectives of jobs and cultural autonomy – about which more in a moment – the minority has to create and enforce solidarity in pursuit of these aims, a solidarity that characterizes serving the dominant majority as a form of treachery and penalizes it. It is no easy task to create and enforce this solidarity because the dominant group generally has at its command a substantial array of rewards and penalties with which to tempt and discipline members of the minority.

Mainly for this reason the militancy of the minority is liable to become rather frantic and turn toward violence. Violence in turn has its own self-perpetuating dynamic. It is mainly, though not exclusively, an activity pursued by young men. For a young man it is much more fun to prance around with a gun, or to kill several enemies with a bomb, than it is to sit at a desk day after day, bored by a dead-end job. That is especially true when there are no jobs anyway for thousands of youngsters with a university education. Opening the universities has had the dangerous result of creating a mass *lumpen intelligentsia* in the Third World and elsewhere. But it is hard to demonstrate that a refusal to open the universities would have had better results.

Turning briefly to the cultural and emotional aspects of these movements, it requires no great perspicacity to see than in an apparently hopeless situation ethnicism and/or nationalism provide a welcome purpose for living and dying. Without such a purpose many human beings will just shrivel and die. Such deaths occurred on a wide scale in the Nazi concentration camps, where even the purpose of survival was hard to sustain. Furthermore, ethnicism and nationalism provide an explanation for everything that seems wrong or feels painful in the current situation. Thus these explanations deflect blame away from the self. It is hardly necessary to add that in a good many cases the explanations have a rather high truth value. Histories of exploitation and cruelty generally reveal truths unwelcome to society's rulers. On account of the elements of truth in these doctrines, and especially on account of the psychological reassurance they give, these doctrines can be almost completely immune to rational criticism and contrary evidence.

We now turn to an examination of the social trends and situations that put an end to ethnic and nationalist movements, or, at the very least, damp down their rhetoric.[24] Undoubtedly the most important of these has been the creation, mainly by royal authority, of the modern territorial state. As Bismarck once sarcastically observed, this was a set of political issues solved with blood and iron, not by rhetoric. In the world as a whole in premodern times there must have been thousands of separate jurisdictions, large and small, each for a time proud of their rights of rule or misrule in their own territories. Central governments ground up and destroyed most of these. Often this destruction left a

---

24 For a differing interpretation see Donald L. Horowitz, *Ethnic Groups in Conflict* (Berkeley 1985), 598-680. This book is an almost superhuman effort to find scientific order and rational hope in a huge mass of refractory facts about ethnic conflicts, mainly in Africa, the Middle East, and Asia. The author deserves very high marks not only for industry but also freedom from positive and negative preconceptions. Yet the combination of parochialism, triviality, and cruelty described over and over again in a book of nearly 700 pages numbs the brain. One needs a Swift rather than a social scientist to do justice to this material.

legacy of bitterness that survives to the present day. Ireland is only the best known European example.

This process, which we can somewhat inaccurately call the creation of royal absolutism, had by the seventeenth century gone about as far as it could under pre-industrial conditions. By then there were huge territorial states ruled, more or less, by a king or an emperor. They covered large parts of Europe and most of Asia. Despite this apparent similarity of outcomes by the seventeenth century, there were variations in timing and degree of success that were to have enormous political consequences later. China achieved unification first in 221 BC under the emperor Shi Huangdi, to my knowledge the first despot to burn books and slaughter intellectuals. This unification never completely disappeared. India, on the other hand, never achieved unity under an indigenous ruler. In Europe, to mention just one more example, German unification was long delayed and deflected by German rulers' preoccupation with Italian affairs during the Middle Ages and beyond. Hence German-speaking territories were a temptation for France and in a different sense for Austria. Except for a brief time under Hitler these territories have never been united under one political roof.

If the rise of the powerful centralized state suppressed a large number of local loyalties and aspirations, it also created the social carriers for the doctrine of nationalism. I will discuss only one form of this: the Jacobin variety which proclaimed that French liberation was a gift to the rest of human society. As is well known, French hopes were thoroughly disappointed. French patriotism stimulated German and even Russian patriots, which contributed to the defeat of France in 1815. In a more general sense, nationalism, unlike democracy, can never have a universal appeal since it always glorifies a particular state. But the Jacobin notion that 'what we have achieved is so good for us you have to try it too' underwent a major mutation in the nineteenth century. It lost the specific connection with France or any other existing country and came up with the idea of a worldwide revolution against capitalism. Neo-Jacobinism, mutated into Communism, had a distinguished career, now at an end.

It is enlightening to look at the consequences of centralization from another standpoint. At the end of the eighteenth century the formation of the modern state still had a long way to go. In the vivid expression of Eugen Weber, peasants had to be turned into Frenchmen. In other words, human beings had to lose their rough angularities of *patois* in speech and singularity in modes of daily work as modernization rolled over them and processed them to turn out citizens. During the eighteenth and nineteenth centuries the main processing agents were the conscript army and compulsory education. Standard English, Metropolitan French, Hochdeutsch (in itself a regional dialect that may have acquired precedence by being the King of England's German), and the Russian of 'Peterburg' became the models of educated speech, crowding aside numerous dialects. Changes in language were part of a general smoothing out of regional peculiarities during the nineteenth century. Newspapers, radio, and later television intensified the process during the twentieth. So did the reduction in cost of travel in the form of railroad and automobile.

Industrialization and modernization have been very unkind to the social enclaves that provide the basis for ethnic movements and demands. Though the melting pot has long been recognized as an exaggeration, there has been a great deal of melting. Immigration, to be sure an integral part of industrialization, has created regional possibilities for ethnic mobilization, especially in the United States. But they didn't amount to more than ethnic voting blocs. There are other cases such as Quebec where industrialization has passed by, leaving an area with a somewhat distinctive culture as a good home for perpetual complaint. Vermont is somewhat similar now. Well colonized by discontented American romantics, it has not yet generated any threat to the unity of the United States. In Western Europe and North America ethnic patriotism still is no more than a minor threat. More severe threats could arise from the strong demand for foreign labour. So far, however, that is a rather small cloud on a huge horizon full of more severe threats to civilized existence.

But – and this is a very big but – if ethnic demands have largely disappeared from within advanced industrial states, they have somehow fused to create virulent currents of chauvinism and nationalism in the external policies of modern states. This virulent nationalism is even more prominent right now in the economically backward areas of the world, where it is in large measure a hostile reaction to the hegemony of the wealthy states. To put the point in capsule form, the decline of ethnic movements has helped to produced an explosion of virulent nationalism. Thus the distinction between 'ethnic' and 'nationalist' is merely the distinction between an aggressive chauvinism directed by a minority against the state and the same kind of chauvinism carried on by the state itself. As the example of the Nazis shows, ethnic chauvinism can become a very vicious foreign policy by capture of the state.

The noticeable continuity in hostile emotional climates, despite the apparent historical changes in their causes and targets, provokes the suspicion that Freud got it completely backwards when he tried to explain what holds human societies together. It is not libidinal ties at all, no matter how sublimated. It is just plain hate that holds people together. More specifically, shared hatreds play a crucial role in social bonding all the way from small groups of friends up to membership in big states and even empires. We shall come upon further evidence along these lines as the argument proceeds.

Now that we have seen how the consolidation of the modernizing state undermines ethnic loyalties at home but intensifies xenophobic nationalism, we may look more closely at how these ethnic movements change their targets or even die out. There are similarities to state formation in the first two examples. In these two, changes in ethnic attitudes come about 'from above' through the acts and decisions of rulers.

Take first the simple case of a change of enemies: for instance, think of two countries with a long and deep-rooted tradition of mutual enmity, embroidered with decorative touches of mutual contempt. The long history of Anglo-French relationships provides a good example, and incidentally proves that such mutual hostilities are not the product of eighteenth-century nationalism or industrial capitalism. Evidently human beings don't need grand historical forces to teach them how to hate each other. That lesson they can learn on their own with minimal instruction. At any rate Anglo-French hostility can be traced back to the Hundred Years War (1337–1453), and continued through the French Revolution and the Napoleonic Wars. In a milder form it continued well into the nineteenth century.

The hostility clearly began to subside after 1890 in response to the emerging German threat to both England and France. That, of course, was and remains the key to the whole process. Hostile countries bury their mutual antagonisms when a third party appears that is a threat to both of them. Hostility as such does not disappear; there is merely a change of target.

The second constellation of circumstances that has occasionally put an end to ethnic rhetoric can be called controlled irredentism. At any given time the map of European states has shown blocs of territory inside each state with language and customs that differ from the surrounding state. Usually such ethnic blocs are the result of a previous conquest, sometimes in the quite distant past. Often enough political leaders arise in these areas to play on local grievances and thereby win support for claims that the territory really belongs to another state or just itself, that is, it should be one more independent state. Looking more closely we can see that most if not all irredentist movements depend for their support and existence on the benign attitude of a great power. The role of the great power is to make the local irredentist agitation sound like the result of an intolerable abuse. Rarely if ever does an intolerable abuse end on account of the moral outrage it produces. Instead it fades out of 'informed' public awareness when a change in the structure of big politics renders the agitation a nuisance to new or changed players on the stage of world politics.

The complicated issue of Danish and German rights in Schleswig-Holstein took up a large amount of European statesmen's time and thought in the latter part of the nineteenth century. It was perhaps the last of the thorny dynastic issues, exacerbated by the entrance of nationalist masses onto the political scene. Its main importance was probably geopolitical since the area under dispute controlled the entry to the Baltic. Palmerston is said to have remarked at one point that only three men really understood the issues. Two of them were now dead, and Palmerston himself was the third. But he had forgotten most of the story.

With the German defeat in World War I, the Schleswig-Holstein issue simply disappeared from 'informed' public view. It ceased to be a political issue. Hardly anyone except a specialist would be likely to know the disposition of this territory at the end of the war or its subsequent fate. (By plebiscite in 1920 the Danish sector voted to return to Denmark).

Alsace-Lorraine, in German Elsass-Lothringen, is the name of another territory that was once a major political issue and then ceased to be one when Germany lost the power to keep it alive. Louis XIV seized the territory as a prize of war, one of the few 'permanent' acquisitions of an expensive, belligerent reign. Subsequently French influence became predominant, though without completely destroying the German element. In the nineteenth century the German government decided to make an issue out of the area, and took it back after defeating France in the Franco-Prussian War of 1871. Thereupon a number of French intellectuals turned in a fine performance, making the status of Alsace-Lorraine into a major grievance against Germany. A French author wrote a widely read and moving short story, 'La dernière classe,' about the lesson in the French language before German authorities took charge. In the Place de la Concorde, where France's major cities were personified in handsome female statues, those of the two cities in Alsace-Lorraine were permanently draped in flowing black robes of mourning throughout the inter-war years. All this was part of a wave of 'anti-Boche' sentiment. At the end of World War II and the defeat of Nazi Germany the territory once again reverted to France.

The disappearance of the issue from international politics did not have altogether happy results. Evidently human beings sometime learn to hug their grievances, especially when they have lived with them for several generations and the grievances themselves have not been overwhelmingly painful. In addition, the end of specific grievances can create utopian hopes about the end of all grievances, as de Tocqueville pointed out about revolutionary hopes. Whatever the exact reasons, not long after the return of Alsace-Lorraine to France a movement in favour of autonomy grew up. It was not the only one. There has also been one in Brittany. Autonomy has become a major all-grievance demand in the latter half of the twentieth century. Outside of France it has emerged with ethnic overtones in Scotland, Northern Ireland, and Quebec. So far these movements for autonomy have accomplished nothing beyond stirring up emotional demands almost certain to be disappointed.

Perhaps the most frequent way for ethnic quarrels to end, or at least to dull their militant edge, is the following. At some point in their history ethnic minorities are likely to become quite militant. Otherwise we would never hear about them. Over a longer period, however, they may succumb to what I would call competing attractions, especially if the dominant society can demonstrate a few routes to prosperity and social respect, and also if its repressive features are on occasion held in check by the laws of the land. Militant minorities lose their doctrinal purity by reluctantly adapting to the world around them, including all of its temptations and corruption. That is true even of religious groups that refuse to give up their organizational identity, such as some monastic orders. The choice for the monastic orders was between doctrinal purity that led towards extinction or taking up sin to keep the place going.

With only slight oversimplification one could describe the monastic dilemma as 'assimilate or die.' I suggest that the same dilemma applies to the Jews, though on a vastly wider and more tragic scale. As mentioned earlier, an ethnic identity is especially important for any ethnic minority. It provides a purpose for living, rules about how to live, and hope for the future in the face of horrible misfortunes. All that is under stress in even the most successful assimilation. A loss of faith is hard to bear under any circumstances. In the case of the Jews, fears about losing religious identity contributed eventually to the creation of the state of Israel, a state that has played the secular and amoral game of power politics with commendable skill. Along with the rise of religious chauvinism all over the world, this conflict between faith and reality has become more acute.

Emphasizing examples of successful assimilation will certainly distort one's perception of the varied and hotly debated situation of the Jews. To go back only slightly in time to Germany before Hitler, Jews had already won considerable acceptance. In some cases it was an acceptance acquired well before the First World War, one upon which their children could build. Social and economic barriers certainly were still present.[25] Yet Jews could prosper in business and lead a patrician life without fear of molestation. In some cases, as I learned from German Jewish friends, a child could grow up to adulthood with no more than very minor awareness of being Jewish or what that could mean. Then came the slaughter and the gas ovens of the Holocaust. After that experience would not a great many Jews say to themselves and one another, "We tried assimilation and look what it brought us"?

Still another way for ethnic-nationalist conflicts to come to an end is through a peace of mutual exhaustion. After years of armed struggle

---

25 For a crisp analysis of anti-Semitism's powerful influence in Germany from Martin Luther (d. 1546) to Hitler, see Franz Neumann, *Behemoth* (Oxford University Press 1944), 108-11.

some combatants do get tired of the fighting and destruction that fail to achieve any desired goal. This seems the least likely way for hostilities to end, though not an impossible one. Something of the sort is obviously at work in the conflict over the status of Northern Ireland as well as the Palestinian-Israeli conflict. There are even indications of a similar development in Yugoslavian fratricide.

A key factor in such a turn of events is the drying up of social support for militant action on the part of those seeking to change the status quo, and likewise support for police repression on the part of the authorities. There is increasing worry on the part of the authorities about the human and material costs of putting down the uprising. On the other side local supporters of the uprising become horrified at the brutal murder of innocent civilians among their opponents. Moral outrage cannot be sustained forever at a high voltage. All these trends and considerations promote an inclination to try negotiations along with guns instead of guns alone.

The immediate hindrance to the establishment of a relatively peaceful *modus vivendi* is the fact that on both sides a relatively small number of individuals command the means of violence. Intentionally or unintentionally one or more individuals on either side can create, and have created, an episode that sets off a new round of violence. The danger is greater on the side of the uprising. As pointed out earlier, there is liable to be a set of militant young radicals among the supporters of the uprising for whom violence is a preferred way of life. They can and do terrorize peacefully inclined inhabitants in contested areas and thereby create the illusion of mass support for violence. This kind of revolutionary bullying takes place in great upheavals as well as small ones. For the young militant peace means the end of all the hopes that made life worth living.

There has long been a widespread common sense opinion about how ethnic hostilities come to an end, indeed about how to bring them to an end: grant a complaining minority its justified demands. Doing that will supposedly make the minority's leaders stop their militant complaints and speed up the assimilation of the minority into the ranks of the dominant society. Evidence from the recent past indicates that this complacent generalization is utterly misleading.

The reverse is closer to the truth. Satisfaction of their demands – mainly for political independence and indeed political autonomy – has led to severe disappointment in the modern history of nationalist and ethnic movements. India is a painfully obvious example where the democratic and secular legacy of Nehru is by now widely discredited. Algeria is another, where turning the country over to the nationalists of a generation ago has led to the near victory of a savage Islamic fundamentalism in the present generation. In Africa as a whole the only 'successful' transition to a black nationalist regime has been in South Africa. There, too, it is rather early for judging success. We often hear that the main economic issues have still to be faced. On the other hand the evasion of issues by common consent is, up to a point, an essential element in a stable democratic government. The rest of Africa is spotted with petty dictatorships, horrifying bloodshed, and if anything even *more* horrifying poverty, more horrifying because it is man-made.

To understand this huge tragic mess is a daunting challenge. We have to learn where the different forms of disappointment come from. It won't do to place all the blame on imperialism and its legacy. That claim won't wash in the corrosive acid of the evidence. The inhabitants of many, perhaps most, of the new African states were better off under British and possibly even French imperialism, which at least provided a fair simulacrum of peace and order. Instead of satisfaction, disappointment intensifies, and radicalizes ethnic demands that are still perceived as the really effective solution. India, for example, now has a vicious Hindu nationalist movement complete with street thugs able to intimidate the whole city of Bombay. "Throw out foreigners and unbelievers. Then all will be well." Such, alas, is the result of satisfying 'reasonable' nationalist demands. Yet the refusal to satisfy them is hardly likely to produce socially constructive results.

Political autonomy by itself does not give a social group either the will or the means to resolve internal conflicts peacefully. In fact by reducing access to economic goods and services political independence makes the situation worse. That is obvious in connection with the most intractable problem of all, one faced by 'old' societies as well as 'new' ones: the distribution of jobs among different sectors of the population. On this score resentments can smoulder indefinitely. At any given moment there is only a limited number of available jobs in the society. Hence for every one of 'theirs' that lands a job to remedy current and past injustices, one of 'ours' will have to be passed over. Because white jealousy and resentment at the good fortune of their patronizingly designated brown, black and yellow co-workers are not feelings to be expressed openly – after all they are vicious and ugly sentiments – they may well fester till they explode.

For this situation it is as easy to see a cure as it is impossible to carry it out. All one needs to do is (1) cancel the newly won political autonomy and put this area back under the former government, and (2) change this government so that it has a strong commitment to balanced economic growth with (a) an increase in jobs worth doing, i.e., not just make work and leaf raking, and (b) a strong commitment to jobs for the previously disadvantaged minority, but so far as possible not at the expense of hard-working individuals from the majority. Here of course is the main difficulty. It was resolved fairly well in the USA for Scandinavians, Germans, Irish, and Italians, but not nearly as well although with a noticeable degree of success for African-Americans and Hispanics. Despite these indications that such a proposal is not altogether fantastic, there is no use developing the argument further. For the foreseeable future it remains politically unthinkable.

Before ending this inquiry it will be useful to step back and look at ethnic-nationalist movements from a wider perspective. This we can do by comparing them with the series of world revolutions that began in the sixteenth century with the Revolt of the Netherlands, continued through the French Revolution, the American Revolution, and more significantly the American Civil War, to end, I believe, permanently, with the Bolshevik Revolution in Russia and its successor, the Communist Revolution in China. (Parenthetically one may observe that only after the great wave of revolution had subsided did revolution become an active topic for academic study, justifying once more Hegel's remark that the owl of Minerva flies forth only at dusk. Understanding always comes too late.) All of these revolutions took place in the name of pan-human ideals, the end of the divine right of kings and of slavery, freedom of conscience, liberty, equality, and fraternity, the end of capitalist oppression, etc. A nationalist-ethnic revolution, as the term indicates, is not and cannot be a pan-human undertaking even if on occasion it may borrow pan-human slogans. A nationalist-ethnic uprising seeks the liberation of an Israel, a Sudan, an Ethiopia, a Northern Ireland, fighting fragments of what was once Yugoslavia, a central Asian province of what once was the Russian Empire, etc., etc. Bloody, passionate, cruel, and violent the uprising often is. But despite the blood and passion a strong odor of provincialism emanates from all these struggles. Victorious or defeated, they are not going to change the world or the way we think about it very much. They will do very little to reduce the sum total of human misery, which at least was the ostensible object of the great world revolutions. Where the main force behind an ethnic-nationalist uprising is a fundamentalist and obscurantist religious chauvinism, a movement not confined to the Islamic world, the effect is liable to be an *increase* in human misery as part of a general destruction of what still can pass for human civilization.

To summarize this essay in accord with its title, we have called attention to six distinguishable ways in which ethnic-nationalist enmities come to an end, or at least have their militance seriously blunted. There are two ways in which they fall victim to external forces: (1) an organization such as the Inquisition, specifically designed to destroy them, can succeed in so doing, as happened to the Cathars, and (2) the creation of the modern territorial state, at first under a single political and religious authority, obliterated numerous culturally distinct regional units. But this process by no means obliterated all of them and left behind nests of grievances and special loyalties to plague the central authority down to modern times. The Russian empire, the creation of a long history of successive and successful conquests, is the most striking example of this process.

Nationalist hostilities also come to an end, as we saw in the case of long lasting Anglo-French rivalries, (3) when a new threat appears on the scene that makes them join forces. There is also the situation (4), labelled controlled irredentism, in which minority grievances appear and disappear at the convenience of the major powers and *their* rivalries.

There are also several cases where factors internal to the militant movement have played a major part in reducing the level of militance. One is (5) the emergence of peace out of mutual exhaustion. Something of the sort seems to be taking place in what used to be Yugoslavia, and also in Israel-Palestine, as well as Northern Ireland. The story is not over yet, and conceivably may never come to an end. But if these three inflamed areas somehow heal to the point of a stable peace, the result will be an encouraging transformation of world politics, the likes of which we have never seen before in human history.

The last one to be mentioned here is much less dramatic but probably the most important in terms of potential for peaceful change. I refer here to the role of (6) competing attractions, to deliberately use a Hollywood expression. In capsule form it describes the way the attractions and concrete rewards of the dominant society undermine the militant and separatist faith of a discontented minority. One reason we don't hear more about this assimilation is that historians of oppressed minorities are generally ashamed of the process. They would prefer to forget about it. Instead they choose the usual historical gambit of creating useful ancestors, heroes who overcame oppression to become bigger than life figures on literary pedestals. That is the way to make a reputation – by keeping the home fires of indignation burning.

Finally it is necessary to recall that what on *a priori* grounds looks like the most effective way of ending ethnic anger, the granting of political independence, has in recent times not succeeded at all. At first glance, it seems that the explanation might be that human beings cherish their grievances. Especially if the grievances have existed for a long time and served to orient the individual in many decisions of daily life such as whom to hate and whom to trust, their sudden disappearance can be upsetting if not disabling. However, these psychological factors, I suggest, play only a secondary role in the disillusionment with independence. The basic source derives from the fact that political independence does not bring with it the economic resources and skills that can do something about massive unemployment and rural poverty, the fate of most of the so-called Third World. If anything, independence and pseudo-autonomy make the situation worse.

CANADIAN JOURNAL OF PHILOSOPHY
Supplementary Volume 22

Nations and Social Complexity

ROBERT WARE
University of Calgary

Some Problems with Thinking about Nationalism

In the last three decades, we in the West have seen nationalism turn from an apparently progressive force, as in Cuba, Vietnam, and many countries in Africa, into a negative force of degenerating chaos, as in Yugoslavia, the Soviet Union, Sri Lanka, and Rwanda. Elsewhere, during the same decades, the record of nationalism has been, or at least been perceived to have been, more mixed, for example in Belgium, Canada, and India. The assessments themselves are uncertain and suspect, however. Maybe nationalism was not so clearly progressive or so clearly retrogressive where we had previously thought it so. Maybe we misjudge its ambivalence elsewhere. Maybe we are not even dealing with the same kind of phenomenon.

More generally, we have yet to understand the role of nationalism in two world wars and countless imperialist incursions. We have only the vaguest ideas of its connection to social ideologies and movements like racism, fascism, and Nazism and little understanding of its relevance to economic systems like capitalism and socialism. There is no settled view about what roles, past and present, nationalism has played, although most would agree that nationalism has been a changing phenomenon with diverse roles. We are equally in the dark about what the role of nationalism will be in the future, although there is little reason for complacency.

Some have said that the twilight of nationhood is approaching.[1] Perhaps the recent havoc brought by nationalism is in fact a death rattle of an obsolete phenomenon. At the very least, nationalism and nationalities are again being brought into question. In my view, nations and nationalities will not end with the millennium, and nationalism will not be extinguished by globalization. Economies and cultures continue to extend their domination, but there are underlying complexities of social reality that resist obliteration while fostering competing cultures and economies.

Unfortunately, the complex reality of nationalities is obscured by overly simple views. The problems with our thinking about nationalism, and nations, arise partly out of our vague conceptualizations of nationalism that are applied diversely to a variety of changing phenomena in different societies. There are conceptual confusions to eliminate, a task that is made easier by using a less simplistic and more realistic understanding of the nature of society than heretofore. Nationalities and nations are different things, differently understood for different reasons. The differences are clarified when we attend to the complex differences of real social entities and social structures.

I contend that underlying some of the obscurities of the term 'nation' is an ambiguity between nationalities and bearers of nationhood, roughly between peoples and countries. Nationalities, or peoples, have linguistic, cultural, ethnic, and/or religious determinants. On the other hand, nations as countries (bearers of nationhood), what are usually called 'nation-states,' are members of a world institutional and territorial system. The existing nations, of both sorts, are socio-historical entities which take different forms in different eras and in different places. Because of the variations, there is a lack of clarity about the nature of the related phenomenon of nationalism and our competing conceptions of it or even whether the term is negative or positive. I think it can be used positively, but we have to know what we mean by the relevant terms.

---

1 See E. J. Hobsbawm, *Nations and Nationalism since 1780: Programme, Myth, Reality* (Cambridge: Cambridge University Press 1990), 179ff.

Nations and Nationalities

Nationalism has been spawned by national groups of diverse kinds. National groupings do not come in just one form. They are not natural kinds with a stable essence determined by natural law. It is not just that there is a multiplicity of criteria that we apply in speaking of nations – although differences of language are widespread. It is also important to recognize that the kinds of groupings, collectives, and institutions that are created in forming a people or a country varies from one society to another. Different societies create different institutions and different forms of community. The language is constantly contested, and the reality is continually changing. Competing conceptions crosscut alternative institutions and forms of community, giving rise to vague and obscure concepts.

Consider first the principal ambiguity of the term 'nation.' There are two basic concepts, the concept of a people, a societal grouping, and the concept of a country with its state, a political entity.[2] In both meanings of the term 'nation,' people are of one nation if they have the same nationality, ethnic identity in one sense and citizenship in the other. It is misleading to think that these are competing definitions of the same phenomenon, such as ethnic vs. civic definitions of 'a nation.' A political entity with its state is a different sort of thing from a community of people grouped, for example, by culture or religion.

It is now more common to think of nations as nation-states or countries, historically the second but now the principal meaning of the term 'nation.'[3] Nations, as we usually think of them, are what become members of the United Nations and are the basis of international activity. It is the recognition and role of the nation as a whole rather than the

---

2 Only occasionally is this distinction noted. For example, see Stanley B. Ryerson, 'Quebec: Concepts of Class and Nation' in Gary Teeple, ed., *Capitalism and the National Question in Canada* (Toronto: University of Toronto Press 1972), 211-27. Ryerson distinguishes 'a political entity' from 'a community of people' (212).

3 Confusions are compounded by nation-states often being thought of as states with a single nation in the sense of a societal group. Is there any state composed solely of people of one nationality?

characteristics of the individual people in it that are determining factors. Nations in this sense necessarily have territories and governments, and they require political recognition by other nations and international groups. The bantustans of South Africa did not achieve nationhood, at least partly because they failed to receive political recognition from established nations. On the other hand, Slovenia and Croatia quickly gained national status through almost immediate international recognition of their aspirations for independence. Nations as countries are real entities in the international political domain.

It is misleading to use the term 'nation-state' because of the ambiguity of 'state,' which refers either to the country or to its government and the political apparatus, including the police and the courts. The government is the institution that manages the political affairs of the country through legislation and enforcement. The state (in the sense of the government and its agencies) is made up of 'representatives' of the territorial state in the sense of the country. A nation in the political sense is not to be identified with its government or state. I will speak of political nations, which achieve nationhood (we also say 'statehood'),[4] as a way of distinguishing them from societal nations, which are nationalities.[5] I will also speak of nations as countries versus nations as peoples.

Turning to societal nations, the determining factors are mostly the characteristics of the people making up the relevant group. A variety of characteristics are prominent in determining sameness of nationality. People of one societal nation generally speak one language, have a similar culture (sometimes including religion), come out of a cohesive tradition and history, and are often thought to have a consciousness of themselves as a group. Their existence as a nationality is a matter of fact rather than recognition. There may be disputes about the concepts used, but no matter what is said there are groupings of people of various kinds. Political nations, on the other hand, depend largely on the

---

4 Notice that 'nationhood' (like 'statehood') applies to the country as a whole (collectively) rather than to its individual citizens (distributively), *contra* David Miller in *On Nationality* (Oxford: Clarendon Press 1995), for example on p. 17.

5 The term 'nationality' is often applied to citizens of political nations as a modifier designating country of origin, but when it refers to a group it is about a societal nation. I use the term 'nationality' to refer to a societal group.

recognition of other nations. This reflects a collective/distributive distinction. Political nations depend on recognition of the whole (collectively), while societal nations depend on the characteristics of the individual members (distributively).

The members of a societal nation can be dispersed or in other ways have no territory of their own. It is sometimes said that a nationality (societal nation) must be capable of forming a nation-state (political nation, in my terms), but this usually confuses matters. It is quite possible that there are some national groups which are too small, too weak, or too uninterested to establish a country, or it may just be that the established nations (countries) simply refuse to accept the existence of yet another nation (country).

Many use the term 'a nation' in the sense of a societal group, synonymously with the term 'a people.' Both are understood ethnically as a way of classifying people into groups independently of their political organization or geographical location. Nations (or peoples) can be dispersed without being any the less an identifiable group. And they can establish one, several, or no states (or other political units). They are like an aggregate of people classified together.

Yael Tamir, however, distinguishes between a nation (in the sense of a societal group) and a people. She regards a nation as a group of people who are conscious of their shared culture, while a people is an ethnic group (perhaps depending on blood, among other things), not requiring awareness of membership.[6] This corresponds to ideas about the spirit of a nation (but not of a people) and national feelings, ideas which play a role in nationalism as usually understood. National feelings are thought of as nationalist feelings, even if they are sometimes below the level of consciousness. A national culture is part of the conscious life of the nationals and often consciously recognized as such.

Thoughts about national feelings, to follow a related but dangerous line of thought for a moment, lead some to ideas about national sentiments and passions in contrast to reason. We do not talk about national reason or the rationality of a nation. Consequently, nationalism becomes suspect for letting passions predominate, especially in collec-

---

6 Yael Tamir, *Liberal Nationalism* (Princeton, NJ: Princeton University Press 1993).

tive forms. Dark passions are contrasted with the light of reason. (This is the beginning of a theorist's overintellectualizing and of over-individualizing going astray. Individual reason is pitted against collective passion.) Much has been said about such conscious and semiconscious spiritual and cultural aspects of nationality. These aspects are important but outside my focus here.

I return to the ideas of Tamir about a nation involving people who are conscious of their culture, to be distinguished from a people who may exist independently of any awareness, even by themselves, of their identity. I myself find little difference between being a people and being a nation, with most of the difference deriving from the vagueness of both terms. There are no strict criteria for nations and peoples. Instead there are changing ideas about collective spirit, cultural traditions, shared characteristics, and racial distinctions[7] that advance or recede in the characterization of both nations and peoples. Both are terms for similar concepts clustering a variety of features together. The one clear but small difference is that a people can contain several nations, as do the Celts and the Crees, and, perhaps, less than a whole nation if the people maintains a subculture.

Whether a societal group is a nation (or people) or not is much contested wherever the question is significant, but the language shifts from one concept to another. Tamir speaks equally of communities and cultural groups.[8] Sometimes such groups are called 'national minorities' and sometimes 'nationalities.' The language is neither constant nor stable.

Some Differences between Nations and Nationalities

There are many differences between a political nation and a societal nation. (I will generally speak of the former as a 'nation' or 'country'

---

7 In this context it is especially important to recognize the unscientific nature of the concept of race. Confusions about race have complicated conceptions of a nation or people. On race, see Nancy Holmstrom, in Mohan Matthen and Robert Ware, eds., *Biology and Society*, Supp. Vol. 20 of the *Canadian Journal of Philosophy* (Calgary: University of Calgary Press 1994), 69-105.

8 See Tamir, *Liberal Nationalism*, 26.

and the latter as a 'nationality' or 'people.') A political nation (or country) is not the sort of thing to be dispersed (as is a nationality),[9] but nations (as countries) can lose their cultural cohesiveness and linguistic unity without losing their status as independent nations (unlike nationalities). Most nations (in this sense of a country) are multinational (with respect to societal groupings). A linguistic clue to the difference between political nations and societal nationalities is that the former have citizens or nationals (but not members) and the latter have members (but not citizens, and probably not nationals). Dual nationality is about citizens (with two passports) of political nations but not about members of societal nationalities, who might, however, be of mixed nationality (with a mixture of traditions). Nations and nationalities are different.

Nations and nationalities can also be distinguished by the possibilities of combination and separation. Separate countries can be combined into one country, as in the case of Tanzania. Recently, countries have more often been formed through separation, for example the separation of Norway from Sweden or the individual republics of the former Soviet Union or Yugoslavia. Those were political changes recognized by the international political community. They occurred basically without any cultural, linguistic, or religious changes of the individual people involved.

The combination and separation of nationalities (societal groupings), on the other hand, are social processes that occur over a longer period. Such changes depend on the development or evolution of cultures and traditions. In the case of nationalities, combination is probably the more common case, at least in the modern world. Societal groups are assimilated into other societal groups to form one people or nation. For example, Manchurians have become a part of the Han nation. Separations occur whenever complex societal groups split into two or more nationalities.

Even more distinctive is that nations as countries can clearly be 'identical twins,' although this is not so clear for nationalities, or peoples. The reality of nations as countries is such that two countries can be

---

9 Of course, a country can be discontinuous, even encompassing an archipelago, but not through a process of dispersing.

formed out of the split of a single homogeneous country. Norway and Sweden did not have to be different for there to be a split. Or, perhaps because of overwhelming cultural influences, one country can become identical to another in all significant ways except for territory. One could imagine this happening to the Rest Of Canada (without Quebec) in its relation to the United States. It is possible for the weaker nation to be formed in the image of the stronger. Nothing even excludes the possibility of a second identical nation being created or formed by accident. Nothing makes it impossible for two nations in the United Nations to be identical in all relevant respects. The reality of one allows for the reality of two nations that are alike in all relevant characteristics, as long as they are both recognized as nations.

The same appears not to be the case for nationalities as peoples. There being two nationalities with the same language, culture, and religion seems conceptually odd. It is plausible to say that two groups of people with the same essential features are in fact one people/nationality, even if the different groups came to have the same features over time. This would be especially true if nationalities were defined solely in terms of shared values or beliefs of the individuals. (This would make it conceptually impossible for everyone in two nationalities to have the same values and/or beliefs.) It might be possible to imagine separate but identical nationalities (or societal groups) if they were defined in terms of a social history or cohesive culture taken in a holistic way, i.e., applying to the nationality as a whole.[10] In such a case, there would be identical cultures applied separately to two separate groups. This would be most unlikely and perhaps conceptually impossible. In any case, it would be very different from separate but identical nations as countries. There are two different concepts of a nation: that of a country and that of a nationality.

This difference is probably the source of a common confusion about distinctness. As is obvious, two things can be distinct without any difference of properties (other than space and time), i.e., they do not have to be distinctive. In much of the literature on nationalism, there is a

---

10 Do the individuals partake of the culture that the nationality as a whole has, or is the culture of the nationality the aggregate of the culture of each individual?

slide from talking about distinct societies to talking about what must be distinctive about them. Because of the nature of things, this may be true of nationalities (as societal groups), but it certainly does not have to be true of nations (as countries).

If nationalities depend on the common characteristics of the individual members, then different nationalities will be distinctive. They will be identified by their distinguishing characteristics (again, other than space and time), and will thus necessarily be distinctive. Of course they will also be distinct, because they are separate. Nations (as countries), on the other hand, can be distinct without being distinctive. They can be boringly alike as long as they are recognized as separate nations, with a particular group of people on a particular territory. It may be that all nations are distinctive (from all other nations) and that it is easier to gain nationhood if the people are distinctive, but distinctiveness is not a necessary condition for being a nation. However, it is a simple point of logic that a nation is distinct.

There is another related difference between nationalities as societal groups and nations as countries. Societal groups that are nationalities appear to be homogeneous, because of the members' common properties. People in a single nationality normally speak the same language, are similarly cultured, and share the same basic beliefs and values. An appropriate homogeneity seems sufficient for being a single nationality. However, homogeneity is certainly not necessary (or sufficient) for forming a single political nation (or country), and it is a rarity in the contemporary world. Many, and perhaps most, countries are multilingual, multicultural, and radically pluralistic in beliefs and values. Like most holistic entities, countries do not gain their unity from homogeneity. They exist because of their international role.

The central notion of a nation is that of a political nation, but there is usually a loose connection with that of a nation as a societal group (probably the source of the now central notion). A nationality is often said to be a cultural group (further qualified) which is capable of forming a nation-state. It begs the question, however, to make the capability to form a state an essential feature of a national group. It is true that culture, language, and territory are all important to nations in both senses, but in different ways. Sameness of culture and language are virtually essential (or criterial) for being a nationality as a societal group, while territory is at most important. On the other hand, territory is essential for being a nation as a country, while a single culture and language may be useful but are in no way essential. Nations as societal groups are different from nations as countries, and it is the latter that tends to prevail in the international context.

The Changing Forms of Nations

There have not always been nations, of a societal, political or any other form. People have not always formed nations, nor do people even to-day everywhere fit naturally into nations. The concept of a nation, and the corresponding social structure, was a European creation of the eighteenth century,[11] when countries (i.e., nations) were created by establishing boundaries. France was united to form a nation only two centuries ago, and at the time when few of the people actually spoke French, although commonly a unifying language is considered a determining factor in constituting a people, the supposed basis of a nation.

Germany and Italy entered into nationhood less than a century and a half ago. Numerous countries have followed the path to nationhood in the past half century, with 185 now being members of the United Nations. Many of them, especially in Africa, have adopted the language of their colonizers rather than that of any of their peoples. In the last decade, many nations have begun to split into numerous other nations, and throughout the world social movements within nations are struggling for national self-determination of their own. In the meantime, most nations have created large bureaucracies and have taken on new functions never even considered early in the century.

Nevertheless, with the growth of transnational corporations, many observe a declining power and importance of nations, and others predict their obsolescence[12] or call for their abolition. At the end of the twentieth century many large corporations are larger and economi-

---

11 See Isaiah Berlin, 'Nationalism: Past Neglect and Present Power' in *Against the Current: Essays in the History of Ideas* (Oxford: Clarendon Press 1991), 345. See also Hobsbawm, *Nations and Nationalism since 1780* and Benedict Anderson, *Imagined Communities: Reflections on the Origin and Spread of Nationalism*, rev. ed. (London: Verso 1991).

cally more powerful than most of the political nations in the United Nations. "Of the 100 largest economies in the world, 51 are now corporations" and the "Top 200 corporations' combined sales are bigger than the combined economies of all countries minus the biggest nine; that is, they surpass the combined economies of 182 countries."[13] Globalization of corporate economies raises questions about the relevance of nations as countries. Certainly the role and influence of nations has changed drastically since they were formed a century or two earlier.

I am sure a similar story of other changes could be told about the history of nationalities during the last few centuries. Nationalities have been variously attached to religion, to cultural resurgence, to movements for autonomy or self-determination, to modernization, to territorial expansion, and to resistance to imperialism in various forms. The nationalism that has been sponsored by various nationalities has varied according to the dominant social, cultural, and political goals. According to Isaiah Berlin, the "first true nationalists – the Germans – are an example of the combination of wounded cultural pride and a philosophico-historical vision to stanch the wound and create an inner focus of resistance."[14] But other nationalities with other forms of nationalism have certainly existed.

In the mid-twentieth century in Africa, nationalism was an anticolonial force, a story well told by Basil Davidson.[15] As Davidson says, "African nationalism was the product not of a Kleistian chauvinism but of a mixture of antiracism and, which amounted in practice to the

---

12 See Basil Davidson, *The Black Man's Burden: Africa and the Curse of the Nation-State* (New York: Times Books 1992), especially in his 'Conclusion,' on the nation-state as a devil to be overcome in Africa as well as elsewhere.

13 Canadian Centre for Policy Alternatives *Monitor* **3:8** (Feb. 1997) 12, using 'The Top 200: The Rise of Global Corporate Power' by Sarah Anderson and John Cavanagh, Institute for Policy Studies, Washington, DC. For other relevant figures, see David C. Korten, *When Corporations Rule the World* (San Francisco, CA: Berrett-Kochler 1995), chap. 17.

14 Berlin, 'Nationalism,' 350. The very change that I am discussing contradicts the idea that there is such a thing as *true* nationalism.

15 See Davidson, *The Black Man's Burden*.

same thing, of anticolonialism."[16] Moreover, the nationalism of Africa germinated in very different sociopolitical structures with different institutions and goals. Some of the differences existed before the arrival of the Europeans, others were imposed by them. Of course, the Europeans also found nations of a very different sort from their own amongst the people of the first 'nations' in the Americas.

In the late twentieth century, nationalism has often been seen as anti-imperialist. As Shashi Joshi says of India, "Nationalism as an emotive force is intrinsic to being a victim of national oppression."[17] As Partha Chatterjee puts it, "[t]he history of nationalism as a political movement tends to focus primarily on its contest with the colonial power in the domain of the outside, that is, the material domain of the state."[18] In each case nationalism is related to various social forces with political goals of creating or developing an independent country with a state. In the colonized countries, however, this contest is fought out with indigenous structures against colonial conceptions and models of what nations and nationalities must be.[19] In much of the world, national movements are also struggles against European conceptions of nationalities and nations. The legacy of this diverse history of nationalities is a diversity of national forms in the contemporary world. Nationality still takes many different forms.

That there is more conceptual singularity about nations as countries is a product of a single international system structured by international law and practice and world institutions. Even so, there are groups that claim to be nations despite this modern 'world order.' From the Cree Nation to the Queer Nation, there are diverse groups to be recognized.

---

16 Davidson, *The Black Man's Burden*, 165

17 Shashi Joshi, *The Colonial State, the Left and the National Movement*, 1: 1920-1934 (New Delhi: Sage 1992) as quoted in Gail Omvedt, *Dalits and the Democratic Revolution* (New Delhi: Sage 1994), 15.

18 Partha Chatterjee, *The Nation and Its Fragments* (Delhi: Oxford University Press 1995), 9.

19 For a good discussion of this see Chatterjee, 'Whose Imagined Community?' in *The Nation and Its Fragments.* "Even our imaginations must remain forever colonized," he says. (Chatterjee, 5)

With such diversity, no wonder that it is so unclear what nations are and that our theories of nationalism are in such disarray.

Thinking about the Real Social World

Part of the problem with our social theories[20] is that we avoid full-fledged recognition of social entities. There really are nations – and nationalities. Social phenomena are shaped by national and international activity. Nations restrict trade and control union activity. They fight wars against each other and force restructuring of other nations and their economies. Nations are as real as families, which raise and comfort us, and as real as corporations, which structure production and make investments. There are also nationalities, which form associations and foster cultural practices and artistic productions. Nationalities give vision and understanding to their members, the people they embrace. They promote aspirations and sometimes discourage alternative understandings.

Nationalities and nations are different, but they are equally real and similarly large and encompassing. They span whole cultures and everyone within their domains or borders. Their practices reach to the heart and soul of every member or citizen, and they colour and structure the surrounding environments. Nations set up immense institutions and cover vast tracts of land with security forces, taxation procedures, and other systems. Their representatives and functionaries contact and direct everyone. The citizens of nations and the members of nationalities can have their influences in return, of course, but often with disappointing insignificance.

Nations and nationalities are real things constituted by real collec-

---

20 It should be obvious that my use of the term 'theory' in this context is broad, covering the diverse kinds of understanding that we find in social studies. My inclination is towards rigorous and more specific descriptions of social phenomena and their mechanisms. I would countenance social laws except that the social sciences appear to be like the biological sciences in their paucity of laws. I hope that what I have to say in this discussion of nationalism and related phenomena will be mostly independent of particular theories and metatheories, other than the points about referring to social entities.

tives, but there are also many other social entities that are among what must be understood in the social scene. In recognizing such social things, I am a holist. Holism, as I understand it, is the contradictory, rather than the opposite, of individualism. According to holism, individuals are not the only entities in society, although undoubtedly they are the most important. There are also nations, real nations with real, if diminishing, influences. There are also various middle-sized social objects. Everyone recognizes the reality of families, and little can be done in social theorizing without mentioning clubs, courts, and corporations, which are only at the beginning of the spectrum of 'holistic' (i.e., nonindividualistic) entities. Holistic entities are not the most important entities, but they are not to be ignored either.

Recognizing the existence of holistic entities does not, of course, establish their *unreducibility* – although personally I cannot imagine their being reduced and have argued for their unreducibility. It is enough for now that we take nonindividualistic entities seriously. I will leave it to others to struggle with formulations of reductive theories in terms of individuals alone. What is important for me here is to show that a serious recognition of the existence of nonindividualistic entities helps reveal the complexity of society and the ways in which that complexity is important with respect to nationalism.

I contend that a holistic approach to society gives a better perspective and a superior understanding of social phenomena. Part of that superiority comes from the aspects that are revealed and the questions that are asked. Charles Taylor suggests this in his clarification of the liberal-communitarian debate. I agree with Taylor that "once you opt for holism, extremely important questions remain open on the level of advocacy; at the same time, your ontology structures the debate between the alternatives, and forces you to face certain questions."[21] The only way to establish this is to consider the results of adopting such an ontology. If I make some progress here on understanding nationalism and related phenomena, it will be partly due to thinking about real social entities like nations and nationalities, but also corporations, associations, regions, etc.

---

21 Charles Taylor, 'Cross-Purposes: The Liberal-Communitarian Debate' in his *Philosophical Arguments* (Cambridge, MA: Harvard University Press 1995), 202.

Nations as Social Kinds

Nations seem a strange sort of thing, whether they are countries or societal groupings, nations or nationalities. We have difficulty deciding what they are, and there is little consensus about their nature. Sometimes it is thought that they do not have any real nature at all, that they are vague, subjective, or imagined entities. They are certainly formed, in various ways, by social groupings, perhaps under the influence of social structures, neighbouring peoples, and environmental factors. Once formed they are real social entities that influence and sustain us.

It is thus wrong to say "that nations are not things that exist in the world independently of the beliefs that people have about them, in the way that, say, volcanoes and elephants do."[22] Verificationism shows when Miller adds that elephants are known simply by observation.[23] Nationalities are identifiable things that exist in the world. Even if they are reducible they are not eliminable. (I continue to leave reductions to those who fancy attempts at reformulating nonindividualistic accounts.)

It is even more obvious that nations as countries exist. Countries occupy territory, establish governments, wage wars, colonize other countries, join the United Nations, and in general carry on international activities.[24] The reality of nations (as countries) should not be in doubt. What is in doubt, and probably wrong, is that they form natural kinds of the sort we find in the classification of particles or of the animal kingdom.[25] Nations have not always existed, and they do not fit

---

22 See Miller, *On Nationality*, 17. Of course, many or most of the people in a nation (or nationality) will have beliefs about the nation of which they are members, but the existence of the nation does not depend on the beliefs of its nationals, as is suggested in the passage.

23 I am not sure that nations cannot be observed – countries certainly can be – but I am sure that they do not have to be observed to be known to exist.

24 Different things have to be said about the Queer Nation or the Nation of Islam, although they are real forces to contend with and the structure of their reality is similarly gained through assertiveness, activity, and recognition.

25 There are important suspicions about there even being natural kinds of animals. See John Dupré, *The Disorder of Things* (Cambridge, MA: MIT Press 1993).

into any known general theory of social phenomena. They appear in diverse forms with no indication that they are formed according to natural forces and phenomena. They are social things constructed in a variety of ways by diverse societies.

Nations and nationalities can be thought of as social kinds, to use a concept similar to Ian Hacking's useful concept of human kinds.[26] Hacking applies the notion of a human kind to individuals, using classifications of people that take into account their behaviour and temperament. What distinguishes human kinds from natural kinds is that we create new classifications of people that, in turn, affect the people classified and how we think about them, looping back and giving further reason for human classifications. Hacking uses 'child abuser' and 'homosexual' as examples. The classification itself creates new behaviour and thus has a looping effect.[27]

Society constructs social entities, including nations and nationalities, but also cities, corporations, and parliaments, and in so doing creates social kinds. The social kinds then have a new influence through new activities which in turn affect society and create (with other forces in society) still other kinds. Societies create corporations which bring about stock exchanges which change corporations, and then trade organizations are established, and so on. There is a continuing looping effect that means that social kinds are in constant flux, bringing about not only social change but also conceptual change.

Nations and nationalities are real and varied, but they are also variously regarded. Some of the variation in the discussions of nations is to be accounted for by the variation in nations themselves, through the looping effects of social kinds. Different classifications (of the very same social reality) can be used; groupings can be delineated differently in

---

26 See Ian Hacking, 'The Looping Effects of Human Kinds' in Dan Sperber, David Premack, and Ann James Premack, eds., *Causal Cognition: A Multidisciplinary Debate* (Oxford: Clarendon Press 1995), 351-94.

27 See Hacking, 'The Looping Effects of Human Kinds,' 366-70. A current example that fits Hacking's analysis is that of whiteness. Recent studies try to explain the importance of being white, of thinking about the property of whiteness, as a way of better understanding classifications in a racist society.

different societies. The concepts are as malleable as the social entities are transitory. It should be noted that different sets of classifications can be equally applicable to the same social reality. Social phenomena are complex, with varying salient features, and thus can be described in different ways. There is the same underlying reality, only differently described and consequently with the possibility of different looping effects. The social classification used has social effects.

The concepts of nationality and nationhood are, consequently, contested concepts. These concepts are constructed, consciously or unconsciously, to fit contested values and ideologies. Many of the constructions will depend greatly on the particular salient characteristics that distinguish a familiar societal grouping. People have a variety of legitimate reasons, and some illegitimate ones as well, to focus on one concept or another. Even so, some conceptualizations are less descriptively adequate than others to the various shifts in social kinds. And of course some conceptualizations are less appropriate to some cultures and societies than others, which is the source of cultural and conceptual imperialism in dealing with nationalism elsewhere.

The Construction of Nations and Other Social Kinds

Much of the diversity of conceptions of nationalities can be attributed to the diversity of the real phenomena. People focus on different aspects of existing nationalities, which themselves vary. Among the diverse distinguishing factors in various concepts of nationality, language is usually important, although the Han people (nationality) has no single language. (There is a single script but the spoken languages, especially Cantonese and Mandarin, are not mutually intelligible.) Culture is widely thought to be equally crucial to nationality, although 'culture' is a vague term and variously applied. A culture can encompass an all-engrossing religion and little else, or it can encompass several religions in a secular society with other cultural preoccupations. Culture can be as minimal as American culture or as narrow as the car culture. Identifying and individuating cultures, which can encompass other cultures and/or ways of life, is far more difficult than individuating languages. Still, various nationalities do form around cultural aspects of societies.

Ethnicity, whatever it is in its various guises, is also thought to be a factor. Having a shared history, where the individuation is even more vague, is also mentioned in the literature. The self-perception or self-identity of (some) members is often relevant to some degree. Living with others of the same group in one territory can help in developing this self-perception. All of these various characteristics of whole groups and of their individual members are unified by religious, legal, and mass media institutions. Sociopolitical institutions are unifying forces which bring people together in various 'national' groups.

Which factors are operative or even important varies from one nationality to another. Most peoples have a shared language. Some peoples have little if any religion, and even where there is religion the differences in religious beliefs and practices are vast. The structures of the law and media vary greatly as do the structures of culture. All peoples have a culture (however structured), but some societies, and not just individuals, can be less cultured than others.

In the case of a political nation, having a territory is a crucial factor. Language becomes important for effective operation of the political institutions, although many multilingual states easily pursue their national interests. Political nations (or countries) pursue common interests, the commonweal of the people, and these common interests themselves help strengthen the nation (as well as solidifying a nationality). There is no reason why nationhood could not rise out of common projects, given of course the necessities for communication and for collective pursuit of them. People form real groups in a variety of ways and for various reasons. Western structures and contemporary capitalist interests may be dominant, but they are not the only kind, as is clearly seen in a cursory glance at other continents. Nations in various parts of the world take different forms with different social structures.

It is common to see a nation as a homogeneous group of individuals who have a common or shared set of beliefs and/or values. There are several things wrong with this view of a nation. For one thing, beliefs and values usually do not distinguish groups along national lines. The people of one nation have vastly different beliefs and values. Consider, for example, the differences between the people of the city and those of the countryside in most nations and nationalities. Moreover, there is often greater similarity across national borders than within them, but the borders are nonetheless real.

Wayne Norman has persuasively argued against the 'ideology of shared values' as a basis of unity, and presumably of separate nationality.[28] In the world today, many countries share values, without there being any reason for erasing international borders or obliterating differences of nationality. Norman, and Will Kymlicka,[29] think it is better, instead, to appeal to a sharing of identity, rather than values. People (individually) identify with others in a group or community, and the political unit is determined by the shared identity. Although this proposal has some merit, I think it suffers from some of the same problems of another well-known source of nationality: imagination. Benedict Anderson defines a nation as 'an imagined political community.'[30] It is not so much what individuals think or do – homogeneously or not – whether that is having values, identifying with a group of people, or imagining some community, but what the societal entity as a whole does.

Any such homogeneity of individuals necessary for forming a political or national community is rarely if ever found. An appeal to such a 'construction' of nations trades on stereotypes of individuals more than the rich diversity of interesting national groupings. Nationalities may be 'constructed' by the people but not by sharing values or imagining borders. It is more important that the people have common (joint) projects and set up institutions for the society as a whole. Still it should be remembered that in different parts of the world people will set up different kinds of nationality with different characteristics and institutions. The reality of societies, historically and contemporaneously, is one of diversity in kinds of nationality.

---

28 Wayne Norman, 'The Ideology of Shared Values: A Myopic Vision of Unity in the Multi-nation State' in Joseph H. Carens, ed., *Is Quebec Nationalism Just? Perspectives from Anglophone Canada* (Montreal: McGill-Queen's University Press 1995), 137-59.

29 See Will Kymlicka's review of Carens' book in 'The Paradox of Liberal Nationalism,' *The Literary Review of Canada* **4:10** (November 1995) 13-15.

30 Anderson, *Imagined Communities*, 4. But it should be noted that Anderson also gives weight to the importance of functionaries, the media, and various structures of the state. See, for example, *Imagined Communities*, 65 and 160. It is not simply a matter of imagination for him.

There appear to be degrees of being a nationality. Nationalities can be more or less cohesive and beliefs and cultures more or less shared. Religions are variously adhered to. Even common languages can have great variations of dialects. Some nationalities will form mostly on the basis of a religion. Some will depend on one or two aspects of culture, while other nationalities will depend on a rich diversity of aspects. The aspects will also be variously emphasized and developed more or less consciously. The varying cohesiveness or well-formedness in no way impugns the reality of nationalities.

In the case of nations as countries, nationhood is not a matter of degree – at least not in any significant way. Countries are either recognized or not in the international domain. There is no partial membership in the United Nations, and no nation is more of a nation than any other. There is only at most a question of how many nations recognize the nationhood of a polity. Only a few nations recognize Taiwan as a nation. There is also the occasional marginal case of a territory that claims nationhood and carries out some of the activities of a nation, such as printing stamps and minting coins. I would say that the aboriginal 'First Nations' of Canada and the 'Queer Nation' are differently formed rather than being less well formed or nations only to some degree. They are just different kinds of nations.

It is important to note that the world is made up of much more than nations and nationalities, of whatever diversity. There is a glaring contradiction between the simplicity in our treatment of momentous sociopolitical problems and the complexity of sociopolitical systems. Our minimalist perspectives are desperately inadequate for understanding the organizational and structural complexities of late capitalist societies and contemporary world systems. The world is complex in the social kinds that it contains. There are suprasocietal distinctions that are relevant to global changes and have an historical role of their own. We are all familiar with the developing European Union and various trade regions, such as those organized by the North American Free Trade Agreement and Southern African Development Coordination Conference. But there have long been empires (the British and the Inca, for example), commonwealths, and confederacies.

At the societal level, the important divisions vary from one country to another. The Soviet Union and Yugoslavia were wracked by the fragmentation of nationalities. In India the fragmentations are regarded as communal, under the pressure of communalism with strong religious divisions. Africa has seen tribalism move from an indigenous to a colonial nature. Native groups in all countries have various forms of confederacy and decentralized leadership and/or guidance. Nations and nationalism take on various forms in different parts of the world.

There is also a rich diversity in each separate society. Societies are filled with communities, minorities, subcultures, extended families, associations, security forces, management teams, Mafia families, co-operative societies – groups of all kinds. People live in neighbourhoods, communities, cities, townships, counties, arrondissements, villes (of various kinds), prefectures, environs, dioceses, constituencies, etc. All societies have complex structures, and most are very different. All are real entities of a social kind. In order to see the reality of social entities that are non-national and the complexity of their construction, one merely has to think of the struggle that ensued over the attempt to form a 'megacity' (a new social kind?) around Toronto.

The world is not divided between the individual and the nation, or the individual and the society (as it is often put). A nation is not composed simply of individual nationals. People are parts (members, citizens, or whatever – there is also no one kind of membership) of many different societal groupings and organizations with very different institutions. There are many ways for people to combine, develop visions, pursue common projects, and secure recognition. The differences need to be reflected in the construction of theory and reality. The study of nations is only a part of the study of societies and needs to be integrated into the study of the other parts.

Nationalism and Nations

The recent rise of nationalism has sent shockwaves around the world. Recognized nationalities and established nations have not found it easy to deal with the promotion of new nationalities and nations. Nationalism is seen as a destructive force, a negative phenomenon. It changes the circumstances for existing nations and nationalities and usually fragments or even eliminates another nation or nationality. In the last decade the process has been especially violent, destructive, and even genocidal. It should not be forgotten, however, that the competition of established nations had an important part to play in two world wars and ever since has been a factor in imperialist aggressions and invasions. Imperialist nations wreak havoc even more through the long, slow process of economic exchange. New and old nations alike are the source of destruction and chaos.

Because of the prevailing role in the world today of countries over societal groupings, nationalism tends to be tied to political nations and their states. Nationalism gets attached to national flags and armies and is whipped up into chauvinism and war. In the western context it is mostly a state phenomenon which is often connected with imperialism and the imposition of national cultures, institutions, and economies on other peoples or countries. But as we have seen above, it is also a means of resistance to dominant global forces. For nationalities that seek recognition and societies that want nationhood, nationalism looks a lot more positive. From their perspective, it is good to promote nationality and nationhood.

In a world of nation-states, it is important to be a nation to secure the favored institutions, positions in international organizations, and goals of the societal group(s). It is still true, as Delaney wrote in 1859, that "the claims of no people are respected until they are presented in a national capacity."[31] This unfortunate reality was the basis for bloody struggles up and down Africa and is now the source of daily frustrations for social movements seeking recognition throughout the world. The contemporary world has to find a way to recognize nations without allowing the dysfunctions of states brought about by the contradictions of the global economic systems. There can be countries without the present international politics, but the search for international peace cannot be a reason for denying recognition of new nations. It would be best to have nationalism without coercive states, but in the modern world every nation needs a protective state, protective against other

---

31 Quoted in Davidson, *Black Man's Burden*, 43. Cf. Isaiah Berlin's claim that "no political movement today, at any rate outside the western world, seems likely to succeed unless it allies itself to national sentiment" (Berlin, 'Nationalism,' 355).

nation-states as well as other international forces. The nationalism that establishes nations is a legitimate force.

Nationalism can be seen to be a very negative thing from one perspective but a positive thing from another perspective. Not all -isms are alike. Sexism is universally considered a bad thing – it wrongly promotes one sex over the other. Racism is almost universally bad, although I know people who seem to honestly see it as neutral as long as one 'race' is not thought to be superior. What we think of speciesism seems to depend on whether we think it is acceptable to see one species as superior to others. Humanism and environmentalism are generally thought to be positive. It is good to promote human or environmental values.

What about nationalism? Should we promote nations and nationalities? I do not see why we should promote one nation or nationality *over* others, but to promote nations and nationalities does not in any way imply the superiority of one nation or nationality over others. Unfortunately it is always possible for one person, group, or kind to *claim* their superiority, and worse, to wage wars over it. That is reason to establish institutions for international order and not to deny recognition to societies with good and peaceful national aspirations. Nations and nationalities still have the function of providing the associations and institutions that give people's lives form, context, and security.

Because nations and nationalities are different, nationalism is bound to take different forms in the two cases. A nationalism that promotes a nationality will normally promote one or more of the many diverse factors that determine nationality: language, culture, religion, ethnicity, or whatever. These are central aspects of human civilization. These factors can be promoted or secured without the group being imperialistic or evangelistic in any of those respects. The factors of nationality can also be promoted within and/or without the political institutions of a country, i.e., a nation in the political sense. However, if they are not secured without a defending country, then reasons for establishing a defending country, i.e., a nation, will be strong.

Because nations and nationalities are both transitory and diverse, nationalism, with respect to both social kinds, has to be understood in its particular circumstances, historically and geographically. We should avoid locking any group into historical anomalies and alienated ideologies. This is a message from non-Western sources that is at last breaking through.[32] Nationalism connected with nations can be more or less state oriented, because of the established global 'order,' but it can also be focussed on cultural developments of various kinds and to various ends when it is attached to societal groupings of various kinds.

Nationalism is not the only kind of social movement that promotes a part of society. Chauvinism, for example, attaches generally to different groupings, including cities, states, and regions. Some forms like Eurocentrism have a name, while others escape a nomenclature. It is probably best for a negative force to go unnoticed. From racism and sexism to elitism and corporatism, differing groups are promoted. Various instances of 'groupism' have had the negative role of promoting the superiority of one group (of the relevant kind) over others. But many groups have also been the focus of movements to promote a firmer and larger vision of the group concerned, including an understanding of similar movements promoting visions for other groups. There is every reason to promote goals, institutions, and cultures for groups that will be integrated into the rich complexity of diverse groups, internal and external to a society.

If national visions are developed socially for societal groups as opposed to the chauvinist forces that are attached to contemporary countries and their states, the world would avoid conflicts of states in order to achieve a multiplicity of languages and cultures. There is every reason to allow aspirations of political nationhood while discouraging the political nationalism of warring governments. There is also every reason to allow nationalist movements that encourage social development without political divisions of hierarchy and conflict. But political units are significant and legitimate parts of the international order.

It is not a matter of nature nor is it obvious what kind of political units will best secure the various determining factors of nationality whether or not they apply to a particular nationality. Of course if existing political units do not secure the language or culture or other social features, then that will be reason to find other political units to do so. It should also be obvious from the complexity of nationalities that the securing of only one feature, just language or just culture or just reli-

---

32 In this context, see Davidson, *The Black Man's Burden*, and Chatterjee, *The Nation and Its Fragments*.

gion, will likely be insufficient. Simply having multilingualism or multiculturalism alone is not enough. A nationality is not secured when only one of its determining factors is secured. Equally obvious is that few if any countries, i.e., political nations, contain only one nationality. So the role of the nation is to help secure all of the determining factors of nationalities important to everyone. It may even have the goal of securing multiculturalism and multinationalism. These are, of course, complex political goals facing even more complex social realities.

The legitimacy of a nation, however, does not require that it protect and secure distinct national characteristics. A nation does not have to be distinctive in order to be separate. Protecting distinctive character- istics can be a reason for establishing a nation, but having a distinctive nature is not a defining feature of a nation. The autonomy of a nation is like that of an individual. In both cases, the life is its own without *nec- essarily* being different. A nation merely requires having a role in the international political context. Nationhood is decided by the will of the people and the politics of the world around them.

Some would say that distinct societies are legitimate candidates for national existence, for achieving nationhood. That may be true but we know so little about what a society is, as well as what a distinct society is.[33] It is true that separate nations have distinct, i.e., their own, socio- political institutions. In some social groupings, even within existing nations, there are institutions that are distinct and even distinctive. This appears to be the case for Quebec and for (some?) First Nations in Canada. This gives the beginning for the establishing of nationhood. The rest is a matter of the will of the people and the politics in the existing world 'order' – no small matter, of course. The future will emerge from organization and negotiation over the preservation of real nationalities and the recognition of real nations.[34]

---

33 For a discussion of our ignorance about this social kind, i.e., societies, see Claude Denis, *'Quebec-as-distinct-society* as Conventional Wisdom: The Constitutional Silence of Anglo-Canadian Sociologists,' *Canadian Journal of Sociology* **18:3** (1993) 251-69.

34 For critical comments and useful discussions about nationalism and nations, I thank Jocelyne Couture, Diana Hodson, Kai Nielsen, Peter Okeke, and Michel Seymour.

PART II

Probing the Orthodox Dichotomy

Democracy and Nationalism*

ANDRÉ VAN DE PUTTE
K.U. Leuven

In 1789 Sieyès defined the nation as *"un corps d'associés vivant sous une loi commune et représentés par la même législature."*[1] In so doing, he gave expression to an idea that would follow a remarkable historical course and develop a complex and ambiguous logic.[2] In this study we attempt to clarify this ambiguity, thereby gaining some insight into the complicated relationship between democracy and nationalism.

I   The Revolutionary Idea of the Nation

The revolutionary idea of the nation, expressed by Sieyès, did not come out of thin air, but arose within a process of social and political transformation which began long before the French Revolution. By attempting to establish its sovereign power and found a state, the French monarchy came into conflict with regional and other traditional powers with whom it had previously shared power as *primus inter pares*. The absolutist state founders discovered how important it was to have the community united behind them, so they sought to create feelings

---

* Translated from the Dutch by Dale Kidd.

1 "[A] body of associates living under a common law and represented by the same legislature." E. Sieyès, *Qu'est-ce que le Tiers état*, critical edition with an introduction and notes by R. Zapperi (Genève: Droz 1970), 126

2 A. Renaut, "Les deux logiques de l'idée de Nation," in *Cahiers de philosophie politique et juridique*, 1988, nr. 14, 7ff

of national unity that would transcend the old regional loyalties and make France a 'patria' in the minds of the people, with the king as its incarnation and guarantor. They linked formation of a state with formation of a nation. In this way, a united civil society arose through a long process of (economic) community formation in which regions and classes converged. Along with this, there was a growing sense of individualism. By breaking the bonds of feudalism, the kings released individuals from traditional ties while ensuring at the same time that individuals would see themselves more and more as members of a nation. The new society less and less resembled an articulated body characterized by traditional ties and *'corps intermédiaires,'* becoming more and more a formless mass of atomized equal individuals.[3] Under the *ancien régime* this development was actually only present as a general tendency: the nation was still articulated and diversified, even after the king's sovereignty was no longer in dispute. National feeling was still linked to the existence of *'corps intermédiaires,'* a plurality of estates (nobility, church and *'la nation'* – the third estate), and provincial particularism.

The French nation that arose in this way grew out of a process of modernization, bureaucratization, and rationalization imposed on the country by autocrats. In Meinecke's words, it was a *Staatsnation* and not a *Kulturnation*,[4] since it had its origin not in a communally experienced cultural patrimony, but in a common political history. The sense of community characterizing such a nation grew out of the state-building activity of the political power brokers. The nation united around strong political figures who incarnated it and who became the object of political loyalties.

And yet, under the *ancien régime*, one cannot yet speak of a French *nation*, for the term is really only applicable to a world of citizens and

---

3 J.E. Acton, "Nationality" [1862], in his *Essays in the Liberal Interpretation of History: Selected Papers*, ed. and with an introduction by W.H. McNeill (Chicago: University of Chicago Press 1967), 140

4 Fr. Meinecke, *Weltbürgertum und Nationalstaat* [1908] (München: Oldenbourg 1969), 10ff. Meinecke admits that he does not intend this distinction to be absolute. Pure cultural nations with no contribution by political factors are as rare as state nations with no cultural element.

not to a world of subjects.[5] A group of people that is only integrated by some central authority is not a nation, and so not every state is a nation-state.[6] Without a *"Sinn für selbständige politische Überzeugung und freiere politische Tätigkeit,"*[7] and without the rise of a constitutional government through which the people (in the first place the civil elite) participate in political life, no nation can exist.[8]

By the end of the eighteenth century, the French kings had done their job so well that the nation became aware of itself, claiming for itself sovereignty and the right to self-determination. The 'nation' became a battle-cry against absolutist society. After having been constituted by the kings, the nation completed its emancipation by demanding a nation-state, control of the government, and the right to determine its own fate.

***

This sketch of the historical background was necessary in order to bring to light the inherently political meaning of Sieyès' definition. The nation cannot be considered in isolation from the aspiration for democracy, emancipation, political participation, and self-determination. The

---

5   "A state becomes a nation when instead of its members being primarily divided between sovereign and subject, government and citizenship become a common task, demanding not passive citizenship but active cooperation from all." A.D. Lindsay, *The Modern Democratic State* (London: Oxford University Press 1943), I, 151, quoted in R.A. Nisbet, "Citizenship: Two Traditions," in *Social Research* **41** (1974) 614-15.

6   The fact that states are often called nations, as in the expression "United Nations Organization," does not contradict this but is a result of the modern principle of legitimacy which accepts only the nation-state as a legitimate state, i.e., the state which has become a state of *some* nation. Cf. Meinecke, *Weltbürgertum*, 286; Th. Schieder, *Nationalismus und Nationalstaat. Studien zum nationalen Problem im modernen Europa*, O. Dann and H.-U. Wehler, eds. (Göttingen: Vandenhoeck and Ruprecht 1991), 17.

7   "Sense for autonomous political conviction and free political activity"

8   Meinecke, *Weltbürgertum*, 17, 31, 37; W.J. Mommsen, "The Varieties of the Nation State in Modern History: Liberal, Imperialist, Fascist and Contemporary Notions of Nation and Nationality," in M. Mann, ed., *The Rise and Decline of the Nation State* (London: Basil Blackwell 1990), 210-11

nation is created in a sort of self-proclamation in which the citizens proclaim themselves to be sovereign, the source of all power, a historical and political agent empowered to act politically, both internally and externally.

In this study our attention will be directed primarily to the implications of the idea of the nation for the social life of the citizens, and only secondarily to its international dimension. What characterizes the nation is the political will of its citizens to link their fate to one another. This is why Sieyès uses the term *'associés.'* It is this political will that establishes a social bond among them, making them a *'corps d'associés.'* The social bond, consequently, is not pre-political; it is not a religious, cultural, or ethnic communality or affection which objectively characterizes them and which they have not chosen, but a bond of mutual recognition of one another as legal subjects and fellow citizens. The integration displayed by a nation is that of a legal community (*vivant sous une loi commune*) of citizens who direct themselves by participating in the life of the state through representation (*représentés par la même législature*). Of course, such a juridical and political integration of the social body is quite abstract when compared with the integration of an emotional community characterized by alliances which have developed naturally. In opposition to these alliances, the nation expresses the will and ambition to transcend all social, religious, regional, and ethnic bonds, and to integrate all individuals into a single, joint political and juridical space. The secularism and neutrality which the nation ascribes to itself express the idea that the bond which links the citizens is no longer religious or ethnic, but national. Also fundamental to the idea of a nation is the distinction between a public space in which everyone may participate and in which issues of general concern are discussed, and the many private spaces where natural solidarities and alliances are maintained.[9] The nation, as such, is the expression of a

---

9 "What the civic sense more than anything else seems to involve is a definite concept of the public as a separate and distinct body and an attendant notion of a genuine public interest, which though not necessarily superior to, is independent of and at times even in conflict with both private and other sorts of collective interest." C. Geertz in C. Geertz, ed., *Old Societies and New States: The Quest for Modernity in Asia and Africa* (New York: The Free Press 1963), 156.

new ethos. Recognition of the value of others, and their reception within the bonds of solidarity are no longer dependent on their membership in a family or ethnic group, but only on their abstract qualities as human and citizen. So the idea of a nation also implies that individuals are capable of the reasonableness which the nation demands of them and that, through political education, they can be shown the way beyond the natural solidarity linking them with their ethnic group toward an abstract solidarity with their fellow citizens and countrymen.

***

This initial outline should make it sufficiently clear why and in what sense the social contract metaphor was so appropriate for theoretically legitimating the nation's political emancipation.[10] This metaphor represents individuals in the state of nature not as bound by natural ties but freely in control of themselves. In social contract thought, individuals are not seen as concrete beings marked by particular facticity, but as abstract individuals, pure representatives of humanity. The only relevant characteristics taken into account are those which J. Rawls has recently summarized in his political concept of the person: rationality and reasonableness, freedom and equality.[11] The ascription of these characteristics to individu-

---

10 Although this process of emancipation was carried out in the name of universal claims, the natural rights of individuals, and the sovereignty of the people, in reality it was from the outset the emancipation of a particular group which identified itself with the nation. As already mentioned, the nation was originally seen as equivalent to the third estate, even to the extent of excluding the nobility and clergy insofar as they refused to subscribe to the terms of the social contract and the universal principles of the revolution. There is little doubt that this identification of the nation with the bourgeoisie influenced the attitude of socialists and Marxists toward nationalism. In 1848-9, the workers still supported the national struggle. They believed a solution to the national question was a precondition for solving the social question. However, when the bourgeoisie rejected the notion that national emancipation also entailed the emancipation of the fourth estate, the workers turned against national movements. But 1914 demonstrated once more that this was more an appearance than a reality.

11 J. Rawls, *Political Liberalism* (New York: Columbia University Press 1993), 29ff., 48ff., 79

als is sufficient to found the ideal of a society that would generate solidarity and cooperation among heterogeneous peoples.

In social contract theory, then, a legitimate political society results from the free consent of such individuals. The nation is therefore artificial, not natural. It is an *association* arising from a social contract, an act of will by sovereign individuals. The social bond is not a natural fact, but rather the result of a wish, inspired by reasonableness, to integrate everyone into a single political space, even those we experience as *foreign* because we feel no natural link with them. Enlightenment philosophers saw this idea of the nation as the realization of the moral principle of universality. This principle requires that I should be able to universalize whatever I undertake to do; that I take others – *all the others* – into account from an impartial standpoint; that I consider things also from their point of view, with an *'erweiterte Denkungsart'* ['enlarged way of thinking'] (Kant). Society therefore ought to rest on principles that everyone can reasonably accept, not on conceptions that refer to a particular form of life. And the standpoint one occupies can no longer be ethnocentric – valid for all those who are like me, who share the same identity – but must be universalistic – valid for all reasonable beings and all possible societies. Laws and institutions are only legitimate if they meet with the reasonable consent of all members of the political community, thus implying everyone's recognition.

However, since this recognition is no longer based on a particular shared conception of the good life, it can only be *abstract* and *formal*. That is to say, it can only be the recognition of every person's *equal freedom* to lead their lives according to their own convictions. The social contract, then, is an agreement by which individuals undertake to live together in an association that respects and safeguards everyone's natural freedoms. Universality also demands recognition of the equality of freedoms, and therefore it must be restricted by the law, since it is only the form of the law – i.e., the law's universality and abstractness – that can guarantee the equality of freedoms. The law's form refers in a formal manner to a successful universalization, and universalization and abstractness preclude arbitrariness and establish legal certainty. The social contract, as a result, includes the consent and submission of everyone to a communal *law*. And yet, the universality of the law is still insufficient to secure its legitimacy. In a kind of reflexive movement, universality makes a further demand, that the law itself should result from a process of legislation in which everyone may take part unhindered. Consequently, individuals must not only recognize one another as free and equal legal subjects, but also as free and equal participants (through representation) in the legislative process. They must constitute a public space that can be understood as an institutionalization of the *erweiterte Denkungsart*.

The revolutionary idea of the nation is thus constructivistic, individualistic, and voluntaristic. What constitutes, animates, and maintains political society is the *general will*, the consent and free choice of radically autonomous individuals to recognize one another and live together. It is this that makes them a nation, not a shared history nor ethnic or linguistic determinations. In the words of Renan, it is *'le plébiscite de tous les jours'* that continually recreates the nation.[12] All those who subscribe to the conditions of the social contract are members of the nation; they give their consent to the constitution, which embodies the universal juridical principles of the democratic constitutional state. The nation is not a body to which one naturally belongs by fate; nationality is not a natural determination. The integration and sense of community which characterize the nation are that of an abstract legal community that does not exist by nature, but is only constituted in and through the mutual recognition of one another's rights. The integration of a nation is not mediated by a shared ethos or form of life, but by the law. One becomes French by a voluntary act of adhesion, not by birth or because one happens to speak French. What is necessary and sufficient for determining to which nation a group or individual belongs is not any objective characteristics or historical claims, but a plebiscite.[13] A nation has no natu-

---

12 E. Renan, *Qu'est qu'une nation* (Paris: Calmann Lévy 1882), 27. In the words of Meinecke, *Weltbürgertum*, 12: *"Nation ist, was eine Nation sein will"* ["A nation is what wants to be a nation"].

13 The abstractness of this point of view can be seen from the fact that a people must first be identified before a plebiscite can be taken (J. Mayall, *Nationalism and International Society* [Cambridge: Cambridge University Press 1990], 41). Furthermore, a plebiscite will never solve the problem of minorities. Despite the theoretical acceptance of the principle of nationality in 1919, the map of Europe was redrawn according to pragmatic strategies and political criteria. Even in those states which were decolonized after World War II, borders were frozen without a plebiscite. Cf. Mayall, 56.

ral borders based on language, race, or ethnicity, but only political-moral borders, and they reach only as far as the principles of the social contract hold. In the revolutionary conception, 'nation' and 'people' have a purely political and constitutional meaning. Nationality is nothing other than citizenship. The nation does not precede the contract which founds the state as if it were some pre-political entity rooted in nature or history and which, once aware of itself, strives for self-determination.

The republican nation is, in principle, an open society of anonymous and abstract individuals united by a contract. It is not an exclusive club open only to those with identical natural characteristics, but is ready to admit anyone who accepts its principles. Because of its universality, the idea of a nation refers ultimately to all people, and is an appropriate idea for any society whatever its place in history might be. Since a nation's right to self-determination is legitimated by universal postulates of reason, the nation will appear as a subsection of humanity,[14] as a practical link between the individual and humanity at large, and as the most comprehensive empirical approximation of humanity that is possible in everyday life. In principle, then, the nation possesses hardly any particularity which would distinguish it from other nations. It could at any moment expand into a world republic of all humanity if everyone would subscribe to its humanistic principles. Yet the proponents of this revolutionary idea of the nation did not extend its universality. Their 'realism' ensured that they continued to situate the nation within the old traditional limits of the state. It is important to emphasize this, since it reveals something that remains largely unthought: the contingency of history, the fact that an actual nation grows out of history and, as such, is a social and historical entity separate from other such entities, as 'we' from 'they.'[15] The national bond would then ap-

---

13 Meinecke, *Weltbürgertum*, 71. According to Meinecke, this "formalistically" conceived idea of national sovereignty is blind to the nation in a historical, "substantial" sense.

14 For many commentators, the absence of a "they" at this level is an argument supporting the view that belonging to humanity can never be a truly subjective, existential feeling, but only a rational construction of the mind. See, most recently, D. Schnapper, *La communauté des citoyens. Sur l'idée moderne de nation* (Paris: Gallimard 1994), 183.

pear to be more complex than the revolutionary idea of the nation suggests. Despite its being open in principle, in reality its limits are not abolished, and historical alliances still play a part.[16]

Because the proponents of the civil nation were blind to this unthought-of element of their beliefs, they were able to point confidently to the eternal peace and friendship among nations that would take shape once the Europe of nations replaced the Europe of monarchs. They were able to interpret the revolutionary and messianic war of *'la grande nation'* as the fulfillment of a mission. When the French nation waged war, they were able to think that this was done not as a historical nation, but as the representative of a universal culture propagating the natural legal principles of correct state organization, of freedom and self-determination. This is not, at least in principle, a natural entity's cult of vital expansion and hegemony, or will to live, but rather a patriotism in which the promotion of one's own nation coincides with the promotion of universal human ideals and the institutional framework of a democratic state, and where ethnicity and language are irrelevant. In this way, one could be both a patriot[17] and a citizen of the world.

II   An Untenable Abstraction?

In the preceding section we examined the ideal type and the specific logic of the political idea of the nation. This analysis, however, also brought to light something unthought of, indicating that reality is more

---

16 This "realism" is also apparent in the way in which a people's right to self-determination was conventionally interpreted after the Treaty of Versailles. It was reserved for the peoples of the disintegrating multinational Empires, and (later) for ex-colonies. Cf. Mayall, *Nationalism and International Society*, 50ff.

17 The term "patriot" did not originally refer to someone who professed blind allegiance to his country ("my country, right or wrong"), but rather to someone who worked to renew and reform the nation according to the principles of natural law. Americans and Dutchmen used the term in this sense, around 1780. The "patria" which is the object of a patriot's loyalty is no existential, pre-existing unity, but a nation to which its members can consent. Cf. E.J. Hobsbawm, *Nations and Nationalism since 1780: Programme, Myth, Reality* (Cambridge: Cambridge University Press 1990), 87.

complex. Are we not in fact dealing with an untenable abstraction when we assume that pure, unsituated freedoms can bring about a society characterized only by conformity to abstract postulates of reason, postulates lacking any reference to particular natural determinations, to a shared past, or to feelings of unity? Does this not overlook the one-sided and the particular, the 'earthly' love for a landscape, for the sound of a language, for a way of life that, produced by habit, characterizes all groups and individuals? It was clear even to Renan, despite his emphasis on the importance of the plebiscite for the nation, that nations are also marked by objective facts, a history, a tradition.[18] Can reason, freedom, and choice really be dissociated to such an extent from facticity, determination, and nature? We should not forget that the revolutionary French nation was a product of the kings' state-building activity. Even the new nation has roots in a historical process; it does not exist merely in the continuous present of ever-repeated consent. Even the French nation led a quasi-vegetative existence before coming to consciousness and willing itself into political unity.[19] This conclusion casts a different light on the revolutionaries' self-interpretation that the French nation could be a creation of the will, a *Vernunftstaat* [a state produced by reason], and not the product of historically determined forces.

Indeed, the revolutionary nation appears not to have been immune to ethnic and cultural nationalism. As already explained, the revolutionary nation tries to exclude in principle any reference to particular alliances, in order to establish a social bond which would be based solely on the political will to mutual recognition and solidarity. In reality, however, it quickly became apparent that there was a latent nationalism at work even at the heart of the revolutionary nation.[20] Already with Jacobin nationalism, the principles of the revolution were naturalized. The revolutionary concept of the nation did not really succeed in excluding all particularity. In fact, constitutional patriotism turned out to be supported by alliances referring to culture and history. Dur-

---

18 Renan, *Qu'est qu'une nation*, 26

19 Fr. Meinecke, *Weltbürgertum*, 248-9

20 Mayall, *Nationalism and International Society*, 92

ing the revolution there arose a compromise between liberal rationalism and historical essentialism that provoked, in Europe, an immediate counter-nationalism.[21] How are we to understand this?

As already mentioned, the nation is constituted and maintained by the unanimous will of its members. This general will is the life principle, as it were, the nation's soul. This confronts the nation and particularly the nation-state – as the instrument of the nation – with a specific problem. It must somehow manage to perpetuate the general will, and somehow manage to integrate all its members into the nation and awaken in them the social dispositions required by mutual recognition and solidarity. But the creation and permanence of the general will is threatened by the abstract, liberal-individualistic assumptions which we have seen reflected in the metaphor of the social contract. What is to prevent the society of the daily plebiscite from falling apart into its atomic elements and becoming an instrument of private interests? After all, the nation conceives individuals to be both reasonable and rational. The former assumes that individuals are capable of acting in the general interest and making public use of their reason, thus creating political bonds among them. The latter, however, implies that individuals have their own aims and are able to act strategically for their own good, or the good of those with whom they feel most closely connected. This presents the democratic nation with a paradox. On the one hand, the democratic legal order permits the freedom and goal-rationality of strategically acting subjects within the framework of binding laws. On the other hand, it also appeals to the citizens to let themselves be guided by reasonableness in their actions, i.e., to make public (not strategic) use of their reason. The nation cannot, however, compel this kind of behaviour, for the citizens' rights of participation can only be institutionalized in the form of political rights of freedom which leave the citizens free either to publicly make use of or not to make use of their reason. Rawls' duty of civility can therefore never be more than a moral duty.[22] And the law, as distinct from morality, can never compel the public use of reason even though this is presupposed

---

21 Mayall, *Nationalism and International Society*, 57

22 Rawls, *Political Liberalism*, 217, 253

in the very idea of democracy, and even though, without the public use of reason, the institutions of freedom would collapse. The ethos of a nation seems paradoxical in a world populated by unconnected individuals. Free consent and the general will which constitute the nation will be shaky and uncertain unless the problem of the unity, homogeneity, and universality of the wills that create the nation can be resolved. In addition, the public space of legislation must provide room in which individuals can consult, understand and persuade one another; this presupposes that they share a certain frame of reference. According to the principle of a nation, this framework should be purely political: a public language, the political values and principles of universality, the distinction between the public and the private, and a political culture that goes along with all this. In this sense, the state must educate the nation's members in order to perpetuate their general will.

In reality, however, the nations' attempts to deepen and strengthen the intimate bond between individuals and their nation went much further than a strictly political education. Apparently their trust in the solidity of a purely abstract, political bond was not very great. The nations often referred to a sense of community and a frame of reference linked with emotions, feelings of connectedness, and an identity, all of which emerged out of the contingencies of history and concerned the fact that a nation is never simply a community of citizens, but always a historical and cultural singularity as well, distinct from other such singularities.[23] In this manner, they hoped to bring about a sufficiently unified and homogeneous frame of reference with sufficiently strong feelings of solidarity, in order to provide resistance to states that were unified by bonds less abstract than merely political ones, based on reasonable will and choice.

***

Hobbes and Locke had already found themselves confronted with the problem of civil-mindedness in a society based on liberal, individual-

---

23 Schnapper, *La communauté des citoyens*, 155

istic foundations.[24] But it is especially in Rousseau's writings that we are faced with the question of how to ensure that the citizens act as one people and not as an aggregate of individuals, that their wills are directed to the general interest, and that the general will has a chance to be heard. This question had a decisive influence on Rousseau's conception of democracy. For Rousseau, the political body must not be fragmented into parties and interest groups; all intermediate bodies which would hinder the individuals' direct involvement with the general interest must be abolished. Furthermore, there must be a sufficient degree of equality among the citizens, and the sovereign must demand of all subjects a unanimous participation in a *'religion civile.'* Rousseau is quite aware that a democratic nation cannot be artificially constructed in just any society whatsoever. 'Democracy' presupposes a population of perfect beings, of gods, and among human beings a relatively poor and simple society characterized by sufficient socio-economic and moral *homogeneity*. If this is lacking, the people will have to be educated and the conditions created to give the will of the people a 'correct' and 'unified' determination.[25]

For Rousseau, then, the individualistic foundations of contract theory are converted into a collectivism. The social contract gets the meaning of an existential act of identification with the community whereby, in a single movement, the individuals are metamorphosed into citizens and are absorbed by 'the people,' understood as a natural substance. In this metamorphosis they disappear as individuals possessing subjective rights of freedom, and they acquire (positive) freedom. Critical observers of the French Revolution such as Burke, de Tocqueville and Lord Acton have noted that the Revolution was driven less by the idea of freedom than by that of unity, equality, and homogeneity; that the

---

24 This problem is also I.G. Fichte's starting point in *Reden an die Deutsche Nation*, in *Fichtes Werke* (Hrsg. I.H. Fichte), Bd. VII, *Zur Politik und Philosophie der Geschichte* (Berlin: De Gruyter 1971), 26ff.

25 P. Alter, *Nationalism* (London: Edward Arnold 1990), 39. Later, the republic will in fact take on the task of forging this unity and determination of the will via republican education in J. Ferry's *école laïque*. Although in principle, this indoctrination does not refer to language and soil, but to the values of the republic, in reality the reference is to *"la France"* and *"la République"* simultaneously.

Rousseauist majority democracy did nothing other than extrapolate the logic of centralization and bureaucratization begun by the French kings; that the sovereignty of the people was just as intolerant of intermediate powers separating itself as a sovereign from itself as a subject; and that the Revolution ultimately led to a totalitarianism of *'la nation une et indivisible,'* egalitarian and homogeneous, prepared to nip in the bud any dissent, any pluralism, any federalism, or any autonomy.[26] Lord Acton in particular has shown how, in the transition from individualism to collectivism, revolutionary discourse became permeated with references to a collective identity of language, history and culture.[27] For this to occur, it was enough that the conception of 'the people'

---

26 Alter, *Nationalism*, 39

27 Undoubtedly, Rousseau is thought of in the first place as a promoter of republican patriotism. Nevertheless, there are already announcements of this transition in his thinking. In his *Projet de Constitution pour la Corse* (in *Oeuvres Complètes*, T. III, Ed. de la Pléiade [Paris: Gallimard 1970], 913) he states: *"La première règle que nous avons à suivre est le caractère nationnal. Tout peuple a ou doit avoir un caractère nationnal et s'il en manquoit il faudroit commencer par le lui donner"* ["The first rule to be followed is the principle of national character; for each people has, or ought to have, a national character; if it did not, we should have to start by giving it one"]. And in his *Considerations sur le gouvernement de Pologne et sur sa réformation projettée* (in *idem*, 960) we read: *"La vertu de ses Citoyens, leur zèle patriotique, la forme particulière que des institutions nationales peuvent donner à leurs âmes, voila le seul rempart toujours prêt à la défendre, et qu'aucune armée ne sauroit forcer [...] Ce sont les institutions nationales qui forment le génie, le caractère, les goûts, et les moeurs d'un peuple, qui le font être lui et non pas un autre, qui lui inspirent cet ardent amour de la patrie fondé sur des habitudes impossibles à déraciner, qui le font mourir d'ennui chez les autres peuples au sein des délices dont il est privé dans le sien"* [The virtue of its citizens, their patriotic zeal, the distinctive form which its national institutions may give their soul, this is the only rampart that will stand ever ready to defend it, and which no army could subdue by force ... It is national institutions which form the genius, the character, the tastes, and the morals of a people, which make it be itself and not another, which inspire in it that ardent love of fatherland founded on habits impossible to uproot, which cause it to die of boredom among other peoples in the midst of delights of which it is deprived in its own"]. For an examination of the ramifications of these texts within the thought of Rousseau, see R. Derathé, "Patriotisme et nationalisme au XVIIIe siècle," in M. Albertini *et al.*, *L'idée de Nation* (Annales de Philosophie Politique, 8) (Paris: PUF 1969), 69-84.

– understood as a natural substance into which individuals are absorbed in order to become themselves – was interpreted ethnically, that it was ascribed an ethnic character. According to Acton, the Rousseauist understanding of democracy ensured that the idea of nationality could be grafted onto the idea of people's sovereignty,[28] that *dèmos* and *ethnos* could become intertwined. After having subjected the individual to the collective will, the revolutionary system subjected the collective will to the contingencies of a historically arisen identity.[29]

Faced with the resistance of other European states, it was not difficult for Jacobin nationalism to tap the hidden forces lying dormant in proto-national feelings of natural alliance, race, language and culture. The one, indivisible republic became the incarnation of a pre-political, natural unity. Although in principle one could be a Frenchman without knowing French, there quickly arose an unmistakable pressure in the direction of linguistic uniformity.[30] References to ethnic ties were integrated into, and became the central emotional component of, republican patriotism. And insofar as they did not exist, they had to be constructed. Feelings of existential identification with *'le pays natal'* were projected onto the country as a whole; the heritage of the different regions is combined into one national heritage; a single, universal republican culture was constructed out of diversity.

This is why the integral nationalism of Maurras and *l'Action française*, to which Jacobin nationalism can be seen as a prelude, was from the beginning an intrinsic *possibility* of the republican nation-state. This integral nationalism opposes everything that might cause division: party politics, individualism, foreigners and Jews, international socialists and cosmopolitan capitalists – anything that might threaten the unity, singularity, and purity of the nation. It propounds an ideology

---

28 "The theory of nationality is involved in the democratic theory of the sovereignty of the general will." Acton, 'Nationality,' 147.

29 "Thus after surrendering the individual to the collective will, the revolutionary system makes the collective will subject to conditions which are independent of it, and rejects all law, only to be controlled by an accident." Acton, 'Nationality,' 159.

30 For an example of an early mixture of both concepts of nationhood, see Hobsbawm, *Nations and Nationalism*, 20ff.

of integration which attempts to fashion a firm, unanimous will by returning to the spiritual force of the nation's authentic origins. As a 'civil religion' with a cult of the soil and the dead, it presents the nation as absolute: we owe everything, not to God, but to the nation. National-istic rituals celebrate a shared way of life, a shared identity, and ultimately the community itself.[30] In this way, the nation that initially situated itself on an abstract, political level and claimed to have substituted religious ties for abstract, political ones, ends up by sacralizing itself.

One objection to this interpretation is that it took nearly a century, after the short period of Jacobin nationalism, for the integral nation-alism of Maurras and *l'Action française* to arise, and that it was never as virulent as other nationalisms.[32] But it is precisely this fact that con-firms our suspicion of there being a secret link between the sovereign people's majority democracy and nationalism for, as is well known, the nation that rises up against the kings is the original third estate. It is only very gradually that electoral democracy and the (common) people fully arrive on the political scene. Until that time, Risorgimento nationalism was able to quell the dangerous tendencies apparent in Jacobin nationalism. As long as 'the people,' in a political sense, re-main a small group, it makes very little difference that only a few of them consider themselves to be Italian. Only later, with increasing de-mocratization and mass politics, is it necessary to create Italians and to turn peasants into Frenchmen,[33] binding everyone to the nation and the flag. The nationalistic trend toward homogenization can thus be

---

31 This intertwining of nationalism with (pseudo)religious language has been noted by C.J.H. Hayes. See his *Nationalism: A Religion* (New York 1960). The relation between nationalism and religion (or fundamentalism) is in fact extremely complex. Often religion competes with the nation by claiming exclusive loyalty. See, for example, Hobsbawm, *Nations and Nationalism*, 67ff., 168ff.

32 This difference in virulence most likely has to do with the fact that nations which can count on a sufficiently high degree of internal cohesion can also afford to tolerate more liberal and subjective elements in the state. If this is not the case, unity and homogeneity must be compelled by force.

33 E. Weber, *Peasants into Frenchmen: The Modernization of Rural France, 1870-1914* (Stanford 1976)

seen as the reverse side of the process of gradual democratization.[34] The more a political nation comes to coincide with the people as a whole, the greater the need to impose a sense of national and ethnic unity on all its citizens.

***

What this analysis shows is that with the attempt to establish a democratic nation, nationalism can come into the world. Nations set out on the political project of uniting the national-political with the cultural-ethnic. The basis for this was the widely accepted belief (by J.S. Mill among others) that a population's social and cultural homogeneity is a necessary condition for political stability, and hence for peace, happiness, and welfare, and that the elimination of social and cultural differences is the most economic and efficient means of realizing the idea of a nation. Nevertheless, as our analysis of the idea of a nation has shown, the assumption of objective socio-cultural homogeneity is not part of the concept of a political and democratic nation.[35] The idea of a nation does not exclude diversity. The political project of nationhood is motivated by the ambition to transcend particular rootedness, not to destroy it. The fundamental distinction between the public domain, where individuals recognize one another as citizens, and the private domain, where they can live in their particularity, makes their coexistence possible in principle, precisely by first separating them. Citizenship in a community does not in principle presuppose a shared cultural identity or form of life. The nation in its pure form is not fated to clash with cultural groups. As a political reality, it moves on another, more abstract, level. Nonetheless, it would appear that this abstraction, especially under critical circumstances, is untenable. We have seen the

---

34 W.J. Mommsen, 'Varieties of the Nation State,' 215ff.; Hobsbawm, *Nations and Nationalism*, 80ff

35 "*La coïncidence entre unité politique et communauté culturelle a été l'idéal politique de la nation, ce n'en est pas pour autant le type-idéal, au sens analytique du terme*" ["The coincidence of political unity and cultural community has been the political ideal of the nation. It was, however, not its ideal type in the analytical sense of the word"]. Schnapper, *La communauté des citoyens*, 43.

private sphere of culture, history, and identity return to occupy the political domain. And this ethnicization of the political nation signifies, perhaps inevitably, the introduction of a foreign body, a pre-political idea within an essentially political idea. With nationalism, the nation abandons faith in its foundational idea and in the universal and formal principles it imposed upon itself. While harbouring the ambition to transcend all ethnicity, it becomes an ethnic group itself, united by feelings of historical community and identity. This reversal can easily be seen in shifting educational practices. The nation takes the idea of its citizens' perfectibility for granted, the idea that citizens can acquire the political virtues and reasonableness that nationhood demands. It is from this that the nation claims its right to provide a national-political education. But when the reversal takes place, the nation illegitimately extends this education to include the stirrings of cultural-political identity, thus emotionally fusing individuals into a cultural-political unity.

We will have an opportunity later to ask if this incursion of a pre-political idea does not threaten to destroy the political-juridical bond and, in so doing, abolish the public domain. At this point it is enough to conclude that the nationalism of the nation seems to indicate that there are some obvious limits to the political project of transcending particular rootedness. Not only are the citizens apparently unable to live according to this ideal when they surrender to favoritism and patronage, but the nation also betrays itself by evoking specific emotionality. Sociologically speaking, then, there exists no nation that answers to its own idea. They are all situated along a continuum stretching from nationhood to ethnicity, mixing both extremes in constantly changing proportions. The revolutionary nation is only opposed to the ethnic community as an idea, not as a concrete historical reality. It is not only *"transcendance par la société politique abstraite, mais aussi réalité sociale concrètement inscrite dans le temps et l'éspace."*[36] Because it is also the latter, it awakens feelings which are typical of ethnic belongingness. People will adhere to what is familiar and, as a result, the familiar attains a kind of naturalness and determines them in turn. One must not forget

---

36 ["transcendence by the abstract political society, but also a social reality concretely inscribed in time and space."] Schnapper, *La communauté des citoyens*, 82.

that one consequence of the nation's universalizing ambition to bring everyone into ties of solidarity is that the nation encroaches deeply into the lives of the people. Its growing omnipresence creates favourable conditions for transferring ethnic feelings to the nation. This is how for many people the nation could become a focus of loyalty.[37] But, at the same time, this encroaching presence of an ethnicized nation, with one dominant culture over its entire territory, contributes to its being perceived as a threat to those enclaves where minorities could live relatively undisturbed in pre-national times, according to their own way of life. The nation then provokes fear and suspicion among minorities, when its original intention was to free them and bring them into the public domain. Increasingly, the nation meets with the resistance of ethnic groups, particularly those who have attained a certain degree of self-awareness. Once the nation begins incorporating these ethnic elements, the nationalistic principle of unifying the national-political with the ethnic-cultural prevents it from placing national minorities on an equal footing with the ethnic nation constituting the state, for then it would cease to be national.[38] The fusion of state patriotism and ethnic nationalism eventually turned out to be politically risky. The identification of the political and the cultural left a portion of the citizens alienated from the nation, refusing assimilation, with the result that the nationalism of the nation generated counter-nationalisms, no longer directed against multinational empires but against the nation itself.

---

37 In this connection, it should not be overlooked that the idea of nationhood sets in motion a dynamic which moves in the direction of the welfare state. Indeed, the very idea of integrating all individuals into one single political bond has consequences not only for the diversity of ethnic groups and regions, but also for social and economic disparities. The principle of the equal value of every citizen which forms the basis of the logic of the nation may not be contradicted by too great a social or economic inequality. A generalized citizenship cannot really, nor symbolically compensate for this. The nation-state, therefore, has felt itself to be increasingly responsible for the economic and social development of the nation.

38 Acton, 'Nationality,' 157

III The Romantic Idea of the Nation

Before pursuing this idea further, we must first make an attempt to see what significance the idea of a nation acquires, and according to what logic it develops, when it assumes an ethnic content and incorporates pre-political alliances. It might seem inconsistent to use the term nation in this case, given that we are dealing with the introduction of a pre-political, foreign element into the idea of a nation. It is generally accepted, however, that in opposition to the revolutionary idea of the nation, there is another conception, which I shall call 'Romantic.' The use of the same name indicates that the Romantic idea of the nation emerges from within the the framework of problems set forth by the revolutionary idea, and that the debate between the two takes place against the background of the modern problem of a people's right to self-determination.[39]

***

The historical context from which the Romantic idea of the nation arose is not that of an already constituted state, as in Western Europe. In Central Europe, for various historical reasons, no stable states came into being as in the West. The empires of Central Europe made no attempt to bring about a unified 'imperial consciousness' in their populations. They made no efforts toward centralization, uniformity, or assimilation. As a rule, they would tolerate significant ethnic, religious, and cultural differences only as long as the essential demands of the authorities were met.[40] The sovereign might change as a result of the fortunes of war or succession, but most ethnic groups remained virtually untouched within their traditional borders.[41] Consequently,

---

39 This explains why the thought of Herder and Fichte also contain references to humanism and universalism. Similarly, Renan was not insensitive to the ethnic element in the concept of a nation. Just as in the first section, then, this is also a description of an ideal type.

40 Mommsen, 'Varieties of the Nation State,' 214

41 Because of this, Theodor Schieder believes that the nationalist politics of these empires has not been correctly evaluated (Schieder, *Nationalismus und Nationalstaat*, 30ff.).

in the historical consciousness of the Central European inhabitants, cultural belonging was experienced as separate from political organization.

When the (Western) notion of a people's right to self-determination spread through Central Europe, it encountered a world of *Kulturnationen*, not *Staatsnationen* as in Western Europe. The result was that Central European nationalists appealed to shared cultural, linguistic, and historical ties in order to strengthen their claims to nationhood and self-determination. The meaning of nationalism, for them, was that a people, aware of itself as a unique and specific cultural nation, had the right to form a state as a precondition for the nation's realizing its full potential and taking its place within the concert of nations. So while the theoreticians of the revolutionary nation stressed the transcending of particular rootedness by means of citizenship, the defenders of the Romantic nation interpreted the term 'nation,' right from the start, in terms of ethnic particularity, exalting the power, value, and authenticity of rootedness. The natural and the historical, rather than being suppressed, were explicitly advanced as legitimizing the claim to state formation.

The cultural history of the Romantic idea of the nation is rooted in a movement of growing interest in the rediscovery of everything ethnic and historical. This interest can be traced back to Herder and the *Sturm und Drang*, as well as to Montesquieu, Hume, Vico, and the conservatism of Burke. All these authors reacted against the rationalism of the Enlightenment, and its exaltation of freedom as freedom of choice. They saw the social bond not as something political, rooted in will and choice, but rather as a natural, affective bond, preceding every choice and defining the individual's identity and objectives. They not only drew attention to the irrational elements in society – the power of tradition, morals, instinct, and prejudice – they also gave these a positive value as expressions of a higher wisdom. For this reason, they did not consider it important to emancipate individuals from this context, but

---

On his view, the dynastic principle and personal union offered more possibilities for freedom and plurality than the idea of the self-determination of a fictive *"einheitlich nationale Demokratie"* [unitary national democracy"] (Schieder, 21). In such a case, the sovereign can appear as a neutral (non-national) mediator who, far removed from social and national groups, can apply justice.

rather to better integrate them into it, since it is only within such a context that individuals can attain positive freedom and fulfilment, and become who they are. In these thinkers there arose a sense of the characteristic, a sense of the uniqueness and particularity which typifies the products of an irreducible history. They came to view the world as a swirling plurality of personalities, each one marked by its own *Sonderleben*, each one unique and distinct rather than an exemplar of the same thing. Similarly, the nation came to be seen also as a personality, characterized by spontaneity and autonomy, and by the drive to self-preservation, self-determination, and expansion of power. The nation is not an abstract legal or political reality, but a separate, specific, and vibrant unity, a *living body* that bears witness to vitality and spirit in all its members and functions. Just as with individuals, a nation also has the right to its own life, freedom, and welfare, and this should not be violated by the incursion of foreign elements.[42]

***

What constitutes the nation's uniqueness, then, is not the general will of the individuals, *le plébiscite de tous les jours*, but the sustaining *Volksgeist*, a dark and impenetrable womb, some hidden Thing that works in secret and only becomes manifest in the features of private and public life: morals and customs, language, literature and poetry, law and institutions, state and political life, even science.[43] All these features are national insofar as they are intrinsically linked to one another and to the *Volksgeist* which, as the impersonal principle of national life, is difficult to circumscribe and capture in words.[44] It is this

---

42 Thus, paradoxically, modern individualism acquires more depth. Cf. Meinecke, *Weltbürgertum*, 168ff.; L. Dumont, *Essais sur l'individualisme. Une perspective anthropologique sur l'idéologie moderne* (Points) (Paris: Editions du Seuil 1991), 134ff.

43 Meinecke, *Weltbürgertum*, 19-20, 189; The state is national because it is the product of a specific national soul or *Volksgeist*, not of the will of the people. In the same sense, the Historical Law School opposes the doctrines of natural law. According to this school, all law arises intrinsically from customs, tradition, and popular belief. On "national" science, see Meinecke, *Weltbürgertum*, 125ff.

44 Meinecke, *Weltbürgertum*, 247-8

secret, spiritual Thing that precedes every constitution and animates all its forms.[45] It is active through generations, linking them all to the hidden, distant *origin* from which the nation cannot be separated without losing its uniqueness, soul, and power.[46] While the revolutionary nation is witness to the continual novelty of the daily renewed plebiscite, the Romantic nation emphasizes rootedness in the past.

The Romantic nation is a pre-political entity. Nationality is a naturally determined fate, not the outcome of a free choice. One is born German, and one bears Germany within, whether one wants to or not.[47] The nation is a *Schicksalsgemeinschaft* [community of fate] to which one is bound by deep and unbreakable affective ties. It is not the individual's *Selbstbestimmung* [self-determination] that has the upper hand, but rather *Bestimmtheit* [determinacy]. Instead of voluntarism and constructivism, instead of a free choice made by rational and (as yet) undetermined individuals, it is now a matter of the contingent finitude and specificity rooted in age-old ties which have *always* determined the individual's sense of belonging, and which are not the result of a choice, but determine all further choices. The nation is not a free association of individuals, but a comprehensive living totality, a historically evolved organism. It is not a contract but a moral bond underlying all positive contracts; it is the very atmosphere of individuals' existence, making them who they are. One's ties to the nation, then, are more spiritual than political, and this makes the Romantic nation an exclusive and closed cultural community. It is not open to whoever may subscribe to its principles, for individuals bear their nationality within the objective features of their existence. Nationality, as a natural

---

45 L. Von Ranke, *Politisches Gespräch* [1836], quoted in Meinecke, *Weltbürgertum*, 246-7

46 Fichte, *Reden an die Deutsche Nation*, 313ff., 359ff

47 *"Hier heiszt es nicht: Eine Nation ist, was eine Nation sein will, – sondern umgekehrt: Eine Nation ist, mögen die Einzelnen, aus denen sie besteht, ihr zugehören wollen oder nicht. Sie beruht nicht auf freier Selbstbestimmung, sondern auf Determination"* ["Here we do not say: a nation is what wants to be a nation. The contrary is true. A nation exists whether the individuals wish to belong to it or not. It is not rooted in free self-determination but in determinacy"]. Meinecke, *Weltbürgertum*, 247. As a result, revolutionaries consider this view to be undemocratic and irrational.

or quasi-natural reality, is distinct from citizenship. One cannot acquire it nor relinquish it, just as one cannot join or resign from a family.[48] The difference with the revolutionary nation is now quite apparent. We have seen that the revolutionary nation was in principle open, but in reality characterized by inclusion and exclusion, just like any (political) organization. But even so, because it tries to conceive of itself primarily in political and legal terms, it is able to set up a legal framework for taking in foreigners according to criteria that are, in principle, largely political and juridical. A nation that conceives of itself in exclusively ethnic terms would have no basis for this.

Contract theory works from the assumption of abstract and atomic individuals, disembodied and undetermined freedoms, and representatives of universal humanity who establish a political society on reasonable grounds, free of all contingent determination and finitude. Against this individualistic and political foundation for society, the proponents of Romanticism stress humanity's fundamentally social nature. A person is not an abstract individual, stripped of all particularity and solidarity, but rather someone whose identity is profoundly determined by community and culture. A person can only be a person in accordance with the ever contingent and one-sided mode of personhood derived from society. One can only be a person as, e.g., a German. A person is not a universal being who is primarily a member of humanity and only secondarily a member of one of its parts. One is an immediate member of a particular nation, and only mediately a member of humanity as a whole. Instead of being derivative, society and the culture one shares with others are primordial. The nation is the environment addressing the totality of the person. Once separated from it, the individual loses his or her identity and sense of life, for a person without a country, '*sans lieu ni feu*,' is incomplete, less then human. The nation's emancipation, then, does not necessarily go together with the individual's emancipation from social ties, for individuals owe their existence

---

48 Assimilation is, on this view, impossible. Nationalists of the Romantic nation saw the high degree of assimilation by the German Jews as proof of their perfidy and of the extent to which they had already compromised the purity of the Volksgeist. On this point, see Z. Bauman, *Modernity and Ambivalence* (Cambridge: Polity Press 1991), 102ff., 121.

to the nation, as to a mother or father. The individual is always indebted to the nation. The ethics of the revolutionary nation, which we sketched out earlier, was an ethics of autonomy in the Kantian sense: the individual's submission to the universal law of reason which it finds within itself. Against this demand for reason, the Romantic nation makes a demand for authenticity. In both cases the demand is for loyalty to the deepest self: in the case of the revolutionary nation, to the noumenal self, to the reason that I share with everyone; in the case of the Romantic nation, to the unique self whose identity and objectives have been formed in and through membership in the nation. Authenticity demands that I consciously recuperate, in an existential act, that which always already marks my unique personality. Only by piously communing with the nation, by preserving its unique singularity, and by working to enrich it, can individuals remain true to themselves, repay their debt to the nation, and give genuine meaning to their lives.

It is evident that these considerations give the nation a very particular ontological density. Individuals seem to dissolve into the collective individual whose irreplaceable uniqueness, specificity, geniality, distinction, and often higher value are extolled. While the revolutionary nation, as the closest empirical form of humanity, is scarcely distinct from other such nations, the emblem of the Romantic nation is difference and the irreducible particularity and plurality of nations. This is why each nation must be judged and understood according to its own foundations and internal laws. And this is why every abstract humanism or cosmopolitanism, every reference to what links people together, every introduction of foreign or universal institutions, customs and laws is perceived as a threat.[49] The more conservative a nation is, and the more it taps its origins and keeps its source of life pure, the more it is a nation.[50] For the Romantic nationalist, therefore, in order to pre-

---

49 Meinecke, *Weltbürgertum*, 130. The introduction of a British-style parliamentary democracy would therefore be like planting a foreign (British) flower on German soil. At the same time, the liberal constitution is identified with a materialistic, utilitarian bourgeois society, such that loyalty to the *Volksgeist* entails loyalty to a way of life which transcends egoism.

50 Meinecke, *Weltbürgertum*, 78

serve its own essence and purity, and come to full self-possession, a nation must be able to take free and independent decisions, without the meddling of foreigners, and it must enjoy the right to self-determination and to recognition as a nation, not as an ethnic group. Nationality and the *Volksgeist* are thus not irrelevant when it comes to building a nation and delimiting its borders; to the contrary, they are the natural foundation of the state. This *"natürliche oder historische Volksverband"* ["natural or historical union of a people"] must be taken into account when redrawing the map of Europe.[51] The nation is then no longer thought of in terms of the realization of a *Vernunftstaat*. It is the needs and singularity of the nation as a natural, historical reality that determine the nation-state's character, shape and policy.[52] What provides a guideline is not the regulative juridical ethic that decrees recognition of one another's equal, natural rights, but rather the *Volksgeist*, the law which the nation discovers within its own vital nature. This must be protected and strengthened. Political power reverts to those who are most closely connected to the nation's unique spirit, those who can decipher and interpret the most profound singularity of the people, and who are thus able to determine what is necessary for the nation's survival and prosperity.

Like every emanation of national spirit, the nation-state is defined by the nation to which it belongs and from which it emerges. Yet the nation-state is not only a determination *of* the nation, it is also the nation's own *self-determination*. In the nation-state, the 'spirit' of the nation is more strongly expressed, delimited, and clarified. The secret Thing supporting the nation becomes aware of itself. State formation is thus a movement from the impersonal to the personal, from being determined to inner self-determination. In the nation-state, the still obscure and vegetative identity of the nation is articulated and appropriated, and in this process of self-clarification, the nation more effectively isolates itself.[53]

---

51 Meinecke, *Weltbürgertum*, 225-6

52 Fichte, *Reden an die Deutsche Nation*, 384ff

53 Meinecke, *Weltbürgertum*, 252. It is the task of the intellectuals to keep the nation alive and guide it by interpreting its deepest nature and singularity.

While from the revolutionary viewpoint eternal peace formed the horizon of the revolutionary nation, from the Romantic perspective conflict appears never to be far off. Preservation of the nation and protection of its purity and singularity are sacred duties for each individual, and can lead to repression and intransigence against minorities and foreigners. Moreover, nation-states must coincide with their natural borders, for it is only when the national organism is undivided and inviolate that it can further develop. In this way, the international stage becomes a forum for those claiming the *irredenta* (exclaves) and the heartlands once occupied by ancestors, for the supremacist affirmation of the nation's will to live, and for a competition between collective individuals where one flourishes at the other's expense. In such a context, war can easily seem justified as being rooted in a developing personality's inner drive toward growth, and no longer as the arbitrary whim of a monarch. For nations who believe they have a unique place and mission in world history, to subject and conquer can appear to be an ethical act, one that includes the total engagement of the people in a freedom and identity which can only be achieved through a struggle of self-affirmation with others.

IV   Nations Between Universality and Particularity

From the moment that a nation makes the turn to nationalism, the idea of a political nation is supplemented by the concept of the people as a substantial unity, a quasi-metaphysical reality, and a subject characterized by a unique and particular essence. An organicistic and holistic concept is grafted onto the purely political, individualistic, and rationalistic idea of the nation. The *'corps d'associés'* of Sieyès metamorphoses into a *living body* with its own irreplaceable uniqueness. The people's right to self-determination is no longer the right of individuals to freely link their fate to one another and to direct their own affairs, but rather the right of this living substance to take up its own place in the concert of nations. Similarly, sovereignty of the people, as Rousseau's thought already announced, becomes the sovereignty of this metaphysical entity transcending individuals, into which individuals must be absorbed in order to be truly free. In this way, the unity that is rooted in the freely assumed political responsibility of individuals for one another is replaced by the fused unity of a homogeneous entity in which individual autonomy is relinquished.

In our discussion of the revolutionary nation, we mentioned that it is essential to this idea of the nation to distinguish between the public and the private. In the public domain, all particular alliances are transcended, whereas the private is the domain of natural ties and solidarities. In comparison with the pure idea of the revolutionary nation, then, the nation's ethnicization can, in a certain sense, be seen as an obliteration of the distinction between the public and the private. In the ethnicized nation, the political space in which individuals should attain a universal *Verständigung* [agreement] and give shape to their universal solidarity is done away with and replaced by a substance in which everyone is fused and moulded without diversity. *Sameness* replaces *togetherness*. And as Arendt – from whom we borrow these terms – has written, "this unitedness of many into one [sameness] is basically antipolitical; it is the very opposite of togetherness prevailing in [...] political communities."[54] Yet this does not mean that no public discussion takes place in the Romantic nation. As we have already seen, the nation-state is the place where the nation articulates its still obscure and vegetative identity, in order to consciously appropriate it. One could say that the Romantic nation's 're-privatization' will result in the public discussion being limited to an exposition and interpretation of the identity of the people. And, as a rule, this activity will remain a privilege of the leaders, who maintain close connections with the essence of the nation and are in a position to decipher and interpret its unique identity. The discussion will remain within these particular limits, excluding any wider public (or universal) perspective.

The nationalism of most actual nations is undoubtedly far removed from the ideal type sketched out here. Nevertheless, the introduction of ethnic elements into the political idea of the nation signifies, to a greater or lesser degree, the introduction of references to a communal identity and essence, encompassing everyone, and functioning as a frame of reference for the community and a focus for feelings of loyalty. To the extent that every nation is situated along a continuum

---

54 H. Arendt, *The Human Condition* (Chicago-London: University of Chicago Press 1958), 214

stretching from the revolutionary nation to the Romantic, they all have in some measure posed the question of their identity as a socio-historical reality. We have already indicated that a nation is never merely a transcending of ethnic particularities, but always a historical reality as well, a 'we' that comes into relief against a 'they.' Because of this, questions of identity can never be completely banished from political life, as the political nation tried to do, and a really universal political space is in fact an impossibility. In its attempt to transcend particular belongingness, the political nation was inspired by the hope that it would not have to pose questions of identity, that it might limit itself – in the words of Habermas – to *moral* questions, questions of justice, and to the problems of interpreting the demand for universality and the demand to recognize everyone as both individual and citizen. It had hoped that no *ethical* questions – in which the authentic meaning of a form of life is under discussion – would have to be posed. Our analysis of the ethnicization of the nation has shown that wherever there is a 'we' that has to take political decisions, there will also arise questions of identity, questions which refer to a shared ethos, a shared culture and form of life, a belongingness that precedes all choice and that must be hermeneutically clarified before correct political decisions can be made. This has also been recognized by Habermas.[55] One could say that the Romantic nation makes absolute this aspect of every political society by cutting off the discussion about identity from any critical questioning of the traditional ethos, and from any comparison of this ethos with the universal critical principles of the Rights of Man or of the constitutional state.

***

In our examination of the revolutionary nation as the result of a free choice by abstract, non-situated individuals, we mentioned that this concept of nationhood expressed the central theme of the Enlightenment: the separation of freedom (reason) from all-encompassing nature,

---

55 J. Habermas, *Faktizität und Geltung. Beiträge zur Diskurstheorie des Rechts und des demokratischen Rechtsstaat* (Frankfurt am Main: Suhrkamp 1992), 190ff

the exaltation of the negative power of freedom, and the idea of a practical reason that, being external to nature, believes it can find every resource within itself. The revolutionary nation is inscribed in the project of modernity: the emancipation from all natural ties which envelop and determine humans, in order that they may be fully self-determining. In this sense, the nation is fundamentally a project directed against nature.

However, our analysis has exposed the limits of this project and, thereby, the limits of the entire project of modernity. It seems that the nation is unable to fully escape from ethnic and emotional ties. We have seen that nature and the past were not so easily dispelled, often quickly returning to provide a basis for unity and mobilization. Modernity establishes its own naturalness and emotionality. It seems impossible to form a society purely on the principles of a universal juridical ethic because, as already mentioned, nations are also social entities, affirming their particularity against all others. Nations, just like individuals, are partisan and arbitrary, marked by the unconscious of nature and history.

It is precisely these aspects of facticity, fatality, and finitude that the Romantic nation emphasizes. It does not cut us off from the past and from nature. Yet this does not mean that we should refrain from critically questioning this idea of nationhood. On this view, nationality is a natural objective determination, a given particularity, from which the individual cannot free himself or herself. While the revolutionary conception upholds freedom, indetermination, and constant novelty and represses finitude, particularity, and tradition, what tends to be forgotten in the Romantic view is freedom, openness to the universal, and the possibility of self-determination and critical distancing. But is one ever completely imprisoned within the horizon of culture and feelings of loyalty? Does not human existence consist of always being critically involved with one's facticity and finitude, with one's given objective features, in order to accept them, give them meaning, or reject them? The Romantic nation risks surrendering individuals to the given, to what we have simply because we have it. It threatens to place individuals in the service of the mere development of their national spirit, foreclosing the possibility of taking a critical position that might be able to renew their destiny and fate. This conception does not uphold the negative power of freedom, but suppresses it, fully inscribing individuals in the particular (private) horizon of tradition.

190

What is at stake philosophically in the controversy between these two conceptions of the nation is the relation between reason and freedom on the one hand, and nature and determination on the other. One side absolutizes freedom, cutting humanity off from nature, from what always already determines their identity and ties them to a larger whole. This assumes that one can live in a totally public reality, constructed purely by reason. The other side pins humanity to the particular, as if they would have no access to the universal, not even in thought. It seems that what is needed is to maintain the tension between these two extremes. Humans live, and must live, in the particular, but are at the same time endowed with formal knowledge of the universal and of the requirements of reason. As a result of this formalism, reason cannot provide any content, and must renounce the rationalistic hope of generating everything from out of itself. Similarly, rational freedom cannot imply a complete negation of nature. It cannot be a disembodied freedom, transcending time and history, but a freedom inscribed in nature, a *'distance à la fois nulle et infinie'* ['a distance which is at the same time null and infinite'] whereby openness and relative autonomy are created, but not so as to separate us from what is given. Humanity's genuine home is within this tension. Although we live in a particular world, we can still aim toward a juridical ethic that would function as a *critical authority* against the history which determines us so deeply.

What is decisive for the problem of nationalism is not whether questions about identity can be kept out of the political debate, but rather how a nation is to deal with these questions. What is decisive in answering these questions and in appropriating one's identity is the ability to maintain at the same time a sufficiently universal and public point of view. Every nation carries with it a tradition that is wider than a strictly political tradition. The important thing is that political discussion about the tradition should be carried out openly, and that those who were not involved in creating the tradition – minorities of every kind – should be able to voice their opinion of the tradition and its effects on their lives, whether it subjugates or emancipates them. The important thing, in other words, is that the inevitability of these identity questions should not lead us to preclude a questioning of their impact on everyone, inside or outside the nation, nor should we neglect to always check tradition against the universal reasonableness which we found at the heart of the political nation. In this manner, the essence expressed by the idea of a nation can be carried over to a world characterized by particularity, facticity, and finitude. Likewise, the nation can give political form to the fundamental anthropological fact that a human is both particular and universal. It clears the way, and awakens respect for history and naturality, for the various loyalties tying people together, but simultaneously makes room in its constitution for the critical power of the universal principles of law and reason. Only a society that is 'open' in this sense can answer to human nature: not a prisoner of the past, but neither situated within an undetermined choice; never unlimited, but also never entirely limited. It combines the ethics of autonomy with the ethics of authenticity in a fruitful tension which is loyal to reason and freedom as well as to our particular ties. Only within this tension and its dual loyalty is it possible to make something moral and political out of what would otherwise remain a mere instinctive affection and preference for the private. Only in this way can individuals escape the tyranny of natural feelings, of the natural community's self-concern, and bring to it a moral content. Who is finally more loyal to the fatherland: one who surrenders to it in a blind *Nibelungentreue* [Nibelungen-faith], or one who critically appropriates their attachment to it?

***

The discovery that not every reference to natural ties can be banished from politics, and that the nation can never completely distance itself from the particular, must now lead us to another conclusion. We have already stressed that the nationalist project does not aim at the destruction of ethnic particularities. On the contrary, the political nation is fundamentally pluralistic and multicultural. However, this pluralism is included in the project of transcending the particular, and separating the public from the private. Everyone has the right to cultivate their own particularities in private and in *civil society*, as long as they respect the rules of public order. The fact that the nation itself inevitably displays an ethnic and historical particularity – that of the dominant particular group – raises the question whether mere recognition in private law of diversity and particularity is really sufficient. Once it is apparent that the nation has to exist in a world of particularities, does not the very idea of a nation require it to make room for the recognition of particularity within public law? Aware of its own inevitable arbitrariness, the nation must, as it were, protect itself from its own nationalism by limiting its power and by giving the diverse particularities their own public status.

We have already seen how Rousseau's understanding of democracy led him to resist any division of the political body into parties and interest groups. In attempting to safeguard the universality of the will, he rejected all *'corps intermédiaires'* and called for exclusive loyalty to the nation, a fusion of everyone in 'the people' as a kind of natural substance.[56] Such a conception of sovereignty, however, can only be experienced by minority groups as the tyranny of the general will and as an infringement of their particularity and freedoms. In his critique of Rousseau, Acton countered absolute democracy's claim to supreme, exclusive loyalty with the concept of a 'divided patriotism' in which individuals can by loyal both to particular groups as well as to the nation.[57] In the name of freedom, he championed a limited democracy where there is room for orders, bodies, classes, and particular groups, and which is based on the idea that freedom can only be safeguarded through the creation of counterforces, through respect for particular attachments and belongings. Such a democracy renounces the ambition toward a fused unity of the will, accepting instead diversity and heterogeneity. It no longer condenses all sovereign power in 'the people' understood as a substance, but in the *constitution*, understood as the articulation of groups and interests, and in the *togetherness* of individuals – not just abstract individuals, but individuals marked by deep ties. The social nature of people implies that individual and collective recognition will coincide. As long as individuals sense that they are not being recognized as a collective, there will be a feeling of humiliation and exclusion, preventing them from being recognized as individuals

---

56 It is a strange but perhaps not entirely fortuitous coincidence that Rousseau's project, which tries to elevate the "public" into a completely transparent nation, seems so easily to undergo a reversal into a completely "privatized," ethnic nation. The totalitarianism of universality seems here to touch on that of particularity. It seems that only a simultaneous recognition of particularity and universality can shield us from totalitarianism.

57 Acton, 'Nationality,' 149

also. This does not mean a rejection of the idea of a civil nation and the introduction of other ideals, for instance, the ideal of diversity. It is rather an institutionalization of the *erweiterte Denkungsart* in a public space where everyone's point of view can have a chance, an institutionalization of the nation in the real circumstances of life where a nationalism of the nations seems inevitable. It emerges from the recognition that politics and culture cannot be completely separated, so culture must be admitted within politics, but in such a way that its plurality and diversity are also recognized.

This recognition in public law of the limited sovereign right to self-regulation by particular groups cannot be dissociated from the central idea of a nation: the unity and integration of a public space, a space of solidarity transcending all particularities. Without this public space, the diverse groups become separated and the threat of a nationalistic logic of homogeneity can only increase, providing little opportunity for a federal and pluralistic organization of the state.[58] Even in a pluralistic nation the state must direct its efforts toward the integration of public space, seeking a balance between the recognition of autonomy for particularities and the maintenance of a communal political space and solidarity.

Precisely where this balance between cohesion and autonomy lies is difficult to determine in the abstract. What is certain is that the promotion of the nation's principles will inevitably imply a political acculturation for the diverse peoples and cultures. Even if the nation clings anxiously to the purely political logic of its principles, avoiding any identification with ethnic elements, it is still representing the universal ethic of the Rights of Man and the principles of the constitutional state. So the pluralistic nation cannot tolerate every group and incorporate them into its public space. Indeed, its political assumption of the equal value of its citizens also implies that legal inequalities of status in other areas of social life (e.g., family life) are excluded. As a consequence, the nation is not compatible with every tradition, even though in principle

---

58 This is indirectly confirmed by the thesis that the functioning of consociative democracies presupposes a sufficiently unified elite with a "common background and outlook." Cf. A. Lijphart, *Democracies in Plural Societies: A Comparative Exploration* (New Haven: Yale University Press 1977), 168.

there is no opposition between diversity and the idea of nationhood. The nation remains the protector of the universal ethic of autonomy which, as we said earlier, must function as a critical authority for the ethnic and cultural traditions. It will protect the public domain, insofar as this is humanly possible. Then, if it can succeed in fully suppressing its nationalism, it will become the mediator promoting justice among ethnic and other groups.

This idea of a voluntary self-restraint of the nation will likely not convince those who believe that the population's social and cultural homogeneity is a necessary precondition for stability. Won't the pluralistic and limited nation be unstable and vulnerable as a result of greater freedom and diversity and less efficiency and bureaucracy?[59] It seems that stable nations built out of heterogeneous populations are rather few in number, and are the outcome of a long history in which they learned to respect one another and to put in place the political institutions that would objectify this respect. A federal, pluralistic nation cannot be improvised, and there is simply no getting around this fact. Such nations are continually evolving; every system of competencies and jurisdictions is only a phase or moment in a process of seeking balance. This is why they exhibit an intense political life, thus only reconfirming Arendt's thesis that a unified, homogeneous nation's 'sameness' is fundamentally anti-political. But when a consensus and mutual recognition comes about, in and through political discussion, then the nation will be supported by everyone. There seems no reason to think that pluralistic nations will be less powerful than homogeneous ones, whose politics of identity incite resistance. The contrary rather seems to be the case, at least if they can succeed in creating political space and solidarity for all groups, where everyone feels they are recognized and, in turn, can recognize one another.

---

59 Acton, ('Nationality,' 150ff.) sees the coexistence of several nations in a single state as a source of progress. Diversity and difference are "resources" and "incentives." When national and political borders coincide, society is at risk of sclerosis, of reverting to itself.

In Search of a Post-National Identity: Who are My People?

FRANS DE WACHTER
Catholic University of Leuven

The Nation as Philosophical Problem

The problem of the nation is well articulated in a speech given in 1985 by then president of the Federal Republic of Germany, R. Von Weiszäcker:

> I belong to a people, the German people. What are the characteristics which we Germans share as a people? What does it mean to belong to such a people? What does the fact that I am German have to do with my identity as a person? Does this fact place a claim on me? Does it mark me? Does it include responsibilities for me? Does it include obligations to me as a German, obligations which I would otherwise not have to fulfil? (...) It is up to us to give content to the term 'German,' a content with which we ourselves and the world would like to live in peace.[1]

This is not a psychological comment. It is not about the deep-seated need of people to express feelings of collective identity. The question of the nation here is asked from a normative perspective. That will also be the starting point of this study. The question concerns what a good society should represent, at least in its political shape. A democratic state should refer to universal principles, that much is certain. It is directed to a general good, and it must protect the rights of citizens and promote their welfare. With respect to this, the English state must live up to the same norms as the French. Yet in modern times the state is considered to be a 'nation-state'; it refers to a particular, 'national'

---

1 R. Von Weizsäcker, 'Die Deutschen und ihre Identität,' *Von Deutschland aus. Reden des Bundespräsidenten* (München: Deutsche Taschenbuch-Verlag 1987), 39 and 61.

distinctness. Belonging to the English people is *not* the same as belonging to the French people. The reference here is to the spontaneous cohesion of a group which sees itself as *this* people and not another. At first sight, this cohesion is not situated at the level of political principles but rather in the domain of daily life: shared traditions, memories, historical experiences, language, religion.

The philosophical problem involved in this concept of the nation-state concerns the relation between the national and the state dimensions. More generally it concerns the relation between the pre-political and the political. The spontaneous, pre-political, socio-cultural, and affective distinctness and cohesion of a group is different from the political entity that is based upon rational principles of public regulation. The issue is precisely the relation between these two. In the context of the problem of the nation it is useful to define nationalism. By nationalism we mean the ideology which pursues congruity between both the political and the pre-political. This definition has the operational advantage that it dovetails with the common definition of Gellner.[2] It also has the advantage that it is a purely political definition and so dissociates itself from more extreme meanings. Extreme meanings appear, for example, where there is excessive idolatry of one's own group or when all particular relations (family, class, religion) become subordinate to interests which are shared with members of the nation. We wish to avoid our study becoming an archaeology of extreme meanings. It is not about the issue of the particular and the foreign. It is about the relation between the political and the non-political. If politics is not only a matter of general moral principles but also of historical effectiveness and plausibility in a concrete community, is it possible to concretely think about it without the pre-political, particular unity which is the nation? Or can I think of a modern state – that is a state which grants people rights independent of their social or cultural position – as a 'national' state in the sense of a uniqueness which is precisely defined by such a position?

---

2 E. Gellner, *Nations and Nationalism* (Oxford: B. Blackwell 1983) 1: "Nationalism is primarily a political principle, which holds that the political and the national unit should be congruent." This formulation is adopted by many well-known authors, for example by E.J. Hobsbawm, *Nations and Nationalism since 1780* (Cambridge: Cambridge University Press 1990), 9.

This is a difficult problem. In order to be able to solve it one must accept the problem of nationalism as it is. It is not a tribal regression to an archaic type of society. Neither is it, at least not primarily, the disguised expression of conflicts of a different (for example, psychological) order. Nationalism is essentially a modern political ideology that offers its own answer to the question concerning the relation between the political and pre-political order. And its answer is that both should be congruent. Loyalty with respect to the particular pre-political distinctness of the unity of the nation is the necessary foundation for political loyalty and legitimization. Where does this answer come from? Is it a good answer? Can one think of a better one?

It is important that the question of the nation be taken seriously as a normative-philosophical question because in political philosophy it has been stigmatized for a long time. The first reason for this stigmatization is that political philosophy, not only Marxism, presupposed an ideology of progress. Nations (and the related ideology of nationalism) were quickly seen as belonging to the pathology of history, as something that again and again thwarted the high expectations of a universally tolerant humankind with an always recurring violence of tribalistic group loyalties. But the non-national forms of globalization would free us from this pathology.

The second cause of the stigmatization was situated in the internal methodology of political philosophy itself. It was used to treating normative questions from the perspective of universal reason: what is the meaning and the foundation of (*the*) constitutional state, (*the*) democracy, (*the*) civil rights? This is why democratic philosophers had difficulty situating and valuing the attachment to *this* particular nation, at least as long as people like Walzer, Rorty, Scruton, or Taylor had not yet spoken. Similarly, philosophers have filled libraries with theories about man as a linguistic being, and about the importance of language itself, but there is hardly any serious contemporary philosophical reflection on what it might mean that I speak *this* language and not another one.[3]

---

3 An exception to this is the series of lectures Derrida gave in Toronto. J. Derrida, 'La philosophie dans sa langue nationale,' *Du droit à la philosophie* (Paris: Galilée 1990), 283-309.

Frans De Wachter

The Nation, Child of Democracy

The philosophical problem becomes clearer when we realize that the nationalistic principle is not a tribalistic regression to an archaic type of society, but a modern form of cohesion, the meaning of which is related to the problem of democracy.

On the political scene, 'the people' appear only in the eighteenth century. Of course people have always felt a certain connectedness via religion, city, or class, and especially via their personal loyalty to a monarch ('*Kaisertreue*'). But only in the eighteenth century does a bond come into existence based upon a common belonging to a nation or a people. This is a rather unusual development. Until then, monarchs commonly ruled over very heterogeneous populations, as in the Ottoman and Habsburg empires. But then, at the moment that people democratically freed themselves and developed a tolerance for differences, their political forms of organization tended towards the homogeneity of 'a people.' Why? Why did the democratic state need the nation?

The democratic formation of a state means the exclusion from political relevance of all pre-political liaisons and loyalties. It is as a citizen, as a naked individual, that I obtain my rights, not, for example, because I am a member of a certain social, ethnic or religious group. In that sense the political totality becomes an aggregate of undefined individuals. Yet there must be a unity. The democratic state is also an historical subject. It must make decisions and it must exercise authority. Citizens must not only be able to rebel, they must also be able to obey. They have to develop a loyalty to the totality which is stronger than their loyalty to other intermediate structures. To that end the political entity must not only *be* a unity, but also manifestly express itself as such. It must put forth a figure of unity or an image of its distinctness. This face of unity is the nation. It is a principle that transcends the divisions, not in an abstract structure but in a collective life: a life that is broad and anonymous enough to bear the political unity; a life that is at the same time motivationally and affectively strong enough to generate a real loyalty in the face of the totality. The nation is not an irrational passion for the tribal, but a modern form of socio-political cohesion and loyalty.

Where does this feeling of unity come from? Can it come from the political itself? Each young, beginning democracy enthusiastically believes it can. It believes that the people can be a people because they assemble themselves around principles of equality and sovereignty. Here 'nation' is not used to refer to a particular uniqueness, but only to the totality of the citizens as the bearers of equal rights and responsibilities, the bearers of the sovereignty of the people.[4] The unity of the people refers to no other source than the political process itself. This people does not exist before it founds itself in a political act of self disposition. There is still no reference to the uniqueness of a cultural or social group. The nation represents precisely the opposite: unity around the rejection of the political relevance of uniqueness. The state is not an embodiment of a pre-political identity, but of the political principles of the common good. And the nation is not a prepolitical given, but the solidarity which comes into being around these principles. One is not born a Frenchman, as if there were a natural or cultural determinism, but one becomes one (as Jeremy Bentham or Thomas Paine) through an act of free choice for these principles, which are summarized in the declaration of human rights of 1789. The fatherland is then the land where these rights are recognized, and the *'enfants de la patrie'* are they who bear this universal inheritance. The only attribute that the group must share in order to be a nation is the will to cluster around the universal reasonableness of democratic principles.[5]

---

4 It is the famous definition of Abbé Sieyès from the time of the French Revolution: "La nation, c'est un corps d'associés vivant sous une loi commune et représentés par la même législature."

5 This meaning was also present in 'patriote' or 'patriot' which means 'warrior for the nation' in the universal sense of warrior against tyranny, for freedoms and constitutional rights. This was also the acceptable meaning, not only during the English and American revolutions, but even in England at the beginning of the nineteenth century. The term was then mostly used by and for the Chartists, who in their fight for radical social and economic reformation were at an earlier stage even internationally oriented. Only later in the century would the term obtain nationalistic connotations. Cf. M.G. Dietz, 'Patriotism,' in T. Ball, J. Farr, and R.L. Hanson, eds., *Political Innovation and Conceptual Change* (Cambridge: Cambridge University Press 1989), 177-93.

From Nation to Nationalism

This original concept of people or nation seems to be at odds with the concept with which Gellner's definition works. In the latter view nation is particularistic and pre-political. From where does this second notion come? It is certainly not a return to a pre-democratic and premodern form of feudalism or tribalism. It relies in a certain sense upon democratic considerations. The 'French' version (Rousseau) holds that the construction of a state must be based upon universal principles. But principles alone do not contain enough organic connection to the real social life of the group. They have insufficient power to call forth into the political sphere concrete historical ties, loyalty, and identification. Even the significance of democracy is obtained only via the mediation of concrete practices and institutions, that is, in culture. The state must create for itself a national culture. This culture must penetrate the fibre of the entire society, and apply the principles of reason to all the remote corners of life. The universal must become embodied. This leads almost necessarily to a Jacobinic centralism. The goal is the conversion of political unity into the unity of a French nation which is indeed conceived of as particularistic and culturalistic. Thus the French language is seen as the bearer of universal reason. What occurs outside of the homogeneity of French culture is identified with the dark regions of particularism, of local superstition, of *esprit de corps*, and must be brought back to universality: the peasants, the Jews, languages on the periphery. They must be saved from their dark feudal bonds which prevent them from associating, as free and equal citizens, with all other citizens.[6]

Against this enlightenment ideal, as is well known, an alternative romantic ('German') version of the nation-state developed. The middle-European peoples knew no political unity. Therefore they tried to

---

6 At the same moment that Abbé Sieyès in 1789 wrote his universal outpouring on human rights, Abbé Grégoire wrote his famous texts: *Essai sur la régénération physique, morale et politique des Juifs* and *Rapport sur la nécessité et les moyens d'anéantir les patois et d'universaliser l'usage de la langue française*. For an analysis see M. De Certeau, *Une politique de la langue. La Révolution française et les patois* (Paris: Gallimard 1975); P. Caussat, *De l'identité culturelle. Mythe ou réalité* (Paris: Desclée de Brouwer 1989), 66-76.

compensate by having as their point of departure a purely cultural concept. The nation is primarily the culture to which one belongs, not by rational adhesion or civil upbringing, but from a natural givenness, into which one is born (*'hineingeboren'*). This alleged naturalness of the German cultural nation is even thought to be more in line with democratic principles than the French version. The argument that the French language is a universal 'lingua franca' is turned around with the observation that it is derived from Latin, a foreign, dead language, and thus is not really a genuine language of the people. In contrast, the German language originated from its own people, namely the Goths![7] Such discourse was very popular, and even people such as Fichte were guilty of indulging in it. However linguistically absurd this might be, it does express the positions well. German authors believe that French political unity is based in abstract ideas and only afterwards is the cultural unity of a nation founded. This artificiality is then seen as a democratic shortcoming because the people will never be able to completely recognize themselves in it. Only when rooted in the spontaneously given naturalness of cultural nations, prior to politics, can non-alienating democratic entities be formed. That is why such nations are required to strive for the formation of a state. A more dramatic example of the difference between both versions is the reactions to groups that fall outside the mono-cultural fabric. In French texts the Jews are accused of irrational forms of particularism.[8] In many German texts the opposite occurs. Jews do not appear as people who hold too much to their traditions or particular identity; rather, their fault is that they have no traditions or identity at all. They are seen as a wandering people, cosmopolitan but without roots, businessmen in the international market. They are described not as a type, but as the absence of every type, the bastard par excellence.[9] Here we see how ethnic obsessions or identity problems often translate themselves into patterns of ridicule concerning non-ethnic collectives.

---

7   Caussat, *De l'identité culturelle*, 77-81

8   Caussat, *De l'identité culturelle*, 66-69

9   Ph. Lacoue-Labarthe and J.-L. Nancy, *Le mythe nazi* (La Tour d'Aigues: Editions de l'Aube 1991), 57-58

Yet the contrast between the two versions, however polemically and belligerently they have been used, is for the most part deceptive. 'A people' as cultural identity is just as artificial and just as modern as the democratic state. The ideology serves precisely to suggest and invent an alleged naturalness. 'A people' is, however, not a sleeping beauty which wakes up at a certain moment.[10] Jacobinic and romantic nationalism (civic and ethnic nationalism), seen politically, have the same goal: the formation of a culturally homogeneous national and political entity. That the point of departure is in one case the state, and in the other case culture, is irrelevant. The political principle is the same.[11] What must be sought after is the congruence of state and nation, of the political and the pre-political terrain. It is understandable that both versions continually demonize each other. The rejection of the other form of nationalism as thoroughly reprehensible suggests that one's own form is respectable and good. It distracts attention from a discussion of the basic idea itself. Let us return to the basic idea and investigate the philosophical implications and normative legitimacy thereof.

Nationalism as Philosophical Principle

The basic idea can also be formulated negatively. It is impossible and undesirable that a state should want to realize its integration primarily around political principles. Impossible, because a merely moral assent to political principles generates insufficient loyalty and civil virtue.

---

10 Gellner, *Nations and Nationalism*, 43. Even in the cradle of the romantic version there was, in spite of the communal language, no feeling of national unity. This occurred only after Bismarck, thus after political unity. One thinks precisely of the cult of the Gothic. In this way a Flemish and Walloon national feeling has only developed after, within, and thanks to the Belgian context that historically represents a much older unity.

11 The double movement is possible also at the level of supra-national structures. In so called Euro-nationalism, Europe is presented as a super-nation with its own national (and also socio-cultural) identity. This can be interpreted in two ways. Either political union is the expression of the unity of the nation (the Christian inheritance, for example), or a politically unified Europe must make of itself a cultural unity (via, for example, educational policy).

Undesirable, because a political unity which exhibits no real connection with the concrete socio-cultural life of the society is external to that life, is something which is forced upon it, and is in a certain sense oppressive and undemocratic. This definition transcends the opposition between civic and cultural nationalism. It has no interest in how the feeling of historical solidarity in a certain society has come about, and whether this is a result of political action, cultural processes, or even ethnic factors. What this ideology comes down to is that political connections must not be considered abstractly or apart from the factual or quasi-spontaneous connections which are already present in the society. The political community offers sufficient binding only when it is based upon a shared cultural life-world, and this cultural life-world is only liveable (that is, effective in the exchange of meanings) if it is embodied politically.

Formulated in this way, nationalism is more than an ideology. It is a thesis which is philosophically discussible. Even more, the underlying thought is, in its philosophical form, due for a revival. Enlightenment-critique calls into question the ethical effectiveness of universal humanism, and senses danger in the rationalistic and technical aspects thereof. The insight is growing that it is insufficient for freedom and self-determination to free ourselves from all possible codes. There is also a certain anchoring necessary *in* these codes. Attachment to the local group, to one's own ethos, even ethnos, to one's own culture is no longer considered as a form of folklore or dubious narrow-mindedness, but as an important support in human existence. In contemporary normative thinking the central position of the notion 'society' appears more and more to be replaced by that of 'culture.' Our skepticism concerning the enlightenment causes philosophy in all its forms (not only in ethics but also in metaphysics and logic) to shift to variations of the philosophy of culture. The culturalization of the philosophical project might be the ideological horizon of forms of culturalistic over-definition of the political, to which nationalism must be seen to belong.

The philosophical questions finally are these: what is genuine communality, what is a genuine community, and what are the conditions thereof? Tnse are old questions which were already central to Aristotle's *Politics*. They were also central questions for Rousseau, administered, moreover, in a certain homesickness for the old *polis*. For him a 'genuine' community must be more than the outcome of balanced interactions between individuals and groups. It must be the expression of a deeper unity, of an indivisible popular will. Those who accept the social contract do not carry with them their individualistic entitlements into the political situation, as Locke thought, but receive a new identity: that of a citizen who can think from the perspective of the universal and who can vote for the common good. This argumentation, based upon the genuine community, reappears in contemporary communitarian literature. A genuine community must be more than an instrumental service: it must be foundational for the identity of its participants. What brings us together in a communal identity can never be a 'willed' political construction, such as association in a democratic state. What really brings us together is the ability to share in professed meanings and agreements. The nation is an elementary example of this.[12]

What is actually at issue here is the question concerning whether moral principles can be foundational for genuine communality. For Sandel this is impossible. All morality is a reflexive construction. But communality is only experienced as such when it is experienced as *given*, not as willed, not as a demand, not even as a moral demand. Or still more: the state cannot generate sufficient loyalty by an appeal to morality, or by trying to consciously orient citizens by, for example, upbringing in civil virtue and respect for the basic laws. Attempts at rational legitimization do not bring about unity. On the contrary, they cause rational discussions to break out, differences of opinion, plurality, not unity. A national identity is a pre-contractual given, and is not subject to our opinions.

This communitarian perspective builds into politics, a place of conflict, the attractiveness of a me-transcending context which, precisely because it is pre-given, co-operates in the constitution of the identity of my existence and my existing together with others. But there is more. The thesis appears attractive, not only for our feelings of solidarity and loyalty, but also with respect to democratic legitimization. If an authentic experience of unity can never be political, but only social, then politics is indeed never capable of generating our deeper forms of

---

12 See M. Sandel, 'The Procedural Republic and the Unencumbered Self,' *Political Theory* 12 (1984) 1, 81-96.

loyalty, even those concerning the state itself. If the state is to acquire recognition without recourse to force in order to legitimate itself democratically, then this is not possible except from outside a bond which was already present before the state was. This is the nation. Put another way, the democratic legitimization of the state is connected with its capability to recuperate non-political, pre-contractual bonds. In this way Roger Scruton attempts to make plausible the Thatcherite fear of Europe. He shows how important it is that the British keep their own national traditions, namely for the functioning of their democracy. A construction of European political unity which is disconnected from British traditions must be rejected as an obtrusively bureaucratic creation of Brussels. For the same reasons a plea is made for a limitation on immigration which would threaten those same British traditions.[13]

Here it becomes even more clear how the nationalistic thesis does not necessarily have to do with extremist positions and can also be argued from democratic motives. But not enough has been said about the validity of the thesis itself. Is the presupposition as such correct? Do the bonds of communality necessarily run via our membership in this pre-given cultural context? This thesis is problematic, for the following reasons.

Perhaps a community which comes about from factually shared cultural values and aims is not really a community. If one shares values and aims but there is no reason why they *must* be shared, then such a community excludes those who, for whatever reason, do not find themselves sharing the same values; such a community exists in fact as a definite community by the grace of this exclusion. Finally, what divides us are *not* differing empirical aims (customs, ways of life, culture); therefore, these are not what unites us. What would really divide us is a situation in which we elevate these empirical givens to the main source of our practical principles, because then there would no longer be fundamental rights and duties in which we would be compelled to unite. What makes us a community is not the factually cultural identity in which we are rooted. The person is not a tree, and humanity is

---

13 R. Scruton, 'In Defence of the Nation,' *The Philosopher on Dover Beach* (Manchester: Carcanet 1990), 299-328

not a forest.[14] What makes us a community is not the anchoring in a sedentary location, but a task of justice which we must fulfil together.

The Dutch philosopher Peperzak articulated this idea in a text in which he, against the ethos-concept of Heidegger, clarifies the universal content of the moral dimension, as well as the moral deficiency of merely particularistic positions. From a phenomenology of the greeting he makes plausible that the moral relation precedes language, and that belonging alone, for example to a culture, cannot be foundational for morality. Against Heidegger's use of ethos, Peperzak evokes an ethos of the desert:

> An open space is there: its openness is desert-like; too many possibilities of being human, too many characters, symbols, signs, languages, myths, and civilizations have become known to us. No longer do we belong firmly to any one of the peoples, cultures, or beliefs that form the museum of our past. No one of them can save us (...) for it would separate us from other communities with their peculiarities and not guide us in our communication with human beings as such – unless the ethos we are looking for includes, at least as an element, a universal hospitality with regard to all other wanderers and strangers with their peculiarities. The barrenness of a desert guarantees its openness to all possible determinations and differences.[15]

Belonging does not alone found community. Something else is also necessary: the barrenness of the desert, or more prosaically, the bare abstraction of the constitutional state and its basic laws, through which I, torn loose from each particular qualification, find access to the others.

The nationalistic thesis contains the danger that the concept of community rests so strongly upon the givenness of the belonging that the normative content is threatened with erosion. This extreme consequence is illustrated in the positions defended by Bernard Willms, the famous Hobbes exegete. For him the nation is the only bond which is no longer subject to the subjectivity of opinions. Democracy, on the other hand, is the work of people. Parties and their ideas are possibilities, possible ways to think, and therefore sources of arguments, disagreement, and destruction of real cohesion. Only the nation, speaking socially, is neces-

---

14 E. Levinas, *Difficile liberté. Essais sur le judaïsme* (Paris: Albin Michel 1976), 40

15 A. Peperzak, 'From Utilitarianism to Ethics,' *Algemeen Nederlands Tijdschrift voor Wijsbegeerte* **83** (1991) 4, 271

sary and is thus the source of what he calls "substantial communality." In his vision, therefore, one may not interpret the Second World War as the battle of democracy against fascism. The Allies represented the (liberal or Marxist) ideologies, the kingdom of 'opinions,' the non-nations. They fought against the embodiment of the idea of nation. It was a battle of non-nations against nation. To express it more strongly, as the nation is the only bond which happens to me from 'the real' it demands a loyalty which is erected on the other side of good and evil, because each value that addresses me from outside the nation consists only in one or the other partisan 'opinion.' The only relevant distinction, applicable also to thinking, is finally that there is a nation which is mine.[16]

This position is extreme and is not necessitated by Gellner's classical definition of nationalism. This definition proclaims only the congruence of politics and culture. Culture, particular as it may seem, always possesses universal moments. First, there is the element of language. Language can to some extent be communicated and translated. Herder was a great translator. Second, there is the fact that all culture, as a symbolic form, is marked by the distance between signifier and signified. For this reason a national culture finds a more authentic representation in the work of great artists, critical and subversive as they may seem, than in trivial uncritical works of kitsch. Consequently, J.-L. Nancy rightly suggests that Nazism not be considered as a form of nationalism.[17]

Between Internationalism and Nationalism

Have we won a moral or moralistic position too cheaply? We have argued that as citizens we can better think of our communality as a

---

16 B. Willms, *Idealismus und Nation. Zur Rekonstruktion des politischen Selbsbewusstsein der Deutschen* (Paderborn: Schöningh 1986)

17 *Le mythe nazi*, 61. In Nazism, the political cannot be viewed as an articulation of pre-political or cultural identities, because this would presuppose a universal moment. Nazism is the negation of *all* universality. For that reason it is not even about language or cultural identity. It is about the completely singular and the completely incommunicable. It simply marks its own soil with its own blood.

solidarity achieved through shared ethical ideals – human rights for example – than as a solidarity achieved through culture, language, and origin. Are we ourselves not neglecting the political aspect of the problem, the problem of the definiteness of the political? Are we ourselves not slipping into a naïve universalistic construction that has no connection with the meanings of our life-world?

One often hears this accusation concerning the term 'post-national identity' which is used in this connection by authors such as Habermas or Jean-Marc Ferry.[18] The term sounds extremely universalistic because it is formed analogously to Kohlberg's concept of post-conventional morality: phases five and six of moral competence in which the child is capable of judging using abstract considerations that are no longer dependent upon the particularity of the group. The dream would then be a society which publicly identifies itself not around a socio-cultural particularity, but purely on the basis of universalistic principles. These can be moral in nature, such as basic rights. But one can also dream of a universal society guided by entirely different universal principles, the principles of the techno-economy or of the market. Or, perhaps the two belong together as is often heard in the comment, 'Europe is the market plus human rights.'

Is such internationalism not naïve, in the sense that it forgets the problem for which the nation was an answer, namely the problem of the concreteness of politics? It would then not be an appropriate reaction to nationalism. To put it another way: internationalism and nationalism could both be signs of the same thing, namely of the erosion of politics.

The techno-economy expressly chooses this erosion as a necessary condition for a rational, prosperous, and non-oppressive society. Its rejection of nationalism is, as is the case with Hayek, also a rejection of politics as such. Society neither can nor should, in any way whatsoever, provide for a collective will. I no longer actually need to be a citizen, but only a consumer in the international market. The status of

---

18 J. Habermas, *Eine Art Schadensabwicklung*, (Frankfurt a. M.: Suhrkamp 1987), 135, 171; *Die nachholende Revolution* (Frankfurt a. M.: Suhrkamp 1990), 135. J.-M. Ferry, 'Qu'est-ce qu'une identité postnationale?' *Esprit* **164** (1990) 80-90; 'Pertinence du postnational,' J. Lenoble and N. Dewandre, *L'Europe au soir du siècle* (Paris: Editions Esprit 1992), 39-58.

my national identity is reduced to something less than a cultural expression. It is merely a product for purely private consumption, a folkloristic or gastronomic identity.[19]

Also possible is a moralistic version of this internationalism, namely in a philosophy of difference. Here each political form of identity would be rejected as a form of substantialism, appropriation, or over-determination, because every determination is already an over-determination. Political unity would then only lie in the recognition of difference. The only connecting bond is the difference, a difference between us which we recognize as the fractures that we also experience in ourselves. Upon this recognition, solidarity can be built. If I am also a foreigner to myself then there are no more foreigners; a paradoxical community of foreigners is founded.[20]

But perhaps this is not a good alternative to nationalism. Both the market and moralism are forms of denial of the definiteness of the political. They offer no answer to the question: how do dispersed modern individuals gather as citizens in an experience of loyalty and solidarity? In the presence of this question it could be that this concept of the 'nation-state' is too weak, at least in the sense that the political makes its presence known insufficiently as a concrete form, or is unable to satisfactorily present an image of its unity.

This could be a dangerous situation, because this sort of erosion creates a vacuum which can easily be filled by more extreme forms of nationalism. The nationalist and the technocrat easily live in the same soul. The technocratic demolition of the political dimension creates a post-ideological situation in which only nationalism is capable of actually interpreting solidarity, because it is the appropriate ideology when there are no longer any other ideologies. The only thing left to defend when there are no more ideas to defend is the idea of 'we' against the others. If the people no longer have anything to worship, then they worship themselves, their own image. It becomes enthusiastic via its

---

19 This seems to be suggested in F. Fukuyama, *The End of History and the Last Man* (New York: The Free Press 1992), ch. 25.

20 See the last pages of J. Kristeva, *Etrangers à nous-mêmes* (Paris: Fayard 1988), 287-90.

own enthusiasm. The definiteness of the political project is replaced by the feeling of identity that is no longer supported by any content but has become tautological: we are we. We are those who have always been. We must be what we have always been. We must be what we already are. We endlessly carry on with the story of our we.[21] The erosion of the possibility of experiencing integrative moments in the political arena can express itself in the crumbling away of our capability to be interested in the political debate. This debate consists precisely in the fact that we learn to handle differences in a democratic manner, that we search for every possible solution, and that in this communal search we experience solidarity and cohesion. When the capability to do this is eroded, differences become no longer the creative source of democracy, but a poor alibi to retreat into the pre-political we-feelings of homogenous subgroups that entertain the illusory feeling of being a community without differences.[22]

It is somewhat ironic that the nationalistic ideology, which dissociates itself from the problem of the abstraction and lack of meaning in modern democracy, is itself in its extreme form absolutely abstract and lacking in concreteness. This is also logical. Respect for the given, in its historical purity, when it respects nothing other than the given, cannot be supported by the content of what is given, but only by the fact *that* it is given to us and that we find ourselves within it.

Nationalism and naïve internationalism seem thus to reflect the same emptiness, the same formalism and the same erosion of the political. When we think of the concreteness of the political order from the givenness of the national, we risk losing sight of the specifically political character of this concreteness. Our political identity is then a product of culture, and through this the content of the project of society is

---

21 The expression comes from J.-F. Lyotard, *Le Différend* (Paris: Editions de Minuit 1983), 216-17.

22 It is conspicuous how Belgium, after becoming a federal state a number of years ago, still finds it difficult to discuss important political problems (for example, the efficient working of social security or of justice). Just as a discussion is begun, another party proposes that the competence in the matter be divided up and referred to the regional governments. This type of splitting up has now acquired the status of 'political solution.'

emptied of normative meaning. Nationalism is then a culturalistic over-determination of the political arena. But if we consider the content of the political merely as the demands of human rights and as the technical imperatives of the market, we likewise run the risk of losing sight of the specifically political dimension, because this demands an historical concreteness, effectiveness, and plausibility.

Is there no other way? The debate between communitarianism and liberalism has wrongly created the impression that there are only two polarized positions possible. On the one hand, we have the instrumental, liberal-procedural society, which is only the manager of individualistic interests and the regulator of conflicts concerning individualistic rights. Thus this is not a 'genuine' society in which identity, loyalty, and solidarity are possible. On the other hand we have a 'genuine' society which is a closed substantial unity with a shared culture and shared conceptions of the good. The question is whether this polarization is correct. Perhaps a political society is thinkable that arouses this solidarity and citizenship, but not merely on the basis of the fact that we share the same culture, language, or past. A political society can concretely make its presence known without being the expression of a pre-political substance. A political society can be a 'nation' (at least in the sense of image of unity) without drawing this image simply from a pre-political life-world. In what follows two approaches are proposed to implement this way of thinking.

The Land of the People

One approach is that of the constitutional state. The citizen understands the constitutional sphere not merely as a catechism of general principles, but as the possibility for all particular and private bonds. It is misleading to suggest a contradiction between the state, that cold and abstract region of calculating justice-seeking citizens, and the nation, that warm region of affectivity and feeling at home. Such a suggestion is part of the nationalistic rhetoric. The nation does not, after all, have a monopoly on solidarity. Our attachments might be better protected by the abstract laws of the constitutional state than by the cultural homogeneity of a nation.

The abstract constitutional sphere of rights seems to be a source of frustration for citizens themselves. A minority group understands itself on the basis of unique characteristics. The more unique these characteristics, the better they are at defining the group against others. That which is most unique is most valuable to the group. Because, after all, this is the ultimate legitimization of its existence, the reason why the group is this group and not part of another. Yet a minority derives its rights, not from that which is unique, however important that might be, but from an abstract principle which negates each particularity and is valid for all. This is a frustrating situation. It implies that a minority, even in full possession of its rights, will not be fully appreciated for its uniqueness. From its point of view it is being recognized for the wrong reason.

In a famous speech at his acceptance of an honorary doctorate in the United States, then-Czechoslovakian president Vaclav Havel was confronted with this frustration. His compatriots had seemingly accused him of emphasizing too strongly the importance of citizenship, and thus diminishing the value of belonging to a nation, to a people.[23] In his speech he answered that what he called 'the civic principle' was the possibility condition for all other bonds. While belonging to a people or to a culture is only one form of attachment, citizenship and the rights that go with it make possible many forms of attachment, be they family, church, professional grouping, language group, or regional or supra-regional communities. Havel is right. Those searching for 'a fatherland to love' too quickly believe that this can be found only in a political entity which coincides with a more substantial life-world, such as the cultural nation. But it is better that the political sphere *not* precisely coincide with a particular attachment, because it must be the public possibility of all forms of attachment by all sorts of people in a multicoloured life-world. The cultural nation is only one aspect of this, however important it might be.

Some believe that a state which does not coincide with a 'people' or a cultural nation is missing the warm heartbeat of concrete society and thus is no more than a formal skeleton. Such a state would have only an instrumental meaning. It would regulate the economy and provide

---

23   V. Havel, 'On Home,' *New York Review of Books*, 5 December 1991, 49.

procedures for resolving conflicts. Presumably there is a misunderstanding here. Such a state is indeed capable of 'being loved,' because it can be the state 'of the people' in a very rich way. Of course one must no longer understand 'people' in the massive and homogeneous sense which it has in the modern concept of nation. The question is precisely whether a people, as a homogeneous mass of contractors or sharers of culture, really is such a genuine, warm, life-filled entity. A people really lives only there where, amongst the teeming multiplicity of life attachments, they are more than members of an homogeneous culture group: father, artist, church-goer, shopkeeper, city dweller.... The possibility and organization of this variety comes into existence via the constitutional state, not in the nation which is only one of my many identities. In this sense a land is more 'of the people' in its constitutional principle than in its national principle. A fatherland is capable of being loved precisely because it does not contain some massive form of determinedness. It is *our* land, the land of everyone of us, precisely because it belongs to no one exclusively. In this sense the state is 'de-nationalized' or 'post-national' (Ferry). But it is not an abstract or cold state. Real coldness exists only when all life is thought to be the same, nothing more than the expression of one identical culture substance, and when it seems it may only be judged upon this basis.

There is another suggestion within Havel's text. The civic principle is not seen as congruent with an attachment to a specific content-definite group. Therefore it is the only principle that regards humankind in its full sovereignty: expressly *not* as members of a group, but as pure bearers of rights. This means that *in* the civic principle itself there is a transcendent moment. The general thesis which we encountered in the communitarian perspective, is of course true, namely that a merely willed, purely contractual order cannot fully bind. But what transcends our wills must not be sought in the moment that the state is a people in the sense of the givenness of the nation. Finally, the nation is itself the work of people, the result of all sorts of historical machinations and imaginations. What does transcend our wills must be sought *in* the political moment itself. This moment institutionalizes and makes public our sovereignty and our dignity as a person. Such a state is not a skeleton. It is a place of life and dignity.

The Land of Our Ancestors

But does not such a state remain abstractly universal, disconnected from concrete culture? In this case the problem of the concreteness of the political, which we have called the kernel of the nation problem, is not really solved, unless a moment of concreteness within the constitutional realm itself can be shown.

Rights and constitutions are not just general principles which fall from heaven in order to be concretely applied. They come to be only in concrete democratic action. We ourselves organize them. We fight about them. We formulate them. They are not separate from a concrete democratic culture within a concrete political space.[24]

The post-national identity must be much more concrete than a bundle of rules. Freedom can be an effective principle only if it is also a practice. There are concrete traditions of freedom. Even liberalism has the form of a tradition and not a bundle of principles. This historical concreteness is inherent in the term 'constitutional patriotism' ('*Verfassungspatriotismus*'). This term is usually used, and Habermas sometimes seems to suggest this, to denote a purely universalistic principle. But that is incorrect.[25] It is not just my willingness to direct my loyalty exclusively to universal fundamental rights. It is, for example, the most concrete manner, and the only concrete manner, in which German citizens can still be German citizens. A collective identification can no longer occur for them on the basis of the mere narration of a historical-national continuity, because this has been irretrievably damaged. Their formation of identity can thus only occur via a certain distance, a distance which exists precisely in the expressed agreement with democratic principles: the basic rights contained in the constitution. Germany is the nation whose uniqueness consists in no longer being able to be a

---

24 Sociologists such as Gabriel A. Almond use the term 'political culture.' It is useful here in expressing the fact that groups embody and institutionalize very specific forms of political conduct and notions. Thus a form of national integration, in the political sense, is possible which does not coincide with the ethnic or cultural unity.

25 Habermas has emphasized this himself in his interview with Ferry (*Die nachholende Revolution*, 149-56).

nation in the 'German' sense of that word.[26] It is the post-national identity of a land that has won its democratic conscience through a totalitarian experience. A very different identity is developed in countries that have not known such an experience.

In this scheme a multiplicity of national identities is good. If the political becomes a completely cosmopolitan and decentralized space, it is only a complicated technical network and an opaque multiplicity of levels of decision making. In this case a formal condition for democratic participation disappears. Then there is no longer an *agora*, no longer a privileged public space which summons us. Then there are insufficient strategic places, insufficient frames of reference, insufficient points of recognition, and insufficient traditions of discussion. Participatory citizenship needs a place where it is at home, a local history and a local language. This is a form of concreteness that one could call 'nation.' This concept must not be understood as a culturally homogeneous group, but rather as the structure and the centring of this public space – a post-national nation.

The externality of law is overcome, not by 'virtue and terror' (*'die Tugend und der Schrecken'*), as is the case when it falls down from a universal heaven to a society with which is has no connection, and not because it would be the articulation of an imagined cohesion already present in the nation. The externality is overcome because my freedom has a history. I can relate myself to this history, not in a merely narrative way as in the cultural nation, but in a participatory, argumentative, and quarrelling way as true citizens are wont to do. Who are my people? We are the people.

---

26 Sociological research has shown that in the Federal German Republic the dominant feelings of collective identity have shifted from a cultural identity to a collective pride in their democratic and economic achievements. H. Honolka, *Die Bundesrepublik auf der Suche nach ihrer Identität* (München: C.H. Beck 1987).

Beyond the Opposition:
Civic Nation versus Ethnic Nation

DOMINIQUE SCHNAPPER
École des Hautes Études en Sciences Sociales, Paris

The political and scientific debate surrounding the concepts of nation, ethnicity, and nationalism is so deeply loaded with values and passions that it should be the sociologist's highest priority to define those terms as precisely as possible in order to distinguish a new debate from the common discourse and to subject the definitions to scrutiny. It is often acknowledged that a clarification of the terms used in the debates of ethnicity, the State, the nation and nationalism is necessary, but such work is rarely done. It is important to make a distinction between the term 'nation' and other terms with which it is often confused – and differently in the different nations – and to clear up the ambiguities that affect the political, ideological, and scientific discourse. In the common discourse and even in the scientific literature, such terms as 'ethnic' and 'national' are often used indifferently, and the 'nation' is subject to contradictory criticisms as it is sometimes understood as referring to the 'nation' and sometimes to the 'ethnic group.' There is always a connection between the concepts used by a given author and that author's theoretical frame of reference. It is the sociologist's task to explicate the vocabulary used in the debates that take place in social life and to ask the right questions after clearing up the pointless controversies about words. This task is all the more important as words are not only the instruments, but also the very objects of political and scientific discussions.

I will define 'nation' as a specific type of political unit characterized by the sovereignty exerted to integrate the nation's populations at home and to play its role as a historical subject on the international level, the world order being based on the existence of states and the relationships between them. Its specific trait is the existence of a community of citizens legitimizing the policy of the state both at home and abroad. This type of political entity can be designated equally as 'nation,' 'democratic nation,' or 'civic nation.'

'Nation' and 'state' are often confused because most of the states since the Second World War claim to be the expression of a democratic nation. The reason for the ambiguous use of the term 'nation' in social life is that it is intimately linked to the modern principle of political legitimacy and to the source of social fabric. This is why the democratic nation has remained an implicit model, to which references are constantly made in political life, even if in many cases it is only in a purely symbolic way.

It is usually argued that there are two conceptions of the nation. The way they are expressed differs between countries, according to intellectual tradition and the researchers' background, but the distinction remains. Roughly speaking, one definition refers to the 'civic' nation, the other to the 'ethnic' nation. This dual conception pervades any discussion of the term 'nation.'

It is this duality that I wish to question here. The opposition is both historical and ideological, but from an analytical point of view I will argue that there is only one idea of nation. Analytical thought should not consist in using words and arguments from nineteenth-century ideological disputes and European international conflicts, whilst giving them a scholarly or obscure form. The 'pre-notions' of social life, to use Durkheim's words, should not be confused with analytical concepts. There have indeed been two trends in the history of the formation of the nations – the 'French' or 'American' trend and the 'German' one, or, to use another type of vocabulary, the 'Western' and 'Eastern' ones. There have also been two types of nationalist ideologies. But one cannot deduce that there are two – analytically distinct – ideas of nation. One should resist the temptation of a Manichean duality, however attractive it may at first appear.

I History of Western and Eastern Europe

In Western Europe, political unity had been created long before nationalism emerged in the nineteenth century. Kings had reunited a territory on which they exerted authority. The political union of England, later Scotland and Ireland was completed by the English monarchs. For centuries kings progressively united the provinces, which were to form the national territory, into the small kingdom of France, following military conquest and a cunning policy of marriages, exchanges, and negotiations. State institutions emerged slowly from the Middle Ages onwards in France, England, and Spain, prompted by the need to keep an army, which imposed a heavy burden on the population. The kings' officers levied taxes, enlisted men, and requisitioned goods. The profit gained from taxes was first used to wage war, then to enable the state to consolidate the royal territory, to centralize administrative organization, and to differentiate state control and the instruments of coercion. "War made the State and the State waged war."[1] Against feudal power and popular uprisings, the kings' civil servants, lawyers, and military progressively built the State, closely related to the nation. The first manifestations of national feeling appeared in France as early as the thirteenth century;[2] the idea of nation was born in England and France as they fought the Hundred Years War, and in Spain during the Catholic *Reconquista* at the end of the fifteenth century, with the deportation of Jews and Muslims in 1492 being both its instrument and symbol. The French nation-state, born out of a process stretching across centuries, existed in a monarchic form long before the nationalist idea of the peoples' right to self-determination was expressed. Monarchy was so much merged with the nation that, as Renan noticed, when France turned into a Republic, the nation remained: "This great French monarchy was so highly national that when it fell, the nation was able to stand without it."[3] France and Britain experienced a parallel history in the birth of the idea of nation and the creation of political and State structures which, inside relatively stable borders, embodied and symbolized the unity of the nation.

The deeply interwoven dynastic and religious entities intensified each other's integrationist effects: religious unity increased royal power.

---

1 Charles Tilly in Charles Tilly, ed., *The Formation of National States in Western Europe* (Princeton, NJ: Princeton University Press 1975), 42

2 Colette Beaune, *Naissance de la nation France* (Paris: Gallimard 1985)

3 Ernest Renan, *Oeuvres complètes*, T. 1 (Paris: Calmann-Lévy 1947 [1882]), 894

Following the model of the dual – human and mystical – nature of Jesus Christ, the doctrine of the King's Two Bodies created a real royal christology. By developing the fiction of a mystical royal body distinct from but mysteriously united to the natural body of the king, English lawyers moulded the abstract idea of a monarchy whose existence transcended the king himself. Thus secular power asserted itself against the Church while regarding the State as, by its very nature, above and independent from its agents. The king, an image of God and His instrument in the world, tended to put himself at the head of the religious organization in his Kingdom. The king of France, who had expelled the Jews and the Protestants from his kingdom, held power by divine right. The Spanish Catholic monarchs had based their political legitimacy on the religious unity of their kingdom. "The State became more and more a quasi-Church or a mystical guild on a rational basis."[4] But at the same time, faced with the political ambitions of the Church, the king of divine right had set up and guaranteed the independence of the political body as "wholly one, essentially distinct from the Church."[5]

In 1414, at the Constenz synod, the five leading Western European nations – Italy, France, England, Germany, and Spain – showed themselves as steady and recognized political entities. But over the following centuries, the imperial ambitions of the Holy Roman Empire, which only ceased officially to exist in 1806, and the Ottoman invasion prevented stable national units from appearing in Central Europe. From the Baltic sea to Sicily, in what S. Rokkan and D. Urwin called the 'polycephalous' Europe, city-states, independent cities, kingdoms, ecclesiastical and dynastic principalities perpetuated themselves under the aegis of the imperial dream up to the nineteenth century. In the German and Italian historical conscience, cultural identity has always been separated from political organization. Germany and Italy were only constituted as nation-states, albeit imperfect ones, after 1870. It was a German, Meinecke, who in 1907 elaborated the distinction be-

---

4 Ernst Kantorowicz, *Les Deux Corps du Roi* (Paris: Gallimard 1989 [1957]), 146

5 Pierre Manent, *Histoire intellectuelle du libéralisme, dix leçons* (Paris: Calmann-Lévy 1987), 29

tween the nation-state *(Staatsnation)* and the cultural nation *(Kulturnation)*. More or less voluntarily the Germans experienced at different times in their history different situations in which nation and state were separated, either 'two States, one nation' or 'several States, one nation.'

Between this polycephalous Europe and Central and Eastern Europe, the Austro-Hungarian empire was still in 1914 a "conglomeration of heterogeneous States devoid of any internal cohesion."[6] The Habsburg monarchy, a depository of the old imperial dream, was supranational in its very principle. Charles I, the Austrian emperor and Apostle King of Hungary, was also King of Bohemia, Dalmatia, Croatia, Slavonia, Galicia, Lodomerya and Illyria, King of Jerusalem, Archduke of Austria, and so on. The Emperor could not or would not associate himself with a specific national aspiration. The Austro-Hungarian empire, established in its last political form by the 1867 Austro-Hungarian Compromise, gathered peoples who were diverse in their historical conscience and religious beliefs, and convinced of their unique destiny. The Catholics, Protestants, Orthodox, and Muslims constituted a medley in which the churches divided the peoples instead of uniting them. As far as the distribution between majority and minority languages was concerned, Western Europe seemed to head towards unity and Eastern Europe towards dispersion. These different types of diversity could hardly be transcended by a national aim since the troubled history of the area had prevented a free bourgeoisie from emerging. The feudal tradition had remained strong, setting the nobility in opposition to the peasants, without any political society with bourgeois citizenship.

The peoples, confronted with invaders from the East, subjected to conquerors, could not be organized into independent political units nor separated by lasting borders. Whereas between the fifteenth and eighteenth centuries the modern state appeared in the big Western monarchies, Germany and Italy remained politically split and the Turks destroyed the national institutional framework of Hungary and

---

6 Istvan Bibo, *Misère des petits Etats d'Europe de l'Est* (Paris: L'Harmattan 1986 [1946]), 144

Bohemia and the medieval kingdoms of Serbia and Croatia. When nationalism spread through the Central European countries in the nineteenth century, ethnic differences could not be overcome, all the more so as the borders' instability had impeded the birth of true political institutions. They had neither capital nor state apparatus, autonomous economic organization, national elite, or political culture. Furthermore, in the nationalistic age, the Romanians or Germans living, say, on Hungarian soil, had no reason to accept the Magyars' domination in the name of the peoples' right to self-determination. Historical peoples could not agree to give up their political independence, as had done Brittany in the sixteenth, Alsace, Artois, and Roussillon in the seventeenth, or Scotland in the early eighteenth century, with the 1707 Treaty of Union and Home Rule.

Eastern European nationalists, while putting forward the Western European principle of the peoples' right to self-determination, justified their demands with ethnic and linguistic arguments. They asserted their historical specificity by hating their immediate neighbours, as shown by the Romanians and Hungarians, or the Hungarians, Croatians, and Serbs. Isaiah Berlin was not the first one to notice that nationalist excesses are "less felt in the societies which have benefited from political independence over long periods of time."[7] The fear for the very existence of the national community, deeply internalized by collective conscience, nourished collective hysteria and exacerbated groundless national pride. It set peoples against each other and prevented a democratic nation from emerging.

One would not understand how nations appeared if one neglected the link between domestic integration and external sovereignty. Spain, Portugal, England, the Netherlands and France were conquering nations: they explored the non-European world and built large colonial empires throughout the world. External power could not but reinforce the process of internal integration. On the contrary, Eastern European countries were conquered by non-European invaders who came from the East. In the whole of Central Europe and the Balkans, populations

---

7 Quoted and translated in Gil Delannoi and Pierre-André Taguieff, *Théories du nationalisme* (Paris: Kimé 1991), 318

were shifted, deported, subjugated, and borders moved to and fro following the Turkish advances or retreats. The peoples, submitted to an outside power, were subjects of large, partly non-European empires for centuries. They could not turn into communities of citizens within a few years.

II   Western Ideology and Eastern Ideology

It is from this double experience of European history that the nation was thought out. The arguments put forward by the militants during the nationalist conflicts – the eighteenth-century conflict between England and its American colonies, then between France and Germany from the revolutionary wars until the annexation of Alsace to the German *Reich* in 1870 and the First World War – were transformed into Ideas.

Indeed, nineteenth-century thinking was still influenced by the political and ideological struggle between the French *Grande Nation,* stemming from the revolution, which referred to the new principle of legitimacy, and the old 'nation,' in the medieval sense, or the empires derived from a dynastic or religious history. But the new principle itself could be interpreted in two ways. The peoples' demand for self-determination could be legitimized either in the name of a people of citizens or of a people resulting from an original history and culture. Though referring to the same revolutionary principle, two ideologies of the modern nation were elaborated. One cited the will of men, the other cited their ethnic and linguistic identity. The French conception, born of the Enlightenment and the revolutionary experience, was political, individualistic, rationalist, and voluntarist. On the other hand, the Germans defined their nation against the French, in organicist terms, following their 1806 and 1807 military defeats. The ethnic nation based itself on a community of an original people (*Urvolk*) sharing the same ancestry, the same culture, and the same past, imposed on individuals.

After the 1870 war, the controversy between French and German historians raised to the level of classical tragedy what appeared as the opposition between two ideas of the nation, which was held as essentially 'ambiguous.' On one side, Theodor Mommsen justified the Bismarckian annexation policy by the ethnic, linguistic, and cultural

Germanness of Alsace, whatever the provisional will of its inhabitants. On the other, the French argued that "neither race nor language makes nationality" (Fustel de Coulanges), cited the revolutionary principles and, in the name of the legitimate "wishes of the nations" (Renan) and the 'will' and 'free consent' of the peoples, argued that Alsace was "French by nationality and love of homeland" (Fustel de Coulanges). The role played by the annexation of Alsace in the reflexion on the nation in Germany, France and even Italy shows how controversy and analysis were indissolubly linked.

These ideologies, which had been moulded by the nationalists in order to justify and lead collective action, were then accepted as ideas in the analytical sense. The two ideas, formulated first by the German Romantic thinkers to build their own nation against the French, became accepted as obvious; they were analyzed by theoreticians, then sanctioned by the historians of nationalist ideas.

In different national and scientific languages, the nation according to the 'French' (or 'Italian,' or 'American') ideology would always end up being distinguished from the nation according to the 'German' ideology, or 'Western' nation as opposed to 'Eastern' nation, civic nation to *Volk*, 'Nation-state' *(Staatsnation)* to 'cultural nation' *(Kulturnation)*, citizens to ancestor worship, political will to organic nation, elective nation to ethnic nation, nation based on contract to nation-genius, civism to populism, the individual to the nation as collective individual, the enlightenment to Romanticism, or, lastly, individualism to holism. Behind these various terms lay always the same elements. The first great historian of nationalism, Hans Kohn, had already set this opposition in historical science by arguing that "freedom for the Germans was based on history and particularism, as opposed to reason and equality in France."[8] When a Hungarian historian put forward the idea that there was a 'third Europe,' referring to Bohemia, Hungary and Poland, he characterized it as being born between the 'Western' type and the 'East European' model.[9]

---

8 Hans Kohn, *The Idea of Nationalism: A Study in its Origin and Background* (New York: MacMillan 1944)

9 Jenö Szücs, *Les Trois Europe* (Paris: L'Harmattan 1985)

This series of dual oppositions was all the more rooted in the minds of historians as they recalled nineteenth-century thought on the new society born of the industrial and political revolution and of modern political legitimacy. They were also part of the more general philosophical discussion on liberty and necessity.

The move from historical description to theory, which characterized the reflexion on the nation, still has repercussions today. After he described the two historical 'trajectories' which actually led to the building of nations, Anthony Smith drew the conclusion that there are two 'concepts' of the nation, a territorial-civic one and a genealogical-ethnic one: "The concept of the nation is found to be inherently unstable and dualist."[10] John Plamenatz, by contrasting nineteenth-century German and Italian nationalism to the Balkan peoples' demands, also referred to the double idea of the nation: the former, already united around a great culture, demanded to be recognized as an independent political entity and to form a civic nation ; the latter, in search of a common culture, with unstable and changing historical and ethnic allegiance, aspired to form an 'ethnic' nation.[11]

One should note that, in practice, every national tradition is dual – whether it be intellectual history or historical reality. Not all the Germans ignored the political conception of the nation: Louis Dumont recalls that "Herder's mention of different cultural communities is one aspect of German acculturation to the developed form of individualism and combines a holistic aspect with an individualistic one."[12] In France, anti-revolutionary writers like Joseph de Maistre or Louis de Bonald followed Burke's passionate criticism of the revolutionary idea of the nation *à la française*. But these very criticisms imply that there actually are two ideas of the nation, even if they may be combined in concrete historical nations.

---

10 Anthony D. Smith, *The Ethnic Origins of Nations* (New York, London: Blackwell 1986), 4

11 J. Plamenatz in Eugène Kamenka, ed., *Nationalism: The Nature and Evolution of an Idea* (London: Edward Arnold 1976)

12 Louis Dumont, *L'idéologie allemande. France-Allemagne et retour* (Paris: Gallimard 1991), 24

This intellectual tradition perpetuates itself today, even more so as it may be a tool to analyze some present realities. Comparative analysis of citizenship laws and immigration policies in France and Germany, for instance, shows that the opposition between the nation-contract and the nation-genius has not lost its appeal, that it still permeates the minds and is expressed in law. Comparing the French and German citizenship laws is revealing. In France, the automatic or quasi-automatic ways of acquiring citizenship, the importance of mere declaration (for instance for French people's foreign spouses) and the right to be reintegrated (for those who have lost citizenship), give some rights to the individual against the state. The small cost of application and the liberal implementation of the nationality laws in practice still give wide access to French citizenship not only to the individuals born and educated in France, but also to almost all the foreigners settled in France for a long time who apply for it. French policy still aims at integrating the populations of foreign origin in the name of citizenship. The Germans, on the other hand, maintain an ethnic conception of the national link. Many contemporary authors still evoke the linguistic and historical community rather than political will. The 'German blood' idea is still alive among the population. The almost exclusive respect of *jus sanguinis*, expressed in the citizenship laws based on a 1913 law, results in refusing citizenship to foreigners even when they have lived in Germany regularly and for a long time, sometimes two or three generations, even if they are acculturated to German society and culture, whereas it is granted to those living in Poland, Russia, or the Sudeten who can claim German ancestors, even if they don't know anything about German language and culture.[13]

Thus European history crystallized into a fundamental and insurmountable ideological opposition – defined as a system of ideas and values turned into political action – what had been mainly a result of

---

13 Dominique Schnapper, *La France de l'intégration, Sociologie de la nation en 1990* (Paris: Gallimard 1991), 51 ff.; Schnapper, *L'Europe des immigrés. Essai sur les politiques d'immigration* (Paris: François Bourin 1992); William Rogers Brubaker, *Citizenship and Nationhood in France and Germany* (Cambridge, MA: Harvard University Press 1992)

different histories. The socially constituted ideas of the nation have been used as instruments of nationalist struggles in Europe since the French revolution. Although ideas are necessarily objects in history, insofar as they are a means used by social actors to conceive and build nations, their study ought not to be confused with sociological analysis. "Binary oppositions are an analytical procedure, but their usefulness does not guarantee that reality can thus be divided. We must be suspicious vis-à-vis anyone asserting there are two kinds of people, two kinds of reality or process."[14]

III   A Single Idea of Nation

The intellectual and political legacy is not enough to explain how entrenched this opposition is. Not only are binary oppositions comfortable, but the 'theory' of the two ideas of the nation is based on the very features of a democratic nation.

The founding principle and the ideal of the democratic nation consists in integrating the different populations, no matter what their ethnic identity may be, in a community of citizens. The democratic nation is characterized by its ambition to transcend through the notion of citizenship all particularities, whether they be biological (or perceived as such), historical, economic, social, religious, or cultural. It defines the citizen as an abstract individual, without particular identification or label, below and beyond all his concrete characteristics.[15] Every citizen has the same rights and the same duties, and is subjected to the same laws as all the others, no matter their race, gender, religion, socioeconomic status or ethnic identity. What makes the modern nation specific is that it integrates all populations into a community of citizens and it legitimizes the action of the State – its instrument – by this

---

14   M. Douglas (*Daedalus*, Fall, 1978), quoted by Dumont, *Essais sur l'individualisme. Une perspective sur l'ideologie moderne* (Paris: Seuil 1983), 15

15   Schnapper, *La Communauté des citoyens. Sur l'idée moderne de nation* (Paris: Gallimard 1994)

community; so it implies universal suffrage – *all* citizens[16] are involved in choosing their governments and judging the way power is exercised – and conscription – *all* citizens are involved in common defense or foreign intervention. This double participation is undoubtedly true, but it first and foremost symbolizes political legitimacy.

Secularism, particularly, is an essential attribute of the modern state because it transcends the numerous religious identities, shifts religious beliefs and practices into the private sphere, and turns the public sphere into a religious-free space to which all citizens belong, whatever their religion. Needless to say, *in concreto*, there are all kinds and degrees of recognition and negotiations between the secular state, the churches, and the religious groups, which are different in every nation according to their traditions and history. But, whatever its historical forms, secularism is at the core of all democratic nations; it shows that the social link is no longer religious but political, and therefore, until now, national. The national project is universal not only because it is meant to encompass all those who are in the same nation, but also because going beyond particularities through political means can in principle be adopted in any society. Universalism is the long-term objective of the ideology of liberty and equality, a basis for the idea of the democratic nation.

The national idea does not prevent individuals from referring to multiple cultural or ideological identities. Historically nations have emerged from one or more pre-existing ethnic groups. The nation transcends the ethnic groups, but they exist just the same. The multicultural character of social life is implied in the very definition of the democratic nation. This should encourage sociologists to reformulate the language used in the often obscure and passionate controversies that take place in both Europe and America about the meaning and value of multiculturalism. The real question is: to what extend could or should the fact of multiculturalism be recognized in political life? How far can this recognition go without challenging the necessary political unity of

---

16 Even if in practice the conception of the universal 'citizen' evolved since its 'reign' was proclaimed. See Pierre Rosanvallon, *Le sacre du citoyen* (Paris: Gallimard 1992).

the nation? Of course the answer is different in different countries with different traditions.

The notion of citizenship is central to the democratic practice which characterizes political modernity. Its basic tenet is that beyond their differences, all men are born equal in dignity and must be treated as such legally and politically – dignity is the value of democratic societies. To be as faithful to such an ideal as possible, efforts are made in democratic nations to transcend ethnic or ethnic-religious passions and to solve conflicts by resorting to the laws. Citizenship is a constructive utopia. By definition it has never been and cannot be totally implemented in real life.

The universal quality of the republican idea of the 'civic nation' according to Kant, combined with the particular aspect of the ethnic groups from which the nation was built and which are still alive under more or less recognized forms, explains the tension between universalism and particularism, which is a constituent of the nation. The variety of cultural and ideological references is implied by the very definition of the nation. Nations were historically built from one or several pre-existing ethnic groups. Insofar as it transcends pre-existing ethnicity, 'protonationalism,' nationalities, or religions according to specific modes and political traditions, each nation is unique.

On the other hand, the state, whose institutions and ideology tend to assimilate the population to the national culture, reinforces this uniqueness. Indeed, asserting the principle of citizenship would not be in itself sufficient to create a community of citizens. Sovereignty and citizenship are fictions. You cannot rally individuals to such abstract ideas. They can only be actually integrated if some concrete realities, values, and interests justify the inevitable constraints of collective life and their adherence to foreign action – which may entail the loss of their lives. Their integration can only be achieved as a result of the continuous action of common institutions, in the wide Durkheimian sense of the word – constituted forms of practice through which generations pass on the ways of being and living together which characterize a specific historical society.

The democratic nation, even though it is founded on the notion of citizenship, cannot but maintain the ethnic dimensions of collective life. There is an essential tension between, on the one hand, the formally rational and abstract ideal of citizenship, of a political and legal

231

nature, and on the other hand the necessity in every society to create a social link that is necessarily 'ethnic' or 'community-oriented,' that is direct and emotional, between the citizens. The democratic nation strives to conciliate the rational character inherent with a political organization founded on law, political and legal equality with the inevitable human passions. In other words, it aims to create a paradox: a community of citizens. Consequently, it is essentially fragile, as are all human creations appealing to reason rather than passions.

The social functions of education exemplify this tension. The aim of schooling is to form citizens, but at the same time, it has to create a sense of historical community at the national level, which is directly expressed in ethnicity. To form future citizens, education creates an abstract locus in which all pupils are treated equally, no matter what their social characteristics may be, as are the citizens in the political society. This locus, both abstract and real, is meant to compensate for the actual inequalities of social life and to resist the potential disruptions initiated by civil society. The prevailing order at school is impersonal and formal, as is that on which the idea of citizenship is based. Confronting the abstraction prevailing in the school system makes the child ready to achieve understanding and mastery of the abstraction which characterizes political society. But the school simultaneously conveys and nurtures the ethnic ideology of the nation. Interpreting real facts, historians have developed the myths of the glorious birth of Western democracies, the tragic birth of Israel, and the municipal freedom of the 'small European nations' such as the Netherlands, Belgium, or Switzerland. In the heyday of nations and nationalisms, before World War I, the role of the narrative of past historical events was to motivate the young generations, heirs of a glorious past, to maintain this legacy and to continue common action. In all European nations, national history showed the building and triumph of the nation and imposed the idea that the nation should be the exclusive object of the individual's loyalty at the expense of any form of identity. More generally, the state has always aimed at reinforcing the nation's particularity through the promotion of the national language and symbols.

The permanent tension between the nation's self-proclaimed universality and the specific pre-national ethnic groups that government policies tend to reinforce explains why the opposition between the 'two ideas' of the nation remained for so long. The advocates and the theoreticians of the civic nation would stress the uprooting of specific bonds through citizenship; the advocates of the ethnic nation would put forward the strength, value, and genuine nature of these roots.

If one agrees to define democratic nation by the never-fulfilled aim of creating a political society by transcending concrete roots and specific membership, there are not two ideas of nation, but one, unevenly and differently achieved, following an ever-different pattern according to the political project which is at the basis of nation-building. The different nations are all both 'ethnic' and 'civic,' but are differently 'ethnic' and 'civic.' In every national tradition, there are different means and institutions to transcend the ethnic realities of the society by the civic principle of the political domain.

The nations which were traditionally called civic, Western, *'à l'américaine'* or *'à la française'* according to countries and intellectual traditions, insofar as they were true to their logic and their proclaimed ideal, were close to this idea or ideal-type, for they saw political society and citizenship as the principle organizing social life. This is not a value judgment asserting the moral or political superiority of the political nation over the ethnic nation, but conclusions drawn from an analytical definition.

Of course I am not arguing that the French example is the universal model for the nation. It is only an illustration, for historical reasons. The idea of the civic nation has been invented by the English. But, whereas the English nation was born of an endogenous process and of pragmatic adaptation of the political organization to the necessities of democracy, the civic nation suddenly broke out as a revolution in France. It was immediately reflected on and staged. The principles of nation-building were thought out in France as in no other country and the republican, integrationist, and universalist model was constantly referred to in public and scientific life. The legitimacy and sovereignty of the nation, the need to submit specific identities and cultures to it and secularism, have been proclaimed there with more vigour than elsewhere; since the Revolution, the nation and its features have been uninterruptedly debated. England practically invented the idea of nation as a community of free and equal citizens; the French endlessly theorized the individual citizenship and universality of political society and strived to build it in a voluntarist way – which does not mean, as American scholars often remind us, that they were always faithful to their own theories. One can even wonder whether they haven't proclaimed the principles all the more as they were not always easily implemented.

The nationalists and ideologists of ethnic or '*à l'allemande*' nation cited pre-national values and not *specific* or *characteristic* values of the nation, a particular form of political organization of the democratic age. Ethnic-nation ideology was a means of justifying the failure of the nation in Central and Eastern Europe. If Central European nationalism can indeed be described as ethnic, as much by its features as by the arguments the nationalist thinkers used, it does not follow that there is an ethnic idea – in the analytical sense – of the nation. By insisting on pre-existing ethnic links rather than on the objective of creating a political society, the advocates of the "ethnic nation" failed to grasp what really defines national ambition, the momentum, albeit imperfect, towards overcoming particularism and ethnic loyalty, even if it expresses itself in a tension between universality and the state keeping national features alive. They discarded the main characteristic of the democratic national idea: the effort to transcend the level of concrete identities and ethnic solidarities through citizenship. This scheme is bound to remain unfulfilled, but this effort characterizes the democratic nation's project.

PART III

For and Against Nationalism

CANADIAN JOURNAL OF PHILOSOPHY
Supplementary Volume 22

Liberal Restrictions on Public Arguments: Can Nationalist Claims be Moral Reasons in Liberal Public Discourse? *

GENEVIÈVE NOOTENS
Université du Québec à Chicoutimi

I Introduction

Asserting the relationship between liberalism and nationalism is no easy matter. Liberal philosophers have been very suspicious of the phenomenon of nationalism, partly for historical reasons (e.g., national socialism) and partly for philosophical ones (amongst which a belief that liberal principles would override people's need for identification with ethnocultural communities). But even if some still consider the expression 'liberal nationalism' to be an oxymoron,[1] most of current Anglo-American liberal work on the subject leans toward a more nuanced approach, trying to specify how hospitable liberalism should be to nationalistic claims. The challenge, from this point of view, is to explain why and how political philosophy can incorporate national attachments to a *moral* argument on people's identity and distributive justice. In fact, it seems that nationalist rhetoric has found in identity politics a rather safe (even if narrow) way of entering liberal discourse.

---

* I wish to thank the Social Sciences and Humanities Research Council of Canada for providing the postdoctoral fellowship which has made this essay possible. Thanks are also owed to Jocelyne Couture, Kai Nielsen, Wayne Norman, Michel Seymour, and the participants to the ERES seminars (Winter 1996), for helpful and judicious comments on an earlier version of this article.

1 Sanford Levinson, 'Is Liberal Nationalism an Oxymoron? An Essay for Judith Shklar,' *Ethics* **105** (April 1995) 626-45

Nonetheless, liberalism still encounters great difficulties in dealing with nationalism, partly because nationality-based arguments are grounded in claims that are not reducible to distributive justice, but also because they appeal to people's cultural identity as a basis of settling conflictual claims. Nationalist arguments therefore come forward as a competing way of justifying political legitimacy. A nationalist government may, for example, want to ensure by the legislative process that people (citizens as well as immigrants) are going to live and work mainly within the nation's language, so as to ensure its survival for future generations. For example, Quebec's *Charte de la langue française* (usually referred to as *Loi 101*) aims at "making French the language of the state and the law, as well as the usual language of work, education, communications, commerce and business." But the legitimacy of such a will is far from being widely accepted; some dispositions of that law (notably the ones concerning education and commercial posting) have given rise to strong opposition.[2]

There are several questions related to the status of nationalist claims, such as the consistency of nationalism with liberal demands of neutrality, the value of national identities to individuals, the relation between the evaluation of nationalism and minority rights, the content of national identities, and the terms of inclusion into a national identity. Although they are closely linked, each of these topics would require an article of its own. In this paper, I want to tackle the question of whether liberal public discourse can grant a moral standing to nationalist claims. This question raises a twofold problem. First, the *nature* of such claims

---

2 *Charte de la langue française*, L.R.Q., c. C-11. Commercial signage, for example, has been an important source of conflict and judiciary debate in Quebec. The original version of the *Charte de la langue française*, adopted in 1977, imposed French as the exclusive language of public signage and commercial advertising (article 58). In 1988, the Supreme Court of Canada concluded, in *Ford*, that the prohibition of any language other then French in public signage and commercial advertising was contrary to freedom of expression. The National Assembly then resorted to a constitutional dispensatory clause to maintain the exclusive use of French in exterior signage; but in 1993 article 58 was modified in such a way as to ensure the predominance of French without prohibiting the use of other languages, so as to avoid resorting to the dispensatory clause relative to freedom of expression (Law 86, 1993, C. 40, article 18).

seems to differ from the nature of the arguments usually giving rise to legitimate moral claims in the liberal view and delimiting the boundaries between public and nonpublic reason. Second, as a corollary, these claims appeal to what seems to be a *competing standard of legitimacy*. I shall show however that there is no *a priori* compatibility or incompatibility between liberalism and nationalism, although liberalism cannot provide any moral justification for nationalism itself; such a justification would imply an assumption about the ethical character of national communities, a claim that liberal theory, whose fundamental concerns are individual well-being and social justice, cannot accommodate.

I will first make clear what I mean by nationalism. Then I will explain why the question of whether a claim can be given a moral standing in the public forum of a liberal polity is important. I will draw a distinction between the arguments we can invoke to sustain our claims in matters of political justice, on the one hand, and the rationale sustaining the political settlement of such claims, on the other. For this purpose, I will use an example focused on the distinction between secular rationale and religious motivation. I will start from that example to clarify how distinct nationalist claims are from religious ones and which category of these nationalist claims, if any, can legitimately be invoked in the liberal public forum. I hope to sketch an approach that would neither draw merely from a conception of minority rights as a remedy to unequal circumstances, nor from a theory of nationalism built on a right to culture.

II Nations and Nationalism

Current literature on nationalism generally defines a nation as a group of people sharing a set of 'objective' characteristics (such as language, territory, religion, race), and 'subjective' characteristics (such as myths, a sense of solidarity and of historical continuity, common beliefs). This definition is deliberately vague: as Yael Tamir stresses, no nation will have all of these characteristics, but only some of them, together with the existence of a national consciousness.[3] In some cases, the objective

---

3 Yael Tamir, *Liberal Nationalism* (Princeton, NJ: Princeton University Press 1993), 65; Wayne Norman, 'Prelude to a Liberal Morality of Nationalism,' in S. Brennan,

characteristics can be easily identified (the case of a colonized nation is an appropriate example); while in others, the Jewish diaspora for example, the subjective identification with the group, the sense of solidarity and of a common history and fate, are the most significant factors. The objective characteristics of a nation (some of its institutions and practices) may not distinguish it from other comparable groups, if it were not for the distinctive way in which conationals interpret their common life. The shared sense of a common identity thus reveals itself to be more significant than the distinctive character of 'objective' practices, although there also must be some number of such objective characteristics; a mere will to form a national group would not suffice to qualify as such.[4]

Nations are not necessarily highly organized and institutionally integrated societies. Using an institutional criterion to delimit the concept of a nation can be misleading: some institutionally organized (sub)cultures (such as gay and lesbian culture, or some religious groups) would not qualify as nations; while some loosely institutionalized groups actually constitute nations (again, think of the Jewish diaspora). Nonetheless, 'modern' nationalism seems to be characterized by close links between culture and politics.[5] But if this is the case, we need a definition of the nation that will help us in distinguishing between nations and other cultural groups. As Brian Walker rightly suggests, cultural environment is much more complex than the identification with a national group.[6] Many factors, issued from experiences of socialization

---

T. Isaacs, and M. Milde, eds., *A Question of Values: New Canadian Perspectives in Ethics and Political Philosophy* (Atlanta: Rodopi 1997 [Value Inquiry Book Series #40]); David Miller, 'In Defence of Nationality,' *Journal of Applied Philosophy* **10:1** (1993) 6-8. See also Charles Taylor, 'Why Do Nations Have to Become States?', in Stanley G. French, ed., *Philosophers Look at Canadian Confederation* (Montreal: Canadian Philosophical Association 1979), 33.

4 Tamir, *Liberal Nationalism*, 66

5 Tamir, *Liberal Nationalism*, 66; Bernard Yack, 'Reconciling Liberalism and Nationalism,' *Political Theory* **23:1** (February 1995) 180; F.M. Barnard, 'National Culture and Political Legitimacy: Herder and Rousseau,' *Journal of the History of Ideas* **44:2** (1983) 231-53

6 Brian Walker, 'Culturalist Dilemmas: On Some Convergences between Kymlicka

and people's self-representation, come into play in the constitution of individuals' identities. Only some of them depend on belonging to a nation. People participate in several cultural (and subcultural) levels and groups (civilization, society, nationality, religion, etc.)

Moreover, a culture is not a stable, fixed, univocal conceptual framework. As Daniel Weinstock emphasizes, from the point of view of the people participating in it, a culture is not to be compared to an *episteme*, but rather to *phronesis* (practical knowledge):

> [it is] a set of aptitudes, symbolic orientations, and tacit knowledge which constitutes [an individual's] capacity to participate in the complex network of practices and language games which make up his cultural life (...) It is less a set of statements about the world than a kind of transcendental condition of our apprehension of the world, of formulating epistemic as well as axiologic positions.[7]

Thus, although the content of the identity which unites a cultural group may change, the sense of a shared identity may still remain. For example, before the *Révolution tranquille* (the turning point which initiated a general movement of modernization and secularization of the Québécois state in the 1960s), religion was a very significant cultural characteristic of Québécois society; but the Québécois's sense of a distinctive identity persisted in a secularized context.

In our world, the specificity of the nationalist phenomenon pervades political discourse with such collective identity features. This does not necessarily raise claims to statehood. But it certainly bears on the organization of the common life of conationals. And it does so in a rather different way than do the identity-based claims of groups such as gays and lesbians, which can fit rather well in the conventional liberal logic

---

and the French New Right,' presented at the CPSA Annual Meeting, Montreal, 1995, and 'John Rawls, Mikhail Bakhtin, and the Praxis of Toleration,' *Political Theory* **23**:1 (February 1995) 112-16

7 Daniel Weinstock, 'Le nationalisme civique et le concept de culture politique commune,' in François Blais, Guy Laforest, and Diane Lamoureux, eds., *Libéralismes et nationalismes. Philosophie et politique* (Sainte-Foy: Presses de l'Université Laval 1995), 99-100 (translation is mine). See also Amelie Oksenberg Rorty, 'The Hidden Politics of Cultural Identification,' *Political Theory* **22**:1 (February 1994) 156, and 'Varieties of Pluralism in a Polyphonic Society,' *Review of Metaphysics* **44** (September 1990) 5.

of rights. As F.M. Barnard emphasizes, the 'cultural nationalism' tradition initiated by Rousseau and Herder points to a profound change in the source of political legitimation:

> Culture now emerges as something not only potentially relevant to politics but as something indispensably *necessary*. A nation is no longer simply a group of people owing political allegiance to a sovereign but a community bound by spiritual ties and cultural traditions. Indeed, I would suggest that it is precisely the infusion of culture with political content and the infusion of the political with cultural content, which characterizes modern nationalism. Nationalism, on this view, is untenable without the appeal to some cultural values.[8]

This link seems to support the view that nationalist arguments make use of a particular rhetoric and mode of political justification. Although I shall follow here C. Taylor and W. Norman in adopting such an interpretation of nationalist rhetoric, I want to specify that this point of view is of course issued from a specific intellectual tradition and historical journey (the liberal-democratic one). Therefore, I will not vouch for its applicability to possible modes of national affirmation that would not have been touched by, or pervaded with, this tradition and the way it interprets culture and its significance. Also, I will introduce in sections 2 and 3 some requirements of a moral position, in order not to reduce legitimacy to such a specific type of political consciousness, which may confuse historical and moral reasoning (facts and values).

A mere alleged partiality towards one's co-nationals is not sufficient to identify the specific character of nationality-based claims. As W. Norman suggests, there is a set of beliefs (such as more extensive duties to one's co-nationals, limits on immigration, or defense against foreign aggression, for example), almost universally held by citizens of contemporary liberal democracies, and which (to the eyes of these citizens) legitimate a departure from moral impartiality on the ground of membership in a state. This set of beliefs therefore fails to distinguish nationalists from non-nationalists. Norman suggests that we rather distinguish nationalists from non-nationalists on the grounds of the kind of political rhetoric and justification nationalists appeal to:

---

8 Barnard, 'National Culture and Political Legitimacy,' 250-1. See also Taylor, 'Why Do Nations,' and Yack, 'Reconciling Liberalism and Nationalism,' 180.

> Normally in a liberal state competing parties debate the merits of policies in terms of their impact on justice and individual well-being (...) Nationalists, however, appeal to considerations or sentiments that cannot be directly reduced to these terms. In addition to the question of justice or material benefits of a policy, they care about what it does to the nation's soul, or so to speak. Is it consistent with the nation's identity? Will it threaten the possibility of future generations having the same identity? Will it make the nation less distinct from others?[9]

Yet such considerations often themselves involve issues of justice. For example, decisions about adopting a public language may have a significant impact on justice (think of those co-nationals whose language is not the one adopted as the public, common one, as in the case of anglophone Québécois). In such cases, conflictual claims must be carefully weighted. Hence, Taylor's claim that nationalism *modifies* the other modes of political justification[10] seems more appropriate than the claim that these different modes of political justification *compete* with each other.

There is one last consideration I want to point out before discussing the requirements of liberal public morality. I can see no way of justifying national fellowship at the foundational level of morality. T. Hurka tries to defend national partiality inside the liberal framework through an argument based on the goods that may be produced by co-nationals' interaction in a system of cooperation. According to him, people whose history involves closer relations and whose interactions produce more goods have stronger duties of partiality toward one another.[11] But the justification of such an argument at the foundational level of morality would require an additional premise, namely, that one's interaction with her co-nationals in a system of social cooperation produces goods that are also globally significant, or significant in themselves, so that partiality can be considered a good in itself. This may condemn us to the very same confusion for which Hurka criticizes cultural perfectionism, that is, a confusion between the form and

---

9 Norman, 'Prelude,' 12-13

10 Taylor, 'Why Do Nations,' 24ff

11 Thomas Hurka, 'The Justification of National Partiality,' in Jeff McMahan and Robert McKim, eds., *The Morality of Nationalism* (New York: Oxford University Press 1997)

content of ethical concern. Moreover, a deeper concern for one's co-nationals is not the prerogative of nationalists. Finally, I could reasonably consider myself as having more duties to very disadvantaged people who are not my co-nationals than to people with whom I share the benefits of social cooperation.

For the purposes of this paper, I will mean by 'nation' a group of people united by some shared sense of a common identity, whose focus may be qualified as cultural, and acting politically in such a way as to maintain/develop that identity. Nationalist claims are not necessarily claims to political sovereignty and statehood; they focus on that identity which is at the heart of identification with one's co-nationals. From such a point of view, the political legitimacy of co-nationals' common life takes its sense, at least partly, from the preservation of that shared sense of identity. The idea of the nation has an inescapable political dimension, because political institutions and governmental decisions are the essential means by which a people can ensure the flourishing and survival of a culture. Decisions about the language of schools, courts, and government services, immigration and naturalization, or school curricula are but a few examples of the crucial role of the political apparatus in ensuring the viability of a culture.[12] Concerns with a nation's cultural identity therefore give rise to claims in the public forum, for example about what may appropriately be done to protect the nation's language. The nature of such debates obviously depends extensively on geopolitical and sociological factors determining the degree to which a nation controls its destiny (either in a national or a multinational state), the degree to which its culture seems imperiled, and the way people perceive, and react to, these facts. By nationalist (or nationality-based) claims, I will mean a specific type of political argument. Such arguments (1) originate in the significance of belonging in a national group, (2) introduce considerations related to national identity, and (3) are offered in the public forum as a consideration modulating conventional liberal considerations of distributive justice in the settlement of political issues. I will thus focus on nationalist claims as a basis of justification in the public forum.

---

12 Will Kymlicka, 'Misunderstanding Nationalism,' *Dissent* (Winter 1995), 136-7

III   Moral Claims in the Liberal Public Forum

One of the main tenets of contemporary liberalism is that despite their sometimes very deep disagreements over moral life, citizens agree on common norms by which they can settle their conflictual claims in matters of basic justice. The political sphere thus specifies the morality which characterizes the common life of citizens. It is not a mere *modus vivendi*: the common norms and principles on which citizens agree play a motivational role, which depends on the conception of the citizen that defines the political ideal. As moral agents, citizens must be motivated by the principles of justice and the ideals from which they arise.

This convergence on principles, as well as on some reasons to respect them, appears to be essential in regard to the liberal principle of legitimacy: when citizens settle political issues, they want to invoke reasons that can be recognized by their fellow citizens as being authoritative and as having moral weight according to the principles that define political reason. In other words, they look for reasons that can be given a moral standing in the policy-making process and the adjudication of conflictual claims. If a claim is granted such a moral standing (in other words, if it is recognized as a *reason*), it has more weight in public discussion, justification, and adjudication. Whether some considerations can be qualified as being moral constitutes an essential step in their entering the public forum as issues (on which citizens can agree or disagree), and, at a latter stage, in their capacity to play a role in legitimating some public policies. Considerations related to individual freedom and autonomy constitute a broad category grounding most adjudications of conflictual claims in a liberal polity. Liberal public reason is mainly made of the principles of justice, the guidelines of public inquiry, and the political values falling both under the principles of justice (equal political and civil liberty, equality of opportunity, social equality, and economic reciprocity) and under the guidelines of public inquiry (reasonableness, publicity, duty of civility, virtues of citizens).[13]

We must distinguish two types of arguments when evaluating publicly admissible considerations. On the one hand, we want to clarify

---

13   John Rawls, *Political Liberalism* (New York: Columbia University Press 1993), 223-7

the type of claims citizens may legitimately invoke to sustain their claims in matters of political justice. On the other hand, we have to specify what can ground the rationale of the political settlement of those conflicting claims. These two types of claims must be distinguished: people can invoke arguments that their fellow citizens may recognize as reasons but that in the context of moral pluralism ought not to found the public rationale for adopting specific policies.

For a position to qualify as 'moral' and sustain reasons citizens may present in the liberal public forum, it must meet some criteria. From the point of view of liberal public reason, we generally agree to reject considerations referring to interests based only on the self-interest of a particular group, rationalizations of non-moral premises, and appeals to authority that close off any possibility of publicly asserting or interpreting the content of claims put forward.[14] We also exclude from a moral position prejudices, emotional reactions, implausible propositions of fact challenging the minimal (generally accepted) standards of evidence and argument, and parroting others' reasons. These are not *reasons*.[15] The second broad requirement to make a moral position out of a conviction is the ability to defend it from a disinterested perspective.[16] This does not require us to share the reasons and the motivation of our fellow citizens, but it appeals to a capacity to understand that *from their point of view*, they have good reasons to defend their convictions. Finally, "any premises in the argument that depend on empirical evidence or logical inference should be in principle open to challenge by generally accepted methods of inquiry" (although premises for which such empirical or logical reasoning is not appropriate should not be considered implausible from the outset).[17] The basic principles of our com-

---

14 Amy Gutmann and Dennis Thompson, 'Moral Conflict and Political Consensus,' *Ethics* **101:1** (October 1990) 69-70

15 Ronald Dworkin, 'Lord Devlin and the Enforcement of Morals,' in Richard A. Wasserstrom, ed., *Morality and the Law* (Belmont: Wadsworth Publishing Company, 1971), 55-72. Sincerity and consistency are also important elements in evaluating whether one's position is moral or not (ibid.).

16 Gutmann and Thompson, 'Moral Conflict,' 71

17 Gutmann and Thompson, 'Moral Conflict,' 17

mon political morality help us in delimiting the boundaries of liberal toleration towards some doctrines (racism, for example).

Particular reasons may intervene in political discussion, provided they respect some limits. As long as individuals are morally motivated to accept a common criterion of political rationality, there is no justification to prevent them from invoking particular reasons (e.g., religious reasons) to sustain their moral position in the public forum. For example, one can legitimately support the restriction of abortion because one believes that human life has an inherently sacred meaning, being given by God. This is a moral reason, and it moves that person. However, she cannot impose this particular reason as the public rationale for restricting abortion. In other words, a person can be moved by religious considerations, as long as she does not coerce her fellow citizens on the basis of these beliefs and recognizes that these convictions should not determine the public rationale for adopting a policy.

Let us take the case of religious convictions. Robert Audi has suggested that in matters of policy restricting the scope of liberty, citizens have an obligation to support their claims with secular reasons understood not as rationalizations of religious motivations but as being in themselves motivationally sufficient to support a (proposed) conduct. Audi defines a secular reason as

> one whose normative force, that is, its status as a prima facie justificatory element, does not (evidentially) depend on the existence of God (for example through appeals to divine command), or on theological considerations (such as interpretations of a sacred text), or on the pronouncements of a person or institution qua religious authority.[18]

Audi does not consider it sufficient that one can propose a secular rationale to support a conduct or a policy: he argues that the motivation itself must be secular, and cannot be a mere rationalization, that is, a purported justification intended to conceal the real motivation.[19]

---

18 Robert Audi, 'The Separation of Church and State and the Obligations of Citizenship,' *Philosophy and Public Affairs* **18:3** (Summer 1989) 278

19 Audi, 'Separation,' 281, 284, 295

But this way of stating the requirements of public discourse would compel people to choose between having secular motives to oppose abortion (for example), or being denied the right to oppose it in the public forum. It seems quite right to say that to count as a reason (for which we usually claim normative authority), the rationale supporting my claims must motivate me: a reason must have normative force, it cannot be a mere rationalization, intended to disguise the real motivation. But this does not imply that we must exclude from the public forum, from the outset, reasons linked to particular moral doctrines. Motivating reasons are themselves dependent on people's situations, experiences, and natural psychological traits as well as self-representations (for example, the way people believe they have to fulfill their social roles). There is a wide diversity of experiences and points of view. At the policy-making level, reasons certainly have to go through a kind of universality test. But we can consider a reason 'adequate' for some people in a certain situation and be moved by our concerns for these people's intrinsic well-being rather than by the reasons motivating them. We can perfectly well recognize the normative value a reason has from someone else's point of view, without being similarly motivated. Is not reasonable pluralism workable precisely because we (as citizens of liberal democratic societies) share some background values enabling us to understand and, at the same time, dispute some judgments and interpretations? In such a context, as Barry Stroud stresses,

> if I do not agree with a person's evaluative judgment, I can still correctly attribute to him and understand what it is for him to hold that view, because of my own general competence in the language of evaluation and my knowledge of the evaluative features of the environment – what things are good or bad, better or worse than others.[20]

---

20 Barry Stroud, 'The Study of Human Nature and the Subjectivity of Value,' *The Tanner Lectures on Human Values* (Salt Lake City: University of Utah Press 1989), 234. Joseph Raz suggests the following test of publicly acceptable reasons: "If p is an acceptable reason for a certain action, or for the adoption of a certain principle or the institution of certain political arrangements, then while there may be disagreement over whether p is the case, whether it is or [is] not overridden or defeated by other reasons, and so on, it is nevertheless agreed that p, if true, is a reason for the claimed conclusion. When the reasons proposed for coercive political action meet this test they are acceptable reasons (...) Of

Moreover, a person can employ secular arguments because she accepts a secular criterion of political legitimacy; she is thus moved by a moral value, and her reasons for employing secular arguments are also moral, not only prudential. Hence, a person can be moved by a moral reason to conform to a secular criterion of political legitimacy.[21] I believe that we do not necessarily deal here with a second-order moral argument. Of course, understanding how someone can be morally motivated to adhere to a secular criterion of political legitimacy while defending a point of view based on religious considerations raises a complex question of moral motivation and psychology. Undoubtedly, if a liberal polity is to be just and stable, people must demonstrate an appropriate motivation for doing what justice requires.

Actual liberal theory is rather unclear as to how this priority of justice is embedded in the motivational structure of individuals. For example, Rawls assumes that political values trump other values. But as Daniel Weinstock emphasizes, Rawls is not clear as to the sense in which we should understand this argument: we can understand this assumption as a conceptual claim implying that political values are categorically superior to all other values, or as an empirical hypothesis to the effect that people realize that they are better able to pursue their own life-plans in liberal institutions.[22] But neither interpretation seems to fit the motivational structure of actual people. Of course, civic education plays a fundamental role in instilling liberal principles and virtues into new generations. We may hope that when reasoning morally, citizens will recognize the regulative role of the principles of justice. From the point of view of moral psychology, such education to the moral values

---

course, that does not guarantee actual agreement. We may not agree on this particular reason, but we may nonetheless recognize it as a reason." Joseph Raz, 'Facing Diversity: The Case of Epistemic Abstinence,' *Philosophy and Public Affairs* **19:1** (Winter 1990) 39.

21 Paul J. Weithman, 'The Separation of Church and State: Some Questions for Professor Audi,' *Philosophy and Public Affairs* **20:1** (Winter 1991) 61, 63; Audi, 'Separation,' 282-3

22 Daniel M. Weinstock, 'The Justification of Political Liberalism,' *Pacific Philosophical Quarterly* **75** (1994) 179-80

of a liberal society is essential, for the way people self-represent themselves plays a significant part in their motivational structure.[23]

Yet, as we cannot assume that people will always conform themselves to principles as categorical imperatives (not to mention, as Lawrence Kohlberg's work has shown, that people are situated at different levels of moral 'development'), we must conceive of a mediation, or interface, between the priority of justice and people's motivational structure. Thus, it is likely that the commitment to the overriding role of political values is best expressed by the content and form of public reason. This 'mediation' is not purely categorical, nor strictly empirical; it appeals to moral motivation, but plays its role through practical mechanisms such as public discussion, constitutional clauses, and the courts of justice.

IV Private Reasons, Public Rationale, and Nationalist Claims

The example drawing on the distinction between secular motivation and secular rationale shows that the range of reasons citizens can appeal to in order to sustain their claims in the public forum is wide enough to make room for their nonpublic reasons, provided this public affirmation of their nonpublic reasons does not undermine the conclusions of public reason and the requirements of political legitimacy. It is now time to clarify the moral status to which nationalist claims can aspire in a liberal theory of justice.

If we were to apply to nationalist claims the same reasoning we use to judge the appropriate place of religious convictions (that is, that they may move a person but not legitimately determine public policies), we would conclude that people may present their nationalist claims in the public forum but cannot ask their fellow citizens to recognize the grounds of these claims as a common, legitimate basis for settling conflictual claims in political matters. The reasonable, religiously mo-

---

23 See for example Owen Flanagan, *Varieties of Moral Personality. Ethics and Psychological Realism* (Cambridge, MA: Harvard University Press 1991), 138-9: he stresses that "the self as represented often has motivational bearing and behavioral effects," and that self-represented identity draws on available theoretical models about the nature of the self.

tivated person of our example recognizes that the grounds of her motivation cannot constitute a common, public point of view, because faith and religion are the objects of long-lasting reasonable disagreement amongst citizens. We agree on this, although we also recognize that she is morally motivated.

But nationalists obviously believe that nationality represents a legitimate basis for sustaining some public policies. Nationalist arguments are intended to be moral claims appealing to people's national identity as a legitimate common point of view for settling (potentially) conflictual claims and orienting public life. For example, nationalists may argue that a people's language expresses its identity, and therefore ought to be the language of public life, work, and education. Or they may support some social and economic institutions which are seen as characteristic of the nation's sense of identity and solidarity. As Norman recalls, we encountered such arguments in the Canadian debate over the North American Free Trade Agreement (NAFTA): some people may have worried about the way membership in NAFTA would erode the ability of the Canadian state to provide its citizens with quality health care; others went further, arguing that providing such services was in fact a significant part of the Canadian's national identity.[24] It is as if our religiously motivated citizen, in the example above, would rather argue that her faith constitutes an appropriate and legitimate basis for publicly settling the abortion debate. From the point of view of public reason, we would consider her argument to be unreasonable. I want to argue that there are two levels of arguments at which we may grant the public legitimacy of some nationality-based claims. First, the intellectual journey of liberalism authorizes the interpretation of a clear-cut difference between the *diktat* of religion and the realities of cultural belonging.[25] Second, we can, in some cases, elaborate an argument for

---

24 Norman, 'Prelude,' 13

25 By pointing to what seems acceptable or not in our liberal democratic societies, I want to stress that such 'agreement' is the result of a specific historical and intellectual journey, but that this should not close the door to judgments of practical reason as to the worth of these achievements. The point of view from which we proceed to such judgments will always be ours; but we should not give up the quest for objectivity.

nationality-based claims respecting the requirement of a disinterested perspective. We will examine both in turn.

Let us begin with considerations about the distinction between nationality-based claims and religiously motivated arguments. What makes nationalist claims different from the religion-based motivation of our example? As I said above, nationality involves some shared cultural traits, and there are very close links between political power and culture. The state cannot remain neutral on the main cultural issues such as language and school curricula, although it may aspire to a relative neutrality towards citizens' religious convictions as long as these do not violate fundamental liberal principles; the state sometimes restricts the expression of some religious convictions, but it does not promote particular religious beliefs.[26] As Kymlicka explains, the model of religious toleration based on the separation of church and state hardly provides a model for dealing with ethnocultural differences. The category of human rights is unable to resolve some of the most controversial issues relating to cultural minorities (in our case, national groups):

> [W]hich languages should be recognized in the parliaments, bureaucracies, and courts? Should each ethnic or national group have publicly funded education in its mother tongue? Should internal boundaries (legislative districts, provinces, states) be drawn so that cultural minorities form a majority within a local region? Should governmental powers be devolved from the central level to more local or regional levels controlled by particular minorities, particularly on culturally sensitive issues of immigration, communication, and education? Should political offices be distributed in accordance with a principle of national or ethnic proportionality? Should the traditional homelands of indigenous peoples be reserved for their benefit, and so protected from the encroachment by settlers and resource developers? What are the responsibilities of minorities to integrate? What degree of cultural integration can be required of immigrants and refugees before they acquire citizenship?[27]

---

26 See for example the decisions of courts in the following cases: *B. (R.)* v. *Children's Aid Society of Metropolitan Toronto* [1995] 1 S.C.R. 315; *Wisconsin* v. *Yoder* 406 U.S. 205; *Mozert* v. *Hawkins County Board of Education* 827 F. 2nd 1058 (6th Cir. 1987).

27 Will Kymlicka, *Multicultural Citizenship: A Liberal Theory of Minority Rights* (Oxford: Clarendon Press 1995), 4-5

A national group that cares about the survival and flourishing of its culture will be very concerned with state legislation about those fundamental matters. Nationality cannot remain private; it expresses itself in the public, common life of co-nationals.

Yet, such an acknowledgement does not justify giving a moral value to national or cultural belonging. Universalists may argue that such belonging does not possess any moral meaning. And indeed, the fact that questions of cultural identity have been politically problematized does not necessarily justify giving moral significance to such issues as the survival of a language or the survival of some historical community. As Owen Flanagan emphasizes, the fact that identity conditions give each life its meaning does not imply that these conditions set some baseline constraint on ethical theory.[28] This observation, together with the fundamental liberal concern for individual well-being, explains why liberal theory cannot provide a justification for nationalism at the foundational level of morality. Moreover, serious communitarian attempts to provide phenomenological and ontological arguments that would justify encumbering morality in cultural belonging have not succeeded.[29]

If this is so, what can be argued against arguments such as the ones developed by Habermas and his colleagues against national identification? Kymlicka's theory about cultural belonging is a step toward the recognition of the moral significance of claims issued from national belonging. Recall that Kymlicka argues that since cultural belonging appears to be essential for an individual's self-respect and autonomous definition of a life-plan, there are moral reasons to ensure that people live in a secure cultural framework.[30] Therefore, there is a component of people's self-respect that would justify expressing some traits of a shared identity in public institutions.

---

28 Flanagan, *Varieties of Moral Personality*, 82

29 See my 'Ontologie, philosophie et politique: la critique de la tradition épistémologique chez Charles Taylor,' *Dialogue* **35:3** (1996), 553–569.

30 Will Kymlicka, *Liberalism, Community, and Culture* (Oxford: Clarendon Press 1989), 164-6, 178

However, the fundamental liberal concern for individual well-being generally impedes liberal theorists from conveying the full significance of national/cultural belonging. Liberals may recognize that the expression of national/cultural identity cannot be relegated to nonpublic life; but the collective meaning of national belonging reveals itself to be more problematic for liberal theory, which usually grants legitimacy to claims related to individuality understood as the separation of consciousness and one's capacity to develop one's own life-plan. Kymlicka, for example, is thus confronted with the following paradox: he considers cultural belonging as playing an essential, significant role in ensuring individuals' self-respect, but his theory cannot sustain the significance of belonging to a *specific* historical community, which is precisely what actual individuals care about.[31] Liberals should not give up the categorical constraints required to ensure the equal respect of all individuals. But if we really want to understand the legitimacy of some nationality-based claims, we must go a step further than Kymlicka does: if there are moral reasons to respect the significance a shared cultural identity has for individuals, then these require that we respect both the cultural structure providing individuals with meaningful options and the significance of sharing some conditions of identity. From the individual's point of view, both of these facts contribute to the significance of national/cultural belonging.

Explaining the distinct nature of nationality-based claims may not absolve nationalists in the eyes of 'universalist' liberals. These liberals could still argue either that nationalist claims refer to considerations based on the self-interest of a particular group, or that they are based on mere emotional reactions. These objections, if well-founded, would make any nationalist claim no moral position at all. Thus, the possibility of justifying such claims (or some of them) from a disinterested perspective turns out to be significant. If we cannot justify nationality-based claims from the point of view of a disinterested perspective, we may not be able to support respect for the shared identity of a national group with moral reasons, except in cases of flagrant injustice (genocide, for example).

---

31 On this paradox, see also John R. Danley, 'Liberalism, Aboriginal Rights, and Cultural Minorities,' *Philosophy and Public Affairs* **20:2** (Spring 1991) 180-1.

Arguing for some nationality-based claims from a disinterested point of view can be done in several ways, although for the purposes of this paper I will only outline three such strategies.

1. One can conceive of cultural belonging as a primary good, as Kymlicka does, and proceed with an argument linking self-respect to identity conditions rooted in belonging to a cultural/national group. Whatever the merits of Kymlicka's work, I would not suggest adopting the characterization of cultural belonging as a primary good, for (as I hinted above) cultural belonging fits rather uneasily in that Rawlsian category.

2. One may imagine that some parties founding a multinational state would, at the second stage of some original position, propose a constitutional secession clause in case they would think it necessary to part (because they would not know which group they represent). Wayne Norman suggests such a strategy,[32] and in fact, it may be useful as a device for clarifying actual reflections on secession. Using such a device requires specifying (amongst other things) why a state would want to include a right to secession in its constitution, and which entities would be represented in discussions. I won't discuss this view in detail here, since I do not assume that nationalist claims are necessarily secessionist claims or claims to statehood. But I nevertheless want to stress that the needed specifications I mentioned shall be argued for from a moral point of view, a task a procedural device cannot perform alone.

3. To argue for a nationality-based claim from a moral point of view, one may have to appeal to an empathic understanding of impartiality emphasizing that many people do strongly value their national/cultural belonging, not only because it provides them with meaningful options about how to lead their lives, but because they value the sense of a shared identity. Therefore, respecting their interests as individuals requires taking the meaning of such belonging as a significant moral issue. The first step towards a recognition of nationalist claims as moral reasons is thus linked to what I said above about tolerance and respect requiring a

---

32 Wayne Norman, 'Domesticating Secession,' unpublished paper

capacity to conceive that my fellow citizens may have good reasons, *from their point of view*, to defend their convictions, since each person's motivation is related to her own point of view. I can recognize that my fellow citizens' reasons are morally motivated without sharing that motivation. Such an empathic point of view recognizes not only that there is no standpoint completely independent of who we are, but also that a disinterested perspective does not require disengagement nor impersonality. Of course, any further development of this position involves discussing the wider issue of the justification of norms and principles, a task I cannot tackle here.[33]

If we agree on such reasoning, then, as a corollary, we need not consider nationalism as a purely emotional (and irrational) reaction. As Ronald Dworkin explains in his critique of Lord Devlin's *Enforcement of Morals*, a position based on an emotional reaction must be rejected, because although a moral position can justify an emotional reaction, a mere emotional reaction cannot justify a moral position. This does not mean that moral positions are unemotional, but rather that we must produce reasons explaining the emotional reaction if it is to demonstrate a moral conviction.[34] If we agree that there are moral reasons to respect the shared identity of a national group, some nationalist claims need not be considered as purely emotional, non-moral, reactions.

---

33 For example, Habermasians may argue that such a point of view confuses the justification of norms with their applicability, whereas we have to keep these issues separate.

34 Dworkin, 'Lord Devlin,' 63. Kedourie's *Nationalism* is a good example of an emotional characterization of nationalist aspirations: "It is at these extremes of human nature which they knew so well how to explore, where horror and delight, love and hate, cruelty and tenderness are indistinguishable, that the Romantics sought a heightened, transformed, superhuman existence, which might abolish life as it is actually lived; nationalism is the political expression of this quest." Elie Kedourie, *Nationalism* (London: Hutchinson 1966), 87. In the same vein, Ignatieff writes that "As a moral ideal, nationalism is an ethic of heroic sacrifice, justifying the use of violence in the defence of one's nation against enemies, internal or external." Michael Ignatieff, *Blood and Belonging: Journeys into the New Nationalism* (Toronto: Viking 1993), 3. He also blames romanticism for this 'dark' side of nationalism (see, for example, 4 and 63-64).

This is an important (though primary) step for any debate on nationalist claims. For it opens the door to moral debate on nationalist claims in the public forum and to the recognition of these claims as moral ones. As Gutmann and Thompson write, "[A]cknowledging the moral status of a position that one opposes requires, at a minimum, that one treat it as a moral rather than a purely political, economic or other kind of nonmoral view. This acknowledgment in speech begins with the recognition that an opponent's position is based on moral principles on which reasonable people may disagree...."[35] Once nationalists have offered moral grounds on which they found considerations that are not antithetical to fundamental liberal principles, the public forum should be opened to their claims.

Determining which concrete nationality-based claims are actually acceptable cannot be done entirely from a philosophical point of view; each case is peculiar, and our judgment shall depend on these peculiarities. However, if what I have suggested is correct, we have at our disposal some guiding principles, issued from moral reasoning. First, respecting the value and significance that a shared national identity has for the individuals participating in it may be expressed as a component of the equal respect due to all persons; this can be argued for from a disinterested perspective emphasizing an empathic point of view. Second, the requirements of a moral position define criteria by which we may judge the public legitimacy of nationalists' claims. To qualify as moral, and thus to legitimately enter the public forum, nationality-based claims must respect these criteria. My point against universalists was to argue that such claims cannot be *a priori* ruled out as self-interested, simplistic, or emotional merely because they build on particular communal attachments. Finally, the very same criteria used to qualify a moral position set limits to acceptable claims. Some claims are obviously unacceptable: forced religious conversion, 'ethnic cleansing,' suppression of civil and political liberties, and manipulation of history are but a few examples of pretensions that do not meet the requirements of a moral position necessary to sustain arguments in the public forum. However, limits on immigration, language rights,

---

35 Gutmann and Thompson, 'Moral Conflict,' 79

devolution of powers, international recognition, and, in some cases, claims to statehood may be acceptable, depending on the extent to which such measures respect individual rights and freedoms (especially with respect to citizens that do not share the sense of a common national identity), as well as the requirements of liberal public reason.

V Conclusion

Does this mean that we accept a two-levels moral discourse, that is, on the one hand, a public morality articulated around a more fundamental level concerned with liberal principles, and, on the other hand, moral commitments related to nationalist or culturally oriented settings which are specific to each political community (this particularity may take the form of civic patriotism, as in the United States, of a well-established national consciousness, as in France, or of a conflict of nationalist aspirations, as in the Canadian case)? In a sense, that two-levels picture can be misleading, for these two levels do not simply coexist; they act in conjunction one with another. When an American, a French person, or a Québécois adheres to liberal principles, she does so in ways specific to the community to which she belongs. Specific cultural elements pervade every polity's public reason and discourse, and this is in fact what deeply determines people's identification with their common institutions.[36]

---

36 Liberals such as Norman and Kymlicka recognize that the stability of liberal institutions depends on the sense of a shared identity that an abstract justification of moral principles alone cannot generate. Taylor has been defending such an argument for a long time, although from his point of view legitimacy, rather than stability, is the crucial issue relative to identification; see for example his 'Alternative Futures: Legitimacy, Identity and Alienation in Late Twentieth Century Canada,' in Alan Cairns and Cynthia Williams, eds., *Constitutionalism, Citizenship and Society in Canada* (Toronto: University of Toronto Press 1985). The problem of the interplay between abstract moral principles and the embeddedness of their signification in concrete settings would be a fruitful way of assessing the relationships between liberalism and nationalism from the point of view of moral psychology.

As liberals, we should be inclined to respect the significance national belonging may have from the individuals' point of view; since the nature of this belonging is such that its expression cannot be relegated to nonpublic life (it expresses itself in the public life, the common institutions), it may claim some legitimacy in the process of settlement of some political issues. Nationalist claims are based on the will of a people for their culture to survive and flourish, as well as on their will to control their destiny (either in a national or multinational state). I hope to have shown that these claims can stand morally in the public forum, in two senses: that they may express legitimate concerns serving as a base for moral arguments; and that there are some issues the settlement of which they can guide. Nationality-based arguments can play a legitimate role in adjudicating political matters relative to crucial cultural-political issues. We thus have good reasons to think that *to some extent*, nationalist claims can interact with, or modulate, 'traditional' liberal preoccupations in settling political conflicts.

From a liberal point of view, however, this legitimacy depends mostly on the particular *content* of these claims and the form they take. The content of specific nationalist claims and the extend to which they respect fundamental liberal rights determine how acceptable they are from a liberal point of view. In liberal states, nationality-based arguments cannot override liberal constitutional essentials, and even a tight equilibrium between nationalist claims and liberal rights will never free the public forum of tensions and disputes. The resolution of any tension between nationality-based moral claims and liberal principles depends in a significant way on the concrete political settings used to deal with cases in which nationalist claims interpellate liberal principles, as well as on the extent to which a community's public reason conceives of such an interaction. It is not futile to recall that our conception of legitimacy is closely linked to liberalism's intellectual and historical journey. This journey may explain why we are ready to accept some nationalist claims (for example, the ones based on language), but not some others (for example, race-based nationalism). It also explains why the recognition of nationality-based claims does not necessarily require a defense of moral partiality. But this is another matter. For now, I have only clarified the possibility of a moral recognition of nationalist claims in the liberal public forum. I surely have settled no concrete case; this was not my task. However, establishing a coherent theoretical view, emphasizing the significance both of 'our' fundamental principles and of the cultural-political issues which are at stake in nationalist demands, represents a basic and non-negligible step for any liberal anxious to deal with nationalism.

CANADIAN JOURNAL OF PHILOSOPHY
Supplementary Volume 22

Secession and the Principle of Nationality*

DAVID MILLER
Nuffield College, Oxford

The secession issue appears to many contemporary thinkers to reveal a fatal flaw in the idea of national self-determination. The question is whether national minorities who come to want to be politically self-determining should be allowed to separate from the parent state and form one of their own. Here the idea of national self-determination may lead us in one of two opposing directions. If the minority group in question regards itself as a separate nation, then the principle seems to support its claims: if the Québécois or the Catalans come to think of themselves as having national identities distinct from those of the Canadians or the Spanish, and to seek political independence on that basis, then if we are committed to national self-determination we should support their claims. But we then face the challenge that once national identities begin to proliferate there is no feasible way of satisfying all such claims, given elementary facts of geography and population spread. As Allen Buchanan, citing Gellner, puts the point, "the normative nationalist principle is a recipe for limitless political fragmentation."[1] And he rightly points out that this process may bring with it

---

* An earlier version of this paper was presented to the Roundtable on National Self-Determination and Secession, American Political Science Association Annual Meeting, San Francisco, 28 August – 1 September 1996. I am grateful to the participants in that meeting for their comments, and also to Michel Seymour for writing to me at some length about the case of Quebec.

1 A. Buchanan, *Secession* (Boulder: Westview Press 1991), 49

quite unacceptable moral costs, in the form, for instance, of the disruption, displacement, or even annihilation of communities that turn out to be territorially in the wrong place.

On the other hand, the idea of national self-determination may be appealed to in defence of the political status quo. The Canadians and the Spanish have a claim to be self-determining too, and a claim to determine the future of the territory that has historically been identified as Canada or Spain. If the principle is used in this more conservative way, it is subject to a different critical charge: that it turns out in practice to call for self-determination for *states*, not nations, or at least for states that are territorially compact.[2] Self-determination comes to mean the claim of a state to exercise sovereignty within its established borders, not to be invaded or coerced by its neighbours, for instance. But interpreted in this way the idea loses much of its original moral appeal, which came from the vision of a body of people sharing a common identity and wishing to be associated with one another deciding on their own future. The second reading collapses the crucial distinction between nations and states by treating 'the nation' simply as the set of people who fall *de facto* within the jurisdiction of a particular state.

The charge, then, is that the issue of secession reveals the idea of national self-determination either to be a recipe for political chaos and human bloodshed or to be a conservative defence of the rights of established states. My aim here is to see whether it is possible to develop a coherent position on the issue that avoids both extremes, starting out from the principle of nationality that I have defended elsewhere.[3]

---

2 Under international law, regions within the main body of a state have for some time been regarded differently from geographically separate territories, such as colonies. The 'right of self-determination' that international bodies such as the UN sometimes proclaim has only been taken to support independence movements in the latter case. In the case of a territorially compact state, it does not imply a right of secession for any part of the state, but the right of the population as a whole to determine its form of government. See J. Crawford, *The Creation of States in International Law* (Oxford: Clarendon Press 1979), esp. ch. 3.

3 Most fully in *On Nationality* (Oxford: Clarendon Press 1995). See also D. Miller, 'In Defence of Nationality,' *Journal of Applied Philosophy* 10 (1993) 3-16, reprinted in P. Gilbert and P. Gregory, eds., *Nations, Cultures and Markets* (Aldershot:

I Why Do We Need a Theory of Secession?

Before we embark on matters of substance, it is worth pausing to ask what purpose we intend our theory of secession to serve. Some writers have proposed that we should be seeking to define a quasi-legal right of secession that might be inscribed in the constitution of a state, or in the charter of an international body such as the United Nations.[4] In other words, we should try to identify a set of conditions that might be formally codified, and that any group attempting to secede from an existing state might appeal to in order to justify its claim. This proposal has some obvious attractions. It holds out the promise that secessionist claims might be treated in a detached way by a constitutional or international court, rather than being fought over with words or guns. But this promise comes at a price. First, the conditions justifying secession would need to be stated in a form that a judicial body could apply, and this immediately slants the discussion in favour of certain criteria and against others. For instance there is likely to be a bias in favour of procedural criteria (is there a majority in favour of secession in the territory in question?) whose application is relatively uncontroversial, and against substantive criteria whose application may depend upon difficult and contested matters of judgment (is the existing state suppressing or eroding the distinct culture of the minority applying to secede?). Second, as Buchanan points out, we have also to think about the incentive effects of different definitions of the right of secession; we have to ask how inscribing one or another version of such a right in a constitution would alter the behaviour either of the existing state or of the would-be secessionists.[5] For instance, would the effect be to make established states less willing to devolve power to regions which might subsequently foster secessionist demands? But it seems to me a mistake to allow our thinking about the secession issue to be dominated

---

Avebury 1994); D. Miller, 'On Nationality,' *Nations and Nationalism* 2 (1996, 409–21).

4   See Buchanan, *Secession*, ch. 4, and W. Norman, 'Domesticating Secession' (unpublished).

5   A. Buchanan, 'Theories of Secession,' *Philosophy and Public Affairs* 26 (1997), 31–61

by such considerations. We should establish the basic principles first, then ask what effect the public promulgation of these principles might have on the behaviour of different political actors.

In contrast to the legalistic approach sketched in the last paragraph, I believe that a theory of secession should be seen as a political theory, meaning one that articulates principles that should guide us when thinking about secessionist claims. 'Us' here means the would-be secessionists, non-secessionist citizens of the relevant state, and members of the international community who may be called upon to intervene on one side of the other. We are looking for guidance when we have to decide (say in a referendum) whether to vote for secession or for remaining in association with a larger state. Equally we need guidance about how to respond, as British citizens say, to demands for Scottish or Welsh independence. We likewise need to know whether to recognize and support a Slovenia that has chosen to sever its ties with the rest of the Yugoslav federation. A theory of secession should tell us in broad terms when secession is justified and when it is not.

Some critics might argue that the questions I am raising here are insubstantial. If a referendum is being held on secession, then I should vote for secession if I want it, and against if I do not. The issue is settled procedurally, by a majority or a qualified majority, or however. It is irrelevant to ask about the principles that might guide me when casting my vote. But notice that this is not how we think about democratic decision-making in general. We agree, of course, that the party which wins an election should form the government, or that when a referendum is held the result should be adopted as policy, but that does not deter us from putting forward principles which we think voters ought to follow – principles of social justice for instance. Sometimes we will say that the voters got it wrong, that they supported the party whose policies were less just, or less in their interests, than the opposition's. We can say this while still thinking that the democratic procedure should be followed. How are things different when the issue is one of secession? Even if we come to believe that such questions should be resolved procedurally, there may still be good grounds and bad grounds for secession, and it is surely not irrelevant to try to spell these out.

It is in any case implausible to think that a purely procedural theory of secession could be satisfactory. If we say, for instance, that a majority vote to secede is sufficient to justify secession, this immediately raises the question of how the constituency for the vote is to be established, and how the territory which the seceding group would take with them is to be defined. In practice we are likely to think of regions like Quebec which are already administratively defined, and where we can pick out a 'people,' the Québécois, among whom a referendum might be held. Here we are tacitly invoking a background theory about the circumstances which make a referendum on secession appropriate: whether on balance we think the secessionist claim justified or unjustified in this case, we can at least recognize it as a plausible candidate. If, by contrast, someone was to propose holding an independence ballot among the Jews of Montreal, we would immediately recognize this as a not-very-serious proposal and react accordingly.

A substantial theory of secession is not likely to be simple. To break up a state and create a new one is a serious matter. It raises questions about political authority, about historic identities, about economic justice, and about the rights of minorities. Any adequate theory must address all of these issues, and this means that it will have to be multicriterial. Instead of looking for a set of necessary and sufficient conditions to justify a secessionist claim, we must accept that the different criteria may pull in opposite directions, and so to reach a verdict on any concrete case we are likely to have to balance conflicting claims. Keeping that in mind, what guidance can an appeal to nationality offer us?

II The Principle of Nationality

The principle of nationality I defend holds, as one of its three elements, that where the inhabitants of a territory form a national community, they have a good claim to political self-determination. Although a sovereign state is not the only possible vehicle of self-determination, both now and in the past it has been the main vehicle, and so this principle grounds a claim to secession made by a territorially compact nation which is currently subject to rule by outsiders. I say 'a claim' rather than 'a right' in order to signal that the claim in question is not necessarily an overriding one, but may be defeated by other considerations that we shall come to in due course. This is not the place to set out the reasons supporting self-determination; I want instead to consider some of the ramifications of this apparently simple principle.

As has often been pointed out, territories occupied by homogeneous nations are very much the exceptions in today's world. Let me say, very briefly, what I take a nation to be: a group of people who recognize one another as belonging to the same community, who acknowledge special obligations to one another, and who aspire to political autonomy – this by virtue of characteristics that they believe they share, typically a common history, attachment to a geographical place, and a public culture that differentiates them from their neighbours.[6] If, with this definition in mind, we look inside those entities popularly described as 'nation-states' we are likely to find some combination of the following: (1) minority groups (especially immigrants) who do not see themselves as sharing in the national identity of the majority (e.g., Turkish immigrants in Germany); (2) regionally gathered minorities who see themselves as forming a separate nation and who aspire to a greater or lesser degree of autonomy (e.g., Kurds in Turkey); (3) regions with intermingled populations identifying with different adjacent nations (e.g., Rumanians and Hungarians in Transylvania); and (4) regions in which a substantial part of the population bear a dual or 'nested' identity, as members of a national minority within a larger nation (e.g., Catalans in Spain).

If we want to apply the principle of nationality to cases fitting one or more of these descriptions, our question must be: what structure of political authority will best fulfill the principle for each community, given that the simple solution (homogeneous nation/unitary state) is not available in these circumstances. This involves first of all making qualitative judgments about how people conceive of their identity, and how the identity of one group relates to that of to others. Compare, for instance, the position of the Kurds in Turkey with that of the Catalans in Spain. Although the Catalans regard themselves as a distinct people, there is no deep-seated hostility between them and the Spanish people as a whole. There is a considerable cultural overlap (in religious belief, for instance), living standards are somewhat higher than the Spanish average (traditionally Catalonia has been one of the more prosperous regions of Spain), Catalans are not held in low esteem elsewhere in Spain, and so on. In these circumstances, it is not problematic

---

6 I have given a fuller account of nationality in *On Nationality*, ch. 2.

for Catalans to regard themselves as both Catalan and Spanish, as many of them do.[7] The Kurdish case is in many respects different: per capita income in the Kurdish region of Turkey is less than half the national average, the Kurdish language and culture are vigorously repressed by the Turkish state, and there is a long history of armed conflicts and massacres between the two communities.[8] Furthermore the Turkish leadership has for many years been committed to the ideal of a unified, homogeneous Turkish nation which leaves no space for cultural pluralism. Given these differences, the Kurds have a claim for independence that is qualitatively different from that held by the Catalans. Short of a dramatic reversal in mainstream Turkish attitudes, there is no chance of the Kurds achieving cultural recognition in a Turkish state, nor of Turks and Kurds working together to achieve political democracy and social justice. This is not to say that full secession would necessarily be the right solution for Turkish Kurdistan. Various practical considerations count heavily against this solution, and it seems that few Kurds themselves are actively seeking secession.[9] My point is that to apply the nationality principle to this problem, we have to begin by looking at the actual content of group identities, in order to discover whether group X has a distinct national identity whose substance places it at odds with that of group Y to whose political institutions it is presently subjected. To the extent that this is so, any claim that the group may make for political independence is strengthened – which is not to

---

7 I have drawn here on the discussion of Catalonia in M. Keating, *Nations Against the State: The New Politics of Nationalism in Quebec, Catalonia and Scotland* (Basingstoke: Macmillan 1996), ch. 5.

8 See D. Mcdowall, *The Kurds: A Nation Denied* (London: Minority Rights Group, 1992); P.G. Kreyenbroek and S. Sperl, eds., *The Kurds: A Contemporary Overview* (London: Routledge 1992).

9 It should also be said that some Kurds have chosen the route of assimilation, forgoing their Kurdish identity in favour of a Turkish one. The important contrast with the Catalan case is that a Kurd in Turkey is more or less forced to make a choice between these two identities, whereas for a Catalan in Spain a hyphenated identity is easily available, and indeed a large majority of Catalans describe themselves in these terms (for instance as ' Equally Spanish and Catalan,' 'More Catalan than Spanish,' etc. – see Keating, *Nations Against the State*, 129-34).

say that its claim is decisively vindicated, for, as indicated above, it may eventually be defeated by countervailing factors.[10]

One such factor which we must now consider is the competing claim of group Y, the larger nation whose present territory would be broken up if the secession were to go ahead. Do they not have a claim which is at least as strong as that of the would-be secessionists? Here we need to take account of the following empirical fact: in most of the cases under discussion, there will be an asymmetry between the way the smaller group sees its relationship with the larger and the way that the larger group sees its relationship with the smaller. The larger group will play down the distinctness of the minority: rather than regarding them as a nation with a separate identity, they will tend to see them as one variation on a common theme: not as distinct Xs, but as Ys who speak a different language or have their own quaint folk culture. Thus whereas the Québécois tend to see themselves as belonging to a nation separate from the rest of Canada, Canadians at large are likely to regard the Québécois just as French-speaking Canadians, and parallels to this case can be found in many other places, for instance between the Scots and the English or the Macedonians and the Greeks.

There may be a temptation to think that in such instances the majority has simply got it wrong – that if the Xs no longer identify themselves as Ys, then for the Ys to assert a common identity with the Xs amounts to ignorance or a refusal to face up to the facts. But the issue will very rarely be as clear-cut as this. Assuming that the Xs and the Ys share a single citizenship and have been associated politically for a substantial period of time, they do indeed have a good deal in common. And the Xs themselves are very likely to recognize this when not actively waving their nationalist banners – for instance by acknowledging the two-sidedness of their national identity, as do most Catalans and most Scots. So the issue is how best to interpret a complex state of affairs in which the minority group has both a distinct identity and a

---

10 Nor is it to say that secession is only justified when there is a sharp conflict of national identities: national groups may decide to separate by mutual consent, as the Norwegians and the Swedes did in 1905, and here the depth of the antagonism between them is largely irrelevant. I am considering the much more common case where the Xs wish to secede but the majority Ys oppose this.

sense of belonging to the larger community. Members of the majority group are very likely to be unperceptive and to behave in ways that are insensitive to the minority, but this does not mean that they are simply in error when they invoke a shared identity in order to resist the Xs' claim to secede.

A second tempting error is to think that if the seceding group wants to break up the political union, the majority's sense of identity is irrelevant. Some authors draw a parallel with individuals divorcing: if Anne decides she no longer wants to be married to Brian, then Brian's belief that they are still a viable domestic unit is neither here nor there. The union must rest on the continuing consent of both parties.[11] This analogy cannot be sustained, however. Most obviously, nations are not individuals with a single will. They are likely to embrace a wide range of opinions about how national identity is best expressed – through union with a larger nation, through devolution, through an independent state, and so forth. This point hardly needs to be laboured: it raises issues that I return to in the following section. A bit less obviously, secession does not only involve a political separation, but also a partition of territory. Here we must address the difficult question of how best to understand the rights of peoples to the territory that they occupy.

We might think initially that what is at stake here is an aggregate of property rights: I own this plot, you own that, and so all of us together own the territory that we call Britain.[12] If that were the right way to think about the problem, then a secessionist group occupying a compact area would simply have to assert their joint property rights to establish a conclusive claim to the land they want to take with them. But, as Buchanan has argued, the relationship between a

---

11 See. for example, K. Nielsen, 'Secession: the Case of Quebec,' *Journal of Applied Philosophy* **10** (1993) 29-43; D. Gauthier, 'Breaking Up: An Essay on Secession,' *Canadian Journal of Philosophy* **24** (1994) 357-72.

12 According to Hillel Steiner, for instance, 'since nations' territories are aggregations of their members' real estate holdings, the validity of their territorial claims rests on the validity of those land titles' (H. Steiner, 'Territorial Justice,' in S. Caney, D. George, and P. Jones, eds., *National Rights, International Obligations* [Boulder, CO: Westview Press 1996], 146).

people and their territory cannot properly be understood in these terms.[13] When we say that Iceland belongs to the Icelanders (to take a simple case), we do not mean that they own it as property: we mean that they have a legitimate claim to exercise authority over Iceland, to determine what happens in that island, including what individual property rights there are going to be. (If they were to decide to leave it as common land, that would be their prerogative.) This authority is exercised in practice by the state on the people's behalf, but the Icelanders' claim to authority is not reducible to the authority of the Icelandic state, as we can see if (*per impossibile*) we were to imagine a revolutionary upheaval in that country which established an entirely new set of political institutions. The Icelanders' claim to control Iceland would survive such a political cataclysm.

How are such claims established? The people who inhabit a certain territory form a political community. Through custom and practice as well as by explicit political decision they create laws, establish individual or collective property rights, engage in public works, and shape the physical appearance of the territory. Over time this takes on symbolic significance as they bury their dead in certain places, establish shrines or secular monuments, and so forth. All of these activities give them an attachment to the land that cannot be matched by any rival claimants. This in turn justifies their claim to exercise continuing political authority over that territory. It trumps the purely historical claim of a rival group who argue that their ancestors once ruled the land in question.[14]

If that is the right way to understand territorial claims, let us now return to the case of a divided community where a minority of Xs wish

---

13 Buchanan, *Secession*, 107-14

14 If one group occupies the territory previously held by another, then, *ceteris paribus*, the strength of its claim to exercise authority will increase with time. At a certain point – impossible to specify exactly – it will have a stronger title than the original inhabitants. This may sound uncomfortably like a version of 'might makes right,' but I cannot see any reasonable alternative to the view that it is the occupation and transformation of territory which gives a people its title to that territory, from which it follows that the competing claims of the present and original inhabitants increase and diminish respectively with the passage of time.

to secede (with the territory they occupy) from a majority of Ys. Can the Ys make a valid claim to continued control of the territory in question? The answer must depend on how the relationship between the two groups has developed historically. At one extreme we might have a case where the Xs were always the unwilling subjects of the Ys whom they regarded as an occupying force: the relationship between the native populations of the Baltic states and the Russian majority in the Soviet Union may have been close to this extreme. Here there has been no real political community between the Xs and the Ys, no freely undertaken collective projects, and it is hard to see the Ys having a legitimate claim to the territory occupied by the Xs except insofar as they have, say, invested physical capital in that territory (in which case some compensation may be due if the Xs secede).[15] At the other extreme we find the case where the Xs, although perhaps always having certain features that distinguished them from the Ys, have been free and equal partners in the building of the community. Their new-found nationalism is a result not of historic exploitation but of cultural developments that make them now want to have greater control over what happens in their particular territory (for instance, their language is in danger of being eroded). Here I think the legitimate demand of the Xs does have to be set against the equally legitimate demand of the Ys not to be deprived of part of the territory which they and their ancestors have helped to shape, and which they quite naturally think of as theirs. In a non-economic sense, the Ys will be poorer if the Xs secede. If no compromise is possible the Xs' demand may finally prove the stronger, but in such a case there is a powerful reason to find a solution that gives the Xs a form of autonomy that falls short of independence. This argument applies, I believe, to groups such as the Scots and Welsh in Britain, the Catalans and Basques in Spain, and the French-speaking communities in Canada.

To conclude this part of the discussion, if we appeal to the principle of nationality to ground the case for self-determination, then we shall want to apply two criteria to any group of would-be secessionists. The

---

15 This brings into play questions about distributive justice which I shall address later.

first is that the group should form a nation with an identity that is clearly separate from that of the larger nation from which they wish to disengage.[16] The second is that the group should be able to validate its claim to exercise authority over the territory it wishes to occupy. These criteria can't be applied mechanically or by counting heads; their application requires judgment and a degree of historical understanding. But if both criteria are met, the group in question has a serious claim to be allowed to secede. This is still not a conclusive claim, however, for there may be other factors weighing in the opposite direction, but *prima facie* the group has a good case. Let me now turn to explore some of the other factors that may count in the final judgment.

III Minorities and Numbers

Up to this point I have been considering the artificially simple case of a nationally homogeneous group of Xs occupying a discrete piece of land and attempting to secede from a state in which the Ys form a majority. In any real case that we might wish to consider, matters will not be so clear-cut. Within the territory that the Xs are claiming (a claim we are supposing to be legitimate by the criteria set out above) there are likely to be a number of Ys, and also members of other minorities who are neither Xs nor Ys. Within the borders of the remainder state, likewise, there may be found some Xs and also members of other groups. Secession does not simply mean shifting from a nationally heterogeneous community to one that is nationally homogeneous; it means replacing one heterogeneous pattern with two different (but still to some extent heterogeneous) patterns.

The assumption guiding our discussion is that there is a value to each member in being a citizen of a state that embraces your nation; to be part of a minority, although by no means always a disaster, is generally a worse option. So how should we compare the state of affairs prior to secession with that which would obtain afterwards, using this principle? One proposed criterion is that we should simply count up

---

16 Though note the qualification recorded in f.n. 10 above.

the numbers of people who live in a state in which they form a national majority.[17] In the case envisaged, this criterion will favour secession, on the assumption that the Xs form a majority in the territory which they are claiming. If the new state is formed, it will contain more Xs who now meet the criterion than Ys who now fail to meet it (they become a minority in the new state); the position of the Xs who remain in the Y state is unchanged; and so is that of the other minorities in both states.

But this proposal takes too little account of the political realities of secessionist movements. It assumes, in particular, that the treatment of national minorities in the new X-state will be no worse than their treatment in the original Y-state – for instance that whatever degree of autonomy was given to the Xs in the original state will be matched by the autonomy granted to the Ys in the new X-state. But in many cases this assumption is highly unrealistic. The sociologist Donald Horowitz has argued that secession nearly always intensifies conflicts between groups.[18] The Xs, in order to justify their secessionist demand, may have to exaggerate the features that differentiate them from the Ys. If they are successful, they are likely to want to purge the new state of the baneful influence of the Ys by cultural repression or, at the extreme, ethnic cleansing. Furthermore a side-effect of secession may be the stimulation of new group conflicts: Horowitz points out how, in Africa and elsewhere, new ethnic cleavages have almost always developed following the break-up of larger states. Differences that had little salience in the bigger unit may come to loom large in the smaller one, so that the vision of a culturally homogeneous political community gives way to infighting between the sub-groups.

---

17 Margaret Moore argues for the relevance of numbers in 'On National Self-Determination,' *Political Studies* 45 (1997), 900–13, and in 'Miller's Ode to National Homogeneity,' *Nations and Nationalism* 2 (1996), 423–9. I am not sure, however, that she would endorse the criterion I am discussing in its crude form because she also speaks about 'utilitarian calculations' which suggests taking into account intensities of feeling as well as the sheer numbers who are satisfied or dissatisfied with a proposed boundary redrawing.

18 D.L. Horowitz, 'Self-Determination: Politics, Philosophy, and Law,' in I. Shapiro and W. Kymlicka, eds., *Nomos XXXIX: Ethnicity and Group Rights* (New York: New York University Press 1997)

It is also false to assume that there is no change in the position of those Xs who, as a result of living in the wrong place, find themselves citizens of the rump Y-state. Most obviously they now form a much smaller minority and will have less political influence than previously. There may no longer be any constituencies regularly electing members of X to parliament, for example. Special rights which may have been in place before, such as rights designed to protect the X-culture, may now be dismantled on the grounds that there are too few Xs left to bother about. Furthermore political leaders in the Y-state may argue that the very existence of the X-state provides ample protection for that culture. It is hard, for instance, to imagine a Canada shorn of Quebec accepting responsibility for preserving French language and culture in North America. Finally the creation of the X-state inevitably alters the political identity of those Xs who remain outside it. Although their sense of self-worth may in some ways be enhanced by its existence (as the self-esteem of many Jews has been bolstered by the creation of the state of Israel), they may also feel more estranged from the Ys, and this feeling may be reciprocated ('If you don't think you belong here, why don't you move out to X-land?'). On balance, therefore, the position of the stranded Xs is likely to worsen as a result of the secession.

For these reasons, the proposal to settle the minorities issue by counting heads seems to me seriously inadequate. Once again qualitative judgments about how the status and welfare of different groups would be altered by the creation of a new state must be made. How can the principle of nationality guide us here? Let me make it clear first of all that the principle as I understand it does not advocate the creation of states that are culturally or ethnically homogeneous through and through. To say that fellow-citizens should as far as possible share a common national identity leaves space for a rich pattern of social diversity along lines of religion, ethnicity, and so forth. So alongside the principle of nationality we may – and surely should – hold other principles that protect the rights of minorities – principles of human rights, of equality, and so forth. These principles must also be brought into play when judging a claim to secession. Looking at the facts of a particular case, we have to try to estimate whether minority rights are likely to be better or worse protected if the secession goes ahead.

Such estimates are clearly difficult to make. One thing we cannot do, however, is simply to take whatever reassurances the secessionists may give at face value. Political philosophers writing on this topic are prone to say, in effect 'let the secession go ahead provided that those who form the new state undertake to respect the rights of minorities within it.'[19] But how should we apply this conditional to an actual case? How are we to judge the real worth of such an undertaking? It is important to bear in mind here that once the new state is formed and recognized, powerful norms of international non-interference come into play. As the experience of former Yugoslavia demonstrates, it is very difficult to control from the outside even massive violations of the rights of minorities. So there is a serious risk that in permitting the secession to occur, we (as third parties to the conflict, say) may be tacitly condoning maltreatment of minorities in the newly-formed state, which at a later stage we will be unable to do anything about.

The principle of nationality itself may guide our thinking in one further respect. Recall that the underlying vision is of a state whose citizens share an inclusive national identity that makes room for cultural differences. How far this ideal vision can be realized in any particular case will depend on the character of the identity in question – for instance, how far it includes elements that are tied to the culture of a particular ethnic group. If the national identity of the Ys is relatively amorphous whereas the identity of the Xs contains a much stronger ethnic or religious component, say, then there is clearly a much better chance of a common identity in which the Xs (and others) can share evolving in the Y-state than there is of the reverse happening in the X-state. This criterion does not necessarily tell in favour of the status quo, but in many cases it will, especially where the existing state is long-established, and over time has developed mechanisms for coping with cultural pluralism. If we consider the case of Quebec, for instance, it is reasonable to expect that an independent Quebec would protect the private rights of its English-speaking minority at least as effectively as Canada has so far protected the rights of French speakers. On the other

---

19 See, for instance, D. Philpott, 'In Defense of Self-Determination,' *Ethics* **105** (1994-95) 352-85. 'In a heterogeneous candidate territory, the decision [to secede] rests with the majority of the territory's inhabitants, with the qualification that under the new government, minority rights – including Kymlickan cultural rights – are guaranteed' (380).

hand it is hard to imagine that it would evolve a national identity that was as hospitable to English-speakers in Quebec as Canadian identity has become to French-speakers throughout Canada, since the active promotion of French language and French culture would necessarily be a central component of that identity.

There will, however, be some tragic cases where the project of reconciliation is simply not feasible. These are cases where two physically intermingled communities cannot live together peacefully because of ingrained mutual hostility, and where there is no reason to believe that under any division of the territory the rights of the minority groups will be respected. Here I think it may be necessary to contemplate some exchange of populations so that two more or less nationally homogeneous entities can be created. Most liberals will baulk at this suggestion, because it brings to mind the horrifying spectre of forced ethnic cleansing, and indeed there is no doubt that historically most population shifts of this kind have taken place more or less under coercion. But it is at least possible to envisage an internationally supervised operation in which people are given financial incentives to exchange their homes and their land, and if the alternative to this is a continuation of events such as those we have witnessed in Bosnia, or indeed on a much smaller scale in Northern Ireland, we should be prepared to contemplate it.[20]

---

20 Perhaps the most interesting example of an exchange of this kind occurred between Greece and Turkey in the 1920s. Under the terms of a formal agreement between the two states, some 200,000 people of Greek descent living in Turkey were required to emigrate to Greece, and about 350,000 Turks were required to move from Greece to Turkey. Alongside the formal exchange, however, much larger numbers of Greeks – perhaps about one million – emigrated to Greece either voluntarily or as a result of Turkish oppression, and a further 100,000 Turks moved in the opposite direction. There is not a great deal of hard evidence about the overall impact of the transfer on the people who experienced it, but, focussing on the Greek side, the following four statements appear to be true. (1) Materially speaking the infrastructure and investment provided by the internationally-funded Refugee Settlement Commission allowed large numbers of immigrants to settle and flourish in their new places of residence. (2) The exchange appears also to have had a strongly positive effect on the overall economic prosperity and sense of national identity in Greece. (3) The refugees experienced psychological difficulties in adjusting to their forcible translation and continued to harbour hopes of a return to their birthplaces at least up until

In tackling the minorities issue, therefore, the principle should not be to allow secession whenever a territorial majority favours it, but to judge which outcome offers the best chance of creating states with national identities which are relatively congenial to internal minorities, and which are likely to protect their cultural and other rights. Numbers should count to some extent, but insofar as they are predictable overall consequences should count for more. Where the consequences for minorities look very bad wherever the boundaries are fixed, some people – as few as possible – may have to be encouraged to move their abode.

IV Distributive Justice

When secession occurs, it is likely over time to alter the pattern of economic distribution both between and within the new-formed and remainder states. So ought we to judge secessionist demands by applying principles of distributive justice to them – favouring secession when it seems likely to be justice-enhancing, and disfavouring it in the opposite case? Several recent discussions of the question have followed this strategy, giving principles of justice a more or less prominent place in the theory of legitimate secession.[21] How far, then, should we modify the conclusions already reached to take account of such considerations?

World War II. (4) Over the same period there were significant social divisions between natives and refugees in Greek towns and villages. To arrive at a balanced assessment, these pluses and minuses would need to be set against the likely fate of the minorities, particularly at the hands of the Turkish authorities, if the transfer had not occurred. For descriptions of the exchange, see S.P. Ladas, *The Exchange of Minorities: Bulgaria, Greece and Turkey* (New York: Macmillan 1932); D. Pentzopoulos, *The Balkan Exchange of Minorities and its Impact upon Greece* (Paris: Mouton 1962); J. A. Petropulos, 'The Compulsory Exchange of Populations: Greek-Turkish Peacemaking, 1922-1930,' *Byzantine and Modern Greek Studies* **2** (1976) 135-60.

21 Including Buchanan, *Secession*, ch. 3; Gauthier, 'Breaking Up: An Essay on Secession'; C.H. Wellman, 'A Defense of Secession and Political Self-Determination,' *Philosophy and Public Affairs* **24** (1995) 142-71.

David Miller

As Buchanan points out, the first issue that has to be settled here is the scope of the principles in question.[22] Should we see principles of distributive justice as applying globally (though no doubt given practical application through more local institutions) or do these principles themselves have a restricted scope? Buchanan analyzes this issue by drawing a contrast between 'justice as reciprocity' and 'subject-centred justice,' the former holding that obligations of justice hold only between the contributors to a co-operative scheme, the latter imposing no such restriction. I want to propose a somewhat different view. Principles of distributive justice, and especially *comparative* principles, such as principles of equality, need, and desert, do indeed have a restricted scope, but the limits are not set by the bounds of a co-operative practice for mutual advantage; rather they are set by the bounds of a community whose members recognize one another as belonging to that community. This view avoids what Buchanan takes to be the major weakness of justice as reciprocity, namely that it cannot recognize obligations of justice towards those who are unable to contribute to a scheme of social co-operation, such as the seriously disabled. If instead the scope of principles of justice is determined by the boundaries of the relevant community, then these principles will embrace members of the community who for one reason or another cannot contribute to the social product; for instance principles of equality and need will apply to them. And I take it that although nations are not the only communities that will count from this perspective, they are arguably the most important.[23]

If that picture (which I state rather than defend here) is right, then how should we judge the justice of a claim to secession? We begin with a single political society whose institutions are governed more or less closely by principles of justice which citizens of that society – or perhaps

---

22 Buchanan, *Secession*, 114 ff

23 I have set this argument out more fully in 'The Limits of Cosmopolitan Justice,' in D.R. Mapel and T. Nardin, eds., *The Constitution of International Society: Diverse Ethical Perspectives* (Princeton: Princeton University Press, forthcoming) and in 'Justice and Global Inequality' in A. Hurrell and N. Woods, eds., *Inequality in World Politics* (Oxford: Oxford University Press, forthcoming).

some portion of them – endorse. If secession occurs, we now have two political communities within which, again, each set of members' sense of justice will be more or less closely embodied. It is impossible to say in general terms whether the cause of justice is likely to have been served by the secession. In favour of the secession, it can be argued that the discontented minority – the Xs, to return to earlier terminology – will probably have suffered injustice in the large state, either because the principles they subscribe to were not adequately reflected in the state's policies, or because principles which they share with the Ys were implemented in a discriminatory way.[24] Against the secession, it can be argued that the pooling of resources that the larger state made possible served to protect the members of both communities against hardship of various kinds. What cannot be argued, though, is that the bare fact that the Xs as a group and the Ys as a group receive different treatment from their governments and other institutions after the separation is a reason against it. This follows from the premise that comparative principles of justice apply within communities rather than between them. Just as it is no injustice that the Germans enjoy on average higher incomes or better medical care than the Spanish, so if the Basques were to separate from Spain it would be no injustice if they proceeded to enjoy a higher (or lower) living standard than their erstwhile compatriots.

In general, this means that the argument from justice will tend to reinforce, rather than offset, the original argument from national self-determination. Where a state presently contains two communities whose collective identities are radically at odds with one another, this is very likely to mean that the minority community gets treated unjustly for one or both of the reasons set out above. Contrasting national identities are likely to mean contrasting public cultures, and therefore

---

24 These two grounds do not necessarily coincide, as the Scottish case illustrates. In recent years many Scots have felt that their public culture and sense of social justice is increasingly at odds with the Thatcherite ideas that have infected some parts of British central government and administration. On the other hand, Scotland has for some while been a net beneficiary of the British system of public finance, so it would be hard for Scots to claim that they are victims of discriminatory treatment.

somewhat different understandings of what justice requires. Equally where there is a good deal of hostility between the communities, political leaders in the majority community will feel strongly tempted to practise discriminatory policies in favour of their fellow-members, as Protestant leaders in Northern Ireland did for many decades. Where, on the other hand, group identities converge more closely at national level, neither the principle of nationality nor distributive justice are likely to support a secessionist cause.[25]

So are there no circumstances in which justice can be appealed to in order to contest a secessionist case which otherwise seems well-founded? I can think of two such instances. First, as several other commentators have observed, a secession might be unjust if it deprived the remainder state of some valuable resource that had been created collectively – for instance if the pre-secessionist state had made a large capital investment in a power station built in the territory to which the secessionists lay claim. In principle this problem is soluble by a transfer payment from the X-state to the remainder Y-state, though it may prove hard to agree precise terms. It is possible that a similar argument might apply when the Ys have taken decisions premised upon continued co-operation with the Xs, as Gauthier suggests.[26] If the Ys suffer as a result of the Xs' withdrawal in circumstances where they could legitimately expect the cooperation to continue, they may have some claim to compensation which tapers downwards over time. These, however, are best regarded as transitional issues of justice, and should not be conflated with the idea, rejected above, that the relative position of the two communities formed by secession can be judged by applying comparative principles such as equality across both.

Second, a secession might conceivably leave the remainder state so depleted of resources that it was unable to secure its members' basic

---

25 There may be cases – blacks in America come to mind – in which groups suffer from injustice at the hands of the majority without having or developing a separate sense of national identity. But where a minority group is territorially concentrated, the experience of injustice has a strong tendency over time to foster such a separate identity, so that once again the cause of justice and the cause of national self-determination are fused.

26 Gauthier, 'Breaking Up: An Essay on Secession,' section III

interests, and so was forced to contract an alliance with some colonial power or other neighbouring state. This could happen if a rich secessionist region chose to cast off an impoverished fringe area – not a likely scenario, perhaps, but one that is worth contemplating briefly for the light it can shed on the general principle at stake. The principle here is that the pursuit of national self-determination and justice for the Xs should not lead to a state of affairs in which the Ys are so deprived that they cannot achieve justice among themselves, and as a result have to give up a large measure of self-determination as well. This is a bit like Wellman's condition that both secessionist and remainder states should be "large, wealthy, cohesive and geographically contiguous enough to form a government that effectively performs the functions necessary to create a secure political environment,"[27] though I do not think we can insist that each state should measure up to some pre-formed standard of liberal legitimacy. What matters is that both the Xs and the Ys should have territory and resources from which a viable political community can be created; how this is done in practice may depend upon the differing political cultures of the two groups.[28]

V Conclusion

I have tried to show that the principle of nationality provides us with a perspective on the secession issue that can avoid us having to condone a secessionist free-for-all without forcing us to defend existing state boundaries regardless. Sometimes these boundaries need changing, but we can decide whether they do by applying relevant criteria, not simply by listening to how loud the clamour for independence has become. It is far too crude to suggest that any territo-

---

27 Wellman, 'A Defense of Secession and Political Self-Determination,' 161-2

28 So, for example, I think that the Slovenian secession from Yugoslavia could not be condemned on the grounds that it made the achievement of liberal democracy in Yugoslavia as a whole less likely. We ought indeed to try to promote liberal and democratic ideals externally, but I don't think that our duty in this respect is so strong as to oblige us to remain in political association with groups whose culture or identity we find uncongenial.

rial majority that wants to secede has a right to do so. Instead we need to measure the strength of its claim by looking at how far different groups have or have not evolved separate national identities, at how minorities are likely to fare under various possible regimes, and so forth. Admittedly this is demanding in terms of the level of knowledge that outsiders may be called on to acquire. But only by getting to grips with the facts of each particular case in this way can we decide whether outright secession is justified, as opposed to the many other forms of partial autonomy – consociationalism, federalism, local autonomy, etc. – that a constitutional settlement within existing state borders may provide.

CANADIAN JOURNAL OF PHILOSOPHY
Supplementary Volume 22

What's So Special About Nations?

ALLEN BUCHANAN
University of Arizona

I Introduction

Until quite recently, most Anglo-American political philosophers have
had little if anything to say about national self-determination.[1] However, a growing number of prominent political philosophers are now
endorsing national self-determination. This new-found enthusiasm is
surprising if not ironic, since it comes at a time at which genocidal
ethno-nationalist conflicts (in the Balkans, in Rwanda and Burundi,
etc.) might seem to lend credence to the view that the doctrine that
every nation should have its own state is both impractical and dangerous, and that the nationalist mentality is often racist, xenophobic,
exclusionary, and morally regressive. In this essay I will question the
wisdom of this new-found enthusiasm for national self-determination.
I will probe what I shall call the Strong National Self-Determination
Thesis (or, more briefly, the Strong Thesis). This is the assertion that
every nation as such has a right to some substantial degree of self-government
and there is a presumption that every nation as such has a right to its own
independent state (where this includes the right to secede from another state).
I call this the Strong Thesis because it is more robust than the thesis
that nations have a right to some form of self-government.

---

1 Charles Beitz, in his excellent book *Political Theory and International Relations*
(Princeton, NJ: Princeton University Press 1979), is a notable exception.

An even Stronger Thesis would remove the qualifier in the second clause, stating flatly that every nation as such has a right to its own independent state. I shall not focus on the Stronger Thesis, however, for two reasons. First, it has fewer takers than the Strong Thesis in the current literature. Second, if I am successful in refuting the Strong Thesis, the Stronger Thesis will fall *a fortiori*.

Although the Strong Thesis, or something close to it, is often advanced and nowadays, perhaps, less frequently attacked, there remains considerable confusion about what sort of right this alleged right of national self-determination is and about what kinds of justifications might be enlisted in its support. The problem lies in part with the much-used but ambiguous phrase 'the right to self-determination.' Sometimes this phrase is used to refer to the right to some form or other of self-government *including* independent statehood under some circumstances; sometimes to the right to determine *whether* to have some form of self-government short of sovereign statehood or to choose independent statehood. To avoid these ambiguities, I have framed the Strong National Self-Determination Thesis as having two distinct parts: (1) a statement that nations as such have a right to some (substantial) form of self-government, where this right does not itself entail a right to independent statehood, and (2) a statement that there is a presumption that nations, as such, have a right to independent statehood (and hence to secede when they find themselves part of states that are not exclusively controlled by themselves).

In what follows I will first distinguish Strong National Self-Determination from other views about national self-determination that do not in fact ascribe rights of self-determination of any kind to nations *as such*, as distinct from nations that have suffered certain injustices, including the unjust annexation of their sovereign territory. I will then consider two powerful objections against the Strong Thesis about national self-determination, one based on the unacceptable consequences that would most likely result where the Strong Thesis is accepted, the other on the view that singling out nations for rights of self-government is arbitrary and this arbitrariness violates the principle of equal respect for persons. Then I will offer a taxonomy of justifications for the Strong Thesis, distinguishing those that present rights of self-determination for nations *as such* as *basic* rights, grounded in the direct contribution which membership in a nation makes to individual well-being and autonomy, and as *derivative* rights, whose exercise facilitates the implementation of principles of democracy or distributive justice. Next, I will show that the most influential arguments in favour of rights of national self-determination, whether as basic or derivative rights, are weak and at best inconclusive. Finally, I will argue that these arguments for rights of self-determination for nations as such cannot be repaired without embracing some of the most repugnant tenets of nineteenth-century nationalist doctrine. These include the thesis that nations have a moral standing to which individual autonomy and all other allegiances and sources of identification are properly subordinated, and the belief that there is an inevitable competition among nations such that the globe eventually will be divided among a relatively few 'great' nations, with 'lesser' nations dying out or being assimilated into the 'great' ones. Because neither of these tenets is in the least acceptable to an even minimally liberal political philosophy, I conclude that efforts of some contemporary liberal thinkers to embrace rights of self-determination for nations as such are doomed to failure.

II   Strong National Self-Determination

The Strong National Self-Determination Thesis ascribes a right of self-government, and a presumption of a right to secede in order to establish a sovereign state, to nations *as such*. In other words, it is simply by virtue of being a nation that a group has this right (to some substantial form of self-government) and this presumption of a right (to secede). This is important to keep in mind, since one can reject Strong National Self-Determination and yet maintain that nations sometimes have a right to self-government of some sort and even a right to secede.

More specifically, one can hold that there are *remedial* rights of self-government and of secession, and that nations sometimes have these rights. The idea of a remedial right of self-determination is straightforward: It is the idea that a group can form its own political unit and secede from another state if necessary, in order to escape serious injustices that are being inflicted on it, at least if there is no other recourse.

If a group occupying part of the territory of a state is subject to persecution or systematic discrimination, then it makes sense to ascribe to that group the right to secede, at least if creating their own independent state is their best prospect for escaping these injustices.[2] Similarly, if a state is unjustly annexed by another, then the right to secede from the conquering state may again be understood as a remedial right, in this case one whose exercise simply rectifies the unjust taking of territory.

In the former case, that of secession to escape gross violations of human rights, the persecuted group may or may not qualify as a nation, but this is immaterial to its having the right to secede. In the latter case, where secession is the remedy for unjust annexation, the people of the sovereign state whose territory was taken may be one nation or their state may have been multinational, but the basis for ascribing the right to secede has nothing to do with nationality as such. Nevertheless, in either of these cases of the right to secede, understood as a remedial right, the group that has the right may qualify as a nation. Thus one can agree that nations sometimes have the right to secede, but deny that nations *as such* have this right.

To summarize: the thesis that nations as such have a right of self-determination and a presumptive right to secede must be understood as including the assumption that these rights are *not* remedial rights. Otherwise, 'the right of national self-determination' is no more than a misleading way of referring to the right of existing *states* (or rather their citizens) to recover unjustly taken territory or the right of aggrieved groups (which in some cases happen to be nations) to escape injustices by establishing their own state.[3] So from here on I shall assume that those who advance the Strong National Self-Determination Thesis are

---

2 For a developed account of the right to secede as a remedial right, see Allen Buchanan, *Secession: The Morality of Political Divorce from Fort Sumter to Lithuania and Quebec* (Boulder, CO: Westview Press 1991).

3 Of course, if one *assumed* that every nation as such has the right to its own state, then any nation that did not have its own state would be treated unjustly, and then the right to secede could be understood as a remedial right. However, since what is in question is *whether* every nation as such has a right to its own state, it makes sense to distinguish between the view that nations have a right to independent statehood *only* as a remedial right in the sense of a right to recover the independent statehood of which it was unjustly deprived or as a remedy against other, independently characterizable injustices (such as genocide) and the view that every nation as such has a right to its own state.

asserting that nations have these rights even in the absence of being the victims of injustices such as the violation of human rights and even if the nation did not previously have its own sovereign state that was unjustly annexed. The thesis I wish to criticize, then, is that nations have a nonremedial right to some substantial self-government and that there is a presumption that nations have a right to independent statehood, and hence to secede, independently of any remedial justifications for doing so.

Before we proceed, however, we must fix upon a definition of 'nation' that is at least roughly serviceable. Doing so is not without risk, considering the multitude of definitions that have been proposed. Nevertheless, we can begin with a characterization proposed by Margalit and Raz according to which nations are 'encompassing cultural groups,' defined as large-scale, anonymous (rather than small, face-to-face) groups that have a common culture and character that encompasses many important aspects of life and which marks the character of the life of its members, where membership in the group is in part a matter of mutual recognition, is important for one's self-identification, and is a matter of belonging, not achievement. In addition, like virtually all other writers on nationalism, Margalit and Raz emphasize that the identity of the encompassing cultural group includes the idea of an historical attachment to a particular territory, the notion of a homeland.[4] This last element is important; without it the distinction between nations and nonnational, for example, ethnic or religious, groups that sometimes have the other features of 'encompassing cultural groups' would be lost.

What is lacking in this characterization, and what is emphasized in the preponderance of scholarly writing on nationalism, is that among the members of the group there is an aspiration for some form of self-government for the group. Or, as David Miller puts it, that nations are 'inherently political' (in their aspirations).[5] For brevity we can say that nations are encompassing cultural groups that associate themselves with a homeland, and in which there is a substantial (though not nec-

---

4 Avishai Margalit and Joseph Raz, 'National Self-Determination,' *The Journal of Philosophy* **87** (1990), 439–61

5 David Miller, *On Nationality* (Oxford: Oxford University Press 1996), 11

essarily unanimous) aspiration for self-government of some kind (though not necessarily for independent statehood).

Given this relatively uncontroversial conception of what a nation is, it is not difficult to see how intuitions about rights of self-determination of nations *as such* might be mistaken for intuitions about *remedial* rights of self-determination. Consider Will Kymlicka's conception of a nation as an 'institutionally complete' cultural group (what he also calls a 'societal culture') that occupies a particular territory.[6]

Kymlicka seems to agree with Margalit and Raz that nations are 'encompassing' cultural groups – that they are cultural groups whose cultures pervade the whole range of an individual's major life activities and function as an important source of self-identification. Kymlicka apparently also believes, however, that a culture can be encompassing only through being embodied in a comprehensive system of institutions – hence the requirement that nations be cultures that are 'institutionally complete.'[7]

---

6 Will Kymlicka, *Multicultural Citizenship* (Oxford: Oxford University Press 1996), 11

7 Kymlicka's view seems to shift between his *Liberalism, Community, and Culture* (Oxford: Oxford University Press 1989) and the more recent *Multicultural Citizenship*. In the former he unambiguously asserts that belonging to a culture is necessary for having a meaningful context for choice; in the latter he sometimes says that belonging to a 'societal' (institutionally complete) culture is necessary for having a meaningful context for choice. If his considered view is the latter, that *only* 'societal' (institutionally complete) cultures supply the needed context for meaningful choice, then there are two difficulties. First, he must somehow counter the many apparent counterexamples to this sweeping generalization – the many cases, as Waldron notes, in which individuals seem to exist, and to thrive, while partaking of two or more cultures without being full-fledged members of any one 'societal' culture. And he must do so without making the notion of a 'societal culture' so expansive and accessible that everyone, including the member of a minority nation in the midst of a dominant culture that is not their national culture, is a member of some 'societal' culture or other. Second, Kymlicka must show that the ethnic cultures of immigrant groups, which he believes are not 'societal' cultures and hence are not capable of providing a meaningful context for choice, still matter so much for individuals that justice requires the various minority rights which he endorses for these groups.

Now from the claim that nations are institutionally complete cultures to the claim that at one time or another they must have had some form of self-government is only a short step, given a reasonably broad conception of 'institutional completeness' as including political institutions. But if we assume that nations are cultural groups that at one time enjoyed self-government, then we are already well on the way to concluding that they have a *remedial* right to self-government – a right to the restoration of their former self-government. All that is needed to yield this conclusion is the additional assumption that the group's loss of self-government was unjust – through forcible annexation of their territory or by some deal among heads of dynasties in the past which by no stretch of the imagination represented the will of the people.

This slide (via the notion of institutional completeness), from the definition that nations are encompassing cultures associated with a particular territory to the conclusion that they are formerly self-governing groups, has an unfortunate effect: It blurs the distinction between self-determination as a right of nations as such and self-determination as a remedial right which nations may sometimes have (if they were previously self-governing and lost their self-government through injustice).

The confusion is fostered by Kymlicka's choice of examples. After giving his characterization of nations as institutionally complete cultures, he argues that nations have rights of self-government, appealing to cases in which previously self-governing groups, such as native peoples in Canada, lost their self-government by being unjustly incorporated into settler states.[8] What is most appealing about these cases – what gives the group's claim to self-government plausibility – is the clear injustice of the conquest of peoples who had been self-determining, who had their own forms of government, in a territory they had occupied since time immemorial. One need not embrace the view that nations as such have a right of self-determination in order to say that these groups have a right to self-government – unless one simply stipulates that all nations were previously self-governing and that no nation loses its self-government justly. Rather, all that is required is a

---

8 Kymlicka, *Multicultural Citizenship*, 12-13

commonsensical belief that justice requires restoring groups to their previous, self-governing status, when they were unjustly conquered.

If the thesis that nations have a right of self-determination is to be of much interest – if it is to be something other than a misleading way of attributing remedial rights to previously self-governing groups – then it cannot be part of the definition of 'nation' that the cultural group in question was self-governing at some time in the past. That is why it is better to say, as most definitions of 'nation' do, that nations *aspire* to self-government, not that they were previously self-governing.

On the other hand, suppose that one were convinced that a culture can only become what Raz and Margalit call an 'encompassing group' through an institutional embodiment that includes self-government. On *that* definition of 'nation' the issue of whether nations as such have a right of self-determination turns upon what the correct theory of remedial or rectificatory justice is. And this theory has nothing to do with nationalism *per se*. For presumably any group whose government was usurped by unjust conquest – whether the group is a nation or not – has a remedial right of self-determination. For example, a multinational group, or a collection of ethnic and/or political groups that had legitimately formed a state would also be entitled to this remedy. The crucial issue for a theory of remedial rights of self-determination is not 'Was the group whose self-government was destroyed a nation?' but rather 'Was the government of that group legitimate?' and 'How far back in the past do we go in recognizing remedial rights for the restoration of self-government?'

It is important to understand which definition of 'nation' we are dealing with if we are to sort out our intuitions. If, like Kymlicka, in order to marshal intuitions to support the thesis that nations have rights of self-government, we appeal to cases where self-governing groups had their territory unjustly incorporated and suffered the destruction of their self-government, then we cannot confidently draw any conclusions about the rights of nations as such, understood as nonremedial rights. Because I believe that the interesting thesis about nations and self-determination is the Strong National Self-Determination Thesis, understood as the view that nations have a *nonremedial* right to self-government and a presumptive *nonremedial* right to independent statehood, I will thus operate from here on with the preceding definition of 'nation,' which does *not* include the condition that the cultural group in question at one time had its own government. And I will simply set aside appeals to intuitions about national rights of self-determination concerning cases that involve self-governing groups that were unjustly incorporated into other political units. Once we remove from consideration those cases in which nations have remedial claims to self-government, the view that nations as such have rights of self-determination becomes considerably less plausible, especially once the objections to it are articulated.

III   The Case Against (Nonremedial) Rights of Nations to Self-Determination

The Infeasibility Objection. The most familiar objection to the idea that nations as such have rights of self-determination is that there are too many nations, whose members are mixed together, and too few territories capable of being viable states.[9] Call this the Infeasibility Objection.

It should be clear that the Infeasibility Objection is most powerful against the Stron*ger* Thesis, according to which nations as such have a right to independent statehood, not just a presumption of such a right. And it is against the Stronger Thesis that it has mainly been wielded.

However, as David Copp among others has noted, even if it were universally acknowledged that every nation has the right to its own state (not just the presumption of such a right), it does not follow that every nation would try to exercise the right.[10] So we should not assume that we would face the catastrophe envisioned by those who raise the Infeasibility Objection – a global scramble for territory, with national groups everywhere trying to kill or drive out others occupying 'their' territories, or at the very least trying to reduce them to the status of resident aliens without full citizenship rights. Similarly, to acknowledge that every nation as such has a right to self-government of some

---

9   Ernest Gellner, *Nations and Nationalism* (Oxford: Blackwell 1983), 2

10   David Copp, 'Do Nations Have a Right of Self-Determination?' in Stanley G. French, ed., *Philosophers Look at Canadian Confederation* (Montreal: Canadian Philosophical Association 1977), 71-95

sort and a presumption of a right to independent statehood (the Strong Thesis) would almost certainly not result in every nation attempting to exercise the right or act on the presumption.

Copp's criticism shows that the Infeasibility Objection must be developed with some care if it is to be telling. Perhaps we should not assume that there can be a right to something only if the consequences of *everyone* who has the right acting on it would be acceptable. Yet surely the consequences of the acknowledgement of a right has *some* significant bearing on whether there is such a right. Rights must in some sense be practicable: The exercise of a right by some must not be systematically and pervasively thwarted by the efforts of others who have the right to exercise it also.

Properly developed, the point of the Infeasibility Objection is not that the globe does not contain enough useable land so that it could *in principle* be parcelled out to provide viable territories for each nation (which may or may not be true – much would depend upon what institutions of international distributive justice were available). Rather, the point is that because nations are so intermingled in most parts of the world and because there is no international institutional order capable of imposing a peaceful relocation of groups according to some master plan, the likely effect of legitimizing the idea that every nation has a presumptive right to its own state would be to exacerbate existing territorial disputes and ethno-national conflicts.

In other words, properly explicated, the Infeasibility Objection rests on the claim that whether a given normative principle such as the Strong Thesis is justified depends in part upon whether general acceptance of that principle would create expectations that cannot be satisfied without unacceptable moral costs – in this case the costs to human rights that would result from nations striving for the independent statehood they are supposed to have a presumptive right to. If we add one more assumption, we can conclude that the moral costs of general acceptance of the Strong Thesis would be considerable: Historically, nationalist groups have not been distinguished by a willingness to compromise their perceived interests nor, in many cases, even to recognize that other national groups could make claims that are as legitimate as theirs.

Of course the proponent of the Strong Thesis might reply that nations *need not* exhibit bellicosity, exclusiveness, and intractability in attempting to achieve self-determination – that there is nothing in the definition of nationalism stated above that requires these destructive attitudes. That is certainly true, but of very limited relevance. The question is whether there are enough national groups in the real world, our world, that will exhibit these destructive attitudes to make the moral costs of the general acceptance of the Strong Thesis intolerably high.

Even when understood in this more sophisticated fashion the Infeasibility Objection still is not a debate stopper. It does not show conclusively that the Strong Thesis is wrong. It does, however, accomplish at least this much: Given the likelihood that general acceptance of the Strong Thesis would at the very least help perpetuate existing nationalist conflicts (if not exacerbate and multiply them), *very weighty moral reasons in favour of the Strong Thesis must be adduced if we are to accept it.* Shortly I will examine the reasons that have been offered in support of the Strong Thesis, and I will find them wanting. But first I will consider a quite different objection to the Strong Thesis, one that is entirely independent of the soundness of the Infeasibility Objection.

The Equal Respect Objection. The Infeasibility Objection challenges only one part of the Strong Thesis, the claim that nations as nations have a presumptive right to independent statehood. A second objection targets as well the first part of the Strong Thesis, the claim that nations as nations have the right to self-government (short of independent statehood). According to this second objection, to single out nations as such for rights of self-government that are denied to other groups is morally arbitrary, and this arbitrariness violates the principle that persons are to be accorded equal respect.[11]

The Equal Respect Objection to the Strong Thesis assumes a background of what might be called *dynamic pluralism*: Society is composed of numerous groups and individuals with numerous life-projects or conceptions of the good. Moreover, given that the society is at least minimally liberal – in which there is substantial freedom of religion, of expression, and of association – pluralism will continue, with new

---

11 Most recently Harry Brighouse ('Against Nationalism,' this volume) has raised this objection, but in one form or other it has been advanced by a number of authors. See, for example, Kymlicka's discussion of the 'benign neglect' view in *Multicultural Citizenship*.

groups and new conceptions of the good emerging over time. Some groups will attract or hold members, flourish for a time, then lose their grip on individuals' allegiances and identities, just as individuals will revise and in some cases abandon their initial conceptions of the good.

In such a society individuals not only sometimes change allegiances, they also have multiple allegiances, and these give rise to complex self-identifications. Even more importantly, there is no uniformity as to the *priorities* persons attach to their multiple identifications. Some think of themselves first as fathers or mothers or members of a family, and second as Swiss, or Americans, or Blacks, or Hispanics, or Christians. For others their primary self-identification is religious or political-ideological. (I recall meeting a man in Apartheid South Africa at a social gathering who introduced himself as follows: "I'm a bloody Communist; my name is Sam _____, and I used to be a professor before I went to jail."). Finally, there are some individuals for whom there is no *one* identification that is more fundamental than all others – for example, being a mother is no less and no more important than being Swedish, or being a socialist, or being an artist.

The crucial point is that in pluralistic societies nationality will be only one source of identification and allegiance among others, and for some people it will be of little or no importance relative to other sources of identification and allegiance, whether these are cultural or occupational or religious or political or familial. For example, for some people – perhaps millions at present – being Muslim is more important than being Iranian or Turkish or Kurdish. While some religious groups (e.g., Hindus who support the BJP in India) may count as nations because they satisfy the condition of identifying with a homeland, others, like Christians or Muslims, do not.

In a society characterized by dynamic pluralism, singling out nations as such as being entitled to self-government is nothing less than a public expression of the conviction that allegiances and identities have a single, true rank order of value, with nationality reposing at the summit. So to confer a special right of self-government on those groups that happen to be nations is to devalue all other allegiances and identifications. And to devalue these other allegiances and identifications is to show less than equal respect to those persons whose allegiances and identifications they are.

This last point cannot be overemphasized. To confer special rights of self-government on nations as such is an act of society as a whole, given the liberal assumption that government acts as the agent of the people.[12] Hence the implied judgment that nationality is superior to other allegiances and identities is also a public judgment. As such it is an insult to the equal status of every citizen whose primary identity and allegiance is other than national and to all who have no single primary identity or allegiance. In a word, singling out nations for self-government is a form of *discrimination* and like all discrimination violates the principle of equal respect for persons.

Sometimes this point is made by saying that giving special political recognition to nations violates the 'liberal principle of neutrality.' There are two reasons why I have chosen to avoid this familiar phrase. First, the notion of neutrality is ambiguous. Second, even if a clear and relevant sense of neutrality can be identified, the fundamental moral issue is equal respect for persons – neutrality on the part of the state is only a vehicle for its expression.

In addition to constituting a public ranking of the value of nations relative to other sources of identification and allegiance, according nations as such rights of self-government (and a presumption of a right to independent statehood) also facilitates the domination of nationality over other sources of allegiance and identification. When nations have powers of self-government, but other groups (cultural, religious, political-ideological) do not, the latter groups are thereby disadvantaged. They lack a powerful resource for pursuing their ends which nations have been given. And when this disadvantage comes as the predictable result of public action (through conferring rights of self-government on nations), this disadvantage itself constitutes a violation of equal respect for persons, and hence an injustice.

I have used the term 'dynamic' to qualify pluralism to emphasize three types of change. First, groups (ethnic, religious, national, political-ideological, etc.) change over time; the values and practices that give them their distinct identities are not fixed. Second, individuals' conceptions of the good change over time, sometimes in accordance

---

12 Harry Brighouse, 'Against Nationalism'

with changes in the values and practices of the groups of which they are members, sometimes in relative independence from the character of any particular group they participate in. Third, groups change in the extent to which they command the allegiance of individuals, in the degree to which individuals identify themselves as members of the group, and in how deeply the groups' values penetrate individuals' conceptions of the good. Once we appreciate the dynamic nature of pluralism in a minimally liberal society, the thesis that nations ought to be singled out for rights of self-government and that they have a presumptive right to their own states becomes all the more dubious.

Suppose, however, that we grant for a moment what I believe to be patently false – that for most individuals *at present* nationality is the most important source of allegiance and identification and exerts the strongest influence on the character of their conception of the good. There is no reason to believe that under conditions of dynamic pluralism nationality would *maintain* this preeminence, unless nations were singled out for special treatment by conferring rights of self-government on them.

Given the pluralism of even minimally liberal societies and given that this is a dynamic pluralism, it will be very difficult, to say the least, to show why nations as such, among all the different sources of allegiance and self-identification, have rights of self-determination. For to confer such rights on them not only ignores the fact that there are many individuals for whom nationality is not so important but also ignores the fact that whatever importance nationality now possesses may change through the free interaction of individuals and groups over time.

A proponent of national self-determination might at this point object that I have misunderstood the notion that nations are encompassing cultural groups. What makes nations, as encompassing cultural groups, special is not that they are, or should be, winners in competition with other sources of identification for the allegiances of individuals. Rather, the point is that national identity functions to 'encompass' other identities by integrating them and making them cohere. Thus national identity is not on an equal footing with, say, religion, or motherhood. Instead, it provides a kind of integrating structure for these and other identities, and it is this function that gives nations a distinctive normative status.

This objection achieves at best a pyrrhic victory for national self-determination. For if by an 'encompassing cultural group' one means a group that serves as the primary source of self-identification for individuals and that provides a coherent structure to unify and integrate whatever other self-identifications individuals may have, then we cannot assume that only nations are encompassing cultural groups. Membership in a religious group can and does play this same role for some individuals in cases in which it makes no sense to talk of the group as being a religious *nationalist* group or a religious *nation*. For some individuals their religion may serve as both their primary source of self-identification and a way to integrate and render coherent their other identifications (as fathers, daughters, professionals, etc.). Yet this 'encompassing' character of their religious community need not, and in most cases will not, be accompanied by either of the other two features that are supposed to distinguish nations from other cultural groups: the identification with a homeland and the aspiration for some form of self-government. For some Christians and for some Muslims (or Buddhists, etc.), their religion is an encompassing culture in this integrative sense, yet the idea of a religious homeland plays no role whatsoever in their religious identity. Similarly, while it may be true that to be an encompassing group a religious community must have some form of political authority over its members, this is not to say that its members aspire to, or that it must have, self-government in the sense relevant to nations, which includes some form of political authority over territory.

From a liberal standpoint, then, singling out nations for political self-determination is problematic for two reasons. First, it imposes as a matter of public judgment a rank-order among sources of allegiance and identification that is incompatible with equal respect for persons, given the fact of pluralism. And this is true even if what is said to be special about nations is that they provide unity and integration for, rather than compete with, the other identities that individuals may have. Second, it ignores the dynamic nature of pluralism, erecting barriers to changes in individuals' conceptions of the good and disadvantaging all the other potential sources of identification and allegiance that might become important for individuals were not nations given a position of privilege in the political order.

It is worth emphasizing that those who have been the most vigorous proponents of the view that nations as such have rights of self-determination have often held very strong and very illiberal beliefs about just how important nations are and about the permanence of their importance. In the heyday of nationalist fervor in the late nineteenth and early to middle twentieth centuries, especially in Germany and Italy, nationalist doctrine often included the assertion that allegiance to the nation *is* morally primary, because *nations* are morally primary.

The most extreme nationalists held that the individual, the family, the church, and so on all have value only insofar as they serve the life of the nation, understood as a kind of transgenerational super-subject. Moreover, their view of history did not allow the possibility that nationality would become less rather than more important, at least for the foreseeable future.[13] Few contemporary defenders of nationalist self-determination would wish to play these cards, at least not publicly.

If they are liberals to the extent of acknowledging the permanence and dynamic nature of pluralism and the moral primacy of equal respect for persons, proponents of national self-determination face a difficult task. They must show why nations – among all the various sources of allegiance and identification – deserve this very strong form of political recognition, and they must do so without deifying the nation at the expense of the other allegiances and identifications which individuals in a pluralistic society value and without denying the possibility that under liberal conditions whatever importance nationality has for some individuals may be reduced as other attachments become more significant for individuals.

There are two strategies for attempting to do so. The right of self-determination, understood as encompassing the right to self-government and the presumptive right to independent statehood, can be justified as a *basic* right or as a *derivative* right. As a basic right, at least in the liberal tradition, the right of self-determination for nations is said to be grounded in the special value that belonging to a nation has for individuals. In other words, the right of self-determination for nations is justified on the grounds that self-determination for nations directly promotes the autonomy or well-being of individuals. As a

---

13 Heinrich Gotthard von Treitschke, *Selection on Politics*, Adam Gowens, trans. (New York: Frederick Stoke's Co. 1900), 29-30

derivative right, the right of self-determination for nations is grounded in the ways in which this special political recognition for nations serves important moral-political values, in particular distributive justice and liberal democracy.

IV   The Case for National Self-Determination

As a basic right. Perhaps the clearest and most forceful contemporary exponents of the basic right approach to justifying a (nonremedial) right of national self-determination are Will Kymlicka, especially in his book *Multicultural Citizenship,* and Avishai Margalit and Joseph Raz in their article 'National Self-Determination.' Though there are significant differences, what Margalit and Raz have in common with Kymlicka is the view that the liberal emphasis on the moral primacy of individuals lends direct support to the principle that nations are entitled to self-government. Moreover, both Kymlicka and Margalit and Raz are committed to the second part of the Strong Thesis as well, that there is a presumption that nations have a right to full self-government and independent statehood.[14]

Kymlicka contends that cultural membership is a necessary condition for individual autonomy because one's culture provides a meaningful context for choice, and without a meaningful context for choice autonomy is impossible or at least valueless.[15] Jeremy Waldron has seriously challenged this contention. He argues that all that is necessary for meaningful choice and hence for individual autonomy is access to coherent cultural materials, which may originate in a number of different cultures. There is therefore no necessity for an individual to have access to a complete or whole culture, and *a fortiori* no need for her to maintain membership in her culture of origin.[16] Waldron's point is all

---

14 Kymlicka, *Multicultural Citizenship,* 27; Margalit and Raz, 'National Self-Determination,' 439-40

15 Kymlicka, *Multicultural Citizenship,* 50-1

16 Jeremy Waldron, 'Minority Rights and the Cosmopolitan Alternative,' *University of Michigan Journal of Law Reform* **25** (1992) 784-6

the more plausible if we assume that all individuals enjoy the standard liberal civil and political rights, including preeminently the rights to freedom of expression, religion, and association, and that they have access to a decent education and to a wide range of cultural goods, originating in various cultures, through some appropriate combination of private resources and public institutions such as libraries and art galleries.

Although I find Waldron's objection telling, I will not pursue it further here. Instead, I want to focus on a serious problem for Kymlicka's defense of national self-determination as a (nonremedial) basic right that arises if we grant his premise about the indispensability of cultural membership for individual autonomy. The problem is that Kymlicka has great difficulty explaining why only nations, among all the various types of cultural groups (religious, ethnic, political-ideological), are entitled to self-government, without relying on claims about remedial justice and without making exaggerated claims about the importance of nations for individual autonomy.

Recall that it is supposed to be membership in cultural groups, not just membership in those cultural groups that are nations, that is essential for meaningful choice and hence for individual autonomy. But if this is so, then, so far as meaningful choice and autonomy are concerned, either all cultural groups require self-government or those cultural groups that happen to be nations do not require it.

Kymlicka, of course, does not hold that all cultural groups require self-government. Instead, he believes that what he calls ethnic groups, as distinct from nations, only require various 'polyethnic rights,' which include minority language rights and special exemptions from legislation in deference to religious practices, and so on.[17] His argument for 'polyethnic rights' is straightforward: Because cultural membership is necessary for meaningful choice and hence for individual autonomy, justice (which ultimately comes down to the equality of persons as choosers of ends) requires these rights so that members of minority cultures will not be disadvantaged in having access to a meaningful context for choice.

---

17 Kymlicka, *Multicultural Citizenship*, 30-1 and 33

But if 'polyethnic rights,' which do not include rights of self-government, suffice for cultural groups that are not nations, why are they not sufficient for nations as well? Either 'polyethnic rights' protect a culture well enough so that it can supply a meaningful context for choice for its members or they do not. If they do, then why do any cultural groups, including nations, need rights of self-government in addition? If 'polyethnic' rights do not protect cultures well enough to provide a meaningful context for choice, then every cultural group must have self-government, and 'polyethnic rights' are simply a waste of time. This latter consequence Kymlicka rightly rejects. But he does not contend, and should not contend, that every cultural group must be self-governing.

Of course, there is one difference among various cultural groups that provides a principled reason for according some of them rights of self-government: Some were previously self-governing but lost their self-government through injustices. If, in the end, this is Kymlicka's only reason for ascribing rights of self-government to nations, then he does not endorse *national* self-determination as such; he is a remedial right theorist.

I have taken some pains to determine whether Kymlicka's emphasis on the importance of cultural membership for individual autonomy can provide a case for national self-determination because I believe its failure to do so is revealing. What is revealed is the difficulty of showing what, aside from remedial considerations, is so special about nations, among various groups, that entitles them to self-government and to a presumption of independent statehood.

The same conclusion emerges, I believe, if we examine Margalit and Raz's argument for national self-determination. Like Kymlicka, Margalit and Raz try to argue for national self-determination on liberal-individualist grounds, strictly eschewing any appeals to the nation as a moral subject in its own right. Their view is that in the case of nations the interests and self-respect of individuals are importantly bound up with the flourishing of the group and that the best protection for the interests and self-respect of individuals who belong to nations is that nations be self-governing.[18]

---

18 Margalit and Raz, 'National Self-Determination,' 448-9

Margalit and Raz are committed to the Stronger Thesis – that nations have a right, not just a presumption of a right, to independent statehood. However, they heavily qualify this supposed right: Nations only have the right to secede to form an independent state where their doing so does not 'endanger' the fundamental interests of those in the remainder state or of minorities in the new state. They do not, however, provide an account of what constitutes endangerment and which interests are fundamental. Because this broad qualification on the right to independent statehood is so unspecified and potentially so limiting, I shall proceed as if Margalit and Raz's view is equivalent to the Strong Thesis, that their reservations about the right to independent statehood can be expressed by saying that there is a presumption of a right to independent statehood for nations. If I can show that there is no such presumption of such a right, then *a fortiori* I will have shown that there is no right.

Margalit and Raz's argument faces the same difficulty as Kymlicka's: how to single out nations, among other cultural groups, as entitled to rights of self-government, without either devaluing those other groups or overstating the importance for individuals of belonging to nations. Suppose we grant Margalit and Raz's premise that the *best* protection for those interests of individuals that are served by belonging to a nation is for the nation to have its own state. That might be true as well for a number of other types of groups – religious, political-ideological, ethnic, and so on.

But even if it were true that it is only for nations that independent statehood provides the *best* protection, why is the *best* required? If the answer is that nations can only survive if they have their own state, this may be true of other groups as well. And even if it were true, and uniquely true, of nations that they require their own states in order to survive, we would still need an account of why the survival of *this* particular kind of cultural group – this particular focus of identification and allegiance – deserves this special protection.

Why should the survival of nations alone be guaranteed? The answer cannot be that nations are uniquely vital to individual interests and self-respect as Margalit and Raz seem to hold, since membership in other types of cultures or communities can do this also. To deny that they can is to inflate enormously the importance of nationality relative to all the other sources of allegiance, self-identification, and fulfillment in dynamically pluralistic societies. Liberalism, as opposed to the illiberal nationalist theories of old, simply cannot explain why individuals cannot achieve, and are mistaken to expect, fulfillment through other sources of identification and allegiance.

So far I have examined, and attempted to cast doubt upon, the claim that there is something about nations that makes belonging to them so important for individuals that nations have special rights to self-determination. I have argued that neither appeals to individual autonomy (Kymlicka) nor to self-respect and other interests that depend on how one's nation fares (Margalit and Raz) show that nations are so special as to deserve self-government in the absence of valid remedial claims. And I have also argued that unless some weighty reason for giving nations this special treatment is supplied, singling out nations as such for rights of self-government violates the principle of equal respect for persons, who, in a pluralistic society, will have a variety of identifications and allegiances, and divergent priorities among them.

As a derivative right. Now I shall examine the other main type of argument for national self-determination (understood according to the Strong Thesis, *not* as a claim about remedial rights). This second type of argument includes several variants, but the most famous is offered by Mill in *Considerations on Representative-Government* in a section entitled 'On Nationality.'[19] Unlike Kymlicka and Margalit and Raz, Mill does *not* argue that membership in a nation itself directly contributes to individuals' well-being and autonomy. Instead, he argues that democracy ('representative institutions') is essential for individual liberty and that democracy can only flourish where "the boundaries of governments ... coincide in the main with those of nationalities."[20] Mill's contention is that where there are two or more nations within the state, public opinion will lack the unity necessary for free political institutions to work.

Interestingly, Mill stops short of the conclusion that nations as such have a right of self-determination, including a right to their own independent state, even though his argument seems to require it. Perhaps he

---

19 John Stuart Mill, *Considerations on Representative Government*, Currin Shields, ed., (Indianapolis: Bobbs-Merrill, 1958), 229-37

20 Mill, *Considerations*, 232-3

did not think that every nation was entitled to a state – only the 'great' ones. Members of lesser nations (e.g., Bretons and Basques), he tells us, should be content to be absorbed into the great nations.[21]

This latter view, redolent with national chauvinism as it is, is no more easy to square with the liberal principle of equal respect for persons than would be the claim that members of minority religious sects should throw in their lot with large, well-organized, 'high-culture' religions. But it would probably be a mistake to assume that Mill thought that members of 'lesser' nations *ought* to assimilate into 'great' nations. Instead, it is more likely, given the pervasiveness at the time he was writing of views of human progress that were heavily influenced by social Darwinism, that he believed that it was *inevitable* that the 'lesser' nations would disappear. His point is that this is not to be lamented, even from the standpoint of the members of the 'lesser' nations, for they will gain by partaking of the 'greater' cultures.

Assuming that only a relatively few 'great' nations among all the nations of the earth will require their own state is wonderfully convenient for the proponent of rights of national self-determination. For this assumption takes much of the sting out of the Infeasibility Objection encountered earlier. If members of 'lesser' nations will bow to the inevitable and assimilate willingly into the 'greater' nations, then perhaps there will eventually be a harmonious world in which every nation has its own state, and representative institutions can flourish.

However, if we do not assume that the destruction or decline of minority nations is historically inevitable (or morally justifiable as a deliberate undertaking), the matter is not so neat and simple. We are faced with a painful dilemma: Either we must acknowledge that some nationalities will not have their own states, but will be submerged to create mono-national states so that democracy can flourish, or we must forgo progress toward democracy in the name of equal consideration for nations by recognizing the multinational character of most existing states.

The painfulness of this dilemma should lead us to question its premise more closely than Mill and his contemporary followers have

---

21 Mill, *Considerations*, 234

done. Is it in fact true that democratic institutions cannot flourish where the state contains more than one nation?

Those who doubt this generalization point to apparent exceptions: Canada, Belgium, and perhaps Switzerland (depending upon whether one thinks the latter is truly multinational or merely multi-ethnic). One might also add the United States, since a number of American Indian tribes have a legal status that approaches that of an independent state and at least approximate the common definition of nations as encompassing cultures associated with a particular territory. Of course, modern-day proponents of the Millian view would be quick to point out that the continued unity of Belgium and Canada is very much in doubt, and might also argue that the circumstances of American Indians are so anomalous as to not constitute a serious exception to the generalization that democracy cannot flourish in multinational states.

The best reply to the Millian argument, however, is not only to cite these apparent exceptions to its premise, but to point out that it is simply too early to tell whether the acknowledged presence of more than one nationality within the borders of the state will undermine democratic institutions. The lamentable fact is that until very recently there have been almost no serious attempts to develop democratic states that recognized a plurality of nations.

Given that we can no longer console ourselves, as Mill may have done, with the belief that the number of nations will conveniently diminish to the point at which it will be feasible to have only one nation per state, and given that general acceptance of the presumption that each nation must have its own state is therefore likely to perpetuate if not inflame existing conflicts, we had better have very good reason to believe Mill's generalization. If we do not, the more responsible course is to explore the possibilities for multinational democratic states more fully than has been done heretofore.

Recently David Miller has advanced a different argument for national self-determination as what I have called a derivative right. He holds that nations should have their own states because only nationality can provide the kind of unity that is required for success in achieving the redistribution of wealth that justice requires.[22]

---

22 Miller, *On Nationality*, 11

There are two serious objections to Miller's view. First, whether or not nationalism will facilitate or block large-scale redistributions of wealth will depend upon the character of the nationalism in question. As socialists from Marx onward have observed, the privileged minority has often been quite adept at appealing to nationalism to counteract the redistributive impulse. Second, even in cases where nationalist sentiment facilitates redistribution, one must ask: What *else* does it facilitate? Miller frequently appears to argue from the fact that a morally pristine sort of nationalism would facilitate worthy social goals (such as distributive justice) to the conclusion that nations *as such* ought to be accorded their own states. But of course, we have many historical instances in which the sort of nationalist unity that Miller assumes will be harnessed for the pursuit of justice is in fact ferociously directed toward conquest and against non-nationals and dissenting members of the nation itself.

Whether one believes this risk is worth taking will depend upon two factors: how great the risk is – and this will depend upon how dangerous one thinks states tend to be when they are empowered by a deeply motivated and highly unified majority – and how ambitious the demands of distributive justice are. Lord Acton, among other liberals, was deeply impressed by the risks of abuse of power in mono-national states and less convinced than Miller that distributive justice is so demanding that it cannot be adequately approximated without harnessing the motivational power of a single nationality for all citizens. Indeed, he believed that the presence of more than one nationality within the state was desirable because it impeded the formation of such a high degree of political unity as to confer dangerous powers on the state.[23]

Once we acknowledge that nationalism (rather than some varieties of it) has no particular penchant for distributive justice, that it has in fact often been used to block redistribution, and that the political unity nationalism achieves can be and often is used for quite different and in some cases downright evil purposes, the second argument for national

---

23 Lord Acton, 'Nationalism,' in J. Figgis and R. Laurence, eds., *The History of Freedom and Other Essays* (London: MacMillan 1922), 285-90

self-determination as a derivative right appears to be far from compelling. It does not seem strong enough to rebut the combined weight of the Infeasibility and Equal Respect objections to the Strong Thesis.

V Conclusions

I have argued that, at least from a broadly liberal perspective, nations as such have neither rights to self-government nor a presumptive right to independent statehood. My strategy was to start with two powerful arguments against rights of national self-determination, the Infeasibility Objection and the Equal Respect Objection, and then examine two influential arguments in favour of rights of national self-determination, one which presents these rights as grounded directly in the value for individuals of membership in nations, and another which holds that national self-determination furthers the attainment of distributive justice and the functioning of democracy.

I have argued that unless contemporary liberals are willing to embrace two repugnant and eminently illiberal tenets associated with the least respectable forms of nineteenth-century liberalism, neither type of argument for the rights of self-determination for nations as such can succeed. The first of these illiberal tenets is that nations have a unique moral status such that other cultures and communities, as well as individual autonomy, ought to be subordinated to the nation; the second is that the principle that every nation ought to have its own state is practicable because the 'lesser' nations will be weeded out or assimilated into the 'greater' through an inevitable process of consolidation.

Unless the first of these tenets, or something very like it, is adopted, it is not possible to show, using liberal premises, that nations are so especially important for individual well-being and autonomy that nations as such have rights of self-determination. Unless the second tenet is adopted, acceptance of the principle that nations as such have a presumptive right to independent statehood would most likely help perpetuate if not exacerbate unacceptable levels of nationalist conflict, owing to the intermingling of nations, the sheer number of nations, and the utter lack of an international institutional mechanism for peacefully allocating territories to nations.

In addition, I have suggested that much of the intuitive appeal of the idea of national self-determination may result from a confusion between remedial and nonremedial rights of national self-determination. The former have much intuitive appeal, resting as they do on relatively uncontroversial notions of rectificatory justice. Moreover, remedial rights of self-determination for those groups that happen to be nations can be advanced without exaggerating the importance of nations to individuals and without ignoring the dangerous impracticality of encouraging each nation to have its own state by indulging in social Darwinist fantasies about national consolidation.

I would like to stress that I have *not* argued that nations do not have rights of self-determination; only that nations *as such* do not. I believe that nations often do have remedial rights of self-determination. Furthermore, although I have argued against the view that nations as such have a right to secede, I do not wish to deny that nations can, through negotiation, come to have rights to secede, even in the absence of the sorts of grievances that ground a remedial right to secede. There may in fact be cases in which the members of one nation morally ought to agree to the aspirations of another nation for independent statehood, and my personal opinion is that this is true in Canada and in Belgium. But whether the Québécois or the Flemish have a right to secede simply by virtue of being nations is something I doubt.

Finally, nothing I have said in this paper is inconsistent with there being constitutional arrangements which confer *legal* rights of self-determination, including the right to secede, upon nations. The particular circumstances of a given multinational state might make it not only wise but necessary to guarantee such rights of self-determination to minority nations. (In fact, this was done in the 1993 Ethiopian Constitution.) My point is that whether legal rights of self-determination ought to be accorded to a nation or nations will depend upon the particular features of the case, not upon the mere fact that the group or groups in question are nations. In sum, I have not argued against secession by nations, only against the idea that nations as such, in the absence of remedial grounds and without negotiated agreements or constitutional provisions, have the right to secede.

There are many reasons why particular groups ought to have legal rights of self-determination short of the right to independent statehood – from various rights of self-government to special rights of representation in central legislative bodies. In some cases such rights of self-determination will be justified as a way of achieving efficiencies that are not available in centralized regimes. In other cases, conferring rights of self-determination on minority groups will enhance democratic participation. Often these and other reasons in favour of legal rights of self-determination will apply with particular force to the case of groups that are nations. But this is not to say that it is by virtue of their being nations that these groups ought to have these rights of self-determination or that only nations ought to have them.

CANADIAN JOURNAL OF PHILOSOPHY
Supplementary Volume 22

The Nation-State as a Political Community: A Critique of the Communitarian Argument for National Self-Determination

OMAR DAHBOUR
Colorado State University

The principle of national self-determination has usually been justified by extending to national groups an entitlement that individuals are regarded as having, namely, to the conditions necessary for their self-development. In order to extend the concept of self-determination to nations in this way, an argument that it is important for nations to exist within their own political communities must be given. In this essay, I describe and criticize one type of argument for such a principle of national self-determination – what I will call the communitarian argument.

Contemporary communitarians (such as Michael Walzer and David Miller) usually contend that determining who rightfully has membership in a political community must precede the allocation of rights and responsibilities between members.[1] Community is understood to mean a national community; membership in communities therefore results from the ascription of national identities to individuals and to the consequent sorting out of loyalties that follows from this ascription. A right of self-determination for nations is required, on this view, in order to

---

1 The relevant writings of Miller and Walzer will be cited below. While Miller openly acknowledges his political philosophy to be communitarian, Walzer is somewhat more circumspect. He seems to view communitarianism as a supplementary theory to liberalism; nevertheless, he sees liberalism as requiring 'periodic communitarian correction.' See David Miller, *Market, State, and Community: Theoretical Foundations of Market Socialism* (Oxford: Oxford University Press 1989), ch. 9, and Michael Walzer, 'The Communitarian Critique of Liberalism,' *Political Theory* **18:1** (Feb. 1990) 21.

ensure that political communities are legitimately formed in accordance with national identities.

In this essay, I do not contest the idea that community is a positive good independent of and conceptually prior to norms of justice or rights. But I contend that communitarians are wrong to regard nation-states as the most legitimate form of political community. This is the case for three reasons: (1) national identities cannot serve as the legitimate basis for political life, (2) assertions of national rights are disruptive of relations between different peoples and states, and (3) nation-states do not ensure the real conditions for self-determination. I conclude by suggesting that an idea drawn from theories of urban and environmental planning – that of ecological regions – provides a conception of community that avoids the problems of the nation-state while still embodying a robust notion of communal life. National identities are not, therefore, an adequate foundation for political community, and a principle of national self-determination cannot accordingly be justified on communitarian grounds.

I Definitions and Justifications

The *principle of political self-determination* can be defined as *the right of a person or group of persons to participate in decisions made by the government that exercises authority over them.* National self-determination is the application of this idea to nations. Nations themselves are to be understood as distinct from states. A *nation*, strictly defined, is *a group of people who believe they share, or are believed by others to share, a common kinship or ethnicity,* whether or not they also share citizenship in any particular state.[2] The *principle of national self-determination* therefore constitutes *the right of nations to govern themselves* – that is, to be ruled by states of their own.

It is important to distinguish this idea from political self-determination as such – that is, the idea that people have a right to some participation in political life. The principle of national self-determi-

---

2 This definition is loosely based on the one given by Walker Connor in his book, *Ethnonationalism: The Quest for Understanding* (Princeton, NJ: Princeton University Press 1994), xi.

nation is indistinguishable from such a concept unless there is a difference of some kind between nations and states. Otherwise, self-determination for a nation would simply mean self-government for the persons who are already citizens of a particular state. To maintain a distinct concept of national self-determination, nations must already be thought to be communities in some sense prior to their claim to or attainment of statehood.

Thus, nations cannot simply be 'nationalities' in the sense of persons affiliated by citizenship in an already existing state. For instance, those who are citizens of Canada or India would not necessarily constitute a Canadian or Indian nation. Only if there was some prior specification of membership in these nations (e.g., of language or ethnicity), and all those who were citizens fit this specification, would they then be equivalent.

It would be more appropriate to call nations 'communities of character';[3] and it is the fate of these communities – rather than the right of people to engage in political life – that is at stake in discussions of national self-determination. One thing that this form of self-determination amounts to in practice is the right to specify that the conditions of citizenship in a state are to be restricted to those who have a particular national identity.

But this requires further consideration of what constitutes a national identity. A *national identity* may be defined as a *set of personal characteristics ascribed to individuals denoting their kinship, ancestry, or origins*. To reiterate the definition of a nation given above, nations are 'ascriptive groups' – groups comprising all those to whom a particular (national) identity has been ascribed.

When nations are understood in this way, it is easier to see the difference between nations and the citizenries of states. The ascription of national identities is a process by which we "are defined in relation to how others identify us, and they do so in terms of groups which are

---

3 This term originated in Otto Bauer, *Die Nationalitätenfrage und die Sozialdemokratie* (Wien: Wiener Volksbuchhandlung 1907); excerpted in Tom Bottomore and Patrick Goode, eds., *Austro-Marxism* (Oxford: Clarendon Press 1978), and has been used by Walzer, among others; see, Michael Walzer, *Spheres of Justice: A Defense of Pluralism and Equality* (New York: Basic Books 1983), 62.

always already associated with specific attributes, stereotypes, and norms...."[4] Thus, nations are formed by processes of group and individual identification which are *in theory* prior to political choices or acts that individuals might take. Nations are not constituted by individual choices to enter into political associations, but by the ascription of identities to persons by others.

II Individualism, Communitarianism, Nationalism

To the extent that a principle of self-determination is applied to collective entities such as national groups, a break must be made with the strain of individualism that has been dominant in political philosophy since the development of social contract theory.[5] This is not to say, however, that national self-determination cannot be given an individualist justification.

There are two ways in which this has been done: (1) by maintaining that a principle of self-determination for national groups is beneficial to individuals as members of these groups, and (2) by arguing that national self-determination constitutes a means of democratically determining who rightfully has membership in which political associations.[6] In the first case, the idea that nation-states are beneficial to

---

4 Iris Marion Young, *Justice and the Politics of Difference* (Princeton, NJ: Princeton University Press 1990), 46

5 The classic discussion of individualist political philosophy is found in C.B. MacPherson, *The Political Theory of Possessive Individualism: Hobbes to Locke* (Oxford: Oxford University Press 1962); see also the various writings of Charles Taylor, particularly the essays in his *Philosophical Papers, 2: Philosophy and the Human Sciences* (Cambridge: Cambridge University Press 1985).

6 Charles Taylor, in 'Why Do Nations Have to Become States?' in Stanley G. French, ed., *Philosophers Look at Canadian Confederation* (Montreal: Canadian Philosophical Association 1979), 41, distinguishes several types of argument for a principle of national self-determination based on individualist ideas of rights, welfare, or self-government. But he sees the 'communitarian' argument (from the espousal of national identity) as a 'deeper' justification based on a questioning of personal identities (44-45). For another perspective on the different types of justification for a principle of national self-determination, see Omar Dahbour,

individuals relies on a perfectionist conception of well-being that values membership in national groups.[7] In the second case, the contention that national self-determination is an extension of a right to political self-rule depends on a libertarian view of democratic rights that regards national groups' consent to membership in a state as an essential part of democratic legitimacy.[8]

While the philosophical basis for both of these justifications is individualist, the arguments ultimately depend on communitarian assumptions about the importance of national identities and the necessity of nation-states for their realization. In particular, these assumptions are: first, that nations have a reality independent of their existence within particular states, and second, that national identities, as important features of a full human existence, need states to ensure their flourishing. Neither belief, however, can be easily demonstrated on individualist premises, while both are central to the case for national self-determination that has been made by 'political' communitarians.[9]

'A Critique of National Self-Determination' (PhD dissertation, City University of New York, 1995).

7 See Joseph Raz, *The Morality of Freedom* (Oxford: Clarendon Press, 1986), and Avishai Margalit and Joseph Raz, 'National Self-Determination,' *Journal of Philosophy* **87** (Sept. 1990) 439-61; see also Yael Tamir, 'The Right to National Self-Determination,' *Social Research* **58:3** (Fall 1991), and *Liberal Nationalism* (Princeton, NJ: Princeton University Press 1993).

8 See Harry Beran, *The Consent Theory of Political Obligation* (London: Croom Helm, 1987), as well as Harry Beran, 'Self-Determination: A Philosophical Perspective,' in W. J. Allan Macartney, ed., *Self-Determination in the Commonwealth* (Aberdeen: Aberdeen University Press 1988); see also, e.g., David Copp, 'Do Nations Have the Right of Self-Determination?' in French, *Philosophers Look at Canadian Confederation*. It ought to be mentioned that the libertarianism of this approach tends to be unacknowledged.

9 The reasons that individualist concepts of self-determination cannot justify these assumptions are too involved to summarize here; see Dahbour, 'Critique of National Self-Determination,' esp. chs. 2 & 3. This paper is concerned with the 'political' communitarians – David Miller and Michael Walzer – rather than 'moral' communitarians such as Alasdair MacIntyre and Michael Sandel (and, to some extent, Charles Taylor). On this distinction, see Walzer, 'Communitarian Critique of Liberalism,' 21, where the latter are characterized as concerned with

The development of a theory of political communitarianism is an important part of the contemporary revival of interest in the idea of community. This idea is one that, with the rise of social contract theory, has tended to be displaced by a focus on the bases of social trust or agreement between self-interested individuals. Individualists from Hobbes to Rawls have largely accepted the seeming incommensurability of personal goals and have sought some way of reconciling them without specifying particular values or identities that should underlie a legitimate political community.

In contrast, the fundamental claim of political communitarians is that a social contract between self-interested individuals cannot adequately characterize what it means to establish a political community – that it fails to explain the background assumptions or common identities that enable individuals to assume the minimal trust necessary for establishing mutual relations. Instead, communitarians have devoted attention to defining the prepolitical basis of political community.

On their view, political community cannot be defined without either a particular account of what constitutes the good life or the ascription of a communal identity to particular groups. What are crucial here are the reasons that individuals come to feel obligations to others. While individualists commonly rely on a notion of rational self-interest to explain the possibility of obligation, communitarians maintain that a more deep-rooted identification with other persons is necessary before obligations can obtain.

The political expression of this distinction is the difference between a view of community as based on individual consent to a social contract or political regime and one in which a common identity underlies any feeling of trust or obligation. Miller makes this point by arguing that it is 'identity' (of groups, and by extension, of individuals) rather than 'will' that is important in defining the nature of communities (and specifically, of national communities).[10]

---

the 'constitution of the self' while the former seek to theorize the 'connection of constituted selves.'

10 David Miller, 'In Defence of Nationality,' *Journal of Applied Philosophy* **10** (1993) 12

The main concern of communitarians in stressing the importance of political community is the need to find a basis for solidarity in modern societies.[11] In a world of territorial states, every community must, on this view, confront the problem of how to mobilize its members to fulfill duties to other members or to protect the community as a whole. The nation-state is regarded as the best means of solving this problem.

Such a view of the importance and role of nationality in ensuring the solidarity of people within a state can be regarded as communitarian inasmuch as it focuses on the connection between a nationality as an already existing community and the state as the political means of expressing the identity and interests of that community. Communitarians argue that political communities cannot be constituted solely on the basis of voluntary association – that something more is required for communities to cohere in a morally satisfactory way.

From this perspective, existing communities inevitably constitute the context within which society rightfully grants rights or goods to its members. But such communities – generally conceived to be nations – can only flourish if their identities are accorded due recognition. This is why nations must have the right to obtain their own states, for this is the best way to ensure such recognition.[12]

The nation-state, as a number of scholars have argued, is the conception of political community inherent in modern society.[13] While political action has thus seemed to impose the nation-state as the in-

---

11 Miller, 'In Defence of Nationality,' 9

12 The basic case for a communitarian approach to social justice and human rights is made by Taylor in his articles, 'Atomism' and 'What's Wrong with Negative Liberty,' both in *Philosophy and the Human Sciences*, and by Walzer in his book, *Spheres of Justice*. The case for a socialist communitarianism is made by Miller in his article, 'In What Sense Must Socialism Be Communitarian?' *Social Philosophy and Policy* 6 (1988-89) 51-73.

13 See, e.g., Ronald Beiner, *What's the Matter with Liberalism?* (Berkeley: University of California Press 1992), 123; Ross Poole, *Morality and Modernity* (London: Routledge 1991), ch. 5; Tamir, *Liberal Nationalism*, ch. 6; and Anthony Giddens, *A Contemporary Critique of Historical Materialism*, 2: *The Nation-State and Violence* (Berkeley: University of California Press 1987).

evitable context for all modern political theories, communitarians at least have the virtue of being aware of the necessity for specifying a normative conception of the nation-state as a political community.[14] If they are to generate a conception of community (rather than merely the *need* for a conception of community), the nation-state seems the obvious choice. And to the extent that it is seen as embodying the essential nature of political community, the claim that the principle of national self-determination ensures the 'communal autonomy' necessary for communities to flourish is justifiable.[15]

The connection between communitarianism and nationalism (whether as a concept of community or as a principle of self-determination) seems to be the necessity, in both theories, of positing community as a basic good of some kind. As previously indicated, this is what distinguishes a communitarian argument for national self-determination from individualist ones. But even if the good of community is taken as a first premise, one is still left with the task of arguing that nations are the best manifestations of community. Nevertheless, the case for national self-determination seems to be more easily made from a communitarian position.

There are, however, two views that are skeptical about the purported affinity of communitarianism with nationalism. One view is that a conception of community can in fact be derived from individualist premises. This idea is sometimes put in terms of a theory of 'civic

---

14 Poole, *Morality and Modernity*, 105; Tamir, *Liberal Nationalism*, 139. Both Poole and Tamir make the important point that the nation-state is the largely unacknowledged form of community implied in individualist accounts of supposedly universal conceptions of justice or rights. It remains unacknowledged because a privileging of national affinities seems to violate the fundamental individualist commitment to neutrality with respect to conceptions of the good life. Despite this, attempts to derive a universalistic account of distributive justice necessarily presuppose particular territorial states within which distributions take place. But if, as Poole and Tamir contentiously maintain, the nation-state is the only form that such territorial states can (currently) take, then even universalistic theories must implicitly assume their legitimacy.

15 Michael Walzer, *Just and Unjust Wars: A Moral Argument with Historical Illustrations* (New York: Basic Books 1977), 90

republicanism.'[16] In any case, the argument is that individualism requires a stronger conception of community than 'universalistic' theories of justice have generally allowed. But this does not mean that this stronger conception involves fundamentally different principles of political legitimacy (such as the assertion of the independent value of community).

The limitations of this approach can be seen in the claim of, e.g., Andrew Mason, that, "Although it is perhaps plausible to regard mutual concern as partially constitutive of the good life for everyone ... [it] is difficult to see how the view that community membership is an essential ingredient of the good life can be defended...."[17] On the individualist account, community can therefore be seen as *a* good, but not as *the* fundamental good with which other political norms are to be reconciled. So, while individualism might be able to generate a justification for community as an elective virtue, it does not seem to be able

---

16 On civic republicanism generally, see Adrian Oldfield, *Citizenship and Community: Civic Republicanism and the Modern World* (London: Routledge 1990); and on the problem of finding a realizable concept of what he calls 'civic identity,' see Ronald Beiner, 'Why Citizenship Constitutes a Theoretical Problem in the Last Decade of the Twentieth Century,' in Ronald Beiner, ed., *Theorizing Citizenship* (Albany: State University of New York Press 1995), and Beiner, *What's the Matter with Liberalism?*, passim. Walzer points to a limitation of civic republicanism when he writes that, "A revival of neoclassical republicanism provides much of the substance of contemporary communitarian politics.... [But] there are virtually no examples of republican association and no movement or party aimed at promoting such association" ('Communitarian Critique of Liberalism,' 19). The recent work of Stephen Macedo seems designed to answer – at least in the realm of theory – Walzer's charge against civic republicanism by arguing that 'liberal constitutionalism' does in fact embody substantive civic values. As Macedo writes, "Communitarian values are implicit in the idea of a pluralistic community governed properly by liberal justice" (*Liberal Virtues: Citizenship, Virtue, and Community in Liberal Constitutionalism* [Oxford: Clarendon Press 1990], 203). I cannot deal further with this controversy here other than to say that Macedo does not seem to separate the problem of how to define the conditions of membership in a community – whether on grounds of national identity or in some other way – from the question of the values that underlie the constitution of a state.

17 Andrew Mason, 'Liberalism and the Value of Community,' *Canadian Journal of Philosophy* **22** (June 1993) 232

to justify a conception of community in the strong sense that would yield, for instance, a principle of national self-determination.

A different view of the relation of nationalism to communitarianism is held by Will Kymlicka, who argues that the nation-state is *in*compatible with communitarianism, since the latter emphasizes the need for shared *moral* values, which can only be found within *sub*national communities, not entire nations.[18] While this may be true, it does not necessarily contradict the communitarian idea that in order to constitute a *political* community a particular national character is required. National identities, Kymlicka admits, "must be taken as givens";[19] yet, if this is so, these identities are equivalent to 'national characters' that do embody common *political* or public virtues, values, or goods which can serve as the basis for political institutions. The theory of political communitarianism and the institution of the nation-state do therefore seem to be closely connected.

Before considering the specific communitarian argument for national self-determination, it is worth noting that it shades imperceptibly into a case for the inevitability and desirability of the nation-state. On the one hand, this is because the communitarian argument accords no particular importance to rights-claims as such. Rights are invoked – to the extent that they are invoked at all – when they are warranted by the intentions or desires of a community. But then the rights are only a kind of name for those (justifiable) intentions.[20]

On the other hand, once the communitarian definition of a nation is accepted, the idea of self-determination for nations follows inexorably. For instance, Walzer defines a nation as "a historic community, connected to a meaningful place, enacting and revising a way of life, *aim-*

---

18 Will Kymlicka, *Multicultural Citizenship: A Liberal Theory of Minority Rights* (Oxford: Clarendon Press 1995), 92-93

19 Kymlicka, *Multicultural Citizenship*, 184-5

20 The communitarian view of rights is expressed, e.g., by Walzer (in *Spheres of Justice*, 153), when he states that rights (at least some of them) are not 'natural or human rights' but are "derived from the social meaning of offices and careers and vindicated in the course of long political struggles." But the case for the second-order character of rights (that is, as dependent on the values of a given political community) is more often assumed than argued for by communitarians.

ing at political or cultural self-determination...."[21] By defining nations in this way, the need for a distinct argument for a right of self-determination is avoided; the work has already been done in the act of definition. As Miller writes, "the thesis that a nation should want its own state is at one level tautological, since the ambition to be politically self-determining is built in to the very idea of nationhood."[22]

III The Communitarian Argument for National Self-Determination

The communitarian justification of a national right of self-determination has two aspects; one concerns the importance of nations for establishing the legitimacy of states and the other concerns the necessity of nations in ensuring solidarity within states.[23] Both result in the affirmation of a principle of self-determination for national groups.

In arguing, first, that nations are the necessary foundation of political legitimacy, communitarians must define nations as being distinct from the populations of already existing states. Walzer, for instance, maintains that nations "share a wide range of cultural artifacts" – including a 'sense of place' – that generate the feeling of being a distinct nationality. The result of this common identification is that an "emergent nation-state ... can be viewed by its members as an appropriate and already familiar framework for the exercise of autonomy and the formation of attachments."[24] A political right of self-determination for nations is generated, in the manner mentioned

---

21 Michael Walzer, 'Nation and Universe' (Tanner Lectures on Human Values, Oxford University, May 1989), 554 (italics added)

22 David Miller, *On Nationality* (Oxford: Clarendon Press 1995), 90

23 These two aspects will be dealt with here by focusing, in the first case, on Walzer's argument for national self-determination, particularly in his books, *Just and Unjust Wars* and *Spheres of Justice*, and in his 1989 Tanner Lectures, 'Nation and Universe,' and in the second case, on Miller's argument, particularly in his recent book, *On Nationality*.

24 Walzer, 'Nation and Universe,' 538

above, from this very national identity, since nations, by adopting particular ways of life in particular places, inevitably seek independence.

This connection of a community to a place is what enables Walzer to argue for the importance of territory in establishing communities. It is certainly the case that nationalities are sometimes tied more or less closely to regions, lands, or territories. But Walzer goes beyond this truism. The fit of nations and lands is much closer; fundamentally, nations are defined as those communities that *already* have countries (in the geographical sense) of their own: "Nations look for countries because in some deep sense they already have countries: the link between people and land is a crucial feature of national identity."[25]

Of course, the sense in which nations already have countries is that of their cultural affinity with a place; the political problem still to be settled is the means by which a nation could come to govern a territory encompassing this country. Emphasizing this close link between nations and lands means that a major reorganization of boundaries and territories may be warranted. This is because it is only the correspondence of boundaries with nations that establishes the legitimacy of states existing within those boundaries: "It is the coming together of a people that establishes the integrity of a territory."[26] Absent this 'coming together,' boundaries and territories are apportioned to states and rulers by contingent historical events, without any rights necessarily following from them.

This view of political community implies that nations are entitled to protect their communal integrity by whatever means are necessary – particularly by establishing independent states of their own. Only then can nations create the conditions under which they can live out their own understanding of what constitutes the good life. Furthermore, only by maintaining control over the entry and exit of people into a community can such a life be cultivated.

For instance, the achievement of any degree of social justice requires the ability to set limits to the scope of mutual obligations, limits be-

25 Walzer, *Spheres of Justice*, 44

26 Walzer, *Just and Unjust Wars*, 57

yond which communities cannot be expected to have responsibilities.[27] This is what Walzer means by the primacy of 'membership' – the fact that in a world of territorial states, claims for justice have a necessarily limited scope. Political wisdom consists in accepting this and making the best of it.[28]

In determining what goods there are and how they ought to be distributed, therefore, the first good to be distributed is that of membership itself.[29] Once they possess citizenship, individuals may claim other goods. But the first matter to be settled is whether such individuals are, or can plausibly claim to be, members of the nation at all. On this view, only if nations have the means to determine and then enforce decisions about membership can they be assured that their communities and ways of life will be secure.

This is why, according to communitarians, nations can legitimately claim a right of self-determination. In claiming self-determination, nations assert their right to determine their own boundaries, as well as the citizenship requirements that obtain within them. Both are designed to protect the autonomy and integrity of nations from their domination or dilution by other states or groups.

A right of nations to possess the territory that constitutes their homelands implies that state boundaries are an important means for protecting the autonomy that nations require. Sovereignty is constituted principally by secure state boundaries. But how are the boundaries determined? Walzer admits that, while some boundaries are necessary for a nation's self-determination to be assured, where the boundaries should be is not a matter that is easily settled.[30] He maintains that a partial solution may be found by a presumption in favor of separatism

---

27 This is what Miller calls the basis of a 'universalist case for nationality' – the need for delimited communities within which redistributions of goods in favor of greater equality can be mandated. See David Miller, 'The Ethical Significance of Nationality,' *Ethics* **98** (July 1988) 661.

28 Walzer, *Spheres of Justice*, 31

29 Walzer, *Spheres of Justice*, 31

30 Walzer, 'Nation and Universe,' 554-5

and partition, other things being equal.[31] Yet, political independence is not always the best outcome for ensuring the continued existence of national groups.[32] Nevertheless, whenever separatism is popularly supported by a national group, it is prima facie warranted.

Once the boundaries of a state have been determined, the question of who is entitled to citizenship arises. It is axiomatic on the nationalist view that since, in Walzer's words, "There is no easy way to avoid the country (and the proliferation of countries) as we currently know it,"[33] this question can only be answered by nation-states themselves. Without a right of 'admission and refusal,' no nation could maintain its national identity in the face of migrations and other changes in population. So nation-states must determine their own conditions of membership, including the circumstances warranting exclusion or expulsion of non-nationals. As Walzer puts it, "The distribution of membership is *not* pervasively subject to the constraints of justice ... states are simply free to take in strangers (or not)...."[34]

Are there limits or restraints on the rights of nations to determine the boundaries of their territory and the characteristics of their members, on the communitarian view? Certainly there are no limits severe enough to override the right of self-determination itself. The rights of nations are not abrogated because a nation might abuse such a right by claiming too much territory or excluding too many people.[35] In settling national disputes over territory or people, there is not only a presumption of the justifiability of separation – that is, the separation of nations from one another into nation-states wherever possible. A ready means – that of (further) partition of land – is also available for the settlement of disputes that still may arise.[36] In both cases, the

---

31 Michael Walzer, 'The New Tribalism: Notes on a Difficult Problem,' *Dissent* (Spring 1992), 169

32 Walzer, 'Nation and Universe,' 554-5

33 Walzer, *Spheres of Justice*, 44

34 Walzer, *Spheres of Justice*, 61-62 (italics added)

35 Walzer, 'Nation and Universe,' 519

36 Walzer, 'Nation and Universe,' 548

communitarian view is that it is better that nations separate from one another, or that they partition disputed lands into separable entities. Only in this way can national communities maintain their integrity.

But *which* nations may legitimately claim states? After all, many nations have never had states, and others might be too small, weak, fragmented, or dependent to warrant a claim to sovereignty. Walzer, however, argues for the maximum possible extension of the principle of national self-determination. Not only should it apply to 'captive' nations that at one time possessed sovereignty, but it should also apply to nations that 'ought to have been independent.'[37]

The first part of the communitarian argument for national self-determination, therefore, starts with the idea that a nation is entitled to a state on the condition that it demonstrates its identity as a distinct community based on a common land and ancestry. If this is the case, then a nation may justifiably claim that it has a right of self-determination; furthermore, it is entitled to take whatever actions are necessary to establish a nation-state, ensure its sovereignty in relation to other states, and enforce citizenship policies that will guarantee the continuation of its distinct national identity. It follows from this contention that states are fully legitimate only when they are in turn based on nations which have attained this consciousness of their own existence and rights.

The second aspect of the communitarian argument builds on the claim that nations are not only the most legitimate form of political community, but in fact "are the only possible form in which overall community can be realized in modern societies."[38] One important consequence of this supposed fact about modern political life is that the self-determination of nations is mandated by the need for communal and solidaristic relations.[39] It is only when states embrace a national community that they can embody 'trust' across society (and particularly, among different social classes).[40]

---

37 Walzer, 'New Tribalism,' 166

38 Miller, *Market, State, and Community*, 245

39 Miller, *On Nationality*, 11

40 Miller, *On Nationality*, 90

The reason for this is that nations are 'ethical communities' in a way that transnational groupings – not to speak of the human race as a whole – are not. It is an inevitable feature of modern politics that we feel that we have duties to other members of our national group that we do not have to others.[41]

This feeling is rooted to a substantial degree in 'prior obligations of nationality' – obligations that obtain prior to those that may arise between citizens of states. It is, in fact, only when these latter obligations are congruent with already existing sentiments of national solidarity that, generally speaking, they are politically actionable.[42]

The effects of this disjunction are felt in two different domains of contemporary politics. First, the basis of specifically political trust in democratic political processes must be founded upon the faith that there are potential grounds for agreement among citizens. In modern states, it is only a common nationality that makes this 'sense of solidarity' possible.[43] Second, in attempts to use the state to ensure a measure of social justice, particularly through redistributive taxation or welfare policies, it is only when such policies can be conceived to be national – that is, designed to better a national community within which some sense of obligation *already* obtains – that they have a possibility of acceptance and success.[44]

The proper fit between nations and states – something which the principle of national self-determination is designed to ensure – is thus essential in strengthening sentiments and institutions of democratic legitimation and redistributive justice without which modern societies are increasingly vulnerable to domination by political elites and exploitation by the global market.[45] Nations require self-determination because states "with strong national identities and without internal

---

41 Miller, *On Nationality*, 11

42 Miller, *On Nationality*, 72

43 Miller, *On Nationality*, 98

44 Miller, *On Nationality*, 93

45 Miller, *On Nationality*, 187

communal divisions" are more successful in achieving social justice within their borders.[46]

IV National Identity versus Political Legitimacy

The key to determining whether nations must form the basis for the legitimacy of states – and therefore that national self-determination is an important principle of political life – lies in examining the relation of political to nonpolitical identities in the formation of states. The idea that a community must be based upon some underlying conceptions or ideas that are shared by its members is a commonplace of political philosophy. But the extent to which a political community must be rooted in nonpolitical ideas or meanings that are held in common by members of the community is what is at issue. The communitarian view is that political communities must also be national communities (in some distinct sense) in order to obtain the minimal amount of agreement that ensures a commonality of purpose. This view challenges the belief of philosophers such as Rawls who have argued that only the most minimal agreement on specifically political matters (such as constitutionally guaranteed rights or rules of democratic procedure) is needed for a political community to cohere.[47]

But while political individualism does not provide a satisfactory account of why political communities should take the forms that they do (i.e., particular territorial states), the communitarian view is flawed in not recognizing what makes political identities distinct from national identities. While political identities may have antecedents in nonpolitical forms of life, they cannot be simply the expressions of those forms of life, for the reason that this would rid them of exactly that feature that makes them 'political' – their formation through acts of choosing, deciding, associating, and so on. Our political identity is constituted by choosing to see ourselves in certain ways, not by accepting

---

46 Miller, *On Nationality*, 96

47 John Rawls, 'The Domain of the Political and Overlapping Consensus,' *New York University Law Review* **64** (1989) 235

or acquiescing in a pregiven identity formed by custom or prejudice. And it is this associative aspect of political identity that enables political communities to attain cohesion and solidarity.[48]

Nationalists might argue that this emphasis on choice or commitment in the formation of political communities is precisely the function of principles such as self-determination – to give shape and expression to the political commitments of a national group seeking its own state. But this idea actually exists in some tension with the communitarian version of nationalism, since it is an important part of this theory that, as Miller writes, "nations *really* exist [and] identifying with a nation, feeling yourself *inextricably* part of it, is a legitimate way of understanding your place in the world."[49]

However, while nations may initially be formed from a putative ethnic identity, Miller also wants to argue that "nationality becomes a self-defeating idea if it is not accommodating" – i.e., if it does not grow to include different peoples within a given territory.[50] But defeat is only assured if nations are unwilling to take the harsh steps necessary to secure their national homelands – steps (from restrictive immigration laws to 'ethnic cleansing') that may strike some as unjust but that are nevertheless not proscribed by a principle of self-determination. If nations are 'real,' then they will not be able to accommodate – except at the cost of weakening their own identity – non-nationals within a political community. But if they are not real in this sense, then there is no mandate for a principle of self-determination that distinguishes nations from whatever peoples happen to live in existing states.

So not only do nations actually exist on the communitarian view, but they must exist, at least to some extent, prior to political action (including claims to self-determination). This has to be the case even if nations do tend, by their nature, to seek states of their own. What has come to be called the primordialist theory of nationality – the idea that national identities have deep roots in historically ancient, or 'primor-

---

48 Oldfield, *Citizenship and Community*, 7

49 Miller, *On Nationality*, 10-11 (italics added)

50 Miller, *On Nationality*, 92

dial,' circumstances – is assumed in the communitarian account.[51] Even when, as in Miller's view, nations are defined by common beliefs, historical 'continuities,' and 'national characters,' rather than ethnic origins per se, these must have their sources in *some* form of prepolitical experience if they are not to become synonymous with membership in already existing states.[52]

The problem with this view is that it tends to take for granted the existence and historical solidity of national identities and, above all, their separation from the political process of group identity formation. The implausibility of this account is the reason that the dominant tendency in the contemporary historiography of nations and nationalism is not primordialist, but 'modernist' – that is, one that sees national identities as formed contingently through particular political experiences (usually conflictual ones).[53] As John Breuilly puts it, "Once one concedes that people have a 'need' for national identity, the study of nationalism ceases to be one based on rational and demonstrable criteria ... 'national identity' is just one particular role which people play, a role whose character and significance changes with circumstances."[54]

---

51 The primordialist account of national identity can be found, e.g., in the numerous works of Anthony Smith (for example, *The Ethnic Origins of Nations* [Oxford: Basil Blackwell 1986]), as well as in John Armstrong, *Nations before Nationalism* (Chapel Hill: University of North Carolina Press 1982).

52 See Miller, *On Nationality*, 22-25, for his definition of national identity, which is in most respects similar to that given by Walzer.

53 For this modernist view, see, among others, the following works: Peter Alter, *Nationalism*, tr. Stuart McKinnon-Evans (London: Edward Arnold 1989); Benedict Anderson, *Imagined Communities*, rev. ed. (London: Verso 1991); John Breuilly, *Nationalism and the State* (Chicago: University of Chicago Press 1982); Ernest Gellner, *Nations and Nationalism* (Ithaca, NY: Cornell University Press 1983); William McNeill, *Polyethnicity and National Unity in World History* (Toronto: University of Toronto Press 1986); and Hugh Seton-Watson, *Nations and States: An Enquiry into the Origins of Nations and the Politics of Nationalism* (London: Methuen 1977); as well as the previously cited works by Connor and Giddens.

54 John Breuilly, 'Nationalism and the State,' in Roger Michener, ed., *Nationality, Patriotism, and Nationalism in Liberal Democratic Societies* (St. Paul, MN: Professors World Peace Academy 1993), 38

So the communitarian account of national identity is faced with a dilemma: either it concedes the political nature of national identities, as most historians have done, thereby forfeiting the exclusive claim of nations to self-determination, or it must hold on to some version of the distinction between primordial national identities and modern political citizenship, but at the cost of allowing claims to national rights to override the claims of non-nationalistic groups or individuals to political association, when they conflict.

In addition, it is important to note that political identity is characterized not only in terms of its associative features, ones that cannot be coextensive with already existent 'national characters,' but also by the legitimacy of the choice or commitment that constitutes such an identity. Thus, while political communities have sometimes been formed by the demands and actions of nationalities, the question is whether they can *legitimately* be formed on this basis.

Here thought should be given to how a specifically political association is constituted. Ronald Dworkin and Jürgen Habermas, among others, have described significant features of what constitutes political associations. Dworkin, for instance, has emphasized the importance of what he calls 'integrity' in the formation of political communities. On the one hand, he does concede that political communities may be formed through the organization and incorporation of persons possessing particular characteristics; these are what he calls 'bare' communities. But to form a 'true' community – that is, one in which the community constitutes a true associative relation – some means of determining the integrity of the relations within the community must be found.[55]

It is only what Dworkin calls a 'community of principle' that can fulfill the conditions of being a community with integrity – of embodying truly associative relations. Communities of principle are to be distinguished not only from bare communities based on pre-existing or historically derived ties (e.g., national communities), but from communities constituted by adherence to a set of rules designed to produce political compromises between competing groups. Communities may be said to have integrity only when they are organized on the

---

55 Ronald Dworkin, *Law's Empire* (Cambridge, MA: Belknap Press 1986), 201

basis of principles that have gained common acceptance. Political community is therefore rightfully a community of *principle*, not a community of *character*.[56] If a community essentially consists of those to whom a particular identity is ascribed rather than those who adhere to certain principles, then definite limits are placed on the ability of the community to achieve the goals implied in the original commitment to form an association.[57]

A crucial feature of political community has often been thought to be a commitment to common, joint, or collaborative actions or enterprises. In other words, the idea of cooperation is intrinsic to the idea of community.[58] The way in which this notion of community differs from the communitarian view is that the latter posits nonpolitical (especially national) identities as constituting the primary basis of political identities. Yet, if political community is constructed through the execution of cooperative tasks, the extent and membership of a community cannot be legitimately determined in advance according to nonpolitical criteria. A people's choice to associate should be a function of their attraction to enacting certain ideas or principles in a joint enterprise;[59] this enterprise cannot be limited to an already constituted group of people who may or may not have joint tasks to perform. The communitarians seem to have gotten the process of forming a political community backward; rather than being based on common identities, political communities form identities through a process of commitment to common goals. But how then do the common goals that define a political community become established in the first place?

Habermas' concept of a 'communication community' is helpful here. His basic idea is that a political community is defined by a process of

---

56 Dworkin, *Law's Empire*, 211

57 This is a quandary for any theory of political representation that neglects consideration of the consequences for those represented; on this point, see Raz, *Morality of Freedom*, 55.

58 Charles Taylor, 'The Nature and Scope of Distributive Justice,' in *Philosophy and the Human Sciences*, 311

59 Haskell Fain, *Normative Politics and the Community of Nations* (Philadelphia: Temple University Press 1987), 102

communication within which a normative ideal of mutual understanding is embedded.[60] This process of communication necessarily involves an attempt to 'harmonize' individual goals through joint actions based on 'common situation definitions.'[61]

Political identities cannot therefore be formed on the basis of primordial national identities, which may be the result of custom, prejudice, or oppression, but only through a process of communication and mutual agreement. Political communities are necessarily associations created for the achievement of common goals; restrictions on membership in them cannot legitimately follow from delimiting potential members' nonpolitical identities or characteristics.[62]

The communitarian idea that a national identity must serve as the basis for legitimate political identities does not account for a fundamental feature of political identity – its associative, principled, and communicative nature. The 'nation' that is legitimately coterminous with the state is one that is formed through agreement about common goals, an agreement achieved communicatively. Nations cannot serve as the *necessary* basis for legitimate political communities, since they are usually defined by customary or prejudicial ascriptions of identities, rather than through a cooperative process of communication concerning needs or interests.[63]

This is not to say that the communicative features of political life can provide us with a *sufficient* definition of political community.[64] For

---

60 Jürgen Habermas, 'Legitimation Problems in the Modern State,' in *Communication and the Evolution of Society*, tr. Thomas McCarthy (Boston: Beacon Press 1979), 188

61 Jürgen Habermas, *The Theory of Communicative Action*, 1: *Reason and the Rationalization of Society*, tr. Thomas McCarthy (Boston: Beacon Press 1984), 285-6

62 Jürgen Habermas, 'Citizenship and National Identity: Some Reflections on the Future of Europe,' *Praxis International* **12:1** (April 1992) 17

63 Habermas, 'Citizenship and National Identity,' 3

64 As Brian Barry puts it, "Why should anybody form an attachment to an administrative apparatus with a monopoly of legitimate force within a certain territory? ... what is important is not the machinery of government but that the people should have a sense of shared political destiny with others, a preference for being united with them politically in an independent state, and preparedness

how are specific communities that engage in rational communicative practices or that endorse a similar set of principles to be differentiated from one another? Actual political communities cannot be defined only by a set of constitutional principles, however legitimate.[65] What is required, as will be argued below, is a concept of community based on regional identities that is particularistic yet still capable of incorporating the principled or communicative aspects of political identity. In any case, the idea of a 'community of character' cannot do this, since it relies on a notion of ascribed national identity in order to differentiate communities from one another in a way that precludes principled – and thus legitimate – discursive agreement about rights or goods.

V Communal Autonomy versus Political Sovereignty

Once the concept of community has been equated with that of the nation, communitarians assert the desirability, on the one hand, of ensuring the autonomy of communities as the only available means for legitimating sovereign states with recognized international boundaries and, on the other hand, for ensuring the solidarity of the members of a political community (Walzer emphasizes the importance of the first, Miller the second). When communitarians use national identities to determine political sovereignties, the problem does not lie in using a *general* justification of national self-determination to establish a *general* claim by nations to sovereignty over territory. Communitarians link nations with territory by defining nations in part through their connection to particular homelands. From this perspective, a nation is

---

to be committed to common political action" ('Self-Government Revisited,' in David Miller and Larry Siedentop, eds., *The Nature of Political Theory* [Oxford: Clarendon Press 1983], 140-1).

65 The root of the problem with theories of 'constitutional patriotism' – to use Habermas' phrase – is that they fail to posit substantive values that can serve as a basis for deciding upon particular principles. On the idea of 'constitutional patriotism,' see Habermas, 'Citizenship and National Identity,' 7; on how this problem affects the foundations of Habermas' theory of procedural legitimacy, see Agnes Heller, *Beyond Justice* (Oxford: Basil Blackwell 1987), 236-40.

regarded not simply as a collection of individuals but as a conglomeration of a land with a people. A general connection between nations and territories is thus clearly established.

The problem with this view lies in specifying a means by which one could determine *which* nations have rights to *which* territories. The communitarian view cannot provide such a means since it accords rights to territory to any nation that claims them. Walzer attempts to deal with the resultant problem of territorial disputes in three ways: (1) by maintaining that the exercise of popular choice is a presumption that trumps other claims, (2) by arguing in favor of partition, other things being equal, and (3) by establishing a principle of mutual consideration of other nations' claims.[66]

In the first case, Walzer states that, "I would be inclined to support separation whenever separation is demanded by a political movement that, so far as we can tell, represents the popular will. Let the people go who want to go."[67] Does this settle the issue? According to a leading scholar of international law, Wentworth Ofuatey-Kodjoe, "to assert that the right of self-determination means the right of a group to choose the sovereignty under which it shall live is simply incorrect."[68] This is because the principle of self-determination has historically and legally been considered to be applicable to a people only when that people is "under the subjugation of another community."[69]

The obvious case in which self-determination is clearly justifiable is that of colonies whose populations are denied any political rights. But nationalists seek to extend this idea of self-determination to all nations seeking states, whether subjugated by another state or not. Walzer replies that, "[in some societies] the only way to avoid domination is to

---

66 Taylor adds a fourth possible solution – a federal system. But this is, as with Walzer's palliatives, too little, too late, and, in any case, lacks any theoretical justification from communitarian premises. See Taylor, 'Why Do Nations Have to Become States?,' 57.

67 Walzer, 'New Tribalism,' 169

68 Wentworth Ofuatey-Kodjoe, *The Principle of Self-Determination in International Law* (New York: Nellen 1977), 164

69 Ofuatey-Kodjoe, *Principle of Self-Determination in International Law*, 162

multiply political units and jurisdictions, permitting a series of separations."[70] While this may be true in some instances, it does not entail a general right of nations to determine their own territorial boundaries.

Furthermore, there is the problem of defining the appropriate unit within which to determine the 'will of the people.' By referring the resolution of disputes over sovereignty to mechanisms such as plebiscites for determining the 'popular will,' the dispute is simply pushed back one step to a dispute over the appropriate territory in which to conduct such a referendum. As Ivor Jennings famously stated this dilemma: "the doctrine of self-determination [on] the surface ... seemed reasonable: let the people decide. It was in fact ridiculous because the people cannot decide until somebody decides who are the people."[71]

Walzer takes another tack in arguing that partition, in and of itself, constitutes an adequate solution to most disputes over territory.[72] Unfortunately, this view must seek to counteract the more fundamental principle established previously – that of the right of nations to determine their own boundaries. The latter idea would seem to provide a justification for different nations *not* to settle for partition of their countries or homelands. Partitions cannot be presumed to solve territorial disputes, since there is no particular principle on which they are based that could override or counteract the justification nations might feel in continuing to pursue the unification of their presumptively divided territories or homelands.

Finally, it might be maintained that some principle of the mutual consideration of nations for one another might be combined with a principle of self-determination without contradiction – or at least this is what Walzer contends in maintaining that nations seeking states ought to respect the rights of other nations to have their own states.[73] But it is central to the communitarian view that communities cannot

---

70 Walzer, 'New Tribalism,' 166

71 Ivor Jennings, *The Approach to Self-Government* (Cambridge: Cambridge University Press 1958), 56

72 Walzer, 'Nation and Universe,' 548

73 Walzer, 'Nation and Universe,' 535

be judged by standards external to them. In seeking to resolve the conflicts that he admits accompany the struggle for autonomy by nations, the idea that each nation's claim to a state might be respected by all other nations seems a pleasing possibility, but unfortunately little more than that – since the self-limitation of nationalist aspirations is in no way entailed by or even consistent with communitarian advocacy of the rights of nations.

The fundamental problem with the communitarian's use of the idea of communal autonomy is the lack of reasons why nations seeking their own states should pause to consider the needs or interests of other national groups. Without such reasons, communitarians will be unable to offer a way to resolve the conflicts that inevitably arise when different nations seek sovereignty over the same territories and when different nationalities live within the same state. Yet, these are the hard cases that are also frequent cases in international relations, and it is these cases that communitarians fail to address.

Walzer seems to think that nationalist revanchism need not be a fundamental problem for his view of self-determination, but rather something that could be dealt with peacefully through international forums. But he overlooks the political motivation given to revanchist movements by the very concept of national self-determination that he espouses.

What is missing is some rationale for why nations might come to renounce or modify their claims to states. This is a result of the first problem with the communitarian argument: it implies a conception of political community that is in important ways 'antipolitical' in that it leaves no room for the virtues of political judgment, debate, or compromise. Why would a nation seeking a state accept anything less if it regarded its right to one to be rooted in the very structure of political life? A philosophy that begins with a commitment to the autonomy and integrity of national cultures is going to be unable to provide much guidance in developing a procedure to determine legitimate sovereignties and to settle territorial disputes between rival nationalities.

From a theory in which the right of national groups to political power is accepted as bedrock principle, it becomes very hard to derive a means of restricting and limiting such a right in order to reconcile conflicting nationalist claims. By legitimizing every nationalist claim to a state, it prevents, rather than contributes to, development of a theory of political sovereignty as a means of determining legitimate territorial boundaries.

VI   The Nation-State versus Communal Self-Determination

While the problems with using national self-determination as a principle for determining just boundaries may seem insurmountable, if nation-states are the only effective forms of political community that can ensure some measure of social solidarity, then the cost in potential international conflicts may be one that will simply have to be accepted, as Walzer suggests. But nation-states are, in fact, neither necessary for social solidarity nor even particularly conducive to it. This is so for several reasons, but most especially because there is simply no general connection to be made between nations – when they are defined by reference to ethnicity or kinship – and what underlies solidarity, that is, the satisfaction of people's welfare, interests, or needs. Brian Barry has made this point in stating that the trouble with ethnonational criteria for establishing political communities is that "there is no necessary connection between descent, which is a matter of biology, and interest, which is a matter of the fulfilment of human needs and purposes...."[74]

Miller would undoubtedly reply that nations and ethnicities are separable and that nations not strictly based on ethnicity can be vehicles for satisfying needs. But the problem with this modification of the nationalist concept is that it is not modified enough to salvage the idea that the nation-state is the necessary context for political programs committed to social justice through economic redistribution.

If the idea of national identity is *completely* abandoned in order to focus the energies of the state on justice, then the political system has become the constitutionalist one that Dworkin and Habermas espouse, but that Walzer and Miller reject as unlikely to produce sentiments of communal solidarity. But if the ethnonational identity of the state is *not* completely abandoned, then the connection between community and justice is, to that degree, undermined – since, as Walzer maintains, the specification of membership in the community cannot itself be subject to considerations of justice. This limitation will easily lend itself to 'offloading' social problems from the community, as has happened in many states that exclude noncitizens, resident aliens, and guest workers from full citizenship and thus from the social benefits of membership.

---

74   Barry, 'Self-Government Revisited,' 135

What then is the exact connection between redistributive justice and the nation-state, on the communitarian view? It turns out to be a conditional one; as Miller puts it, "*Provided* ... that we endorse ideals of social justice, and recognise that these take hold mainly within national communities, we have good reason for wanting the political systems that can realize these ideals to coincide with national boundaries."[75] But there is nothing in the principle of national self-determination that mandates a commitment to social justice in the first place – and there are reasons to think that such a principle tends to prevent it.

While communitarians maintain that the nation-state is the best vehicle for social equity based on a concern about the power of international capital, they fail to note three problems with this view. First, nation-states frequently act in concert with transnational economic interests rather than opposing or limiting them in various ways. This is the result of the too little noted fact that nation-states can only exist within an international *system* of political sovereignties that affords them recognition. This system, which has been called that of 'internationality,'[76] is not necessarily at odds with that of the global market, especially to the extent that nation-states seek full recognition in the international arena. The real conflict exists between nations and various supranational corporations or agencies, on the one hand, and social movements, cities, or regions seeking development or autonomy, on the other. It is one result of advocacy of national self-determination that the legitimacy of non-state-oriented political actors is put in question. Yet, it is these actors that historically have provided the impetus for achieving more egalitarian social institutions.[77]

---

75 Miller, *On Nationality*, 85 (italics added)

76 Jonathan Rée, 'Internationality,' *Radical Philosophy* **60** (Spr. 1992) esp. 10-11

77 Warren Magnuson, 'The Reification of Political Community,' in R.B.J. Walker and Saul B. Mendlovitz, eds., *Contending Sovereignties: Redefining Political Community* (Boulder, CO: Lynne Rienner, 1990). It is also important in this regard to realize that contemporary social movements that oppose the unrestrained global market are increasingly transnational; for examples, see Jeremy Brecher and Tim Costello, *Global Village or Global Pillage: Economic Reconstruction from the Bottom Up* (Boston: South End Press 1994).

Second, while the relation between nation-states and social justice is surely at most an elective one, it is important to realize the role that the nation-state actually plays in relation both to other states and to subnational communities. In the first case, nation-states function primarily not as welfare states but as 'warfare states.' The reason for this is the need to position the (new) nation-state within the international system so as to demand due recognition from other states.

This fact was, unfortunately, more generally recognized in the last great period of nationalist resurgence, the 1930s, than it is today. Lewis Mumford, in his great book from that period, *The Culture of Cities*, notes that

> Only in times of war, when frontiers are closed, when the movement of men and goods and ideas across 'national' boundaries can be blocked, when a pervading sense of fear sanctions the extirpation of differences, does the national state conform to its ideal pattern.[78]

Today, movements for national self-determination continue to seek to attain a state power modelled on that of already existing states. This leads them to seek national armies, patrolled borders, and immigration controls, as well as an industrializing economy that can produce or buy the weaponry and other technologies needed for these features of modern statehood.[79] There is, consequently, an intrinsic connection between nationalist movements for self-determination and the construction of a militarized state.[80]

In the second case, nation-states play a parasitic role in relation to subnational regions and cities. It is here that the importance of regions

---

78 Lewis Mumford, *The Culture of Cities* (Westport, CT: Greenwood Press 1981 [originally published, 1938]), 349; another interesting, but forgotten, critic of the nation-state from this period, who makes some of the same points as Mumford, is Rudolph Rocker; see his book, *Nationalism and Culture*, tr. Ray E. Chase (Los Angeles: Rocker Publications Committee 1937 [originally published, in Spanish, 1936]).

79 Giddens, *Nation-State and Violence*, 254

80 Maria Mies, in Maria Mies and Vandana Shiva, *Ecofeminism* (Atlantic Highlands, NJ: Zed Books 1993), 128

becomes manifest – for these are an alternative locus of community that does not eventuate in the drive for states and is not based on ethnic or kinship relations or beliefs. As Mumford pointed out, the realities of regional economic and cultural development are obscured by adopting the "mythology of the national state."[81] Nationalism inevitably colonizes local life on the basis of the dominance, enforced by the state, of one region over others: "'nationalism' is an attempt to make the laws and customs and beliefs of a single region or city do duty for the varied expressions of a multitude of other regions."[82]

Third, the social solidarity of the nation-state is a replacement – partly mythological, partly created – for the real solidarities of the region or city. The reality of regional solidarities is based on their arising from the actual means of satisfying human needs, rather than from a belief in a common ancestry that characterizes national loyalties. From the perspective of needs-satisfaction – and from a concern for social justice – the region (and, more precisely, the ecological region) is the best form for achieving communal self-determination.[83]

A concern for social justice cannot be served via the policies of the nation-state, as communitarians suggest, because nation-states exploit and even destroy the means of sustainable and self-reliant development found in regional and urban life. It may even be the case that an inverse relationship exists between the ability of regions to support their populations and the creation of national identities – only when the first is destroyed does the second become attractive. This is because oppressed peoples must then "struggle to compete for a place in the only social space that remains – the social space defined by the modern state."[84]

---

81 Mumford, *Culture of Cities*, 354

82 Mumford, *Culture of Cities*, 349

83 Mumford, *Culture of Cities*, 367; in this passage, Mumford is concerned to point out that regions are partly natural, partly created by humans. The region, he writes, is a 'collective work of art.' For recent discussions of Mumford's concept of regions, see Donald Alexander, 'Bioregionalism: Science or Sensibility?' *Environmental Ethics* 12 (Summer 1990) 161-73, and Mark Luccarelli, *Lewis Mumford and the Ecological Region: The Politics of Planning* (New York: Guilford Press 1995).

84 Vandana Shiva, in Mies and Shiva, *Ecofeminism*, 112

An alternative means of self-determination would have to be based upon a reawakened attention to regional and urban solidarities 'below' the nation-state, so that "those who struggle for ethnic and national identity would accept an economic policy of self-sufficiency and restraint."[85] While the communitarians are correct in criticizing the inability of individualists to specify the bases of political community, the nation-state is also an unsuitable specification because it inhibits the ability of localities and regions to meet human needs through policies of sustainable development.[86] This realization suggests that there may be a 'third way' beyond the insufficiency of liberal constitutionalism and the undesirability of a nation-state – that of the ecological region.[87]

The ecoregional perspective, first formulated by Mumford and revived today by the environmental movement, may give rise to a new conception of community that is opposed to the creation of nation-states.[88] While regional communities would not seek to *replace* states, they would work for substantial autonomy within them, in order to pursue goals of self-reliance and sustainable development. Self-

---

85 Mies, in Mies and Shiva, *Ecofeminism*, 129-30

86 On the contradiction between nationality and locality, see Rée, 'Internationality,' passim, as well as Jonathan Rée, 'Cosmopolitanism and the Experience of Nationality,' in Omar Dahbour, ed., *Philosophical Perspectives on National Identity*, a special issue of *The Philosophical Forum* **28:1–2** (Fall-Winter 1996–97), 167–79.

87 On the need for a 'third way,' Beiner writes that, "we are left deprived of a suitable vision of political community unless we can come up with a third possibility that is neither liberal nor nationalist, and that somehow escapes the liberals' arguments against nationalism and the nationalists' arguments against liberalism" ('Why Citizenship Constitutes a Theoretical Problem,' 16). One example of this third way is the revival of the idea of the city-state; see Daniel Kemmis, 'Focusing the Countryside: The Rebirth of the City-State,' *Orion* 13 (Autumn 1994), 14–17, and Neal R. Peirce, *Citistates: How Urban America Can Prosper in a Competitive World* (Washington, DC: Seven Locks Press 1993).

88 For a thoughtful discussion of different concepts of community in contemporary environmentalism, see Robyn Eckersley, *Environmentalism and Political Theory: Toward an Ecocentric Approach* (Albany: State University of New York Press 1992) esp. ch. 7.

determination is better realized, on this view, by establishing communities on the basis of a "biotic, not merely ethnic" sense of "rootedness that also encourages planetary interdependence and cultural exchange...."[89]

Two political consequences follow from this ecoregional approach to communal self-determination. First, political communities would be seen as institutions with overlapping sovereignties that rely on mixed loyalties – some to the city or region, others to the country or state. Second, only in cases where regions were systematically deprived of the ability to support themselves, and to devise unique forms of accommodation to their ecosystems, would statehood become an issue. Thus, regional self-determination would be served by political secession only in cases of what Allen Buchanan calls 'discriminatory redistribution.'[90] Needless to say, the ethnonational identities of peoples would not be a consideration in this respect.

The nation-state is a type of community that undermines the self-determination of actual communities in important ways. This is true not only of national groups that are threatened by the irresolvable nature of nationalist conflicts over territory, but also of the local, regional, and urban communities that have historically served as the real focus of needs-satisfaction and development. A concern for communal self-determination cannot, therefore, be the basis for a principle of national self-determination, since such a principle gives reasons for destroying the autonomy of the subnational (and multinational) communities within which people actually live.

---

89 Morris Berman, *The Reenchantment of the World* (Ithaca, NY: Cornell University Press, 1981), 297-9. For the historical origins of an ecoregional conception of community, see Robert A. Nisbet, *The Social Philosophers: Community and Conflict in Western Thought* (New York: Crowell 1973), esp. 382.

90 Buchanan defines 'discriminatory redistribution,' which he applies to groups rather than regions, as "implementing taxation schemes or regulatory policies or economic programs that *systematically work to the disadvantage of some groups, while benefiting others, in morally arbitrary ways*" (*Secession: The Morality of Political Divorce from Fort Sumter to Lithuania and Quebec* [Boulder, CO: Westview Press 1991], 40). On his account, this is the clearest case of a justifiable claim to secession; claims based primarily on the assertion of a right of self-determination for nations, however, are illegitimate (50-51).

The communitarian argument for national self-determination is an attempt at reconciling rival claims to political authority by providing a standard – national identity – for determining sovereignties and boundaries. To reiterate, the problems with this argument are three-fold. First, affirming a principle of self-determination for ascriptively defined national groups leads to the construction of communities that lack essential features of legitimate political associations. Second, there just is no way to definitively settle disputes that arise between nationalities once states are viewed as mutually exclusive entities founded on distinct group identities. Third, viewing self-determination as a means of obtaining nation-states overlooks the ways in which these states prevent or undermine the real bases of community in urban, local, and regional ecologies. Consequently, the communitarian assumption that states must maintain an uncompromised territoriality – and that this is the only way to ensure the autonomy of political communities – is unwarranted.

Recognizing the deficiencies of the communitarian argument for national self-determination should lead to a rejection of the elusive goal of a world divided without remainder between nation-states. Acceptance of the desirability of limited and overlapping sovereignties in a world political system based on regionally autonomous and self-reliant communities would probably be more conducive to a truly equitable political life and to defusing conflicts over territory and membership than attempting to universalize the nation-state through advocacy of a right of self-determination for nations.

CANADIAN JOURNAL OF PHILOSOPHY
Supplementary Volume 22

Just Nationalism:
The Future of an Illusion

ANDREW LEVINE
University of Wisconsin–Madison

Until quite recently, political philosophers routinely ignored national-ism. Nowadays, the topic is very much on the philosophical agenda. In the past, when philosophers did discuss nationalism, it was usually to denigrate it. Today, nationalism elicits generally favorable treatment.[1] I confess to a deep ambivalence about this turn of events. On the one hand, much of what has emerged in recent work on nationalism ap-pears to be on the mark. On the other hand, the anti- or extra-national-ist outlook that used to pervade political philosophy seems as sound today as it ever was, and perhaps even more urgent in the face of truly horrendous eruptions of nationalist hostilities in many parts of the world. What follows is an effort to grapple with this ambivalence. My aim will be to identify what is defensible in the nationalist idea and then to reflect on the flaws inherent in even the most defensible as-pects of nationalist theory and practice.

To this end, I will investigate two loosely related issues.[2] First, I will examine nationalism in light of current understandings of what justice

---

1 See, for example, Michael Walzer, 'Nation and Universe,' in G.B. Peterson, ed., *The Tanner Lectures on Human Values*, vol. xi (Salt Lake City: University of Utah Press 1990); Charles Taylor, *Multiculturalism and 'The Politics of Recognition,'* Amy Gutmann, ed. (Princeton, NJ: Princeton University Press 1992); Will Kymlicka, *Multicultural Citizenship* (Oxford: Clarendon Press 1995); David Miller, *On Nationality* (Oxford: Clarendon Press 1995).

2 I will not have much to say about historical and sociological studies of national-ism, but I should note that the reflections that follow have been influenced

requires. Then I will reflect on nationalism from the standpoint of certain views of moral and intellectual progress, which I will endorse. It will be instructive, in both cases, to meld together philosophical considerations and historical ruminations. Thus I will, from time to time, invoke Enlightenment and post-Enlightenment ideals of the good society and also seventeenth- and eighteenth-century republican notions of civic virtue and patriotism. I aim to show how it is possible to accept many of the pro-nationalist positions defended in recent philosophical investigations of the topic and still endorse a cosmopolitan worldview in which nationalist aspirations ultimately have no place. Nationalism, I will argue, is a flawed idea, in much the same way and for much the same reason that theistic religion is, according to Freud's well-known account.[3] It is an *illusion*, a term that I will presently explain. But, unlike the idea of God, it is an illusion grounded in historically transitory conditions. As such, its future depends, in part, on the persistence of these conditions. I would venture that a post-nationalist future is eminently likely, and that an unequivocally cosmopolitan stance will one day become morally possible. But now and for the foreseeable future, ambivalence about nationalism is a reasonable, if not entirely satisfactory, response to the situation we actually confront.

Nationalism and (Liberal) Justice

In order to gain a purchase on *just* nationalism, it will be useful to think about the place of religion in liberal theories of justice. The analogy is imperfect, but instructive nevertheless.

The idea that religion would wither away or at least assume a nontheistic form as civilization develops has been a tenet of important

significantly by some important contemporary accounts – especially Ernest Gellner, *Nations and Nationalism* (Oxford: Blackwell 1982), Eric Hobsbawm, *Nations and Nationalism since 1780* (Cambridge: Cambridge University Press 1990), and Benedict Anderson, *Imagined Communities*, rev. ed. (London: Verso 1991).

3 See Sigmund Freud, *The Future of an Illusion* (1927) in James Strachy, ed., *The Standard Edition of the Complete Psychological Works of Sigmund Freud*, vol. xxi (London: Hogarth Press 1961).

strains of progressive theory at least since the Enlightenment.[4] Needless to say, nothing like this has happened yet. Instead, in recent years, secularism has suffered serious defeats, and almost everywhere religiosity appears to be on the rise. Nevertheless, throughout much of the world, religion has effectively migrated from the public arena to the sphere of private conscience. Its political impact has therefore lessened – especially, but not only, in the Western liberal democracies and the formerly socialist countries. At the same time, a broadly secular worldview has become part of the commonsense of many of us. There are even sizeable numbers of people who, like myself, are unable to identify with religious sensibilities experientially. For us, the world of the faithful seems both exotic and ridiculous. It is accessible to us only in the way that, say, Greek mythology is; from the *outside*. We know that religions have millions of adherents, many of whom are ardent believers, just as we know that belief in the exploits of Zeus was once fervent and widespread.[5] But in neither case can we understand the phenomenon empathically. Before the Enlightenment, most people experienced non-belief as a failing to be overcome.[6] Nowadays, many

---

4 Since 'religion' can legitimately assume a variety of meanings, I should say that it is mainly theism that I have in mind. In this respect, Emile Durkheim's *The Elementary Forms of Religious Life* (New York: The Free Press 1965) is exemplary. For Durkheim, 'religion' designates the cement of society, the mechanism(s) through which societies cohere. As such, it can no more wither away than society itself can. But a key aspect of religion, so conceived, is its system of 'collective representations.' In Durkheim's view, collective representations take on a theistic ideational content as human civilization advances beyond its primitive, 'elementary' stage. But the further advance of civilization will, in time, cause theistic ideation to give way to a broadly secular and naturalistic worldview. Durkheim surmised that, by his time, theism was already on the wane. In this respect, he shared the fate of many other progressive nineteenth-century thinkers who may well have been right about humanity's prospects but who were woefully wrong in estimating its rate of progress.

5 For an illuminating discussion of this phenomenon, see Paul Veyne, *Did the Greeks Believe in their Myths: An Essay on the Constitutive Imagination*, Paula Wissing, trans. (Chicago: University of Chicago Press 1988).

6 Emblematic of this state of mind was Pascal's agonized but successful attempt to instill belief in a God whose existence he thought improbable – through ratiocination ('the wager') and indirection (as in the injunction to 'practice first'). See

non-believers experience the inability to understand belief empathically as a triumph. We consider ourselves *beyond* theism. This is precisely the *desideratum* articulated by Freud in *The Future of an Illusion*. For Freud, 'illusion' has a technical meaning. The term designates a belief held not in consequence of rationally compelling reasons but as an expression of an unconscious wish. In Freud's view, illusions are generated by infantile desires that properly matured minds would have set aside or mastered. They are produced and sustained by the same mental processes that generate neuroses. Freud's account of theism stands or falls with the tenability of his causal hypotheses. But specifically psychoanalytic considerations aside, Freud's aim is entirely consonant with the Enlightenment imperative, epitomized by Kant in the slogan 'dare to know.'[7] The point is to face the world as it is, without benefit of comforting but indefensible illusions that represent only how we would like the world to be.

Does the existence of genuinely secular mentalities in the modern world vindicate the hopes of Freud and other progressive post-Enlightenment thinkers? Or was their faith in the universal maturation of human mentalities itself an illusion? No doubt, it is too soon to tell. The world today falls short of their expectations. If we assume a short-term perspective, it can appear that humanity is moving in the wrong direction. But we need not therefore conclude that theirs was a utopian dream. Some of what they had in mind has already come to pass. Perhaps the rest will eventually follow. The vicissitudes of recent history notwithstanding, it is hardly beyond the realm of possibility that humanity will eventually release itself entirely from its 'self-incurred nonage' in matters of theistic belief.[8]

However uncertain the future of *that* illusion may be, I think it is fair to venture at least one prediction – that the 'migration' of theistic belief from the public arena into the private sphere, a trend that has

---

Pascal's Pensées, Martin Turnell, ed. and trans. (New York: Harper & Bros. 1962).

7 See Immanuel Kant, 'What Is Enlightenment?' in *Kant's Political Writings*, Hans Reiss, ed. (Cambridge: Cambridge University Press 1970).

8 See Kant, 'What is Enlightenment?' 'Self-incurred nonage' was Kant's expression for the antithesis of the Enlightenment ideal.

long been evident throughout much of the world, is probably irreversible. Theistic religion is destined to become everywhere what it already largely is in the liberal democracies and the formerly socialist countries, a matter of private conscience only. To be sure, anti-secularists seek to interject religion back into the public arena everywhere, and 'fundamentalisms' of various kinds are rampant in many parts of the world. The *privatization* of religion could therefore fail to proceed. But it does appear to be a long-term and welcome trend. In any case, as religion has in fact moved into the private sphere, *nationalism* seems to have taken its place in public life. Nationalist identifications now fuel political passions in much the same way that religious convictions once did. Wars of religion tore early modern Europe apart; nationalist struggles today threaten similar horrors on a global scale. It is not surprising, therefore, that attitudes towards religion have counterparts in debates about nationalism. Cosmopolitanism, after all, is as much an Enlightenment legacy as secularism is; from a cosmopolitan standpoint, nationalism appears to be yet another 'infantile disorder.' This assessment is nearly as old as nationalism itself. It is epitomized in a telling phrase uttered some years ago by Albert Einstein who called nationalism "the measles of the human race."[9] It is no doubt wise to avoid the condescension implicit in this remark, tempting as it may be for those of us whose intuitions it captures. But, of course, it is well too, even for militant atheists, to avoid condescension in matters of faith. The best post-Enlightenment critics of religion were exemplary in this regard. Marx, for example, acknowledged that religion, "the opium of the people," is also "the sigh of the oppressed creature, the heart of a heartless world ... [and] the spirit of spiritless conditions."[10] He therefore implied that, in a heartless world, religion cannot be rejected outright and that it is wrong and even dangerous to try to do so prematurely. The point instead is to 'overcome' religion by altering the heartless

---

9   Cited in H. Dukas and B. Hoffman, *Albert Einstein: The Human Side* (Princeton: Princeton University Press 1979) and in David Miller, *On Nationality*, 5

10 Karl Marx, 'Contribution to the Critique of Hegel's *Philosophy of Right;* Introduction,' in Joseph O'Malley, ed., *Marx: Early Political Writings* (Cambridge: Cambridge University Press 1994)

earthly conditions that make it necessary. Non- and anti-nationalists would do well to adopt a similar stance. But an 'understanding' attitude is not the same thing as an empathic understanding, and neither does it imply support for what is understood. For many of us, real empathy with the sentiments that make nationalism attractive is simply not accessible. If I may generalize from my own experience, we are glad that it is not, just as most non-believers today are glad not to be tempted by faith. What I shall go on to say about nationalism – the phenomenon and the ideology – reflects this attitude.

The idea that nationalism is, at best, a passing phase in humanity's progress towards something more 'mature' has been a long-standing feature of major strains of both liberal and socialist thought. Thus the superiority of a genuinely *cosmopolitan* world outlook is probably even more deeply entrenched in progressive political theory and practice than opposition to religion is. This is one reason why political philosophers have ignored nationalism. But it is not the only reason. Of perhaps even greater importance is the fact that, throughout what Eric Hobsbawm has aptly called the 'short twentieth century,'[11] nationalisms of different sorts have taken on a variety of political colorations as they have aligned themselves with larger political struggles or figured inadvertently in the unfolding of world events. Thus even those of us who think of nationalism as a vestige of humanity's 'nonage' cannot deny that, for as long as the phenomenon has existed, some nationalisms have played positive roles in world affairs. Until recently, most progressive thinkers may have held nationalism in contempt, if they thought of it at all, but in practice progressives have never been able to condemn the phenomenon altogether. Nationalists have too often been the agents of progressive social change. Nationalism has been an especially potent weapon in struggles against imperial domination – of smaller countries by larger ones, of colonies by colonizing powers, and of the Third World by the First World. Political movements motivated, at least in part, by nationalist aspirations also played important roles in the Cold War. It is already very clear that the Cold War profoundly affected the world's national-

---

11 Eric Hobsbawm, *The Age of Extremes: A History of the World, 1914-1991* (New York: Pantheon 1994)

isms. It affected theoretical reflections on nationalism too, causing almost everyone who did not ignore the phenomenon completely to subsume it under other, ostensibly more pressing, concerns. The end of the Cold War has left us without larger contexts, and has dissipated most of these other concerns. It is hardly surprising, therefore, that in the face of rising nationalist sentiments we find ourselves without conceptual bearings. Needless to say, this is just the kind of situation that calls for a philosophical response. It is only to be expected, therefore, that a response has been forthcoming.

It is fair to say that the aim of most philosophers who reflect on nationalism nowadays is to determine what justice requires or at least permits with respect to individuals' identifications with nations. This question is mainly investigated from within a theoretical framework shaped by John Rawls's accounts of justice and political legitimacy.[12] Accordingly, long-standing liberal views about religious toleration and the rightful place of religion in public life, filtered through the prism of Rawlsian theory, serve (usually implicitly) as models for determining how nationalist aspirations ought to be treated. As remarked, many pre-Rawlsian liberals evinced hostility towards religion at the same time that they promoted religious toleration. Rawlsian liberals are more at peace with religious worldviews, deeming them 'reasonable' in light of what Rawls calls "the burdens of judgement." They even insist that religious 'comprehensive doctrines' are unlikely ever to expire for want of popular assent. But whatever their attitudes towards religion may be, the relevant point, for writers influenced by Rawlsian positions, is that religions are of deep importance in many peoples' lives – that they are constitutive, in some cases, of long-term projects and plans of life, and that they serve as elements in the construction of particular personal identities. Because they are so fundamentally important, legitimate institutions are obliged to protect them wholeheartedly and fairly – without favoritism to some religions over others or even to religion itself over

---

12 See John Rawls, *A Theory of Justice* (Cambridge, MA: The Belknap Press of Harvard University Press 1971) and *Political Liberalism* (New York: Columbia University Press 1993).

non-belief. National identifications, it is claimed, are or can be similarly fundamental. They are therefore to be accorded comparable protections.

The analogy, however, is far from perfect. It is sometimes argued, for example, that states have positive duties to promote nationalist attachments – at least in cases where persons of a particular nationality have been involuntarily incorporated into a political community dominated by persons of a different nationality or when individuals belonging to different nationalities 'confederate' voluntarily on the understanding that their respective national identities will be protected.[13] No liberal would argue in favor of comparable claims for particular religions or for religion in general. But the idea that nationality fundamentally matters and that its protection must therefore be of paramount concern in any just society does represent a rationally compelling extension of the liberal consensus on religion into this secular domain. The implication is that a just society cannot rightfully repress nationalist aspirations and that it must be fair to competing nationalist claims. If the analogy with religion breaks down, as it does when the issue is positive support for nationalist identifications, it is only because fairness has different implications in the two cases.

There is no inconsistency in holding the view that justice sometimes implies support for nationality and a cosmopolitan world outlook too. Nor is there any inconsistency in insisting that a just society should protect and in some cases even reinforce nationalist aspirations, while hoping, at the same time, that humankind will grow out of its nationalist phase. In this respect, the parallel with religion is clear. One can disparage religion and still consider it a phenomenon important enough to merit unqualified protection by the state. Thus Rawls insists that even the most ardent atheist should advocate public neutrality with respect to religious commitments in precisely the way that liberalism has always maintained. To do otherwise would be inconsistent with

---

13 Cf. Kymlicka, *Multicultural Citizenship*. Immigrant groups, in Kymlicka's view, do not have similar claims, no matter how large they may be, because immigrants *choose* to join political communities in which their particular nationalist attachments are alien. However, the distinction is not always clear; thus immigrants can settle or be settled in ways that effectively (re)constitute a national community and thereby acquire the various rights which that status confers.

the equal respect Rawls thinks persons are due as a condition for both *de jure* and *de facto* political legitimacy. Similarly, there is nothing inconsistent in believing both that nationalist identifications are 'the measles of the human race' and that justice requires their defense. If an atheist can support religious toleration, a cosmopolitan can support the wishes of a national minority to maintain and strengthen its nationalist identifications. A cosmopolitan can even support the right of a national minority to secede from the larger political community into which it is incorporated – provided, of course, that the conditions that render secession defensible, whatever they might be, obtain. This is a matter, as Rawlsians might say, of *political* morality – in which extra-political convictions have no legitimate role to play. In sum, respect for nationality at the political level, like toleration for religious doctrines and practices, is compatible with virtually any assessment of the merits of these positions or of the sentiments that make them compelling to the people who hold them.

Liberal justice accommodates to the world as it finds it. What matters from a liberal point of view, therefore, is only that many people find religious ideologies and nationalist sentiments central to their plans of life, their conceptions of the good, and their personal identities. Questions about the merits of these views are relegated to another terrain, outside the political arena. Thus liberalism dissolves the tension between a broadly cosmopolitan worldview and a sense that the new philosophies of nationalism are generally on track. As a matter of *political* principle, the widespread belief that nationality matters, whatever its merits, must be accorded its due. We who disparage this idea can rightfully pursue our own agendas and convince whomever we can, just as we who disparage the claims of the faithful can rightfully inveigh against theistic beliefs and their associated practices. As Mill would have it, we are free to remonstrate, reason, persuade, or entreat those with whom we disagree, but we are not free to compel anyone or "visit ... (anyone) with any evil in case he do otherwise" – whether through statist means or by "the moral coercion of public opinion."[14] The Rawlsian version of this idea is, if anything, even more emphatic.

---

14 John Stuart Mill, *On Liberty*, Currin V. Shields, ed. (New York: Bobbs Merrill 1956), 13

Whatever matters fundamentally, provided it is not wildly irrational or blatantly incompatible with the stability of liberal regimes, merits protection by public institutions – provided, of course, that in conferring the requisite support, liberal norms themselves are not transgressed.

Enlightened Nationalism?

Nationalism and religion have much in common from the standpoint of liberal justice. But there is also a significant disanalogy that warrants reflection. I have suggested that religious convictions, especially if they are theistic in nature, are at odds with the Enlightenment imperative to face the world as it is, without illusions. But even those who disagree with this assessment of religious belief should agree that nationalism bears a far more complex relation to the Enlightenment tradition than religion does. There can be little doubt about what Freud, for example, *wants* the future of religion to be. The corresponding hope for nationalism is far less clear. On the one hand, nationalism is plainly at odds with the aspiration to universality that important strains of Enlightenment thought took over and adapted from earlier philosophical traditions. Cosmopolitanism expresses this universalizing impulse. On the other hand, it is far from clear what a genuinely universalistic perspective on human affairs implies. No important Enlightenment figure or heir to the Enlightenment tradition has ever claimed that it implies the illegitimacy of special loyalties, for example, to family and friends. Similar considerations have always been understood to apply among citizens as well. We owe our fellow citizens more than we owe people in general, and we can legitimately expect more from them in turn. But if philosophers in the Enlightenment tradition are prepared to concede this much to particularity, what is to prevent them from endorsing nationalism as such? For whatever else a nation may be, it is a kind of community in which individuals stand in special relations to their fellow nationals. Indeed, by most accounts, nationalism is the distinctively *modern* form of *political* community – a form especially conducive, in real-world conditions, to the kind of economic and social development characteristic of the modern period.[15]

---

15 The mainstream view, at least since Gellner's pioneering work (see note 2), is

If this view is right, nationalism and the Enlightenment are creatures of a common cause. I would go further and contend that nationalism is virtually implied by some of the core political ideas that motivate the Enlightenment aspiration to authentic cosmopolitanism, conjoined with real-world historical conditions. My claim, then, is that nationalism expresses a sound and important idea, but in a fundamentally unsound way. Just as Freud thought religion an illusory and therefore inauthentic response to a genuine human need for solace and meaning in a meaningless and hostile universe, I would propose that nationalism represents an illusory solution to an increasingly pressing problem – the need for real community. In support of this contention, I will try to identify and reflect upon the aspect of the nationalist idea that is unequivocally consistent with Enlightenment aspirations. Doing so will, again, involve mixing straightforwardly philosophical considerations with some relatively uncontentious historical reflections.

First, however, some terminological clarifications are in order. I will stipulate, in accord with common usage, that *nationality* is a matter of culture. Individuals share a nationality insofar as they are members of a community constituted by certain generally recognized cultural similarities and insofar as they share certain social 'meanings.'[16] Of course, it is appropriate to identify distinctive 'cultures' at virtually all the interstices of social life. Thus we talk about the cultures of particular organizations and family units. Individuals who have similar occupations can have distinctive cultures; miners, for example, or merchant seamen. There is a 'gay culture,' a 'culture of poverty,' and so on. We even talk about cultures that are global in scope – the culture of capitalism, for example, or (not long ago) of Communism or of modern industrial society. With respect to nationalism, the relevant cultures are, of course, national in character. It would be pointless to try to specify necessary and sufficient conditions for *nationhood*. The idea is too fluid.

---

that nationalism is indispensable for modernization; it supplies a cultural context within which strangers can interact in the ways they must if genuinely national economies are to develop.

16 *The Oxford English Dictionary* defines 'culture' as 'the intellectual side' of 'civilization.' In *The Future of an Illusion*, 5-6, Freud declared his intention to use 'culture' and 'civilization' synonymously.

But there are well-known and generally acknowledged features that cluster around the concept of nationality. Thus people who live in the same geographical territory, who speak a common language, and who share fundamental values and beliefs, including religious beliefs, are likely to claim a distinctive national identity. Another relevant factor is common descent (real or imagined). In accord, again, with common usage, I will use the term *ethnicity* to designate the latter idea. Ethnic identifications frequently motivate a sense of nationhood. But common nationality and common ethnicity are not the same thing. Not all nations can claim common descent. To cite some conspicuous European examples, the people of Great Britain and France compose nations, not ethnic groups. On the other hand, for the Jews dispersed throughout Europe and elsewhere, a belief in common descent and also, of course, a set of common religious convictions and practices was sufficient for forging a nationalist political movement, Zionism, and eventually a national identity for the Jews who settled in Palestine and founded the state of Israel.

As remarked, nationhood is intimately connected, in both history and logic, to the principles, themselves dimly understood, that sort individuals into distinct political entities. Thus from the very beginnings of the modern state, the typical state was a *nation state,* a state whose boundaries coincide with the boundaries of nations. It is because nationality and political citizenship are so closely linked that there is at least a *prima facie* case for according political autonomy or self-determination to national groups. But no one would propose that all nationalities ought in principle to have their own states. In any case, such a proposal would serve no purpose; moreover, if implemented, it would rip apart the existing world system of states, with dire consequences for social stability and peace. Therefore, in practice, the borders of nations and the borders of states seldom coincide. The German 'nation,' for example, is not ruled by a single German state, even now that East and West Germany have unified. And there are political communities that are multi-national – Switzerland and Belgium are examples – not because they are vestiges of older, multi-national empires, and not because individuals of different nationalities have immigrated in, but because these states were founded as multi-national unions.

The political dimension of *nationality* is crucial to its 'rational kernel.' It signals a connection with another idea with which nationalism is easily confounded, *patriotism*. By 'patriotism,' I mean support for the political community of which one is a part, for its fundamental constitutional arrangements, irrespective of the ethnic or national composition of that community. Patriotism is a very old idea. Its roots lie in the political philosophy of the ancient world. It is a cardinal virtue, accordingly, in the *republican* tradition in political theory and in the sources on which republicanism draws. Patriotism and nationalism have been confounded for as long as nationalism has been a political phenomenon. It is nowadays widely believed that German Romanticism is to blame for conflating these ideas.[17] But whatever the cause, patriotism and nationalism are effectively fused almost everywhere that nationalist aspirations are a potent political force. It is patriotism, not nationalism, that, suitably qualified, can be a component, perhaps an indispensable component, of a defensible political morality. I argued in the last section that respect for nationalist aspirations can be defended in more or less the way that respect for religious beliefs and practices can: as a joint implication of the fundamental moral idea that persons ought to be accorded equal respect and the empirical fact that, in the world as it is, many people are bound to be afflicted by this "measles of the human race." To defend patriotism, however, we need concede nothing to the 'spiritual' immaturity of the human race.

In support of this contention, it will be instructive to turn, briefly, to Rousseau's political philosophy.[18] Rousseau was hardly a typical Enlightenment thinker. But he did provide an especially clear purchase on patriotism from the universalizing perspective of Enlightenment thought. For Rousseau, the just state rests upon a social contract that is "always and everywhere the same," even if it has never anywhere been

---

17 Martin Thom argues persuasively that the rejection of republicanism, a reigning doctrine in revolutionary France, and its replacement by the various strains of nationalism that the Romantic movement developed was, in large part, an expression of revulsion towards the more radical phases of the French Revolution, especially the Great Terror. See *Republics, Nations and Tribes* (London: Verso 1995).

18 I elaborate on the claims advanced in this paragraph in *The Politics of Autonomy* (Amherst, MA: University of Massachusetts Press 1976), *The End of the State* (London: Verso 1987), and *The General Will: Rousseau, Marx, Communism* (Cambridge and New York: Cambridge University Press 1993).

'formally enunciated.' This contract requires each individual "to place himself under the supreme direction of the general will."[19] But, as Rousseau was painfully aware, this notional possibility can actually govern human affairs only if there is a high degree of civic *virtue*, a deep and extensive sense of identification with one's fellow citizens. For unless individuals are virtuous in this republican sense, unless they are disposed to place the good of 'the whole community' above their own private goods, they will not in fact make the general will their own. They will instead act according to their private interests, and the (notional) possibility of *de jure* authority will therefore be undone. Then the just state will remain an unrealized human possibility. This is why, although the social contract itself is universal and unique, the states it (notionally) legitimates must be structured in ways that attend with the utmost sensitivity to geographical, historical, and cultural particularities. Rousseau was very doubtful that *de facto* sovereignty could ever be legitimate *de jure*, given the degree to which real-world history had already 'corrupted' humankind. But if we nevertheless attempt to envision a world of just states, we would have to imagine them as varied as the world's peoples in their fundamental characters and institutional arrangements. Their principle of legitimacy, the social contract, would be the same everywhere, but they would differ profoundly in almost every other respect. For Rousseau, then, particularity is indispensable for universality. This is why he would have all the institutions of society conspire together, as it were, to foster patriotism. It is patriotism that sustains the historically contingent particularities that make general will coordination possible.

Of course, Rousseau's conception of patriotism is in many ways anachronistic. When he reflected on ways to promote this disposition, he assumed, among other things, that states are very small, and that they superintend homogeneous societies, distinguished by 'simplicity' of manners and morals. But the core idea remains applicable in a world of large states that superintend complex and heterogeneous populations. The idea is just that patriotism matters – instrumentally, not intrinsically – whenever and to the degree that it lends support to

---

19 *The Social Contract*, Book I, ch. 6

regimes worth supporting. A just state is plainly worthy of support in Rousseau's view; it is the condition for the possibility of our becoming the autonomous beings Rousseau believes we essentially are. But it is not necessary to embrace Rousseau's stringent and idiosyncratic conditions for political legitimacy to accept the idea behind this thought. Patriotism is a condition for the survival and flourishing of political regimes. It is instrumentally warranted if and only if the regimes it serves *deserve* support. To put it differently: as a political virtue, patriotism is accessible only to people fortunate enough to be citizens of states that ought to survive and flourish. Therefore, a rationally defensible patriotism is a human possibility, but its feasibility in particular circumstances is a matter of luck, *political luck*.[20]

Since, under real-world conditions, nationalism and patriotism have become profoundly and, in some cases, inextricably intertwined, it follows that the normative assessment of particular nationalisms also depends on luck. But, where nationalism is concerned, political luck has an ineluctable historical dimension. In assessing nationalisms, therefore, the exigencies of real-world politics, usually at a global or at least at an international level, almost always take precedence over ahistorical and localized judgments about particular institutional arrangements. This is why it has generally been in the framework of views about human history and its trajectory that cosmopolitans have found particular nationalisms progressive. Thus the conviction of many socialists a quarter century ago that Vietnamese nationalism was defensible while Taiwanese nationalism was not, was not, in the main, a judgment about the timeless properties of the institutional arrangements in

---

20 In *Democracy and Education, Middle Works*, vol. 9 (Carbondale: University of Southern Illinois Press 1979), John Dewey argued, for this reason, that American patriotism is justified because Americans live under generally progressive and democratic institutions. Needless to say, this assessment depends on accepting a construal of American history that stresses the democratic aspects of the American experience, while discounting or ignoring, among other things, America's treatment of indigenous peoples, slavery, economic exploitation, imperialism, and so on. But whatever the merits of Dewey's historical assessment, the theoretical principle he assumes is essentially identical to the rationale for republican patriotism.

place in these countries. Rather, the idea was that, in the conditions that obtained at the time, Vietnamese nationalism was instrumental for advancing defensible internationalist objectives, while Taiwanese nationalism was regressive from that vantage point. It was, in fact, the conviction of many progressives at the time that Vietnamese national-ism was instrumental for moving human civilization closer to its ra-tional 'end'– and therefore to a social order in which, among many more important things, the nationalist temptation itself would pass into obsolescence. Nowadays, of course, erstwhile socialist internation-alists have lost their bearings, and so-called 'grand narratives' of the kind that are able to sustain such convictions have fallen into disre-pute. But the general point survives these *fin de siècle* phenomena: na-tionalisms that serve causes worth defending are defensible

Still, nationalism is objectionable in a way that patriotism is not. The difference is that patriotism can be a rational response to real-world conditions – to the fact, should it ever be the case, that existing institu-tions are justifiable in their own right. In a word, patriotism can be rational. Nationalism, on the other hand, can never be rational, even when it is incontrovertibly 'progressive.' It always bears an irremedi-ably non- or extra-rational dimension. It rests upon beliefs that are dubi-ous at best, and conjures up feelings that lack rational grounding. However intensely they may come to be experienced, nationalist sentiments are always to some degree contrived – not just in the way that all social iden-tities are 'socially constructed,' but in a more straightforward way.

Nationalism is a comparatively new historical phenomenon because national identities themselves were only recently imagined – in response to historical exigencies that have only recently developed.[21] Impelled by this context, the beliefs and affects that underlie nationalist ideolo-gies are 'illusions,' in just the way that Freud thought theistic convic-tions were. I would venture, in fact, that this conclusion applies in the nationalist case, even if Freud was wrong about theism. For the nation is nothing if not an expression of a wish, a wish for a community that extends throughout time, uniting generations, and across space, incor-porating strangers. But this wish is always at least somewhat at odds

---

21 For corroborating evidence, see, among others, the sources cited in note 2.

with the facts. Thus, for nationality to seem psychologically real, it is necessary, as Ernst Renan shrewdly observed, that people "forget a great deal."[22] Of course, nations cannot be fabricated out of thin air; there are limits to forgetfulness. But national communities are always, in Benedict Anderson's expression, 'imagined.'[23] But, in contrast to the theistic case, it is not just trans-historical facts of human nature and the human condition that stimulate the imagination in nationalist directions. It is human nature in the context of the deep historical processes that have shaped the modern world: above all, the rise of the nation state and the dissolution of feudal solidarities. In these conditions, there is, at once, a material cause and a psychological need to forge new solidarities – at the level of the national economy itself. Thus nationalism is a product of deep and long-standing, but ultimately transitory, social processes. This is why nationalism is ultimately a less vexing problem for cosmopolitans than theism was for Freud. A yearning for community fuels the nationalist project, but there are no ahistorical psychological mechanisms that threaten to bring nationalist illusions to human consciousness in perpetuity, as there are in the case of theistic belief. In fact, nationalist ideologies seldom arise *spontaneously*, except insofar as peoples innocent of nationalist illusions may be tempted, unconsciously, to mimic their nationalist neighbors or, more often, their colonial masters. Typically, nationalisms are deliberately contrived and promoted. They are the work of political entrepreneurs who mold popular longings for communal forms appropriate to modern life in nationalist directions.[24] In short, it is real-world politics, not unadulterated psychological necessity, that explains this distinctively modern way of valorizing an illusion. The remedy for theism is intellectual maturity. But, if Freud was right, it will always be a struggle to make this remedy hold in the face of the crushing burdens of human existence and

---

22 See Ernst Renan, 'What is a Nation?' in Alfred Zimmern, ed., *Modern Political Doctrines* (Oxford: Oxford University Press 1939).

23 See Anderson, *Imagined Communities*.

24 Some case studies are sketched in Ernest Gellner, *Encounters with Nationalism* (Oxford: Blackwell.: 1994), and in the sources cited in note 2.

the inexorable facts of human psychological development. Intellectual maturity is also a remedy for nationalism. But it is only needed because we now live under historical conditions that failed to obtain for most of human history and that could well cease to exist again.

The state system predates the emergence of nationalist ideology, but the nation and the state have come to be joined indissolubly. So long as the conditions that sustain this connection remain in force, the two are likely to remain inextricably linked. For better or worse, therefore, nationalism is likely to remain a fact of political life for some time. We who identify with the Enlightenment injunction to face the world as it is, without illusions, may bemoan this fact. We may regret that universalist aims must sometimes be pursued through nationalist means. But now and for the foreseeable future, we often have no choice but to accede to nationalist aspirations, and sometimes even to support political movements organized around them.

Conclusion

I have tried to reconcile the idea that nationalism is always non- or extra-rational with the political judgment that there can be nationalisms that merit support in ways that exceed what (liberal) justice requires. In this respect, nationalism is like the republican patriotism it has largely superseded. How it is assessed depends on the ends it serves. But, in contrast to patriotism, a truly rational nationalism is an impossibility, even in principle. Rational patriotism, however, is an idea of only limited applicability. Its very ahistoricity undermines its usefulness in shaping both quotidian and long-term political practice. Thus we can imagine a patriotism that supports, say, fundamental constitutional forms and national symbols and holidays, but not one that underwrites a full-fledged politics responsive to the exigencies of real-world conditions and events. Nationalism, on the other hand, *is* a genuine political ideology suitable for guiding political practice in the short and long run. But because it is based on a wish, not a reality – because the nation is not found but imagined and sometimes even deliberately contrived – it rests on a flawed idea. Thus it is an unseemly instrument, even when it is instrumentally defensible. Nationalism is a fact of political life that just polities must accommodate. But it is a fact that humankind would do well finally to render unnecessary and obsolete.

What might then supersede nationalism? What remains when nationalist illusions are finally overcome? At a very high level of generality, the answer is clear: real, not imagined, communities. But from a less abstract vantage point, there is much philosophical work to do. We know, of course, a great deal about what community involves. The issue is an important concern in many of the strains of political philosophy that, until recently, denigrated or ignored nationalist ideas. Real-world politics has impelled many of us to turn away from traditional treatments of the topic. It has put nationalism on the philosophical agenda. But if we are to build communities without illusions – or, rather, to become more clear about what this goal implies – some of us, at least, must resist the pressure to remain fixed on the nationalist idea. Our task is to resume the journey it interrupted. The detour has been worthwhile. It has forced philosophers to see things that would otherwise have gone unnoticed. It has enriched political philosophy, and will undoubtedly continue to do so. But if we are ever to free humanity from its 'self-imposed nonage' in this domain, we must not let the nationalist turn lead us off track or indeed anywhere other than back to the path it distracted us from.

CANADIAN JOURNAL OF PHILOSOPHY
Supplementary Volume 22

Against Nationalism

HARRY BRIGHOUSE
University of Wisconsin, Madison

A recent resurgence of interest within analytical political philosophy in the status of ethnic and national minorities coincides with the re-emergence of national identity as a primary organizing principle of political conflict, and with an increasing attentiveness to identity and recognition as organizing principles of political struggle. The recent theoretical literature within political philosophy has focused very much on recognizing the importance of national identity, and allowing attention to national sentiment to inform the design of social institutions.

In this paper I shall state the case for a version of the position which Will Kymlicka has dubbed 'benign neglect' toward cultural identities. Benign neglect is the position that the state should, as far as possible, be neutral among the cultural (and hence national) sentiments of its citizens. The position is, I think, implicit in the theoretical work of many contemporary liberals, and also in much socialist theory and some socialist practice.[1] But it is rarely defended explicitly. Liberal theory is generally developed on the unrealistic assumptions that the society to be regulated is closed and coincides with the membership of a single nation. Under that assumption the problems associated with the exist-

---

1 It is hard to infer positions on this question by attention simply to practice, especially to socialist practice which has hitherto been (and will for the foreseeable future be) explicitly rectificatory. Nevertheless many (though probably not most) socialist currents have been hostile to national sentiment both because it is a barrier to immediate political projects and because it is desirable to do away with it in the long term.

ence of national minorities do not arise. So the treatment of national status as just another kind of ideological commitment or preference, with the same standing as other commitments and preferences, does not require defence by the theorist attempting to develop a political morality.

The particular variant of benign neglect I shall advocate is friendly to but not identical with a moderate cosmopolitanism. A moderate policy of cosmopolitanism would aim to make national and ethnic identity less salient to relationships within and across political units by promoting a loosening of cultural boundaries. I shall defend cosmopolitanism briefly at the end of the paper, but my main aim is to show that liberals have not been given sufficient reason to forge lasting accommodations of national and ethnic identities.

Consideration of the following complaint of nationalist and anti-liberal Roger Scruton will help clarify my position:

> It is neither polite nor politic for those brought up in Western liberal tradition to defend the 'national idea' as the foundation of political order. Or rather, you can defend that idea on behalf of others - at least if they're engaged in some 'struggle for national liberation' - but not on behalf of your own community and kind. Indeed you should be careful not to use words like 'kind', 'race', or 'kin'. Loyalties, if they are not universalist, must be expressed surreptitiously, in the self-deprecating language of one confessing to a private fault.[2]

Scruton appears to be accusing liberals of making three claims. First, that it is impermissible for 'dominant nations' to use the 'national idea' as part of the basis of the justification of the political order. This I endorse. The second is that 'subordinate nations' are exempt from this stricture. This I deny. Finally, that liberals are or should be intolerant toward non-universalist loyalties such as national sentiment. This, again, I deny. Not only might a liberal state legitimately endorse some particularistic loyalties (such as family loyalties), but it should *tolerate* many such loyalties. Scruton's and my national loyalties should be tolerated by the state, but they should be tolerated in exactly the same way that our loyalties to our favoured cricket teams are tolerated – as the private loyalties of private citizens which have no business informing the design of social institutions.

---

2 Roger Scruton, *Philosopher on Dover Beach* (London: St. Martin's Press 1988), 299

Having stated the position and the prima facie case for it, I shall first consider William Galston's challenge to the kind of liberalism which underlies my position. I then consider two arguments against my position. The first argument challenges the universalistic outlook of anti-nationalists, and claims that a particularistic ethic would give a more central place to nationality, and adds that a common nationality within a state is valuable for the delivery of other liberal commitments, so that the liberal state should foster a common national identity. The second argument says that the state should grant some 'group-differentiated rights' to some ethnic and national minorities as a precondition for preserving the autonomy and equal status of the members of those minorities.

I National Sentiment

Someone who fondly remembers 1966 as a golden moment in English football displays national sentiment. So does the voluntary recruit to the U.S. Armed Services who enthusiastically anticipates the opportunity to fight for his country. The British racist who proposes forcible 'repatriation' of Indians resident in Britain displays national sentiment. So does the internationalist socialist who looks back with shame at the British government's actions when it precipitated the war over the Falkland Islands.

What these examples share is a sense of identification with a *nation*, a sense that one's own life is somehow made better or worse by the activities and constitution of the nation (or other members of the nation) to which one belongs. It would be too strong to call this sense a *belief*, as the internationalist socialist example helps to show. The socialist may well *believe* that her well-being is entirely unaffected by the status of her country's actions, and is likely even to deny that the country is in any interesting sense 'her' country. She nevertheless, despite herself and in the face of her rational judgments, feels diminished and shamed by the behaviour which she actively opposed of a government which she has devoted much of her life to campaigning against. She does not feel the same sense of shame and diminishment when the U.S. government funnels military support to the Contras in Nicaragua, even though she regards these actions as equally wrong, and even more detrimental to the long-run success of the socialist project. The explanation is that she feels national sentiment toward the British nation.[3]

So national sentiment need not be revealed in the beliefs or the desires of the agent in whom it resides. It *can* be, and often is, of course, revealed in beliefs and desires: the belief of the racist that Indians are not British and his desire to keep Britain white both reveal his national sentiment.

Lack of space prevents me from giving a full definition of the nation, which anyway is not necessary for my argument.[4] But some characteristics should be mentioned. Most of our fellow nationals are just as much strangers to us as are foreigners. We do not know them, we know little about them, and we have no personal reason for caring more about them. Increasingly we interact in morally significant ways with many foreigners more than we do with many of our fellow-nationals. The liberal theoretical model of a closed system of social cooperation does not describe any country in the world: international trade now reaches even into Albania. Through that mechanism, as well as imperialist and colonial relationships between countries, we all come to have morally important relations with foreigners.

Nations are defined, in part, subjectively. A nation cannot be identified independently of the sentiments of its members concerning nationhood. The Welsh are a nation, but the Cornish are not, even though both groups have a distinct language, a distinct history, and a distinct geographical location, and almost certainly share the feature that they could not sustain themselves as a political entity entirely separate from England. What explains the difference is just that (a good number of) the Welsh think of themselves as a nation, whereas the Cornish do not.

---

3 I do not mean to imply that all internationalist socialists will feel this way. I am just describing what seems to me a possible (and, for some people, actual) psychological scenario.

4 See Allen Buchanan, *Secession* (Boulder, CO: Westview Press 1991); David Copp, 'Do Nations Have a Right to Self-Determination?' in Stanley G. French, ed., *Philosophers Look at Canadian Confederation* (Montreal: Canadian Philosophical Association 1979), 71-95; David Miller, *On Nationality* (Oxford: Oxford University Press 1995) for more elaborate characterizations of nations.

A shared belief in nationhood is not *sufficient* for nationhood. Were the residents of Northern California, or of South Yorkshire, to start to think of themselves as members of a distinct nation, they would not thereby constitute a nation. They lack the relevant kind of history which enables a group to be constituted as a nation. They, and their forebears, have not been defined by others in terms of their common characteristics, nor have they developed institutional ways of treating each other differently from how they treat others.

Again, it is too strong to say that nationhood needs to be something that all fellow nationals believe in. There has to be some critical mass of members of the group who regard one another as fellow-nationals, and who have some common view about who else counts as a member. It should be possible for the unsentimental internationalist socialist to be a member of the British nation even though she does not share any of the relevant beliefs or sentiments.

II   The Case Against Special Attention to National Sentiment

Liberals endorse a number of values which, together, support a prima facie case against giving special status to national sentiment in the structure of the state. I shall review these values, which are quite closely connected, and show how they support the case.

(1) *Liberal Legitimacy.* Liberals are typically not content with social institutions that merely deliver liberal justice. They usually believe that the state must do more – it must also be *legitimate.*

There is no consensus on exactly what constitutes liberal legitimacy. But three features are common to many accounts. The primary concern is with the consent of the governed. If legitimacy rested on unanimous consent, that would give a veto power to the unreasonable, which may, in turn, make it impossible for liberal arrangements ever to be legitimate. So the consent requirement is usually spelled out in terms of some hypothetical contractual condition: the state has to be such that it would be endorsed by all reasonable and well-informed people who are interested in moral terms of association.

Just as unanimous consent is too stringent a condition to be plausible, the hypothetical consent condition can look trivial. So it is usually strengthened by some concern that the state aspire for the actual consent of at least a majority, and preferably the vast majority, of citizens.[5]

Finally, conditions are placed on the means by which the state can permissibly seek the consent of the governed. In particular, liberals prefer that actual consent, where it exists, is robust against critical scrutiny. If it is the result of adaptive or accommodationist processes, or simply conditioned by manipulation or coercion by the state itself, it has no standing as actual consent. This is not to say that the consent must have been arrived at through a process of critical evaluation – it may be that the citizen assents largely without thinking, or because of loyalties passed on through family or enthusiasms shared with friends – but the consent should be such that if the citizen were to scrutinize it rationally and freely she would not revoke it. This condition is threatened if the state or state policy is designed to promote loyalty to the existing order, which policy is likely to promote consent without any reference to critical reasoning.

Liberal legitimacy therefore counts strongly against according special status to national sentiments. While according special status might well be supported by neutral arguments, a distortion is introduced in the process of the formation of the consent of citizens if granting special status leads to measures and policies which promote loyalty to the de facto state. This concern comes out most clearly in thinking about the way that public institutions present the history of the nation. If public institutions – especially museums and educational institutions – are subjected to patriotic and nationalistic pressures then they will present history in ways that are designed to support the reproduction over time of loyalty to the nation and, usually, the state. Consider contemporary 'culture wars' concerning the educational curriculum in the United States. Those who object to the presentation of the founding

---

5   This corresponds to the idea in Joshua Cohen's description of the ideal procedure in a deliberative democracy that "On the deliberative conception it is important that collective choices be made *in a deliberative way*, and not simply that those choices conform to the preferences, convictions and ideals of citizens," 'The Economic Basis of Deliberative Democracy,' *Social Philosophy and Policy* **6:2** (1987) 25-50 at 33. It is important for liberal legitimacy that assent be actually achieved, and not simply be consistent with people's preferences, convictions, and ideals.

fathers as slaveholders do not dispute the historical facts, nor do they dispute the relevance of those facts to historical interpretation and explanation. Instead, they argue that presenting those facts in that way inhibits the development of national loyalties. As William Galston puts it:

> rigorous historical research will almost certainly vindicate complex 'revisionist' accounts of key figures in American history. Civic education, however, requires a nobler, moralizing history: a pantheon of heroes who confer legitimacy on central institutions and are worthy of emulation. It is unrealistic to believe that more than a few adult citizens of liberal societies will ever move beyond the kind of civic commitment engendered by such a pedagogy.[6]

Consider also the recent furor over the Enola Gay exhibit in the Smithsonian Institution. The Enola Gay exhibit was to have included a text which gave the full historical record of the decision to bomb Hiroshima and Nagasaki, as well as a well-documented account of the political consequences of the bombing and the consequences for the victims of the bombing. Most opponents of the exhibit did not deny the truth of what was said, nor did they deny the accuracy of the historical interpretation. Rather they complained that including careful documentation of the suffering of the victims implied criticism of the decision, and that the effects of the exhibit would be to inhibit the development of national sentiment.

The problem is that Galston's nobler and more moralizing pedagogy, and the new Enola Gay exhibit, deliberately withholds relevant information and thus distorts the development of national loyalties. The state involves itself in deliberately trying to condition consent in a way that bypasses the critical faculties of its citizens and future citizens, thus undermining its own capacity for legitimacy.

(2) *Autonomy.* Liberals typically endorse an ideal of personal autonomy. The idea is that the way people live their lives should be in some deep sense genuinely their own. This does not imply that their choices about how to live should not be caused by external factors, since that is an unavoidable fact of human life. Nor does it imply that their choices should only count when made through a process of care-

---

6 William Galston, *Liberal Purposes* (Cambridge: Cambridge University Press 1991), 243-4

ful rational scrutiny. But it does imply that they should have the opportunity to make those choices which can be expected to have lasting effects on their lives in conditions where careful critical scrutiny over the range of options is a realistic possibility for them. The interest in autonomy supports the rights to freedom of conscience, association, and expression, and also, according to many theorists, supports a right to some basic level of access to resources.[7]

Liberals disagree about how much weight autonomy should be given *vis-à-vis* other values.[8] In so far as it is important, though, it conflicts with giving special attention to national sentiment in a number of ways. One fear is that granting special rights to national minorities will allow them to organize themselves in ways that violate the autonomy-supporting rights of some members of the minority. At the limit of granting special rights, secession, members of the nation from which secession occurs relinquish their power and obligation to protect the autonomy of the less powerful members of the seceding nation against predatory intrusions from more powerful members of the nation. Less extensive special rights, especially where they include rights to national self-government, jeopardize autonomy in so far as they cede discretion to the more powerful members of the minority group to limit the autonomy of their fellows.[9]

Of course, the argument above is only persuasive in so far as multinational political arrangements can be expected to protect the autonomy-supporting rights better than the exclusive political arrangements would. So, for example, there is no reason to suppose

---

7 See David Copp, 'The Right to an Adequate Standard of Living: Justice, Autonomy, and Basic Needs,' *Social Philosophy and Policy* **9:1** (1992) 231-62 for an account of how our interest in autonomy supports rights to access to a basic level of resources.

8 Some self-described liberals accord it no formal weight at all, for example, William Galston.

9 This worry might be dealt with in practice by making the right to secede conditional on the new state recognizing that minorities within the new nation have more limited rights of self-determination. See Allen Buchanan, *Secession*, especially ch. 4.

that a self-governing Scotland would do worse with respect to the autonomy of Scots than does the central government in Britain.

The argument may also sound somewhat paternalistic. The tendency to think of small nations as less careful than large nations concerning autonomy (especially given that the small nations we are concerned with have, in addition, often been objects of oppression by large nations) is a habit that exposes liberals to ridicule by defenders of small-nation nationalism. But, when the qualification explained in the previous paragraph is made clear, the argument is not paternalistic. The claim is that national sentiment should be granted no special status, whosoever national sentiment it is. And the claim is made in the broader moral framework which asserts that all of us have the obligation to provide one another with conditions conducive to the development of autonomy, which obligation is carried out through authoritative bodies such as the state. This obligation holds among co-nationals, and it also holds between members of different nations. As moral members of one nation (majority or otherwise) we should see the emergence of new terms of association as constrained by our obligation to ensure that all can be autonomous. We may be permitted to accept new terms, and, once we have acceded, the new terms may make it impermissible for us to interfere to promote autonomy. But for precisely that reason we must expect that the new terms provide properly for autonomy. The liberty of some to secede is not limited by a concern with *their own good*, but by the interest of others – who do not wish to exercise their liberty to secede – in autonomy.

The liberal approach is also less patronizing than it might seem. We can see this when we recognize that the obligation to provide autonomy-supporting conditions to others is universal. All moral persons owe it to all others. Therefore, the members of minority nations seeking new terms of association also owe it to members of majority nations. Just as members of majority nations should be concerned to ensure that members of minority nations have autonomy-supporting conditions preserved, so should members of minority nations do the same for those with whom their terms of association are changing. It is hard to think of real-life examples, especially because in actual historical cases there is almost always a relationship of injustice holding between nations which renegotiate their terms. But the basic idea can be illustrated by considering the standing of the Scots within the British national state.

It is commonly remarked that if Scotland seceded then the rest of the U.K. would be consigned to permanent government by the Conservative Party. If this is true, and if Conservative Party government is considered to be bad for the autonomy of whoever is ruled by it, then in seizing rights to self-government the Scots would be jeopardizing the autonomy of the English and the Welsh. It cannot be objected that the English and Welsh bring the harm on themselves, for while Conservative voters may deserve whatever happens to them, the same cannot be said of anti-Conservative voters. By quitting, the Scots would be leaving their erstwhile co-voters in a permanent minority and hence damaging their prospects for autonomy.[10]

(3) *Neutrality*. Liberals often argue that the state should be neutral among conceptions of the good life. They acknowledge that in modern societies there will be a plurality of ways of life and conceptions of how best to live, and they say that the state should not favour some at the expense of others. Neutrality could constrain the state in several different ways, of which only one is a live option. We could mean something like *neutrality of effect*, which would imply that the state must not act in ways that actually make it easier for some conceptions to be realized and more difficult for others. For example, a policy subsidizing the maintenance of outdoor parks and the planting of trees would make it easier and less expensive to live a rambler's life but more difficult (because, by hypothesis, the trees cause interference with reception) and expensive to live the life of a ham radio operator. Such a policy would be prohibited by neutrality of effect unless it was matched by other policies which would exactly compensate the suffering parties. The example should make it obvious why such a constraint would be impractical – it would require a level of monitoring of the effects of policies which seems unfeasible.

But a more powerful case against neutrality of effect is that the reasons supporting neutrality support a different interpretation of the constraint, as *neutrality of justification*. Neutrality of justification prohibits that policies be *justified* on the grounds that they favour one con-

---

10 This example has limited force because the case involves only harms and bads, and not the cessation of guarantees for autonomy-supporting conditions.

ception over another. This version of neutrality does not scrutinize the effects of policies but instead the reasons for them.

What makes a neutrality constraint appealing? If we accept what Rawls calls the fact of reasonable pluralism – the idea that a free society will inevitably be characterized by reasonable disagreement among its citizens about the good, leading to a multiplicity of competing, conflicting, and sometimes incommensurable conceptions of the good – then we should be concerned that the state not presume the falsehood or wickedness of the deepest moral commitments of its reasonable citizens. As the holder of a monopoly on legitimate coercive force, and as a mechanism which is supposed to be accountable to all citizens, the state should pass as little comment as possible on the content of the ways of life of its own citizens.[11]

---

11 It is important to note that my use of the term 'citizen' does not reflect any commitment to any sort of national identity. Saying that citizens of a state owe these obligations to one another carries no implication that they owe any less or any different to citizens of other states. Nor does it imply that they have any right to determine the conditions of entry to or exit form citizenship. Anti-liberals are prone to accusing liberals of inconsistency when they use the language of commonality or citizenship. Roger Scruton says,

"Nor are liberals consistent in their repudiation of the national idea, as is shown by a characteristic liberal attitude to immigration ... The argument is advanced that we have no right to close our doors against immigrants from our former colonies, since it was we who exploited them, or reduced them to the state of economic and cultural dependence which ensures that their best – perhaps their only – prospects are now on British soil. If you examine the use of 'we' in that sentence you will find the perfect instance of the national idea, as I have described it: the idea of moral unity between people, based in territory, language, association, history and culture, and so bound up with the self-consciousness of those who are joined by it, as to make subsequent generations answerable for the sins of their forefathers..." Roger Scruton, *Philosopher on Dover Beach*, 320.

Scruton does not *quote* a liberal anti-nationalist, so his attribution of inconsistency is only to a statement which he has made up himself. But even on the way he has construed the position it does not take a great deal of charity in interpretation to render the position consistent. The first 'we' in his sentence refers only to the group of people who have the de facto control of the gates. The subsequent uses of 'we' and 'our' are indeed careless (though, as I say, the carelessness is that of a liberal in Scruton's imagination), but they are a shorthand for the individualist idea that we, the de facto controllers of the gates, are,

A clarification about the role of the state is in order here. The liberal democratic state is properly seen not as an outside agent, but as a corporate agent through which citizens carry out their obligations to one another. The obligation of neutrality, then, is an obligation which citizens have to each other. Nevertheless, the constraint on the state is stronger than the constraint on individuals. As individuals we have no obligation to refrain from personal comment on the ways of life that others select. We may disagree and disapprove of the behaviour and moral commitments of others, and we may – and sometimes should – give expression to this comment. What we should refrain from is co-ercing or manipulating others into behaving as we would have them behave. The state, though, as a corporate agent, is incapable of passing personal comment, and its coercive functions are so integral to its identity that even when it passes comment in a way that is neither coercive nor manipulative it will generally be easy for citizens to reasonably believe that coercion or manipulation is taking place. Even if they do not believe that, they may still feel that they are devalued and not treated with equal respect.

The basic idea behind the value of neutrality, then, is that non-neutrality is an unwarranted sign of disrespect to the person whose views are being disregarded. In treating that person's conception of the good as inferior to others, the state is (and fellow citizens through the state are) treating that person, effectively, as worthy of lesser respect. If the ideal of respect for persons supports the value of neutrality, the version it supports is neutrality of justification. Neutrality of effect makes no reference to any kind of comment on the commitments of citizens. It is not disrespectful to another if I simply take actions which make it more diffi-cult for them to fulfill their aims, for in doing so I am not commenting on

---

unjustly, the beneficiaries of a current distributive injustice which was caused by the behaviour of past de facto controllers of the gates who also, coincidentally, were our forebears (or some of our forebears). We do not owe anybody anything just because our forebears did wrong to their forebears. We owe things to them because we are currently on their wrong side, which situation was indeed brought about by the actions of our forebears. The appeal to groups here, furthermore, is not a fundamental appeal to group identity, but a convenient appeal for the sake of social policy, which must always be applied to well-defined groups, even though it must fundamentally be justified on individualist grounds.

the aims themselves. It is only if my reason for doing so is my attitude toward that person or their aims that I am according them disrespect.[12]

It should be obvious how neutrality of justification would prohibit special attention to national sentiment. In any free society not only can pluralism about ways of life be expected, but so can pluralism about the nation. Citizens will be loyal to different nations and will have different levels of loyalty toward their nation, and some will have no loyalty at all. To make decisions about institutions which deliberately favour the sentiments of some rather than others on the grounds that the loyal citizen's sentiments are superior would violate the constraint: it would be disrespectful toward the disloyal or indifferent citizen. Similarly, to make decisions on such grounds within the state in public policy areas – for example, to spend tax money on the upkeep of national heritage collections – violates the constraint.

It might be less obvious why the devolutionary measures of establishing special rights to national minorities would violate the constraint. After all, the decision to do this could be based on any of a number of grounds, and will rarely be based on the view that the sentiments of some national minorities are superior to those of others or the majority. But such measures are often based on a view that national sentiments are important in a way that other sentiments (say, political, or merely regional, sentiments) are not. Usually, if the sentiments of the merely regional secessionist movement are not given the same weight in the same circumstances as the national minority secessionists, their own identities would be treated as having less significance than those of the national minorities.

There are two qualifications to the power of neutrality to bar the promotion of national identity or the establishment of special rights.

---

12 In fact, violations of neutrality of intent sometimes make it easier for the victims to fulfill their conceptions of the good. Obvious cases are conceptions of the good which see persecution as a precondition of demonstrating full faith. Less obviously, cultures which suffer mild persecution are sometimes artificially sustained by the resistance that persecution provokes. That said, when a policy has publicly demonstrated negative effects on a particular conception of the good for some lengthy period of time it is sometimes reasonable for those who are disadvantaged by it to feel devalued even when in fact the justification of the policy was neutral.

Neutrality of justification, as I have said, comments only on the justification of a policy, and never on the content of the policy itself. So, while it does rule out special attention to national sentiment in *justifying* policies, if other justifications can be given for promoting some national identities or granting special rights, then the *measures* may be permissible by the constraint. For example, a proposal that English be the official language of the E.U. is susceptible of at least two justifications. The first would be non-neutral – it is a superior language, reflecting a superior culture, to those of other European nations. But a neutral justification is also possible – that it is already the second language of more E.U. citizens than any other language, and would therefore be the most administratively convenient.[13]

The second qualification is that neutrality of justification is implausible if it is supposed either to be a foundational constraint or to have wide scope. While Nazis should have the same rights and liberties as all other citizens, there is no reason to grant their values exactly the same status as other people's values in thinking abut how to design social institutions. Neutrality has narrow scope, in the sense that the state should be neutral within a range of acceptable conceptions of the good (which should, in turn, be a wide range). There are, furthermore, other values, which like neutrality emanate from the more foundational value of respect for persons. Neutrality is one among several values to be applied at the point of institutional design, and a defensible theory of neutrality would tell us exactly how to balance it against other values.

Non-neutral arguments for attending to national sentiment, then, may be acceptable because they fall outside the scope of the neutrality constraint. Equally, there may be quite serious arguments for special rights or national identities which are in the relevant sense neutral.

---

13 Of course, if the neutral justification were proposed by Baroness Thatcher no one would believe that she was being sincere. Discussions of justifications of policies are usually highly stylized because it is difficult in practice to establish the *real* justifications of any given measure. Not only are people often insincere about the public justifications they offer, but even when they are not, in democratic processes the supporters of any measure or package of measures typically diverge in their motivations. I address this issue in 'Neutrality, Publicity, and State Funding of the Arts,' *Philosophy and Public Affairs* **24:1** (1995) 36-63.

Although I shall ultimately reject both of them, I think the argument considered in section 5 falls into the second category, while the argument in section 4 falls into the first.

(4) *Equality and Arbitrariness.* The final liberal concern is one of justice. Contemporary egalitarian liberals are committed to a principle of equality, which says that how the benefits and burdens of social cooperation are distributed should not be affected by features of persons' situations which are arbitrary from the moral point of view. The best known elaboration of this principle is that of John Rawls, who uses it to generate his two principles of justice. In particular, he argues for the Difference Principle on these grounds.[14]

National membership is for the most part morally arbitrary. We did not choose our nation from a range of serious options any more than we chose our race or sex, or the class position of our parents. It seems arbitrary to allow national membership to affect our prospects, and this arbitrariness seems objectionable when it is feasible to design institutions or promote policies which will ameliorate the effects of national membership on our life prospects.

Granting national sentiment a special status in the determination of policy will often render our prospects unequal. Having the government sponsor the identity of the greater nation risks two particularly worrying effects. The first is that members of minority nations within the larger polity may have their self-respect undermined by the promotion of the greater national sentiment, and thus be rendered less capable than others of taking advantage of opportunities which are formally available to all. The second is that within the majority national identity people who are already less advantaged than others will be made more manipulable by those who are more powerful within the nation. Special rights for minority nations within the polity also jeopardize equality. In particular, as I shall argue later, special language rights can risk the equal advantage of members of the minority national group. To put it starkly, children growing up as monolingual speakers of a minority language are usually at a tremendous dis-

---

14 John Rawls, *A Theory of Justice* (Cambridge: Harvard University Press 1971), esp. 75-90, 100-8

advantage as against children growing up speaking a majority language. Language provides access to opportunities, and for most people their native language is that with which they most readily identify. If we consider competitive opportunities in the economic marketplace this should be obvious: other things being equal, a larger economy provides more, and more diverse, opportunities for individual economic actors than smaller economies. The problem here is with the predictable effects of giving national membership special status.

III   Against the Diversity State

The first position I shall consider does not directly advocate giving national sentiment special status, but repudiates the version of liberalism I have relied upon in section 2. One reason for giving special attention to national sentiment is the emergence of 'diversity' as a progressive value. Respect for diversity requires that we take seriously people's deepest sense of identity; and nationality, like sexuality and gender, is privileged as a source of identity.

William Galston attempts to systematize the vague sense that diversity should be respected into the basis of a theory for the liberal state. He contrasts the diversity-based approach, which is continuous with the Reformation project, with the autonomy-based approach deriving from the Enlightenment project. While the Enlightenment project emphasizes *individual autonomy*, and regards state legitimacy in terms of free and reasoned consent of citizens, the Reformation project emphasizes *personal commitment*, and regards legitimacy in terms of the scope permitted for diversity. The problem for liberalism is that of managing differences – primarily, but not exclusively, religious differences – and the most effective strategy for this is by 'managing diversity through mutual toleration.'[15] The autonomy-based liberalism I relied on in section 2 is self-defeating:

> any liberal argument that invokes autonomy as a general rule of public action in effect takes sides in the ongoing struggle between reason and faith, reflection

---

15   William Galston, 'Two Concepts of Liberalism,' *Ethics* **105:3** (1995) 516-34 at 526

and tradition. Autonomy-based arguments are bound to marginalize those individuals and groups who cannot conscientiously embrace the Enlightenment Project. To the extent that they identify liberalism with the Enlightenment Project, they limit support for their cause and drive many citizens of good will – indeed many potential allies – into opposition.[16]

Galston's primary theoretical concern is to vindicate allowing great scope for religious commitment. He does not explicitly address the question of nationality (at least in his explicit discussion of the Diversity State[17]), and I doubt that his view directly implies that national sentiment should get special accommodation. But since respect for, or the preservation of, diversity is so often used to justify special accommodations of nationality, and since Galston offers a systematic account of diversity as a political value, it is worth looking at his argument for 'taking diversity seriously.' He offers three basic reasons for placing diversity at the center of liberal theory.

First, the fact of wide diversity could only be overcome by degrees and kinds of coercion that both would have disastrous effects for civic peace and might be unacceptable on independent grounds. Second, we could recognize diversity as instrumentally valuable, either for the Madisonian reason that it acts as a bulwark against tyranny, or for the Millian reason that the availability of options both makes possible experiments in living and makes more meaningful those commitments we adopt. Third,

> we may embrace diversity as an intrinsic value. One variant of this is the thesis ... that our moral universe is characterized by plural and conflicting values which cannot be harmonized in a single comprehensive way of life.... Another form ... appeals to the necessarily diverse experiences and standpoints of different groups within a social structure and to the desirability of public institutions that conduce to the expression, rather than the coercive suppression or covert homogenization, of such differences.[18]

---

16 Galston, 'Two Concepts of Liberalism,' 526

17 Galston does appear to put forward a proposal favouring large-nation national sentiment in his account of civic education. See *Liberal Purposes* (Cambridge: Cambridge University Press 1991), 243.

18 Galston, 'Two Concepts of Liberalism,' 527

But none of the above reasons support giving diversity a central place. The first concern is not a reason for caring about diversity per se, but for respecting certain basic liberties. If respecting liberties leads to diversity, so be it, but if it were to lead to ideological convergence, we would have no reason for trying to disrupt that process. Consider the second reason proffered. Whether a particular diversity has Madisonian or Millian benefits depends on the content of the different commitments that it contains. A diversity of authoritarian and fundamentalist sub-communities, coexisting uneasily only because of the heroically well-constructed design of the institutions governing their interactions, might make for much less experimentalism than a less diverse array of overlapping and more liberal subcultures. Similarly, if the only way that one could adopt another way of life would be by completely cutting one's ties with one's parent community, it is not clear how the existence of other formal options confers value on one's continued commitment to the original way of life. Of course this is an unrealistic picture – in modern societies different fundamentalisms are buffered by a wide array of ways of life which are committed to toleration, autonomy, and experimentalism as values in themselves. But it is the existence of *these ways of life* that enables the others to be part of a diversity which contributes instrumentally to Madisonian and Millian goals.

Finally, and most tellingly, the reason Galston gives for intrinsically valuing diversity is deeply problematic. Take the first version of the view. The fact that our moral universe is pluralistic does not make *diversity* intrinsically valuable. A narrow world, in which most people live only a few of the available valuable lives, is no less valuable than one in which more of those available valuable kinds of life are lived. That world is more desirable, furthermore, than one in which a narrow range of the available good lives are lived as well as a diverse range of bad lives. The value here is not of *diversity*, but of the realization of the *valuable* values. The second version of the idea, that it is valuable that those lives that are lived should be expressed, again does not make diversity intrinsically valuable in any interesting sense. It supports the standard liberal freedoms of conscience and expression. But it also supports the much less clearly liberal idea (which finds no place in Galston's theory) that people should be actively encouraged to express their ways of life. And in neither case does it support *diversity* as a value; it merely supports accommodation of whatever diversity there is.

So the reasons offered do not support giving diversity per se the central place that Galston claims for it in liberal theory, although they certainly do support making available some of the standard freedoms common to all versions of liberalism, which freedoms can be expected to produce some diversity. Nor is the case against autonomy-based liberalism as strong as Galston suggests. An autonomy-based liberalism does not aim to obliterate (nor would it have the effect of obliterating) ways of life involving unreasoned faith. Instead, it aims at ensuring that no one falls into (or is conditioned into) such a way of life without there being available to them other real options. By facilitating autonomy, through appropriate requirements on the mandatory educational curriculum, through regulating the provision of information to consumers, and by other measures, the liberal state gives meaning to its promise that citizens will be free with respect to the variety of available ways of life. Recognizing the truth of Berlin's claim that there are plural and incommensurable values does not prejudice the liberal against autonomy – indeed it is precisely the value of the skills associated with autonomy for negotiated plural and conflicting values that leads some theorists to give it a central place in liberalism.[19]

IV Miller on Nationality

The first direct challenge to the standard liberal position I consider has been recently made by David Miller. Miller argues for an ethical particularism which implies that national membership carries with it special ethical obligations:

> Nations are ethical communities. In acknowledging a national identity I am also acknowledging that I owe special obligations to fellow members of my nation which I do not owe to other human beings.[20]

---

19 See Joseph Raz, *The Morality of Freedom* (Oxford: Oxford University Press 1987). I discuss autonomy-facilitation as an element of liberalism in 'Is There a Neutral Justification for Liberalism?,' *Pacific Philosophical Quarterly* **77**:3 (1996), 193–215, and 'Egalitarian Liberals and School Choice,' *Politics and Society* **24**:4 (1996), 457–86.

20 David Miller, *On Nationality* (Oxford: Oxford University Press 1995), 49

Miller describes ethical particularism as follows:

> [Ethical particularism] holds that relations between persons are part of the basic subject matter of ethics, so that fundamental principles may be attached directly to these relations ... agents are already encumbered with a variety of ties and commitments to particular other agents, or to groups or collectivities, and they begin their ethical reasoning from those commitments.[21]

How does ethical particularism support nationality? The idea is that attachments to groups such as nations may play a legitimate role in reasoning about fundamental principles. It is proper for me to think of myself as having distinctive obligations to my parents, co-workers and fellow members of my local community, and I should similarly think of myself as distinctively obliged to my co-nationals.

Miller does not provide an argument for the connection between particularism and nationality. He appears to think that if it is true that distinctive moral obligations arise simply from membership in a community then membership in a nation, which is a community (albeit of an unusual kind), similarly gives rise to obligations. He treats it as a given that people *will* feel national attachments, and says that "the potency of nationality as a source of personal identity means that its obligations are strongly felt and may extend very far."[22] The resultant obligations will differ from nation to nation depending on the content of their public culture, and will be somewhat indeterminate, reflecting the indeterminacy of any national culture.[23] Nevertheless, the resultant obligations are in an important sense objective:

> It [the indeterminacy of the obligations] certainly does not imply that my obligations *qua* member of nation *A* are merely whatever I take them to be. The culture in question *is* a public phenomenon: any one individual may interpret it rightly or wrongly, and draw correct or incorrect conclusions about his obligations to compatriots as a result.[24]

---

21 Miller, *On Nationality*, 50

22 Miller, *On Nationality*, 70

23 Miller, *On Nationality*, 70

24 Miller, *On Nationality*, 69

Would it follow from our owing distinctive obligations to our fellow nationals that national sentiment ought to be given a special status in determining political arrangements? This depends on how we understand national membership. For Miller there are five distinctive characteristics of national communities. They are constituted by belief; they embody historical continuity; they embody an *active* identity ("nations do things together: they take decisions, achieve results."[25]); they are connected to some geographical area; and they have a national character and a common public culture: there is a "sense that people belong together by virtue of the characteristics they share."[26]

It is not clear from his characterization of nationhood whether Miller regards national membership as voluntary in the weak sense that those who decide they do not want to belong can withdraw from the nation (without withdrawing from whatever state they belong to). If membership were voluntary in this sense, then the obligations to fellow-nationals would also be voluntary: having withdrawn from membership, one would no longer have the obligations. The emphasis he places on the *feeling* of national membership does suggest that membership is voluntary in this sense. But there is a problem here. If national membership is fully voluntary, then it is not clear how to justify giving national membership the political salience which Miller suggests (let alone how to do it in practice). If national membership is voluntary then one can jettison the putative obligations it grounds simply by giving it up. But political institutions which enforce the obligations of nationality will thereby provide a strong incentive to give up membership, as well as confronting the difficulty of distinguishing members from non-members at any given time. Rather than having the state enforce these obligations it would make more sense to allow for voluntary civic organizations within which those who think of themselves as national members (and hence bearers of mutual obligations) can deal freely with one another.

The idea that membership is fully voluntary is, anyway, counterintuitive. The alienated American is still an American, however much

---

25 Miller, *On Nationality*, 24

26 Miller, *On Nationality*, 25

she repudiates her national membership, and this remains true even if she succeeds in giving up her citizenship and taking on another.[27] If the intuitive idea that people can be members of their nations even if they do not themselves identify with the nation is correct, then the idea that we have distinctive obligations to our compatriots does give a special place to national sentiment. The sentiments of nationalists trump those of their co-nationals who are anti-nationalist or internationalist. Those who recognize their obligations toward their compatriots must be allowed to carry them out; and it may be that those who do not recognize them must be forced to carry them out.

Miller offers a particular way in which national sentiment should be accommodated: through national self-determination. Nations should be allowed to be politically fully self-governing entities.[28] National self-determination is desirable from the perspective of the national members because it gives them a vehicle (the state) for the central coordination of their obligations to one another, and for the maintenance of their national culture.[29] It is also an expression of collective autonomy: people 'have an interest in shaping the world in association with others with whom they identify,' and making the main direct coercive mechanism through which they have influence one through which only their fellow nationals also have influence fulfills this interest.[30]

This defence of national self-determination suggests a second way in which national sentiment should be treated specially. Not only should it be accommodated by allowing (and where appropriate forcing) people to deliver on their distinctive obligations to their compatriots,

---

27 I do not mean to preclude the possibility of successful assimilation, but, at least for adults, it takes a very long time and considerable good fortune.

28 He explicitly distinguishes national self-determination from the view that every nation should have a state, though he is friendly to that idea. Miller, *On Nationality*, 80.

29 Miller, *On Nationality*, 83-86

30 Miller, *On Nationality*, 88. Notice that this advantage, unlike the other two, requires that the state be democratic. Whereas mediating our distinctive obligations and protecting our national culture can be done by an authoritarian state, it is meaningless to say that we are exercising collective autonomy unless the mechanism by which we are doing this is responsive to our demands.

but it should also be actively fostered to ensure that national ties are felt, thus enabling the state to pursue its central functions effectively.

Miller's defence of nationality is flawed in a number of ways.

First, of course, there are the difficulties with ethical particularism. It is a standard move against impartial or universalistic theories of ethics that they have difficulty dealing with attachments. But once a universalistic standard is abandoned the particularist has to give an account of *which* ties and attachments should be privileged by theory. The difficulty is how to abandon universality without conceding to arbitrariness. One reason why universalistic theories of ethics have been seen as more secure bases for liberalism is that moral theories which make arbitrary features of our lives figure centrally in the determination of rights and obligations will have difficulty giving a principled account of the freedoms and rights associated with liberal democracy.

Even if we concede Miller's particularism, there is difficulty showing that the nation is one of the relevant particulars. As I noted, he does not really provide an argument for this connection. There are two natural candidates to serve as bases for particularistic moral obligations. The first, which universalistic theories notoriously have great difficulty with, is intimacy.[31] Friendship and family relationships are difficult to account for, since although strangers are often in greater objective need than our friends and family members, it seems wrong of us to abandon our friends or children, or even to make our attachment to them contingent on them having needs we can better fulfill than those of others. But nations are not families – they are not intimate in the way that poses this difficulty for universalists. The nation is, simply, a group of strangers. So intimacy cannot be the basis of the special status of the nation.

The second natural candidate would be our distinctive impersonal cooperative and mutually beneficial interactions with our fellow nationals. There are two serious difficulties with this. First, whom we interact with is to a large degree the *result of* (and hence not grounds

---

31 The problems are not, in my view, insuperable. See for example Barbara Herman, 'Agency, Attachment, and Difference,' *Ethics* **101:4** (1991) 775-97 and Peter Railton, 'Alienation, Consequentialism, and the Demands of Morality,' *Philosophy and Public Affairs* **13:2** (1984) 134-71.

for designing) the boundaries and structure of political institutions. Secondly, even in a world with fairly well-defined and limitedly permeable national boundaries, we interact just as significantly with members of other nations as with our fellow nationals. The Detroit autoworker interacts as closely with her Japanese counterpart as with the Vermont organic farmer. The Scots fisherman interacts more with the Icelandic fisherman than with the East Grinstead stockbroker. We live in a world of complex interactions among strangers – and these interactions do not track nationality, except where the design of political boundaries along national lines constrain them to.

The third problem with Miller's defence of nationality is that Miller works with an extremely benign nationalism. In an earlier paper he quotes the Rat's expression of a peculiarly English insularity:

> Beyond the Wild Wood comes the Wild World. And that's something that doesn't matter, either to you or me. I've never been there, and I'm never going, nor you either if you've got any sense at all. Don't ever refer to it again, please.[32]

He argues that nationalism is not necessarily illiberal, and that while "it is descriptively true in many historical cases" that "national identities are ... biased in favour of the dominant cultural group, the group that has historically dominated the politics of the state," "it is not integral to national identities that they should be loaded in this way."[33] But this is not sufficiently reassuring – he is claiming that *nationality* has a special importance that should inform institutional design, not just those nationalities which lack dominating and oppressive dynamics. Many national identities in fact include within them the notion that they are superior to others in a way that justifies overriding the interests of nonnationals as well as some of the claims of national members. Perhaps the Generals who plotted to kill Hitler were being 'good Germans' – but perhaps they were not. It is possible that 'Labour's thirteen traitors'[34]

---

32   David Miller, 'In Defence of Nationality,' *Journal of Applied Philosophy* **10:1** (1993) 3-16 at 3

33   Miller, 'In Defence of Nationality,' 11

34   These were the thirteen Labour MPs identified by *The Sun* as opponents of the war against Argentina over the Falkland Islands.

and the few thousands of people who protested against the British military action were being good Britons – but it is more likely that Mrs. Thatcher and her supporters were. If national identities are privileged, malign national identities are included, and this puts other centrally important values (including individual freedom, democracy, and distributive justice) at risk. At least Miller owes some additional account which both shows why malign national identities are excluded from his special importance and does not make reference to national identity redundant.

An associated concern is that national cultures will be promoted in a coercive and oppressive manner. Uncoordinated market forces are liable to establish incentives which lead to the national culture being undermined in ways that no one wants. As Miller says,

> We may all value a landscape in which small fields are divided by hedgerows rich in animal and bird life, but each of us has commercial reasons for rooting out hedges and creating agricultural prairies. As owners of television stations we may sincerely want to make high-class dramas and probing documentaries, but in a competitive market we may have to buy imported soap operas in order to survive.[35]

Miller claims that "very often this [protection of the national culture] can be done by inducements rather than by coercion: farmers can be given incentives to preserve their hedgerows; the domestic film industry can be subsidized out of cinema revenues; important works of art can be purchased for national collections; and so forth." But the mechanisms he describes *are* coercive. Certainly, they do not coerce the farmer and the broadcast company owner; instead they coerce the cinema-goer and the taxpayer. And they coerce these people in the name of a culture for which they do not express an interest in their behaviour as consumers. When inducements are established they have to be inducements to do (or avoid doing) *something*. What the content of that something is depends on the content of the culture envisaged. Those who establish the inducements guide the direction of the culture, and in the course of doing so they coerce some of the participants in the culture. It is hard to see in what sense they can 'provide an environ-

---

35 Miller, *On Nationality*, 87

ment in which the culture can develop spontaneously,'[36] since their inducements must be guided by non-spontaneous views about the direction the culture should take.

That some measure involves coercion is not, in itself, an objection to it, and my main point here is just to show that coercion is not avoided even by mechanisms which offer inducements. Coercion is legitimized when it is necessary in order to provide justice (e.g., taxation to provide education for children and to redistribute wealth in an egalitarian direction), and it is also often legitimized by being the outcome of democratic procedures. But Miller makes no argument that the protection of the national culture is a requirement of justice. And even if inducements and coercion to protect the culture in various ways are the result of a democratic vote, they are still problematic in that they involve the democratic majority in coercing the minority with respect to the way of life they prefer to lead. The minority, presumably, either does not concede the importance of protecting the culture or does not believe that the proposed measures will do so effectively. Coercion, at least in the former case, goes to the heart of dissenters' views about the good life, coercively redistributing resources which they would have used to live their lives the way they sought to, and deploying those resources both to supplement the resources others have for living a different way and to shape the cultural environment in a way that the dissenters find unacceptable.[37]

Finally, it is worth examining Miller's non-particularistic argument that national self-determination enables the state to function more effectively, especially in its redistributive functions.[38] He argues that since

---

36 Miller, *On Nationality*, 88

37 I have discussed the issue of state funding of the arts in 'Neutrality, Publicity, and State Funding of the Arts,' *Philosophy and Public Affairs* **24:1** (1995) 36-63. I think that the moderate argument I make there against state funding of the arts applies even more compellingly to state support for a particular national culture. For more discussions of state funding of culture, see Ronald Dworkin, *A Matter of Principle* (Cambridge, MA: Harvard University Press 1985), ch. 11; Noel Carroll, 'Can Government Funding of the Arts be Justified Theoretically?,' *Journal of Aesthetic Education* **21:1** (1987) 21-34; and Samuel Black, 'Revisionist Liberalism and the Decline of Culture,' *Ethics* **102:2** (1992) 244-67.

38 Miller, *On Nationality*, 90-92

much state activity requires voluntary cooperation of citizens, and since in democratic states majorities have to be forged in favour of just policies, a certain level of trust has to be present among the citizens of the state. "Ties of community are an important source of such trust between people who are not personally known to each other and who are not in a position to directly monitor one another's personal behaviour" and "the importance of national communities here is simply that they are encompassing communities which aspire to draw in everyone who inhabits a particular territory."[39]

Note that this argument is not one for giving national sentiment a special place. Special place is given to distributive justice, and national membership is deployed in a systematic way to advance that goal.

The empirical evidence for Miller's claim that nationally homogeneous states are better equipped to deliver justice is far from clear. The most assimilationist national identity in the world, that of the 'American,' dominates the culture of a country which has, among advanced industrial nations, singularly failed to establish robust economically egalitarian institutions.[40] Some historians claim that the content of the national identity has at least some small explanatory role in this failure.[41] The successful establishment and maintenance of welfare states, which has certainly been carried out within nation states, owes a great deal to *class* solidarities and the capacity of different class agents to build lasting class coalitions through the ingenious design of policy. Whether a common national identity facilitated the establishment of those coalitions is, at least, an open question.[42]

---

39 Miller, *On Nationality*, 92. See also 'In Defence of Nationality,' 9-10.

40 See Andrew Shapiro, *We're Number One* (New York: Vintage Books 1992), Edward N. Wolff, *Top Heavy: A Study of the Increasing Inequality of Wealth in America* (New York: Twentieth Century Fund 1995), Nancy Folbre, *The New Field Guide to the U.S. Economy* (New York: The New Press 1995) for some evidence of this failure.

41 See, for example, Mike Davis, *Prisoners of the American Dream* (London: Verso 1984).

42 See, for example, Gosta Esping-Anderson, *Politics Against Markets* (Princeton, NJ: Princeton University Press 1985) and *The Three Worlds of Welfare Capitalism* (Princeton, NJ: Princeton University Press 1990); Adam Przeworski, *Capitalism and Social Democracy* (Cambridge: Cambridge University Press 1985).

Miller also neglects the frequent disruptive effects of national identities on class solidarities, and hence on redistribution. National identity is often used with some success in capitalist democracies to persuade working people that they should moderate their demands, and to impugn the responsibility of political agents who advocate a more militant stance.[43] If national identity is to be advocated for its effects on the functioning of the state, all potential effects, good and bad, should be taken into account.

Of course egalitarians are in practice remarkably tolerant of national boundaries, and argue for redistributive measures within rich nations which fall far short of the wholesale redistribution egalitarian justice appears to require if we owe nothing distinctive to our fellow-countrymen. This tolerance can be endorsed without contradiction. Egalitarians can only effect full-scale redistribution if they are able to win wide support for it, so they have to concentrate on redistributive policies for which support can be won in the social institutions within which they operate. They do not believe that redistribution within rich countries works to the detriment of egalitarian redistribution from rich countries to poor countries, and they are empirically supported by the fact that the more egalitarian wealthy countries tend to give a higher percentage of their GDP in foreign aid, with fewer 'national interest' conditions attached to the aid. So realistic egalitarians with long time horizons can accept the conditions in which they operate as given in the short term, and seek changes within those institutions, without compromising their long-term aim of transforming them.[44]

---

43 'The state of the nation is all my concern
When I'm gnawing a crust for my dinner
I can't afford meat on the money I earn
And I'm growing steadily thinner
But its all for the good of the nation.

The Nation the nation
The nation is in such a terrible state
Stagnation, inflation
If we all pull together we'll once again make Britain Great.'

Leon Rosselson, from 'The Good of the Nation,' lyrics printed in Leon Rosselson and Jeff Perks, *For the Good of the Nation* (London: Journeyman Press 1981).

44 See Robert Goodin, 'What's So Special About Our Fellow Countrymen?,' *Ethics* **98**:4 (1988) 663-86 for a careful defence of a universalist approach to nationality.

V Kymlicka's Liberal Objection

Will Kymlicka has recently developed an argument in favour of granting special rights to minority nations from within the autonomy-based liberalism which usually underlies opposition to such measures. His argument is extremely important, and, in my view, the most promising, since it uses the very premises on which liberals tend to base their hostility to granting national sentiment special attention. I shall review the argument in some detail. Having done so I shall identify three key problems. Although I think that the objections to Miller are decisive, I am less sure that those for Kymlicka are. But I do think that the problems I raise at the very least show that his argument has application only in a very limited range of circumstances.

The central argument proceeds in two stages. Kymlicka argues first that membership in a cultural community should count as a primary good (in the Rawlsian sense of a good that any rational person would want whatever else she wanted), and second that its status as a primary good justifies some special cultural rights and protections which conflict with and override some standard liberal rights.[45]

The first stage of the argument proceeds by analogy with Rawls's argument for the Liberty Principle. Rawls identifies self-respect as a good crucial to the ability to pursue our conception of the good whatever that is. But we can only have self-respect, and the confidence in ourselves and the conception of the good which accompanies it, if we have a conception of the good with which we can identify. In turn, this requires that we have the conditions in which we can realistically form and revise our beliefs about how to live. This interest in the capacity to form and revise our conception of the good supports the Liberty Principle; in particular it supports very firm guarantees for freedom of expression, freedom of association, and freedom of conscience.

---

45 Most of my discussion focuses on the arguments made in Will Kymlicka, *Liberalism, Community and Culture* (Oxford: Oxford University Press 1989), and developed in *Multicultural Citizenship* (Oxford: Oxford University Press 1995). A distinct argument, concerning the importance of societal, or institutionally complete, cultures, is developed in *Multicultural Citizenship*. See Allen Buchanan's contribution to this volume, 'What's So Special About Nations?', for criticism of this argument.

But, Kymlicka adds, the ability to form and revise our conception of the good is not just dependent on our own capacities and guarantees of freedom. It also depends on there being background cultural and intellectual institutions which we can realistically draw on in developing our beliefs. We do not spontaneously form our beliefs about the good life – we take up and scrutinize ideas in our cultural environment. The background culture provides a 'context of choice' without which the liberty to form and revise our conception of the good cannot serve the interest which justifies it. The cultural structure provides a context of choice which is essential for self-respect.[46] So membership in a cultural structure is a primary good in much the same way as are some of the basic liberties protected by the Liberty Principle.

The mere fact that people have an interest in cultural membership does not suffice to justify any special rights. The second stage of Kymlicka's argument tries to establish that there are indeed special rights or protections supported by this interest, and that when they conflict with standard liberal rights the special rights sometimes take precedence. The argument proceeds as follows:

1. For liberals the interests of each member of the community matter equally.[47]

2. Egalitarian political and economic procedures (constitutional democracy and constrained markets) *generally* support outcomes which are fair in the sense that they count each individual's interests equally.[48]

3. But small cultural communities can be outbid in markets and outvoted in majoritarian democracies on matters which are crucial to their survival as a cultural community.[49]

---

46 Kymlicka, *Liberalism, Community, and Culture*, 166; *Multicultural Citizenship*, 82-84

47 Kymlicka, *Liberalism, Community, and Culture*, 182-3

48 Kymlicka, *Liberalism, Community, and Culture*, 183

49 Kymlicka, *Liberalism, Community, and Culture*, 183. See also *Multicultural Citizenship*, where he says 'The viability of their [national minorities'] societal cultures may be undermined by economic and political decisions made by the majority. They could be outbid or outvoted on resources and policies that are

4. The liberal theory of equality supports claims based on *unequal circumstances* but not on *differential choices*. So any special rights claim must be grounded in the former and not in the latter.[50]

5. But aboriginal special rights claims *can* be based in unequal circumstances, because the choices of surrounding cultures render, say, the survival of aboriginal languages vulnerable in a way that is not reciprocal.[51]

Therefore, according to Kymlicka, there will be circumstances in which the liberal principle that individuals should be compensated for their unequal circumstances justifies recognizing group rights over culture.

In his most recent book Kymlicka explains that his argument justifies only group rights of a certain kind – rights which 'reduce a minority's vulnerability to the decisions of a larger society,' or 'external protections.'[52] External protections are contrasted with "'internal restrictions' – that is, the demand by minority culture to restrict the basic civil or political liberties of its own members ... in short a liberal view requires *freedom within* the minority group, and *equality between* minority and majority groups."[53]

One difficulty in evaluating Kymlicka's argument is that the obvious real-world cases in which his argument would apply are cases where the potential recipients of the group right are people who are currently living with the unjust legacy of past infractions of liberal principles of justice.[54] Most liberal commentators are willing to countenance granting some group differentiated rights to current victims of injustice if they are persuaded that such measures will help to overcome the

---

crucial to the survival of their societal cultures. The members of the majority do not face this problem. Given the importance of cultural membership this is a significant inequality which, if not addressed, becomes a serious injustice,' 109.

50 Kymlicka, *Liberalism, Community, and Culture*, 185-6

51 Kymlicka, *Liberalism, Community, and Culture*, 187

52 Kymlicka, *Multicultural Citizenship*, 152

53 Kymlicka, *Multicultural Citizenship*, 152 (emphases in original)

54 Buchanan makes and elaborates this point in 'What's So Special About Nations?'.

(liberal) injustice.[55] Most liberal defenders of affirmative action, for example, take this view.[56] Such willingness to grant the group rights which Kymlicka advances does not signify agreement that national (or ethnic) identity merits special attention as a matter of justice – it just acknowledges that attending to groups defined that way can, in some circumstances, be instrumentally effective in addressing standard liberal injustices.

Kymlicka is not, however, making the relatively unobjectionable claim that rectificatory measures should be taken for members of groups that have suffered standard liberal injustice, as he makes clear with his shipwreck example, which is a modification of Dworkin's initial auction and which I shall quote at length:[57]

> Two ships, one very large and one quite small, shipwreck on an island, and to ensure a smooth auction, they proceed by entering bids into the ship's computers without ever leaving the ship.... The auction proceeds and it turns out that the passengers of the two ships are very similar in the distribution of ways of life chosen.... Finally the resources are all bid for, but when they disembark from the ship they discover for the first time, what had been obscured by the use of a common computer language, that the two ships are of different nationalities. Assuming, as is reasonable, that their resources are distributed evenly across the island, they will now be forced to try to execute their chosen lifestyles in an alien culture – e.g., in their work, and, when the state superstructure is built, in the courts, schools, legislatures, etc.[58]

The disadvantage faced by members of the minority nation is that the majority members 'possess and utilize their resources within a certain

---

55 Aboriginal peoples in the U.S. have been subjected to massacres, thefts, juridical inequality of liberty, political inequality, and inequality of opportunity, and hardly any living North American descendants of American Indians who were resident at the time of the worst infractions have avoided the consequences. Even on Robert Nozick's view living North American Indians merit substantial compensation.

56 See Dworkin, *A Matter of Principle*, chs. 14 and 15.

57 For Dworkin's version of the initial auction see 'What is Equality Part 2: Equality of Resources,' *Philosophy and Public Affairs* **10**:3 (1981) 283-345.

58 Kymlicka, *Liberalism, Community, and Culture*, 188. For a less formal rendering of the main argument I am discussing here see *Multicultural Citizenship*, 108-15.

context, i.e., within their own cultural community',[59] whereas the minority members have to utilize their resources within a cultural community which is not their own. In the absence of other special measures designed to protect their culture they would have to purchase and settle a separate part of the island to secure their cultural community – and this is an extra 'cost which members of the majority community do not incur, but which in no way reflects different choices about the good life (or about the importance of cultural membership within it).'[60]

There is no history of standard liberal injustices to rectify here. The thought experiment is supposed to show that special measures can be justified not only for purposes of rectification, but as measures which are, in themselves, required by justice – in particular by the standard liberal conception of equality.

It is worth noting that for Kymlicka the notion of a secure cultural context of choice is, fairly clearly, a threshold notion. Were the minority culture secure, there would be no case for redistribution even if fewer resources were being devoted to its culture than to the majority culture. Security is all that is needed. How much it takes to secure a culture will depend on the circumstances, including the ability of proponents of other cultures to reach into the minority culture and attract supporters from it.

Most of my argument against Kymlicka will focus on the case for special rights and the shipwreck example. But there is a difficulty with the first stage of his argument: the claim that a cultural context of choice is needed for individual autonomy. This claim seems true, but partly because it is not clear what it would mean to lack a cultural context of choice in a society.[61] To take the most extreme case, a monolingual individual moves to a foreign culture with a foreign language. She lives within a cultural context which sets the background for her choices. She brings with her internal personal resources informed by her own

---

59 Kymlicka, *Liberalism, Community, and Culture*, 188

60 Kymlicka, *Liberalism, Community, and Culture*, 189

61 I suppose that children growing up in the wild lack a cultural context of choice, but also that there is nothing that can be done about this except searching for them and placing them in societies.

culture. *That* culture, of course, is no longer reinforced by her daily experiences, but a new culture does interact with her own culture to give meaning and content to her choices.

I do not mean to underestimate the extreme difficulties facing the person whose situation I have described – of course, she faces a massive set of disadvantages which it is entirely unreasonable to expect any but the most robust and cheerful personalities to deal with well. But the point is that even in this case it is not clear that the person lacks a cultural context for choice. And if she doesn't lack a cultural context of choice, it is not clear what lacking a cultural context of choice means.

Suppose that the idea of lacking a cultural context of choice makes sense. The main difficulty with Kymlicka's argument for group differentiated rights comes from the fact that the design of institutions has a dynamic effect on the reproduction of culture. The shipwreck case looks plausible as long as we consider culture to be static and relevant only to the adults landing on the island. But instituting special rights will affect how the two cultures develop, how the relationship between them develops, and which cultures the children of the shipwreck survivors will opt for. Suppose a set of special rights designed to protect the minority culture is implemented, and is successful. The survivors themselves will then be able to live out their lives in their original culture. But such rights may also artificially support the culture by channelling the survivors' children into it. The most obvious case is that of special language rights – say, allowing parents to send their children to schools in which all subjects are taught in the minority language, and providing through public funds a minority language TV and radio service. If children do not learn the majority language as children they will have great difficulty entering the majority culture as adults.[62] But suppose that the majority economy contains a more diverse set of opportunities than the minority economy. Then the children of the minority have available to them fewer economic opportunities than the children of the majority. Equal opportunity for the children is compromised in favour of the cultural membership of the parents.

---

62 Allen Buchanan makes a similar point in *Secession*, 101-2.

An example, slightly adapted from reality, makes this vivid. Today Welsh is a minority language even in Wales. But it was not always so. One hundred fifty years ago the vast majority of inhabitants of Wales were Welsh-speakers, most of them monolingual. Yet Welsh was, even then, a language spoken by very few people compared with English. In fact, English was forced on the Welsh by comparatively mild violations of liberal justice – Welsh was prohibited from schools and courts, setting up distorted incentives for parents to force their children to learn English.[63] But consider two counterfactual histories. In both, no violations of liberal justice, but in History *A* special language rights are granted to the Welsh in the late nineteenth century along the lines that have been recently granted, while in History *B* no special rights are granted. In History *A*, many young people who currently grow up speaking only English, or both English and Welsh, would have grown up instead as monolingual Welsh speakers. They would have far fewer cultural and material opportunities than they do as English speakers. They would have realistic access to a much less diverse range of potential life-partners, access to a much less rich body of literature, drama, scholarship, and popular culture in their own language, and access to a much less extensive and diverse range of well-paying and rewarding employment opportunities. There are good reasons for thinking that in History *B*, by contrast, young Welsh people would be in much the same situation as they are now. In short, it is reasonable to think that the mild violations of liberal justice made these people much better off than they would have been in the presence of the special rights Kymlicka recommends.

Kymlicka understands that other strictures of liberal justice will sometimes conflict with the special cultural rights he recommends.[64] He places a premium on the liberal individual freedoms which protect the individual's ability to rationally reflect on and revise her conception of the

63 For discussion of the state of English and Welsh in Wales, see Max Adler, *Welsh and the Other Dying Languages in Europe: A Sociolinguistic Study* (Hamburg: Helmut Buske Verlag 1977), and Nikolas Coupland, ed., *English in Wales: Diversity, Conflict and Change* (Bristol, PA: Multilinguistic Matters Ltd. 1990).

64 Kymlicka, *Liberalism, Community, and Culture*, 194-5; *Multicultural Citizenship*, 152

good life, since these are preconditions for living a good life: "Liberals can and should endorse certain external protections where they promote fairness between groups, but should reject internal restrictions which limit the right of group members to question and revise traditional authorities and practices."[65] But beyond that there is no reason, for Kymlicka, to suppose that standard liberal prescriptions always take precedence over the special rights justified by his equality argument.[66]

There are two problems here. First, our ability to revise our practices and question authority depends crucially on what other opportunities are available to us. If I have a realistic option of exiting Culture *A* to Culture *B* that not only sets up another option for me outside Culture *A*, but it also generally sets up for me a more diverse range of options within Culture *A*: the traditional authorities have more incentive to bend to my demands for revision in order to keep me within Culture *A*. The degree of permeability of boundaries between cultures affects what goes on within them, including the extent to which members of cultures can be restricted. The best examples can be given by analogy with religion. If a particular Christian church is protected by a strongly religious state, then there is little reason for its doctrines and practices to evolve; such churches tend to stagnate. If, however, the church is surrounded by other sects of freely practising Christians it will evolve and respond to the expressed interests of its congregations. This fact compromises Kymlicka's crucial distinction between internal restrictions (designed to protect a culture from the recalcitrant choices of its members) and external protections (designed to protect the culture from the choices of non-members). The interest in having conditions in which we can rationally exercise our capacity to reconsider and revise our conception of the good supports an interest in cultural membership and also supports the ban on internal restrictions. But it also supports an interest in having permeable boundaries between our culture and other cultures. And since the permeability of boundaries will predictably be limited by many external protections,

---

65 Kymlicka, *Multicultural Citizenship*, 37. See also 81-82.

66 Kymlicka, *Liberalism, Community, and Culture*, 196; *Multicultural Citizenship*, 153

especially special language rights, the permissibility of those protections is threatened.[67]

The second problem is that many of those children whose futures will be shaped by group rights are, like their parents, already on the receiving end of standard liberal injustices. For the most part, in the U.S., Australia, and other countries which feature heavily in Kymlicka's discussion, the liberal injustices they face are not primarily violations of the liberties which protect the ability to choose how to live and the interest in being able to revise one's choices, but they are the injustices of unequal resources and unequal material opportunities. If these inequalities are not only not corrected, but actually compounded by special rights, those special rights should be viewed with considerable suspicion.

Neither of these problems are decisive against Kymlicka's case that group differentiated rights are *compatible* with liberalism. But they do point us in a different direction from Kymlicka's. The natural question raised in the face of these problems is: why not design a cultural policy aimed not at protecting any particular culture but at the long-term integration of different cultures, so that it is easy to move between them and perhaps even difficult to differentiate between them? Such a policy – let us call it cosmopolitanism – would promote equality of opportunity without obviously depriving individuals of their interest in a cultural context for choice.

There are two obvious answers to that question. I shall show that neither is successful, although I shall raise reservations of my own.

One answer might be to make a pessimistic induction, and claim that since no such policy has been successful, none can be. History is replete with efforts to inculcate a single culture into a culturally diverse population. Despite the best efforts of the British to eliminate them, Welsh and Irish culture have persisted. The ethnic and national conflicts in the former Soviet Union and Yugoslavia both suggest that large-nation nationalism has difficulty getting hold even when the state has available to it considerable powers of repression.

---

67 Allen Buchanan has pointed out to me that while some proscriptive minority language rights, like Bill 101 in Quebec, are external protections, they are also internal restrictions, since they are binding on the members of the culture as well as on non-members.

This response faces two problems. First, the historical precedents are of governments attempting to impose a single culture rather than, as I am suggesting, trying to make more permeable the boundaries between cultures (without privileging a single culture over others). Second, the historical means used to achieve this have been violations of standard liberal justice – restrictions on freedom of expression and religion, violations of the liberties associated with the rule of law, etc. – and they have been accompanied by other violations of liberal justice expressing contempt for the individuals involved regardless of their culture (non-democracy, unequal distributions of resources, violations of equal opportunity, etc.) It may well be that illiberal mechanisms designed to achieve rapid assimilation are doomed to failure – but more long-term means which carefully respect the strictures of standard liberal justice can have more success.

A second objection is suggested (though not made explicitly) by an argument Joseph Raz makes in favour of multiculturalism. Raz says that membership in cultural groups is vitally important for individuals because such membership makes available mastery of 'the dense webs of complex actions and interactions' which constitute the 'core options which give meaning to our lives' but 'defy explicit learning or comprehensive articulation' and are available only to those who 'have or can acquire practical knowledge of them.'[68] Membership in a cultural group, therefore, has profound effects on one's life prospects because it 'determines the horizons of one's opportunities,' that is, it provides you with what might be thought of as the internal resources to take advantage of some formal opportunities, and fails to provide you with the internal resources to take advantage of others.

But cultural membership also has powerful effects on the kinds of relationships available to us. As Raz says:

> A common culture facilitates social relations and is a condition of rich and comprehensive personal relationships. One particular relationship is especially sensitive to this point ... in one's relations with one's children and with one's parents a common culture is an essential condition for the tight bonding we expect and desire. A policy that forcibly detaches children from the culture of their parents not only undermines the stability of society by undermining people's ability to

---

68 Joseph Raz, 'Multiculturalism: A Liberal Perspective,' *Dissent* Winter 1994, 67-79 at 71.

sustain long-term intimate relations, it also threatens one of the deepest desires of most parents, the desire to understand their children, share their world, and remain close to them.[69]

This suggests the second objection to cosmopolitanism – that in the early stages of such a policy children might quit the culture of their parents, thus depriving their parents of fulfillment of one of their deepest desires and undermining the capacity of the children for meaningful relationships.

Raz emphasizes that this is a bad consequence of a policy of 'forcible' detachment, but a policy of gentle detachment could equally well have similar consequences: at least the problem of nonfulfillment of the parents' desires comes from the fact that the children cease to share the culture of their parents rather than the process by which they leave it.

How much should the frustrations of current parents constrain a national policy? I would argue that it should not constrain the policy. One of the risks of parenthood in any free society is that the child will 'get away' from the parent. Even in societies where cultures enjoy considerable external protection some children have rotten relationships with their parents, and of course some will leave their parents' culture. In a more fluid cosmopolitan society, as I have argued above, rebellious children may well stay within the culture as it adapts to the perceived outrageousness of their generation. As the culture adapts, so the parents may come to have a better understanding of their children.

In the short term parents *may* have to bear a significant cost which others do not. But this is only likely when a genuinely cataclysmic cultural change occurs. Cataclysmic change is probably rare when the constraints of liberal justice are carefully obeyed, but even implementing group-differentiated rights of the relevant kind do not eliminate the possibility of cataclysm: even closed cultures sometimes endure rapid change. Concern for the costs which parents will bear may support a preference for group-differentiated rights over cosmopolitanism when there is a high probability that cosmopolitanism will spur sudden change. But it is reasonable to speculate that such circumstances are rare (in the absence of violations of liberal justice), and anyway compensatory programs, and policies which attempt to guide people

---

69 Raz, 'Multiculturalism,' 71

through the change by making publicly transparent the changes that occur, may be preferable.

The second part of Raz's point is more troubling – if sharing a common culture with one's parents is a precondition of being able to participate in lasting intimate relationships, then it is tremendously important. Again, Raz emphasizes the malign effects of forcible detachment, and in this case it seems right that the *manner* of detachment is more significant than the *fact* of detachment. Sharp ruptures of the relationships between children and parents which inhibit the ability of the children to reflect on the relationship, the reasons for its end, and other features are disruptive of their ability to form and maintain healthy relationships.

But the cessation of the relationship need not be disruptive. If the conditions supporting cool reflection are maintained, and if cultural barriers are very permeable or extremely vague, then children can experiment 'outside' their culture without leaving it. They can test the barriers and test their parents, and if rupture occurs it is less likely to be traumatic or permanent than if it occurs either forcibly or in the face of force.

In short, while Kymlicka makes a strong case for the *compatibility* of group-differentiated rights with liberalism, it is much less clear that a policy of permitting group-differentiated rights should be preferred by liberals to a policy of promoting cosmopolitanism in ways compatible with liberalism. Of course, cosmopolitanism as I have described it is itself a policy which gives a special place to national sentiment, in that it deliberately tries to erode the significance of national sentiment within civic life. This is consistent with the view that national sentiment should not be given special status in the same way that affirmative action is compatible with the view that social institutions should be race-blind. But, that said, I suspect that an adequate policy for promoting cosmopolitanism is simply implementing the demands of standard liberal justice (including its demands with respect to the distribution of resources and opportunities), which we have grounds independent of attention to national sentiment for doing.

VI   Concluding Comments

While acknowledging a good deal of power in Kymlicka's case for the compatibility of liberalism and group-differentiated rights, I have tried to argue that an alternative policy, a cosmopolitan version of benign neglect, is a more suitable liberal policy. Kymlicka, however, argues that the liberal idea of benign neglect is not only mistaken, but is actually incoherent.

> The whole idea of benign neglect is incoherent and reflects a shallow under-standing of the relationship between states and nations. In the areas of official languages, political boundaries, and the division of powers, there is no way to avoid supporting this or that societal culture, or deciding which groups will form a majority in political units that control culture-affecting decisions regarding language, education, and immigration.[70]

Kymlicka is right that decisions have to be made regarding language rights and the boundaries of political subunits, and that these decisions will affect the prospects for the relative success of different cultures as well as the directions taken by each of the cultures. But, as we saw in section 2, neutrality of *justification*, and the other fundamental liberal values, are the motivating principles behind benign neglect – not, as suggested by Kymlicka's comments, neutrality of *effect*. The government will (usually) give a boost to the cultures whose languages it recognizes as official, and benign neglect just says that that boost should not play any part in the justification of granting official status. If benign neglect limits its version of neutrality of justification it saves itself from incoherence, but it does so at the cost of indeterminacy – there are many different policies, and different justifications of policies, which will be compatible with it, many of which may be objectionable on other grounds. I have suggested a principle to guide policy, which I believe is compatible with benign neglect – that in areas where government decisions are liable to have a considerable impact on culture and cultures, we aim at making more permeable the boundaries between cultures so as to facilitate the realization of the values of autonomy and legitimacy over the long term, as well as equality between individuals across *and* within cultures.[71]

---

70 Kymlicka, *Multicultural Citizenship*, 113

71 I am grateful to Darrell Moellendorf for extremely valuable discussions and for suggesting that I write this paper, and to Allen Buchanan for extensive comments on it. I'm also grateful to Jonathan Barrett, Lynn Glueck, and Andrew Levine.

CANADIAN JOURNAL OF PHILOSOPHY
Supplementary Volume 22

National Identity, Multiculturalism, and Aboriginal Rights: An Australian Perspective

ROSS POOLE
Macquarie University

My main concern in this paper will be with questions of national identity, multiculturalism, and aboriginal rights as they have emerged in Australia, especially over the past twenty or so years. The issues are not, of course, unique to Australia: similar questions have arisen in other places, including Canada, New Zealand, and the United States. However, each place has specific problems, and while I hope that much of what I say has relevance to these countries, I will not try to establish this here.

The paper falls into two parts. In the first, I argue for certain limits on the practice of multiculturalism. The basis of this argument is a concern for national identity – especially for what I will call 'national sovereignty.' This is a familiar conservative position; however, I hope to show that it is one which liberals and those on the left should take seriously. In the second part of the paper, I distinguish the issue of Aboriginal (or indigenous) rights from multiculturalism, and try to establish that the basis of these rights is a principle very similar to the notion of national sovereignty. I conclude by discussing the role of the concept of national identity in conveying the specific responsibility of present and future Australians and their governments to make reparation for the immense wrong inflicted on the indigenous people of their country.

I The Limits of Multiculturalism

Shortly after the Second World War, the Australian government initiated a programme designed to encourage large-scale immigration. The date is significant: White Australia had always been conscious of its position as a rich but sparsely populated country on the edge of Asia. This insecurity had been intensified by the Second World War when Japanese forces reached perilously close to the Australian continent. One of the primary motives for the postwar immigration programme was to build up the population and economic strength of Australia to provide it with a better capacity to resist a future threat from Asia.

The results of this programme have been dramatic.[1] The population of Australia in 1945 was around 7.5 million; it is now over 17 million, and 40% of that increase is due to migration. The Australia of 1945 was predominantly of English or Irish origin, and the original intention of the migration programme was to keep it that way.[2] However, though the United Kingdom has remained a major source for immigrants, it quickly proved inadequate on its own. The programme was extended to include the Scandinavian countries and Central and Eastern Europe – people who were considered both racially and politically appropriate for Australia. When this source began to dry up in the 1950s, the programme was again extended to include Italy, Greece, and Malta. Initially, Asians and Africans were kept out by the 'White Australia' policy. However, this policy was relaxed in the late 1960s and formally abandoned in 1972, and non-European migration began. This started as a relatively small part of the total intake but, with the acceptance of refugees from Lebanon and Vietnam, the proportion increased, and this increase has continued, partly as a result of a policy which gives some priority to family ties. Somewhere between 35% and 45% of the current immigration intake is from Asia.

Many of the results of the immigration programme are contrary to those originally intended. Instead of securing a culturally homogene-

---

1 The information in the following paragraphs is largely drawn from Stephen Castles, *The Challenge of Multiculturalism: Global Changes and the Australian Experience* (Wollongong, NSW: Centre for Multicultural Studies, University of Wollongong for the Office of Multicultural Affairs, Department of the Prime Minister and Cabinet, 1992), ch. 1, and Uldis Ozolins, 'Immigration and Immigrants,' in Judith Brett, James Gillespie, and Murray Goot, eds., *Developments in Australian Politics* (Melbourne: Macmillan 1994).

2 According to Castles, the first Minister for Immigration, Arthur Calwell, "promised the Australian public that there would be ten British immigrants for every 'foreigner'," *The Challenge of Multiculturalism*, 8.

ous society, Australia has become one of the most heterogeneous societies in the advanced world. The five million immigrants who have settled in Australia since the war come from around 100 different countries. Australia now has a greater proportion of its population made up of recent immigrants than any other advanced country (around 40% of Australians were born overseas or have at least one immigrant parent). And instead of the immigration programme protecting a white Australia from Asian incursions, Asia is now one of the most significant sources of new immigrants. If current policies continue, this is likely to increase in the foreseeable future.

The term 'multiculturalism' entered Australian politics in the 1970s, shortly after it made its appearance in Canada and the United States. Initially it was used to signal a greater involvement of the government in problems that immigrant communities faced: unemployment, discrimination, educational disadvantage, and so on. However, it quickly came to mean an end to the assumption that immigrants would or should merge into an existing national identity and the adoption of government programmes designed to recognize and even protect the distinct cultural identities which migrants brought with them. Some form of multiculturalism in this broader sense is now taken for granted in mainstream Australian politics, with both major political parties in Australia claiming to be 'multiculturalist.'[3]

Given the political currency of the term, it would be foolish to assign too precise a meaning to it. Sometimes, it is used simply to assert that Australia is in *fact* a culturally diverse society, comprising people from a variety of different backgrounds, who are likely to speak different languages, practise different religions, have different social

---

3 There is disagreement about the extent to which the policy is accepted by the population at large (opinion polls give different results depending on the questions asked), and attempts are often made to challenge the consensus in the name of 'ordinary Australians.' The most intellectually respectable of these was the historian Geoffrey Blainey's *All for Australia* (North Ryde, NSW: Methuen Haynes 1984). Recently, strong opposition to multiculturalism has been voiced by elements within the conservative government and by some independent members of parliament. While the government is maintaining an official – though somewhat muted – commitment to multiculturalism, it is taking the opportunity to cut back on multicultural programmes.

conventions and rituals, eat different foods, and so on. However, those who claim multiculturalism as a fact usually do so in order to assert multiculturalism as a *value*: that it is a good thing, and that living in a multicultural society allows for a richer and more interesting life than is possible in a culturally homogeneous society, such as Australia before the Second World War. Migrant communities have contributed to Australian life, it is argued, precisely because they have *not* assimilated to a pre-existing Australian identity. Finally, and for present purposes most importantly, multiculturalism is a *political principle* which claims that the government should act so as to protect and sustain this social diversity: at the very least by preventing discrimination on the basis of cultural identity and not discriminating in its own practices ('negative multiculturalism'), and perhaps also by acting positively to ensure the continued viability of minority cultures ('positive multiculturalism').

One way to defend multiculturalism as a political principle is by reference to multiculturalism as a value. For example, the form of liberalism affirmed in John Stuart Mill's *On Liberty*, or easily derivable from it, identifies variety as a crucial constituent in a conception of a life worth living.[4] For Mill, the choice of one way of life over others is enriched by the awareness of alternatives. Without this awareness, informed choice and commitment is not possible. Social diversity is thus a condition of autonomy, and a liberalism which is committed to autonomy must also value diversity. But liberalism of this kind is rejected by many contemporary liberals precisely, if paradoxically, because it is incompatible with a proper recognition of the extent of cultural diversity. Mill's liberalism values diversity because it is an intrinsic element in the good life, and for those contemporary liberals influenced by John Rawls, the affirmation of *any* conception of the good life, even one with diversity as a crucial element, is incompatible with those conceptions of the good which do *not* value diversity. Thus, a liberalism based on

---

4 See John Stuart Mill, *On Liberty*, in *Utilitarianism; Liberty; Representative Government* (London: Everyman Library 1957), especially chs. 2, 3. For some discussion of Mill in this context, see C.L. Ten, 'Multiculturalism and the Value of Diversity,' in Chandran Kukathas, ed., *Multicultural Citizens: The Philosophy and Politics of Identity* (St. Leonards, NSW: The Centre for Independent Studies 1993).

the value of cultural diversity is too restrictive ('sectarian' is Rawls' phrase[5]) for a multicultural society. Since it is the task of liberalism to seek principles of justice which as far as possible neutral between different ways of life, it should not favour one conception over another. On this view, cultural identity is a private concern, a matter of individual choice or commitment, not a question of public policy. The liberal state will treat culture, as it treats religion, as falling within the sphere of individual right, a sphere which should be protected and not interfered with by the state.

It is important to be clear about what is at stake here. Culture exists in the language we use, the forms of social interaction in which we are at home, the symbols we recognize as ours, even in the food we eat and the games we play. It is one of the most significant determinants of our identity. If humans are, in Charles Taylor's perspicuous phrase, 'self-interpreting animals,'[6] then the forms in which we interpret ourselves are those provided by our culture. We are born into a culture: we acquire it through the family, social interaction, and education. Normally, we do not choose to acquire a culture, nor can we choose to give it up. It is rather that our cultural identity provides the context within which we choose, and sometimes the criteria on which we choose; it is not itself an object of choice. Culture in this sense is embodied in our sense of individual identity and in the social practices within which we exist. Where these two coincide, our individual identity is confirmed and reflected in our social life, and as we express our identity, we reproduce that form of social life.

Will Kymlicka has argued that liberals should recognize the importance of culture just because it is a precondition of individual freedom.[7]

---

5 See John Rawls, 'The Idea of an Overlapping Consensus,' *Oxford Journal of Legal Studies* 7 (1987), 1-25; see p. 6. The distinction between 'toleration' liberalism and 'autonomy' liberalism is criticized in Will Kymlicka, *Multicultural Citizenship* (Oxford: Clarendon Press 1995), ch. 8. The passage from Rawls is cited and discussed on 163-4.

6 See Charles Taylor, 'Self-interpreting Animals,' *Human Agency and Language: Philosophical Papers 1* (Cambridge: Cambridge University Press 1985).

7 See Will Kymlicka, *Liberalism, Community and Culture* (Oxford: Clarendon Press 1989), ch. 8. Kymlicka reiterates this position in *Multicultural Citizenship*, ch. 5,

In order to exercise our capacity to choose between options, to conceive and reconceive our various projects, we need a secure sense of who we are and of the kinds of things which give our lives significance. We need, in other words, a cultural identity. Kymlicka's argument provides an important reminder of the cultural conditions of autonomy; but it hardly provides a defence of those many forms of culture which do not themselves value or encourage freedom of choice. It may be, as Kymlicka would argue,[8] that a liberal should not be in the business of defending those cultures which do not value autonomy, but we still need an account which explains why those cultures are so important to their members. Further, Kymlicka's argument does not explain the importance of retaining one's *existing* cultural identity. If culture in general is a precondition of autonomy, then it does not matter (within broad limits) *which* culture an individual has. But much of the moral force and political intensity of multiculturalism resides in the desire of people to retain their own culture.

A better account of the importance of culture lies in the notion of identity. If my identity is formed within a certain culture, then it defines my fundamental perspective on the world, constitutes me as a member of a community, it provides me a set of memories and aspirations, and thus with a past and a future, and it gives me a place which is mine. My cultural identity defines who I am; when I envisage the loss of that identity, I am confronted with the thought that I will lose

---

80-94, but in the exposition moves towards the position – discussed below – that culture is important for our sense of identity.

8 As mentioned above (note 5), Kymlicka argues elsewhere against 'toleration liberalism' that autonomy should be the fundamental value for liberals; so that for him, liberal toleration should not be extended to those cultural minorities which restrict the civil liberties of their members. See Kymlicka, *Multicultural Citizenship*, ch. 8. While I am sympathetic to this argument, there are some difficulties in applying it. It may be that a cultural group (e.g., a religion) does not restrict the *civil* liberties of its members; but because it controls certain resources which are of profound importance to their members (i.e., the promise of salvation), it is able to restrict their liberty in important ways. A culture may not only determine the importance of individual liberty, but may also determine what counts as a constraint on it (e.g., the threat of damnation hardly affects a nonbeliever).

my sense of self and cease to be what I am. It is important now, and it will be important later, to recognize that such losses can occur – and in certain cases be voluntarily incurred – and that I will in fact continue to exist. However, the loss is a considerable one and usually carries with it a continuing and deep sense of dislocation and alienation. It is because culture is so important to identity in this sense that the claim of the individual to his or her own culture has so much force.[9]

To what extent can this claim be met within the framework of a liberalism which claims neutrality between conceptions of the good, and thus, presumably, between the ways of life associated with various cultures? Chandran Kukathas has recently argued that a liberalism of this kind can provide all the protection that cultural identities can reasonably – and legitimately – want.[10] The claims of diverse cultures are, he argues, protected by one of the most fundamental rights in the liberal lexicon, the freedom of association. So long as this right is protected by the government, it will secure the existence of those cultures which continue to attract the support of their members. Kukathas recognizes, of course, that most cultural groups are not associations which people voluntarily join. People are typically born into a culture and acquire their cultural identity through upbringing, education, and

---

9 For persuasive accounts of the importance of culture to identity, see Avishai Margalit and Joseph Raz, 'National Self-Determination,' *Journal of Philosophy* **87** (1990) 439-61, and Avishai Margalit and Moshe Halbertal, 'Liberalism and the Right to Culture,' *Social Research* **61** (1994) 491-510. Margalit and Halbertal draw a distinction between the 'metaphysical individual' – identified by them with the 'person' – and the 'anthropological individual' – the 'personality.' In their terminology, when I lose a certain cultural identity I cease to be the same 'personality' though I remain the same 'person.' In 'On Being a Person,' *Australasian Journal of Philosophy* **74** (1996) 38-46, I argue against the reification of the concept of a person, and suggest that the concept should not be understood as designating a metaphysical substratum (what we essentially are beneath various social identities), but rather as one of the social identities which are available to us.

10 See Chandran Kukathas, 'Are There Any Cultural Rights?' *Political Theory* **20** (1992) 105-39; reprinted in part in Will Kymlicka, ed., *The Rights of Minority Cultures* (Oxford: Oxford University Press 1995). Page references here will be to the latter.

social interaction, not through a voluntary act of affiliation. Kukathas argues, however, that just so long as one has a 'fundamental right' – the 'right to be free to leave' the community – then one's association with it can be conceived as voluntary to a 'small' but – presumably – sufficient extent.[11] An implication of this position is that a liberal polity may include cultural communities which are not themselves liberal. These retain their place just so long as their members are entitled to leave.

Kukathas recognizes that many minority cultures are under threat in the modern world, but argues that it is not the appropriate role of governments to protect them; when they attempt to do so, they interfere with the processes of change and development which are necessary for a culture's well-being. The health of a culture, and its ultimate survival, depends on the commitments of its bearers, not on government policy.[12] The crucial problem with this is that Kukathas does not consider the effects of cultural inequality. Where there is a dominant culture – the culture, say, of economic life and social interaction – then a minority culture will be under threat just so long as it remains a matter of private commitment. In practice, most people have little choice but to participate in the dominant culture if they are to have jobs and participate in social and political life, and those who find their identity in a minority culture must be disadvantaged. It is for this reason that members of cultural minorities have asked that the state intervene to protect it from the normal pressures of the economic and cultural market place, perhaps by the provision of subsidies or by making special legal provision or exemption for them. And to liberals such as Kukathas who are reluctant to allow the state to intervene in this way, they have a powerful response: the state itself is complicit in their cultural marginalization. No state in the modern Western world is as culturally neutral as the post-Rawlsian liberal argument requires. Almost every

---

11 Kukathas, 'Are There Any Cultural Rights?', 238

12 Kukathas, 'Are There Any Cultural Rights?', 234-7. Kukathas' arguments here are overstated. That it is difficult to put in place government policies which foster a healthy and independent cultural life does not mean that it is impossible. For example, one such policy might be to secure the right of internal disagreement and criticism. If the right to leave is the only right of protest that members of a community have, then internal criticism and reform will be stifled.

state carries on its political and legal affairs in a national language, exercises its authority through rituals and procedures which are imbued with a particular national culture, and administers an educational system which gives priority to one language, one history, and – as one might say – one people.[13] So the request for cultural protection is for the redress of an existing imbalance, a redress which – it would seem – can easily be justified in the name of liberal egalitarianism. If the state functions to protect and perpetuate one culture, then surely liberal justice demands that it protect and perpetuate others as well.

But paradoxically, this argument is too strong: if it exposes an enormous blind spot in one liberal position, it also brings out a limitation in multiculturalism. For the fact that modern states favour one culture over others is not a mere contingency which might be changed, but is essential to their practice. As Ernest Gellner has argued, *any* state which is functionally appropriate for an industrial society will provide a unified educational and administrative system which will inevitably favour one culture over others.[14] Further, and this is a separate argument, there are good reasons why this should be a requirement of a *liberal* state. Liberalism requires that the state define and protect a range of rights for the citizen; that it provide due legal process through which its members may secure justice; that it conduct its political affairs in ways which are open to scrutiny and criticism; that political matters be open to widespread discussion; and that the state provide an education which allows its citizens to participate in basic social, economic, and political activities. As John Stuart Mill recognized, it is not possi-

---

13 As Will Kymlicka notes, the analogy between religion and culture does not work: "It is quite possible for a state not to have an established church. But the state cannot help but give at least partial establishment to a culture when it decides which language is to be used in public schooling, or in the provision of state services" (*Multicultural Citizenship*, 111).

14 See Ernest Gellner, *Nations and Nationalism* (Oxford: Basil Blackwell 1983), ch. 3. Needless to say, the scope of this argument is limited to *modern* states. In premodern societies it was perfectly possible to have multicultural states in which the culture of the ruling classes was quite different from those over whom they rule. Indeed, this was probably the norm. See Gellner, *Nations and Nationalism*, ch. 2.

ble for a genuinely liberal and democratic state to be culturally neutral.[15] The key connection here is *language*. Where a state is multilingual in its operations (Switzerland is the usual example of this), it has to make special provisions for this to work (Switzerland has an unusually strong set of civic practices; it works in many ways like a federation, rather than a unified state). Without special provisions – and perhaps other favourable conditions (Switzerland is both small and very wealthy; it runs very tight immigration policies) – multilingualism in the operation of the state would stand in the way of its performing some of the key functions demanded by the liberal. While it is a mistake to identify language with culture, it is clearly a crucial constituent. When one also considers the requirement that the state attract the allegiance and commitment of its citizens, it is hard to imagine a modern state which did not appropriate to itself the further cultural resources necessary for this. The state will exercise authority through symbols and rituals which have a resonance with the traditions of the country; it will legitimize it through a historical narrative and a characterization of the land and the people which it claims as its own. In other words, the integrity of the body politic, and more especially of a liberal polity, requires the existence of a preferred *public culture*, and this will inevitably occupy a privileged position with respect to other cultures.

It is, perhaps, a further argument – also to be found in Mill – that a modern society requires the elements of a common culture if it is to maintain the minimal level of the trust and fellow feeling necessary for even the most impersonal forms of social life. I would not want to press this argument too far. The demands on social cohesion differ in different contexts; some modern cities show that a semblance of social life can continue without much by way of trust and fellow feeling. However, in circumstances which require commitment, sacrifice, or joint

---

15 See John Stuart Mill, *Representative Government*, in *Utilitarianism; Liberty; Representative Government*, ch. 16, 361: "Free institutions are next to impossible on a country made up of different nationalities. Among a people without fellow feeling, especially if they read and speak different languages, the united public opinion, necessary to the working of representative democracy, cannot exist.... The same books, newspapers, pamphlets, speeches, do not reach them."

action, there will need to be a strong sense of community and common cultural identity. It is no accident that many of the elements of the welfare state are argued for in the name of the nation (e.g., 'national health'), rather than an abstract principle of social justice. Sensitivity to the plight of fellow citizens is at least in part carried by the sense of a shared national identity, and it is because of this that we have been prepared to empower the state to provide a basic standard of well being for all citizens.[16]

The idea that the modern state should in principle be neutral between different cultures is a liberal fantasy, though a surprisingly widespread one.[17] It ignores the fact that state power in the modern world necessarily has a cultural dimension.[18] This means that the characteristic modern form of the state is the *nation state*, i.e., the state whose legitimacy depends on its claim to represent a community defined by its culture.

---

16 This point is made by David Miller; see *On Nationality* (Oxford: Clarendon Press 1995), ch. 3, esp. 70-73.

17 For example, Joseph Raz writes: "A political society, a state, consists – if it is multicultural – of diverse communities, and belongs to none of them." See 'Multiculturalism: A Liberal Perspective,' *Dissent* (Winter, 1994), 67-79, 69. Jürgen Habermas argues that the liberal-democratic state – the proper object of 'constitutional patriotism' – should be differentiated both in theory and practice from the cultural community – the object of nationalist sentiments; see 'Citizenship and National Identity: Some Reflections on the Future of Europe,' *Praxis International* **12** (1992) 1-19. Chandran Kukathas does discuss the issue of Australian national identity, and – not surprisingly – argues for a 'weak' understanding of this notion – comprising a 'shared history and common legal and political institutions.' See Kukathas, 'The Idea of an Australian Identity,' in Kukathas, ed., *Multicultural Citizens*. But even this 'weak' understanding (which ignores language) is incompatible with the demand of liberal neutrality.

18 To avoid misunderstanding, let me repeat (see note 14) that this claim only applies to modern states, where the nature of state power and the scope of its interventions in the lives of its subjects are enormously different from that, say, of the vast multi-ethnic empires of the premodern world. No doubt most of these were at least as 'multicultural' as any modern state; as argued, for example, in William H. McNeill, *Polyethnicity and National Unity in World History* (Toronto: University of Toronto Press 1986). But the issue of multiculturalism takes on a different meaning in the modern world where the idea of a common culture plays a key role in the legitimation of the state.

Curiously, Kymlicka, who recognizes the cultural dimension of state power, is reluctant to draw this conclusion. For Kymlicka,

> [A] 'nation' means a historical community, more or less institutionally complete, occupying a given territory or homeland, sharing a distinct language and culture.[19]

And he concludes from this that many modern states are not genuine 'nation states,' but are multinational in that they include more or less well defined nations within their borders. For example, Canada consists of three nations – the Anglophone majority, the Québécois, and the indigenous people; the United States of many – including various Native American communities, Puerto Rico, Hawaii, etc.; Switzerland of three – the French-, German-, and Italian-speaking communities; and so on. But Kymlicka does not notice than his 'multinational states' *also* satisfy his criterion of nationhood; indeed, they do so quite as much as his preferred 'subnations.' The United States, for example, is an institutionally complete, historic community with a given territory and a distinct public culture and language, even though it also contains smaller nation-like communities within it. So, too, to use an example he does not mention, is Great Britain. The point is that cultures, and the communities they define, are not discrete entities, but may overlap, or nest within each other. The fact that Scotland and Hawaii may satisfy the condition of cultural and territorial unity so as to count as nations on their own does not mean that they cannot be parts of larger nations (or, for that matter, contain smaller nations within them). One individual can be *both* Scottish *and* British, or *both* Hawaiian *and* American. The challenge that these 'multi-national nations' must meet is that the central state attract the cultural resources necessary to service its operations, but this is compatible with a degree of cultural diversity – even nationhood – elsewhere.[20] Of course sometimes multinational

---

19 Kymlicka, *Multicultural Citizenship*, 11

20 It was one of the great imperial achievements of the English to create a concept of 'Britishness' which encompassed, and to a certain extent even fostered, subordinate Scottish and Welsh identities. On the eighteenth century, see Linda Colley, *Britons: Forging the Nation 1707-1837* (New Haven: Yale University Press

nations do not meet this challenge, and a national minority will strike out for independence – as have the Basques in Spain and the Québécois in Canada. But that some multinational nations are under strain does not mean that there are none.[21]

The modern state operates through an officially recognized and supported public culture, comprising a recognized national language, a history, a range of cultural traditions, publicly accepted rituals, and so on. There may well be disputes about various aspects of the national culture, for example, about what should be emphasized in the national history, or about exclusions and prejudices that are associated with it. Its content is subject to debate and change. A national culture – any culture for that matter – is something like a tradition in Alasdair MacIntyre's sense: it is a story of change and evolution, not a fixed essence.[22] Nevertheless, there will be those from outside that tradition, whose identity lies elsewhere, members of minority cultures who find

---

1992), and on the nineteenth century, see the essays in E.J. Hobsbawm and Terence Ranger, eds., *The Invention of Tradition* (Cambridge: Cambridge University Press 1983).

21 It may be that this is a matter of definition, with Kymlicka requiring a high degree of cultural and linguistic homogeneity within a community before it is to be counted as a nation. But if this definition is accepted, it is not clear whether there will be *any* nations. Certainly the Anglophone majority and the indigenous minority in Canada will not count as such. I see little advantage in employing a definition of 'nation' which would exclude the United States, France, Britain, and perhaps even England. Kymlicka argues that we "should distinguish 'patriotism,' the feeling of obligation to the state, from national identity, the sense of membership in a national group" *(Multicultural Citizenship*, 13).While this distinction is important in some contexts (the patriotism of the ancient world was not national identity), it is dubious whether it has much application in the modern world where mass allegiance is carried by a sense of belonging to the same culture (even when, as with Great Britain, Canada, or the United States, this culture contains diversity).

22 For MacIntyre's account of tradition, see *After Virtue*, 2d ed. (Notre Dame: University of Notre Dame Press 1984), ch. 15, and *Whose Justice? Which Rationality?* (London: Duckworth 1988), ch. 18. It should be noted that MacIntyre himself would not count a national culture as anything more than a debased tradition; see 'Is Patriotism a Virtue?' *The Lindley Lectures*, The University of Kansas, 1984.

themselves without public confirmation of their identity and apparently excluded from the dominant culture. What is their place in the political and social order of the nation state? Can we provide an understanding of multiculturalism which recognizes the significance of this alienation, as well as the need for a dominant public culture?

Let us consider the situation of people who decide to leave a country which, we may suppose, provides the necessary sustenance for their own identity in order to settle in a country which does not. One consequence of this decision is that they can no longer claim to have their identity affirmed in the public culture of the country in which they will live. For many this will mean an alienation from the prevailing public culture which may well last their lifetime, and it also means that they will know that their children and grandchildren will grow up in a culture which is not theirs. There is loss, even tragedy, in this. However, this must be regarded as an inevitable consequence of the decision to migrate. Those who make this choice must be aware (and should be made aware) of what it means. They, or at least their children, must learn the national language and come to terms with the characteristic forms of social interaction if they are not to be disadvantaged. Of course, the nature and extent of the loss may be much greater than could be envisaged; so the choice to return home should be available (and very many migrants do choose eventually to return to their home countries). But there are strong liberal and democratic reasons why this loss should be borne. A citizen of a democratic country should be able to understand the main issues of political debate and policy; be prepared to participate in political life; accept – within reasonable limits – the results of the democratic process; and commit him- or herself to the common causes and responsibilities of the new country. A national identity is not an optional extra to these commitments, but is involved in them. The decision to immigrate must be understood as involving a commitment to share some elements of the identity and culture of the host country. It is, of course, a corollary of this that the host country allow that commitment and not conceive the immigrants as second class citizens, forever excluded from full participation in the culture and politics of their new country.

There are complications which will need to be taken into account. The decision to migrate is not always as voluntary as I have pretended. People choose to leave their own country not merely because another offers better prospects for them and their families, but because they must escape from intolerable circumstances. But whoever is responsible for the circumstances from which they are escaping, it is unlikely to be the government and people of the country where they intend to settle.[23] A national government may, and certainly should, accept some refugees, knowing that their identity and commitments will continue to lie with their native country, and that they will not become full members of the host society. But the normal case is the one in which the immigrant desires permanent settlement, and in this case, they should be treated as potential citizens They should be expected to participate in the public culture of their new country, and provided the means and the opportunity to do so.

This may seem like a return to assimilation. However, a liberal state will also recognize that the process of change should involve the national culture as well. Multiculturalism in the context of the nation state is the idea that the cultural identity which informs the political structure be understood in such a way that it both allows for the existence of cultural diversity and is open to influence by that diversity. The dominant public culture – the nation's self-understanding – is susceptible to change, and minority cultures should contribute to that change. This means that cultural groups should be given the freedom to form associations, language schools, lobby groups, and so on. If they are to contribute to public debate, they must be able to sustain a sense of their own cultural identity, and it may well be that the government should play a role in encouraging, sustaining, and financing these endeavours. The contribution of cultural minorities to public life may eventually transform the national culture beyond recognition. But it remains the case that they will contribute to that change from a position of inequality. The culture to which they are contributing is public and central; theirs is and will remain private and marginal. They cannot and should not expect that their culture should take its place on the public stage on an equal footing with the existing public culture.[24]

---

23 See Kymlicka, *Multicultural Citizenship*, 98-9.

24 The point here is not that the culture of immigrants is in some sense inferior *as a culture* to that of their host country. The inequality is political and contextual: their language is not the language of public debate, their history is not taught in

Migration inevitably involves alienation. However, it should also carry with it a commitment to participate in the public culture of the nation which will be one's new home, to acquire a new national identity, and also – something I will say more of later – to assume the responsibilities which go with this. This does not rule out the state involving itself in multicultural practices. There is a kind of practical inevitability with which a liberal state will need to learn the language and cultures of its minorities. Its welfare agencies, education departments, police forces, and law courts will have to deal with their ethnic constituencies differently from those of the dominant cultural group if they are to reach some semblance of liberal equality of treatment. But this is, or ought to be, informed by the idea that individuals should be treated equally, not that all cultures are on an equal footing.

Behind this argument stands the assumption that states have the right to set the terms of immigration. Legally, the assumption is unproblematic: it is a condition of sovereignty that the state has the right to police its borders and set the terms of entry. But it raises troubling moral issues. There is, at the very least, a tension between the principles of liberalism and the claim that states have the right to control entry.[25] If the freedoms of movement and occupation are important liberal rights, it is not clear why they should stop at state borders. Given the enormous inequalities in the way in which the world is divided up and the differences in life expectations between states, there is little doubt that if people were allowed to move as they wished and work where they found employment there would be a massive movement of the world's population across existing borders. The main thing that stands in the way of this redistribution is the right of states to restrict entry into their territory.

---

schools, and so on. Their culture does not enjoy the same public status, but will become a matter of private choice and commitment. This contextual inequality would be reversed if migration took place in the other direction.

25 Liberal arguments for a radical easing of restrictions on entry are presented by Joseph H. Carens, 'Aliens and Citizens: The Case for Open Borders,' *Review of Politics* **49** (1987) 251-73; slightly abridged version reprinted in Will Kymlicka, ed., *The Rights of Minority Cultures* (Oxford: Clarendon Press 1995).

The issue is complex, and I can only touch on one aspect of it here. But one of the principles underlying legal sovereignty is that members of a nation have a privileged relationship with a certain territory and through their state the right to set the terms of entry to it. Each nation has its 'homeland,' and this provides – or promises – members of the nation a special place of belonging. This principle – that of *national* sovereignty – has played an enormous role in the history of the past two hundred years and continues to do so. If it has not been properly discussed in much philosophy and political theory, this is because of the dominance of a narrowly economic understanding of the relationship between people and their physical environment. This economic understanding is inadequate even for individual property. We do not conceive our home and personal possessions primarily as exchangeable objects of utility; they are tied to our sense of self and they are exchanged only with considerable sense of loss. But the economic understanding is even more inadequate for the sites, areas, or territories to which members of various groups claim a special affiliation. It may well be that *every* significant identity carries with it a sense of place and provides its bearers with a special relationship to that place. In the case of nations, the territorial affiliation is obvious and crucial. It defines a 'homeland' which is the ground, in a near literal sense, of its members' sense of self. This extension of territorial identification from locality to national homeland is undoubtedly a product of the modern world, reflecting increased mobility, the emergence of national cultures, and changes in the extent and nature of state.[26] But it has a powerful presence in everyday moral consciousness, and it is undoubtedly this sense of place, which defines England for the English, Australia for Australians, and no doubt

---

26 The most impressive recent accounts of these developments are Ernest Gellner, *Nations and Nationalism,* and Benedict Anderson, *Imagined Communities: Reflections on the Origin and Spread of Nationalism,* 2d ed. (London: Verso 1991). For appropriation and criticism, see Ross Poole, 'Nationalism and the Nation State in Late Modernity,' *European Studies Journal* **10** (1993) 161-74, and 'Nationalism: The Last Rites?' in Aleksandar Pavkovic, Adam Czarnota, and Halyna Koscharsky, eds., *Nationalism and Postcommunism* (Dartmouth: Aldershot 1995).

Kurdistan for the Kurds, which underlies the claims of a people to sovereignty over their national homeland.[27]

It may be that the doctrine of national sovereignty is no longer sustainable. An exclusive attachment to a homeland is – poignantly and tragically – incompatible with the existence of competing claims to the same national homeland. However, those of us who live in the economically advanced and politically stable countries of the Western world should remember, as we condemn the attempts to apply this principle in the former Yugoslavia and Soviet Union, that we also rely on it to secure a comfortable refuge against the demands of the poor and needy beyond our borders. Though the doctrine rationalizes violence and barbarity in the one place, and complacency in the other, it cannot and should not be rejected out of hand. The sense of place has deep cultural and emotional roots, and these need to be explored and understood, not merely dismissed in favour of the deliverances of abstract theory. But abstract theory must have its place too. Though we should recognize the moral force of national sovereignty, considerations of need and equity also have force. The desire of an existing national community to maintain its relationship to a given territory must be balanced against the needs of those living in conditions of poverty or political repression. The claims of national identity deserve a presence in the argument, but they cannot be allowed to settle the issue.

There is no reason to suppose that a morally serious engagement with these issues would not conclude that relatively wealthy and underpopulated countries such as Australia, New Zealand, and Canada should substantially increase their rate of immigration and change the criteria on which potential immigrants are accepted.[28] The doctrine of

---

27 It is puzzling that Margalit and Raz's sensitive discussion of cultural identity in 'National Self-Determination' makes no reference to this. But the relationship of national identity to territory is a crucial component in the claim to self-determination.

28 In recent years, Australia has been admitting between 80,000 and 100,000 immigrants per year, using a mix of economic and social, family reunion, and humanitarian criteria as the basis of admission. The current government has just lessened the overall intake to around 70,000, and changed the criteria so that economic and social criteria (e.g., education, skill, language, financial consid-

national sovereignty would play a dual role in this argument. Continuity of an existing national identity might provide grounds to limit immigration; nation states could ask that their new members to come to terms with the existing national cultures. Under (unlikely) conditions of large-scale immigration, it might even be necessary to take steps to protect the existing national cultures from being swamped by newly emerging majorities. Under ordinary circumstances, however, no such protection is needed or justified: the existing national culture already holds all the important cards. In this case, what is required is a reasonable and humane policy of multiculturalism: the state should allow – in fact encourage – the practice of cultural diversity, and allow this diversity to contribute to its own cultural self-understanding.

II   Aboriginal Rights

I now want to tell a story about another immigration. In 1788, white settlers established a colony on the east coast of the Australian continent. They happened to be English, but there is no reason to suppose that if the English had not arrived, another European power would not have established a colony. Estimates vary as to the number of aboriginal inhabitants, but it is usually thought to be in the vicinity of 300,000-350,000.[29] These people lived in some 500 tribes, and they

---

erations) take priority over family reunion and need. This has the effect of giving preference to those who are already doing reasonably well. It also decreases the need for the government to involve itself in programmes aimed at settling new immigrants into the Australian community.

29 The *Encyclopedia of Aboriginal Australia*, ed. David Horton (Aboriginal Studies Press for Australian Institute for Aboriginal and Torres Strait Islanders Studies 1994), gives the figure of 314,500 for the Aboriginal population in 1788 (Appendix, 1299). However, in *Aboriginal Sovereignty: Reflections on Race, State and Nation* (St. Leonards, NSW: Allen & Unwin 1966), Henry Reynolds remarks that an 1838 estimate of 1,400,000 Aborigines 'may have been too high, but ... was probably closer to present day assessments than the figure of 300,000 accepted from 1930 until recently' (20). This would put the figure as closer to 900,000.

30 New evidence has recently been presented which dates a rock carving discovered at Jinmium in the Northern Territory as 75,000 years old, and other human

ranged over vast areas of what was to become Australia. Archaeological evidence suggests that they had lived there for at least 60,000 years.[30] In terms of any conceivable human experience of time, the Aborigines have been in Australia forever. Over this time, they developed a complex and fascinating culture and mode of living, both with each other and with the environment.

The history of white settlement is the history of the dispossession of these people and their culture. It is also the history of genocide: Aborigines were killed in large numbers, both directly and indirectly as a result of white settlement. At the turn of this century, when the Australian Commonwealth was formed, the Aboriginal population was around 95,000, and by 1930 it was down to 74,000. It was widely expected that they would eventually die out. By 1991, however, it had recovered to around 240,000.[31] Aborigines were denied full citizenship until 1967, and were subject to barbaric and contradictory policies of forced assimilation and social discrimination. Their culture and way of life has been so savagely eroded that in some cases it has disappeared beyond the possibility of recuperation. Today, in terms of every standard measure of well being (health, life expectancy, property, wealth, employment, education, liability to imprisonment, etc.), Aborigines are the most disadvantaged group in the Australian population.[32]

---

traces as between 120,000 and 176,000 years old. See Richard Fullager, Lesley Head and David Price, 'Early Human Occupation of Northern Australia: Archaeology and Thermoluminescence Dating of Jinmium Rock Shelter, Northern Territory,' *Antiquity* **70** (1996), 751–73. Even if this dating is accepted, however, it does not establish continuity with contemporary Aboriginals. There have been invasions and other large population movements since then.

31 Figures from *Encyclopedia of Aboriginal Australia*, 1299. It should be noted that in recent years there has been a marked increase in the number of those who identify themselves as Aboriginal, and this is reflected in census returns.

32 For example: median income of Aborigines and Torres Strait Islanders was two-thirds of the national figure; mortality rates are over two and a half times the national average; life expectancy is 15 to 17 years less than that of the whole population; infant and perinatal mortality rates are three times the national average; rate of imprisonment is eighteen times that of non-Aboriginals; unemployment rates are 35% against the overall rate of 9%, etc. Figures are from the 1991 census, and are contained in Ian Castles, ed., *Year Book Australia 1994* No. 76 (Canberra: Australian Bureau of Statistics 1994), 411-16.

The white advance into the continent was largely rationalized by the convenient myth of *terra nullius*: the claim that the Aboriginal people had no ownership relation with the land, which was thus available for expropriation without consent or compensation. This doctrine was overturned in 1992 in the case of *Mabo vs. Queensland* (the 'Mabo Case'), when the High Court of Australia ruled that Australian common law included the recognition of pre-existing 'native title.' The Court acknowledged the existence, prior to European settlement, of a complex understanding of the relationship of people to the land, an understanding which included – though it went beyond – a set of rights and duties with respect to its occupancy and use. There is, however, an important limitation to the Mabo judgment. If it established legally that members of Aboriginal communities enjoyed property rights over various portions of the Australian continent, it did not establish that the communities also had rights of political and legal sovereignty over that land.

Indeed, it explicitly refused to do this. If in one sense ('property'), the Mabo judgment recognized that Australia had once belonged to the Aboriginal people, in another sense ('sovereignty'), it did not. So when the British Crown claimed sovereignty over Australia (initially over the Eastern two-thirds), this meant that the Crown and succeeding legislatures had the right to annul pre-existing ownership as they saw fit. By the time of the Mabo judgment, most Aboriginal land had in fact been legally appropriated and the original title extinguished. In order for an original native title over land to remain in existence, the Aboriginal people must have maintained an ongoing relationship with it. According to one estimate, this meant that over eighty percent of the Aboriginal population was excluded from the Mabo judgment. And even where native title continues to exist, it can still be nullified by legislation.[33]

---

33 On these points, see Tim Rowse, 'Aborigines: Citizens and Colonial Subjects,' in Judith Brett, James Gillespie, and Murray Goot, eds., *Developments in Australian Politics* (Melbourne: Macmillan 1994), especially 184. The claim that five-sixths of Aboriginals would not qualify for native title was made by Michael Mansell; see 'The Court Gives An Inch But Takes Another Mile: The Aboriginal Provisional Government Assessment of the Mabo Case,' *Aboriginal Law Bulletin* 2:57 (August 1992), 4–7. Since the body of this paper was written, the High Court has determined (the 'Wik Judgement' of December 1996) that native title has not been

This is not the place to pursue the question whether it is legally coherent to recognize pre-existing property rights but to deny sovereignty.[34] Morally, at least, the issue is straightforward. The five hundred or so tribes which inhabited Australia prior to Western settlement had done so without dispute (except, occasionally, with each other) for many millennia. They had not gained possession of the land by the dispossession of some other people (or if they had done so, this was so long ago as to leave no currently identifiable group with a claim to reparation). Their relationship to the land sustained a unique and complex culture, and the culture recognized the relationship to the land as crucial to their identity and well being. Indeed, given the nature of aboriginal property – that the land was used by individuals in virtue of their membership of tribes; that it was not alienable either by individuals or tribes; and that the relationship between tribes was predicated on an understanding of each tribe's prior rights to certain territories – there is no easy way to distinguish the claim to property from the claim to sovereignty. If we are to translate the Aboriginal relation to the land into Western legal categories with a minimum of distortion, then both property and sovereignty will be required. It may be that the Aboriginal people lacked a state – or states – with sufficient power to deter invaders and that their sovereignty was not part of an international framework of reciprocal recognition. But the moral basis of their claim was just as strong as that of every modern state to have its territorial integrity and right to control entry respected. The Aboriginal people were entitled to have their sovereignty recognized in 1788, and it should be retrospectively recognized now.[35]

---

extinguished for large areas of rural land. For these 'pastoral leases,' Aboriginal rights coexist with the rights of farmers to use the land for agricultural purposes. The legal, economic and political implications of this decision have yet to be worked out, but the government is under considerable pressure to legislate to extinguish this residual native title.

34 The argument that it is not coherent to separate the issue of sovereignty from that of property in this way and that the Australian courts should recognize pre-existing Aboriginal sovereignty is powerfully made in Henry Reynolds, *Aboriginal Sovereignty*.

35 These point are well made in Janna Thompson, 'Land Rights and Aboriginal Sovereignty,' *Australasian Journal of Philosophy* **68** (1990) 313-29.

I have been discussing the nature of the dispossession of the Aborigines because it seems obvious that the history is morally relevant, and that in considering what is now due to the aboriginal people, we should not merely take into account their present situation, but also what has happened in the past. This assumption is shared by Aboriginal people themselves. For them it is crucial, both to their own identity and for an understanding of what is due to them, that they are the original inhabitants of Australia.[36] This assertion of the moral relevance of the past is by no means unique to indigenous people: probably every important identity is constructed in terms of a conception of the past, and questions of current well being will often require that some aspect of the past be addressed by way of compensation, retribution, or reinterpretation. The current situation of Aborigines is partly constituted by the history of their expropriation, and we cannot address it without taking that past into account.

Curiously, however, this is denied by Will Kymlicka, who argues that

> it is a mistake ... to put too much weight on historical property rights ... [for] the idea of compensating for historical wrongs, taken to its logical conclusion, implies that all the land which was wrongly taken from indigenous people in the Americas or Australia or New Zealand should be returned to them. This would create massive unfairness, given that the original European settlers and later immigrants have now produced hundreds of millions of descendants, and this land is the only home they know. Changing circumstances make it impossible and undesirable to compensate for certain historical wrongs.[37]

---

36 See, for example, Kevin Keefe, *From the Centre to the City: Aboriginal Education, Culture and Power* (Canberra: Aboriginal Studies Press 1992), 192; Rowse, 'Aborigines: Citizens and Colonial Subjects,' 186.

37 Kymlicka, *Multicultural Citizenship*, 219-20. In a section omitted from the cited passage, Kymlicka argues that claims for compensation do not by themselves justify the self-government rights which are his preferred option for dealing with the claims of indigenous people. He writes: "Many groups have been wrongfully dispossessed of property and other economic opportunities, including women, blacks, and Japanese immigrants.... Each of these groups may be entitled to certain forms of compensatory justice, but this does not by itself explain or justify granting powers of self-government...." At the very least, this argument confuses questions of property with those of sovereignty. I will say something about the self-government option later in this paper. After the passage quoted, Kymlicka argue that indigenous people may themselves have

But Kymlicka's argument is confused. If the 'logical conclusion' of 'compensating for historical wrongs' would be further 'massive unfairness,' then no doubt this should be taken into account in resolving what now ought to be done. But this does not imply that we should ignore or downplay the 'historical wrong.' Rather, we should assess what it is and what might count as addressing it, and *then* consider the costs of so doing. It might well be that the costs in terms of further consequential injustice will severely limit the extent to which compensation is possible. But this should not inhibit the initial inquiry. Indeed the comparison requires that it proceed.

In fact Kymlicka is not consistent on this point. He recognizes, for example, that there is an important moral distinction between the claims of indigenous people and that of immigrant cultural minorities: the first are, he argues, 'national minorities' which have the right of (limited) independence from the state; the second – 'ethnic' groups – have certain cultural rights, but not those of independence, nor even of cultural equality with the dominant culture.[38] But this distinction is itself historically grounded. It is because immigrants (once) chose to leave their own country and settle in a new one that they may be assumed to have voluntarily incurred their minority status, and it is because indigenous people were not given a choice, but had their land taken away from them and their culture destroyed or threatened by foreign settlement, that they retain a claim to sovereignty over traditional lands. Kymlicka is right to emphasize the difference between the claims of indigenous peoples and those of migrant groups, but in order to do so, he must take into account their different histories. Just as the (present) claims of ethnic groups are diminished by a (past) decision to immigrate, so the (present) claims of indigenous people are strengthened by a (past) expropriation.[39]

---

acquired land by expropriation of prior claimants. Whatever the force of this argument in some cases, it has no application to the Australian case.

38 Kymlicka, *Multicultural Citizenship*, 11-26, 61-69, etc.

39 A different but analogous case is that of African Americans whose past is one of forced immigration and slavery. It may be that behind Kymlicka's decision to marginalize the issue of historical wrong is the fear that the very enormity of

It is important, though difficult, to contextualize the moral issues involved here. The invasion of the Australian continent and the arrogation of sovereignty by the British Crown and subsequent Australian governments must be placed in the context of what was and is historically possible. It was nearly inevitable that there would be enormous changes to the situation of Aboriginal people. They were hunters and gatherers, and were able to live, and by their own standards to live well, prior to European settlement. But given the agricultural revolution of some 12,000 years ago, the industrial revolution which was getting under way even as Captain Cook explored the eastern coast of the Australian continent, and the developments in transport, navigation, and trade in the sixteen, seventeenth, and eighteenth centuries, there is no way that this way of life could have maintained itself without fundamental change. There are moral considerations, too. Where between 300,000 and 350,000 indigenous people were able to subsist before white settlement, neither dependent on nor contributing to the rest of the world, modern agriculture and industry now enable the Australian continent to support and contribute to the support of countless millions more. These considerations do not justify, excuse, or even rationalize the brutality, oppression, exploitation, and misery which were the direct and indirect consequence of white settlement in Australia. But one does not have to believe in doctrines of historical progress to think that these should be placed in the context of what was historically possible, and one does not have to be utilitarian to think that the interests and needs of the many must figure in any argument as to the rights of the few.

The moral sovereignty held by the Aboriginal people in 1788 was not, any more than the sovereignty enjoyed by nation states today, an

---

the crime and its consequences may serve to inhibit moral reflection and action. This is a real worry, especially when the results of relatively abstract argument are pitted against the comfortable certainties of everyday morality reflection and the political problems in the way of practical policy. But the problem is inescapable. The other side of this problem is *ressentiment*: the way in which the identity of an oppressed group is constituted by the image of an oppression so vast that it can never be expiated or diminished. See Wendy Brown, *States of Injury* (Princeton, NJ: Princeton University Press 1995), esp. ch. 3. But this problem is one for members of the oppressed group to resolve, not for advice from those implicated in the oppression.

absolute right. It covers a range of factors relating to traditional use of the land, its importance to the way of life and the identity of the people, and the absence of other identifiable claimants. Like the national sovereignty claimed by states in the modern world, it should be taken into account in any argument as to the final disposal of that territory. But it should not predetermine the outcome of that argument. If, as I suggested in the first part of this paper, wealthy nation states ought to adopt immigration policies which take account of the needs of those outside their borders, so too there are moral as well as historical grounds for suggesting that the Aboriginal inhabitants of Australia could not expect to retain sole occupation of the continent.

These considerations are not intended to diminish the responsibility of present-day Australians to make reparations, but to place the origins of that responsibility within an historical narrative rather than an abstract moral discourse of right and wrong. They also indicate some aspects of the reparation which is due. For example, they place the onus squarely on the settlers to come to terms with Aboriginal ways of life and traditions. The conception of national sovereignty at work in the Western world demands no less, and there is no reason to diminish these demands in the case of the moral sovereignty which we can retrospectively ascribe to Aboriginal people. It means that all migrants to this country have the responsibility to come to terms with the culture of the Aboriginal inhabitants. It also means that the understanding of Australian national identity must recognize Aboriginality, and this recognition must have a prominent place in all public and official occasions. The symbols and rituals through which Australians identify themselves as Australians, both to themselves and others, must give priority to the history and achievements of those who have the best claim to this identity.

For many Aborigines, the transformation of non-Aboriginal Australian identity is largely irrelevant. For them, pre-existing sovereignty establishes a claim to their own national identity and national independence.[40] If, it is argued, the Aboriginal people enjoy, not just re-

---

40 See, for example, Paul Coe, 'The Struggle for Aboriginal Sovereignty,' Kevin Gilbert, 'Aboriginal Sovereign Position: Summary and Definition,' and Michael Mansell, 'Towards Aboriginal Sovereignty: Aboriginal Provisional Government,'

sidual ownership, but also residual sovereignty, then it is appropriate to assert that sovereignty in the form of an autonomous Aboriginal state. Though there is an enormous diversity of Aboriginal cultures, the depth and complexity of the relationship to the land is a significant common thread. If there is good reason to extend the Mabo judgment to include sovereignty, self-determination would complete the logic of that recognition. A similar position is proposed by Kymlicka who argues that indigenous people constitute national minorities and have therefore a right to national independence.[41]

Now it may well be that some form of sovereignty is appropriate in many areas and for many Aborigines. It is even possible – and this is the policy of the Aboriginal Provisional Government – that these separate areas could together constitute an Aboriginal nation. But given the relatively small numbers of people involved and the lack of economic resources, it is not likely that full independence would be possible. Indeed, except for occasional rhetoric, it is not clear that this is seriously envisaged. So it is not surprising that many Aborigines and their sympathizers are skeptical of this programme.[42] What is more likely is that some regions will achieve a measure of self-government within the Australian Commonwealth, and that this will extend to different systems of laws and law enforcement. Indeed, forms of self-government are already in place in some areas. While there are formidable political obstacles in the way of this programme, there are legal and political precedents for quite strong forms of indigenous autonomy

---

in *Social Alternatives* **13:1** (April 1994) 10-12, 13-15, 16-18. For a moderate version of the case for sovereignty, see Henry Reynolds, *Aboriginal Sovereignty*.

41 See Kymlicka, *Multicultural Citizenship, passim* but especially chs. 2 and 4. Apart from the problems discussed in the next two paragraphs, it is worth noting that Kymlicka's account limits the options which are available to indigenous people. It may be the case that many do desire national independence. But many do not, and a theory of indigenous rights should provide for this.

42 See, for example, Noel Pearson, 'To Be or Not To Be – Separate Nationhood or Aboriginal Self-determination and Self-government Within the Australian Nation?' *Aboriginal Law Bulletin* **3:61** (April 1993) 14-17. See also Frank Brennan, SJ, *One Land, One Nation: Mabo – Towards 2001* (Brisbane: University of Queensland Press 1995).

(e.g., in Canada and the United States), there are even some precedents in Australia (the Norfolk and Cocos Islands), and the existing federal structure could accommodate it.

Developments along these lines would not achieve full autonomy, but they would be a partial recognition of the strength of the Aboriginal claim to sovereignty. Their attraction is that they promise the space – in a literal sense – in which tribal Aborigines can continue or recuperate their culture on their own terms and provide a political form in which the Aboriginal relationship to the land might be sustained or renewed. The operation of Aboriginal law and custom would be separate, in space if not in time, from that of Western law and custom. But this solution is not available to those Aborigines – almost certainly the majority – who have long been dispossessed of their traditional land and are living in the cities and towns of Australia. For many, land rights are no longer an option; their land has long since been given over to agricultural, industrial or other use, or their own relationship to it has become tenuous and distant. Many have formed a conception of their own lives which does not involve a direct association with traditional land. For these Aborigines, life involves much closer contact with dominant non-Aboriginal forms, and cultural change and renewal must take place in this context. The interaction between different laws and customs takes place in the encounter between Aboriginal and non-Aboriginal people occupying or competing for the same streets, pubs, jobs, unemployment offices, sports fields, and schools. Much more difficult to envisage than land rights and self-government are the conditions which will allow Aborigines the capacity, not merely to sustain past forms of life, but to create new forms of Aboriginal life in a profoundly non-Aboriginal context. The challenge here is to find the political, legal, and social forms in which this can take place.

Discussion of Aboriginal rights almost invariably focusses on those rights which are necessary to recreate or sustain some form of traditional life. These rights – which include land rights and rights of self-government – are very important. But the issue of Aboriginal rights goes much further than these. Those Aborigines, who are not in a position to make use of these rights or who choose not to do so, have just as much a claim as those who do. However important traditional culture is to Aboriginal people, the rights and resources they are provided should not be predicated on the continuance of that culture.[43] And the conceptual and political difficulties in the way of discovering and establishing the legal, social, and political forms in which non-traditional Aboriginals can create and recreate their lives are immense. However difficult they will be to achieve in practice, land rights and self-government for Aborigines are less problematic than changes needed in the town and cities of Australia. The recognition of Aboriginal difference must find a place, not just in the symbols and rituals of the public culture, but in the meanings involved in day-to-day social life.

If by virtue of their history and current position, Aboriginal people have certain rights, it is important to ask: Who do they have rights *against*? The usual and, I think, the correct answer to this question is: non-Aboriginal Australians. But it is important to ask why this should be so. After all, most Australians will never themselves have acted with the intention of harming Aborigines, and most of the worst atrocities were committed in the past. By what line of inheritance do contemporary Australians inherit the sins of the predecessors? And which contemporary Australians? Is it only those of us of Anglo-Celtic stock whose ancestors came to Australia in the nineteenth century? Should we exclude those recent immigrants, especially those whose background is free of the taints of European colonialism and imperialism? And what of those Australians whose ancestors had no choice in the decision to migrate, but were brought over as convicts?

One answer to these questions turns on the issue of benefit. Those who have a special responsibility to make reparation to the indigenous people of Australia are those who have lived and flourished on the land that was taken from them. Many, perhaps almost all, immigrant Australians have benefited in some way from this expropriation, and it is these people who have the issue of reconciliation, compensation, and coming to terms with Aboriginal Australia on their moral agenda. Now I am sure that this is part of the answer, but it is not all of it. There

---

43 Cf. Paul Patton, 'Mabo and Australian Society: Towards a Postmodern Republic,' *Australian Journal of Anthropology* **6:1-2** (1995) 83-93, 89: "… it would be another form of racism to extend protection to indigenous communities only on the condition that they maintained and practiced a traditional form of life."

is a quite distinct moral thread connecting us with the expropriation of the Aboriginal people, and it is important to disentangle it. This is the concept of national identity. We have certain moral responsibilities just because we have a certain national identity.

In the Australian case it is difficult to isolate this because it is inter-twined with the issue of benefit. But that they are separate becomes clear in other cases. For example, the Holocaust has a specific relevance to Germans just because they are Germans. This may not be just the responsibility to make reparation; it is also the responsibility to remember what happened, and why it happened. Habermas, speaking as a German, puts this well:

> Our own life is linked to the life context in which Auschwitz was possible not by contingent circumstances but intrinsically. Our form of life is connected with that of our parents and grandparents through a web of familial, local, political, and intellectual traditions that it is difficult to disentangle – that is, through a historical milieu that made us what and who we are today. None of us can escape this milieu, because our identities, both as individuals and as Germans, are indissolubly interwoven with it.[44]

This is not a matter of whether present-day Germans have benefited from the past actions of their compatriots. This is highly unlikely. It is because they have a certain identity that they acquire certain historical responsibilities and find themselves implicated in actions which they themselves have not performed and, indeed, might never have performed.

A national identity involves, not just a sense of place, but a sense of history. The history constitutes the national memory, and it provides a way of locating those who share that identity within an historical community. The history is not given, but is subject to debate and reinterpretation. For example, Australians of earlier generations grew up with a history of British achievements, the European 'discovery' and 'exploration' of Australia, the trials and triumphs of the early settlers, and

---

44 Jürgen Habermas, *The New Conservatism: Cultural Criticism and the Historians' Debate* (Cambridge, MA: MIT Press 1989), 232-3. It is not clear to me that this passage is consistent with Habermas's 'constitutional patriotism' and universalistic 'discourse ethics.' I discuss this issue in 'On National Identity: A Response to Jonathan Rée,' *Radical Philosophy* 62 (Autumn 1992) 14-19.

so on. It was a history in which Aboriginals were marginal or absent. But this history has been and is being rewritten. It is now recognized that Australia did not come into existence with European discovery; that Aboriginal cultures and ways of life had existed for millennia; that Aboriginal practices had formed the land which was appropriated and exploited by the European immigrants; and that Aborigines had with flair and courage resisted white advances into their country. Australian history is now coming to terms with the suffering, destruction, and human tragedy consequent upon the European settlement of Australia. The details of this history may be debated, but it cannot be disavowed. Acquiring a national identity is a way of acquiring that history and the rights and the responsibilities which go with it. The responsibility to come to terms with the Australian past is a morally inescapable component of what it is to be Australian.

It is in this context that we must understand one of the risks of multiculturalism. Insofar as it involves a weakened sense of Australian historical identity and a strengthened sense of the affiliations which migrant Australians have to the countries of their origin, it also carries with it a weakened sense of the responsibilities which are written into Australian history. Many recent migrants do not feel implicated in it. It is not just that they personally have not been involved with or had direct dealings with Aboriginal people; this is true of most Anglo-Celtic Australians. It is also that their cultural identity implicates them in a different history and, perhaps, with a different set of responsibilities. It is only if they have a sense that coming to be an Australian involves coming to share its history that they will recognize that they have acquired the responsibilities which go with that history.

Though all Australians, even recently arrived ones, have a responsibility to come to terms with the Aboriginal past, present, and future of Australia and to contribute to the transformation of Australian life that this will require, the agency which will be most involved is, inevitably, the Australian government. Yet it has this task at a time when the capacity of all national governments to undertake major tasks is being undermined. Governments are under increasing pressure, from both international and domestic economic forces, to reduce government commitments and expenditure. At the same time, there is widespread cynicism – some of it justified – about the capacity of government policy makers and bureaucrats to carry out effective social interventions, and widespread alienation from the political process. The political climate of the day, in Australia as in most Western countries, is favourable to smaller and less active governments. This provides the context in which multicultural policies have their somewhat contradictory place.[45] Though they may call for greater government involvement, they also help erode the moral basis for that involvement. Governments may legitimately intervene in the business of society only insofar as they have, and are perceived to have, the moral authority to do so. For the past century or so, governments have relied for this on the claim to represent the nation and to embody and protect that culture which forms the day-to-day life of its citizens. In its more radical forms, multiculturalism involves the denial of this claim, and the affirmation of a diversity of culture within the one polity. While the legacy of nationalism is a profoundly ambiguous one, it remains one of the few moral and political resources available to combat the erosion of state authority. If the government ceases to embody the significant identity and thus commitment of its citizens, it will not have the moral capacity to undertake major tasks, especially those which require sacrifice on the part of citizens. If multiculturalism is not to have this effect (and it is in the interests of multiculturalism itself that it does not), the multicultural agenda must be clearly subordinated to the national one. And if the argument of this paper is correct, the most important and difficult item on the Australian national agenda is coming to terms with its indigenous peoples.[46]

---

45 For an enlightening account of the tension between multiculturalism and special recognition of the Maoris of New Zealand, see Richard Mulgan, 'Multiculturalism: A New Zealand Perspective,' in Chandran Kukathas, ed., *Multicultural Citizens*. Mulgan brings out very clearly the way in which multicultural and separationist agendas tend to erode the cultural basis for extensive state intervention.

46 Earlier versions of this paper were read at the Macquarie University Philosophy Society, the Conference of the Australasian Association of Philosophy at the University of Queensland, and the Future of Nationalism and the State Conference at the University of Sydney. I thank the audiences on these occasions for discussion, comment, and encouragement. Thanks are also due to Bernhard Ripperger for research and to Lisabeth During for advice and criticism. Finally, thanks to the Research Management Unit of Macquarie University for support for this and associated projects.

PART IV

Some Consequences of Nationalism

CANADIAN JOURNAL OF PHILOSOPHY
Supplementary Volume 22

Barbarous Nationalism and the Liberal International Order: Reflections on the 'Is,' the 'Ought,' and the 'Can'

CAROL A.L. PRAGER
University of Calgary

> It's a mistake to endow the Holocaust or any other massive case of crimes against humanity with cosmic significance. We want to do it because we think the moral enormity of the events should be balanced by an equally grand theory. But it's not. The attempt to do so is poignant.
>
> *Alain Finkielkraut*[1]

Savage ethnonationalism, dating back to the end of the eighteenth century, and violent ethnic conflict, as ancient as history, are sometimes viewed as if for the first time in the post-Cold War era.[2] Still, it is the case that the end of the discipline imposed by the bipolar international system has permitted temporarily repressed ethnic and nationalist passions to reassert themselves. In response, a vast literature has sprung up discussing what states should do about genocide and ethnic cleansing, the gravest human rights abuses. In what follows I will consider barbarous nationalism in the context of the liberal international order

---

1 *Remembering in Vain: The Klaus Barbie Trial and Crimes Against Humanity* (New York: Columbia University Press 1992)

2 Notwithstanding the general persuasiveness of Liah Greenfeld's contrary position, I shall treat ethnic conflict and nationalism as if they were more or less synonymous. They are not, of course, but they do derive from kindred emotions, representing more or less similar challenges to the international order. It is possible to think of barbarous nationalism as a more evolved form of ethnic conflict. See Liah Greenfeld, *Nationalism: Five Roads to Modernity* (Cambridge, MA: Harvard University Press 1992), 12. But cf. Daniel Patrick Moynihan, *Pandaemonium: Ethnicity in International Relations* (Oxford: Oxford University Press 1993), 197.

put into place at the end of the Second World War, the roles of politics, law and morality forming a subtext to that discussion. One cannot help but believe that unlike many of international relations' more transient issues, those raised by barbarous nationalism and the liberal international order will become an enduring preoccupation, as much on the ethical as on the empirical and policy sides.

The significance and persistence of these questions should not be underestimated. For example, one political scientist has entitled his book on ethnic conflict *Pandaemonium*[3] while an historian sees the increasing expression of barbarous nationalism and the consequent weakening of the state as signifying both the end of the modern era and the dawn of one in which barbarism in the form of vicious nationalism and ethnic conflict will undermine civilization.[4] In addition to ethnonationalism, there are other related, momentous challenges to the international order. One is the appearance, most dramatically in the 1960s and 1970s, of what Robert H. Jackson[5] terms 'quasi-states.' Such states, which have been internationally recognized but lack effective internal sovereignty and legitimacy, are subject to continuous assaults, often from national and ethnic groups, resulting in civil war or low-intensity conflict, the 1990s' characteristic form of violence. In these contexts parties to conflicts – including governments – characteristically resort to large-scale human rights abuses to seize or retain power. The former Zaire and the former Yugoslavia are only the most notable instances.

In other cases 'quasi-states' have fallen into anarchy. Stanley Hoffmann[6] has characterized this phenomenon as the 'chaos below,' caused by the breakdown of political authority, resulting in anomic behaviour. In such settings the anarchy is so total that it becomes impossible to distinguish war from crime, making the distinction between

---

3 Daniel Patrick Moynihan, *Pandaemonium*

4 John Lukacs, *The End of the Twentieth Century and the End of the Modern Age* (New York: Ticknor & Fields 1993)

5 Robert H. Jackson, *Quasi-states: Sovereignty, International Relations and the Third World* (Cambridge: Cambridge University Press 1990)

6 Stanley Hoffmann, 'The Crisis of Liberal Internationalism,' *Foreign Policy* **98** (1995) 168

combatants and civilians impossible to maintain. Intervention in these settings is especially problematic since there is no single point at which intervention can be directed and no clear-cut policy objective to be pursued. Clearly, such states of affairs represent momentous challenges to world order. In this article, however, I shall focus on barbarous nationalism, which can be more sharply defined.

Since nationalism itself springs from a sense of grievance,[7] or as Leah Greenfeld put it, 'ressentiment,' due to oppression, uneven development, and other factors, there appears to be no end to the conditions that create furious nationalism. Moreover, many modern developments serve to fan the flames of nationalism. The homogenizing effects of globalization, for example, have been seen as a source of oppression, leading to heightened nationalism. The economic dimensions of globalization, ironically themselves expressions of liberalism, and their tendency to polarize the rich and poor,[8] have created new winners and losers around the world, increasing the latter's sense of deprivation and grievance. These are magnified by the power of the media to exhibit living conditions around the world, and the growing and often conflictive interdependence which Rousseau presciently identified.[9] One reluctant superpower is left in what has become a 'post-heroic' world in which sacrifice and heroism have little valence.[10]

Clearly, humanitarian crises, and the cries for justice and intervention that go with them, raise issues that profoundly challenge the moral commitments of states. Are states obligated to intervene in such crises? What is the extent of their obligation? Where are we left if humanitarian intervention turns out to be morally required but not possible, or, all

---

7   Kenneth Minnogue, 'Identity, Self, and Nation,' in Guy Laforest and Douglas Brown, eds., *Integration and Fragmentation: The Paradox of the Late Twentieth Century* (Kingston, ON: Queens University Institute of Intergovernmental Relations 1994), 89

8   See Lester Thurow, 'A Surge in Inequality,' *Scientific American* **256** (1987), 30–7.

9   Ian Clark, *The Hierarchy of States: Reform and Resistance in the International Order* (Cambridge: Cambridge University Press 1989), 73-8

10 See Edward Luttwak, 'A Post-Heroic Military Policy,' *Foreign Affairs* **75** (1996) 33-44.

things considered, not morally mandated or desirable? In what follows, I assume that the existence of a moral obligation presupposes the possibility of performing that obligation, and that how possible something is, is an empirical question. If one concludes that intervention is undesirable or virtually impossible, how, if at all, can this be reconciled with the continuing possibility of a progressive, liberal international order? I believe, further, that such issues, like most in international relations, fall into the realm of applied ethics. In other words, moral theories in and of themselves cannot resolve in isolation from political facts and law the ethical dilemmas that arise out of barbarous nationalism.[11]

Nationalism and Barbarous Nationalism

Although until fairly recently the positive aspects of nationalism were salient, today it takes effort to view nationalism in a positive light. There is the sense (difficult to justify completely) that positive nationalism has not only reached the point of diminishing returns but a destructive nationalism has replaced it, threatening to undermine the existing international order with its insatiable regress. Not long ago nationalism was seen primarily as a positive phenomenon that promoted democracy, development, diversity, and experimentation, mobilized the masses, and thwarted imperialism. Above all, it was the vehicle that expressed the quintessentially liberal value of national self-determination. Today it seems important to bear in mind this right of self-determination was not made contingent on admirable or desirable results, but included the right to fail. On John Stuart Mill's account, "(T)he only test ... of a people's having become fit for popular institutions, is that they, or a significant portion of them to prevail in the contest, are willing to brave labor and danger for their liberation."[12]

---

11 Stanley Hoffmann also considers this type of analysis to be applied ethics. He writes: "We all know that no 'ought' can be simply and directly derived from an 'is.' What we have now tells us how difficult it is to go beyond – indeed, how easily things might get worse. It does not tell us where we ought to go." Stanley Hoffmann, *Duties Beyond Borders: On the Limits and Possibilities of Ethical International Politics* (Syracuse: Syracuse University Press 1981), 189-90.

12 Cited in Michael Walzer, *Just and Unjust Wars: A Moral Argument with Historical Illustrations*, 2d ed. (New York: Basic Books 1992), 88.

On the other hand Lord Acton, Elie Kedourie, and others pointed out that the conflicts created by the dispersion of Poles, Germans, Jews, and others throughout Europe drew attention to the fact that minorities often found more freedom in multinational states or empires than they did in self-determining nation-states. Acton contended, "If we take the establishment of liberty for the realization of moral duties to be the end of civil society, we must conclude that those states are the most perfect which, like the British and Austrian Empires, include various distinct nationalities without oppressing them.... A state which is incompetent to satisfy different races condemns itself."[13] Notwithstanding, nationalism has been widely embraced as one of the most powerful engines of liberation.

In the twentieth century's interwar years, however, the darker side of nationalism became plainer, and it was largely in reaction to nationalism's monstrous excrescence of the Holocaust that the post-Second World War's liberal international order was organized.[14] Never again, it was affirmed, would the rest of the world idly stand by as deranged nationalists attempted to exterminate whole peoples. At the time it seemed to many a modest, rock-bottom commitment. At the turn of the millennium, however, the world is awash with ethnic violence and there are no grounds for anticipating an end to it; the commitment not to tolerate genocide no longer seems modest but a hornet's nest of unimaginable and paralyzing complexities.

Call it barbarous, monstrous, 'pathological,'[15] criminal, or simply 'evil' (the word Margaret Thatcher used to describe the ferocious ethnonationalism in the former Yugoslavia), a great deal of ethnic conflict can be tied to the 1989 breakup of the Soviet Union (where Stalin

---

13 Cited by Elie Kedourie, in *Nationalism*, 4th, expanded ed. (Oxford: Blackwell 1993), 128.

14 It can, however, also be argued that Nazi racism was more a form of internationalism than of nationalism. See William Pfaff, *The Wrath of Nations: Civilization and the Furies of Nationalism* (New York: Simon & Schuster 1993), 70.

15 Usage is taken from Donald Rothchild and Alexander J. Groth, 'Pathological Dimensions of Domestic and International Ethnicity,' *Political Science Quarterly* **10** (1995) 69-82.

had pursued a calculated policy of breaking up ethnic concentrations to divide his opposition) and its bloc.

One must dig below the surface of barbarous nationalism to identify the possibilities open to international intervention, and the best place, perhaps, to begin is with the ubiquity of ethnic conflict and cleansing. The first case of ethnic cleansing can be traced to Tiglath-Pileser III, an Assyrian leader (745-727 BC) whose policy it was forcibly to resettle half the people of the lands he conquered, and replace them with populations from elsewhere. The Babylonians, Greeks, and Romans also engaged in ethnic cleansing.[16] In other words, ethnic conflict has been a permanent feature of human history, whereas ethno-nationalism can be traced back only to the late eighteenth century.

There is no need to discuss the sickening atrocities occurring today in the former Yugoslavia, the former Soviet Union (notably the Azeri-Armenian conflict in Nagorno-Karabakh), in Rwanda, Burundi, and other places.[17] It is enough to appreciate that such forms of ethno-nationalism and ethno-conflict are absolutist and pitiless. While it is impossible to deny the evil in these scenarios, some empirical scholars have also regarded them as 'pathological' phenomena to be understood in their own terms. The pathology is first seen in narratives of one's own group which portray one's people as noble and proud but abused, and in stereotypes of enemy groups as inhuman, savage, and treacherous. In reality, however, the actual differences between enemy groups can be slight or imaginary. (This is certainly the case in Burundi and the former Yugoslavia.) Perversely, the smaller the actual difference between peoples, the larger they imagine it to be. Freud had recognized this paradox, which he called 'the narcissism of minor difference.'[18] In the presence of monstrous demons who are prepared to use all their vile and mighty powers to exterminate one's group, resorting to the same

---

16 Andrew Bell-Fialkoff, 'A Brief History of Ethnic Cleansing,' *Foreign Affairs* **72** (Summer 1993) 111-12

17 For a grim recent account of the ongoing slaughter in Burundi see Philip Gourevitch, 'The Poisoned Country,' *New York Review of Books* **43** (1996) 58-64.

18 Michael Ignatieff, *Blood & Belonging: Journeys into the New Nationalism* (Toronto: Viking Press 1993), 14

vicious tactics is entirely justified. It is shocking but instructive that General Ratko Mladic, accused by the war crimes tribunal in the Hague of 'the most horrendous, unimaginable war crimes committed in Europe since the end of World War II,'[19] is a hero to Bosnian Serbs and is quoted as saying "Only my people can judge me."[20] (Interestingly, however, his daughter Ana's 1994 suicide was reportedly caused by her guilt over her father's policies and acts.)[21] 'Ethnic psychosis' gains momentum where there is anxiety and despair; problems that could be solved appear hopeless. That liberalism actually has little to say about pathology is unsurprising. But one might surmise that a liberal account might generally hold that the mad be segregated if necessary so as not to thwart others' liberties, and that they should be given non-paternalistic therapy, to strengthen the reason which might subdue their madness, and to restore them to self-determination.

The essential irrationality of 'pathological' and absolutist ethnonationalism does not, however, preclude ambitious politicians from shrewdly using this madness to serve their own purposes. Nor need it completely obliterate the individual sense of responsibility, sometimes subordinating that responsibility to a 'higher cause,' the achievement of a glorious, if not utopian, future which vindicates nihilism. In a powerful and frightening passage William Pfaff eloquently elaborates on this process:

> War in Yugoslavia has incorporated the attempt to desecrate and eradicate values. This was the rationale for the systematic rape of Bosnian women; doing so desecrated and 'ruined' them. The moral cost paid by the rapist, or the murderer, is recognized, but is assumed. Hamlet's desire was to murder his stepfather in his adultery to be certain he would go to hell, even though this guarantees hell for Hamlet as well. The drunkenness of the militias encountered in Yugoslavia is one product of their fearful commitment to an equivalent proposition, and of their rejection of what they had been before, before they had murdered and raped their neighbors, and become changed men. This was in their faces. It was in the urgent lies pressed upon the outsider by the physicians, university professors and other professionals who led the warring factions. They had put

---

19 Julius Strauss, 'Mladic a Hero to Bosnian Serbs,' *Globe and Mail*, 16 July 1996, A8

20 Strauss, 'Mladic a Hero'

21 Strauss, 'Mladic a Hero'

aside their laboratory smocks and briefcases and professional consciousness to enter a different moral universe of different truth and titanic possibilities – from which one does not return.[22]

Moreover, this fanatically limitless commitment to whatever may be necessary to achieve their ends is seen as manly.[23] It is difficult for liberal outsiders to grasp how minority status in a territory surrounded by historical enemies can make a minority feel menaced (often rightly) by the majority, who typically see the minority as the most serious threat to the integrity of the nation.

What, on this empirical account, can be done to 'cure' pathological or absolutist nationalism? In principle the therapy for 'pathological' ethnonationalism is the same as it is for psychoses in general: confronting the people involved with the genesis and dimensions of their problem. The distorted stereotypes embedded in their narrative's splendid characterizations of themselves as well as of the enemy's irredeemable depravity must gradually be eliminated; the preoccupations of competing groups understood; and civic and legal-rational values promoted. Failing this, international resources may be called into play, controlling violence and creating incentives for cooperation and reconciliation.[24] This rational 'cure' presupposes, on the one hand, motivation, typically impaired in psychosis, to turn away from one's demented behaviour, an openness to external help, as well as a willingness in external actors to assume the risks that intervention on their part may entail. All these preconditions, however, are in doubt when parties are unwilling to question their cherished narratives of themselves, their enemies, and their shared history, all of which have become seared in their identities and are renewed with each fresh atrocity. This process is also thwarted by a refusal to cooperate with state au-

---

22 Pfaff, *The Wrath of Nations*, 229-30

23 Pfaff quotes Isaiah Berlin on the mid-eighteenth century German reaction to the French: "All forms of going to the bitter end were thought more worthy of men than peaceful negotiations stopping half-way; extremism, conflict, war were glorified as such" (*The Wrath of Nations*, 34).

24 Rothchild and Groth, 'Pathological Dimensions,' 82

thorities and other international organizations, as seen in both the Bosnian and the Zairian crises.[25]

Accumulated experience in the former Yugoslavia reveals there is no 'therapy' for absolutist nationalism, nor any alternative realities convincing to the parties. The only factor that has made a difference there is overwhelming force. But today the amount and kind of force required are not generally forthcoming. The Dayton Peace Accords separate the military provisions (for example, stopping the fighting and separating the parties) from essential civilian responsibilities (such as resettling refugees in their former communities, tracking down war criminals, and fostering the development of tolerant democratic institutions and policies). NATO forces have vigorously enforced the Dayton Accords' military objectives, but attached a much lower priority to the Accords' civilian commitments. Given the realities on the ground, this is understandable, but at the same time defeats the purposes of the Accords. The other possibility is the use of inducements: promises of help and rewards. Ultimately this may be the most effective tack. The difficulty is finding rewards attractive enough to offset virulent emotions, force powerful enough to intimidate, and the necessary modicum of reason.

Apart from the intransigence of madness and absolutist nationalism, other factors work against controlling barbarous nationalism externally by intervening states. External powers find compelling reasons not to risk the lives of their young in civil wars. The United States' cautious refusal to commit ground troops in the former Yugoslavia can partly be attributed to its loss of life in Somalia. As a European diplomat has been quoted as saying, "When faced with a choice between renewed conflict in Bosnia and heavy NATO casualties, the Europeans and the Americans will choose conflict in Bosnia. It is sad, but perhaps understandable."[26]

---

25 For a current account of how Serb leaders continue to defy the NATO leadership in the former Yugoslavia, see Chris Hedges, 'Latest Tussle in Bosnia Has Familiar Ring,' in *The Globe and Mail*, 3 July 1996, A10. Hedges describes Radovan Karadzic's transparent manoeuvres to appear to satisfy NATO's conditions, while obviously thumbing his nose at them.

26 Hedges, 'Latest Tussle in Bosnia'

Beyond these responses to barbarous nationalism lies the possibility of ultimate reconciliation, on which arguments for humanitarian intervention finally depend. There are, of course, many factors that work against the possibility of reconciliation, especially where renewed savagery augments the historical record. One is hard-pressed to think of many examples where reconciliation between enemies has occurred. More often than we might care to think, belief in the possibility of reconciliation is based on faith rather than historical experience. Far from being a natural, inevitable outcome, reconciliation has historically been the exception rather than the rule. The most successful reconciliations have occurred in Europe among, for example, the Scandinavian people, and between the German and the French. Even in these cases ethnic stereotypes are not far from the surface in their dealings with each other. Too, changing economic circumstances rapidly bring vengeful feelings back into play. Even the much vaunted American tolerance for diversity can be undermined by the history of the Civil War in which the South was savagely conquered by the North.[27] (Reflecting this sense of hopelessness, Bismarck famously said the Balkans were not worth the death of one Pomeranian grenadier.[28])

In sum, absolutist or 'pathological' nationalism accounts for many of the crises that some liberals argue justify intervention but typically do not lend themselves to 'therapy' or any other kind of constructive intervention. On the contrary, such crises are based on distorted narratives that lead to mass psychosis, absolutism, and barbarity. Nor should anyone deny the outright evil in situations leading up to demands for humanitarian intervention. Certainly the moral revulsion to barbarous nationalism is the most compelling argument for intervention. By the same token, the historical background to such abuses typically is morally ambiguous. In the present Bosnian situation, for example, it is the Serbs who have resorted to the most ethnic cleansing and atrocities, but they have been trying to create an enclave where they are free from Croats, whose Ustashe committed war crimes against them during the

---

27   Benjamin Schwarz, 'The Diversity Myth: America's Leading Export,' *The Atlantic Monthly* **275** (1995) 57-67

28   Charles Krauthammer, 'Bob Dole's Bosnia Folly,' *Time* 12 December 1994, 80

Second World War. Canadian Lieutenant-General Lewis Mackenzie remarked that in the former Yugoslavia we are dealing with the moral equivalent of three serial killers. It must not be forgotten, for example, that Croatian troops ruthlessly displaced ninety percent of the Serbian population in Western Slavonia,[29] or that Bosnian Muslims were often accused of murdering their own people in order to bring about intervention. The inhuman cruelty of the war in Bosnia, which epitomized liberalism's dream of a peaceful, secular, tolerant state, is emblematic of the power of barbarous nationalism. (These considerations affirm the wisdom of the suggestion that intervening contingents should be composed of volunteers who are prepared to fight for their own, including moral, reasons.)

Humanitarian Intervention

Turning away from arguments based on the overwhelming difficulties in affecting the rancorous feelings embedded in barbarous nationalism, the mirage of reconciliation, and the moral ambiguity of the histories involved, I now consider arguments based on liberal internationalism and humanitarianism. Liberalism affirms the legal and moral autonomy of self-determining states, raising the issue of consent to intervention. It is rightly assumed that states are extremely reluctant to agree to this manifest assault on their sovereignty, as the present Rwandan resistance to a multinational force illustrates. But for liberals such as Michael Walzer the required agreement of states is bypassed by pointing to the need for a population's consent to their government. Although there is often no systematic way to verify this, the assumption is made that individuals would not willingly submit to a government's savage and humiliating treatment of them. The sovereignty of states is defended on the ground that states assume responsibility for protecting the security and well-being of its population. In such cases it is taken for granted that a reasonably satisfied population consents to its government. On this account, where it is not external enemies that must be guarded against but the state

---

29   Charles G. Boyd, 'Making Peace with the Guilty,' *Foreign Affairs* **74** (1995) 23

itself, the rationale for the state's right not to be intervened in evaporates. The situation in the former Yugoslavia, however, presents special difficulties because it is hard to decide which is the responsible government. Further, ethnonationalist conflict there has variously assumed the form of civil war and international war following the formal recognition of Slovenia and Croatia, each of which entails a different international response. Significantly, too, under international law humanitarian intervention is generally considered a right, rather than an obligation.

Humanitarianism itself can legitimate humanitarian intervention. In fact, early interventions against massive, systematic atrocities were called interventions 'for the sake of humanity;'[30] crimes against humanity referring only to crimes that are not protected by the laws of the state concerned. A theoretically less elaborate rationale for supporting intervention, humanitarianism is based on an obligation to relieve distress: the more widespread and crueler the distress, the greater the obligation. This humanitarianism is even easier to defend for philosophers like Charles Beitz and Martha Nussbaum, who see humanity as the central moral concept in international politics, and insist that state borders lack moral significance. In his discussion of humanity and economic justice in the global context, however, Brian Barry makes the extremely interesting point that as a general proposition humanitarian obligations do not extend to risking one's life.[31] This explains why it is no part of the responsibility of humanitarian workers for private relief agencies to take chances that endanger their lives.

Moreover, all humanitarian interventions are bedeviled with various dangers: the facts that mistakes can and will be made and that outcomes are unpredictable, and the possibility that the intervention does not reduce the amount of chaos, but increases it. Barbarous nationalism and violent ethnic conflict raise special difficulties for humanitarian intervention. First, most international legal authorities

---

30 See Manouchehr Ganji, *International Protection of Human Rights* (Geneva: Libraire E. Droz 1962).

31 Brian Barry, 'Humanity and Justice in Global Perspective,' *Ethics, Economics and the Law*, J. Roland Pennock and John W. Chapman, eds., Nomos XXIV (New York: New York University Press 1982), 224

conclude that intervention is generally forbidden under international law. The conclusion is based on the violation of state sovereignty, international law's fundamental premise, and the suspicion that intervening states will not be able to resist the temptation to arrange matters in the country intervened in to suit their interests. Since one is hard-pressed to find more than one or two pure, disinterested cases of humanitarian intervention, this apprehension is justified. One legal authority contends, "... (I)t is not possible to construct a persuasive argument to legitimize the use of force for humanitarian purposes *while remaining in the idiom of classical 'international law.'"*[32] Another international lawyer, Ellery C. Stowell, maintains, "However morally justifiable interference for such a purpose might be, it remains an act of policy and must be defended as such."[33] Second, although there is a strong case for Walzer's presumption that victims of systematic, humiliating atrocities do not consent to them, this cannot, nevertheless, be assumed in every case. Moreover, since many such situations are embedded in civil wars in which there is the belief that the outcome should be settled between the parties, there is the strong possibility that intervention could prevent this outcome.

A third difficulty has to do with the lessons of experience in other interventions. Initially, when one thinks of humanitarian interventions, one sees them as short, 'surgical,' and disinterested, scrupulously avoiding involvement in local politics. Not only is this obviously impossible in the case of disintegrating states, I argue that this is also true for humanitarian crises triggered by barbarous nationalism, as can be seen in the former Yugoslavia where the collapse of the peace agreement is widely anticipated when the peacekeepers leave.[34] No humanitarian

---

32 Lori Fisler Damrosch, 'Changing Conceptions of Intervention in International Law,' *Emerging Norms of Justified Intervention*, A Collection of Essays from a Project of the American Academy of Arts and Sciences, Laura W. Reed and Carl Kaysen, eds. (Cambridge: American Academy of Arts and Sciences 1993), 96. Damrosch is stating her agreement with the views of Tom Farer.

33 Ellery C. Stowell, *Intervention in International Law* (Litttleton, CO: Fred B. Rothman & Co. 1983), 150

34 Cf. the rather similar arguments of John Dunn, 'The Dilemma of Humanitarian Intervention,' *Government and Opposition* (1994), 248-61.

intervention, however, can be executed in an apolitical, disinterested way. For example, sheltering and feeding large numbers of refugees for a short time may be a humanitarian act. But continuing the policy for months or years will most likely preclude the return of normal political life and is, hence, a political act. The political aspect of humanitarian assistance was borne out in the former Zaire.

A critical problem is what prevents the violence from continuing as soon as intervenors leave? After all, the conditions produced by clashes of barbarous nationalism are not 'acts of nature' but evidence of deeply rooted anger and vengefulness, as well as of political and economic systems that are falling apart. More and more it becomes obvious that intervention's inevitable corollary obligation is 'nation-building.' This particular slippery slope of attempting to restore the state in question to a stable, peaceful, political society that is reasonably free from the danger of further breakdown, raises the most difficult dilemmas for liberals who might view such attempts as unacceptable affronts to the self-determination of the state involved. In principle nation-building might be achieved by supporting the development of tolerant, democratic governments, returning refugees to their homes, and so forth. In practice, the local government and population are highly likely to strenuously object to such interference in their political life; even with their good will such projects are bound to be problematical.

Post-mortems of the Somalian intervention shed light on why intervention is so hard to conceive and justify. One of the most persuasive declares: "This much is manifest: no massive intervention in a failed state – even one for humanitarian purposes – can be assuredly short by plan, politically neutral in application, or wisely parsimonious in providing nation-building development aid."[35] That there is no such thing as disinterested intervention needs to be recalled; to the contrary, it has also been argued that intervenors should not hesitate to throw their weight behind the side that has been most victimized. The fact that the Dayton Peace Accords, on which the 'peace' in the former Yugoslavia is based, devote scant resources to nation-building is understandable

---

35 Walter Clarke and Jeffrey Herbst, 'Somalia and the Future of Humanitarian Intervention,' *Foreign Affairs* **75** (1996) 71

given the fact that acceptance of the Accords by the parties was at stake. Clearly nation-building, typically involving the state's fundamental institutions, is the most intrusive form of intervention, and the most resented. But at the same time it is clear that 'nation-building' is a residual category to which all the intractable problems and the fundamental causes of the humanitarian crisis are relegated, making such projects immensely more difficult than they already are.

International Liberalism

It is no coincidence that liberalism and nationalism both made their appearance at roughly the same time inasmuch as they were in no small measure reactions to each other. Especially in central Europe nationalism was Romanticism's response to the universalism of the French Enlightenment.[36] On the other hand, international law grew as the Congress of Vienna collapsed after the 1848 revolutions, further entrenching republican and nationalist governments. International law compensated for the loss of cosmopolitanism resulting from the breakdown of the Concert of Europe. But liberalism's demand for tolerance was rooted in Europe's religious wars. Liberalism was in no small part a reaction to intolerance, dogmatism, and the cruelty done in the name of religion.[37] It is difficult to see how liberalism, which is based on reason, could be more opposed to nationalism, which is based on will. In any case, over their relatively brief history, nationalism has always triumphed over liberalism.

In the broadest terms liberalism refers to expanding the liberties available to individuals and restricting the intrusions of groups, especially governments, to a level consistent with maintaining basic government services. But as numerous interpretations of liberalism in domestic contexts abound, they are still more numerous in the case of

---

36 Pfaff, *The Wrath of Nations*, 14

37 Judith N. Shklar, 'The Liberalism of Fear,' in Nancy L. Rosenblum, ed., *Liberalism and the Moral Life* (Cambridge, MA: Harvard University Press 1989), 27

liberal internationalism. Different emphases of liberalism in the international sphere, however, use logics that take them in different directions. International liberalism, for instance, might underscore the
independence of states, or the protection of human rights. In the former,
the issue of consent to intervention is central. But the requirement of
consent creates its own difficulties, the most harassing of which include what the consent of an oppressive regime actually guarantees,
and the high probability that such states will not agree to the protection of human rights. As Lea Brilmayer argues, "[Consent][38] protects
only against abuses by nations that have been high-minded enough to
agree to human rights enforcement in the first place, and leaves truly
outrageous violators free to do as they like."[39]

Wilsonian liberalism was predicated on national self-determination, which Wilson believed would lead to peace and an enhancement
of human freedom, as well as progressive international institutions
such as international law and the League of Nations. From Wilsonian
liberalism comes the belief that only a multilateral international organization can legitimately authorize interventions, even though experience's lesson is that interventions are not likely to occur without
a hegemon's involvement. Ironically, humanitarian intervention was
more widely practised before the progressive United Nations came
into existence.

The experience of the Holocaust was pivotal to the development of
twentieth-century international liberalism. Statesmen affirmed the
world would never again stand idly by in the face of genocide. This
seemed a minimum commitment, an unexceptionable common de-
nominator, a universal norm at the heart of the 'substantive morality'
of states and, in international legal terms, *jus cogens*, which specifies
norms that are binding on states whether or not they consent to them.
(The prohibition against slavery also belongs to this category.) Since,

---

38 Deconstructionists and other critical thinkers have a great deal to say about
   how deconstructing the structures and actors further undercuts the meaning of
   consent.

39 Lea Brilmayer, *American Hegemony: Political Morality in a One-Superpower World*
   (New Haven: Yale University Press 1994), 146

however, international law is overwhelmingly based on states' consent, the category of *jus cogens* is not extensive.[40]

The national interest creates further problems for humanitarian intervention. A major vehicle through which a state asserts its sovereignty and autonomy, the national interest defines what a state's wishes and priorities are. But in practice, and sometimes in theory too, the national interest is not often seen as including an obligation to intervene. (Even U.S. President Clinton's decision to finally send military forces to Bosnia was justified at least as much on humanitarian grounds as on the national interest. It is possible that the national interest could include humanitarian values, but this was not his argument.) This is consistent with the international legal reasoning that intervention is a right and not a duty, but it would conflict with moral theories that argue intervention is a moral obligation. One solution to this problem is Stanley Hoffmann's attempt to redefine the national interest to include 'milieu goals' (in contrast with 'possession goals') and moral obligations.[40] 'Milieu goals' include stability and the level of morality in international politics. It must, however, be admitted that states already have 'milieu goals.' For example, former U.S. Secretary of State Henry Kissinger urged moderate policies on states because they led, he believed, to moderate international relations. Related to 'milieu goals' is the right to stop 'public nuisances,' which in international law are state policies that create serious problems for states nearby, such as huge flows of refugees seeking asylum in other countries. This is part of the rationale for the European Bosnian policy as well as the American policy toward Haiti and Cuba. The abatement of public nuisances, moreover, may include the right to intervene. A second problem with redefining national interest to incorporate 'milieu goals' and moral obligations is on whom would this redefined national interest be binding? But the question remains how broadly 'milieu goals' can convincingly be

---

40 Brilmayer, *American Hegemony*, 164, 166

41 See in particular Stanley Hoffmann, 'The Crisis of Liberal Internationalism,' *Foreign Policy* **98** (1995), 159–77, 'In Defense of Mother Teresa: Morality in Foreign Policy,' *Foreign Affairs* **75** (1996) 172-5, and 'The Politics and Ethics of Military Intervention,' *Survival* **37** (1995-96), 51.

defined. It may please scholars and moral philosophers to conceptualize the national interest in this expansive way. But the people whose decisions bear on defining the national interest in practice – let us say in the case of the United States, the president, legislators, and voters – are more apt to define the national interest in a way that protects their liberties, which is to say, narrowly. Another move by Hoffmann is to assert the need for a theory that completely reconceptualizes the international world as it exists today, including collapsing states and the 'chaos below.' In fact, the work has already been begun. Robert Jackson's discussion of 'quasi-states,' Benjamin Barber's[42] arguments for confederations, and David Held's account of global interrelations[43] come to mind, none of which, however, have had much impact on policy.

There is a final, darker, liberal position on barbarous nationalism and the liberal international order, one that I find convincing. It is articulated by the liberal William Pfaff. Bringing to bear historical perspectives, Pfaff, who sees the 'furies of nationalism'[44] presiding over the collapse of the liberal international order, calls his position 'historical pessimism.' Pfaff is pessimistic because he anticipates neither an end to barbarous nationalism, nor empirical or normative theories that salvage liberal internationalism. Unexamined beliefs are to blame. He writes:

> In defiance of experience, an unanalyzed belief in progress continues to lie at the core of western political thought today, even though there is no longer a generally persuasive 'scientific theory' of social improvement, or transformation. The belief is unanalyzed because its verification and its replacement seem equally impossible tasks. The implication of what has happened in contemporary history, and continues to happen, would seem to recommend an intellectual position of historical pessimism, hostile to social engineering and large programmatic reforms, even when the program is so modest as simply to dethrone *laissez-faire* – which has not worked either. But historical pessimism con-

---

42 Benjamin R. Barber, *Jihad vs. McWorld* (New York: Time Books 1995), 288-92

43 David Held, 'From City-states to a Cosmopolitan Order?' *Prospects for Democracy: North, South, East, West,* David Held, ed. (Stanford: Stanford University Press 1993), 13-52

44 Taken from the title of Pfaff's previously cited book, *The Wrath of Nations: Civilization and the Furies of Nationalism.* This section relies substantially on Pfaff's account.

tradicts the principal assumption of western political society: that it is going someplace, and doing so in an intelligible way.[45]

Pfaff's pessimism becomes all the more persuasive when one takes into account Isaiah Berlin's observation that no theory or reality can embrace all values at the same time and that the salience of one causes another to diminish. It is also the case that there are evils for which there is no clear obligation of redress. Especially in international politics there are appalling atrocities that can be remedied only by an extraordinary heroism, for which there is no moral obligation. Barbarous nationalism and the liberal international order remain at war, morally and empirically. There is no doubt, however, which has triumphed.

Conclusion

Ethical dilemmas in international relations have generally been understood in terms of the debate between realists and idealists, sometimes nuanced by the more moderate position held by Hedley Bull. Such arguments, I argue, are too stark for international politics, where the 'is' and 'ought' are intricately interwoven with each other. Nationalism is a creature of will, liberalism of reason, and international liberalism of faith that the world can be improved. But historically '(t)his national feeling, which is not a practical commitment but a matter of passions, has consistently overridden principles of international solidarity and political or religious universalism.'[46] There is little reason to think it will not again, as the international community continues to play cat and mouse (or, perhaps, rat and kitty) with indicted war criminals.

The fact that one of the main links between nationalism and the international order (i.e., humanitarian intervention) must be consigned to the realm of applied ethics along, I would argue, with most international ethical dilemmas, thus undermining the application of universal moral principles, does not mean that constructive action in the

---

45 Pfaff, *The Wrath of Nations*, 39

46 Pfaff, *The Wrath of Nations*, 24

sphere of international politics is impossible. But it probably is quite different from what we abstractly imagine.

'Reflectivists' (i.e., critical thinkers such as John Ruggie, Haywood Alker, Friedrich Kratochwil, R.B.J. Walker, Nicholas Onuf, and V. Spike Petersen) accuse mainstream thinkers of believing that what is determines what ought to be.[47] This, I suggest, is a caricature. It is much more a case of whatever *is*, constraining to a significant degree what *can be*. In all politics, but especially in international politics, whatever is has to be taken seriously and, in that sense, respected. Stubborn facts such as intransigent barbarous nationalism, the decentralized international political system driven by national interests, and the uneven development of states are powerful drags on progress, keeping international politics stuck in the present. Refusing to assign appropriate weight to those considerations and predicating moral theories on reality's obliteration take us nowhere, politically or morally, that we wish to go. Initially international socialism seemed to persons of good will a powerfully progressive development, but it foundered on stubborn facts. Similarly, refusing to assign proper weight to the pathological hatred between the parties in the former Yugoslavia, or Nagorno-Karabakh, or the Tutsis and Hutus in Rwanda and Burundi, or exaggerating the possibilities for reconciliation is to put us on the road to diplomatic disaster and moral cynicism. The prohibition against the genocides produced by barbarous nationalism is ironically, on the one hand, a fundamental universal prohibition, but empirically the most unrealistic, on the other. Although there is plenty of room for disagreement about what can be, this determination is overwhelmingly empirical.

To the extent that moral progress occurs at all, it comes about obliquely and not through the imposition of ethical principles. Wherever a statesman has real alternatives, she or he can choose to throw their weight behind the more progressive. There is, I argue, a moral obligation, guided by realism, to search for such openings. Rational negotiation typically provides another opportunity. One way to reach

---

47 Lea Brilmayer, *American Hegemony*, 194

agreement in negotiation, as Roger Fisher[48] points out, is to "build on legitimacy," that is, work toward a settlement that incorporates established ethical, legal, and political norms, however variously interpreted and prioritized they may be. Somewhat like natural selection which separates out the fittest for survival, whatever is rational and constructive in this realm, at least, has a tendency to perpetuate itself over time. The fact that even the most reprehensible behaviour of regimes must be justified in such terms to their people and international opinion is not only a source of cynicism but a source of hope because it implicitly recognizes the legitimacy of ethical and legal norms. For example, Nigeria attempted to justify arbitrary executions by pointing to criminal attempts to undermine the Nigerian state. China defends its draconian criminal and judicial systems by asserting its need to protect itself from chaos. These, in the abstract, are legitimate goals of states. Whether the rest of the world is persuaded by these rationalizations in individual cases for the moment is neither here nor there. What matters is the inherent need to assert one's policies' consistency with accepted moral and legal norms, and a certain momentum toward progressive solutions that results. The need to legitimize policies, however cynically it is done, can entrench moral and legal norms.[49]

Finally, the possibility is available to statesmen, especially powerful ones, to establish something new. As Machiavelli understood, when fortune smiles on statesmen they show a latent creativity to establish new precedents and institutions. For example, the European Union was begun largely with the high statesmanship of Jean Monnet, who proposed the founding of the European Coal and Steel Community, with the rationale of putting the war-making capacities of historic enemies France and Germany under the collective supervision and control of themselves, Italy, Belgium, Luxembourg, and the Netherlands. Recent counter-intuitive 'firsts' include the U.S.-supported interven-

---

48 Roger Fisher, *International Conflict for Beginners* (New York: Harper & Row 1969), 128–50

49 Lea Brilmayer makes what seems to be a parallel argument in her discussion of hegemonic rule, suggesting that the accountability of the hegemony helps bridge the gap between the is and the ought.

tion in Bosnia, motivated as much by humanitarian considerations as national interests, and the reorientation of NATO itself to embrace the former Soviet bloc countries, the defence against which was its original rationale. Of course, such initiatives are not always well received or built on. But it will be interesting to see the long-term impact of U.S. President Bill Clinton's decision regarding U.S. involvement in Bosnia and international intervention in Eastern Africa. One suspects that future international politics will accord greater legitimacy to humanitarian reasons for intervening, along with rationales such as the threat to the international order. But the sky is not the limit in such revolutions, as the Europeans are now discovering as they expand and try to implement the Maastricht Treaty; limits are invariably met.

One is left with the reflection that threats of moral collapse tend to engender moral theories of equal dimensions, regardless of the thin ice on which they may actually stand. It is not so much that such moral reactions provide an effective response to evils but that they assert that our compassionate moral selves have not been obliterated by events. The danger, however, is that this edifice can cause us to deceive ourselves about reality. How obviously necessary are universal ethical prohibitions against horrific barbarous nationalism, and how apparent their virtual impotence.

CANADIAN JOURNAL OF PHILOSOPHY
Supplementary Volume 22

The Bounds of Nationalism*

THOMAS W. POGGE
Columbia University

Nationalism is generally associated with sentiments, ideologies, and social movements that involve strong commitments to a nation, conceived as a potentially self-sustaining community of persons bound together by a shared history and culture. Recent empirical and normative discussions have been concentrated on revisionist instances of nationalism, that is, on sentiments, ideologies, and social movements that aim to gain power, political autonomy, or territory for a particular nation. I will here take a somewhat broader view of nationalism, focusing on persons who have a bland and conservative commitment to their own country.[1] Quite content with the *status quo*, these persons view it as legitimate and even admirable that they and their political leaders should show a pre-eminent concern for preserving and enlarging their own collective advantage. Most citizens of the affluent countries – however condescendingly they may regard the revisionist nationalisms of the Serbs, Kurds, Tamils, Irish, and Québécois – are nationalists in this sense, and extreme ones at that.

* Many thanks to Dagfinn Føllesdal for the kind invitation to join him at the Centre for Advanced Study in Oslo, where this essay was written, to the MIT Philosophy Department, where it received a friendly yet severe road test, and to Marko Ahtisaari, Christian Barry, Hilary Bok, Stefan Gosepath, Brian Orend, Guido Pincione, and Ling Tong for further valuable comments and criticisms.

1 This focus will allow me to bypass the already much-discussed questions of what nations are, exactly, and how they differ from modern states.

The prevalence of conservative nationalism can be explained – psychologically, for instance, or historically. I will, however, treat it as a normative position, critically examining the belief that a state's citizens and politicians have such powerful prerogatives and special obligations with respect to the wealth and flourishing of their country and co-nationals. This examination may help moderate conservative nationalism by showing that it has been taken to unjustifiable extremes. Even a slight moderation of this sort could achieve a greater reduction in human misery and premature deaths than could be achieved by the harmonious dissolution of all revisionist nationalist struggles.

We can distinguish straightaway between particularistic and universalistic variants of nationalism. The former hold that nationalist commitments are valuable only when they are commitments to some specific nation (or to one of a specific set of nations). On account of the chauvinist, often racist, distinctions such views invoke, they are not worth serious moral discussion. I will concentrate on universalistic variants of nationalism, which assert that all nations can be valuable communities and can, by realizing this potential, generate the same obligations and prerogatives for their members, when they are similarly placed in the relevant conditions. What more particular prerogatives and obligations emerge may depend to some extent on the unique history, culture, and/or traditional habitat of this or that nation. But we can leave such complications aside by concentrating on two substantive claims – loosely associated with popular talk of 'patriotism' and 'priority for compatriots' – which are at the heart of universalistic nationalism:

Common Nationalism: Governments and citizens may (and perhaps should) show more concern for the survival and flourishing of their own state, culture, and compatriots than for the survival and flourishing of foreign states, cultures, and persons.

Lofty Nationalism: Governments and citizens may (and perhaps should) show more concern for the justice of their own state and for injustice (and other wrongs) suffered by its members than for the justice of any foreign social systems and for injustice (and other wrongs) suffered by foreigners.

In discussing these claims, I will not attend to the desirability of there being states at all, but will treat the existence of states, in roughly their present form, as a given. The discussion will, however, address the character of states, which is affected by the scope and strength of its members' obligations *vis-à-vis* compatriots and of their prerogatives *vis-à-vis* foreigners.

Some such nationalist priorities are evidently permissible, even desirable; so I accept the two claims to be true as stated. Analogous claims would hold with respect to groups of many other kinds, such as families, religious communities, firms, clubs, and associations.[2] It is also evident that the asserted nationalist priorities cannot plausibly be affirmed as absolute: It cannot be appropriate, for instance, in each and every context to put a compatriot's interest, however minor, ahead of foreigners' interests, however vital. This suggests that the interesting question here concerns the weight of the asserted nationalist priorities, and this question has indeed been much discussed lately. Much has been written, in particular, about the relevant similarities and dissimilarities between nationalist commitments and commitments to clubs, neighbourhoods, families, and racial or ethnic groups, and about what bearing these similarities and dissimilarities should have on the weight of nationalist priorities. I will here focus not on the weight, but on the *scope* of the nationalist priorities, arguing that there are firm limits to their application and hence contexts in which they do not hold at all. I believe that these limits are quite general by constraining the priority agents may give to any group or collective enterprise. I will therefore skip all the usual points about how nations and states are much more abstract and contingent than families and thus cannot possibly have the same constitutive significance in human lives and human history. Instead, I will argue that, even if nations had the same

---

2 Priority for one's race and its members has fallen out of favour after having been taken to extremes in colonialism, slavery, and the Third Reich. But it is also beginning to gain new respectability: A great deal of prestige has lately come to be attached to commitments to one's 'ethnicity,' which is more complex than race by involving a certain commonality of culture over and above commonality of descent. And giving priority on the basis of shared purely biological features (such as race and gender) has also become acceptable, provided the group in question is an underprivileged minority within the relevant society. (There are subtle variations in emphasis: Some say that blacks should help *blacks*, others that *blacks* should help blacks.)

constitutive significance, the nationalist priorities would still be limited in scope – in a manner analogous to family priorities.

I Common Nationalism – Priority for the Interests of Compatriots

Can there be any plausible limitations on the scope of the priority that citizens and governments may give to their nation and people or, more generally, on the scope of the priority that agents may give to their near and dear? Reflection on a piece of ordinary moral thinking may suggest the beginnings of an affirmative answer. It is within the family that concentration of concern is most clearly desirable and appropriate, and friends of a nationalist concentration of concern often invoke the family as an analogue or metaphor. But acceptable concern for even very close relatives is in fact thought to be quite strictly circumscribed in public life. For example, it is not merely illegal, but also deemed highly immoral for a state official to favour her son's firm in the application of regulations or in the awarding of government contracts. Why should this be so? To be sure, the woman, as a citizen and employee, owes loyalty to the state. But she also owes loyalty to her own family. Why, then, should she not balance the two loyalties and help her son in cases where this benefits him at no great cost to the state? And why should we not make a comparative assessment of these benefits and costs and then approve of such partiality and nepotism whenever the beneficiary's gains are sufficiently large relative to the costs?

It is tempting to answer that we understand the role of a state official as providing what Raz has called strong and exclusionary reasons, i.e., strong first-order reasons (in one's official capacity) to act conscientiously in the best interest of the state combined with second-order reasons to set aside other first-order reasons that would otherwise be relevant to one's conduct decisions.[3] This is surely true. But it is of no help in our inquiry, because it merely re-describes the phenomenon under examination. The question remains: Why should we understand the role of a state official as providing exclusionary reasons?

---

3 Joseph Raz, *Practical Reason and Norms* (Princeton, NJ: Princeton University Press 1990), ch. 1.2.

One clue toward an answer may be provided by the popular metaphor of a 'level playing field.' Participants in a team sport passionately want their own team to win, and the best of them work extremely hard for this. However, players also want games to be fair, to be structured so that the better team will tend to win. This requires a level playing field (broadly conceived as including fair rules impartially administered). These may not be entirely separate desires. Players do not merely want to beat the other team – they want to *win by playing well*. Since they care nothing about other forms of 'winning,' they are not jubilant to learn that a game has been fixed for them in advance. To the contrary, they are disappointed, because fixing the game destroys their chance of winning properly.

To be sure, with lots of money at stake in the major leagues, this portrait of the noble team player is under pressure in two ways. There are the pressures of outright non-compliance: A few players, hoping for fame and advertising revenue, are prepared to do almost anything – on and off the field – to improve their team's score. They would not hesitate, for instance, to infect their opponents with diarrhoea or the common cold before a match, if only they could get away with it. And then there are the more subtle and more consequential pressures of compliance redefined: Many players, as well as their trainers and fans, now take a strategic attitude toward the rules of the game. They think it all right, for example, to falsely claim a rule violation (so as to induce the referee to penalize their opponents), to conceal or to falsely deny a rule violation (so as to protect their own team from being penalized), and even to commit a violation intentionally (so as to save a dangerous situation or even to cause or aggravate an opponent's injury).[4] They view these stratagems as part of the game, understanding the rule that prohibits and provides a penalty for doing X as meaning, really, that players are given the option to do X while risking the penalty.[5] Since such options are

---

4 All these phenomena of compliance redefined are nicely illustrated, I believe, by modern soccer and basketball.

5 They may take this view with regret: "Too bad that this is what the sport has come to, but, seeing that others behave in this way, we can hardly afford to forego these options." I will say more about this defence by appeal to a 'sucker exemption' at the end of this section.

open to both sides, compliance redefined is compatible with the idea of a level playing field, albeit a lower one. While my portrait of the noble team player may not then be typical of much that goes on in sports today, it nevertheless has, I believe, the kind of reality that matters here: It really is our widely held ideal by reference to which we still judge our athletes. And drawing on it is therefore appropriate to elucidate the political use of the 'level playing field' metaphor.

The metaphor suggests that an analogous ideal is operating in public life. In our example, the state official plays a role analogous to that of a referee. She, as well as her son, should ideally be animated by the thought that, if she were to bend the rules in his favour, the game would be spoiled, rendering his 'success' meaningless or even shameful. This ideal has wide application, because we all frequently play the role of referee when we act as citizens, voters, jurors, and the like. An example can show that, even in these much less official contexts, the ideal has considerable force. By supporting political candidates or even merely through public utterances, many citizens take a stand on whether and how affirmative action should be continued. The ideal requires that they should not base their stance on how affirmative action would affect their own children in particular. And citizens would indeed be widely condemned, by supporters and opponents of affirmative action alike, if they were known to reason along these lines: 'We love our children and, if they were girls or black, we would, of course, support affirmative action very strongly. Our children are, however, white boys, whom affirmative action hurts twice over: by reducing their competitive advantage and by increasing the cost of government. We therefore strongly support its demolition.' The common condemnation of such reasoning manifests, I believe, a widespread commitment to the analogue of the noble team player ideal: It is widely thought that the sons in both examples should desire and strive to *do well in a fair and open competition with others.* And their parents should realize that, even if through partiality they could slant the social order in their children's favour, they would spoil the 'game' and thereby deprive their children of any chance for true success.[6]

---

6 Note that it is not the parents' opposition to affirmative action that makes their reasoning offensive. Citizens may reasonably believe that a level playing field

But wait. Do people really dismiss a good education and income as meaningless so long as some cannot compete for them on fair terms? Clearly, the ideal of a level playing field in public life is under even greater pressure than its athletic analogue. While it is quite conceivable that a player may have no desire at all to see her team 'win' even while she passionately wants it to win properly, it is much harder to conceive of our fictional sons (and their parents) taking no interest in their financial success as such. An extra buck, unlike an extra 'win,' always is, *pro tanto*, a good thing.

There are more contingent cultural pressures as well. It is widely considered acceptable, in the U.S. at least, for companies and individuals to use campaign contributions to influence legislators – for example, to affect their stance on pending legislation or to induce them to intercede with executive officials. But if the rules may be tailored in this way through money, then why not through an old friendship or, indeed, kinship? It is also widely considered acceptable for legislators from underprivileged minorities to vigorously promote the collective interests of 'their people.' And if prioritizing the interests of Hispanics is all right for Hispanic legislators, then why should it not be all right for Hispanic citizens to do the same? And if trying to affect the rules in favour of one's ethnic group is all right for Hispanics, then why not for Caucasians as well? It is not only a general de-moralization of the culture that gnaws away at the level playing field ideal, but also the Anglo-American persuasion that an adversarial clash of conflicting partialities is conducive to substantive fairness. This sentiment makes it possible for partiality – paradigmatically illustrated by prosecutors and defence attorneys doing their utmost to win their cases – to appear

---

does not require, or even rules out, affirmative action. What is offensive is that their political stance is based not on what they conscientiously believe to be right and fair to all, but on what they think will benefit their own children (as brought out by their thought that they would strongly support affirmative action if their own children stood to gain therefrom). The example illustrates then a disposition to slant the social order by tailoring its basic rules. The mother of the previous example, by contrast, slanted the social order by corrupting the administration of its rules. In public life as in sports, a level playing field requires both: that the rules be fair and that they be impartially administered.

as a sacred mission and duty that is required for the sake of the very impartiality that it also persistently assaults through compliance redefined. But even here definite limits are recognized: Lawyers who try to succeed by bribing the judge or by stealing their opponents' evidence are roundly condemned for their excessive dedication.

It is hard in public life, certainly much harder than in sports, for ordinary moral thinking to draw the line between acceptable conduct that seeks success in the game and dubious conduct that seeks to slant the playing field – and hard, also, to distinguish acceptable conduct that seeks to make the playing field more level in favour of one's group from dubious conduct that seeks to slant the playing field in favour of one's group in ways that also happen to make it more level. It is also hard to maintain allegiance to the apparently hopelessly unrealistic ideal that officials and citizens in public life should bracket all their particular interests. In light of these facts, it is not surprising that persons differ in how, and how far, they specify the ideal of a level playing field which rules out certain kinds of partiality altogether. There is still greater international variation, as even the national cultures of developed Western states differ widely in how much explicit and tacit public tolerance they display for various forms of corruption and nepotism. It is surprising, however, that within and increasingly also beyond these countries there is widespread support for the general idea that fairness requires of persons, and especially of officials, that they set aside any loyalty to their near and dear, including even their very closest family members, in certain contexts.[7] Though there is considerable diversity of opinion on *how* partiality is limited in scope, there is firm and widespread agreement that it *is* so limited when the basic justice of the larger playing field is at stake.

It may be possible to deepen this agreement by stating outer bounds, or minimum conditions that any institutional order must meet for it to be considered minimally fair. The widely acclaimed *Universal Declaration of Human Rights* presents itself as fulfilling precisely this function.

---

7 This general idea has truly become global, as abuse of political authority and power to benefit one's friends and family has begun to provoke great moral outrage and resentment in numerous developing countries of Asia, Latin America, and (to a lesser extent) Africa.

Its Article 28 reads: "Everyone is entitled to a social and international order in which the rights and freedoms set forth in this Declaration can be fully realized." In the case of national regimes ('social order'), the logical addressees of this entitlement are the officials and citizens of the society in question. They face outer bounds on what they may do or tolerate by way of efforts to slant the playing field in favour of special interests: Their society must be structured so as to afford all members secure access to the objects of their human rights.[8] In most societies, more will be expected, of course, from citizens and especially from officials. My point is surely not that all partiality not endangering human rights is all right and should be tolerated – rather, it is the converse: Partiality by officials and citizens is morally wrong and must not be tolerated when it seeks to shape a society's ground rules or their administration so as to endanger the secure access by some compatriots to the objects of their human rights.

This minimal constraint on the scope of acceptable partiality, which, I have argued, would find wide international acceptance even in reference to close family ties, should also limit the scope of nationalist partiality, which differs from family partiality by being rooted more in collective self-interest and less in meaningful personal ties. Of course, this limit on the scope of common nationalism is not widely accepted today. But its rejection smacks of inconsistency. How can we despise those who seek to slant the national playing field in favour of their relatives and yet applaud those who seek to slant the international playing field in favour of their compatriots? How can we ask our officials to put their own family's finances out of their minds when deliberating about the domestic economic order (e.g., the tax code) and yet expect

---

8 I assume here that it makes sense to judge how fully human rights *can* be realized in some institutional scheme by how fully they generally are (or, if the scheme is hypothetical, would be) actually realized in it. A full explication, in the spirit of Article 28, of the concept of human rights is presented in my 'How Should Human Rights be Conceived?,' in *Jahrbuch für Recht und Ethik* 3 (1995) 103-120. By following the *Universal Declaration*'s understanding of human rights as outer bounds on institutional schemes, one is not committed to its substantive conception (put forth in Articles 1-27) of what these outer bounds are.

those same officials to have their own nation's finances uppermost in their minds when deliberating about global economic institutions?

It was the basic principle of Part XI of the 1982 *United Nations Convention on the Law of the Sea* that natural resources on the ocean floors beneath international waters "are the common heritage of mankind" (Article 136), to be used "for the benefit of mankind as a whole ... taking into particular consideration the interests and needs of developing States [through an] equitable sharing of financial and economic benefits" (Article 140), which was to have been effected by sharing of seabed mining technologies and profits (Annex III, Articles 5 and 13) under the auspices of the International Seabed Authority, or ISA (Annexes III and IV). Three successive U.S. administrations have tried quite hard to secure the great benefits of the treaty in "protecting and promoting the wide range of U.S. ocean interests"[9] without the sharing regime. Shortly before the Convention was to come into force (on November 28, 1996), the Clinton Administration succeeded in having the sharing provisions replaced by a superseding *Agreement*.[10] This *Agreement* endorses the U.S. view that the common-heritage principle means that the oceans and their resources "are open to use by all in accordance with commonly accepted rules."[11] Accordingly, it frees mining companies from

---

9 Ambassador David A. Colson, Deputy Assistant Secretary of State for Oceans, in testimony before the Subcommittee on Oceanography of the Merchant Marine and Fisheries Committee of the U.S. House of Representatives (April 26, 1994)

10 *Agreement Relating to the Implementation of Part XI of the United Nations Convention on the Law of the Sea of 10 December 1982.* Its Article 2(1) says: "In the event of an inconsistency between this agreement and Part XI, the provisions of this agreement shall prevail."

11 U.S. Department of State, *Commentary on the Law of the Sea Convention including the 1994 Amendments,* 3. "The Agreement fully meets the objections of the United States and other industrialized states to Part XI" (*ibid.,* 2), which were that: "it established a structure for administering the seabed mining regime that does not accord the industrialized States influence in the regime commensurate with their interests; it incorporated economic principles inconsistent with free market philosophy; and its specific provisions created numerous problems from an economic and commercial policy perspective that would have impeded access by the United States and other industrialized countries to the resources of the deep seabed beyond national jurisdiction" (*ibid.,* 2-3).

having to share seabed mining technologies[12] and greatly reduces the sharing of profits.[13] The *Agreement* further accommodates U.S. demands by "1) guaranteeing a U.S. seat in the Council [the executive organ of the ISA]; 2) allowing ourselves and a few other industrialized nations acting in concert to block decisions in the Council...."[14]

In managing to renegotiate the *Law of the Sea Convention* – by pressing the Reagan-era threat of founding a competing seabed resources regime with a few like-minded countries[15] – the Clinton administration won a great victory for the U.S. and any other countries that will have the capital and technologies for profitable seabed mining.[16] The reaction in these wealthy countries was quiet relief. Their governments raised no objections, and their media largely ignored the event. The governments of the poorer countries went along as well in the interest of making the treaty universal. It is the global poor, in any case, who will bear the real loss from this further slanting of the playing field. They are the ones who can least afford being shut out from this common heritage of humankind. For the sake of what for us are distant

---

12 "The provisions of Annex III, article 5, of the Convention shall not apply," Section 5(2) of the Annex to the *Agreement* (cited in note 10).

13 Section 7(1) of the Annex to the *Agreement* (cited in note 10) limits the sharing of profits to "economic assistance" to "developing countries which suffer serious adverse effects on their export earnings or economies resulting from a reduction in the price of an affected mineral or in the volume of exports of that mineral, to the extent that such reduction is caused by [seabed mining]." Section 8(3) halves the application fee for exploration and exploitation of sites to US$250,000 and Section 8(2) eliminates the US$1,000,000 annual production fee as well as the profit-related financial contributions (all of which were mandated in the *Convention*'s Annex III, Article 13).

14 Colson, testimony before Subcommittee on Oceanography (see note 9)

15 Germany and Great Britain were especially willing to go along with such a move. For Canada's position and strategy, see Elizabeth Riddell-Dixon, *Canada and the International Seabed* (Kingston, ON: McGill-Queen's University Press 1989).

16 We can easily imagine Clinton saying, in analogy to our fictional parents, that he would of course have strongly favoured the sharing of technologies and economic benefits, if he had been the president of one of the poorer states. Few would have found such a remark morally offensive.

and trivial advantages,[17] Clinton has taken us a great step away from an "international order in which the rights and freedoms set forth in this [Universal Declaration of Human Rights] can be fully realised."[18] His decision, and our acquiescence in it, stand as a paradigm violation of the outer bounds of permissible partiality.[19]

Did Clinton merely do what he had to do as the elected guardian of the U.S. national interest? One might think that, while nationalist priority should be limited for individuals, governments – whose very point it is to safeguard the interests of their nation – ought to give unlimited priority to their own state and people. Though not unpopular, this view fares no better than the analogous view about lawyers whose very point it is, within an adversarial system, to safeguard the interests of their clients. A democratically constituted government can indeed plausibly be conceived as the agent of its people. But allowing such agents to give unlimited priority to the interests of their clients runs into a fatal trilemma. For such clients

- either must then be permitted to give the same unlimited priority to their own interests even when acting in their own behalf (without an agent),

---

17 At current metals prices, seabed mining is not expected to become commercially viable for another twenty years or so.

18 For an explication and defence of the view that Article 28 requires our *global* institutional order, as well, to satisfy the outer bounds imposed by basic human rights, see my 'Menschenrechte als moralische Ansprüche an globale Institutionen,' in Stefan Gosepath and Georg Lohmann, eds., *Die Philosophie der Menschenrechte* (Frankfurt: Suhrkamp 1998). That essay also seeks to illustrate how the global level of human-rights fulfilment is causally dependent on the structure of international institutions.

19 You may respond that any funds Part XI of the *Convention* might have raised for the least developed countries would have ended up in the pockets of corrupt Third-World politicians and bureaucrats. This is indeed where much 'development aid' ends up – because our politicians and bureaucrats need favours from them, not from the poor. But, surely, the choice of throwing money at corrupt Third-World elites versus ignoring global poverty does not exhaust the available options. Clinton might well have pressed for terms that ensure that the funds raised are spent on effective poverty eradication.

- or must then be prohibited from appointing an agent (here: government) to represent their (collective) interest,
- for otherwise they would be able to circumvent moral constraints that the interests of others impose on their conduct by acting through an agent rather than directly.

All three of these possibilities are quite implausible. There are firm constraints on what persons and groups within a larger social system may do by way of tailoring its rules, or corrupting the application of these rules, in their own favour. They may appoint agents to safeguard their interests, but these agents will be bound by the same constraints. Clinton could not permissibly do for his constituents what they could not permissibly have done for themselves.[20] And if it is not the case, therefore, that democratically constituted governments, who are truly the agents of their people, may give unlimited priority to the interests of their state and its citizens, then, surely, undemocratic governments must not do so either.

A more informal way of confirming this result involves comparing Clinton's hypothesized defence with that of the parliamentary delegation of a middle-class party who says that it is merely doing what it has to do in the best interest of its constituents when it proposes that children from families paying no income taxes be barred from public benefits,[21] such as school lunches or government-guaranteed student

---

20 For a much more detailed elaboration of this argument, see my 'Loopholes in Moralities,' in *Journal of Philosophy* **89** (1992) 79-98. A similar argument is presented in Samuel Scheffler, *Families, Nations, and Strangers* (The Lindley Lecture, University of Kansas, 17 October 1994) as "the distributive objection to associative duties."

21 Note that this initiative is, in one sense, more plausible than Clinton's: One can argue that, since public benefits are generated at the expense of those who pay income taxes, they alone should be eligible for them. Clinton cannot make a parallel argument, because ocean floor resources are not generated at anyone's expense. Of course, such resources will be harvested at the expense of mining firms. But this merely shows that the poor can claim a fair share (not of the extracted resources, but) only of the resources *in situ*. The value of these undeveloped resources could easily be determined through auctions in which competing firms would bid for the right to mine particular resources in particular regions of the ocean floor.

475

loans: "It would be wrong for our constituents themselves to slant the playing field in their favour in this way. But we, as their chosen representatives, may and even must do just that. We must be single-mindedly devoted to advancing the interests of our constituents." This sort of reasoning would hardly find support. And those who reject it while accepting Clinton's defence must then implicitly rely on the moral significance of the distinction between nationalist and other forms of partiality. But why this distinction should be morally significant remains a mystery.[22]

One might think that the prevailing tolerance for common nationalism can be justified by reference to the idea that no one should ask us to subordinate our pursuit of our national interest to a concern for a minimally just international regime so long as other countries are not practising similar self-restraint. This thought invokes a 'sucker exemption': An agent is not morally required to comply with rules when doing so would lead to his being victimized ('made a sucker') by non-compliers. The morally relevant difference between nationalist partiality and, say, family partiality lies in the currently prevailing levels of non-compliance and compliance redefined: We must honour tight limits on the scope of family partiality insofar as most of our com-

---

22 Why this distinction is *thought to be* morally significant is less mysterious. Those who have the opportunity to reflect upon morality publicly, in the media or in academic discourse, are, by and large, well-to-do persons in the more affluent countries. In these countries, the domestic poor have at least some capacity to articulate their claims and some power to make their voices heard. The parliamentary delegation I have imagined would provoke considerable protest and social unrest. The global poor, who labour all day for a few dollars a month, are unable to cause us the slightest inconvenience and unable even to alert us to their plight. Thanks to our military superiority, they fall outside what Rawls has called the circumstances of justice, following Hume: "Were there a species of creatures intermingled with men, which ... were possessed of such inferior strength, both of body and mind, that they were incapable of all resistance, and could never ... make us feel the effects of their resentment; ... the restraints of justice and property ... would never have place in so unequal a confederacy." David Hume, *Enquiries Concerning Human Understanding and Concerning the Principles of Morals* (Oxford: Clarendon Press 1972), 190f. Both Hume and Rawls stress rough equality of powers in the context of seeking to explain, not to justify, the exclusion of the very weak. See John Rawls, *A Theory of Justice* (Cambridge, MA: Harvard University Press 1971), 127.

patriots practise similar self-restraint; but we may violate even the outer bounds on the scope of nationalist partiality because this is what other states are doing as well. If the facts of our situation were reversed, we would be free to violate even the outer bounds on the scope of family partiality while having to honour tight limits on the scope of our common nationalism.

Does such an appeal to a sucker exemption furnish a plausible defence? It is true, of course, that international relations have historically been brutal: The main players – the governments of militarily and/or economically powerful societies and lately also the larger multinational corporations – negotiate and renegotiate the rules of the game among themselves with each pressing vigorously for its own advantage, using war and the threat of war when this seems opportune and showing no concern for the interests or even survival of the weakest 'players.' The brutality of the international scene may indeed support the principle that societies and their governments may, in pursuit of their national interest, seek to achieve or uphold an unjust global regime (under which the human rights of many cannot be realized), if other societies and their governments would otherwise slant the global playing field against them. Invoking this principle, a rich society may decline to introduce unilateral reforms to protect the world's poorest populations (e.g., a national law requiring that its mining firms share with the global poor some of the value of the seabed resources they harvest) on the ground that doing so would put it at a competitive disadvantage against its peers. But if each such society so defended itself by pointing to the others, the reasonable response would surely be to ask them all to work out a multilateral reform that affects all of them equally and thus does not alter their competitive positions *vis-à-vis* one another. Each should propose some suitable reforms and should also conditionally promise to support their implementation if the others will do so as well.[23] Such

---

23 Some reforms designed to reduce the problems of undemocratic government, outsized national debts, and domestic poverty and inequality in the poorer countries are outlined in Pogge, 'Menschenrechte.' See also my 'A Global Resources Dividend,' in David A. Crocker and Toby Linden, eds., *Ethics of Consumption: The Good Life, Justice, and Global Stewardship* (Lanham, MD: Rowman & Littlefield 1998), 502–37.

initiatives would not only promote a more level global playing field, but would also build mutual trust and co-operation, ensuring that the sucker exemption would, in time, cease to apply.

Another appeal to the sucker exemption would claim that we may uphold the extreme inequalities of the present world order because, if the rich societies instituted a more level playing field, then many of the presently poor societies, who are inclined unjustly to slant the playing field in their favour and against ours, would over time become powerful enough to do so. This appeal also strikes me as implausible. There are indeed many authoritarian and aggressive regimes in the less developed countries. But this fact is in large measure a result of our highly unjust world order, and thus cannot serve as its justification: Relative poverty breeds corruptibility and corruption, which tend to degrade or destroy democratic institutions in the poorer societies. Absolute poverty and ignorance make it easy to manipulate people into nationalist resentment. There is every reason to believe that, as the rich countries begin to show genuine concern for global poverty and co-operate in its eradication, more benign and reasonable sentiments and regimes would develop in the poorer countries.

In the last five paragraphs, I have tried to respond to two ways of defending the refusal to impose the same outer bounds on the scope of nationalist partiality which we unhesitatingly impose upon the scope of other kinds of partiality. Perhaps these responses were too brief to be convincing. Or perhaps there are better defences of the asymmetry than the two I have tried to rebut. None of this should detract from the challenge I have laid down in this section: In conducting our foreign policy, and especially in shaping the global order regulating international politics and the world economy, we have taken partiality to extremes that we would find intolerable in any other context. Despite its grievous effects upon the global poor, this exceptional tolerance for *nationalist* partiality is widely approved. But how can this exception be justified?

II Lofty Nationalism – The Justice-for-Compatriots Priority

Section I sought to show that we, the affluent in the developed countries, practise a morally untenable nationalism by coercively upholding a badly slanted global order in which the human rights of millions of foreigners are unfulfilled. To this line of argument, I frequently hear the response that we should forgo grand theorizing about global justice until we have achieved justice at home. So long as we face significant injustice in our own society, we should defer consideration of injustice elsewhere. This response relies upon the second nationalist priority claim. Though rarely articulated, let alone explicitly defended, this claim seems to express a prejudice that is widely held, as can be gauged from the fact that participants in academic (and popular) discourse on justice overwhelmingly focus on assessing the ground rules of their own national society, while the assessment of our global order is largely ignored.[24]

Such lofty nationalism may well be important in explaining why the widespread common nationalism, which Section I has criticized as excessive, is so rarely challenged: Our moralists implicitly assume that, even if massive and severe misery were produced by a heavily slanted global order that we help shape and uphold, such misery would manifest a wrong suffered by foreigners and hence would be of less urgency for us than wrongs suffered by compatriots. If this diagnosis is correct, then the objective of Section I – showing how common nationalism is limited in scope – cannot be fully realized without the objective of the present section: showing the limits of lofty nationalism.

My discussion of lofty nationalism will resemble the discussion of common nationalism. I will, once again, leave aside questions of weight and thus will not ask how much greater wrongs suffered by foreigners must be than wrongs suffered by compatriots in order for their eradication (at equal cost) to be equally urgent for us. I will instead focus on the issue of scope, trying to show that there are contexts in which the asserted priority does not hold at all.

Let us again begin by reflecting on a piece of ordinary moral thinking. This is the widespread view that any moral duty not to wrong

---

24 This huge discrepancy exists in the domain of general theory as well as in that of more concrete (or 'applied') work. Compare the amount of theorizing about domestic justice with that about international justice – or the moral scrutiny lavished on national affirmative-action legislation with that expended on the far more consequential ground rules structuring the world economy.

another person, or not to harm him unduly, is much weightier than any corresponding duty (holding fixed what is at stake for all parties) to protect him against wrongs from other sources. Thus killing an innocent person for the sake of some gain (which may consist in avoiding some cost) is generally thought to be morally far worse than failing, for the sake of a like gain, to save him from being killed by others. In many cases, no corresponding duty is recognized at all: One ought to be willing to bear some cost to avoid causing noisy interruptions of another's sleep; but one has no corresponding duty to bear any cost for the sake of preventing such interruptions caused by others.

The importance in ordinary moral thinking of this distinction – which is a narrower variant of a distinction often expressed in terms of negative and positive duties – suggests that our initial formulation of lofty nationalism requires some refinement. When wrongs (including injustice) are produced by oneself, then showing concern for such wrongs means ceasing to harm others unduly (and perhaps also trying to mitigate undue harms one can no longer prevent). When wrongs are produced by third parties, then showing concern for such wrongs means trying to benefit others by stopping these wrongs (or perhaps also by mitigating their effects).

Once we rethink lofty nationalism to take account of this distinction, we find that the permissibility of giving priority to the near and dear is quite questionable in regard to the first type of concern. This is so even with family ties. Few would mind that, if I come upon a group of children who have been hit by a speeding driver, I attend to my own child first and foremost, even if I could do somewhat more toward reducing the harm another child will have suffered. But this judgment changes if we alter the case so that I am the reckless driver. In this case, it would seem wrong to give such priority to my own child. The priority for compatriots fails even more clearly in analogous cases, when, for example, I have made conflicting commitments to a compatriot and to a foreigner. Perhaps it is all right, when other things are equal, to let the special bond break the tie. But if the foreigner stands to lose more from my breach of commitment, should I not favour her? Or consider a case where your plane's engine fails over the U.S.-Canadian border and you must choose between crashing into a suburban area on the U.S. side, where you will endanger foreigners, or into a somewhat less thickly populated Canadian suburb, where you will endanger (fewer) compatriots. Again, it would seem that you should minimize the harm you will cause others, irrespective of their nationality. And if you act in these ways, your conduct is not viewed as disloyal to your country and does not therefore detract from national fellow-feeling and shared solidarity.

Consider also comparative moral judgments. Without any provocation, Smith has severely beaten a stranger. Is his conduct morally worse if she is a compatriot rather than a foreigner?[25] Or is it morally worse to defraud a poor family in one's own country than an equally poor family in France or India? The much celebrated priority for compatriots does not seem to have force in these cases.

The same point can be made about the conduct of governments. It is no better, morally, for a government to jail without charge, or to expropriate the property of, a foreign visitor than one of its citizens. In fact, there are various harms which it is worse for a government to impose upon foreigners than upon compatriots. Goodin lists seven cases of this sort, which are recognized in international law. In discussing these cases, Goodin invokes a distinction between negative and positive duties, stating that "special relationships have this curious tendency to strengthen positive duties while weakening negative ones."[26] I do not quite share the diagnosis of an inverse priority, which this sentence suggests for negative duties. In my view, negative duties are not, and are not thought to be, weakened by special relationships as such. Rather, some of them can be partly waived through *consent* under conditions of *fair reciprocity*: Relevant harms (such as expropriation or con-

---

25 I concede that his conduct usually *is* morally worse if the victim is his mother. But this may be not because one ought to be more concerned to avoid harming family members than to avoid harming strangers, but because the harm is so much greater: The son is not merely inflicting physical pain without provocation; he is also showing ingratitude toward the person who raised him, deeply hurting her love and trust, and so on. Sam Scheffler holds, by contrast, that, according to ordinary morality, negative duties to strangers are more easily overridden by positive duties or by considerations of cost to the agent than negative duties to associates and family members are. See Scheffler, *Families, Nations, and Strangers*, 5-6.

26 Robert E. Goodin, 'What Is So Special about Our Fellow Countrymen?,' in *Ethics* **98** (1988) 663-86. The list is at 668-9, the quote is from 673.

scription) must be allocated pursuant to a procedure that is consented to by those subject to it and this allocation must be fair so that (at least) participation in the scheme is not irrational *ex ante*.[27] The citizens of a society may then democratically authorize their government to expropriate or conscript under specified conditions. Yet, through such an authorization they may, clearly, render only *themselves*, not foreigners, liable to be harmed in these ways. This is how a government may come to practise a kind of anti-nationalist priority that works against compatriots. The moral situation is thus not quite the one Goodin's sentence may suggest: It is not the case that special relationships imply weakened negative duties, as can be illustrated by a special relationship that fails to satisfy the two provisos. The implication goes only the other way: Weakened negative duties imply a special relationship – for example, the special relationship of reciprocity and joint consent which obtains when the two provisos are satisfied. The contrapositive of this second condition is: Absence of a special relationship implies that negative duties fully apply. This crucial point, which Goodin rightly stresses, can explain why no society may render innocent foreigners liable to conscription or expropriation and why no government may conscript or expropriate them: Foreigners do not stand to gain from such a scheme (reciprocity). Nor have they consented to it – we would have a strange notion indeed of moral duties if we held that those bound by them can weaken or eliminate these duties unilaterally.

This discussion shows that the thesis of lofty nationalism is plausible only in regard to concern for third-party wrongdoing. It is certainly permissible, and perhaps also morally desirable, for such concern to be strongest for the near and dear and to fade outward through a series of concentric circles. But the strength of an agent's moral reason not to harm another unduly does not vary with the potential victim's relational closeness to the agent, and, in particular, does not vary with the potential victim's status as a compatriot or foreigner. Combining

---

27 My formulation of the two provisos is intentionally vague as there is of course no agreement on how they should be specified exactly. Nevertheless, the fact remains that a weakening of negative duties through a special relationship such as compatriotism would be found acceptable in modern Western moral thinking only if it satisfied two substantial provisos of the general form I have sketched.

these findings with our starting point – the deeply entrenched view that any moral duty not to wrong another person, or not to harm him unduly, is much weightier than any corresponding duty to protect him against like wrongs from other sources – we can conclude that (holding fixed what is at stake for all parties) ordinary moral thinking is committed to a hierarchy of moral reasons which has the following form:

(1) Reasons not to wrong (unduly harm) others;
(2a) Reasons to protect one's next of kin from wrongdoing by third parties,
⋮
(2n) Reasons to protect one's compatriots from wrongdoing by third parties,
⋮
(2z) Reasons to protect unrelated foreigners from wrongdoing by third parties.[28]

Acceptable lofty nationalism, as well, is sharply limited in scope. It can distance us from wrongs foreigners suffer only insofar as these wrongs are not our own doing. We consider it wrong to inflict undue harms on foreigners even for the sake of securing somewhat greater benefits for compatriots, just as we consider it wrong to inflict undue harms on strangers even for the sake of securing somewhat greater benefits for family members. And because we understand the unwillingness to inflict such harms to be morally required, this unwillingness is not viewed as showing any disloyalty to our country or family and therefore does not undermine our shared feelings of allegiance and community.

---

28 I hope I have made clear enough that this is not presented as a strict, or lexical, hierarchy. It is generally acknowledged that a higher moral reason can be outweighed by a lower, if more is at stake in the latter. Public reaction to the continuing massacres of the twentieth century shows, however, that the 'exchange rates' are extreme: Sexual harassment in a domestic auto plant engenders a much more powerful response than a genocidal massacre in Africa. Obviously, this hierarchy does not cover the entire domain of moral reason. It leaves out moral reasons to protect persons from harms that do not involve wrongdoing (e.g., natural harms) as well as moral reasons to benefit others. I would think that these are on a par with moral reasons to protect others from third-party wrongs ((2a)-(2z)), but am content to leave this question open here.

Many think about the wrongs (including injustice) that foreigners suffer in our world in terms of positive responsibility and thus put them at the very bottom of their list: "The extreme deprivation of so many children abroad surely manifests an injustice to some extent, and one I could help alleviate. But injustice and other wrongs are rife in my own country and community as well, and I should give priority to combating these, even if those abroad are considerably greater."[29] This may be quite the right way to think when foreigners are suffering home-grown wrongs and even when they are severely disadvantaged in their dealings with us through no fault of ours. But it may not be the right attitude when they are being harmed through a badly slanted global order in whose continuous shaping and coercive imposition we are heavily involved. Such harms may invoke not merely our vague ('positive') responsibility to protect others from third-party wrong-doing, but also our sharper and much weightier ('negative') duty not to harm others unduly, either single-handedly or in collaboration with others. This would be the case, if the moral relation between those who shape and enforce an international order and those who suffer grave injustice through its imposition is one of undue harm and thus not materially affected by whether the former and the latter are of different nationality.

Whether or not we see ourselves as co-responsible for injustice suffered by the global poor makes a momentous moral difference. If we do not, we may place this injustice at the bottom of our list (2z). If we do, we will place some of it at the very top (1). The amount of harm that might be affected by such an upgrade is large, as oppression and poverty abound in this world. Some 20 million deaths per year – mostly female and mostly children[30] – are attributed to global poverty: "Nearly

---

29 Many consider it perfectly all right for donors to favour even relatively trivial or well-supplied domestic causes – one's alma mater, the local park or museum, one's congregation – over relatively cheap life-saving efforts in the Third World: It is good to 'give back' to one's community, and fine to favour the causes one personally cares about.

30 Some 3 million children annually die of simple diarrhoea because their parents cannot obtain a 15-cent oral rehydration pack. Lack of vitamins and antibiotics lead to another 3.5 million deaths from pneumonia, one million deaths from

800 million people do not get enough food, and about 500 million people are chronically malnourished" and about 1.3 billion people – 24 percent of world population – live below the poverty line,[31] which is defined as "that income or expenditure level below which a minimum, nutritionally adequate diet plus essential non-food requirements are not affordable"[32] and currently corresponds to *per capita* purchasing power of US$1 per day.[33]

Given the importance of the issue, it is rather strange that it is so rarely addressed. That global poverty is for us, First-World citizens, a matter of positive responsibility is generally taken for granted on all sides – even by those who have most forcefully presented it as a moral task.[34] My main concern here, once again, is to challenge those who

---

measles, and so on. See James P. Grant, *The State of the World's Children 1993* (New York: Oxford University Press 1993).

31 United Nations Development Program, *Human Development Report 1996* (New York: Oxford University Press 1996), 20.

32 United Nations Development Program, *Human Development Report 1996*, 222.

33 United Nations Development Program, *Human Development Report 1996*, 27. Since the purchasing power of money (converted at market exchange rates) is about five times greater in the poorest countries (from *ibid.* 171, 179, 185), this poverty line corresponds to an annual *per capita* income of roughly US$75 at market exchange rates. If 24 percent of the world's population have less than US$75 annually, we may assume that those in the poorest quintile (20 percent) have on average about US$50 annually. (Mr. Selim Jahan, Deputy Director of the UNDP Human Development Report Office [New York City] has confirmed orally that the $1-per-day figure represents purchasing power, not income. This squares with figures in Partha Dasgupta, *An Inquiry into Well-Being and Destitution* [Oxford: Oxford University Press 1993], 79f.)

34 They have argued that we should focus our beneficence on the global poor because the moral significance of a harm's position in the (1)-(2z) hierarchy is less than ordinary moral thinking supposes and/or because the position of the global poor at the bottom of the list is overcome by the much lower cost/benefit ratio involved in helping them: For the price of enabling one poor local youngster to attend summer camp, we can save many foreign children's lives by giving the money to UNICEF for oral rehydration therapy. Representative examples of such lines of argument are Peter Singer, 'Famine, Affluence and Morality,' in *Philosophy and Public Affairs* 1 (1972) 229-43; James Rachels, 'Killing and

hold this consensus belief to reflect upon it. But I will also try, in what follows, to show how problematic this belief is.

One author who has articulated the consensus view is John Rawls. Agreeing that "it seems plausible to hold that, when the distinction is clear, negative duties have more weight than positive ones,"[35] he explicitly classifies our natural duty of justice as positive.[36] This duty, he specifies, "requires us to support and to comply with just institutions that exist and apply to us [and] to further just arrangements not yet established."[37] As an alternative to this position, let us examine the views that

> (1) in some cases at least, just institutions that apply to oneself generate negative duties of compliance;
> (2) in some cases at least, one has a negative duty to promote the reform of an unjust regime in which one is a significant participant (while one's responsibility to promote the justice of social institutions in which one is not a participant is indeed positive).

Starving to Death,' in *Philosophy* **54** (1979) 159-71; Shelly Kagan, *The Limits of Morality* (Oxford: Oxford University Press 1989); and Peter Unger, *Living High and Letting Die: Our Illusion of Innocence* (Oxford: Oxford University Press 1996). Two notable exceptions are Onora Nell [O'Neill], 'Lifeboat Earth,' in *Philosophy and Public Affairs* **4** (1975) 273-92, and Thomas Nagel, 'Poverty and Food: Why Charity Is Not Enough,' in Peter Brown and Henry Shue, eds., *Food Policy: The Responsibility of the United States in the Life and Death Choices* (New York: The Free Press 1977), 54-62. Both emphasize our active involvement in the production of poverty.

35 John Rawls, *A Theory of Justice*, 114.

36 John Rawls, *A Theory of Justice*, 109. Natural duties to mutual aid and to mutual respect are there called positive, and natural duties not to injure and not to harm the innocent are called negative. Rawls does not make clear how he understands the negative/positive distinction. This does not matter, because I am concerned only with what he implies: that our natural duty of justice has the lesser weight of a positive duty.

37 John Rawls, *A Theory of Justice*, 115; a parallel passage is on 334. See also 246: "as far as circumstances permit, we have a natural duty to remove any injustices, beginning with the most grievous as identified by the extent of the deviation from perfect justice."

Since (2) is what matters most, I will defend (1) only in outline, merely to show that Rawls's position is problematic across the board. Suppose we are born into a world in which a just institutional order is already in place. And suppose that we owe one another a merely positive moral duty to comply with this regime: Non-compliance as such does not count as harming others unduly, though it is good to comply just as it is good to help others. When positive reasons to comply or to help conflict, it would then seem to be permissible, if not praiseworthy, to choose the course of conduct that, all things considered, is better for others – for example, to cheat on one's taxes in order to help someone in need whenever the gain to the recipient(s) outweighs the loss (if any) to one's fellow-citizens.[38] This is surely not the prevailing view. More importantly, this view also undermines a major desideratum within Rawls's theory: Just institutions cannot be stable, that is, cannot maintain themselves on the basis of the moral motives of their participants, if these participants see their duty to support and to comply with the institutions of their society as on a par with beneficence or charity.[39]

The foregoing can show at most that our moral duty to comply with just institutions is believed, like negative duties, to have more weight than the standard positive duties[40] and that this belief is necessary for the possibility of a just social order based on moral motives. But is the

---

38 This loss may come from there being slightly less money available for administering our institutional order and from there being a slightly greater risk of damage to mutual trust from discovered non-compliance. I am assuming, quite in the spirit of Rawls, that the duty of justice is an interpersonal responsibility, a duty owed solely to other persons.

39 Rawls has extensively discussed the problem of stability and tried to solve it by envisioning the citizens of his well-ordered society as having a sense of justice that is effective and normally overriding. See, for example, John Rawls, *Political Liberalism* (New York: Columbia University Press 1993), 141f. The puzzle is how citizens' strong moral desire to comply can derive from their allegiance to a moral conception that recognizes only a weak moral reason to do so.

40 In both cases, it is widely acknowledged that a positive duty can still win out when very much more is at stake. One may usually break a promise, violate a just property regime, or injure an innocent when doing so is necessary to save a human life, for example.

belief plausible? How can we show a person who does not wish to consent to the just order we are maintaining that her non-compliance would unduly harm others?

Kant's justification of perfect duties and of the imposition of coercive legal institutions[41] suggests a plausible line of response. His basic idea is that persons are entitled to equal freedom and should therefore constrain their own freedom so that the freedom of each is consistent with the freedom of everyone else. Acting beyond this limit, one invades the rightful freedom of others. One harms others unduly when the success of one's conduct implies that like conduct by others is constrained.

Since a consistent and equal distribution of freedom can be achieved in various ways, we need shared institutions to avoid invading one another's freedom. And we have a negative duty to comply with such existing institutions whenever non-compliance can succeed only if like non-compliance by others is constrained. Obtaining more resources than one is entitled to under an existing just property regime, or abusing an existing institution (e.g., by making deceitful promises), harms others unduly, because one's success depends on others being denied, or denying themselves, a like liberty.[42] This brief sketch of the Kantian

---

41 Kant bases such institutions on the enforceable imperative: "Act outwardly so that the free employment of your will [*Willkür*] can coexist with the freedom of everyone according to a universal law." Immanuel Kant, *Metaphysik der Sitten*, vol. VI (Berlin: Prussian Academy 1914), 231 (my translation).

42 This proposal does not justify a negative duty to comply with *all* existing just institutions. Success at exceeding the speed limit, or at breaching many social conventions and rules of etiquette, usually does not depend on others being constrained to comply. One may think that this line of argument also fails when a non-complying agent can claim to be in compliance with non-existing just institutions. He takes more freedom or resources than he is permitted to take under the existing just order, but does so in accordance with an equally just, albeit non-existing, regime whose rules everyone could be free to follow. Seeing that others could realize a just order by complying with the scheme he favours, why should he have a negative duty to comply with ours? I cannot answer this objection fully here. But the response must begin with the realization that it is generally not possible for each to take what she would be entitled to under the just order of her choice, irrespective of what order others are observing – whereas it is possible for each to take what she is entitled to under the one existing just order.

strategy shows in outline, I hope, how central cases of non-compliance with just institutions can plausibly be classified as violations of a negative duty. This would defeat the view that the first part of Rawls's natural duty of justice can unequivocally be classified as positive.[43]

It is easier to defend (2). When undue harms are mandated or authorized by a society's institutions (e.g., its laws) and when state officials inflict these harms or protect and aid those who do, then citizens who uphold these institutions through their political consent and economic support contribute to the harms. The horrendous harms inflicted by the Nazis, for example, were not possible without the economic contributions of many citizens (e.g., through the tax system), nor without the legitimacy that Nazi laws and officials derived from the consent many citizens expressed (e.g., by participating in legal and political institutions, and by attending rallies).[44] By lending such support, these citizens, too, violated their negative duty not to harm others unduly.[45] It does not follow that one must then stop contributing to the economy – though it may come to that in extreme cases. One can often continue

---

43 The Kantian strategy avoids the claim, suggested by Rawls, that a duty to comply with institutions can be derived from the mere fact that the institutions are just and (purport to) apply to us. This claim is convincingly criticized in A. John Simmons, *Moral Principles and Political Obligation* (Princeton, NJ: Princeton University Press 1979), 147-56. My sketch of how to justify a *negative* natural duty of justice fits with, and can be enriched by, the response to Simmons given in Jeremy Waldron, 'Special Ties and Natural Duties,' in *Philosophy and Public Affairs* 22 (1993) 1-30.

44 I use 'legitimacy' here in the sociological sense specified by Max Weber. It is of the essence of justice that a majority's consent cannot lend *moral* legitimacy to the mistreatment of a minority. The Nazi case exemplifies harms inflicted by state officials, but essentially the same conclusion holds when the state merely legally sanctions undue harms and protects and aids those who inflict them, as when slavery was legally authorized in the U.S. and slaveholder rights were enforced by state officials, who helped put down revolts and capture fugitive slaves.

45 This conclusion squares well with common convictions, for example, that one has a stronger reason to oppose rules that exclude blacks or women from a club when one is oneself a member of it, even if the very same persons are excluded from other clubs whose rules one could oppose just as effectively.

to contribute and yet avoid collaborating in the undue harming of others by taking compensating action: by making as much of an effort, aimed at protecting the victims of injustice or at institutional reform, as would suffice to eradicate the harms, if others followed suit.

This reflection suffices to establish the existential claim in (2). But does it carry over to the case of unjust *economic* institutions that are *global* in scope? Only if it does can the vast evil of global poverty engage our duty not to harm others unduly, and thus command a place at the top, rather than the bottom, of our priority list.

Here is a straightforward way of arguing that the conclusion carries over: "Insofar as our global poor are worse off than the poorest under some alternative (more egalitarian), feasible global economic order would be, the existing global economic order is unjust. By imposing this order upon them, we are therefore harming them unduly." This easy argument invites controversy on two points. First, it invokes a conception of justice that is highly controversial, especially when applied to the world at large. Presupposing that an economic order is just only if *no* alternative would engender less severe poverty, the easy argument assumes the full burden of defending a globalized version of Rawls's difference principle.[46] Second, since any social order will require a certain degree of coercion (imposition) in its creation and maintenance, the easy argument also assumes that we have a negative duty not to help create and not to collaborate (without making efforts toward reform) in the maintenance of any social order that is less than perfectly just. But this assumption is disputable in light of the fact that even rather imperfect social orders can render their participants better off than anyone would be in the absence of any

---

46 The difference principle requires that "social and economic inequalities ... are to be to the greatest benefit of the least advantaged members of society" (John Rawls, *Political Liberalism*, 6). A global difference principle is rejected by Rawls himself, though others have argued that his theory commits him to accepting it. See T.M. Scanlon, 'Rawls' Theory of Justice,' in Norman Daniels, ed., *Reading Rawls* (New York: Basic Books 1974), 202; Brian Barry, *The Liberal Theory of Justice* (Oxford: Clarendon Press 1972), 128-33; Charles Beitz, *Political Theory and International Relations* (Princeton, NJ: Princeton University Press 1979), 149-76; and my *Realizing Rawls* (Ithaca: Cornell University Press 1989), ch. 6.

social order.[47] How can one be *harming* others unduly by imposing upon them imperfect economic institutions that *raise* all participants' standard of living?[48]

The controversial assumptions of the easy argument are not beyond defence. But it seems more promising to modify the argument: to assert that *this* massive and severe global poverty we face today engages our duty not to harm others unduly without maintaining that *any* avoidable degree of global poverty would do so as well. We saw in section I that the *Universal Declaration of Human Rights* can be understood as exemplifying such a strategy. Its Article 28 can be read as asserting that it violates a fundamental right of persons – and thus counts as harming them unduly – to coercively impose upon them an institutional order under which they avoidably lack secure access to the objects of their human rights. We are now participating in the coercive imposition of an international order under which many avoidably lack such secure access. In particular, many persons are born into such abysmal poverty that their mental and physical development is impaired and they have no realistic prospect of securing even a minimally adequate share of the natural resources of this planet.[49] By asserting that only the coercive imposition of such severely unjust social institutions harms others unduly, one can leave open whether coercively imposing less dramatically unjust social institutions should count as harming others unduly as well.

Such a more modest argument is also better able to withstand the second objection to the easy argument: that we cannot be said to be

---

47 The assumption seems particularly dubious when the injustice in question appears to have the character of an omission. One may agree that a legal order in which inter-spousal violence is not prohibited nor effectively deterred is unjust and nevertheless deny that those who impose such a legal order are harming women unduly (rather than merely failing to protect them from their husbands' wrongdoing).

48 Compare: How can one be unduly *harming* an unconscious accident victim if one does less than would have been possible by way of *improving* her situation?

49 In violation of Article 25 of the *Universal Declaration*: "Everyone has the right to a standard of living adequate for the health and well-being of himself and of his family, including food, clothing, housing and medical care...."

harming others unduly so long as the social institutions we coercively impose upon them raise their standard of living above what it would be in the absence of any social order whatsoever. This objection suggests that – at least as far as the imposition of social institutions is concerned – undue harming be defined in terms of a state-of-nature baseline. I will therefore embed the objection in a Lockean account of economic justice. Locke assumed that, in a pre-institutional state of nature, each person has an equal moral claim on all natural resources. He specified this equal claim as the freedom to take possession of any unowned land, water, minerals, fruits, animals, etc., subject to the constraint, which has come to be known as the Lockean proviso, that one confine oneself to a proportional share. Each person's unilateral appropriations in a state of nature must leave "enough, and as good" for others.[50] Locke thought of this constraint not as a (positive) duty of kindness or beneficence, but as an enforceable (negative) duty that is strictly owed to others. And this makes sense, as those who take more will harm others by cutting into their fair shares. We can put this point in terms of the Kantian idea I invoked above to support a negative duty of compliance with just institutions. Taking while leaving enough and as good for others is compatible with their freedom to do the same and thus does not harm them unduly. But taking more than this can succeed only if others' freedom to do so as well is constrained. Quite apart from whether Locke or Kant would have appreciated it, this affinity is welcome, because it shows that, insofar as our duty of justice is a negative one, its two aspects – compliance with and promotion of just institutions – can be grounded in one fundamental moral principle.

---

50 John Locke, 'An Essay Concerning the True Original, Extent, and End of Civil Government' (1689), in Peter Laslett, ed., *John Locke: Two Treatises of Government* (Cambridge: Cambridge University Press 1960), §27 and §33. Subsequent parenthetical references are to this text. Locke imposes two further constraints on unilateral appropriations, which need not interest us here. One may take possession of any natural resource only by "mixing one's labour" with it (§27) and only insofar as nothing will spoil in one's possession (§31). We can also leave aside the question of how the freedom of unilateral appropriation, and the constraints upon this freedom, can be derived from Locke's fundamental 'Law of Nature' (§6).

There is a compelling reason against making the Lockean proviso sacrosanct. For it may be possible for human beings to create and uphold social institutions that *both* permit disproportional unilateral appropriation *and* render all participants economically better off than anyone would be in a state of nature. To accommodate this possibility, Locke argues for an exemption from the proviso. Human beings may create and enforce economic institutions that permit disproportional unilateral appropriation; but they may do so only if everyone can rationally consent to their introduction, that is, only if everyone will be better off under these institutions than anyone would be in a state of nature. One might call this constraint on institutions the second-order Lockean proviso, because it governs not changes in the property status of resources (through acquisitions and transfers), but changes in the rules that govern changes in the property status of resources.[51]

Locke holds that creation of the institution of money, which he claims happened "out of the bounds of society and without compact" (§50), suspends the Lockean proviso in a way that satisfies the second-order proviso. He writes that "the Invention of Money, and the tacit Agreement of Men to put a value on it, introduced (by Consent) larger Possessions, and a Right to them" (§36). And he goes to some length to show that this invention, although it suspends the enough-and-as-good constraint, does make everyone economically better off than anyone would be in a state of nature – that "a King of a large fruitful territory [in the Americas] feeds, lodges, and is clad worse than a day Labourer in England" (§41, cf. §37).[52]

---

51 The Lockean provisos are not subject to majority rule – undue harms inflicted on a few cannot be justified by the fact that the many want to inflict them (cf. note 44 above). It is rather the other way around: Majority rule is itself an institution whose moral legitimacy depends on everyone's rational consent. Locke argues that majority rule satisfies this condition, while autocracy does not (§93, §137; cf. §20, §§90-6).

52 Could one not rationally agree to the creation of institutions that make persons better off *on average*? Locke has good reason not to argue in this way. Institutions cannot be justified to their present participants by appeal to the actual or hypothetical consent of their ancestors (§73, §121). And if we tell slaves or English day-labourers or the present global poor that *they* could have rationally agreed *ex ante* (in ignorance of their social position at birth) to institutions

It is rather unclear what life in a Lockean state of nature would be like, but let us grant, for the sake of the argument, Locke's assumption that most conveniences and all modern technologies would be lacking in such a state, in which, consequently, only a much smaller human population could sustain itself. And let us also accept this rock-bottom baseline as determining the point at which coercively imposing social institutions upon others counts as harming them unduly. Such institutions must not merely increase economic aggregates or the average standard of living, but must also distribute this gain so as to afford everyone access to an economic position superior to what anyone would have in a Lockean state of nature. In the so-called Third World, millions suffer extreme poverty from birth, with low prospects even of survival into adulthood, while also being forced to comply with existing economic institutions, to observe the property rights that others assert over all the wealth of this world. The question on the Lockean account is whether we can, with any confidence, say to them: "We are not harming you by helping to uphold these institutions, for you are still better off than anyone would be in a pre-institutional state of nature." I see no way of providing a plausible defence of this position and hence of supporting the second objection against the more moderate argument I have proposed. Failing such a defence, we must then conclude that today's global poor are clearly being harmed – and unduly so. Their extreme poverty is foreseeable, avoidable, and cannot be justified by anything they have done (they certainly did not squander their share, but were excluded from birth, if not from conception).

If all this were said in reference to the economic order of a particular country, it would provoke little opposition in the rich societies. Most of us reject as unjust the economic institutions of Brazil, for instance, and agree that the wealthy elite of that country, by imposing these in-

---

under which some may be worse off than persons in a state of nature, they can surely plausibly reply that this hypothetical consent could not possibly have been *theirs*, since they never had a real chance to occupy the better positions. (But see John Rawls, *A Theory of Justice*, 167, making the surprising and unnecessary claim that "the general form of the slaveholder's argument is correct.")

stitutions upon all the rest, is unduly harming many of them.[53] But very few of us who accept these conclusions about Brazil are willing to draw parallel conclusions about our global economic order, which is much more inegalitarian even than Brazil's.[54] The discussion of lofty

---

53 Rawls, if he held his theory of justice to be applicable to Brazil's social order at all, would be an exception, assigning to the Brazilian elite a merely positive duty to further (more) just arrangements. I have chosen Brazil, because it displays the greatest recorded income inequality of any country: the ratio between the top and bottom quintiles exceeds 32:1, and 45 percent of its population live below the international poverty line, despite a generous resource endowment and a *per capita* GNP of US$2,930. (All data in this note are from UNDP, *Human Development Report 1996*, pp. 170f, 176, 186f, 198.) It is sometimes said that extreme inequalities are the price for rapid economic growth which, over time, benefits all. But the available data tell a different story: The high-inequality countries (mainly in Latin America and Africa) have consistently shown very slow or even negative growth in *per capita* GNP, while the developing countries with rapid economic growth (mainly in East Asia) have quintile inequality ratios below 10:1, similar to those in many developed countries. This should not be surprising. When inequalities are very large, those born among the poor often suffer nutritional, medical, or educational deficits or disadvantages that prevent them from effectively competing for the more important positions. More or less by default, these positions then go to persons born among the wealthy and thus attract less talent and effort than they would with a more open competition. Because it tends to reduce productivity and innovation, as well as political stability, radical inequality depresses even the absolute share of the rich over time. Because they care about their relative share or because they care more about smaller near-term advantages than about larger long-term gains, the rich nevertheless often resist reform – as we do on the global plane.

54 "The poorest 20% of the world's people saw their share of global income decline from 2.3% to 1.4% in the past 30 years. Meanwhile, the share of the richest 20% rose from 70% to 85%. That doubled the ratio of the shares of the richest and the poorest – from 30:1 to 61:1." UNDP, *Human Development Report*, 2. Note that the 61:1 ratio provided by the UNDP was calculated from country aggregates. The two relevant quintiles were formed by simply taking the populations of the richest and poorest countries, with each set of countries selected so that it represents one-fifth of world population (according to a written explanation received from Mr. Selim Jahan, Deputy Director of the UNDP Human Development Report Office). But this yields the ratio between the average income in the richest countries and the average income in the poorest countries, not the income ratio between the richest and poorest quintiles of "the world's people." The former ratio is obviously a very bad estimate of the latter: the income of the

nationalism then uncovers another problematic asymmetry of judgments: We say that those who impose, shape, and dominate a national economic order are harming unduly those whom this order subjects to extreme poverty that could be avoided through institutional reform. Yet, we fail to draw the parallel conclusion with regard to the avoidable extreme poverty engendered by the global economic system that we impose, shape, and dominate. This failure is surely convenient, for, if we did accept the parallel conclusion, then global poverty would fall outside the scope of lofty nationalism and its eradication would move to the top of our moral priority list. But convenience alone does not explain why we find it so very easy to disconnect ourselves from global poverty.

---

richest quintile is underestimated, as many poor in the richest countries are much poorer than many rich in non-rich countries (so the latter, not the former, should be included in the top quintile). And the income of the poorest quintile is hugely inflated as the poorest in middle-income countries such as Brazil are excluded in favour of more affluent persons in the poorest countries (among them, for instance, President Mobutu Sese Seko, whose income was a rather considerable part of the Zairean national income). My best guess, based on all the 1993 data in the UNDP report, is that the richest quintile of world population has well over 90 percent of world income (ca. US$20,000 annually *per capita*) and the poorest quintile under 1/4 percent (ca. US$50 annually *per capita*; cf. note 33 above). This would suggest a quintile income inequality ratio around 400:1. Wealth inequality is, of course, considerably greater still, as the rich tend to have much more wealth than annual income and the poor tend to have much less wealth than annual income (with the poorest 20 percent having barely any wealth at all). These estimates may be disheartening by showing that the global poor are so much worse off than we thought, and our global economic order thus so much more unjust. But they should be heartening as well, by showing how much less of a reform than we thought would be necessary to double (even quadruple!) the income of the global poor. Ironically, those who like to claim that eradicating world poverty would impoverish the developed countries do not know how incredibly poor the global poor really are. Thus Rorty, for example, doubts that we are able to 'help' the global poor by appealing to the claim that "a politically feasible project of egalitarian redistribution of wealth requires there to be enough money around to insure that, after the redistribution, the rich will still be able to recognise themselves – will still think their lives worth living." Richard Rorty, 'Who are We? Moral Universalism and Economic Triage,' in *Diogenes* **173** (1996) 14f. Good that Rorty's readers are taught to take his essays as narratives!

III Explanatory Nationalism –
The Deep Significance of National Borders

This ease can be explained, I believe, by our 'nationalist' way of look-ing at the world as a plurality of interacting national systems and, more specifically, at the world economy as a plurality of national economic systems that interact through trade, loans, and foreign investment. This view permeates economists' explanations of poverty. They present poverty as a set of national phenomena explicable mainly as a result of bad domestic policies and institutions that stifle (or fail to stimulate) national economic growth and engender national economic injustice. It is difficult to design policies and institutions that promote both growth and justice (and economists differ on how this should best be done), but some countries have succeeded rather well, and so could the oth-ers, if only they had better economic institutions and pursued better economic policies. If the governments of presently poor countries had done better in these respects, there would now be much less poverty in the world; if such governments were to do better from now on, severe poverty would gradually disappear.

This economists' view is quite true on the whole. But it is also to-tally one-sided. For it holds fixed, and thereby entirely ignores, the economic and geopolitical context in which the national economies and governments of the poorer countries are placed. The modern state, af-ter all, is itself an institution. The land surface of our planet is divided into a number of clearly demarcated and non-overlapping national ter-ritories. Human beings are matched up with these territories, so that (at least for the most part) each person belongs to exactly one terri-tory. Any person or group effectively controlling a preponderant share of the means of coercion within such a territory is recognized as the legitimate government of both the territory and the persons belong-ing to it. It is entitled to rule 'its' people through laws, orders, and officials, to adjudicate conflicts among them, and also to exercise ulti-mate control over all resources within the territory ('eminent domain'). It is also entitled to represent these persons against the rest of the world: to bind them *vis-à-vis* outsiders through treaties and contracts, to regulate their relations with outsiders, to declare war in their name, to represent them through diplomats and emissaries, and to control outsiders' access to the country's territory. In this second role, a government is considered continuous with its predecessors and successors: bound by the undertakings of the former, and capable of binding the latter through its own undertakings.

This global context (of which I could here only sketch a few central features) is of crucial importance for explaining the incidence of unfulfilled human rights and the persistence and severity of global poverty. Explanations by reference solely to national factors and international differences leave open important questions, such as why national factors (institutions, officials, policies, culture, natural environment, level of technical and economic development) have *these* effects rather than others. It is quite possible that, in a different global environment, the same national factors, or the same international differences, would have quite a different impact on human living conditions. Such explanations also leave open why national factors are the way they are in the first place. Global factors significantly affect national policies and institutions, especially in the poorer and weaker countries. It is quite possible that, in a different global environment, national factors that tend to generate poverty, or tend to undermine the fulfilment of human rights more generally, would occur much less frequently or not at all.

Such questions are not especially subtle, and economists are well aware of them in other contexts. They recognize the explanatory importance of global institutional factors, for example, when they try to assess the effects of alternative global trading regimes (Bretton Woods, Uruguay Round, etc.) on trade flows and global economic growth. Why are there no systematic attempts to analyze the effects of alternative global institutions on the incidence of poverty? I will not speculate. But it is possible, at least, that the popularity of explanatory nationalism is related to how it distorts our ordinary moral analysis of global poverty.

Explanatory nationalism sends a message that has become deeply entrenched in common sense. It makes us look at poverty and oppression as problems whose root causes and possible solutions are domestic to the foreign countries in which they occur. To be sure, we deplore the misery abroad and recognize a positive moral reason to help out with aid and advice. When poverty is due to natural causes, we demand that "there should be certain provisions for mutual assistance between peoples in times of famine and drought and, were it feasible, as it should be, provisions for ensuring that in all reasonably developed liberal societies people's basic needs are met."[55] Insofar as "the great social evils in poorer societies are likely to be oppressive government and corrupt elites,"[56] we may be able to help by exerting some pressure on the rulers – perhaps through loans, trade, or diplomacy. But, since we see no causal link between global factors and the incidence of oppression, corruption, and poverty, we will not even ask whether those who shape global institutions and, more generally, the global context in which the poorer countries are placed have a negative moral responsibility for global poverty.

Some quick reflections may show the importance of such causal links. A large portion of the huge quantities of natural resources we consume is imported, much of it from repressive, undemocratic countries. We deplore this lack of democracy and wonder what we might do to help. But, as good explanatory nationalists, we see no connection between the international transaction and the domestic tyranny. The former involves us, but is a fair exchange at market prices; the latter is unjust, but involves us only marginally as potential helpers. This separation again makes it very hard to ask the right questions: What entitles a small global elite – the affluent citizens of the rich countries and the holders of political and economic power in the resource-rich developing countries – to enforce a global property regime under which they can claim the world's natural resources for themselves and can distribute these among themselves on mutually agreeable terms? How, for example, can an ever so free and fair agreement between an oil company and a military strongman create property rights in vast quantities of crude oil, thereby dispossessing the local population and the rest of humankind? How can there be a moral difference between paying the Saudi family or General Sani Abacha – the Nigerian strongman who jailed the winner of the annulled 1993 election and has executed numerous political opponents – and stealing the oil outright? In fact, paying Abacha inflicts a second undue harm upon the poverty-stricken Nigerian population: Not only is the oil taken away for our consumption (and much environmental

---

55 John Rawls, 'The Law of Peoples,' in Stephen Shute and Susan Hurley, eds., *On Human Rights* (New York: Basic Books 1993), 56

56 Rawls, 'The Law of Peoples,' 77

damage done) without their consent, but their tyrant is also propped up with funds he can spend on arms and soldiers to cement his rule.[57]

As ordinary citizens of the rich countries, we are deeply implicated in these harms. We authorize our firms to acquire natural resources from tyrants and we protect their property rights in resources so acquired. We purchase what our firms produce out of such resources and thereby encourage them to act as authorized. In these ways we recognize the authority of tyrants to sell the natural resources of the countries they rule. We also authorize and encourage other firms of ours to sell to the tyrants what they need to stay in power – from aircraft and napalm to surveillance and torture equipment.[58] We might instead work out an international treaty declaring that rulers who hold power contrary to their country's constitution and without democratic legitimation cannot sell their country's resources abroad nor borrow in its name. Such a treaty would not merely end our complicity. It would also dramatically reduce the rewards and hence the frequency of coups d'état and dictatorship in the poor countries.[59]

Once we think about present human misery in global terms, other reforms come readily to mind, for example, a treaty by which states would commit themselves to outlaw bribes paid by their firms to foreign officials. Currently, most rich states do not merely permit their firms to bribe foreign officials, but even entitle them to deduct such bribes from their taxable revenues.[60] The proposed reform would evidently render officials in poor countries more responsive to domestic interests. By greatly

---

57 For some background, see 'Going on down,' in *The Economist*, 8 June 1996, 46-48. The article reports that Nigeria is considered the world's most corrupt country and that its *per capita* income has been stagnant during the last 23 years of army rule, even while it receives oil revenues of about US$20 million per day (22 percent of its current GNP), which could have financed large productive investments in infrastructure and education.

58 See, for example, Amnesty International, *Human Rights and U.S. Security Assistance* (Boston: AIUSA Publications 1996).

59 My essay cited in note 18 develops this proposal in detail.

60 Canada eliminated the tax deductibility of bribes with its 1991 amendments to the Income Tax Act. The U.S. took a hard line with its 1977 Foreign Practices Act, after the Lockheed Corporation had paid a large bribe (ca. US$2,000,000) to

reducing a now customary 'perk' of official positions, it would also alter the pool of office-seekers toward more public-spirited candidates.

That these global factors really have an important influence is indicated by the fact that resource-rich countries tend to have slower economic growth. The factors we examined can explain this. The fact that the *de facto* ruler of a resource-rich country can sell these resources, or use them as loan collateral, provides strong incentives to gain power in such a country, by whatever means. And, since the officials of such countries have resources to sell and money to spend, it is also more lucrative to corrupt them than their resource-poor peers. For these reasons, ample resources can become an obstacle to growth, because they foster coups, oppression, and corruption (as Nigeria illustrates). That they have this effect is, however, a result of the global factors I have mentioned.

Explanatory nationalism traces present human misery to bad national policies and institutions in the poor countries. I have given one response: These national policies and institutions are indeed often quite bad, but this can be traced to global policies and institutions. It is worth showing briefly how global factors would be of great explanatory importance even if the national policies and institutions of poor countries were optimal.

Many governments of poor countries face an acute shortage of investment capital for providing education, roads, safe drinking water, sewers, etc., which could boost economic development. To raise revenues, such governments may well decide, as some economists are urging them to do, to provide tax incentives for foreign investment in the construction of sweatshops or sex tourism resorts. To be sure, work in a Central American maquila or an Asian brothel is badly paid and highly unpleasant. But, as things stand, many poor persons and their families depend on such work for their livelihood. Encouraging such investment may then truly be part of the best development strategy for many of the poorer countries. But this is so only because and insofar as these countries and regions lack other sources of investment capital and the power to mandate minimum working conditions on their own soil. Many of them cannot generate domestic investment

---

the Japanese Prime Minister Kakuei Tanaka. But in Europe, international bribery is only beginning to be addressed.

capital because they struggle under a mountain of foreign debt accumulated by previous dictators and military regimes and must service these debts on pains of being shut out of the international financial markets. And, given their dependence on foreign investment capital, they cannot mandate minimally decent working conditions, because foreign firms can easily shift their investments elsewhere. Global institutional reforms could solve these problems through international law or treaties, by creating a source of investment capital to foster economic development in the poorest regions[61] and by creating global minimum standards for working conditions.

I conclude that explanatory nationalism and the moral world-view based on it do not fit the real world. Global factors are all-important for explaining present human misery, in four main ways. Such factors crucially affect what sorts of persons shape national policy in the poor countries, what incentives these persons face, what options they have, and what impact the implementation of any of their options would have on domestic poverty and human rights fulfilment. Current policies of the rich countries and the global order they impose greatly contribute to poverty and unfulfilled human rights in the poor countries and thereby inflict severe, undue harms on many. These harms could be dramatically reduced through even relatively minor international reforms.

IV Conclusion

I have argued that – acceptable common and lofty nationalism notwithstanding – much of the massive poverty and oppression in the

---

61 It is customary to object at this point that we have tried development aid and that it has failed. This is true enough (though not of the Scandinavian countries and the Netherlands). But conventional development aid is allocated by politicians and has, not surprisingly, benefited those capable of reciprocation: export firms in the donor states and the political-economic elites of strategically important developing countries. Organizations that try to reach the poor and oppressed generally do so very well – though they do, of course, make mistakes occasionally. My essay cited in note 23 offers a detailed proposal for a global institutional reform that would be far more effective in eradicating global poverty than conventional bilateral aid.

poorer countries engages our negative duty to avoid harming others unduly. Standard defences that challenge the adverb 'unduly' have little chance of success. The global poor have done nothing to deserve their position – in fact, most of them are children. Politicians and the more affluent citizens of the rich countries know at least in broad outlines what living conditions are imposed upon the global poor, and we also know, or at least should know and can easily find out, how our national laws and policies affect these conditions either directly or through global institutions. We can then try to initiate appropriate changes in national policies or global institutions – for example, by publicizing their nature and effects and by developing feasible paths of reform. We can also take compensating action through volunteer work or contributions to effective relief organizations (such as Oxfam, Amnesty, or UNICEF) that help protect the victims of current policies and institutions.[62] By continuing to support the current global order and the national policies that shape and sustain it without taking such compensating action, we share a negative responsibility for the undue harms they foreseeably produce.

Some will wonder how we can possibly be collaborating in the starvation of millions, if we have never chosen to do any such thing and our lives feel perfectly fine, morally, from the inside. Many Nazi sympathizers wondered likewise: They, too, had never chosen to support war and genocide, but had merely continued to do their jobs, to follow orders, to attend rallies. Yet, by acting in these ways, they did contribute to the massacres. Given what they knew about the ongoing war and genocide and their own causal roles, they ought to have thought, and chosen, and then to have acted differently.[63] Or so we now believe. And if this is how we think about most Germans in the early 1940s,

---

62 How much should we contribute to such reform and protection efforts? I would think: as much as would be necessary to eradicate the harms, if others similarly placed made analogous contributions. One percent of the income of those in the top quintile of world population (cf. note 54) would suffice to eradicate global poverty within a few years. Of course, one might make an equivalent non-monetary contribution instead.

63 See Hilary Bok, 'Acting Without Choosing,' in *NOÛS* **30** (1996) 174-96.

then this is how we must surely think about ourselves, seeing that we enjoy so much more freedom to inform ourselves and to act politically.

The point of this parallel is not to raise issues of blame or guilt, which I am leaving aside throughout, nor to liken our conduct to that of Nazi sympathizers. The common point is thoughtlessness. Poverty so massive and severe as to cause twenty million deaths a year requires a reflective moral response from each and every one of us. It requires that we morally situate ourselves in respect to it and choose how to act or fail to act in the face of it. That the academic justice industry has, by and large, ignored this phenomenon is a stunning failure[64] – which I have tried to explain by reference to the deeply ingrained lofty nationalism of these moralists as reinforced in turn by the explanatory nationalism propagated by their more hard-nosed economist colleagues. That a number of ordinary people *have* stopped to think is a wonderful triumph of humanity in a still inhuman world.[65]

If we do stop to think and if we do conclude that we have been involved in the undue harming of the global poor, some misguided communitarians and patriots will say that it is magnificent and valuable to love and to benefit one's own country and compatriots even if doing so means death to myriad outsiders. But this is false. Our countries can flourish quite well without depriving the global poor. And our national solidarity and fellow-feeling can thrive lavishly even without our readiness to deprive them – just as your loving bond with your children can thrive fully even without your willingness to kill to get them all the latest toys. We can honour our negative duties and still build the most splendid republic that lofty nationalists, communitarians, and patriots might ever desire. Whether we can build such a republic while the dying continues is at least doubtful.

---

64 Stunning? Seeing that Immanuel Kant, a true giant, did not think to question women's lack of rights in politics and family life, perhaps nothing should surprise us.

65 One of them is the Canadian Craig Kielburger, who, starting at age 12, has been organizing a campaign against bonded child labour in the Third World.

CANADIAN JOURNAL OF PHILOSOPHY
Supplementary Volume 22

Social Movements as Nationalisms
or, On the Very Idea of a Queer Nation[1]

BRIAN WALKER
University of California, Los Angeles

Given the immense mobilizing power possessed by the rhetoric of nationalism, as well as the many resources which can be tapped by groups which successfully establish national claims, it is not surprising that we have recently seen such a resurgence in nationalist discourse. One of the things which may surprise us, however, is the growing breadth in the *types* of groups which now launch such claims. No longer is the discourse of nationalism limited to use by ethnic groups and territorial populations. Recently it has come to be deployed by groups which we would normally tend to look upon as social movements. There has been a growing realization of the way in which constituencies such as Blacks, gays and lesbians, Chicano/as, and so on, make up distinct peoples, with cultures, public institutions, dialects, tastes, and social practices that set them off from the people or peoples around them. This growing sense of peoplehood has been explicitly formulated by groups such as Nation of Islam and Queer Nation,[2]

---

1 I would like to thank Jeremy Webber, Alan Conter, Will Kymlicka and Victor Wolfenstein for comments on an earlier version of this paper.

2 Queer Nation is an activist coalition formed in April 1990 as an offshoot of ACT-UP. Like the former coalition, Queer Nation aims at publicizing what it sees as the criminal slowness of the American government's response to the AIDS epidemic. But it aims beyond that at a more general attack on the homophobia which had such mortal results in the first years of the AIDS crisis, when the latter was still seen as a gay disease. The early pamphleteers of Queer Nation drew an explicit link between their strategies and those of black nationalists. See

but these fringe organizations are less important than the wider social transformations which have made them possible; namely, the creation of alternative sets of institutions which have permitted and encouraged a sense of peoplehood to grow within these social movements, and has allowed the claims of Black and gay and lesbian nationalists to strike a resonant chord.[3]

Social movements which cast themselves as nationalisms raise a host of important questions for students of nationalism. Is the roster of world nations fixed and sealed, or does it hold a place open for the acceptance of new peoples? If so, how do we adjudicate between the needs of nascent nations and the claims of more traditional groups? Are the claims of these new groups invalid because of the sorts of communities they have or the modes of identity they centre upon? And, finally, is there any good reason for believing that the 'contexts of choice' which are forged within social movements are less important and enduring than those which have developed within traditional ethnic communities?

None of these questions would be so pressing were it not for a crucial shift which has occurred in theories of nationalism in recent years. Since the Second World War defenders of nationalism have been forced to abandon the old social-Darwinist picture of a struggle among races for scarce living space and have adopted a defense of nations based on the need to protect fragile cultures.[4] 'Culturalist' defenses of nationalism were developed out of pre-war anthropological theory in a series of influential papers from UNESCO which together served as one of the principal justifications for the nationalisms of the decolonizing period.[5] A version of this culturalist justification has recently been rendered plausi-

---

Esther Kaplan, 'A Queer Manifesto,' quoted in Lauren Berlant and Elizabeth Freeman, 'Queer Nationality,' in *Boundary* 2 (Spring 1992) 149-80, esp. 155-6.

3 I shall argue this point at much greater length below.

4 See Elazar Barkan, *The Retreat of Scientific Racism* (New York: Cambridge University Press 1991), 343-5.

5 See Pierre-André Taguieff, 'Les métamorphoses idéologiques du racisme et la crise de l'antiracisme,' in *Face au Racisme Tome 2: Analyses, hypothèses, perspectives* (Paris: La Découverte 1991), 13-63, esp. 21-25.

ble within analytic legal and political theory by the works of Will Kymlicka, Joseph Raz, Avishai Margalit, Moshe Halbertal, and many others.[6]

The development of social movements which look on themselves as nations poses particular problems for this sort of defense of nationalism because social movements, as Alain Touraine and many others have pointed out, are one of the primary means by which new cultures are created within the modern state.[7] Movements such as the gay and lesbian rights struggle create viable cultures which operate at many different levels and fulfill a broad range of functions beyond those entailed in the fight for basic civil rights (I shall show this below). The gay and lesbian movement has created what is, by even the most standard definition, a culture. So if our primary defense of nationalism has shifted to a culturalist one, then perhaps these groups *should* be looked on as having the rights, and as deserving the powers, of other, more traditional nations. And it is this recognition which pushes us to ask the set of questions which I have set out above.

In this paper I will address issues raised by social movements which take on a nationalistic character, especially the issues raised by the development of nationalistic themes within the gay and lesbian rights movement. Whether or not the nationalistic themes in the homosexual rights movement develop into a full-fledged nationalist movement, the advent of a gay nationalism, and more generally, of other social movements which take on a nationalistic character, forces us to face the question of which collectivities should be the proper focus for the strong rights and political powers we (may) see as the appropriate

---

6 See Will Kymlicka, 'Individual and Community Rights,' in Judith Baker, ed., *Group Rights* (Toronto: University of Toronto Press 1994), and *Liberalism, Community and Culture* (Oxford: Clarendon Press 1989); Melissa Williams, 'Justice Toward Groups; Political Not Juridical,' *Political Theory* **23:1** (February 1995), 67-91; Avishai Margalit and Joseph Raz, 'National Self-Determination,' *Journal of Philosophy* **87:9** (September 1990) 439-61; Avishai Margalit and Moshe Halbertal, 'Liberalism and the Right to Culture,' *Social Research* **61:3** (Fall 1994) 491-510; Vernon Van Dyke, 'Justice as Fairness; For Groups?' *American Political Science Review* (1975), 607-14; Michel Seymour, 'Anti-individualisme, droits collectifs et Etats multinationaux,' *Le defi du pluralisme; Lekton* **4:1** (Printemps 1994), 41-80.

7 Alain Touraine, 'The Idea of Revolution,' in Michael Featherstone, ed., *Global Culture* (London: Sage Publications 1990), 121-41

responses to a collectivity's sense of peoplehood. If, as many writers now suggest, modern states should see their minority peoples as having rights to cultural protection, then we would expect many new groups to arise which will press claims to such rights. If groups such as gays and lesbians talk of their nationhood even within a system centred on individual rights, we can safely predict that there will be even stronger reasons for such claims if culturalist arguments for collective rights are accepted and if nations are seen as having a right to extra political powers above and beyond those to which their members are entitled as citizens of a liberal state. Once we adopt a discursive frame which sees minority cultural communities as the beneficiaries of political rights it will become much more important to determine just which groups should be seen as reasonable claimants of such rights.

Social movements which foster a sense of peoplehood also raise questions about which *sort* of nations should be the beneficiaries of rights. Many advocates of rights for peoples suggest that political powers should be reserved above all for cultural communities which are gathered together in large numbers on a particular territory. The question is whether such a limitation can be defended against the claims of non-territorial, trans-statal cultures such as that of gays and lesbians.[8] The latter are nowhere in a clear majority and have institutions which are scattered across many borders and states; yet their claims to cultural vulnerability are at least as strong, and in some ways stronger, than most other national groups.

The third sort of issue raised by the advent of gay nationalism is that of the role and rights of new nations and cultures in comparison with the rights of more traditional national groups. In the course of history

---

8 I shall use the terms 'trans-statal' and 'diasporic' to refer to the way in which gay culture relates to its territories. I use 'trans-statal' rather than the more usual term 'transnational' in order to avoid several confusions pointed out by Katherine Verdery in her article 'Beyond the Nation in Eastern Europe,' *Social Text* **38** 1-19. 'Transnationality' is generally used to refer to "movements of peoples, commodities, ideas, production processes, capital, images as well as possible political alignments across the boundaries between sovereign states" (Verdery, 1). But, as Verdery points out, 'transnationalism' is thus a misnomer, since what is referred to is not processes which bridge ethnic nations but sovereign states. I follow Verdery in using the much clearer 'trans-statal' instead.

cultures come in and out of existence, with peoples merging into, and fragmenting off from, the larger cultures around them. Certain cultural groups in history have been lucky enough to gain control over states and thus have been able to ensure that a version of their cultural patterns survives from generation to generation over time. Culturalists wish to distribute this integrity-promoting power to more groups than have hitherto profited from it, and they thus advocate forms of de-centralization which would allow local cultures (such as Canada's aboriginal peoples, or French-Canadians, or Arabs and Ultra-Orthodox Jews in Israel) to control their territories. But where does this leave cultures which are in the process of formation, cultures that in some sense have never been traditional, but were, rather, launched by developments in modernity itself? Resources for cultural creation are limited on any given territory, and if only traditional cultural groups are rightful claimants to cultural resources then newly forming groups will be disadvantaged. The preference for traditional cultures may also harm gay and lesbian claims by giving new powers to homophobic groups. Many traditional cultures are deeply homophobic, and if communities are allowed to wield the sorts of dense and far-reaching powers which culturalists advocate, we can easily imagine new cultures like that of gay men and lesbians being squeezed out, with no place to go.[9] Social movements which take on a nationalistic character thus raise a number of important questions for students of nationalism.

These three questions I have just posed about the sorts of nations which merit collective rights are subsidiaries of a broader question I would like to pose about the *dramatis personae* admitted into the language-game of modern nationalism. In spite of the shift which has taken place in recent justifications of self-determination there is still an implicit assumption that the nations we should concern ourselves with are basically the same as before. The groups which culturalist writers such as Kymlicka, Raz, Van Dyke, and others concentrate on are still basically races and religious groups: the collectivities that were the focus of collective rights within the abandoned racialist framework. It is useful to concentrate on the example of gays and lesbians because their

---

9 I have been influenced here by Leslie Green, 'Internal Minorities and Their Rights,' in Baker, ed., *Group Rights*, 112.

Brian Walker

nation is so much unlike any other, not only in that it is vehemently modern, the child of our current rights-system, but also because there is nothing of the racial bond in the collective life that gays and lesbians share. They are held together by strictly cultural means, by institutions and modes of thought which are historically specific and vastly fragile but which find no stabilization in ethnic appeals. Gay and lesbian nationalism thus serves as a test case for those defenders of nationalism who see themselves as having achieved a culturalist shift. The strictly cultural claims of gays and lesbians are undeniable and it would seem one could deny them collective rights only by appealing to an implicit racialist claim, namely the idea that ethnic or quasi-ethnic peoples (such as religious groups which hand down their practices from generation to generation) are the principal foci of collective rights claims.

So I wish to focus on a number of issues raised for students of nationalism by this basic language shift justifying national self-determination. I will first discuss this shift and try to show why the exclusionary functions permitted within the racialist paradigm of nationality can no longer be preserved within the framework of the new culturalist form. I will then go on and look at the gay and lesbian claim to national status at greater length.

Nationality Claims and Intergroup Politics

Groups have a strong interest in portraying themselves as nations. When a claim to the survivance vocabulary of nationalism is successfully justified then one may legitimately take up an intransigent bargaining position with a high bottom line.[10] But this only works so long as the number of groups that can make this sort of claim is strictly

---

10 Claims to the status of nationhood or peoplehood are above all claims about *survivance*. They are claims that one's collectivity has the right and perhaps the duty to resist certain forms of metamorphosis, that one's group can not, and will not, be moved from its integral relation with a certain set of patterns.

   Nationality claims which are successfully established thus rule out as illegitimate the trade-offs which might otherwise be demanded of a group within the terms of pluralist politics, where many groups struggle together for scarce resources. Prior to the successful assumption of the mantle of nationhood one's

510

delimited. If all collectivities could establish claims to nation status then relations between them would either break down (so that force and violence would determine their interactions) or all groups would be forced back into a game of strategic trade-offs. Theorists who defend nationalisms thus have two tasks: a task of justification and a task of exclusion. The first goal is to explain why one set of collectivities is justified in putting itself outside the normal bargaining games of a pluralist society. The second goal, intimately connected to this first, is to show why some other groups which might want to make this sort of claim should not be allowed to do so, should not, in other words, be seen as true nations.

Since the French Revolution we have seen three distinct justificatory matrices which nationalist groups have employed to justify their claims to outgroup members and, at the same time, to suggest where the distinction between real nations and false nations should lie. These justificatory vocabularies draw on over-arching goods shared by significant numbers of members both inside and outside the prospective nation and which thus may be used as a means to ground validity claims going in both directions. The background justifications are, in order of their chronological dominance: the theological argument based on God's will; the biological/racialist argument based on the struggle of races for scarce space and resources; and more recently, the culturalist argument, based on the strong role that cultural contexts of choice play in the formation of personality.[11] Although this is not the place to give

---

collective might be seen as just one more interest group among the many which make claims on common resources. In pluralistic democracies these claims are mediated by central authorities who force strategic trade-offs in the name of the large number of groups fighting for scarce goods. When claims to the status of nationhood are successfully established they lift one's group out of this game of bargaining and strategic trade-offs, and they justify the refusal of certain compromises which might otherwise have seemed reasonable.

11 It might be suggested that the right of democratic self-determination serves as a fourth justification for national self-determination claims, and this is to some extent the case. The right of groups to determine their own future has served, since the French Revolution, as a sort of macro-justification to which all nationalisms have appealed. This aspect of republicanism serves as the *lingua franca* of modern self-determination movements. But arguments for democratic self-

a thorough analysis of the discursive regimes which these justifica-tions permit, a brief sketch will allow me to deepen my explanation of why social movements which cast themselves as nationalisms pose such an interesting problem.

The first means by which nationalists justified their concern for the survival of their local cultures was by a theologically oriented refer-ence to a providential plan. Herder, for example, justified resistance to the ideals of the Enlightenment (which, in his view, was very much the *French* Enlightenment) by reference to the pluralism through which God realizes his vision of the good. Different local cultures represent different aspects of God's divine vision, which is singular in essence but plural in representation.[12] One cannot ask a culture to give up its

---

governance have seldom been a sufficient justification for national self-determination, and that for the following reason.

It is widely accepted that peoples have a right to govern themselves, as long as they accept certain well-known side constraints (that they can achieve au-tonomy without thereby causing unnecessary harm to other peoples, for exam-ple). But there is almost always a great division of opinion on the question of who makes up 'the people' for the purposes of self-governance. For example, if Canadians make up one people *a mare usque ad mare* then the borders of the unit of self-determination are set at the Atlantic and Pacific coasts. The various groups living between – those claiming aboriginal heritage and the French-Canadians – are therefore subject to the decisions of the majority, and are held to the everyday give-and-take of the federal order with their needs being discounted accordingly. However, if Canadians make up one people, and francophone Quebeckers make up another, then the appropriate border of self-government is not that of the coun-try Canada but that of the borders of the territory populated exclusively by francophone Quebeckers, namely the areas outside aboriginal lands and out-side the island of Montreal (which has always been a polycultural city). Or, if all citizens of the current province of Quebec (aboriginal peoples, anglophones, Montreal immigrants, francophones and so on) make up one people then the relevant political unit would be the current border of the province of Quebec. An argument for democratic self-government cannot address the question of the appropriate border of the 'people.' This is why theories of nationalism tend to situate a republican core within a more elaborated justificatory matrix which gives the basic democratic argument a particular valence. It is these latter justi-ficatory systems that I am concentrating upon here.

12 Herder, 'Yet Another Philosophy of History,' translated, edited and introduced by F.M. Barnard (Cambridge: Cambridge University Press 1969), 181-223, esp. 183-5

lifeway without destroying an essential part of the divine vision. One thus has a duty to protect the patterns, customs, and worldview of one's local community.

In the nineteenth century this theological justification gave way to a pseudo-scientific, quasi-biological justification based on the idea of race. The human species was seen as divided up into natural 'races,' each of which exhibited certain characteristic traits (such as 'industriousness' for the Scots, 'spirituality' for the Slavs, 'joie de vivre' for the Latins, and so on) on the basis of which the various races could be ranked in terms of superiority and inferiority.[13] By the middle of the nineteenth century this racialist vision was often given a social-Darwinist spin; these various races were portrayed as made up of struggling populations, each of which was increasing at an exponential rate and fighting for its own survival niche. As the uglier ramifications of this picture became evident a concerted political movement grew up inside and outside the scientific community which was aimed at debunking this pseudo-biological vision of the differences which divided populations.[14] Scientists such as Franz Boas argued that there was no evidentiary backing for such claims, no means to rank cultures in any intellectually convincing way, and they suggested a replacement picture based on the holism and equality of cultural meaning sets. This movement within American and British scientific communities gained wide popular resonance after the negative features of the racialist picture were made so clearly visible in the events leading up to the Second World War.

The debunking of the racialist scientific paradigm, and the recognition of its disastrous consequences for European civilization, led to the second major shift in the justificatory matrix for nationalism. In the post-war period, defenders of the rights of peoples picked up the arguments of the pre-war anthropologists and grounded nationalist claims in arguments about the centrality of culture.[15] The recovery and reformulation of a discourse of cultural survivance was given serious

---

13 See Michael Barton, *Race Relations* (London: Tavistock 1967), 8.

14 See Barkan, *The Retreat of Scientific Racism*.

15 Taguieff, 'Les métamorphoses ideologiques du racisme'

support by the anti-colonialist movements of liberation after the Second World War; one of the best records for the construction of the new political paradigm is in the documents produced by the UN, (particularly by UNESCO) during this period.

Modern democratic theorists who defend robust rights for national groups operate, for the most part, within this post-war culturalist paradigm and share its basic assumptions. Vernon Van Dyke, Will Kymlicka, Joseph Raz, Avishai Margalit, Moshe Halbertal, and Michel Seymour are examples of modern writers who have defended national self-determination based on culturalist grounds. Culturalists justify collective rights such as the right to self-determination (as well as lesser cultural rights) by reference to the need that collectivities have to promote the integrity of their cultures. The world we live in, they argue, does not match up with the thought-experiments of universalists. People live in cultures which are vital to them and crucial to their full flourishing. Cultures are like environmental habitats. If certain institutions deteriorate (if the folk no longer go out fishing, if the religious rituals are no longer performed, if the language ceases to be spoken) then it will be as if some environmental disaster had occurred and everybody had to breathe with less oxygen, with a continual sense of lack. These goods that a culture provides are deep and diverse, and it is often impossible for participants in a culture to give an account of all the things their cultural institutions do for them. But we do know that cultures play a crucial role in developing basic human capacities, and these include the basic moral and political capacities in which liberals put so much trust. For example, it is only cultural institutions of certain sorts which will allow us to develop the complex capacities and practices that allow a system of rights and freedoms to operate.[16] The

---

16 Within analytical legal and political theory we can distinguish two distinct forms of culturalism. The first is based on a transcendental-type argument about the necessary conditions for the attainment of full personhood and moral autonomy. Will Kymlicka is the best-known proponent of this version of culturalism. This school of thought is in many ways the most analytically sophisticated, carefully justifying cultural promotion by reference to egalitarian considerations which are already widely accepted, and, in the end, making cultural rights derivative of liberal rights and freedoms.

plethora of institutions which make up a particular lifeway (that of the aboriginal peoples or of the French-Canadians, for example) are what give people the basic capacities they need to make decisions, elaborate plans, and otherwise take full part in a democratic order.[17] We can imagine cultures being eroded to the point where this sort of socialization no longer would work, where basic guiding norms would break down, and where young people would be cast adrift, thereby falling prey to alcoholism, suicide, and the other forms of anomie which would mark their exile from the polity. Democrats thus need to address the background institutions which undergird democratic practices and insure their ongoing health.

But these backgrounds, culturalists argue, are inherently plural. Individuals do not need just any culture, they need their *own* culture, and it is to ensure the survival of their particular lifeways that collectivities are in need of collective rights. This is where a central difference between majorities and minorities comes into play. Certain

---

The other version of culturalism centres on a right to culture, a right which is itself fundamental and non-derivative of individual rights. In this position cultures are portrayed as possessing rights akin to the rights of persons. Avishai Margalit and Moshe Halbertal argue for this position in 'Liberalism and the Right to Culture.' This latter position attempts to solve a central difficulty with the derivative rights position. If cultural institutions are justified only as a means to develop a particular set of capacities then there is no way to protect particular cultures if other ones offer an equally wide range of means-to-capacities. For example, one homogeneous world-culture with a single language but many highly differentiated institutions might well supply access to full socialization and a very supple and pluralistic set of lifeways. Under the derivative view of cultural rights there is thus little reason to protect particular cultures. Under it people should be allowed to assimilate since by doing so they merely exchange one set of capacities for another. In conditions where this is done over generations with relatively little fuss (the case is quite different if colonialism or other cultural imposition is at work) then this form of assimilation should be seen as non-invidious.

The position which suggests that there are non-derivative cultural rights – were there any good arguments given for us to accept such a position – might be a much more satisfactory source of reasons why we should fight assimilation.

17 See Kymlicka, *Liberalism, Community, and Culture*, 165-6.

collectivities – for example, mainstream anglophone Christians in the United States – have cultures which are replicated and supported by an immense range of institutions and by a huge body of resources. Although individual members of the mainstream may wish that its character were different there is little question but that something like their culture will survive over time, and that ongoing membership in the collectivity that it represents is ensured. But there are certain minority cultures about which this cannot be said. Members of aboriginal communities, perhaps the francophones of Quebec or the Ultra-Orthodox Jews of Israel – all these groups might have legitimate worries about their long-term survival.[18] And if these cultures deteriorate or disappear, the source of full civic empowerment and full self-respect will be cut away from these populations. This is what justifies setting cultural self-determination claims apart as representing a crucially important sort of interest, unclassable with the normal give and take of interest-group politics. At stake here are the background goods which make the bargaining and compromise of everyday politics possible.

This is a fruitful recasting of the justificatory framework for nationalism, and it is not surprising that many democratic theorists have been moved by it to look with considerably more sympathy at movements they once viewed with some disdain.[19] But a question arises. When the justification for nationalism was racialist, for example, there was a criterion for determining which groups were and were not peoples. This criterion was, on the surface at least, relatively straightforward. Peoples were either religious groups (it was at one time common to talk of the Catholic or Protestant peoples) or genealogical descent groups. The function of delimitation which is so central to nationalism was relatively straightforward within the racialist framework, for it showed which groups should be looked upon as peoples and which should not. And modern culturalists tend to write as if the change they make in the justificatory framework of nationalism has no influence on the

---

18 For these examples see, respectively, Kymlicka, *Liberalism, Community, and Culture*, Seymour, 'Anti-individualisme,' and Margalit and Halbertal, 'Liberalism and the Right to Culture.'

19 See Will Kymlicka, 'Liberalism and the Politicization of Ethnicity,' in *Canadian Journal of Law and Jurisprudence* **4:2** (July 1991) 239-55.

groups that we should look at as peoples and nations, the legitimate beneficiaries of cultural rights. But the criterion of 'cultural context' covers many sorts of collectivities which the old frameworks would not touch. Many groups can portray themselves as relying on fragile contexts of choice which could not similarly qualify within the old frameworks. For example farmers, fundamentalist Christians, and lesbians and gays all strike me as being eligible groups within the new paradigm.[20] The criterion of vulnerable background cultures does not allow the same sorts of exclusions that the former frameworks permitted, and this thus opens the survivance vocabulary of nationalism to a much broader range of groups. This is where my example of social movements which cast themselves as nationalisms comes into play. For these are ideal cases for exploring the differences in functionality between the old justificatory vocabularies of nationalism and the culturalist reformulations which seek to recast them in a more palatable post-racialist form. My argument is that it is possible to recast nationalism in such a way, but not without letting in a new cast of characters. It is simply not possible to maintain the exclusion functions of the old vocabulary of nationalism within the new culturalist frameworks. If we accept the culturalist re-writing of nationalist ideology we must greatly expand the number of groups we would see as fitting beneficiaries of national rights. But this is not all. I wish to achieve rather more here than just to argue for the extension of cultural rights to gays and lesbians. I think that the enormous number of groups that would qualify under the 'fragile contexts of choice' argument should lead us to radically rethink the whole culturalist picture, and it is this, most of all, which I wish to show here.

The next step in my argument is to look at some of the strategies by which defenders of traditional nationalisms might try to use current culturalist theory to evade the claim of gay collective rights. I then point out why I believe these strategies fail. My aim throughout is to show that the culturalist criterion is much more radical than its main advocates recognize. I will look first at the claim that a social movement like

---

20 I make this point at greater length in Brian Walker, 'Plural Contexts, Contested Territories: A Critique of Kymlicka' in *Canadian Journal of Political Science* 30:2 (June 1997), 211–34.

the gay rights movement should be classed with interest-group claims rather than with claims to peoplehood. The argument I am rebutting suggests that gay culture does not serve as an important context of choice in the way that, say, French-Canadian or aboriginal cultures do. I will then look at the claim that gays and lesbians cannot make claims to peoplehood because they are not gathered together on a contiguous territory in a way that would make them the fitting subjects of the relevant rights. I suggest that both these strategies of exclusion fail and that they do not stave off the effects of the radical criteria cultural rights theorists have set up.

The Very Idea of a Queer Nation

Many onlookers are likely to react to the adoption of a nationalist symbolism[21] by gays and lesbians with some irony. At first sight gay nationalism may seem like nothing more than a parodistic mimicry of 'real' nationalisms, the most recent, though undeniably one of the more ingenious, examples of gay 'camp.' After all, what is more serious at the end of the twentieth century than the resurgence of ethnic nationalisms and the strains that they produce for the democratic constitutions which attempt to respond to them? The whistles and multi-coloured flags of gay nationalism may strike many as comic relief

---

21 I am referring, for example, to the way in which the gay movement in North America has its own flag, the multicoloured stripes of which fly over numerous parades and rallies which are themselves strongly reminiscent of the mass gatherings in which other nations were forged. I am referring as well to phenomena like the gay Olympics (which for trademark reasons is referred to as the Gay Games), which occurs every two years and which gathers together gay athletes from around the world, and to the increasingly frequent talk of a gay sub-economy, what is sometimes referred to as the economy of 'lavender dollars' and to which, it is argued, gays and lesbians should give preferential treatment. But I am thinking, above all, of the way in which a network of gay institutions (community centres, bars, magazines with their readerships, activist coalitions, NGO's and so on) joins together to make up an alternative gay public sphere, one in which gay culture has been formulated and spread and which has allowed, over time, the creation of a sense of a distinct gay peoplehood.

amidst movements of such dire seriousness. Queer Nation might be seen by some as nationalism's ironic Other, offering a moment of carnivalesque bemusement before we return to the more serious problems involved with weighing the relative merits of real ethnic claims.

But the scholar familiar with the literature of nationalism might find him/herself resisting this temptation to irony. What is most striking when one compares the rise of gay nationalism to the genesis of other national movements is that, far from being a case apart, gay nationalism is a textbook case of a nascent nationalism. The stages which the gay movement has gone through on its way to national consciousness match up, step for step, with the developmental stages we know from many other nationalist movements. All nationalisms started as 'social movements.' A people set apart from those around them by in-group attitudes and discrimination by others comes to develop a sense of itself as having a community and a history.[22] At some key moment a group of intellectuals and members of the middle class give explicit expression to this sense of imagined community and fan its growth. A self-consciously particularist literature is developed which emphasizes the local culture. Histories are written which project the story of the community back through time (in the case of gay nationalism, back to ancient Greece and Rome), tracing the pre-history of the present moment in which it came to consciousness.[23] What was first seen, particularly by outsiders, as a relatively minor difference of attitude or dialect comes to be seen over time as a difference of cultures, and finally as a distinction lying between peoples. Members of the group then begin to see that the only way they can guarantee their survival as a culture is to gain control over certain key levers of the state so that they can fight off the predations of

22 I am influenced in this skeleton history of nationalism by the (very different) accounts given by Benedict Anderson in his *Imagined Communities: Reflections on the Origin and Spread of Nationalism* (London, New York: Verso 1983) and by Ernest Gellner in his *Nations and Nationalisms* (Ithaca: Cornell University Press 1983).

23 See Anthony D. Smith, 'National Identity and Myths of Ethnic Descent,' in Louis Kriesberg, ed., *Research in Social Movements, Conflict and Change*, 7 (1984), 95–130.

519

out-group cultures which want to impose their own standards.[24] This skeleton history of nationalisms could be used to describe that of the Ukrainians or of the Croatians, but it also captures the distinctive phases in the development of gay and lesbian nationalism.

And it is not just the congruence of queer nationalism with the standard histories of such movements which should lead the scholar of nationalism to eschew irony when considering the case of gay nationalism. Irony is a typical reaction to nationalisms in the stage before they consolidate themselves completely and establish enough power to prevent their claims from being overlooked. But scholars of nationalist movements might be moved to resist this temptation because of their heightened awareness of the difficulties of definition attendant on the question of what is a real and what an unreal nationalism. Once we have given up the nationalist's own vision of her actions as the recovery of a pre-existing awareness of peoplehood and see that the sense of being a people is itself something created in history, out of a host of local struggles for recognition, it becomes very hard to determine which groups' claim to be nations should be looked upon as such, and which should not. Our tendency to dismiss gay nationalism as a derivative and parodistic form relies on an implicit distinction between true and false nationalisms which is harder to flesh out discursively than it seems at first. We can see this if we compare gay and lesbian claims to those of more traditional national groups.

The idea of a gay nationality will strike many as unconvincing because they see gayness as at most a lifestyle choice, and find talk of gay 'culture' to revolve around an illegitimate comparison to the values and lifeways of true cultural groups such as the Amish or the Swedes. Gay people, such skeptics might admit, do stand in a relation of difference to the cultures which surround them. But this difference does not amount to a cultural one, certainly not a difference of the depth which would allow it to be seen as the foundation for a nationalism. After all, lesbian and gay culture seems to be centred around a few relatively minor traits and limited to a narrow set of choices about sexual preference. It is misleading and illegitimate to speak of a lifestyle preference

---

24 See Lisa Duggan, 'Queering the State,' in *Social Text* **39** (Summer 1994), 1–14.

as making up a culture. Gays and lesbians, on this view, are a special-interest group at most, and it is entirely illegitimate to see them as making up anything like a nation.

This criticism is based, I believe, on two complementary mistakes. It underestimates the complexity and multi-functionality of lesbian and gay culture, while at the same time overestimating the 'thickness' or density of the cultures which other national cultures provide. I will look at each of these issues in turn.

Gay and lesbian culture is a recent phenomenon, and because we can see its entire history with relative ease we can achieve a clear idea of the condition lesbians and gay men were in before and after the creation of gay cultural institutions. We can thereby gain an appreciation for the full range of functions which gay culture plays, and thus easily see that it is considerably more than just a special-interest group. Gay culture serves as a fundamental context of choice for its members.

Even as late as the 1950s one would have been hard-pressed to speak of a gay culture. There were no newspapers or magazines, only two small organizations with a minuscule membership (the Mattachine Society and the Daughters of Bilitis) and almost no public spaces where gays and lesbians could assemble without harassment. Local communities, often using vague concepts such as 'community standards,' encouraged their police forces to break up all forms of nascent organization among gay people. Basic civil rights were not yet seen as extending to homosexuals, and gay people frequently became pariahs in their communities.[25] Except in a few major urban centres (and indeed even there) gay people had little or no opportunity to come together to talk about common problems. Without institutions to meet in, and lacking a language to describe their experiences, gay people could be picked off one by one by the various bodies by which communities policed themselves.

The history of the creation of a gay culture in the past three decades can be seen as the gradual use of often evanescent rights to over-

---

25 For a brief overview see 'Witch-Hunt: The United States Government versus Homosexuals,' a collection of news stories from 1950s' editions of the *New York Times* and *Post* gathered by Jonathan Katz in his 'Documentary,' *Gay American History: Lesbians and Gay Men in the U.S.A.* (New York: Thomas Y. Crowell 1972).

come the (frequently fatal) atomism which gay men and lesbians suffered in the 1950s. The initial foundation of an enduring gay public sphere occurred in San Francisco in the late '50s and was directly linked to the court decisions in California that "upheld the rights of homosexuals to congregate in bars and other public establishments."[26] In spite of constant police harassment, these bars became a focus of political organization in the course of the 1960s.[27] Meanwhile, relaxed laws about obscenity in the public sphere allowed the publication of a great number of texts about homosexuals. At first these were, for the most part, highly disapproving, but they nonetheless showed many gay men and lesbians that they were not alone in their experiences. Scholars of nationalism have shown that one of the key features in the phenomenon is the creation of an imaginary community whereby certain people begin to see themselves as making up a unit based on common experiences. The triggers for this sense of community are various. Benedict Anderson writes of how the governing elites of Latin America began to see themselves as making up a different people from their Spanish masters because they continually met each other on the circuits of provincial bureaucratic life.[28] Jeremy Webber writes of how the administration of Canada through provincial governments led to the creation of a distinct sense of community in each province just because each region had such intense dealings with its local authorities.[29] The trigger for the sense of a distinctive gay and lesbian peoplehood came through the way nascent institutions and a greater openness in the mainstream public sphere allowed a clarification of local experiences of stigma and harassment. Bit by bit an

---

26 John d'Emilio, 'Gay Politics, Gay Community,' in *Making Trouble: Essays on Gay History, Politics and the University* (London: Routledge 1992), 74-95

27 I am indebted here to an unpublished thesis by Gina Anne Del Vecchio, 'Homosexual; Homophile; Gay; Lesbian; Queer: The Construction of Gay Political Power in San Francisco,' 21-25.

28 Anderson, *Imagined Communities*, 48–53

29 Jeremy Webber, 'Language, Culture and Political Community,' in *Reimagining Canada: Language, Culture, Community, and the Canadian Constitution* (Montreal: McGill-Queen's University Press 1994), 194-7

imaginary community was created through which gay people could link up their local experiences of violence and harassment with the experiences of other gay men and lesbians across North America and come to see themselves as a people set apart.[30]

The key period in the creation of a gay public sphere was the era of urban radicalism at the end of the 1960s. The generally contestatory atmosphere, the sudden surge of voices formerly locked out of the mainstream public sphere, and the swift creation of a host of overlapping alternative publics gave gay people a set of inspiring models for action. Borrowing techniques and insights from Black Power groups, from the women's movement, and from anti-colonialist struggles in the Third World,[31] gay men and lesbians developed the institutions – collectives and discussion groups, bookstores, magazines and newspapers, 'liberation fronts,' and political lobbying groups – which allowed them to exchange common experiences and to determine that what were formerly seen as isolated individual incidents (police harassment, street violence) could also be seen as a broader pattern of structural discrimination. This growing awareness led to a break with the accommodationist policies which had formerly dominated the movement. Early groups like the Mattachine Society had held an explicitly assimilationist agenda. Gay people would be best off if they could hide their difference and fit in with the mainstream. As the full extent of violence against gay people became clear this strategy was abandoned by many. Only specifically gay institutions could work to erode the attitudinal prejudices in society at large and at the same time give gay people a shelter in which they could restore the self-respect

---

30 John D'Emilio, *Sexual Politics, Sexual Communities: The Making of a Homosexual Minority in the United States, 1940–1970* (Chicago: University of Chicago Press 1983), 146-8

31 See, for example, the various writings gathered in Karla Jay and Allen Young, eds., *Out of the Closets: Voices of Gay Liberation*, twentieth-anniversary edition (New York: New York University Press 1992), particularly 'Out of the Closets, Into the Streets,' by Allen Young, 6-31. For a synoptic overview of the relations between the gay liberation movement and radicalism more generally see also the Foreword to that volume by John D'Emilio, esp. pp. xi-xxix.

and dignity that was thwarted in society at large. "If society is going to turn up the heat in the closet you might as well be out."[32]

One creates culture by creating new institutions, and these new institutions in turn make possible new forms of identity. Gay identity and gay institutions grew up together, mutually influencing one another.[33] The gay cultural institutions which were created serve a number

---

32 Alan Conter, 'Pride and Plague; Stonewall Traces,' radio documentary broadcast on CBC *Ideas*, 28 November 1994. But to say that people leave the closet because the heat has turned up there does not necessarily mean that they will go back in if the heat goes down. We know, from the history of other nationalisms, that nationalist movements have their own momentum. This is why gay culture has to be seen as something more than just a stepping stone to a non-homophobic society. Most of the functions of gay culture, it might be suggested, are essentially aimed at combating the homophobia in society at large. Once this is done away with, gay nationalism will have no further reason to exist. It is thus not like Québécois nationalism, for example, which is basically about guaranteeing the survival of a certain form of cultural difference over time. Gay culture, some might argue, aims at making a certain form of difference acceptable within the mainstream, at which point it will no longer be needed and can disappear.

There is, no doubt, a part of the gay and lesbian population that wishes to be seen as exactly like all other North Americans, and longs for the day when being homosexual will be seen as no more serious or meaningful than being left-handed. But there are also many for whom homosexuality or 'queerness' is seen as defining an ethos and a way of life. For these people sexual preference is just one feature of a much broader way of life based on a radical questioning of everyday institutions, gender roles, and so on. For these people queerness is not a transitional way of life for those on their way into the mainstream but a radically different ethos that needs to be preserved. (See Mark Blasius, 'An Ethos of Lesbian and Gay Existence,' in *Political Theory* **20:4** [November 1992] 642-71.) And the disappearance of homophobia is in any case a highly unlikely event, particularly if the sort of strong pluralism that culturalists advocate is successfully instantiated in North America. Many traditional cultures have deeply homophobic patterns and at least some culturalist writers advocate giving groups powers which would allow them to preserve these homophobic attitudes (see my discussion of Margalit and Halbertal, below). If we move beyond a regime of individual rights and give communities the right to protect their cultural lifeways, cultural rights for gays may end up being even more important than they are now.

33 Rhetorical strategies of performance and self-defense which were first developed in the gay enclaves on the east and west coast were broadcast by the new

---

of crucial functions for those gay people who are able to gain contact with it. It offers, first of all, a space of shelter from the homophobia of the surrounding society.[34] Those who grow up in a social atmosphere which systematically undermines their self-respect need a sphere in which they can restore themselves and imagine a life without this stigma. The institutions of gay culture give gay people a sheltered space in which they can work at countering some of the soul-destroying aspects of the public hatred they so often feel outside.[35] "While you're being persecuted, you hate what's happening to you, you hate the people who are making it happen; you're in a world of hate. Why, you wouldn't recognize love if you met it."[36] The invasive atmosphere of social hatred which the gay narrator of Christopher Isherwood's *A Single Man* describes here can be offset by the existence of a network of alternate public spaces more hospitable to gay and lesbian needs.

---

gay magazines and newspapers and made available as resources for those individuals attempting to carve a niche for themselves in more peripheral locales. Adopting strategies developed in the cities allowed more secure identity-formation for (the gay aspects in the character of) non-urban gays, and this new self-confidence, in turn, encouraged the formation of new institutions in small towns. Local entrepreneurs saw a profit to be made from this new identity-cohort and opened up new spaces for them, spaces which were protected on other levels by the work done by increasingly confident gay people in advancing their case among non-gays. These processes concatenated to gradually ameliorate the living conditions of many gay people in peripheral areas. Or at least, where local struggles were unsuccessful, the movement as a whole created an alternative network into which people could escape from the pressure of small towns.

34 Maurice Leznoff and William Westley, 'The Homosexual Community,' in Wayne Dynes and Stephen Donaldson, eds., *Sociology of Homosexuality* (New York and London: Garland Publications 1992), 219-25

35 Stephen O. Murray, 'Components of Gay Community in San Francisco,' in Gilbert Herdt, ed., *Gay Culture in America: Essays from the Field* (Boston: Beacon Press 1992), 107-46, and Martin P. Levine, 'Gay Ghetto,' in Dynes and Donaldson, eds, *Sociology of Homosexuality*, 196-204

36 Christopher Isherwood, *A Single Man*, quoted in Leslie Green, 'Internal Minorities and Their Rights,' in Baker, ed., *Group Rights*, 112

Gay culture also teaches gay people how to ford a number of difficult obstacles that they face. The literature on 'coming out,' for example, shows gay people how best to deal with the dangerous moment when they inform those around them of the nature of their inclinations.[37] Coming-out narratives show gay people how to call on the latent sources of tolerance in those that they encounter. Same-sex preference also unmoors one from the classic gender roles that our society makes available to us; gay culture supplies a rich body of reflections on, and access to an ongoing discussion about, this profound rupture from habitual practices of role-fulfillment and marriage.[38] Gay culture serves as a context of choice which allows gay men and lesbians to navigate the numerous obstacles which they face in trying to form workable lives for themselves and to preserve their sense of self-respect.

The sense of gay solidarity and community is itself an important participatory good for members of the gay community. Since gay men and lesbians are always in a minority on any given territory on which they find themselves they are very frequently the victims of local majorities who believe that gays do not make up part of the local cultural vision.[39] The only hope that the victims of local persecution have is in the solidarity of the community at large, which can attempt through boycotts, the funding of class action suits and so on, to reverse the political decisions of locals.

Another of the participatory goods produced by the existence of a gay culture is that it allows gay people to perform the duty of rescue

---

37 See Gilbert Herdt, 'Coming Out as a Rite of Passage: A Chicago Study,' in Herdt, ed., *Gay Culture in America*, 29-67; also Barry Dank, 'Coming out in the Gay World,' in Dynes and Donaldson, eds., *Sociology of Homosexuality*, 60-195.

38 Joseph Harry and Robert Lovely, 'Gay Marriages and Communities of Orientation,' in Dynes and Donaldson, eds., *Sociology of Homosexuality*, 135-200.

39 In 1994 a record number of American states faced ballot initiatives attempting to restrict gay rights, encouraged by a similar measure passed by Colorado in 1992. (See Stephen Holmes, 'Gay Rights Advocates Brace for Ballot Fights,' *New York Times*, 12 January 1994, A12.) Lisa Duggan points out that the combined budgets of the six largest gay organizations total only about $12 million, compared to more than $210 million in the combined budgets of the six largest right-wing religious organizations (Lisa Duggan, 'Queering the State,' 1).

they owe to new members of their community. The duty of rescue within the gay community takes on a peculiar form due to the oddity of gay ethnicity. The trait of homosexuality arises as a certain statistical percentage of populations which are otherwise heterosexual. Homosexuals are, in this respect at least, essentially scattered. Gay people thus habitually find themselves living surrounded by a majority of non-homosexuals. But this puts young people with same-sex desires at great risk. We know that the suicide rate among homosexual teenagers who do not find positive homosexual role models is extremely high.[40] Gay people and their supporters thus take the duty of rescue toward these people extremely seriously. The centrality of this duty of rescue is one of the principal reasons that gay people advocate so strongly that homosexuality not be condemned on school curriculums and that students be offered positive models of gay life from a very early age. This need of the gay community to reach out and protect its fellow members also explains why gay people cannot leave gay culture as a matter for the private sphere, and why there is such a deep disagreement of principle between them and the right-wing groups which advocate the complete banning of positive representations of gay life from state institutions.

But to reduce any culture to a sum of its functions is to underestimate it. Like most cultures, that of gays and lesbians is valuable just because it exists, and drawing its members together gives participants a sense of complicity, a sense of belonging.[41] With members of one's own culture there are things that one doesn't have to explain, a sense one will share a number of important and formative experiences in common even with people from radically different backgrounds just because they are lesbian or gay.

---

40 Gary Remafedi, James A. Farrow, and R.W. Deister, 'Risk Factors in Attempted Suicide in Gay and Bisexual Youth,' in *Pediatrics* **87:6** (June 1991) 869-75; and Paul Gibson, 'Gay Male and Lesbian Youth Suicide,' in *Report of the Secretary's Task Force on Youth Suicide 3: Prevention of Youth Suicide* (Rockville, MD: U.S. Dept. of Health and Human Services 1989)

41 I am influenced here by a passage in Alberto Melucci's *Nomads of the Present: Social Movements and Individual Needs in Contemporary Society* (Philadelphia: Temple University Press 1989), which points out the importance of such highly general and evanescent goods in modern social movements.

Given the importance of a sense of gay and lesbian solidarity, and of the range of institutions, narratives, and contexts of choice which gays and lesbians have elaborated, we should see gay and lesbian culture as a very strong contender for collective rights. There are certainly few groups whose members are so vulnerable or so constantly the focus of harassment. There are very few gay people who have not at some point in their lives suffered some form of harassment, and most have had some brush with violence.[42] If cultural institutions would help deal with the effects of this violence and perhaps serve as a beachhead from which to fight this deep (and, it seems, deepening) intolerance, then there seems to be a good *prima facie* case for the granting of such rights.

But surely the mere sense of peoplehood and of the importance of one's culture cannot be enough to establish a claim to nationhood. Modern culturalist theorists tend, with good reason, to emphasize the role of more objective characteristics in judging which groups should be looked upon as nations. The lists of criteria that culturalists set out are usually rather conservative – they are based on characterizations of the sorts of groups that we already tend to look at as nations, and they thus show a bias toward groups emphasized by the theological and racialist paradigms – but even under these conservative characterizations of what it is to be a nation, gays and lesbians would be very strong contenders.

Here, for example, is the way that Avishai Margalit and Joseph Raz set out the core characteristic of the sorts of group they see as proper beneficiaries of collective rights, what they refer to as *encompassing* groups:

> The group has a common character and a common culture that encompasses many, varied and important aspects of life, a culture that defines or marks a variety of forms or styles of life, types of activities, occupations, pursuits, and

---

42 Richard Mohr sketches the extent of the problem in a paragraph of his book *Gays/Justice: A Study of Ethics, Society and Law* (New York: Columbia University Press 1988): "A recent extensive study by the National Gay and Lesbian Task Force found that over 90 percent of gays and lesbians had been victimized in some form on the basis of their sexual orientation. Greater than one in five gay men and nearly one in ten lesbians had been punched, hit, or kicked; a quarter of all gays had had objects thrown at them; a third had been chased; a third had been sexually harassed and 14 percent had been spit on....", 27-28.

relationships. With national groups we expect to find national cuisines, distinctive architectural styles, a common language, distinctive literary and artistic traditions, national music, customs, dress, ceremonies, holidays, etc. None of these is necessary. They are but typical examples of the features that characterize peoples ... people growing up among members of the group will acquire the group culture, will be marked by its character ... The types of career open to one, the leisure activities one learned to appreciate and is therefore able to choose from, the customs and habits that define and color relations with friends, patterns of expectations and attitudes between spouses and among other members of the family, features of lifestyles with which one is capable of empathizing and for which one may therefore develop a taste – all these will be marked by the group's culture. [43]

Raz and Margalit list a few additional features of encompassing groups. One enters such groups not by achievement but simply by belonging. This belonging is recognized by other members of the community as well as by outsiders; the standards for membership are relatively clear. Membership in the group is one of the ways in which people are pigeonholed and their behaviour understood.[44]

Gay men and lesbians make up a cultural group clearly perceived by others as such. This perception is often cast in negative terms (as in the populist movement in the United States and Canada to turn back the 'gay agenda'[45]), but the recognition is common and pervasive. The markers of membership are relatively clear and are broadly recognized by both in-group and out-group members. Gay and lesbian culture has its own ceremonies and holidays (Gay Pride, the Gay Games) and a disproportionate number of the century's musicians, playwrights, directors, and other artists have been gay or lesbian. There is a distinctively gay literature, and entire bookstores are devoted to its products. It goes without saying that membership in the gay community has a significant influence on the people one chooses as spouses, or spousal equivalents, as well as on the roles one takes in the resulting relationship. At least in the eyes of outsiders, gay men and lesbians have certain distinctive styles of dressing and patterns of consumption that

---

43 Margalit and Raz, 'National Self-Determination,' 443-4

44 Margalit and Raz, 'National Self-Determination,' 445-6

45 See Holmes, 'Gay Right Advocates Brace for Ballot Fights.'

differentiate them from the peoples around them. And there are few cultures in North America whose importance in defending its members against the intolerance and violence of others is more obvious.

But there are also several other criteria that Raz and Margalit set out which gay culture does not fulfill. For example, being gay does not tell one much about what career one should choose, nor set out a particular pattern for leisure activities (unless a preference for gay and lesbian public spaces would be seen as a distinctive cultural pattern). Nor do gay men and lesbians have a distinctive architectural tradition. Does a low ranking on these criteria mean that gay culture should not be looked upon as an encompassing group and should thus be passed over as a potential recipient of collective cultural rights?

The problem is that many other groups which we would consider to be the sort to merit self-determination – groups like the Québécois, for example – also rank low on many features on the Raz and Margalit list. Being Québécois does not determine the types of career open to one, nor does it determine patterns of expectations between spouses in the ways that a culture with arranged marriages does (or as gay and lesbian culture does). Modern Quebec does not have a distinctive cuisine as Louisiana Cajuns do, nor does it have an architectural style that sets Quebec buildings off from the mainstream of the International Style and its postmodern derivatives. Lifestyle choices in Quebec vary in some small ways from those of people in the provinces around, but an outsider arriving in Quebec from Los Angeles would find herself doing many of the same things she would do back in LA: skiing on weekends, visiting the video store, watching the same movies, being involved in a similar sort of business and social life. There are differences between the Québécois people and those around them – enough that they are widely seen as the sort of group eligible for a collective right to self-determination – but not so deep that they could reasonably be referred to as an encompassing group. So it seems that there must be some space within the culturalist defense of national groups to class therein cultural communities which are deeply important for their members but which nonetheless fall short of being full encompassing groups.

Indeed if the standard for national status or cultural protection were found to lie in showing that the community was an 'encompassing' one, then there would be few which qualify, at least as far as North American communities are concerned. In an era in which standardized bureaucracies and international firms cross the borders of more and more communities, where each local group finds itself surrounded by institutions which were created in other cultures, there are very few cultural groups which continue to draw their most important narratives of guidance exclusively – or even primarily – from in-group repertoires.[46] National groups serve as contexts of choice, but only in some delimited areas of life. Being Québécois may guide one when it comes to election time, or it may suggest certain political strategies to take up in reference to the federal government of Canada. But like most other cultural frameworks (including that of being gay), it covers only some areas of existence and leaves many others unaddressed, leaving people to be guided in their most important choices by their religious groups, by the media, by the meritocratic standards of the institutions they work in, and by the standards of the various other trans-statal and trans-national institutions to which they belong.

In any case, it is not entirely clear from reading culturalist defenses of collective rights just why it is *encompassing groups* which should be given extra political rights and privileges. The answer that is usually given is that members of encompassing groups rely in a particularly strong way on participation in the institutions of their community. Men raised in an Ultra-Orthodox Jewish community would find their sense of personhood deeply shaken if they were not able to spend much of their time in Torah scholarship, or if they were not able to pass their time among other members of their religious community, thereby linking themselves to its history and traditions and language.[47] Encompassing groups merit extra political privileges because of the crucial role their culture plays in individual personhood.

But it is by no means clear why this should be the case. Why should encompassing groups ask the rest of society to make sacrifices so that these encompassing communities can create a sort of institution and a way of life that will disempower their members and make them uncomfortable with very ordinary things that the rest of their society

---

46 I argue this point at much greater length in Walker, 'Plural Contexts, Contested Territories.'

47 See Margalit and Halbertal, 'Liberalism and the Right to Culture.'

does?[48] It is one thing to say that such groups should not suffer any undue obstacles such as racism or religious intolerance and that they should be allowed to build up whatever powers they can through use of the marketplace and the democratic power of their combined voices. It is quite another thing to say that such groups deserve additional powers because of the sorts of culture they have.

There is an example closer to the North American case that might make the issues at stake in this question somewhat clearer, for there is, in Canada and the United States, a minority cultural coalition which wishes to become an encompassing group. This movement is North American Protestant fundamentalism. The goal of Protestant fundamentalists is to erect the institutional infrastructure which would allow their members to live entirely Christian lives. Particularly important is the need to protect children from influence by an immensely seductive but (in their view) highly immoral and autonomy-harming popular culture. True freedom can only come through obedience to God's will, but children will not see this if in their early lives they are bombarded with messages from alien 'liberal humanist' culture. Without a childhood spent in organizations run by, and in a public sphere patrolled by, members of the church, individuals will be cut off from Christian culture, and the most fundamental part of their lives would be radically diminished. A fully Christian life, they would argue, is only possible if all members have access to a full set of institutions in which the Christian option is fully respected and shown as worthy of living. Without access to such participatory goods (goods that only come into play if a threshold-number of citizens take part in them and keep them alive[49]) the chances for Protestants of this sort to lead full lives would, in their eyes, be radically compromised.

The creation of such cultural movements in civil society is one of the many ways in which a liberal society based on individual rights

---

48 For example, the Ultra-Orthodox Jews whom Margalit and Halbertal concentrate upon require that visitors to their neighbourhood refrain from driving on Sundays or wearing short skirts.

49 I am following here an argument made in Denise Rhéaume, 'Individuals, Groups, and Rights to Public Goods,' in *University of Toronto Law Journal* **38** (1988) 1-27.

allows for the flourishing of cultural diversity. But the culturalist advocates of collective rights would make it possible for groups such as Protestant fundamentalists to claim additional rights and powers on the basis of their need to preserve their culture. For example, according to Avishai Margalit and Moshe Halbertal, a group like this could demand of lesbians and gay men that they not display their lifestyle in any ostentatious way on territories controlled by Protestant fundamentalists, since this would make it difficult for these Protestants to maintain the integrity of their cultural project (Margalit and Halbertal see the cultural rights of communities as allowing them to act so as to guarantee a religious 'atmosphere' in the territories central to these groups).[50] According to the criteria that Margalit and Halbertal set out, as long as gay men and lesbians have other spaces in which they can fully express the lives that they want, the cultural rights of the Protestant fundamentalist community would justify their attempt to control the religious 'atmosphere' of their communities.[51] Not all culturalists go as far as Margalit and Halbertal, but any one of the dominant culturalist arguments could be used by Protestant fundamentalist groups to make claims for collective powers.[52] Culturalists do not frequently give rea-

---

50 Margalit and Halbertal, 'Liberalism and the Right to Culture,' 507

51 Margalit and Halbertal, 'Liberalism and the Right to Culture.' Chandran Kukathas makes a similar argument in 'Are There Any Cultural Rights?' *Political Theory* **20**:1 (February 1992) 105-39.

52 It might be thought that a Will Kymlicka's account, which justifies collective rights only for vulnerable minorities, could not be used in this way, since Protestant fundamentalists seem to be part of the mainstream English-speaking culture. But the notion of dominant culture that Kymlicka uses is too broad to serve the theoretical purpose he wishes. Just because Protestant fundamentalists share a language and ethnicity with the culture around them does not mean that they are not a minority with good reason to see themselves as strongly vulnerable within the liberal mainstream. Indeed, because Protestant fundamentalists share a language and many other cultural referents with the 'liberal humanists' whom they see as threatening, they are in many ways more vulnerable than groups protected by a barrier of linguistic and cultural difference; for example, it is doubly difficult for such Christians to protect their children from what they see as the corrupting influences of the mainstream culture, since television shows, music, and so on are all in a language their children understand.

sons why encompassing groups should receive extra powers, apart from the crucial role that such groups play in the lives of their members (and I have suggested that that is not a convincing reason for extending such rights).

One argument that we do find, especially among European culturalists, is that protecting encompassing groups would allow us to protect a particularly deep form of cultural diversity.[53] They suggest that we might distinguish between two different sorts of cultural diversity which we see around us. There is the deep diversity that distinguishes some cultures from each other and which moves us to see a striking contrast among, for example, traditional Thai society, the potlatch culture of the Kwakiutl, and the lifeways of the Berbers in the Atlas mountains. These represent a *deep* diversity whereas the difference between, for example, homosexuals and heterosexuals in America is nothing but a difference between 'consumer tribes' and the lifestyle choices they represent.[54]

With this contrast in mind we might see culturalists as advocating the maintenance of, or the return to, a form of deep diversity. Within the context of a modern society we might attempt to safeguard this fragile multiplicity of lifeways which embodies radically different ways of looking at the world and its wonders. This is one way of making sense of a preference for encompassing groups which might otherwise seem merely puzzling.

But there are serious problems with this sort of argument. First, there seems to be no way to distinguish between shallow and deep diversity in a non-ideological way, since each group has every interest in portraying its differences as being very profound. From one point of view gay life may be looked on as a mere 'lifestyle choice.' But gay men and lesbians could point out, in response, that their lives represent such a profound questioning of society's conception of gender and power that even aboriginal peoples might seem, by compari-

---

53 See Pierre-André Taguieff, *La force du préjugé: essai sur le racisme et ses doubles* (Paris: La Découverte 1987), 326-33.

54 Mark Wegierski, 'The New Right in Europe,' in *Telos* **98-99** (Winter 1993–Spring 1994) 55-69, esp. 68

son, to align with the mainstream.[55] The notion of cultural deepness is an essentially contested concept. Even if there is some non-ideological core to this concept which might be convincingly set out (and this is by no means obvious) it is still unlikely that the criterion of 'depth of diversity' would be useful for discussing the sorts of differences we find among cultural groups in modern societies. All societies in North America, and in the North Atlantic world in general, are post-traditional ones, in the sense that all are influenced by modern states and markets, all have had their modes of cultural transmission profoundly changed by modern technology, and all exist in an environment where the discourse of rights has an important influence.[56] Can we talk about a deep diversity lying among cultures which all use modern technology, which are all influenced by the market system, where a large proportion of the population performs wage labour, and where everybody feels the influence of rights-discourse? Cultural groups within modern states operate in a context of very similar material conditions, which was not the case for groups such as the Berbers, the late nineteenth-century Kwakiutl, or traditional Thais. The material environment (that of a capitalist world system with its ineluctable constraints) in which cultural groups operate constrains the cultural differences which they can express.

And, in any case, this portrayal of difference seems to miss the way in which the ability to express difference is itself a political resource which groups are fighting for. The profound social and technological transformations of the past half century have produced an environ-

---

55 On the essentially contested idea of deep difference see James Clifford, 'Identity in Mashpee,' an account of judicial attempts to deny the difference of aboriginal cultural specificity that in many ways operates like similar attempts to deny gay and lesbian cultural specificity, in James Clifford, *The Predicament of Culture: Twentieth Century Ethnography, Literature and Art* (Cambridge, MA: Harvard University Press 1988), 277-346.

56 On changes in the environmental conditions of modern cultural reproduction see Ulrich Beck, *Risk Society: Towards a New Modernity*, translated by Mark Ritter (Newbury Park, CA: Sage Publications 1992); Ulf Hannerz, 'Cosmopolitans and Locals in World Culture,' in *Theory, Culture and Society* 7 (1990) 237-51; and Kimmo Jokinen, 'Cultural Uniformity, Differentiation, and Small National Cultures,' in *Cultural Studies* 8:2 (1994) 208-19.

ment of generalized cultural risk in which all cultural collectivities are forced to recognize that immense obstacles stand in the way of their attempts to preserve the integrity of their fundamental institutions and values. Not all groups are affected by this general risk in the same ways, but it is not as easy as it might at first appear to say which groups are most disadvantaged and face the greatest risks.[57] One of the common features which we find in many different sorts of cultural groups, from queers to Ultra-Orthodox Jews, is an attempt to create a sense of specificity and apartness which will offer a sense of orientation and guidance within this invasive and disruptive world-system. When individuals feel themselves part of an intermediate community, be it a religious group, a kinship network, an ethnic party, or some new hybrid such as the gay and lesbian rights movement, there are a number of important functions to which people gain access. The intermediate group serves as buffer and protection in a system which can otherwise leave individuals feeling that they have no voice and no place. It can offer protection, orientation, and a manageable focus for one's social

---

57 One of the facts that is little noted in culturalist works is that the same worries that ethnic minorities voice about cultural decay are just as frequently voiced by members of majority cultures, often with just as much reason. The worries of Anglo-Canadian nationalist George Grant about the onslaught of mechanized mass society are almost exactly the same as those voiced by the 1953 *Tremblay Report*, which was one of the key documents of conservative French-Canadian nationalism (David Kwavnik, ed., *The Tremblay Report: Report of the Royal Commission of Inquiry on Constitutional Problems* [Toronto: McClelland and Stewart 1973]). But while French-Canadian nationalists were able to mobilize ethnic solidarity and post-conquest resentment in order to found a nationalist movement which was, for several decades at least, immensely creative as far as the development of new cultural institutions was concerned, the project of English-Canadian nationalist mobilization was much less successful. Minority status brings groups advantages of solidarity and creativity that are frequently unavailable to majority groups, and can thus serve as compensation for the smaller numbers and ostensibly more fragile structures of minority communities. And, as I pointed out above about Protestant fundamentalists, ostensibly being part of mainstream culture may well be a *disadvantage* for some groups. Anglophone Christians find it difficult to filter 'immoral' media out of their homes. English Canadians have more difficulty maintaining their distinctiveness from Americans since they share a language with their American neighbours.

concern.[58] Each and every cultural group in society would greatly profit from a larger share of common resources which they might employ to make their sense of specificity and peoplehood more secure, to increase the diversity of their institutions and thereby expand the possibilities of their particular form of life. Within the conditions of advanced modernity the ability to create and express forms of cultural difference is itself one of the sought-after goals of political struggle, one of the scarce resources which is the focus of politics. But culturalists tend to *essentialize* difference, to say that some groups (religious groups and traditional ethnic groups) are *deeply* different and deserve protection, and that other groups are only shallowly different and thus should be left to scrabble for what they can get. Instead of being seen as a resource for which people struggle, difference is seen as a characteristic which groups possess intrinsically. Culturalism sets up an aristocracy of difference which attempts to naturalize and de-politicize the struggle over the resources required for differentiation and cultural development.

Cultures in Diaspora

Another way in which culturalists might attempt to deny the gay and lesbian claim to peoplehood would be by drawing attention to the scattered and diasporic nature of gay and lesbian communities. Culturalists might eventually be brought to accept that gay and lesbian culture is something more than just leather pants and disco records and be made to see that it plays a vital role in allowing gays to preserve self-respect in a viciously homophobic environment. Yet culturalists might point out that gays and lesbians are not, for all that, a group which could ever govern itself. It is not a nation because it nowhere possesses sufficient concentration on any territory and thus does not have the infrastructural prerequisites necessary to be considered a nation. And the evils that gay men and lesbians face could scarcely be addressed by these means anyway. Even if gay men and lesbians were to take over some part of

---

58 I am indebted here to Donald Horowitz, 'The Utility of Ethnic Affinity,' in *Ethnic Groups in Conflict* (Berkeley: University of California Press 1985), 74-83.

the island of Manhattan or the city of San Francisco, secede from the surrounding states and set up their own republic, this would not do much good for the culture as a whole. An independent city-state in Manhattan might be valuable place of refuge for gay people persecuted elsewhere, and some such source of refuge seems necessary given the current high rate of violence toward gay men and lesbians. But it would still leave unaddressed the needs of the many gay men and lesbians scattered among other cultural communities. Gays and lesbians are not the sort of nation which fits into the culturalist perspective. In the culturalist view preference should be given to the cultural collectivities which are gathered together on a terrain and can protect their culture by making that terrain reflect the values and aspirations of the group.[59] Gay men and lesbians nowhere fill this function and thus cannot be considered to be fitting claimants to the rights of nations.

There seem to me to be two problems with this. First of all, it under-estimates the diversity of forms of nationhood (especially the fact that non-territorial diasporas also make up legitimate nations, even in the most standard accounts of nationalism[60]) and the diversity of forms which collective rights can take. National self-determination may not be a reasonable option for gay men and lesbians, but constitutional veto rights, affirmative gerrymandering, or Senate seats to guarantee political representation could all serve as alternative means to reflect collective rights for gays and lesbians. A lack of territorial concentra-tion does not necessarily mean that a group cannot exercise cultural rights which give it a say in determining its future.

This is closely connected to the second problem I see with the culturalist attempt to limit gay collective rights claims; namely, its pref-erence for territorial collectivities over diasporic groups. I would sug-gest that the emphasis on ethno-territorial models we find within culturalism cannot be justified if we are concerned with the protection of cultural contexts of choice for all cultures, without prejudice between them. The culturalist preference for ethno-territorial models of cultural

---

59 See Margalit and Raz, 'National Self-Determination,' 458.

60 See, for example, the chapter on diasporas in Hugh Seton-Watson's *Nations and States* (London: Methuen 1977).

preservation over looser forms (which do not require a specific linkage to a particular territory) is under-justified given culturalist goals. Once I have set out the problematic features of the ethno-territorial model I hope that gay and lesbian claims to collective rights will no longer seem like deficient forms of ethno-territoriality but rather as *exemplars* of the sorts of collective claim that might be put forward in a regime where the equal cultural needs of all would be respected. Broaching this question forces me to raise questions of land and property which are at the centre of many nationalist claims (though not of the nationalist claims of gays and lesbians) but to which culturalist defenders of nationalism rarely give sufficient consideration.

The ethno-territorial model of nationalism portrays a cultural group as relating to the territory it occupies as if that territory were a form of property belonging to the group in question. The terrain is looked upon as property first of all in the sense that the principal cultural group is seen as having a privileged right to the resources of the territory and to the fruits of the social cooperation of its citizens. For example, when the government of a state or province or country gives primacy to the cultural project of one of its cultural groups, it usually funds this project with tax money and other resources taken from the common pot, with the justification that one particular cultural project has a privileged relation to the territory. For example, in some forms of popular Québécois nationalism there is an idea that the territory 'Quebec' belongs to the Québécois people, this being understood in terms of *francophones de souche*.[61] It is this relation of belonging which justifies the differential promotion of francophone Québécois culture over the equally legitimate needs of anglophone Quebec culture.

Nationalists consider territory as property in another way as well. The national territory takes on the expressive function that property serves, being made to reflect the group personality of the primary cultural group. When an ethno-territorial group gains control of a terrain

---

61 As, for example, in Bloc Québécois MP Philippe Paré's suggestion that Quebec's political future should be determined, not by a vote which includes anglophone and other minority citizens, but exclusively by 'old-stock Quebeckers,' the implication being that the latter alone are the real Quebeckers. 'Bouchard Chastises Two Bloc MPs,' *Globe and Mail* (28 February 1995) A10.

it uses it as a sort of screen on which central in-group myths are projected, thereby permitting an increased sense of community solidarity. If, as Benedict Anderson suggests, a nation is first of all a way in which people conceive themselves, an imaginary community which they project into the world, then it is by projecting this imaginary ideal onto a landscape that a group sees its best chance to concretize the community and solidify it in time.[62] An ethno-territorial group aims to memorialize itself on its landscape by renaming the land in accordance with the in-group myths; giving new names to boulevards, parks, lakes, and regions, raising landmarks for itself, allowing the landmarks of other groups to fall into disrepair and so on. The historical sedimentation of names that one finds on most territories, the palimpsest which signals the historic presence of many different peoples, is replaced by a more singular vision which represents the myths and collective vision of one people.[63] The monuments and landmarks which permitted other groups to have an affective link with the landscape are suppressed or allowed to decay.

There are at least two strong reasons why, in North America at least, we should favour the claims of diasporic nations very highly *vis-à-vis* ethno-territorial groups which require a privileged relation with their territories.[64] Both stem in one way or another from the incompatibility

---

62 Anderson, *Imagined Communities*

63 Every terrain must be named. But there is an alternative to the exclusions fostered by an ethno-territorial regime. A state which attempts to give fair access to the expressive goods of a terrain would, first of all, recognize and respect the fact that territories always already have a dense history of naming, and avoid homogenizing this, wiping out the traces of a history in which numerous groups have occupied and disputed the land over centuries. When new streets are created, when new boulevards are opened up, or when renaming is necessary, concerns of fairness should lead to a recognition that all groups on the terrain should have a say in the process. New names, for example, might be constructed out of the culture that is always created in between groups struggling together on a territory, in the meta-community formed by their struggle for the same resources.

64 By diasporic nations I am referring to groups like the Armenians, Chinese, Sikhs, Acadians, the Jewish people before the founding of the State of Israel, and to the form of nationality established within modern social movements. Each of

of territorial models of nationalism with the goal of equal access to cultural goods. The first problem is that arising from our concerns with justice for all cultural collectivities. Because nations usually share territories with other peoples they cannot pursue privileged use of the common territory without compromising the similar rights to use for other groups. The privileging of the needs of one group may well be done democratically, in that one group may be in a clear majority over another, but this can still be unjust if the equal cultural needs of minorities are not respected. There are, secondly, problems of political instability. The project of groups with ethno-territorial goals lead them

---

these different national groups is organized quite differently and sometimes the differences are important. For example the Acadian diaspora, the Jewish diaspora before the twentieth century, and social movements such as that of gays and lesbians all represent diasporas without homelands. Likewise, the ethnic Chinese in California and South America are part of a diaspora with no real homeland as such; its roots rest in a triumvirate of cities: Hong Kong, Taipei, and Singapore.

Despite their diversity, these nations have enough in common to be referred to under a common term. Diasporic peoples all find themselves in situations where a large part of their populations are forced to share space and political power with other collectivities; a large portion of the population of the nation will be scattered in situations wherein they live as minorities *vis-à-vis* other groups. Diasporic nations are trans-statal nations, and are, for the most part, organized as networks. Population pockets are joined together by circulation systems which bring personnel and cultural resources from one node to another on the network. In recent times diasporas have been greatly aided by access to forms of technologies which allow goods and people to move about much more quickly than they could in former centuries. New technologies also make possible forms of public space which are not geographically dependent; newspapers, magazines, cable television channels, and a range of telecommunications media allow diasporas to create their own public spaces drawing together people who are widely dispersed in terms of geography. Diasporas create a form of civil society which is no longer specifically rooted in one geographic space. With the profusion of communications technologies, we now live in a world where numerous particularist civil societies can exist simultaneously on the same terrain. This means that modern technologies have raised the possibilities for diasporas to have their own specific cultures which differ from those of their homelands. Thus, for example, the East Indian diaspora has important differences from the culture of India, the Irish in America have different perspectives than the Irish in Ireland, and so on.

into a necessary conflict with other cultural groups because the former wish to use common territory as their own cultural property, and this introduces zero-sum games. The cultural claims of a group which needs property-like control over a territory for its aims can only be satisfied by creating a cultural atmosphere on the landscape which reflects particular in-group needs. But because this cultural image is to be that of just one collectivity and not of all the collectivities who live on the terrain, other cultures are forced into a position of defensiveness.[65] This is why ethno-territorial nationalisms produce counter-nationalisms of a particularly militant variety.[66]

Given these considerations, it makes sense to give a privileged hearing, not to collectivities with ethno-territorial ambitions, but to those groups which can preserve their cultures in the way that disaporas do, namely, in situations where they share power with other groups. Diasporas typically have their own cultural spaces – Chinatown, a Jewish graveyard or synagogue, an Irish pub, gay bars and community centres – but they do not need to project their group narratives over an entire territory. Diasporas cut the connection between culture and land which produces ineluctable potentials for unfairness and conflict within the ethno-territorial model. The greater compatibility with the equal cultural needs of all groups gives diasporas a claim to cultural powers that is at least as strong as those of groups which are concentrated on a territory.

---

65 There is also the problem of homogenization. Although ethno-territorial nationalisms may seen to be introducing a form of cultural distinctiveness *vis-à-vis* adjacent territories and thus increasing diversity from one perspective, it is often the case that this distinctiveness is gained at the expense of diversity *within* the nation's borders. The government conceives a vision of what the culture it is protecting should be, and projects this over all the actually existing institutions on its terrain. The anthropologist Richard Handler has, with considerable subtlety, traced this process at work in Quebec in his *Nationalism and the Politics of Culture in Quebec* (Madison: University of Wisconsin Press 1988). Even a state that tries for a rigorous cultural neutrality is prey to such problems, but a state which has a particular *visage culturelle* in mind will have a whole set of additional difficulties.

66 See Daniel Boyarin and Jonathon Boyarin, 'Diaspora: Generation and Ground of Jewish Identity,' in *Critical Inquiry* **19** (Summer 1993) 693-725, esp. 712-14.

Territorial nations always already possess a range of cultural goods and institutions which makes them power-players in the struggle for resources. But threshold nations, those just coming into being, particularly those which reproduce themselves in diasporic conditions, do not possess such strong institutions, and they thus deal from a position of relative weakness. Yet the cultural goods circulated within these threshold nations are just as crucial to members, and just as fragile, as the parallel goods in traditional nations. By concentrating above all on the groups which have already garnered a broad range of powers ('encompassing groups,' 'territorial nations') culturalists tend to side with the culturally powerful and to ignore the particular needs and interests of emergent groups.

Too many current discussions of collective rights assume a traditionalist definition of nationhood and do not recognize the new modalities of peoplehood that are permitted by changed technological and juridical relations. Modern telecommunications permit cultural communities to arise among non-contiguous peoples and likewise permit identity to be formed around characteristics which have little to do with kinship or ethnicity. In a face-to-face society people formed bonds with those closest to them. In the modern world there are new forms of proximity, and individuals frequently find themselves in closer contact with a telephone friend in another city than with the man living in the apartment next door. Our sense of peoplehood has shifted in response to this. But the modern theories of nationalism and collectivity do not take sufficient account of this fact, operating instead with a model which gives primacy to contiguous territorial collectivities as if these were necessarily the primary repository of cultural heritage.

Conclusion

Diasporas represent one of the many ways in which modern technologies and modes of social organization have changed the processes by which cultures can reproduce themselves, and have thereby changed the range of cultures we find around us. When we become sensitive to the range of cultural creativity and innovation that is produced by cultures which take a diasporic form then we are pushed to question the culturalist concentration on territorial ethnic enclaves. My attempt to unpack the functions of the network of institutions around which gay and lesbian identity is formed could be repeated for many other sorts of non-territorial cultural systems.[67] In the contemporary world-system lifeways and modalities of cultural differentiation no longer inhere primarily in the filiations of ethnic and kinship groups, but are carried by an immense range of different institutions.

If one's definition of national belonging is racialist in orientation then this socio-cultural transformation does not matter. From a race-based perspective the purpose of self-determination is to preserve a form of genetic or sanguinary filiation, not just culture, and so the set of groups one considers oneself called upon to protect is delimited from the beginning. It almost certainly does not include groups such as gay men or fundamentalist Christians. But if the race-based perspective is abandoned for a culturalist one then the transformation and extension of the way in which cultures are produced (and lived) matters a great deal. For if our goal is to protect *cultural* sets and the broad diversity of lifeways then the recognition that cultural production is not essentially ethno-territorial, but can also be created in a diasporic mode, becomes theoretically crucial. Once the shift to cultural criteria is fully achieved then a host of new claims are legitimated. Culturalists are forced to deal not only with the relatively limited number of cultural groups represented by collectivities such as

---

67 One could, for example, make very similar arguments for the humanistic culture which is carried by the university system. The institutions which bring people into contact with the centuries-old tradition of humanistic learning make possible forms of identity which are deeply different from those modes of selfhood made possible by the state and market system. Academics make up a caste which stands apart in many ways (though, like most other cultural groups, not in all ways) from the rest of the societies in which they live. The mode of life that the academic system makes possible is not that of an encompassing group, but academic affiliation, like many other forms of corporate affiliation, quickly comes to colour the entire life of the people who hold it. This lifeway has been remarkably responsive to and enlightening about the development of modernity. But the widespread campaign to replace the humanistic focus of the university with a more market-oriented approach poses threats to this lifeway which are similar to those felt by ethnic populations which feel themselves threatened by sociological change.

aboriginal peoples and Québécois, but also with all the other cultural collectivities by means of which people orient themselves in modern society. In the nineteenth century it might have made some limited sense to focus one's concern for cultural protection on ethnic collectivities and religious groups. But it is no longer justifiable to do so in the late twentieth century.

As I stressed above, the recognition of these difficulties within culturalism should be seen as entailing more than just the expansion of culturalist protections to groups such as gay men and lesbians. I think that it should lead us to question the whole idea that we can react to the fragility of our minority cultures by devolving political powers and extending collective rights to a particular subset of cultural collectivities. All of the criteria by which we might determine which groups deserve such rights and powers – considerations such as cultural fragility, cultural importance, depth of difference, and so on – are essentially contested terms. Every cultural collectivity sees itself as fragile and threatened, as needing more resources to protect the heritage of patterns which it sees as representing its particular deeply individual and important contribution to the world's stock of patterns. There are few collectivities in society which would not benefit from a share of the common pot in order to promote their ways of seeing and living the world, thereby increasing their sense of self-respect and well-being. The fight for the resources that might promote such cultural differences is the very stuff of politics. Political and legal theorists can address the conditions of fairness in which the struggle takes place but they cannot set themselves up as cultural gamekeepers deciding which groups should be given the means to help themselves and which should be forced to struggle on their own.

This is not to say that legal and political theorists can afford to abstain from a concern with cultural institutions. The arguments which culturalists make about the connection between rights, liberties, and our potentially fragile background practices links them in with a long line of thinkers, from de Tocqueville to Habermas, who have given ample reasons for such concerns. What I am questioning is whether political and legal theorists should approach this theme in a way that requires them to rank the claims of the various groups which struggle with each other in inter-ethnic politics. Reviving dense and satisfying cultural practices and communities within our new socio-economic order is a problem faced by all collectivities. Each collectivity, of course, has its own specific needs, but there are also institutions which might reasonably be referred to as making up a cultural commons because they respond to needs that all groups have. The fundamental institution of guaranteed rights and liberties, for example, was conceived in an era of confessional strife so that members of diverse religious communities could coexist in relatively peaceful terms. Although these rights and liberties are monitored by measuring their effect on representative individuals, their overall influence has been to foster the development of a diverse agglomeration of communities (as the gay and lesbian example shows). Thus in the countries where these rights and liberties are well protected we see a broad diversity of communities, with Protestant fundamentalists, Catholics, Jews, Muslims, aboriginal nations, Québécois, Chinese, and WASPs all enjoying access to their own communities.

There are many other institutions which similarly serve the cultural needs of all groups in society. For example, under certain conditions, when a country preserves a differentiation between state, market, and civil society, a space becomes available in which local communities have a good chance of making over everyday life in a way they consider appropriate.[68] This differentiation serves all groups in society, and, conversely, all groups suffer when the state or the market invades most areas of social life. There are also specific institutions such as universities which are used by all cultural groups to think about their development and their place in the world, their relation to other groups, and so on. Another example of an institution of the cultural commons is the institution of the eight-hour work day. When a certain amount of leisure time is available to citizens, a minority will usually devote themselves to the maintenance of locally appropriate infrastructures and the development of new cultural institutions. Free time is a central cultural resource and its disappearance or invasion means that an important space for cultural creation closes over. One could list many other such institutions, many of

---

68 This point is well argued by Jean Cohen and Andrew Arato in *Civil Society and Political Theory* (Cambridge, MA: MIT Press 1992), xvi.

which are currently fragile and threatened, which serve the cultural ambitions of most groups in society.

Social movements which cast themselves as nationalisms force us to face an important set of questions about the ways in which the conditions of peoplehood have changed in the contemporary world. Taking gay and lesbian nationalism seriously encourages us to think about the claims of nascent nationalisms and to the weight which we might attribute to their cultural needs and interests. It also moves us to question the valorization of territorial nationalisms which we find in current culturalist theory. But most of all the case of gay and lesbian nationalism forces us to question the aristocracy of difference which is created by the culturalist way of ranking self-determination claims. If we take all these questions seriously I think we will be forced to recognize that culturalism does not represent a successful transposition of nationalism into post-racialist terms.

PART V

A Case Study

CANADIAN JOURNAL OF PHILOSOPHY
Supplementary Volume 22

"Seek Ye First the Economic Kingdom!" In Search of a Rational Choice Interpretation of Quebec Nationalism

JOEL PRAGER
Saskatchewan Finance

In Eastern Europe, when someone dies, the custom is to drape mirrors in the house with black muslin or a dark sheet. According to folklorists, this is done so that the deceased, who is believed to wander through his or her house for nine days saying goodbye to friends and family, will not be frightened when he or she cannot find his or her reflection in the mirror. While it is easy to scoff at such superstitious customs, there is much to learn from them. The draping of the mirrors is a vivid metaphor, but it is also useful when it comes to making a counter-intuitive point: namely, little systematic attention has been paid to the role of economic preferences, markets, and the pace of development in shaping Quebec's nationalist objectives and strategy. And it is this failure to comprehend the impact that economics, from a microscopic and macroscopic level, has had on 'nation-building' and, more concretely, on the October 30th referendum (where in answer to the question "Do you agree that Quebec should become sovereign, after having made a formal offer to Canada for a new Economic and Political Partnership, within the scope of the Bill respecting the future of Quebec and of the agreement signed on June 12, 1995?", 49.5 percent of Quebeckers voted 'Yes') that is tantamount to a 'draping of the mirrors,' of providing an incomplete explanation about the bases of Quebec's nationalism. Both the Canadian confederation and Quebec separatism are far from dead, but our one-sided preoccupation with non-economic explanations inadvertently prevents us from seeing the 'reflection in the mirror,' i.e., fully understanding the nature and appeal of the nationalist enterprise.

To be sure, it can be argued that those Quebeckers who voted 'Yes' were motivated to protect their language, their culture, and their 'distinct society,' but opinion polls do not strongly support such conclusions. This can be seen from a poll conducted by Léger & Léger in June 1995 which focused on individuals whose first language of use at home is French. When asked "If Quebec remains in Canada, do you think that the French language could one day disappear in Quebec?", 13 percent of those interviewed replied 'very likely,' and 23 percent said 'somewhat likely'; 30 percent, however, answered 'not very likely,' and 34 percent said 'not at all likely.'[1] This should come as no surprise. Francophones now control Quebec's economy, and there is no longer a significant income disparity between francophone and anglophone workers. What's more, the number of francophones is greater now than it was twenty years ago, and there are more bilingual speakers in the province than ever before. Given these changes, it is not necessarily a statistical aberration that 64 percent of Quebeckers interviewed by Léger & Léger did not see the French language at risk.

If language was not at risk, what then did Quebeckers fear? What did they want? Ironically, during the referendum campaign Ottawa and the provincial Liberals focused on the grave economic consequences awaiting Quebec if it seceded from Confederation. And a number of books and institutional studies appeared more or less at the same time, for example, Kimon Valaskakis and Angéline Fournier's *The Delusion of Sovereignty*[2] and Alan Freeman and Patrick Grady's *Dividing the House: Planning for a Canada Without Quebec,*[3] warning that the province's standard of living and quality of life would plummet if Quebeckers voted 'Yes.' Was the referendum a case of culture versus economics?

But conventional wisdom now has it that the No forces' focus on the dollar and cents ramifications of a Yes vote was misconceived and

---

1 John Richards, *Language Matters: Assuring that the Cube of Sugar not Dissolve in the Cup of Coffee* (unpublished manuscript, 1996), 45, and Rheal Seguin, 'French in Quebec Called Vulnerable,' *Globe and Mail* (2 February 1996), A1

2 Kimon Valaskakis and Angéline Fournier, *The Delusion of Sovereignty* (Montreal: Robert Davies 1995)

3 Alan Freeman and Patrick Grady, *Dividing the House: Planning for a Canada Without Quebec* (Toronto: Harper Collins 1995)

self-defeating because 60 percent of francophones voted with their hearts and souls, rather than with their heads and pocketbooks. Another view that has lately gained greater prominence is that the close outcome of the referendum vote happened because a majority of francophone Quebeckers still feel an historical sense of humiliation and resentment when they recall that they are not masters in their own house. Finally, some survey analysts have suggested that the Yes vote was the product of a long-term weakening in the attachment of Quebeckers to Canada. Simply put, the sum was no longer greater than its parts. While each of these interpretations may seem to be a variation on a common theme, economic considerations – so it would seem in retrospect – were not as powerful as originally thought, and Ottawa would have therefore been wiser if it had developed a strategy based on "counteract[ing] a dream ... by proposing a better dream."[4] But, of course, this leads to the question: What was wrong with the original dream of Confederation?

Yet the jury is out as to why the referendum was so close. Warnings about economic gloom and doom if Quebec should leave Confederation are not new. During the 1970s and 1980s, for example, Quebeckers had heard similar predictions, but such threats proved to have little credibility. Even with Parti Québécois governments and their avowed commitment to separate from Canada and create an independent Quebec, there were not many negative repercussions. True, a large number of anglophones left the province, but the federal government and the international financial community did not impose harsh economic conditions and Quebec did not experience severe economic dislocations. Many Quebeckers continued to prosper. Sovereigntists, moreover, were sensitive to the economic self-immolation argument and shrewdly replied that after a Yes vote, sovereignty association would soon follow on the heels of the referendum, Canada would quickly enter into economic arrangements with an independent Quebec, and despite the forecasts of economic disaster, it would be business as usual. Canada, economically speaking, needed Quebec as much as Quebec needed

---

4 Edward Greenspon, 'The Battle to Keep Canada Whole,' *Globe and Mail*, 29 June 1996, A1, and Richard Mackie, 'Yes 50.2, No 49.8, Poll Suggests,' *Globe and Mail* (21 October 1995), A1

Canada. In short, the more things changed, the more they would continue to remain the same.

Of course, one poll does not make or destroy a nation. And a careful reading of the Léger & Léger poll does not indicate beyond a reasonable doubt that language does not matter or that culture does not count for Quebeckers, especially when the issue of independence is at stake. Of course they do. The question is how much and whether or not other factors are at work in shaping Quebeckers' responses to nationalist and separatist appeals. The Léger & Léger findings reveal that language does not provide the lone definitive explanation of why so many francophone Quebeckers were prepared to consider leaving Confederation, if 64 percent of those interviewed do not believe that their language risks extinction if Quebec remains in Canada.

But do economic considerations matter? And if so, what role do they play in Quebec separatism? This paper shall argue that economic preferences and expectations do matter and what we presently lack is a coherent, sophisticated, economic interpretation of contemporary Quebec nationalism. It is, however, not my intention to present a comprehensive economic theory or model that purports to explain Quebec nationalism. I have no theory and know of no theory that does this or has the power to do this. In fact, I openly admit that my analysis is not at all rigorous as conventionally understood by economists, and much of it is impressionistic, based largely on a few opinion polls, intuition, and a culling of the literature on rational choice theory and economic nationalism. I also admit to having an intellectual bias that prevents me from taking seriously those who believe one economic theory fits all nationalistic events, regardless of time or place. Furthermore, I do not believe that the social sciences are capable of developing ironclad laws that are universally applicable in time or space. At best, we can talk about necessary conditions, preconditions, and prerequisites, but not sufficient conditions. Mencken must have had grand theorists in mind when he said that "complex problems have simple, easy-to-understand wrong answers."

Nationalism and separation are neither inevitable nor foreordained simply because a common language, culture, or religion exist. Countless case studies have demonstrated this time and time again. It is unfortunate that so much of the history of nationalist movements continues to be seen in terms of absolute turning points, driven by immutable laws and described in an almost linear fashion. Life is much more complex than monocausal explanations would have us believe, and for most of the time, the real world refuses to be put into a theoretical pigeonhole. At the end of the day not only does the devil dwell in details, which are more often than not complex and confusing, but studies purporting to examine the same nationalist movement often contradict one another. A.W. Orridge captures this multidimensional aspect of nationalism when he writes, "[T]here is no indispensable basis of a community."[5] Yet we continue to assume that there is indeed an 'indispensable basis of a community,' be it language, ethnicity, or religion.

I make no special claims about the superior power of economic analysis except that it is no better or worse than competing theories or approaches. It is just a method of analysis that has been fruitfully applied to a wide range of problems, including the understanding of human behaviour and the relationship of means to ends. Economists, try as they may, are not philosopher-kings. Too much meaning has been lost by ignoring historical details, goals, and the context of action. Like George Akerlof, I think that much of economics as it is currently practised is unduly restrictive. Akerlof brilliantly captures this when he writes:

> [E]conomic theorists, like French chefs in regard to food, have developed stylized models whose ingredients are limited by some unwritten rules. Just as traditional French cooking does not use seaweed or raw fish, so neoclassical models do not make assumptions derived from psychology, anthropology, or sociology. I disagree with any rules that limit the nature of the ingredients in economic models.[6]

---

5 A.W. Orridge, 'Separatist and Autonomous Nationalisms: The Structure of Regional Loyalties in the Modern State,' in Colin H. Williams, ed., *National Separatism* (Vancouver: UBC Press 1982), 47. See also Alex Rosenberg, 'The Metaphysics of Microeconomics,' *The Monist* **78** (1995) 352-67

6 George A. Akerlof, *An Economic Theorist's Book of Tales* (Cambridge: Cambridge University Press 1994), 2-3

I A Personal Reminiscence

It may seem strange to include an autobiographical sketch in what is otherwise, for all intents and purposes, a paper interested in interpreting Quebec's resurgent nationalism as a manifestation of economic forces that have been evolving over the past fifty years. Understandably, career bureaucrats like me do not usually talk about their personal experiences, since these are often seen as being extraneous and self-serving. They also risk violating the rule of confidentiality. My reminiscence, however, does not involve a discussion of state secrets. It is really an explanation of how I became interested in Quebec nationalism and economic regionalism in the first place, why both subjects still continue to fascinate me, and why I strongly believe that researchers should focus more of their time and resources on examining the economic dynamics and bases of Quebec's nationalist movement.

My interest in Quebec separatism stems from the days that I worked in Ottawa as part of a small team of researchers and advisors deeply involved in patriating the Canadian constitution. From my privileged vantage point – there were only three of us who reported to a few key Opposition politicians – it soon became apparent that in the rush to patriate the constitution from Westminster many basic political and economic problems were wilfully ignored, in the hope that they would go away. Working side by side with provincial delegations and participating as an observer at *in camera* meetings, I soon clearly saw that there was no such thing as a level economic playing field, and that, with the exception of an economic miracle such as a resource bonanza or a stratospheric increase in the price of wheat, little would change to upset the economic relationship between the have and have-not provinces.

Watching the manoeuvring during the constitutional hearings soon revealed what everybody knew, but turned a blind eye to at public forums and media scrums: that some provinces were much more equal than others, and staying in Confederation was all right as long as it was profitable. Robert Bourassa had been very candid about this cash-nexus federalism when he said in a 1971 interview:

> There must be additional powers granted to Quebec. If they don't understand this legitimate concern of the Québécois, there will be a brutal awakening. But I

must admit that we are ready to show considerable flexibility because it pays financially. Even if we became an independent country, there would have to be a common policy. There are several powers that it is to our advantage to leave to the federal government because it is profitable. In fact, federalism is a technique of administration that can make it possible for us to garner important sums of money.[7]

Of course, Premier Bourassa was not the only one playing the profitable federalism game. All the provincial premiers were involved in the 'gimme game,' although a bystander would have the distinct feeling that as soon as the money stopped, the strains and discontent among the regions and the federal government would reappear with a vengeance and cause serious disagreements that could no longer be swept under the proverbial rug as they had in the past. Intergovernmental politics was not simply driven by competing concepts of social justice or by idealism, but was really economics 'by other means.'

This is not to say that the majority of those attending the constitutional conferences and public hearings were so hypocritical or cynical that they thought they were participating in an elaborate political scam. I recall, especially during the early stages of the patriation debate, that there was a feeling of euphoria among the participants, stoked by the prospect of patriating the British North America Act, writing a new constitution and Charter of Rights, building the groundwork for a more perfect Confederation. The power relationships, institutional arrangements, processes, and the so-called tacit political rules of the games that defined Confederation were not then perceived as being incapable of change. There was a rough consensus that political and economic reform was still possible, and that tough bargaining would lead to creative constitutional engineering and compromise. The idea of a Canadian Confederation still carried with it deeply felt and generally shared feelings of common purpose and nationhood. As much as there was concern to protect provincial rights, economic interests, and sovereignty, there was also a sense of collective responsibility and belonging. Everyone recognized that we were involved in what historians like to call a

---

7 In William Johnson, *A Canadian Myth: Quebec, Between Canada and the Illusion of Utopia* (Montreal: Robert Davies 1994), 108

watershed, a pivotal moment in Canada's history, and we did not want to let it slip through our fingers. But there was no sense that this moment was the last chance of preventing Canada from becoming invertebrate, a victim of its own institutional arrangements.

Since that time I have often asked myself what went wrong. How did we let what promised to be a golden political opportunity to make long overdue institutional reforms slip through our fingers? In retrospect, I think part of the answer lies with our belief that a liberal constitution could effectively control regional alienation and that a Charter of Rights would tighten the bonds of nationhood. In an interesting article on America's turbulent 1960s and 1970s, Louis Menand provides some insight into understanding why liberalism and, closer to home, the Charter of Rights failed to live up to the expectation of diminishing Quebec's separatist aspirations and moderating regional alienation. Menand writes:

> This liberalism failed ... because it prescribed more liberalism for situations in which liberalism was the problem.... And each time liberalism responded to attacks on it with more liberalism, it exposed a little bit more of the vacancy at its heart. For when the crisis is procedural ... liberalism has the answers. But when the crisis is existential, liberalism offers nothing – just due process.[8]

Menand's point is that procedural reforms, while excellent in themselves, cannot help much when what are needed are major structural reforms, i.e., introducing sweeping changes to Confederation's institutional and fiscal arrangements and reapportioning the division of powers between Ottawa and the provinces. This point was brought home by a recent postmortem of the 1995 Quebec referendum. The writer, who is anonymous, notes that Pierre Trudeau's vision of a bilingual Canada:

> ... simply did not address the main issue preoccupying most of the five million French-speakers in Quebec itself. Most were simply not that thrilled by French-speaking postal clerks in Vancouver. Nor did they care how many well-meaning English-speaking parents across Canada were educating their children in French. It was not the general survival of French they were worried about. What they wanted above all was to prevent Montreal from becoming a city in which English-speakers would outnumber those for whom French had become the

---

8 Louis Menand, 'You Say It's Your Birthday,' *The New Republic* (18 April 1988) 38

central characteristic of identity. But Mulroney vastly underestimated the hostility that almost all other Canadians – who had come to accept Trudeau's 1982 Charter of Rights, and who were becoming more and more influenced by the American concept of individual rights in general – would have to any agreement that enshrined a special position for French-speakers as a collectivity.[9]

Nor did English-speaking western provinces want to be treated as supplicant provinces; they resented playing second fiddle to central Canada's economic and political priorities and Ottawa's fiscal imperium.

Not surprisingly, politicians turned a blind eye to fundamental economic problems. The economics of Confederation were never a high priority during the constitutional discussions, despite the fact that Quebec and the western provinces were openly unhappy with the status quo. Interprovincial trade barriers, transportation and tariff policies that openly discriminated against the western provinces, for example, were rarely discussed in detail. Yet they were a constant source of friction between the provinces. For those who think that interprovincial trade barriers were really an inconsequential problem, a sort of tempest in a teapot, Frank R. Flatters and Richard Lipsey's call to arms makes for interesting reading. Writing in 1983, one year after the passage of the Constitution Act, they claimed:

> Our survey of the state of the Canadian market and the divisive forces acting on it leaves us to conclude that sustained effort and foresighted policy measures will be necessary to prevent Canada from being pulled down by these forces. If we do not want the judgement of history to be that the realities of politics and economics were stronger than the vision of nationhood for a people that were neither American nor European but a distinctive third force of their own, then acts of foresight and statesmanship are needed.
>
> The preservation of Canada requires recognition of the pervasiveness of the present divisive forces of apparent provincial and federal self-interest, and the creation of a strong set of institutions that will keep forces in check in the longer run self-interest of all Canadians.[10]

---

9 *Shattered Myths and Failed Incantations: The Meaning of the Quebec Referendum* (Toronto: Brendan Wood International 1995), 6

10 Frank R. Flatters and Richard Lipsey, *Common Ground for the Canadian Common Market* (Montreal: Institute for Research on Public Policy 1983), 45

Lastly, some of the blame must be assigned to Pierre Trudeau's leadership. Trudeau was not out of touch when it came to patriating the constitution and drafting the Charter of Rights without Quebec's consent, as far as most Canadians were concerned. He was, however, blindsided by his own strongly held views on Quebec separatism. He had a narrow view of federalism which, when stripped of rhetoric, closely resembled French *étatisme*. He had little understanding of or interest in the regions outside of central Canada. One story that was popular at the time was about a speech he had supposedly given in Lethbridge, Alberta, during which he imperiously asked: "Why should I be concerned about selling your wheat?" He failed to ask his audience "why should Alberta want to stay in Confederation if I have no interest in selling your wheat?" Trudeau's *modus operandi* was to 'hang tough' and take the offensive. Implicit in this strategy was the belief that sooner or later the recalcitrant regions and their parochial premiers would smarten up and recognize that opposing Ottawa's political, economic, and fiscal agendas was a 'no-win' game. All of this struck me as Ottawa's version of gunboat diplomacy. To make matters worse, the Prime Minister's indifference to fiscal and economic matters appeared to me to be a disaster in waiting. The Prime Minister did not understand or really want to understand the context in which he had to operate. He preferred to ignore it, and when that proved not always possible, he tried to bulldoze his opponents into submission. Trudeau did not walk softly, and was not afraid to use his big stick.

I am well aware that reminiscences are always vulnerable to the dangers of faulty memory, selective amnesia, and 'scoundrel' time. And I concede that they are not a substitute for the more exacting task of analyzing the interplay of culture, language, and economics on Quebec's separatist aspirations and behaviour. The patriation of a constitution is an exquisitely complicated affair at the best of times, but in our rush to bring the Canadian constitution home, we took too many short cuts, and refused to face many divisive issues openly and candidly. Interestingly enough, Joe Clark, who was then Leader of the Opposition, raised the idea of a Canada composed of 'communities among communities,' but it went nowhere. Trudeau, the national media, and much of Clark's caucus were not interested, and the idea of a more decentralized Canada was never developed into an alternative constitutional vision worthy of serious debate.

Ten years later, despite the Constitution Act of 1982, Canada is more divided, more regionalized, more alienated then ever before. Certainly Trudeau's vision failed to bring Quebec emotionally into Confederation. Polling studies show that francophone Quebeckers are now divided into three groups: those who continue to have a strong emotional attachment to Canada; those whose attachment is essentially based on economic advantage; and those who have no attachment at all. Between 1980 and 1991, those belonging to the second and third groups have substantially increased. For example, francophones feeling strongly attached to Canada dropped from 56 percent to 30 percent, and according to Angus Reid, "this correlates with support for sovereignty." Moreover, those identifying themselves as Québécois rose from 21 percent in 1970 to 59 percent in 1990 while those calling themselves Canadian fell from 34 percent to 9 percent.[11]

The increasing loss of francophone attachment to the rest of Canada raises fundamental political and economic questions that sooner or later will need to be addressed. Should an imputed national interest take precedence over a provincial one? Where do the long-term interests of the provinces lie? Above all, what political and economic guidelines should the provinces use in deciding when the national interest is at stake and how much to give up in pursuit of national interest? Is there really such a prize as a 'win-win' solution, one that produces an equal sharing of economic burdens and a more equitable distribution of national income? And if Quebec remains in Confederation because of economic reasons, should other provinces be expected to act differently?

William Watson, a well-known McGill University anglophone economist, recently argued that Canadians must face

> the unpleasant but also the unavoidable fact that many Quebeckers have little if any interest in being part of the Canadian 'sharing community'. That poor people in the Maritimes might be treated better or worse than their counterparts in Manitoba would strike few emotional chords among Quebeckers. For many English Canadians it would be a cause for at least a small scandal.[12]

---

11 In Michael Keating, *Nations Against the State* (New York: St. Martin's Press 1966), 83

12 William Watson, 'Two Thumbs Up for Latter Day Birth (or Death) of a Nation,' *Canadian Public Policy* **18** (1992) 108

There are enough opinion polls to suggest that Watson may not be entirely wrong. But, if he is right, what do we do next? Can Confederation continue to survive if the idea of a sharing community is no longer acceptable to Quebec? Or to Ontario, British Columbia, and Alberta? That what matters is whether federalism continues to be profitable to the provinces? We need to debate these issues, but there is, as of yet, no strong will to do so. Instead, we act as if Confederation is 'in bondage to history.'

Hindsight, it has been said, is an exact science. Whether we could have changed the flow of events with the knowledge we now possess, I do not know, but I doubt it. Still the memory of what we did and what we could have done differently lingers and continues to shape my thinking about the bases of Quebec nationalism, the economics of Confederation, and the continued survival of Canada as a confederal state.

II The Need for Economic Explanation

Why are Quebeckers favourably disposed or opposed to sovereignty? This choice partly depends upon the prospective evaluation of the costs and benefits of sovereignty and federalism. What are the relative contributions of economic and linguistic expectations to this choice? Does the impact of these expectations vary according to the time horizon in which they are set? Our logistic regression analysis shows that the implicit calculation of costs and benefits plays a significant role in the choice between sovereignty and federalism, and that economic expectations influence the formation of opinion to a somewhat greater degree than do linguistic expectations. Moreover, medium-term expectations are more important than short-term expectations and more important than long-term expectations about the situation of the French language in Quebec.[13]

So much has been written about the cultural, linguistic, and ethnic bases of Quebec nationalism that it is easy to miss the forest for the

---

13 André Blais, Pierre Nadeau, and Richard Nadeau, 'Attentes economiques et linguistiques et appui a la souverainte du Quebec: une analyse prospective et comparative,' *Canadian Journal of Political Science* **27** (1995), 637–57

trees, to forget that economics matters and that money counts. Maurice Lamontagne understood the powerful role that economics plays in the politics, perceptions, expectations, and aspirations of *les Québécois* when in 1954, before the halcyon days of the Quiet Revolution, he warned those determined to modernize the Quebec state and preserve its distinctness as a francophone society that:

> We must fully recognize that the large majority of citizens judge a particular political situation according to its concrete results and not in abstract terms, that is, on the basis of the promises of a new ideology. What people really desire is a satisfactory standard of living and it is only when they are convinced that their economic and political institutions are not accomplishing this fundamental objective that they become attracted by new ideologies.[14]

As we shall see, Lamontagne's warning did not fall on deaf ears, and throughout much of the past thirty years Quebec politicians, intellectuals, federalists, and separatists have been aggressively engaged in creating a modern economy for Quebec, developing a new middle class, and building an economic infrastructure and milieu designed to stimulate industry and commerce and reward francophone entrepreneurs. They believed that this was necessary if Quebec was to have the large number of well-paying jobs for francophones and the revenues needed to free the province from its economic dependence on Canada, to enable it to stand up to Ottawa, and to strike out on its own as a modern trading nation-state.

While I have no way of proving this, René Lévesque and Jacques Parizeau (and, for that matter, other prominent separatists) instinctively and intellectually understood that Quebec could not survive as an independent state if it continued to have an underdeveloped economy. They knew that Marx was wrong; that urbanization, industrialization, increasing literacy and communication, and a higher standard of living would not lead to convergence, assimilation, or acculturation, but instead would result in divergence, greater self-awareness, and the confidence to compete in the global marketplace. Both men also recognized that frustration, anger, and a collective sense of relative

---

14 Cited in Michael Behiels, *Prelude to Quebec's Quiet Revolution* (Kingston, ON: McGill-Queen's University Press 1985), 185

deprivation do not automatically produce or sustain an active and powerful nationalist movement. Quebeckers needed to believe that their economic future was secure and promising. Richard Hamilton and Maurice Pinard seem to confirm this assessment. In a 1980 study examining the electoral basis of Parti Québécois support through extensive survey analysis they found that

> Economic and social-psychological grievances amongst Québécois are tempered by fears of possible economic decline accompanying separation, (and) which remind us forcibly that the separatist option is as much an act of faith as it is of cold, calculating reason.[15]

Both men, especially Jacques Parizeau, I suggest, also recognized that economic nationalism based on some form of economic autarky was impossible and ultimately self-destructive, and that Quebec had to diversify its economy and look outward. I would argue that they 'selectively' accepted and developed an economic development strategy based on what I shall call Cobban's Theorem. Cobban made the following points:

1. A state that has political stability and recognized national independence need not fear the existence of economic ties with greater powers. The establishment of closer economic relations is indeed one step towards taking the sting out of the existence of separate political sovereignties.

2. Because small states are economically dependent on greater ones it is sometimes declared that they must therefore be deprived of their autonomy. This is an attitude which should be recognised as unnecessarily provocative.

3. The real choice for the small nations lies between being tossed about helplessly at the mercy of the whim of great powers and the elemental play of uncontrolled economic forces, or joining in a coordinated economic system, in which their voices, if small, will be audible, and their interests taken into consideration.

4. Even at the height states [can]not become self-contained economic units, and the small states that [are] most successfully economically [are] those that (are) able to build up a position for themselves in a wider nexus of economic relations.

---

15 Cited in Colin H. Williams, ed., *National Separatism* (Vancouver: University of British Columbia Press 1982), 13-14

5. It must be recognized that the smaller nations, whether they are politically independent or not are bound to rely economically on their relations with greater units.[16]

One important qualification is necessary. I do not mean to suggest that there has not been considerable diversity and differences of opinion within separatist ranks or that many of the major luminaries of the movement did not differ over timing, tactics, strategy, or policy. They did and still do. Nor do I wish to suggest that Quebec's economic take-off was linear, or primarily the result of the efforts of a few die-hard nationalists following a coherent, comprehensive, master plan specifically designed to generate economic growth and modernization. There were no five-year economic development plans in place or a clear idea of how best to get on with the task of making Quebec an economic powerhouse. As Michael Behiels so aptly observes:

> World War II proved to be a turning point in the history of contemporary Quebec. The renewal of industrialization and urbanization on a massive scale guaranteed the decline of a fragile agricultural society and ensured the demise of a highly mythologised rural way of life. The industrial economy, with its smoke-belching factories, its centralizing and monopolistic tendencies, would henceforth have a predominant role in the development of the province and in the lives of its people. Quebec had experienced significant levels of industrialization and urbanization since the 1870s but these phenomena had never penetrated, to any significant degree, the collective identity of the French-Canadian people....
>
> In the end, it was the social repercussions of industrialization and urbanization that set in motion, fed, and continually reinforced the demand of the new Francophone middle-class intelligentsia for a rigorous examination and eventual reformulation of Quebec's socioeconomic and political institutions, and the ideologies, values, and norms of behaviour underpinning those institutions....[17]

Having said this, it would be wrong to conclude that there was not a rough consensus among many of the leading personalities involved in the separatist movement about what had to be done and what needed to be avoided if Quebec was to reach a stage of economic development

---

16 Alfred Cobban, *The Nation State and Self-Determination* (New York: Thomas Y. Crowell 1969), 280

17 Behiels, *Prelude*, 8, 18-19

Joel Prager

that would make independence a feasible and attractive option to francophone Quebeckers regardless of class or income. It is therefore not surprising that Quebec's political leaders throughout the 1980s and 1990s have looked favourably at some form of sovereignty association and were among the most avid supporters of the Free Trade Agreement between Canada and the United States and the North American Free Trade Agreement that eventually brought Mexico into the pact.

To fully appreciate the strides that have been made in developing Quebec's human, technological, commercial, managerial, and financial resources, it is useful to recall that, according to the 1961 census, francophones living in Quebec and comprising 80 percent of the province's population earned two-thirds of the national average income; more than half of those in the 20-plus age cohort did not have a grade 8 education; and those receiving a university education amounted to a minuscule two percent of the population. The numbers were no better when it came to francophone economic involvement and achievement. Francophones, for example, owned only 20 percent of the province's manufacturing sector and 47 percent of the total commercial sector. Quebec, moreover, lagged in productivity when compared to its neighbour and rival, Ontario. Estimates indicate that Quebec's productivity trailed Ontario's by 15 percent. Despite significant economic changes that had taken place during the 1940s and 1950s, and which have frequently, if not conveniently, been forgotten by many of today's separatists, Quebec was, relatively speaking, still a poor, illiterate, and economically weak province.

Pierre Fortin has noted that during this period, francophone Quebeckers and American Blacks, when compared at the level of educational achievement and income, resembled each other. While one can argue that Fortin's numbers are somewhat misleading because the units they measure are not comparable – that francophone Quebeckers lived and worked in a province governed by their own people whereas American Blacks were scattered throughout the U.S., did not govern themselves, and did much better in one region (for example, in the north) than in another region (such as in the deep south) – he does, however, capture the relative economic positions between anglophone and francophone Quebeckers that existed during this period. Fortin's comparison would be more balanced if he also noted the rate of anglophone emigration from Quebec. According to William Watson, between 1976 and 1981, "the rate of emigration from English Quebec was twice that from Northern Ireland." Many anglophone economists, like Watson, believe that this huge out-migration of English-speaking Quebeckers has contributed to the long-term decline of Montreal's economy and is also responsible for rapidly accelerating the "upgrading of Francophone 'human capital'."[18]

Both Fortin and Watson, regardless of their differences, would agree that Quebec's economy has dramatically changed. To begin with, two-thirds of the productivity gap with Ontario has more or less been closed. Those entering university and post-secondary institutions now comprise over 20 percent of the population while nearly all francophone Quebeckers receive a grade 8 education. More important, approximately 40 percent of the province's post-secondary students are attending business schools or are enrolled in commerce faculties, and equally important, these students now constitute 45 percent of all commerce students in Canada. The income gap between francophones and others has shrunk to roughly 10 percent. Francophones now own 40 percent of the manufacturing sector and 62 percent of the total commercial sector and manage 27 of the 50 fastest growing companies in Canada. Finally, over these thirty years of economic transition, francophone ownership of financial institutions has increased from 26 percent to 58 percent; for mining it has risen from 17 percent to 35 percent; and in manufacturing it has grown from 22 percent to 39 percent. Between 1981 and 1995, Quebec's exports of goods and services to the rest of Canada increased 67 percent. But its exports to international markets during this period rose 208 percent. There is little doubt that a confident, aggressive, and indigenous business class and bourgeoisie have emerged and have changed the nature of Quebec politics, moving the separatist demand, *le Québec aux Québécois*, closer to reality and away from what one writer has called "an astounding syndrome of illusions and mythology."[19]

18 Pierre Fortin, 'How Economics Is Shaping the Constitutional Debate in Canada,' in Robert A. Young, ed., *Confederation in Crisis* (Toronto: James Lorimer 1991), 37; William Watson, 'As Quebec Goes …', *Commentary* **101** (1996) 40; and John F. Helliwell, 'Convergence and Migration among Provinces,' *Canadian Journal of Economics* **29** (1996) 324-30

19 Johnson, *A Canadian Myth*, 400

The consequences of this concerted effort to build what Pierre Arbour[20] has called 'Quebec Inc.' and what Tom Courchene has referred to as 'market nationalism'[21] and how it has affected the force, timing, and direction of Quebec's demands for independence and statehood have been lost, or more apropos, seriously neglected by the majority of writers attempting to explain the dynamics of Quebec nationalism.

There are, of course, some major exceptions, but studies examining the relationship between economic preferences, expectations, and aspirations of Quebeckers, or the impact of rising living standards, or the composition of the labour force, or the macroeconomic changes that have taken place, and support for or opposition to Quebec sovereignty have been far and few between.[22]

It can be argued that it is not simply emotion, demagoguery, or linguistic pride that have motivated more and more Québécois to favour the separatist project of a *Québec libre*; it is rather a strategic calculation based on the perceived costs and benefits of Quebec independence, or what some social scientists would call 'self-interest.'[23] It may well be that the genesis and fate of nationalist movements are not ultimately determined by bread alone, but neither are they free from *les Québécois'* desire to maximize their welfare as they conceive it. National self-determination is not decided by birth or culture or language alone, but by rational choice (i.e., efficiently and purposefully relating means to ends), by citizens *cum* voters "making decisions [to advance their rela-

---

20 Pierre Arbour, *Quebec Inc.* (Montreal: Robert Davies 1993)

21 Thomas Courchene, 'Market Nationalism,' *Policy Options* 7 (1980) 7-12

22 Alain-G. Gagnon and Mary Beth Montcalm, *Quebec Beyond the Quiet Revolution* (Scarborough, ON: Nelson Canada 1989); Kenneth McRoberts, *Quebec Social Change and Political Crisis* (Toronto: McClelland & Stewart 1988); André Blais and Richard Nadeau, 'To Be or Not To Be Sovereigntist: Quebeckers' Perennial Dilemma,' *Canadian Public Policy* 18 (1992) 19-103; and André Blais, Pierre Nadeau, and Richard Nadeau, 'Attentes économiques et linguistiques et appui à la souveraineté du Québec: une analyse prospective et comparative,' *Canadian Journal of Political Science* 28 (1995) 637-57

23 Gary S. Becker, Nobel Lecture: The Economic Way of Looking at Behavior, *Journal of Political Economy* 101 (1993) 385-409; Hamish Stewart, 'A Critique of Instrumental Reason in Economics,' *Economics and Philosophy* 11 (1995) 57-83

tive standing in various hierarchies] ... and by considering only the direct benefits to themselves of their actions, not the indirect costs in terms of reduced relative standing, that those actions impose on others."[24] It is with this in mind that Robert H. Frank reminds us of what seems to be self-evident:

> The market economist's insight that people respond strongly to economic incentives is a powerful one. We generally get better results when we provide people with an economic incentive to achieve a desired outcome than when we require them to follow specific procedures.[25]

Quebeckers, like economists, understand the power of economic incentives and the marketplace. Like 'economic man,' they are not simply consumers of virtue, but of utility as well, i.e., Quebeckers seek to maximize their well-being.

III Creating a New Middle Class and the Importance of Economic Preferences, Aspirations, and Expectations

> I know of no national distinctions marking and continuing a more hopeless inferiority ... if they prefer remaining stationary, the greater part of them must be labourers in the employ of English capitalists. In either case it would appear that the great mass of French Canadians are doomed, in some measure, to occupy an inferior position, and to be dependent on the English for employment. The evils of poverty and dependence would merely be aggravated in a ten-fold degree, by a spirit of jealous and resentful nationality which should separate the working class of the community from the possessors of wealth and employers of labour. (Lord Durham, 1838)

> We are beaten, it's true. But by what? Money and the ethnic vote.... Three-fifths of us ... voted Yes. It wasn't quite enough, but very soon, it will be enough. We'll get our country. (Jacques Parizeau, 1995)

The Quebec economy, as we have seen, has undergone dramatic change since the Quiet Revolution. Lord Durham, of course, did not

---

24 Robert H. Frank, *Choosing the Right Pound* (New York: Oxford University Press 1985), 247

25 Frank, *Choosing the Right Pound*, 247

foresee the transformation of the Quebec economy, and the days of francophone Quebeckers 'occupying inferior positions' and depending on the English for employment are long gone. One of the singular achievements of Quebec's economic growth and development has been the creation of a new and sizable middle class. This new bourgeoisie has confidence in its self, its skills, and its ability to compete successfully in both national and international markets, and it believes those will create a more prosperous Quebec for itself and posterity.

Not surprisingly, as the middle class's confidence and income have increased, so too has its support for separatism and the creation of an independent Quebec. The middle-class character of Quebec's separatist movement has been studied in detail by historians and social scientists. The 1980 referendum, for example, revealed that a substantial number of middle-class francophones supported sovereignty for Quebec. One-third of the Parti Québécois leadership were technocrats, while another third were classified as intellectuals, teachers, and journalists. A study by Maurice Pinard and Richard Hamilton found the *souverainisme* was high among 'semi-professionals,' and André Blais and Richard Nadeau report that administrators and technocrats working in the public sector strongly supported an independence for Quebec: *'ont fortement appuyé le oui.'*[26]

Quebec separatist politicians, we have argued, recognized that their destiny was linked to the creation of a francophone bourgeoisie. They knew that ethnicity and language were not enough to provide them with the votes they needed to win office and a referendum victory that would allow them to sever ties with Confederation. The success of this initiative was not simply in the number of new middle-class jobs created for francophones, but the change in behaviour that followed. Hugh Seton Watson observes that "when there were almost no French-Canadians in the Canadian business world members of this group didn't seem to mind very much. But once a third of good business jobs in Montreal had fallen into French Canadian hands Québécois nationalist leaders found it intolerable that two-thirds were still held by the

---

26 Cited in Kenneth McRobert, 'The Sources of Neo-Nationalism in Quebec,' in Michael D. Behiels, ed., *Quebec Since 1945* (Toronto: Copp Clark Pitman 1987), 107.

city's English-speaking population."[27] At the same time, the public service was rapidly and substantially expanded to produce a 'linguistic division of labour,' group solidarity, and a relatively secure niche for this new class. In 1944 anglophones accounted for seven percent of Quebec's public service; by 1991 the number had dropped to one percent. The creation of a new francophone middle class was a key part of a nationalist mobilization strategy.[28]

Albert Breton was one of the first to call attention to the economic character of Quebec nationalism. In a series of articles published during the 1960s and 1970s, Breton argued that nationalism should be viewed as a collective capital good based on self-interest and the desire to "buy jobs for a number of middle-class French Canadians." He was firmly convinced that Quebec nationalism depended "on the burgeoning of a new middle class," who used the nationalist ethos "to accede to wealth and power." The quest for status, income, and deference, however, resulted in conflict with "the old middle class, which in Quebec was English Canadian."[29] This 'investment in nationality' could only succeed if four objectives were achieved by the Parti Québécois. The first priority was to find a way to increase the francophone share of capital owned in Quebec. The second task was to raise the stock of francophone 'human capital.' The third objective was to raise the proportion of industrial production as a share of total production. And the last goal was to increase exports significantly while simultaneously reducing imports. It was with these priorities in mind that the Parti Québécois developed Hydro-Quebec.

Breton was fairly pessimistic that such nationalistic endeavours would succeed. He had little doubt that such an initiative would redistribute wealth and generate a large number of high-paying jobs, but he was convinced that it would not create new wealth. Quebec national-

---

27 Cited in Jack E. Reece, *The Bretons Against France* (Chapel Hill: University of North Carolina Press 1977), VII

28 Hudson Meadwell, 'The Politics of Nationalism in Quebec,' *World Politics* **45** (1993) 208-15

29 Albert Breton, 'Economics of Nationalism,' *Journal of Political Economy* **72** (1964) 381, 382, 377

ism was not driven by linguistic and cultural desiderata, but by money, opportunism, and middle-class self-interest. He writes:

> The monetary rate of return on this capital takes the form of high-income jobs for the nationals of a given territory.... [F]rom a social point of view, the rate of return in terms of income on this capital is lower than if the resources were economically invested in alternative uses. The question that comes to mind then: Why does society invest in nationality and ethnicity? The answer is to be found in the income redistributing effect of these investments. For even if these investments have a low yield, this yield accrues to a specific society even though that group pays only for a fraction of the cost of investment.[30]

While one may dispute Breton on whether Quebec's investment in nationality has only redistributed wealth rather than generating new wealth, it is, however, fair to say that we lack studies which have systematically tested the validity of Breton's hypotheses. What has happened to this new middle class since its emergence during the Quiet Revolution? Is nationalism a commodity that has characteristics of the market? Is economic nationalism a rational choice for francophone Quebeckers of *all* classes, or does it reward particular groups, such as intellectuals and journalists, occupations whose incomes and status would not be seriously threatened if Quebec separated? And do such investments make language and culture more 'salient' because, to quote Daniel Bell, they "can combine [self-]interest with an affective tie?"[31] Unfortunately, based on the studies we have, we cannot answer these questions.

Fortunately, there are several surveys that provide us with clues about the economic preferences and expectations of francophone Quebeckers and how they may influence the choice for or against separation and independence.

1. André Blais and Richard Nadeau, in a study examining the bases of support for and against Quebec sovereignty, report that while francophone Quebeckers see themselves first and foremost as

---

30 Cited in Thomas Courchene, *In Praise of Renewed Federalism: The Canada Round* (Toronto: C.D. Howe Institute 1991), 69-70

31 Cited in Daniel Patrick Moynihan, *Pandaemonium* (New York: Oxford University Press 1993), 56

Quebeckers and not as Canadians, they have "fears about the economic consequences of separation," and there is "a real possibility, economic considerations will come to play an even greater role."[32]

2. A 1995 survey of francophone Quebeckers by Martin, Nadeau, and Blais asked "if Quebec remains in Canada, do you think that the French language could one day disappear in Quebec?" They found that respondents' answers depended on the extent to which they believed that Quebec would do better economically on its own as an independent state, identified as Québécois as opposed to Canadians, and perceived the French language would be less threatened in a sovereign Quebec.[33]

3. André Blais reports that an "implicit calculation of costs and benefits" greatly influences the choices francophone Quebeckers make between supporting or imposing sovereignty and federalism. Medium-term economic expectations are, he concludes, more important than linguistic expectations.[34]

It would appear that support for Quebec nationalism is strongly linked to perceptions that the province could do better on its own in the future. Economic conditions and expectations about Quebec's economic prospects, in short, affect the level of francophone support for Quebec independence. This point is emphasized by Lysiane Gagnon who reports that a recent poll commissioned by *The Globe and Mail* and *Le Journal de Montréal* found that 65.3 percent of the respondents want Quebec to remain part of Canada, while 54.9 percent among decided voters supports a sovereign Quebec. What was of special interest was the fact that 89.2 percent of those interviewed wanted the first ministers' conference held in June 1996 to concentrate on economic affairs, not on the Constitution. Gagnon concludes that:

> ... the catch word is 'partnership' – le 'partenariat.' This is the miracle concept aimed at convincing reluctant voters that sovereignty means nothing more than autonomy and increased collective pride. This is an ideal set-up indeed – a so-called sovereign Quebec still very much a part of Canada....[35]

---

32 Blais and Nadeau, 'To Be or Not To Be Sovereigntist,' 100

33 Richards, *Language Matters*, 30

34 Blais, Nadeau, and Nadeau, 'Attentes économiques et linguistiques,' 637

35 Lysiane Gagnon, 'Sorry to Be Boring, But Quebec Loves Its Constitutional

Maurice Pinard has examined how francophone Quebeckers react to such terms as 'separation,' 'independence,' and 'sovereignty' and concludes that:

> The data reveal a paradox. Although all the terms used refer to the same reality – the secession or separation of Quebec from the rest of Canada to form an independent sovereign country – levels of support and especially of opposition differ according to terms used, as if they were different options.... It is no surprise, therefore, as an initial observation, that federalists prefer the term separation or even independence, and that supporters of independence mainly prefer to talk about sovereignty.[36]

'Sovereignty,' 'separation,' and 'independence' all have different economic connotations associated with them. They are not synonymous or value neutral as far as Quebeckers are concerned. And this is why the wording of the recent and future referenda questions is so important.

Anthony Downs in his *Economic Theory of Democracy* discusses at length both the cost and dissemination of information to voters and politicians and how these affect perceptions, expectations, and behaviour.[37] Rational-choice explanations of economic behaviour, he suggests, recognize how extremely sensitive economic behaviour is to information that actors hold and act upon. But how this information is acquired and the way it may affect economic behaviour is, in the words of one critic, 'seldom addressed' by economists or political scientists.[38] Thus, those who disseminate and control the distribution of information (for example, intellectuals and the media) can directly influence voter per-

---

Contradictions,' *Globe and Mail* (6 July 1996), D3. Also see Richard Mackie, 'Quebeckers Favour Canada, Poll,' *Globe and Mail* (20 June 1996), A5.

36 Maurice Pinard, 'The Secessionist Option and Quebec Public Opinion, 1988-1993,' *Canada Opinion* 2 (1994) 3

37 Anthony Downs, *An Economic Theory of Democracy* (New York: Harper & Row 1957)

38 Jochen Runde, 'Review of Young Back Choi's "Paradigms and Conventions",' *Economics and Philosophy* 2 (1995) 370. Also see Donald N. McCloskey, 'The Rhetoric of Economics,' *Journal of Economic Literature* 21 (1983) 481-571 and Jack L. Knetsch, 'Assumptions, Behavioral Findings, and Policy Analyses,' *Journal of Policy Analysis and Management* 14 (1995) 69-75.

ceptions, expectations, and preferences. If both these groups favour nationalism, then given their control over resources, there is good reason to believe that they can significantly shape the direction and intensity of nationalist support.

Yet we do not have any studies that examine how these 'information' groups mould the microeconomic perceptions and expectations of Quebeckers.

If, as economists assume, an individual's choices are rational when his or her preferences are purposefully and consistently related to a set of preferences – in this case, maximizing one's welfare – then the ambivalence of Quebeckers is understandable, and not necessarily irrational or hypocritical. It is really a hedging of bets. And there are legitimate reasons for doing this. For example, the Canadian Council on Social Development recently concluded a study, *A Statistical Profile of Urban Poverty*, and reports that four of seven cities with the highest poverty rates are in Quebec, and in Montreal and Quebec City, more than one-fifth of the elderly are poor. By contrast, in Regina, Saskatoon, and Oshawa, less than five percent of their senior citizens are living below the poverty line.[39] If this is not enough, there is Premier Bouchard's austerity budget which, according to *The Globe and Mail*, "will hit everyone in the province – but reach deepest into the pockets of middle-income earners."[40] To add insult to injury, Quebec's payroll taxes are currently the highest in Canada and its real jobless rate (i.e., those unemployed, those who have stopped looking for work or have had to accept part-time employment) is between 18 and 20 percent. Add to these depressing economic facts of life the warning that an independent Quebec would bring with it financial chaos, and it soon becomes understandable why economic conditions affect individual perceptions and expectations and why Quebeckers are at times ambivalent and volatile regarding Quebec independence. Why shouldn't

39 Canadian Council on Social Development, *Communiqué: New Study Compares Urban Poverty Rates* (26 June 1996, 1

40 Rheal Seguin, 'Quebec's Cuts Hit Middle Incomes,' *Globe and Mail* (28 March 1996), A1

they be? It also helps to explain why big business supported the No side in the 1995 referendum.[41]

Yet the fact remains that the majority of francophone Quebeckers are still optimistic about their own and the province's economic future, and why sovereignty association with Canada continues to remain such an attractive option for most Québécois. It is therefore not unreasonable to argue that Quebec sovereigntists have believed as an article of faith that if they first seek the economic kingdom, independence will follow. A 1993 CROP in-depth poll supports this conclusion. Taken during an economic downturn that economists considered among the worst since the Great Depression, only 26 percent of respondents thought Quebec would never achieve independence; 41 percent, however, believed that independence would happen before the year 2000. Equally important, 38 percent of those interviewed were optimistic about the future and thought their personal life would be much better by the year 2000, whereas only 18 percent feared it would be worse. Lysiane Gagnon observes that the poll's findings "may be wishful thinking, or a way of saying that things are so bad they can't get worse, or a genuine feeling that there are reasons for hope."[42] It would be helpful if we had longitudinal studies tracking the economic perceptions and aspirations of Quebeckers. We would then be in a better position to answer Gagnon's questions.

IV   Conclusion

What does Quebec want? The answer is simple: Quebec does not know what it wants. Quebec, caught in contradictions, cannot resolve its ambivalences. Torn between the opposed appeals of liberalism and nationalism, of modernity and atavistic ghosts that still haunt the living, the people of Quebec are not free and

---

41 Bruce Little, 'Quebec Payroll Taxes Highest,' *Globe and Mail* (22 September 1995), B3, and Richard Mackie, 'Quebec Employers and Employees See Gloomy Picture,' *Globe and Mail* (22 November 1995), B3

42 Lysiane Gagnon, 'Quebeckers Think Everything is Coming Up Roses for the Year 2000,' *Globe and Mail* (9 January 1993), D3

will never be free until they have emancipated themselves from the myths that hold them in thrall.[43]

Opinion polls reveal that the bases of Quebec separatism are not simply language, culture, or the need for a more decentralized Canada. Compared to Switzerland, Germany, Australia, and the United States, Canada is much more decentralized. What then does Quebec want? It wants more power. It wants independence and statehood. But bread and butter issues, economic preferences, and expectations matter a great deal. These factors are responsible for the cycles and intensity of Quebec nationalist aspirations and demands. Until recently, economists have often discounted the importance of future costs and benefits associated with nationalism. But empirical studies in other countries indicate that people have widely different time preferences and cost expectations depending on the characteristics of particular issues and events. In understanding the support for or opposition to Quebec separatism, francophone Quebeckers' perceptions of the seriousness of various economic risks based on their expected costs and values must be considered along with the individual's calculation of the probable risk and his or her vulnerability if and when Quebec separates and becomes a sovereign state. How much francophone Quebeckers discount the economic value of gains and losses they associate with an independent Quebec will ultimately determine whether or not they support independence.

Unfortunately, we know very little about this aspect of Quebec nationalist support. We need studies examining preferences, aspirations, and expectations to help us find the answers. We need studies which can better help us understand how individuals connect preferences with action, how they rank these preferences, discount these preferences along a time continuum, and choose what they most prefer. Economists have an important role to play in all of this, and rational-choice theory can contribute to helping us understand the dynamics of Quebec separatism and in appreciating the paradoxes, achievements, and tragedies of nationhood.[44] Thirty years ago Mancur Olson wrote:

---

43 Johnson, *A Canadian Myth*, 400

44 Samuel V. LaSelva, *The Moral Foundation of Canadian Federalism* (Montreal: McGill-Queen's University Press 1996)

> Economic theory is, indeed, relevant whenever actors have determinate wants or objectives and at the same time do not have such an abundance of the means needed to achieve these ends that all of their desires are satisfied. The ends in question may be social status or political power, and the means will be anything that is in fact conducive to attainment of those ends, whether or not these means can fetch a price on the market. This means that economic (or more precisely micro-economic) theory is in a fundamental sense more nearly a theory of rational behaviour than a theory of material goods.[45]

The time is ripe for such an undertaking, and it is my hope that this paper will stimulate further and far more sophisticated research on the dynamics of Quebec separatist support. Only time will tell.

---

45 Cited in Brian M. Barry, *Sociologists, Economists and Democracy* (Toronto: Collier Macmillan Canada 1970), 5-6

CANADIAN JOURNAL OF PHILOSOPHY
Supplementary Volume 22

Afterword: Liberal Nationalism Both Cosmopolitan and Rooted

JOCELYNE COUTURE
Université du Québec à Montréal

and

KAI NIELSEN
University of Calgary and Concordia University

with the collaboration of

MICHEL SEYMOUR
Université de Montréal

I

There are nationalisms and nationalisms, and as nationalisms vary from barbarous and murderous to benign and, all things considered, perhaps desirable, so theories of nationalism vary from irrational or turgid metaphysical accounts to reasonable and carefully articulated and argued theories of nationalism. André Van de Putte has well described some of the former (without at all falling into that category himself) while David Miller, Yael Tamir, Geneviève Nootens, Ross Poole, and Robert X. Ware have carefully argued for some modest forms of nationalism, sometimes explicitly and sometimes only by implication. But there are also, as the reader will have seen, forcefully argued and systematic theories setting themselves against even the most sophisticated and plausible defences of nationalism. The articles of Harry Brighouse, Omar Dahbour, and Andrew Levine fall explicitly into that category and, we would argue, so does Allen Buchanan's carefully wrought article, though implicitly and by implication but not by programmatic intent. Buchanan would so constrain the conditions under which a nation could justifiably secede that, we believe, it would – and so we shall argue – again and again, and in circumstances where this is problematic, render the verdict 'unjustified' to reasonable nationalist claims to secession. It would, if accepted, leave too little space for nations to be self-determining and in this way stand in the way of many plausible nationalist projects as well as progressive reforms. So, whatever Buchanan's intentions, his account, like Brighouse's, Dahbour's and Levine's, is another powerful theoretical account directed against nationalism. But even here, these accounts notwithstanding, we will repeat: there are nationalisms and nationalisms. There is the nationalism of the big powerful states, the superpowers, the United States most paradigmatically, using their economic domination to assert in the face of the world their national superiority in a way that is almost obscene. And there are the nationalisms of the stateless nations, embedded, in various degrees, in repressive states and struggling for emancipation and democracy. There are also the nationalisms of historical nation-states – France and Spain may be examples – whose sovereignty and democratic culture are threatened by the institutions of economic globalization.[1] Among the strongest and most powerfully articulated attacks on nationalism contained in this volume, some can be interpreted as challenges to the first kind of nationalism. Under such an interpretation we completely agree with them.

We, like Miller, Tamir and Ware, would like to make a case for a liberal nationalism that is fully compatible with a universalistic and internationalist cosmopolitan outlook and is, as well, compatible with a socialism which is a form of cosmopolitanism and internationalism. But a plausible cosmopolitanism will inescapably be a *rooted* cosmopolitanism.[2] Martha Nussbaum to the contrary notwithstanding, reasonable versions of nationalism and cosmopolitanism fit together like hand and glove.[3]

We will seek to articulate lines of argument that will vindicate a cosmopolitan liberal nationalism and show, as well, that there are real-

1 Stanley Hoffman, 'Look Back in Anger,' *The New York Review of Books*, **44:12** (1997), 43–50

2 Kwane Anthony Appiah, 'Cosmopolitan Patriots,' in Joshua Cohen, ed., *For Love of Country* (Boston: Beacon Press 1996), 21–9

3 Martha C. Nussbaum, 'Patriotism and Cosmopolitanism,' 3–17, and 'Reply,' 131–44, both in Joshua Cohen, ed., *For Love of Country* (Boston: Beacon Press 1996)

life circumstances in which a good case can be made for the project of such a nationalism being carried through. Quebec is one case, Scotland is another, or at least so we shall argue. And in the past the Norwegian and Icelandic secessions were justified. But, for this argument to be something which will be launched in a fair-minded way, without being *parti-pris*, and facing the discipline of criticism, the central task of this Afterword will be to come to grips with the above trenchant critics of nationalism. We shall set out core arguments by Brighouse, Buchanan, Dahbour, and Levine and then critically examine them. What we think we have established, or at least gone some way towards establishing, by this examination, is that liberal nationalism is alive and well and not only is compatible with, but *requires*, a rooted cosmopolitanism that is also through and through universalistic.

In the rest of this first section, we shall, however, concentrate on a rejection of nationalism that is not to any considerable extent rooted in theoretical considerations but rather in a keen observation of history, society, and the lives of human beings. It is brilliantly instanced in this volume, though in different ways, by the essays of Barrington Moore Jr. and Carol A. L. Prager. They might very well say that fine theoretical constructions of liberal nationalism, however soundly argued as models for justified nationalisms, are all justified solely within the limits of Enlightenment cosmopolitanism. They are in reality no more than the dreams of a spirit seer distant from what massively are, have been, and (we have good empirical reasons to believe) will continue to be the realities of nationalist movements: realities, Carol Prager has it, which are, in contrast with liberalism, rooted in passions and not in reason.

Many modern nationalist movements have reignited old enmities and have, beyond that, generated, where the conflict is sustained, hatreds. Even in such a liberal society as Quebec, the police in Montreal on the night of the 1995 referendum in which the No side very narrowly won had to erect barricades and be out in force to keep partisans of the two sides apart. It was plain for everyone to see the hostility there. Moore argues that between different nations there are typically deep and smouldering enmities, resentments of each other, whether justified or not, but still psychologically very real, which go on from generation to generation. When a nationalist movement arises, these feelings are brought to the surface and intensified. Indeed, he could claim, as others have, no nationalist movement can arise without these resentments.

Moore does not distinguish at all between ethnic nationalism and civic nationalism or clearly between ethnic identities and national identities or ethnicity and nationality. However, when he speaks of there being in premodern times "thousands of separate jurisdictions, large and small" which, as we go into the modern era, get ground up and destroyed by central governments (e.g., peasants made into Frenchmen) in circumstances which "left a legacy of bitterness that survives to the present day," this may illustrate the move from an array of ethnic groups to the creation of nations and nation-states and distinctive national identities. In any event he does not attach much, if any, significance to the difference between a sense of ethnic identity and a sense of national identity. They are, he believes, made of similar psychological stuff, and in his view they have similar ill effects.

In speaking of different ethnic groups, Moore does not speak of immigrants but (for example) of those historically ancient, relatively small, localized peoples of Europe who have been made in a unifying sweep into modern French, Germans, Italians, and the like. Where once there were seventeen distinct languages and the diverse cultural groups to go with them, now there are French citizens with one national language: French. Where such unification went on, there are very frequently smouldering resentments and enmities, frequently not without reason, rooted in historically passed-down memories of time past. As Moore puts it,

> At any given time the map of European states has shown blocs of territory inside each state with language and customs that differ from the surrounding state. Usually such ethnic blocs [they could, as easily, have been called national minorities or even perhaps nations] are the result of a previous conquest, sometimes in the quite distant past. Often enough political leaders arise in these areas to play on local grievances and thereby win support for claims that the territory really belongs to another state or just itself, that is, it should be one more independent state.

Given such circumstances, at "some point in their history ethnic identities are likely to become quite militant." Where before they were quiescent, they become in such circumstances intense and insistent, and sharp ethnic conflicts and hatreds come into being. Throughout much of our history ethnic enmities wax and wane but always remain. Though sometimes rather concealed, as in much of Yugoslavia from 1950-80, they still are there, always ready to erupt into hostilities and hatreds. Moore thinks, consciously or unconsciously echoing Carl Schmitt from whom he is certainly politically distant, that what binds people together is hatred. That is their social bonding, liberal piety to the contrary notwithstanding: a common hatred of what is perceived as the enemy or, less frequently, as one among many enemies. It is arguably a weakness of liberalism that it has never been able to take a proper account of that. The claim is that when in a liberal order a strong nationalist movement arises, given these smouldering resentments and the hatreds that nationalistic rhetoric summons out of these resentments, we have a recipe for intense social conflict that will tear the fabric of liberal society. Where such movements have the numbers and where they are strong and confident, they will, as Carol Prager emphasizes, defeat liberal political regimes as the Nazis defeated Weimar.

In the poorer parts of the world where reasonable nationalist demands are met (say, by decolonization), the hopes for a better life that the push of nationalism expresses (think here of Algeria) will be dashed because of the very great poverty and lack of infrastructure of such countries (*quasi-states* as some have been called). With such a deep disappointment, there emerge group bitterness and hatreds – the bitterness and hatreds resulting from crushed hopes. When this is the case, ethnic demands increasingly lead to a cycle of violence generating still more intensified hatreds between the contending groups. This exacerbates an already dreadful economic situation resulting in economic decline and disruption, even more poverty, and the disappearance of anything even looking like stability. Reasonable nationalist demands have triggered, in such circumstances of poverty, unmeetable aspirations, which in turn, not far down the line, lead to a virulent nationalism and something which comes to approach Hobbes's conception of a state of nature as a war of all against all. This is something like the story that Moore tells.

Carol Prager's thoughtful and insightful essay has a more contemporary focus than Moore's, and different aims, but their essays are revealingly complementary; they come to similarly historically pessimistic political conclusions, and both regard nationalism (to understate how they see it) as a misfortune that, in any of its forms, is devoid of an emancipatory force that could serve the cause of human progress, human autonomy, and self-realization. Indeed their pessimism makes them deeply skeptical concerning even the very modest hopes for progress that some liberals continue to entertain even when they are acutely aware of the horrors of contemporary life.

More definitely than Moore, Carol Prager identifies nationalism with ethnic nationalism: 'ethnonationalism,' as she calls it, following Walker Connor, with nationalism *sans phrase*. Civic nationalism, to say nothing of liberal nationalism, does not seem to her a realistic possibility, though it is not clear that she would deny they are conceptual possibilities. Indeed when she speaks of what she calls 'positive nationalism,' which she thinks is now a thing of the past, we should conclude that probably she would take liberal nationalism to be a conceptual possibility. But her interests are not in conceptual possibilities. Her subject is savage ethnonationalism or, as she alternatively phrases it, barbarous nationalism, as it has emerged in the international world order and as it bedevils liberal internationalism in the post-Cold War era, where the end of the "bipolar international system has permitted temporarily repressed ethnic and nationalist passions to resurrect themselves."

Carol Prager, like Liah Greenfeld, sees nationalism as something springing from "resentment due to oppression, uneven development and other factors." Given these circumstances, she sees "no end in sight to the conditions that create furious nationalism." Indeed the "homogenizing effects of globalization ... have been seen as a source of oppression, leading to heightened nationalism." What she calls "positive nationalism" (that is, a nationalism with on the whole beneficial and progressive consequences) "has not only reached the point of diminishing returns but a destructive nationalism has replaced it, threatening to undermine the existing international order with its insatiable regress." What we have – and this is plain enough for all to see and is not reasonably contestable – is sickeningly barbarous nationalism in Nagorno-Karabakh, Rwanda, Burundi, and much of the former Yugoslavia. These are among the most prominent and extreme cases, but they do not stand alone. And, as Carol Prager remarks, these nationalisms "are absolutist and pitiless."

Like Moore, Prager sees the horrible logic of the thing. Ethnic enmities are usually ancient and continuing, and where there are people in a territory with minority status surrounded by historical enemies they will tend to feel menaced "by the majority, who typically see the minority as the most serious threat to the integrity of the nation." Not infrequently these feelings will not be misplaced. But, misplaced or not, they will be tenaciously held onto by both sides. They will hug their grievances, both imagined and real, and fear attacks coming from their enemies.

Nations, particularly where nationalist sentiments are strong, have what Carol Prager calls "cherished narratives of themselves, their enemies, and their shared history, all of which have become seared into their identities and are renewed with each fresh atrocity." These narratives are, of course, largely, but sometimes not entirely, mythical. They are what some anthropologists call 'just-so stories' but just-so stories with baleful consequences. But, as both Moore and Carol Prager stress, many members of the nations in question (often most members) stick with them through thick and thin. These narratives, as Harry Brighouse remarks as well, are very resistant to critical inspection. Given such sociological and psychological realities, barbarous nationalism is very easily kindled and, while it can sometimes be contained for a time, its recurrence seems impossible to prevent. What Albert Camus said about the plague and what it was a metaphor of, can be said about barbarous nationalism: it is something that in one form or another is always with us.

Carol Prager is concerned with the anomalies of humanitarian intervention. And indeed humanitarian intervention is the first thing that those of us who are very normatively oriented call for when faced with a Yugoslavia, Rwanda, Burundi, or Nagorno-Karabakh. She carefully examines the moral, political, and empirical problems involved here, making it painfully evident that there are no easy solutions. But that concern, although important and the burden of her essay, is not what we shall be concerned with here. We shall instead fasten on what she and Moore say about the pervasiveness and intractability of barbarous nationalism and the threat (possible threat?) it poses for the reasonableness of arguments supporting liberal nationalism. In light of world sociological realities, is liberal nationalism a concept that has much, if any, application in the hurly-burly of the real world? It seems, some would assert, to have little interface with the actually existing nationalisms. Is it the case that ethnic enmities and enmities resulting from, and perhaps fuelled by, nationalist projects, with the hatreds they engender, are just here to stay as part of our very human condition? Or can we reasonably expect their slow attrition and expect, or at least plausibly struggle for, a world not so starkly constituted? And what does this say (if anything) about the justifiability of *any* nationalist project?

Behind the very idea of liberal nationalism is the modest assumption that some limited moral and political progress is possible, that there can be and will be societies where nationalist movements are reasonable, that with them we will sometimes have, all things considered, a justifiable ethical rationale for a nationalist project, and that sometimes an actually existing nationalist project can push this progress along. But should we not, if we are reasonable, have a deep historical pessimism and skepticism about that? Is it not more reasonable to believe, as Carol Prager does, that barbarous nationalism and a liberal national order will "remain at war, morally and empirically" and that barbarous nationalism will continue to triumph? And that, while liberal nationalism is not an oxymoron, it will have no stable exemplification?

If, as many believe, this is so, then we should also realize that no sensible normative political theory can argue that what is impossible should be done. No fundamental 'ought' can be derived from an 'is,' but it is equally true that 'ought' implies 'can.'[4] But, and consistent with this, though less frequently noted, it is also the case, as Carol Prager insightfully observes, in international politics and indeed all politics, that whatever *is* constrains "to a significant degree what *can* be. In all politics, but especially in international politics, whatever is has to be taken seriously and, in that sense, respected." Will accepting this, as we think we must do if we would be reasonable, render any project of liberal nationalism a form of spitting into the wind, both utopian and dangerous, because it is oblivious to its inescapable untoward effects?

This challenge to nationalism is not a conceptual challenge or even a theoretical one. It does not say that the very idea of liberal nationalism or even civic nationalism is incoherent or conceptually or theoretically or ethically untoward, but rather that it is out to lunch with respect to the facts concerning nationalism. The beginning of a response goes like this: there are, as our opening sentence asserted, nationalisms and nationalisms, and while of course there are barbarous nationalisms with their horrendous effects, and while it is also plainly evident that such nationalisms are very widespread (and at least seemingly growing), dangerous and just plain evil, still it is also true that they are not the

---

4 Kai Nielsen, *Why be Moral?* (Buffalo: Prometheus Books 1989), 13–38

only types of nationalisms that exist, for there are also instances of liberal nationalism. In our recent history Norwegian, Icelandic, Finnish, and Flemish nationalisms were instances of such nationalisms and at present Catalonian, Faeroesian, Scottish, Québécois, and Welsh nationalisms are paradigms of liberal nationalism and liberal nationalist movements. The struggle for some form of national self-determination is persistent, sometimes intense, and in all societies in which it occurs, it leads to social conflict, but such conflicts were (are) – some isolated containable hotheads to the contrary notwithstanding – non-violent. Moreover, where some isolated violence did occur it was contained with both sides – a few loose cannons excepted – acknowledging that the dispute and its resolution must proceed within the parameters of a liberal framework. This means that the struggle was not violent and, where it is going on now in the places we just mentioned, will not be violent, and that the matter was settled, is being settled, or will be settled in accordance with liberal democratic principles. There are, of course, often disputes about just how liberal democratic principles and procedures are to be understood and, even more so, about how they are to be applied in those contexts. But what is not in dispute is that the matter must be and will be settled democratically. At the height of the controversy, there will, unfortunately, be a lot of inflamed, partisan and often very silly rhetoric flowing from both sides. But (*pace* Carol Prager) there are real life situations where nationalism does not triumph over, or even trump, liberalism, but is rather strictly *constrained* by it. There is a firm resolve on both sides – indeed it is more like an unquestionable background presupposition – that matters be settled with words not guns, no matter how difficult and protracted the discussion may turn out to be.

There may be no international liberal world order, but in some relatively small but not insignificant parts of the world with a good number of nation-states and still more nations, parts of the world in many ways (though not all) more fortunate than the others, nationalist issues have been, and as far as we can foresee will continue to be, settled democratically. It is not we who are out to lunch about the facts, but those who deny the sociological reality of liberal nationalism or who set it aside. They are suffering from what Wittgenstein called a one-sided diet. A preoccupation with barbarous nationalisms, certainly understandable, and vitally important as it is, should not blind us to the fact that there are actually existing liberal nationalisms and that they do not, whatever other inadequacies they may suffer from, suffer from what is so wrong about barbarous nationalisms. And in describing and interpreting nationalism, in making generalizations about nationalism, and in constructing theories about nationalism, we should not, in doing any of these things, treat a subspecies of nationalism as if it were just nationalism – as if it were the whole of nationalism. That it is the larger and more colourful subspecies is neither here nor there. That fact does not turn a subspecies into a species.

It might be responded that that is all well and good, but it is the case that (1) the instantiations of liberal nationalisms are piddling compared to a world awash with barbarous nationalisms, nationalisms that threaten the stability of the 'international liberal world order,' and (2) the characterization we have given of liberal nationalism in liberal societies is itself one-sided and utopian, failing to come fully into sync with salient realities, including the realities of nationalist movements in liberal societies.

We will turn to (1) first. Seen from a world scale these instantiations of liberal nationalisms may be, so viewed, 'piddling,' but they certainly are not so to the people and societies involved. They were not to the Norwegians, Icelanders, Flemish, and Finns, and they are not now to the Catalans, Faeroesian, Scots, Quebeckers, and Welsh. Moreover, the United Kingdom, Belgium, southwestern Europe, Scandinavia, and northern North America are wealthy, relatively influential, and relatively powerful parts of the world. Not the most influential by any means, but not negligible either. And it should not be forgotten that Scandinavia in particular serves as a beacon for progressive developments (feasible progressive developments) within liberal societies generally.

In turn it might be responded – but this moves over in the direction of (2) – that these societies are all at least relatively homogeneous and wealthy, with high levels of education and (Spain aside) with long histories of stability under liberal, often social democratic, democracies. They are not, given this homogeneity, good models for the whole of the liberal social order, to say nothing of the rest of the world.

We will respond to this by starting our consideration of (2). But let us first press the difficulty a little further. In addition to what was just said above, our characterization of the real world of liberal nationalism, it might be remarked, is one-sided in that it fails to consider that nationalist movements are not as liberal in many reasonably stable liberal democracies as we have given to understand. We mentioned the Catalonians but not the Basques in Spain. And we have ignored the Corsicans and the quite distinct movement of Le Pen in France, nationalists in Italy, and nationalist struggles in Northern Ireland. These nationalisms – nationalism extant in liberal societies – hardly have a liberal face and sometimes are violent. There is a continuum here with barbarous nationalism. Quebec's nationalism is peaceful, working firmly within the limits of liberalism alone, but not a few, and not just anti-nationalists, worry about what might follow hard on a victory for the Yes side in the next referendum. Their concern is that in Montreal, right-wing, largely anglophone, partitionist groups might resort to armed violence in an attempt to destabilize things after a Yes vote. It is difficult to estimate how realistic such speculations are. It is hopeful, but perhaps a sticking of one's head in the sand, to believe that they are not very realistic and even to suspect that they are, in some instance, politically inspired to inflict fear on gullible people. And it is also reasonable to believe that in the eventuality of such violence, the Quebec police forces could contain it and the federal Canadian government, vengeful as it might feel, would not intervene causing mayhem. Its own self-interest would restrain it here. But that aside, what is relevant in the present context is that not all contending forces in liberal societies engaging in nationalist struggles are as liberal as our narrative gives us to understand and that what Moore calls ethnic enmities are deep, ancient, and intractable and generate hatreds and violence in liberal as well as non-liberal societies. To remind us of that, we have the fate of Weimar and the way that the United States, in reality an intensely nationalist society that does not recognize itself as such, in a illiberal way big-brothers the world. There is not here the liberal nationalism of which we have been speaking. Yes, as we have said, there are nationalisms and nationalisms, but liberal nationalism and progressively liberal societies are much more frail than we have acknowledged.

The verisimilitude in this should incline us to share Moore's and Prager's historical pessimism. However, the core of our response to (2) is the following: if we are just betting, it is perhaps safer to bet that things will go badly. But we are also actors in the world; we care about our situation and wish for, and some of us struggle to get, the best outcomes possible. In that context we should remind ourselves of

589

Antonio Gramsci's famous slogan about the pessimism of the intellect and the optimism of the will. Even Carol Prager allows herself a little hope at the end of her essay.

However, hope apart, the situation *may* not be as bleak as historical pessimists portray it. There is the undisputed fact that we have had peaceful successful secessionist movements in Norway and Iceland, a peaceful but perhaps ill-advised partition of the former Czechoslovakia, devolution of powers in Belgium, considerable local autonomy for Catalonia within Spain, and some movement (though not yet nearly enough) toward the recognition of First Nations in Canada, New Zealand, Australia, and the United States. And we had votes in two referenda for devolution in Scotland and Wales, for a Parliament in Scotland and a limited form of self-government in both nations. All of the various things mentioned above have happened, and are happening, in a democratic and basically liberal way, though it indeed required some extra-parliamentary opposition.

Such occurrences and the liberal nationalist theorizing that accompanies them serve as models for what can go on in other liberal societies. Suppose this continues to obtain, as it feasibly could. Suppose further that the productive forces of these societies continue to develop, and with this, as can reasonably be expected, the level of wealth, health, and education in these societies continues to rise, and with that, their productive forces come to be more intelligently deployed. These things, of course, may not happen, but they feasibly could. If they do, it is not unreasonable to believe, or at least to hope, that liberal societies will increasingly go the way Scandinavia has and that with the increased salience of democratic ideas having as a constitutive part the very central idea of national self-determination, the aspirations for self-determination (aspirations of nationalist movements) will be increasingly recognized and, as it used to be said in the days of operationalism, peacefully operationalized.

It is still a long way from there to the illiberal and largely (in varying degrees) impoverished parts of the world where barbarous nationalism is rampant. But again it is reasonable to hope that with increased education and wealth the rich liberal capitalist democracies will in time turn away from neo-liberal and other conservative orientations and increasingly, Scandinavian-style, move toward social democratic and even conceivably liberal and market socialist orientations.[5] Even social democracy, if pervasively and stably in place, will blunt the effects of neo-liberal globalization on the Second and Third Worlds as well as on the First. As we can see from Thomas Pogge's trenchantly argued essay in this volume, with even a very small transfer of resources, at great distance (*pace* Rorty) from anything that would require the impoverishment of the wealthy North or bring harm to even the North's poorest compatriots, not a little of the horrendous world poverty can be eliminated. Cutbacks in military expenses, space exploration, and other similar extravagances would greatly accelerate this elimination of such extreme poverty. It is even within the realm of feasible options, further down the line, that these impoverished Third World societies will slowly move to becoming tolerably wealthy, though probably, at least in the first instance, tolerably wealthy capitalist, societies. And this will provide one of the conditions that Moore describes in which ethnic enmities will slowly die, though we would add as well that often they will also die in time with the recognition of legitimate national aspirations to self-determination where the societies in question are not desperately poor. And where, with their realization, we will get either multinations or nation-states and not the quasi-states of the impoverished Third and Fourth Worlds. However, as Moore also envisages, sometimes ethnic enmities will die because ethnic differences will slowly lose their former importance to people, and, with that, the enmities will slowly wither away. Assimilation can be a tragic thing and is usually not to be desired, but it is not always bad when it is in no way forced. As will be seen when we discuss Brighouse, we will basically agree with Ross Poole that assimilation is generally something to be opposed. We are only claiming here that it is not always bad.

As well, there may be a continued devolution of powers to nations until someday even the United States might devolve into several different nations in some loose Swiss-style federation, thereby giving more autonomy to the inhabitants of the United States and making it a place that is more liberal both internally and externally and thus no longer

---

5   Kai Nielsen, 'Is Global Justice Impossible?' in Jay Drydyk and Peter Penz, eds., *Global Justice and Democracy* (Winnipeg/Halifax: Fernwood Publishing 1997), 19–54

such a danger to and bully of the world. This is very probably a fanciful possibility. Did not their Civil War settle that question in the United States? Fanciful or not, it is, at least arguably, what thorough liberal democratic entitlements would require. And, given what may be the long-run power of democratic ideas, it may someday come to be.

Less fancifully, the narrative of a liberal rendering of the world that we have just gestured at, which includes liberal nationalism as an integral part, *probably* is less likely than one or another of the several narratives of historical pessimism. Indeed it may turn out to be a just-so story. But it is a possible (i.e., a feasible) option that with luck and intelligent struggle might become an emancipatory social reality. For human beings thrust into a world they did not make, it is something for which they can reasonably hope and struggle. Again there is the pessimism of the intellect and the optimism of the will.

II

In this volume, nationalism, including liberal nationalism, has come under vigorous, probing, and sustained attack from Harry Brighouse, Allen Buchanan, Omar Dahbour, and Andrew Levine. We will first recall their key arguments and then see what a reasonable liberal nationalist could say in reply. It is most certainly not the task of this afterword to aim at conclusiveness of argument, but we want to raise issues, show connections between different accounts, query the most crucial arguments set forth in this volume and elsewhere (particularly in relation to other claims that have been made), and make some suggestions about our perceptions of the lay of the land and about what issues we take to be outstanding.

We will first consider some of the arguments of Omar Dahbour. He stands a bit apart from the other critics of nationalism in this volume in that, like a nationalist and a communitarian, he defends the importance of communal identities, though his identities are even more local than those of communitarian nationalists and indeed most communitarians. It is not, in his view, the identities yielded by nations that are vital for solidarity, but those formed by subnational regions (including social movements developing in such regions) and cities. Moreover, he claims that his critique of nationalism does not range over all accounts of nationalism, but only over communitarian defences of nationalism. But his two main targets are the defences of nationality and nationalism of David Miller and Michael Walzer, both of whom are communitarians (though this is a term that Walzer will not accept) *and* liberals. From his footnotes it is clear that Dahbour also applies his critique to Yael Tamir, Avishai Margalit, Joseph Raz, Charles Taylor, and Will Kymlicka, all of whom defend broadly similar conceptions of nationality, and of the right to national self-determination as Miller and Walzer do. But they are all liberals, though sometimes social democratic ones, with some communitarian leanings. Their nationalism, to the extent they have one, is, like Miller's and Walzer's, a liberal nationalism. So Dahbour's critique is broader than what he advertises, and if successful, would undermine liberal nationalism as well as non-liberal and illiberal versions of communitarian nationalism (though *some* of his arguments, as we shall see, only apply to those illiberal forms of nationalism). But other more general arguments cut against nationalism *period*. What crucially distinguishes Dahbour from Brighouse, Buchanan, and Levine is that he argues for the need to acknowledge even more local identities than do nationalists. He no doubt would also defend a cosmopolitanism, but not one that was not also very locally rooted.

Nationalists – or most of them – claim that national identities, in modern societies at least, provide the basis for political life. Many would claim that they are the only secure bases. Dahbour, by contrast, argues that "national identities cannot serve as the legitimate basis of political life." Many nationalists argue that nation-states may ensure the stable conditions for self-determination, if anything does. Against this Dahbour maintains that "nation-states do not ensure the real conditions for self-determination." And Dahbour maintains as well *contra* nationalism that "assertions of national rights are disruptive of relations between different peoples and states." Many nationalists, particularly those with a communitarian bent, including liberal nationalists such as Miller and Walzer, believe that having a secure sense of national identity is an important, indeed a crucially important, element for the very possibility of a full human existence and that we need nation-states to ensure such identities. Dahbour denies this. But he does not, as is often done, deny this on individualistic grounds. He agrees with nationalists that, for there to be a polity of any kind, there must be a firm sense of communal identity for the individuals who are members of that polity. Even liberal constitutionalism *à la* Dworkin, Rawls, and Habermas will, he argues, not suffice. Their constitutionalism is a necessary ingredient in a good polity but it is not sufficient, for it will not yield or sustain *solidarity*. We need those common identities for the minimal trust necessary for establishing mutual relations between human beings. In fine, communitarians are right in thinking that community is a basic good of some kind. But what kind exactly is another and more complicated matter, and to think that community, or for that matter anything else, is *the* fundamental good is absurd. But that it is *an* important good should be uncontroversial. Still, Dahbour argues, it is a long way from there to the nationalist claim that, at least in modern industrial societies, nations are the best manifestations of community. We need some common identities to even have a polity, but why must they be or why should they be or why is it best that they be *national* identities? Dahbour presses nationalists for sound reasons for believing that this is so. What reasons and arguments do nationalists have for that fundamental belief of theirs?

It can be argued that in modern industrial societies national identities are the best manifestation of community because in such a setting they best secure for people the right of self-determination: the right to have control over their lives. They may not gain it anyway – that, unfortunately, is the more likely scenario – but they will certainly not gain it if they lack a national identity and, in the best case at least, a nation-state giving expression to and securing that national identity. Nations are vital, the nationalist claim goes, in establishing the legitimacy of modern states and in securing solidarity within these states. This is of crucial importance as boundaries between states become more and more permeable and as the world is increasingly shaped by decisions taken at a global level. If there is to be democracy in this new world, states and governments have to be firmly guided by national solidarities. The impulse here should come from the nation up. There will be little solidarity in societies that are not nation-states or that are not genuinely multination states that maintain their multinational culture by fully recognizing and empowering its component nations. And without solidarity the lives of people will not be secure and they will not flourish as persons.

We are saying here in response to Dahbour that either nation-states or genuinely multination-states are necessary in the present world-order for solidarity and for democracy and that true solidarity and true democracy are importantly secured by instilling in the population a sense of national identity. There need not be, and indeed should not be, anything sinister, ethnocentric, paternalistic, or incapacitating of our critical faculties about this. All of us get socialized. Some socialization makes for autonomy; some fetters us. It all depends on what kind of socialization it is.[6] Instilling a sense of national identity, as we try to establish in various ways in this afterword, need not fetter at all. Indeed it can, or so we shall argue, importantly contribute to the self-respect and autonomy of people. Having in place one or another of these state forms is also necessary for stability in the society and for a sense of political legitimacy. In medieval societies closely knit local groups provided the bonding necessary for solidarity (though the solidarity was not society-wide nor did it need to be), but in modern societies with the movement of people and the creation of new forms of work the source of solidarity changed. Solidarity was once provided by the social ties rooted in the group-identities provided by local groups. But with industrialization these groups slowly dissolved or were very much diminished. They came to be for the most part replaced by larger groups, groups which became nations, with their identity rooted in their nationality, its common language, and its shared comprehensive culture. Whatever society-wide sense of solidarity and political legitimacy that people in modern societies have is rooted in that and provides the social cement necessary for the society to be stable.

To this Dahbour responds by saying that nation-states, giving expression to a principle of nationality, actually generate more conflict and insecurity than multination states, particularly when these multination states are thoroughly decentralized. (Switzerland is perhaps a good example.) Moreover, as we have seen, he believes that we certainly need a communal identity – we cannot be rootless atoms utterly lacking such identities and still thrive as human beings. Rather than a national identity what we need instead is a secure citizenship in a decentralized multination state, together with a firm sense of our local

---

6 Kai Nielsen, *Equality and Liberty* (Totowa: Rowan & Allanheld 1985), 120–1

identity – far more local than anything a nation and a sense of nationality yield. It is at such a local level that we can exercise real self-governance, but not simply or primarily as citizens of a nation-state with a firm sense of our national identities.

We think that many would simply set aside what Dahbour says as too utopian to be feasible – with its echoes of 'Small is beautiful' and the splendid anti-statist, but still socialist, anarchism of Michael Bakunin and Rudolf Rocker. That anarchist ideal is indeed a very attractive one, but it is utopian in a bad sense, for it neglects, as Marx pointed out, problems of the transition. We should now add that that 'transition' seems at least to be a transition which is not very likely to end, and thus it cannot be a genuine transition. In our skeptical moods, it seems to us that we can no more finally get a classless, stateless society than it will be the case that the series of 'caused-causes' will terminate in that Uncausal Cause that some call God. States seem to be here for good. But that is not quite fair to Dahbour, for he (his sympathies for Rocker notwithstanding) does not think we can dispense with states. What he does think is that it would be a good thing to dispense with nation-states, or at the very least severely tame them, and aim for a world of "limited and overlapping sovereignties in a world political system based on regionally autonomous and self-reliant communities...." The characteristic state form here would be that of a deeply decentralized multination state in a world system of such states, all with mutually limiting sovereignties, and with borders that are much more porous and much less fixed than the borders of the nation-states we now have. This is the real-life second-best to a Bakunian socialist anarchism with a commitment to immediately attaining statelessness.

Still, while Dahbour's conception is not wildly utopian, it is perhaps neither very feasible nor normatively speaking the best alternative available. It still might be viewed as a nostalgic looking backward to times past, failing to take to heart Ernest Gellner's anthropological-sociological arguments about the rise of nationalism with the move from agrarian societies to industrial societies and the irreversibility of that process, barring some nuclear catastrophe.[7] Perhaps Dahbour's

---

7 Ernest Gellner, *Nations and Nationalism* (Ithaca: Cornell University Press 1983)

model is a good one for agrarian societies where there is a lot of local bonding and where in central areas of their lives people have a certain kind of day-to-day control. In such a situation there will be little in the way of *national* sentiment and, where inasmuch as state forms exist at all, the states are loose, non-nationalistic – in effect multigrouped – states tolerating a lot of local autonomy not on principled grounds but because the ways in which such autonomy occurs are largely a matter of indifference to the rulers of such states as long as the people pay their taxes and do not struggle against the state.

But such an arrangement – something like the old Austro-Hungarian Empire or the Ottoman Empire – is not, as Gellner argues, functional for a modern industrial order rooted in wide universal generic education and with a considerable mobility of population. These local communities tend to evaporate with the emergence of an industrial order or at least their influence and appeal are much diminished. People shift around too much to continue to rely on their local dialects, on local ways of doing things, or on connections of kinship and other features of segmented societies. In industrial societies we need some *lingua franca* operating across societies, and not just for a small caste of elite either. It is what Latin once was, then French, and now English is, and perhaps in a couple of hundred years Chinese or Spanish will come to be. In addition, and centrally, for the nation-states of those industrial societies there is as well a need for a common national language (e.g., not a cluster of German dialects but high German) linked with universal literacy and the possession of transferable skills rooted in a common generic education. It is utterly essential for the proper functioning of such nation-states. Such a national language and education are universal in each nation and functional for its internal affairs, but they are also, in some of its elements, functional for transnational affairs. In such a world, local attachments will not supply the necessary social glue – glue that Dahbour, like communitarians, regards as essential for the proper functioning of societies and for human flourishing. But (*pace* Dahbour) the social glue essential in industrial societies for solidarity and the confidence necessary for cooperation within such societies must come from a sense of nation rooted in a firm sense of national identity.

Dahbour could respond that his account is not as nostalgic and backward looking as we are giving to understand. We neglect his stress on *new* local identities such as those yielded by new social movements springing up in both modern societies and modernizing societies. These social movements struggle, sometimes effectively, against the pervasive domination and exploitation of people by an increasingly globalized capitalism and by the nation-states, including, of course, the nation-states of the rich capitalist democracies, in bed with global capitalism. These nation-states, Dahbour has it, are part of the problem and not the surcease from exploitation and domination that communitarians take them to be. To gain recognition, nation-states must be part of "an international system of political sovereignties...." And that system is thoroughly wedded to global capitalism. So a sense of nation and national identity is not a source of struggle for liberation and for people's reasonable control over their own lives. Nations are little more than important cogs in that international system.

A splendid example of what Dahbour seems to have in mind when he speaks of a social movement is the Brazilian Movement of Sem Terra, the Landless Movement. It has in the past, though not without grim and violent struggles to seize unused land in Brazil, gained land that they have turned into highly productive farms. These people, acting resolutely in solidarity, have seized that land for themselves and made it very productive in ways that benefit many people. It has in a few years swelled into a vast movement putting enormous pressure on the Brazilian government to allocate land that was, and still is, grossly underused. In the past six years (we write in 1997) Sem Terra has 'occupied' 518 large ranches and resettled 600,000 people. Their members acting together with determination and in solidarity with others have turned themselves from landless, destitute people into people farming productively. Land that was very under-utilized or not used at all has been turned into efficiently productive farms meeting the needs of people and increasing the productive wealth of the society. This movement, which continues to grow, shows how effective such social movements can be and how they can become a deep source of identity and solidarity. Moreover, as Sem Terra grows, it becomes more diversified. It has come to concern itself with the urban poor (plentiful in Brazil) as well as the rural poor (also plentiful), linking itself with more and more elements of Brazilian society and developing transnational links as well. It is said to now have the support of 90 percent of the Brazilian people and, understandably with such extensive sympathy, is gaining support in government circles (though this is something Sem Terra's members, having been lied to before, rightly remain skeptical about).

Sem Terra started as a relatively small, resolutely militant force without the aid of the government or the support of the Brazilian nation. Indeed, it experienced resistance from the government, but, as it becomes successful, it gains ambivalent government support. Behind that, helping Sem Terra to call the tune, there is now broad popular national as well as international support. Without this Sem Terra would be unlikely to achieve its objectives, though its initial impulse had to come from successful militant action on its own. But to become a successful mass movement, since it was in no position to make a revolution, it had to gain that broad support. Local identities had to rely on eventually gaining support from national identities.[8]

The moral for us is that with Sem Terra we can see the importance of both national identities and more local identities. In a nation containing different local communities within states that are our modern states, there must be a reciprocity between them for things to work well. There must be reciprocity between at least some of the local communities, and there must, as well, be reciprocity between the national and local communities. Local communities, if they are not to be marginalized, must be linked with national identities. Neither can stand alone if anything progressive is to be achieved. Both are necessary and neither alone is sufficient for achieving widespread autonomy and human flourishing. Both national and more local identities are desirable; both can exist within a network of what could come to be decentralized, overlapping, multination states where there is limited sovereignty on all sides. But this would be a system where the several component nations with their multination state would have both sufficient power and powers (in the legal sense) to secure some considerable, though still limited, sovereignty. To be a nation, each nation must carry with it its encompassing culture. The securing of this encompassing culture within the multination state will often, but not invariably, be very central to the securing of their national language. Social movements and similar sources of local identity will not do that, but

---

8 John Vidal, 'Landless on the Long March Home,' *Guardian Weekly* (11 May 1997), 8–9

will in fact presuppose in industrial societies the encompassing culture of a nation; they, in turn, do things that nations do not and perhaps cannot do. Consider again, to illustrate our point, the case of Brazil. The Brazilian nation is not under threat. Its language and the other parts of its encompassing comprehensive culture appear at least to be secure. And to the extent that that is true, there is no need for nationalism or a *stress* on national identity or nationality in Brazil. It is, if what we said is true, simply securely there. The crucial issue in Brazil concerns the vast inequality and dire impoverishment of huge sections of the Brazilian population: there remain powerful class and strata differences that result in the people at the bottom or near the bottom having no possibilities for a decent life. Social movements among the various landless people and deeply exploited workers are front and centre. While in Wales, Quebec, and Flanders there is, to understate it, exploitation and deep inequalities, they are not so deep as in Brazil and, as desperate as the situation of the poor is in Wales, Quebec, and Flanders, there are still in these societies more social safety nets for people than in a society like Brazil. But, unlike in Brazil, their national culture, including their language, are under threat, and issues of national identity and nationalism are front and centre. It is even reasonably arguable that until the people of these countries gain effective control of their nations there is not much hope for an amelioration of the severe exploitation of some people in these societies and the extensive marginalization of others. We should be good pragmatic contextualists and be cautious of wide generalizations. Even within modern industrial societies what we should say of one society or cluster of similar societies, we should not say of others.

We should also see (*pace* Dahbour) that there is no conflict between a liberal nationalism and a respect for and a recognition of the importance of more local communal identities. We think that Dahbour is blind to this because he does not believe, or perhaps even recognize, that there is or even can be liberal nationalisms. All nationalism is for him ethnic nationalism ('ethnonationalism' seems for him also to be a pleonasm), and all national identities are taken by him to be ethnic identities. We think this to be a very fundamental mistake and we turn now to this issue.

We will begin (returning to what we briefly discussed in Section I) by making a distinction that Dahbour unfortunately does not make between ethnic nationalism and liberal nationalism – between plainly bad nationalisms and at least putatively good nationalisms – and relatedly between an ethnic conception of nationality and national identity, on the one hand, and a liberal conception of nationality and national identity on the other. Ethnic nationalism defines membership in the nation in terms of descent: put crudely, in terms of blood. Liberal nationalism, by contrast, defines nationality in terms of sharing a distinctive encompassing and integrative (sometimes called comprehensive) culture which is both cultural and political. What makes the culture a national culture (an encompassing and integrating culture) is that it is the culture of an historical community, either having a homeland (a territory they have historically occupied) or (where the nation is in diaspora) the culture of a historical and political community aspiring to a homeland: some distinctive territory of its own where it will have some form of self-governance. What makes the culture encompassing is that it is integrative of the various institutions and forms of life of the culture and that it includes the whole of the culture, all its varied institutions, social practices, and the like.

Ethnic nationalists and liberal nationalists construe *membership* in the nation differently. Ethnic nationalists determine membership in the nation by blood – by descent; liberal nationalists, by contrast, determine membership by people (various individuals) having a common encompassing culture and normally by their residing as citizens in a territory historically occupied by the nation whose members they are or, where the nation is in diaspora, by being persons sharing the same encompassing culture who aspire to have the same homeland. If the nation has a state, those who are entitled to membership – to become citizens – may come as landed immigrants to the country if they fulfill certain conditions: acquiring (if they do not already have it) the encompassing or comprehensive culture (the language, an understanding of and some attunement to the culture, and a willingness to adhere to the laws of the country). Where the nation does not have a state, or yet a state, those entitled to membership are those who come to live on the historical territory of the nation and acquire something of its encompassing culture. This, in short, is the way they become members – full-fledged members – of that nation: a way that has nothing to do with birth or blood, with kith or kin.

We can also see (*pace* Dahbour) how the cultural nation (or as R. X.

Ware calls it, the societal nation) is also, and necessarily so, a political nation, that is, it must have, or aspire to have, a legal structure, including a constitution or its functional equivalent, a set of legal practices, and in most circumstances an exclusive authoritative control (including control over the means of violence) over a certain territory and the authority to tax, control immigration, determine citizenship, and the like. Such a liberal conception of membership in a nation, unlike that of ethnic nationalism, is not exclusionary; it is open in principle at least to anyone as there are no biological or kinship blocks to citizenship. Impediments to citizenship are not at all a matter of not having the right blood. What you need to become a member of the nation is to learn its language, its customs, something of its history, and be willing to abide by its laws. There are, however, additional conditions as well: citizenship must be open in such a way that people who apply for landed immigrant status (something open to anyone who is willing to meet the aforementioned conditions) *must* (1) be accepted as landed immigrants and (2) can, after a short mandatory residence in the country in question as landed immigrants, claim citizenship and *must*, if they meet the above conditions, be accepted as citizens after going through a formal swearing-in process, where the opportunity to so swear allegiance cannot be denied them if they meet the above conditions. This is something (*pace* Walzer) which cannot be denied them if they meet the above conditions. In that way countries must have open borders.

Ethnic nationalism is centrally a matter of blood and ancestry. Liberal nationalism, by contrast, is centrally a matter of having a distinctive encompassing or comprehensive culture in a polity or in diaspora. Ethnic nationalism is closed, exclusionary, and racist, while liberal nationalism is open and a matter of cultural achievement, residence, and allegiance. The difference is well exemplified in Germany which, anomalously for a Western democracy, has an ethnic conception of citizenship and membership in a nation. The current citizenship law in Germany, rooted in an imperial decree of 1913, bases nationality on German ancestry. Under this principle of inherited nationality, we have the bizarre situation in which millions of ethnic Germans whose ancestors have lived for generations in the Volga region of the former Soviet Union, who do not speak German, and who have little acquaintance with the encompassing culture, count as Germans and upon entering the borders of Germany are entitled to citizenship automatically, while many people of Turkish (or Italian or Spanish) descent, to use examples, who were born and educated in Germany, speak fluent German, work for German companies, pay German taxes, are subject to German laws, and are fully attuned to the encompassing culture do not automatically count as Germans and have great difficulties in gaining German citizenship. With a liberal, non-ethnic nationalism, the situation would be reversed. People such as these Turkish Germans would be automatically entitled to German citizenship, if they applied and were willing to take the oath of allegiance, while ethnic Germans such as those from the Volga region could only come to acquire it by coming to reside in Germany and by coming to adopt its encompassing culture and acquiring some reasonable mastery of its language.

Dahbour does not draw this distinction and in effect treats 'ethnic nationalism,' or what he calls 'ethnonationalism,' as equivalent to 'nationalism.' He defines 'national identity' as a "set of personal characteristics ascribed to individuals denoting their kinship, ancestry, or origins," thus clearly defining 'national identity' in ethnic terms. His conception of nationalism as essentially ethnic nationalism is revealed in a passage he quotes with approval from Lewis Mumford written, revealingly, in 1938. Mumford remarks, "Only in times of war, when frontiers are closed, when the movement of men and goods and ideas across 'national' boundaries can be blocked, when a pervading sense of fear sanctions the extirpation of differences *does the national state conform to its ideal pattern*" (italics ours). But this clearly shows that Dahbour takes it that the 'ideal pattern' of nationalism is that of an ethnic nationalism and a fairly virulent one at that – a nationalism, as he goes on to say, that must lead to a militarized Warfare State rather than to a Welfare State of peaceful social democracies. It cannot, when nationalism conforms to its *ideal* pattern, help but be xenophobic, authoritarian, exclusivist, and not infrequently expansionist as well. Nationalists, on such a conception, will claim that a people should give their highest loyalty to their nation and that the state policy of a nation-state should be above all the pursuit of 'the national interest,' if not national greatness, and that in politics all other interests should be subordinate to its achievement. International treaties, the welfare of other countries and nationals, must give way, no matter how much harm is done to those others, to the national interests and the national projects of one's own nation-state. In short nationalism so conceived, with its communitarian underpinning, has a view of political community in which, as Dahbour puts it, "nations are entitled to protect their communal integrity by whatever means are necessary." Thus the Nazi state, as a one-time embodiment of the German nation, is entitled to exterminate the Jews to maintain its communal integrity, an integrity which requires on their view a *Juden Frei* world. This, of course, is vilely extreme, yet it seems to be sanctioned by such a conception, at least if it is consistently adhered to. But it is just such a conception that Dahbour takes to be inescapable for nationalism; not just ethnic nationalism, but any nationalism. That is to say, someone who accepts that conception cannot consistently reject such revolting exemplifications. Hardly surprisingly, Dahbour firmly rejects it, thinking that in doing so he has rejected nationalism *tout court*. This results from his ignoring both the very idea of a liberal nationalism *and* its sociological reality. But there are actually existing nationalisms fitting the model of liberal nationalism, as Will Kymlicka and Jocelyne Couture have pointed out, as well as Geneviève Nootens in this volume, that are not intolerant or even exclusionist, to say nothing of being bestial as were Fascist nationalisms.[9]

Liberal nationalism, as we have observed, does not determine nationality in terms of descent, and it does not take the furthering of the interests of the nation as justifying the inhuman treatment of people or the running roughshod over their rights. Some 'nationalisms,' Kymlicka remarks, "are peaceful, liberal and democratic, while others are xenophobic, authoritarian and expansionist."[10] Earlier in this century, nationalist movements in Norway and Iceland were peaceful and democratic, fitting in well with a liberal conception of society. So it is

---

9 Will Kymlicka, 'Misunderstanding Nationalism,' *Dissent* (1995), 130–7; Jocelyne Couture, 'Pourquoi devrait-il y avoir un conflit entre le nationalisme et le libéralisme politique?' in F. Blais, G. Laforest, and D. Lamoureux, eds., *Libéralismes et nationalismes*. Coll. *Philosophie et Politique* (Québec: Les Presses de l'Université Laval 1995), 51–75

10 Kymlicka, 'Misunderstanding Nationalism,' 132

(*pace* Dahbour, Shklar, and Barry[11] as well) not nationalism *per se* that should be rejected, but *illiberal* forms of nationalism.[12] Dahbour both ignores the relevant conceptual distinctions and sociological realities and, by a combination of stipulation (selective *persuasive* definitions) and selective examples, makes nationalism look bad. But that is word magic and biased sampling. The reality is that some forms are bad – indeed some forms are plainly deeply evil and destructive – and other forms are not, but are forms of nationalism that under certain conditions arguably (as we shall see) can contribute to greater equality, autonomy, and human flourishing without anyone's rights being trampled on or even troubled.

We will now turn to a crucial specific place where Dahbour is led astray by his failure to envisage that liberal nationalism is a possibility even for those with communitarian propensities such as Walzer, Taylor, and Miller. He makes the point, forcefully made as well by Miller, Walzer, Gellner, and Buchanan, that, since there are more nations than there are territories on which they could form nation-states some nations cannot have their own nation-states. They must settle instead for a form of self-government that is less complete than that of a sovereign state. Indeed nationalists of every nation want, and understandably so, their own nation-state or a genuine recognition within a multination state. *Ceteris paribus* it is within nation-states or such multination states that their nationhood would be most secure. But sometimes there are competing historically based claims to the same territory for a homeland. That is to say, sometimes there is more than one nation on a given territory or aspiring to be on it with a genuine historical rationale. Against that background Dahbour asks the question "Why should nations renounce or modify their claims to be states?" He answers that there is no reason available within nationalism with its communitarian underpinnings for nationalists to modify their claims. Following the

---

11 Judith Shklar, 'Liberalism of Fear,' in N. Rosenblum ed., *Liberalism and the Moral Life* (Cambridge, MA: Harvard University Press, 1989); Brian Barry, 'Nationalism,' in David Miller, ed., *The Blackwell Encyclopaedia of Political Thought* (Oxford: Basil Blackwell 1987), 352–4

12 Yael Tamir, *Liberal Nationalism* (Princeton: Princeton University Press 1993)

'nationalist principle' (see our Introduction, part II) they will simply push for sovereignty and have to fight it out with their opponents where there are such conflicting claims to a territory for a homeland. Their conception of a political community, he claims, is "in important ways 'antipolitical' in the sense that it leaves no room for the virtues of political judgment, debate, or compromise." Why would a nation seeking a state accept anything less "if it regarded its right to one to be rooted in the very structure of political life"?

It should in turn be replied that any reasonable political theory, including robust nationalist ones, will recognize that *any right* is defeasible and can upon occasion be rightly overridden by other normative considerations, including being sometimes trumped by other rights, without that right ceasing to be a right. That is true of rights generally and thus it is true of the right to national self-determination.[13] This will be particularly obvious for nationalisms (communitarian or otherwise) that are embedded in liberal theories. Moreover, if the liberal nationalism is even a reasonably philosophically sophisticated one it will not, as Dahbour makes the nationalists do, accept "the right of national groups to political power" as a bedrock principle. There are no bedrock principles on such an account. To believe there are sits ill with the fallibilism and coherentism and antifoundationalism of a philosophically sophisticated liberal nationalism.[14] There will be a connected cluster of principles embedded in a connected cluster of social practices as part of a web of interconnected beliefs. Some will be more deeply embedded in and more central to the web of beliefs than others, but there will be no supreme principle or set of supreme principles. There will, that is, be no bedrock principle or set of bedrock principles that always calls the tune, in terms of which everything else that is morally and politically relevant must be justified. In some contexts some principles will have greater weight and in others, others will. There is no supreme prin-

13 Kai Nielsen, *After the Demise of the Tradition* (Boulder: Westview Press 1991), 101–24, and *Naturalism without Foundations* (Amherst: Prometheus Books 1996), 229–60

14 Nielsen, *Naturalism without Foundations*, 23–77

ciple to decide everything or even to break what looks like ties. And all beliefs are fallibilistically held; all are subject, as they work together in a coherent pattern of beliefs, including normative beliefs, to modification and revision and even abandonment. Nations have a right to self-determination and because of that they have a right, if the proper conditions obtain, to become nation-states. There is a *presumption* in favour of the claim that a nation, just in virtue of being a nation, has a right to its matching nation-state. But it is just that – a presumption. That claim, however, as all claims, can, and should, upon occasion be overridden.

Suppose for instance that another nation on the same territory has, as far as we can at the time ascertain, an equally valid claim to found a nation-state on the same territory. Then fairness requires that neither side try to establish their state, but that they should seek some other solution. Perhaps the solution should be to accept the idea of their being two nations with more limited sovereignty in a decentralized multination state. Or perhaps partition, where it is practically feasible, should be negotiated between them. Nationalists, if they are at all sensible, will not be, *à la* Bentham or Nozick, one-valued people. They will have a cluster of related values of which the principle of national self-determination is only one. Moreover, if they are also liberals, as Miller and Walzer are, they will also be committed to principles of tolerance, equal respect for all people, *moral* equality (i.e., that the life of everyone matters and matters equally) along with the related belief that the interests of all human beings have in principle an equal right to be satisfied. Similarly, liberal nationalists will have as *a* key (not *the* key) political and moral principle, a principle of equal respect for all peoples. This is a cosmopolitan and internationalist attitude that goes with, not against, their liberal nationalism. They may very well have a maxim 'compatriots first,' but that will be understood as compatriots first, *ceteris paribus*, and it will be recognized that it is often the case that *ceteris* is not *paribus*. (In this volume Thomas Pogge's remarks are very important in this regard.) A reasonable liberalism will be coherentist and non-foundationalist, through and through, claiming no principles to be the supreme overriding principles. There is, that is, no principle or cluster of related principles that always trumps all other principles and always determines which practices are legitimate.

So there is a plain rationale for the nationalist, particularly for the nationalist who accepts the nationalist principle, to renounce or modify, on certain occasions, her claim to a state of her own – a state that is her nation's state – and she can make no claim to an unqualified territoriality. We have just given a rationale for this, rooted in liberal moral thinking of a rather untendentious sort. But there is a compatible prudential rationale as well for such a nationalism, rooted in the sensible wish to avoid intractable conflict and strife and repeated power plays whose outcomes are often uncertain and historically unstable. There are, that is, good Hobbesian reasons for being circumspect and flexible in one's claims for a nation-state to match one's nation. Nationalists should have a proper regard for the welfare and integrity of their nation. But that, if they are reasonable or even just prudent, will not come to pushing for a nation-state no matter what. Neither morality nor prudence recommends that.

This is not all that can or should be said about Dahbour's intricate, extended, well-informed, probing, and original essay. But it is almost all that we have space to consider. In saying the little more that we do – a critical little more – we do not wish to leave the impression that we think Dahbour's account is fundamentally misconceived – that what he says is all dross – or even to deny that with some modifications, amplifications, and perhaps some retractions there may not be resources in his theory to respond to our critique. But we have, we believe, pointed to places where his argument is at least inconclusive and to important roads not taken that makes nationalism a more reasonable alternative than he thinks is the case.

A reasonable nationalism, to start some specification of this, with its principle of national self-determination, should not be committed to what Dahbour rightly calls "the elusive goal of a world divided without remainder between nation-states." We also agree with him that it is not always a good thing that there be a separation of peoples from one another into distinct nation-states. Sometimes, indeed often, that is a good thing, most particularly when the viability of a culture is threatened, but sometimes (though less frequently) even when it is not. We should go case by case. But we do think that it is not infrequently reasonable for a nation to want its own state and that *ceteris paribus* nations ought to have them in those circumstances unless some mutually acceptable arrangements within a multination state could become feasibly mutually advantageous for the component nations.[15] But to claim this is a far cry from making an unconditional and unqualified claim to their own exclusive territoriality and absolute territorial hegemony. Or to a claim, just as absurd, that each nation *must* have its own nation-state.

We also agree with Dahbour that it is a mistake to believe, as Walzer does, that the distribution of membership in a nation-state is not "subject to the constraints of justice" and that "states are simply free to take in strangers (or not)...." If, however, we try to unravel this complicated issue, it cannot be as straightforward as Walzer tries to make it. If applicants for citizenship meet the requirements we characterized a few pages back, then a *just* state – subject (as we did not mention there) to the imperatively realistic constraints of really serious problems of overcrowding or economic undermining – *must* grant them citizenship. There are, of course, fully at play here the realistic type of considerations that John Rawls alludes to when he speaks of "the strains of commitment." Still, if a state fails to grant persons citizenship under the conditions just described, then there is a lapse, though often a very understandable one, in justice. The state, *realpolitik* to the contrary notwithstanding, is not behaving as it *ideally* ought. The claims of sovereignty have no more grounds for being treated as *absolute* (totally unconditional) than any other normative claims. No moral claims have that pristine status, and the claim that the state has such an unchallengeable right (current international law to the contrary notwithstanding) to determine who can enter and who can exit is no exception to that general fallibilism.[16] A reasonable nationalist – communitarian or otherwise – will not take such a claim to be absolute or unconditional. She will recognize that a nation's push for its own nation-state is *sometimes* not justified and that a state's right to control exit and entry is not absolute.

Dahbour argues that "political identities may have antecedents in non-political forms of life." While not dissenting from that, we do not agree that national identities are pre-political. They are, given the closely

---

15 Kai Nielsen, 'Secession: The Case of Quebec,' *Journal of Applied Philosophy* **10**:1 (1993), 29–46

16 Nielsen, *After the Demise of the Tradition*, 101–54

similar conception that Miller, Walzer, and Kymlicka deploy and that we have deployed as well, inextricably both political *and* cultural. More specifically such conceptions are inherently political in the sense that nations aspire to some form or other of political self-government. A nation, as we construe it, is political in the sense that it is identical with some form of political community. Perhaps the modernists are right and we should reject *primordialist* conceptions of nationality, to wit "the idea that national identities have deep roots in historically ancient, or 'primordial' circumstances." Perhaps it would be better for a nationalist to take a view similar to Gellner's, that is to say, a view that regards nations and 'national identities' as comparatively recent phenomena arising with industrial societies.[17] Though no doubt, as nations, national identities, and nation-states were being forged, use was made of cultural materials from earlier societies. There were often, perhaps always, elements of culture there which causally affected the particular forms the various nations came to have. But that is still distant from a primordialist theory or even premodern conception of nationality. We are not saying that the nations were just there from time immemorial. With such a broadly Gellnerish modernist view, we still could, and should, agree with Miller that "nations *really* exist [and] identifying with a nation, feeling yourself *inextricably* part of it, is a legitimate way of understanding your place in the world."[18] Reflecting on this, Dahbour simply foists a primordialist view on Miller. But that is not entailed by what Miller says. For something to exist – even 'really' exist – it need not have existed from time immemorial.

Dahbour remarks, unexceptionally enough, that political identities formed on the basis of national identities *may* be the result of custom, prejudice, and oppression. That is inescapable. But the same thing applies for the more local identities he has appealed to as well. Indeed, the political identities formed by local identities are very likely to be the result of custom, prejudice, and oppression. But we have shown earlier how the nationalist, as well as anyone else, can perfectly well

---

17 Gellner, *Nations and Nationalism*

18 David Miller, *On Nationality* (Oxford: Clarendon Press 1995), 10–11. Quoted by Dahbour and italics added by Dahbour.

use coherentist criteria (say, wide reflective equilibrium) to correct for the distortions introduced by custom, prejudice, and for what has come about as a result of oppression. We are all on Otto Neurath's boat – nationalists and anti-nationalists alike – and we must, being so situated, unable as we are to stand free from our histories, cultures, and practices, plank by plank, always working from inside, repair and refashion the ship at sea. Not being able to stand completely outside of all our practices (the very idea of doing so being unintelligible), but rather at any time having to rely on some of our practices, which on another occasion, using still other practices, we can assess, does not lead us to relativism or ethnocentrism. But it does lead us to contextualism and historicism.[19] Being so inevitably placed inside our practices – there is no other place to be – does not mean that we cannot intelligibly step outside of even a very big hermeneutical circle. Any practice or limited cluster of practices can be criticized by using other practices which can in turn be criticized by using still other practices. What we cannot do is stand free of all practices *at once*. In understanding anything and criticizing anything we must be using some practices.[20] Here John Dewey, Hans-Georg Gadamer, Donald Davidson, and Robert Brandon all make common cause.

Relatedly (*pace* Dahbour) both his more localized communal identities and national identities are "capable of incorporating the principled or communicative aspects of political identity." They can incorporate, that is, such salient conceptions from Ronald Dworkin and Jürgen Habermas. The only reason for denying this of national identities, while accepting it for more local communal identities, is Dahbour's arbitrary identification of nationalism with illiberal nationalism, leaving liberal nationalism out in the cold. It is true that nationalism sometimes "colonizes local life on the basis of the dominance,

---

19 Kai Nielsen, *Naturalism without Foundations*, 25–77

20 Robert Brandon, *Making It Explicit: Reasoning, Representing and Discursive Commitment* (Cambridge: Harvard University Press 1994), 'Replies.' *Philosophy and Phenomenological Research*, **57:1**, 197–204; Richard Rorty, 'What Do We Do When They Call You a Relativist?' *Philosophy and Phenomenological Research*, **57:1** (1997), 173–7

enforced by the state, of one region over others." This indeed is what often spurs secessionist movements and sometimes unfortunately revanchism, and in such circumstances we very often get nationalisms which are illiberal. But to say, as Dahbour does, that it is something that nationalism *not sometimes*, but *inevitably*, does is again simply to ignore the fact of liberal nationalism both as a theory and a *sociological reality*. There have been nationalist movements in liberal democratic states – Quebec and Belgium, for example – that have not dominated, or tried to dominate, the minorities in their territories and have acknowledged their full set of civil and human rights.[21] And this is exactly what liberal nationalism as a theory and as a coherent ideological movement is committed to. Dahbour has given us no reason to think such a nationalism is either impossible or in error.

What we have argued that Dahbour basically fails to see is that communitarianism and liberalism, at least over the issues we have discussed, can coherently go together (there can be a communitarian liberalism, if you will) and that there can be a liberal nationalism, much like that of Miller's and Walzer's, with a conception of nationality and a tandem conception of the central importance of nations in political and social thought, that does not have the untoward features of nationalism specified by Dahbour.

III

Dahbour, as we have seen, defends an appeal to local cultures with smaller, and what he takes to be, psychologically and socially speaking, more rooted units than nations. Harry Brighouse and Andrew Levine, by contrast, as Levine puts it, "endorse a cosmopolitan world view in which nationalist aspirations ultimately have no place." We will restate certain of their core arguments and attempt to show in opposition to them that a *rooted* cosmopolitanism will recognize the deep significance of nationality in making sense of human life in con-

---

21 Kymlicka, 'Misunderstanding Nationalism,' 130–7; Kai Nielsen, 'Cultural Nationalism, Neither Ethnic Nor Civic.' *The Philosophical Forum*, **28:1-2** (1996-97), 42–52

ditions of modernity informed by Enlightenment values.[22] Nationality will appropriately continue to have moral and political force and
not just as a flawed idea of our intellectual and political immaturity
and not just as a historical expediency in a certain phase of modernity. Or so at least we shall argue against Brighouse's and Levine's
powerfully articulated views. Unlike Brighouse and Levine, we shall
contend that the most adequate expression of cosmopolitanism will
make room for a sense of nationality – the sense of nationality captured by liberal nationalism. Levine grants that "ambivalence to nationalism is a reasonable, if not entirely satisfactory, response to the
situation we actually confront." But, he adds, in a reasonable world
with a thoroughly just social order in which we had fully overcome
our 'self-incurred nonage' a sense of nationality would have no place.
In such a situation, he has it, "the nationalist temptation itself would
pass into obsolescence."

Levine develops an extended analogy between the phenomena of
religion and nationalism. He first accounts how, against the background of Enlightenment critiques of religion, Freud developed an
account of how religion – and most particularly theistic religion —
was a flawed idea resting on an illusion grounded in historically transitory conditions. Similarly nationalism, a belief in nationality and the
pressing of nationalist sentiments, Levine claims, rest on an illusion.
If conditions change, theistic religion might – just might – wither
away. In a parallel way, Levine ventures the conjecture that nationalism similarly rests on an illusion and that 1) "a post-nationalist future is a genuine possibility" and 2) an unequivocally cosmopolitan
stance – a stance that he, like Brighouse, takes to be incompatible with
even the maturest forms of nationalism – "will one day become morally possible." But, just as for now and for the foreseeable future religion is with us, so for now and for the foreseeable future ambivalence
about nationalism and even, in some circumstances, acceptance of nationalism is a "reasonable, if not entirely satisfactory, response to the
situation we actually confront." Moreover, just as a fully cosmopolitan
outlook rooted in Enlightenment values and conceptions would be free

---

22 Appiah, 'Cosmopolitan Patriots,' 21–29

of theistic belief, so a fully cosmopolitan outlook would be free of nationalist commitments.

In those parts of the world deeply affected by modernity, Levine remarks, "religion has effectively migrated from the public arena to the sphere of private conscience" and with this, in such societies, religion's "political impact has lessened." Moreover, many people affected deeply by the Enlightenment and modernity "experience the inability to understand [religious] belief empathetically as a triumph." They consider themselves, and without ambivalence, regret, or nostalgia, as *'beyond* theism.' They see religious beliefs as illusions, that is, as beliefs not held in consequence of rationally compelling reasons but because they are expressions of unconscious wishes. Enlightenment thinking in the tradition of Hume-Marx-Freud, and shared by many secularizers, contains the injunction that we should "face the world as it is, without benefit of comforting but indefensible illusions that represent only how we would like the world to be." If we can bring ourselves to follow this injunction we will come to live without theistic beliefs and parallelly, Levine maintains, if we follow this injunction, we will live without nationalistic commitments or any belief in the inherent value of nationality. "Nationalism is at best, a passing phase in humanity's progress towards something more 'mature'."

Today nationalism generally gets a more favourable press than it got in the past. But that notwithstanding, it is Levine's belief, and Brighouse's as well, that this traditional Enlightenment conception is the way we should view things. Indeed a thoroughly cosmopolitan view of the world, they have it, requires it.

However, things are complicated, Levine adds, even for "those of us who think of nationalism as a vestige of humanity's 'nonage'," for we have also seen that *sometimes* nationalisms on the ground – really existing nationalisms – have served as the agent for progressive social change. Beside, those of us affected, as almost all of us now are, by broadly Rawlsian conceptions of justice and political legitimacy will take a somewhat different attitude towards both religion and nationalism than most pre-Rawlsian liberals and radicals did. We will stress, as Rawls himself does, "that religions are of deep importance in many people's lives – that they are constitutive, in some cases, of long-term projects and plans of life, and that they serve as elements in the construction of particular personal identities."[23] Because they are, for many people, sociologically and psychologically speaking, so fundamentally important, legitimate political "institutions are obliged to protect them wholeheartedly and fairly – without favouritism to some religions over others or even to religion over non-belief."

The analogy between nationality and religion is, as Levine recognizes, not perfect, but it is close enough to make rationally compelling the extension of the liberal consensus concerning respect for religion in the public domain to nationality. Nationality, like religion, matters fundamentally to many people and "its protection must therefore be of paramount concern in any just society." A just society "cannot rightfully repress nationalist aspirations and ... it must be fair to competing nationalist claims."

Those, like Brighouse and Levine, who are against nationalism can consistently support such views. "There is no inconsistency," Levine remarks, "in holding the view that justice sometimes implies support for nationality and a cosmopolitan world outlook too." As atheists who are also Rawlsians must and, of course, consistently can support religious toleration, as Geneviève Nootens has well explained in her essay, so a cosmopolitan who is also a Rawlsian must accept the legitimacy of a "national minority to maintain and strengthen its nationalist identifications." In short, as Levine puts it, "respect for nationality at the political level, like toleration for religious doctrines and practices, is compatible with virtually any assessment of the merits of these positions or of the sentiments that make them compelling to the people who hold them."

So, as a matter of political morality, including a very fundamental belief in the respect for persons, someone who accepts a broadly Rawlsian conception of justice and political legitimacy, as both Brighouse and Levine do, will also accept the legitimacy of nationalist aspirations. But why then at a deeper level are they against nationalism? What are the grounds for Levine's claim that "a truly rational nationalism is an impossibility even in principle"? Levine's arguments are more general and more historically sweeping than Brighouse's

---

23 John Rawls, *Political Liberalism* (New York: Columbia University Press 1993)

which emerge in the context of a detailed critique of William Galston's, David Miller's, and Will Kymlicka's defences of nationality. Generally speaking, however, their cases against nationalism mesh and are mutually supportive. We will argue that as probing, nuanced, and in many ways right-minded as they are, they are still seriously flawed and fail to undermine the case for a rooted cosmopolitan liberal nationalism. They fail to show that such a view cannot be through and through reasonable and rational.

While Levine stresses, as we have seen, that "nationalism ... is a fact of political life that just polities must accommodate" and is a "genuine political ideology suitable for guiding political practice in the short and long run," still we will not, he also has it, be nationalists if we will face the world as it is without comforting illusions. Nationalism, as Levine summarizes, "is based on a wish, not a reality – because the nation is not found and sometimes even deliberately contrived."

The nation, on Levine's account, is not just something there in the world to discover, and nationalist sentiments, the notion of a nation and the nation-state, have not always been with us. They are not as old as social life and societal cultures themselves. Levine, in this part of his argument, agrees with Ernest Gellner that these notions emerged with capitalism and modernization and that they are functionally indispensable for modernization. Nations came into being with the nation-state system that emerged with capitalism. And national identities – identifying ourselves as members of a nation and prizing that identification — are essential to produce the social bonding for such national economies so that they will function efficiently and, what is another side of the same coin, so that such nation-states will be stable. Even though nationalism is functional in modern and modernizing societies, unlike patriotism (i.e., the "support for the political community of which one is a part, for its fundamental constitutional arrangements, irrespective of the ethnic or national composition of that community"), nationalism can never be rational, "even when it is incontrovertibly 'progressive'" for a "nation is nothing if not an expression of a wish, a wish for a community that extends throughout time, uniting generations, and across space, incorporating strangers." But this, Levine claims, is an *illusory wish* that is "always at least somewhat at odds with the facts."

However intensely they may come to be experienced, nationalist sentiments, according to Levine, "are always to some degree contrived

– not just in the way all social identities are 'socially constructed,' but in a more straightforward way." "Nationalisms," Levine claims, "are deliberately contrived and promoted." They are, he further continues, "the work of political entrepreneurs who mold popular longings for communal forms appropriate to modern life in nationalist directions." That there are peoples making up such communities is a fabrication of nationalist writers giving people just-so stories about who they are. The old feudal solidarities dissolved with modernizing capitalist economies. They were hardly functional even then. But these new economies (these new modes of production), with nation-states functional for them, had to forge new solidarities to replace the dissolving, now dysfunctional, feudal solidarities at the level of the national economies themselves.

Nations were indeed not, Levine admits, "fabricated out of thin air." They are not *just* creatures of our imagination. There were previously existing cultural materials used in their forging. The French, German, and Italian languages, essential for these nations, were constructed out of different dialects bearing some relation to modern French, German, and Italian, but still these modern languages were constructed and coercively promoted. And not without a point, for the capitalist order and modernity more generally and the systems of general education that went with them, were essential to these nations and to the modern economies of these states. Their respective comprehensive cultures were not just something in some recognizable (though still slowly changing) form, which was always there. The historical conditions that produced them "failed to obtain for most of human history," and they, as Levine puts it, "could well cease to exist again."

Levine ends his essay by asking, "What remains when nationalist illusions are finally overcome?" He responds: "At a very high level of generality, the answer is clear: real, not imagined communities." We need, he tells us, "to build communities without illusions." And the first step here is to become clearer about what this goal implies.

We will query his claim, remembering that validity is independent of origin, that nationalist sentiments, just in being nationalist sentiments, must reflect *illusory* wishes. Sometimes they do and sometimes, we shall argue, they do not. Perhaps nations, like all cultural phenomena, are in some sense 'socially constructed,' but they need not always be imagined, fabricated, or deliberately contrived creatures of political ideology. They, like all cultural phenomena, arise at a particular time,

617

are subject to certain historical vicissitudes and contingencies, change and decline, and answer to certain determinate economic relations. Nation-states, a sense of nation, and nationalist sentiments are functional for certain economic relations, and not for others.[24] But this is true of all cultural phenomena of this very general type – the medieval solidarities and the solidarities of the ancient world as well as modern nationalist solidarities. A sense of national identity need be no more, or no less, constructed than any of the historically previous solidarities. If they are 'imagined' then all cultural phenomena are imagined, i.e., socially constructed, and all cultural phenomena rest on illusions – on a wish fulfilment that is in someway at odds with the facts about people and societies. But this fuses together ideas that should be kept distinct. Being socially constructed, being rooted in wishes, and being at odds with the facts are all different things. Moreover, this renders the very idea of 'a community without illusions,' a Holmes-less Watson, for lack of even a possible non-vacuous contrast. It says, in a misleading way, that *all* cultural phenomena are illusory. 'A non-illusory community,' by implicit *persuasive* definition, becomes an oxymoron. This is a *reduction* that Levine rightly will reject. But then his claim that nations, a sense of nationality, and nationalist sentiments *must* rest on illusory wishes about what some people want, and thus cannot be rationally grounded, is at best false. Levine must show something more straightforward than that these ideas have a determinate historical origin, are functional for a given type of society, and coincide with the aspirations of certain people. He must show that they are illusory wishes answering to nothing in reality. (Moreover, '*illusory* wishes' must *not* be in effect treated as if it is pleonastic). That a person wants a socialist transformation of society is not a good reason in itself to believe that it is unrealistic to believe that a socialistic transformation of society can, or perhaps even will, obtain.

Is there anything more straightforward that Levine could appeal to in order to show that nations are imagined and national sentiments are illusory? Does he have any more specific grounds for his claim that nationalist beliefs are dubious and that nationalist sentiments lack ra-

---

24 Gellner, *Nations and Nationalism*

tional grounding? Well, he could rightly respond that *some,* sometimes plainly, lack such grounding. Many, perhaps all, African or Arabian nations – in some instances nations forged by colonial powers out of disparate groupings of people – are *contrived* communities with no roots in history or determinate long-standing territorial claims. They are the contrivances of the colonial powers. *These* nations are in a more determinate sense imagined than are some other nations which are also simple social constructions as perhaps all cultural groups are social constructions. But to vindicate Levine's strong claim one must go from *some* to *all* and indeed to the claim that there is something about the very idea of a nation that makes it an *illusory* community. But he has done neither of these things.

Levine's argument presupposes that all nations are the creation of an 'ideological state apparatus.' But what about stateless nations, imbedded in a repressive state, and what about nationalist movements aiming at the political sovereignty of such nations? They are not so rare that we should ignore them. These nationalist movements often take the form of an authentic struggle for democracy and justice. Why should we think that they are not, and cannot be, rationally grounded or that they are the creation of the ideological state apparatus? Can they not be movements which are, in Rawls's terms, both rational and reasonable? Moreover, these movements appeal to solidarities based on a common history of injustice, domination, and sometimes exploitation inflicted on peoples because they happen to have certain traditions, culture, language, or sometimes skin colour. To say that these nations are not real is to add insult to injury. And to say that they were 'not found' but contrived by a State which was precisely trying to repress or even eradicate them is something, to understate it, which is not obviously true. It is true that these movements express a wish, perhaps not likely to be realized, for a better society. But so do our aspirations for liberalism or cosmopolitanism. Again, should we abandon our wishes for a better society because that society does not correspond to 'the facts' of our actual circumstances? To claim that is what it is to be tough-minded is a bit of a persuasive definition.

Moreover, over time with the forging of a national language (e.g., French, forged in a territory that once contained seventeen distinct languages) and the comprehensive culture that goes with it, what started out as contrivance can as time passes become rooted in people living in a determinate territory with what has become a common comprehensive culture pervasively adopted in the territory in question. Indeed this has happened again and again. To speak of such communities as 'imagined communities' is not only misleading, it is a mistake. All social constructions are *not* imagined. And what started as contrivance can over time become something very different. Levine here misses the importance of Brighouse's point about attending to the dynamic effect of the reproduction of culture.

Perhaps it is not nationalism or nationalist sentiments that should be said to be illusory, but *a powerful image of the world and ourselves as human beings* that *often* goes with the nationalist project. In an important passage which we have already cited, Levine writes that the nation is a mere expression of "a wish for a community that extends throughout time, uniting generations, and across space, incorporating strangers. But this wish is always at least somewhat at odds with the facts." Levine is surely right, and importantly so, about this. There is, our dreams notwithstanding, no such community that is so transhistorical or indeed in any way transhistorical. Nationalism, *in this sense*, is illusory. It is understandable that we should so wish to escape the vicissitudes of time and deep, typically irreversible, change, but there is no such escape. That is a utopian dream and we should be grateful to Levine for so clearly pointing this out to us.

But we need not give such a utopian range to our imagination – to our humanly understandable wishful thinking. We need not so embellish our sense of being a member of a nation. Is there not a more modest, more realistic, belief in the importance of nations, the significance of national identification, the seeing of ourselves as a people, as members of a distinct nation with its distinctive language and pervasive culture? Is such a conception of nationality at odds with the facts? And is that not something that is important to retain? Is seeing ourselves as Mexicans, New Zealanders, Cubans, or French something that is of no human importance or at least something which would be transcended with greater maturity? Seeing ourselves as *superior* or the ways of our culture to be just the right way of doing things is indeed something urgently in need of being firmly set aside as blindness or arrogant ethnocentrism. Liberal nationalists cannot be committed to ethnocentrism of any kind. Indeed, as soon as a trace of it is recognized, a consistent liberal nationalism must repudiate it. But to have a sense of being a people need not be ethnocentric. And, shorn of dreams of historical transcendence or of mythological self-seeking and self-glorifying national historical narratives (the history of the nation we get taught in school), it need not be illusory. Neither Levine nor Brighouse nor Buchanan, who makes similar points against nationalism, have done anything to show that having a sense of belonging to a group and attaching importance to this group belonging and identification is irrational or something to be abandoned with greater maturity and a 'more universalistic' outlook.

Levine, following Gellner, has claimed that only with the rise of capitalism and modernity does this group identification take the form of national identification. It is the form of group identification that goes with modernity, that is, with capitalist societies and with postcapitalist societies (when we get them), including such socialist ones as might come into being. And given that group identity, of which national identity is a subspecies, is so humanly ubiquitous and taken by almost all human beings to be so important, what is the basis for saying it is illusory? Here is an important disanalogy between nationalism and religious feelings which are also pan-culturally ubiquitous, but which can still be said to be illusory because they rest on *cosmological* beliefs which are at best false.[25] But what are the false *cosmological* beliefs, or even *just false beliefs*, that go with attaching importance to group identity? Levine does not say, and it is, to put it minimally, not evident that there are any.

That nationalism, any form of nationalism, involves such a mythical embellishment of the nation and/or a sense of inherent superiority is also a claim made by Brighouse. Nationalism implies, Brighouse has it, that the "state involves itself in deliberately trying to condition consent in a way that bypasses the critical faculties of its citizens and future citizens." Nationalism, he argues, is committed to manufacturing a kind of mythical history, a 'history' which at crucial points deliberately bypasses, without caring about truth, what rigorous and critical research would put before us and which gives us instead "a nobler, moralizing history: a pantheon of heroes who confer legitimacy on central institu-

---

25 Kai Nielsen, 'Naturalistic Explanations of Religion.' *Studies in Religion*, forthcoming, and his *Naturalism without Foundations*

tions and are worthy of emulation."[26] Nationalists claim, Brighouse also has it, "that nationality has a special importance that should inform institutional design" and that a sense of nationality is crucial for our having firm personal identities. But in achieving that, Brighouse avers, nationalism also carries with it the idea that certain people, as members of a particular nation, "are superior to others in a way that justifies overriding the interests of non-nationals as well as some of the claims of national members."

We cannot but agree that when nationalism leads to such things, then nationalism is bad. It is completely unacceptable for nationalists (or for that matter, anyone else) to argue that students should have a 'civic education' centrally involving a *mythical* history. To do this, to put it bluntly, is to replace history with propaganda. Such 'civic education' fails to respect human beings by paternalistically teaching them 'noble lies' which bypass (or try to bypass) their intelligence and integrity. But while *some* nationalists have argued in defence of such a mythological 'history,' and claimed the inherent superiority of their nation, it is not even remotely, as we said before, a viable option for a liberal nationalism. Institutions which seek to pervert our ability to use our critical intelligence and undermine equal respect for people are completely unacceptable. But such things are not inherent components of having a sense of national identity and are plainly incompatible with liberal nationalism. There are, as we have seen, nationalisms and nationalisms.

Brighouse makes another critical point against nationalism to which any liberal nationalist who is also a socialist must be particularly sensitive. His critical point is that nationalism with its stress on national identities frequently has "disruptive effects ... on class solidarities, and hence on redistribution." He goes on to remark that "national identity is often used with some success in capitalist democracies to persuade working people that they should moderate their demands, and to impugn the responsibility of political agents who advocate a more militant stance." This was dramatically exemplified by all the contesting powers in and around the First World War. And it has been used again

---

26   William Galston, 'Two Concepts of Liberalism,' *Ethics* **105:66** (1991), 516–34

and again both before and since. But it is something that does not, as Brighouse himself recognizes, necessarily go with nationalism. A liberal nationalist must (1) reject this kind of repressive ideology, and this mystifying of people, out of hand and (2) be on guard against its arising in nationalist movements. Though it *has* gone with nationalism it *need* not and *should* not go with nationalism.

Brighouse also objects to nationalism and to having national sentiments because they promote, according to him, loyalty to *the existing order*. Given what most – and perhaps all – existing states are actually like, this is indeed a bad thing. But such a claim shows that Brighouse, no more than Levine, pays attention to the nationalisms of stateless nations, whose aim is to change the existing order. Brighouse, like Buchanan and Levine – but Brighouse in the most detail – also argues that the ethical particularism of nationalism is incompatible with ethical universalism and its commitment to the impartial treatment of all, to equality and to equal respect and freedom for all. One way nationalism can do that is by advocating some 'special obligations' to peoples belonging to one's nation. But here, as Levine well realizes, we must be careful. Many things can lead to overriding a loyalty to a community of which one is voluntarily (in some not very clear sense of 'voluntarily') a member. In this volume Thomas Pogge powerfully and in convincing detail shows the limitations of such loyalties. But limitations are one thing; denial that there are such special obligations is another. *Prima facie* in certain respects, one has special obligations to those people whom one recognizes to be members of one's community that are not the same as obligations one has to others. First, the rationale for the special obligations to one's compatriots need not be, and indeed must not be, that they and you – members of a particular community – are superior. Rather the rationale is that for there to be bonds of community – something which is essential for anything recognizable as human life – there must be such special obligations. Second, this loyalty need not be to the particular government or even to the state of that nation but to the nation – to the people – of which one is a member. And finally, such a loyalty does not, to understate it, override all other moral considerations. One's nation may behave so badly that one leaves or alternatively stays and fights to change it or, if one is weaker or in some other way inescapably encumbered, one enters into 'inner emigration.' And with any of these things one may come to side with a people that have a different national identity. This may earn one the name of 'traitor' – as some Germans spoke of Willie Brandt for fighting against the Nazis in the Norwegian army – but, its negative emotive force notwithstanding, one sometimes can receive that epithet with pride and honour.

If one migrates out, one may in time come to have a different sense of nationality aligned with a different community. This is usually, perhaps always, more difficult and less complete than it is often thought to be. A person without a community is lost, but where this is not her situation and where she sees herself as a 'we,' she has special obligations to that 'we.' As egalitarians we will believe in the equal worth of all human beings, but with that we still can consistently recognize certain people as 'our people.' To which community we belong is, of course, an accident of history. But belonging to some community – the having of 'we feelings' – is essential for human flourishing, and the historical contingency of which community we are a part does not in any interesting or significant sense make that belonging arbitrary.

Buchanan, Levine, and Brighouse all recognize that there are certain particular attachments that are in certain respects privileged. For example, an adequate universalistic ethical theory must acknowledge a special place for friendship and family relationships. As Brighouse well puts it, "Although strangers are often in greater objective need than our friends and family members, it seems wrong of us to abandon our friends or children, or even to make our attachment to them contingent on them having needs we can better fulfil than those of others." Of course, and fortunately, it is not always, or even usually, the case that "we have to abandon our friends or children" in order to efficiently help those who are strangers. But the point here is that Brighouse's belief about it, as difficult as it is to theorize or rationalize, is one of our deeper considered judgments. Is that particularist claim incompatible, as he also believes, with a universalistic ethic? We do not think so; it is perfectly generalizable or universalizable. The claim is that any person x has special obligations to her friends and family rooted in intimacy and sometimes in mutual dependence that that person does not have to others standing in different relations to her. And this is universal. It applies to all persons in their relationships to friends and family. Something very like that obtains between a person (any person you like) and her compatriots. Any person x has special obligations to her compatriots because of their communal relationships and mutual dependence that that person does not have, or does not have as stringently, to others. And this is universal. It applies to all persons in their communal relationships and in their recognition of a common nationality. It is no more morally arbitrary than the special obligations involved in friendships and families.

All of these things are for most people deeply important: they are relationships they care about and would continue to care about on informed reflection in a cool hour. There is no good reason to label them irrational or illusory. However, while this special importance of friends and family cuts across time and location, though, of course, its specific forms will vary from culture to culture and over historical time, national identity, though not group identity, of which national identity is a subspecies adapted to certain historical circumstances, is, as we have seen, something which came into prominence with the modern era and is functionally appropriate to it. Still, for most people in conditions of modernity, it is a vitally important relationship, and modern nation-states and multination-states could not continue to even remotely efficiently function without it.

Brighouse, like Levine, resists this. We have already considered and set out what we take to be a refutation of Levine's argument that national identity is imagined – a product of wishful thinking. But Brighouse here argues differently. He argues that "nations are not families"; a nation, lacking the intimacy of families, "is, simply, a group of strangers." But, while it is true they lack the intimacy of families or of clans in primitive societies, it is at best misleading to say that nations are simply groups of strangers. A nation is a people with a common language and comprehensive culture with distinctive ways of doing and perceiving things that are prized by most of its members and which yield a common form of recognition. They are things into which they are all thoroughly socialized. Such a collection of individuals provide for each other a common sense of at-homeness (in the German sense of *heimat*) that is commonly not felt by these individuals when they are among people with a different language and culture. In these very important ways people with the same comprehensive culture do not face each other as strangers but as members of a common community. This remains so, in a backhanded way, even when some alienated members of the community recognize with distaste their compatriots abroad.

625

It is *ersatz* realism to claim that a "nation is, simply, a group of strangers." Their commonalty carries the sense of at-homeness described above and it yields specific obligations – obligations to, in some way, serve in their common defence, to pay their fair share of taxes, to accept if called to jury duty, and the like. These are obligations, sometimes overrideable, that obtain between compatriots that do not obtain more widely. If they were not in place, nations would be dysfunctional and life in our conditions of modernity would be even more impoverished than it already is.

Brighouse argues that nationalism, because it yields special obligations and is a particularism, is not egalitarian and undermines autonomy. Like Buchanan, he also claims that it undermines the very central liberal norm of equal respect for all people. Again there are nationalisms and nationalisms. To claim that we have special obligations to our compatriots is not to claim that we have *no* obligations to other people. For liberal nationalism, a commitment to equal autonomy and equal respect for all people are such obligations. To remain a liberal nationalism, it must be committed to the egalitarian maxims that the life of everyone matters and matters equally and that each is to count for one and none to count for more than one. These notions of moral equality are key background assumptions as much for liberal nationalism as they are for Rawlsian cosmopolitanism.

There are, of course, severe problems – problems Brighouse adverts to – concerning how to achieve equality – particularly fair equality of opportunity – where in a territory there is a majority language, which is the *de facto* dominant language, and a minority language or languages. The people speaking only the minority language or speaking also, but imperfectly, the majority language cannot but be disadvantaged and this will obtain with even the best will in the world among all the different linguistic groups in such a territory.

The solution in Quebec to these problems seems to us exemplary. (We do not assert that this is only true of Quebec.) French is the language of Quebec (it is the mother tongue for over 80 percent of the population), but there is a sizeable, historically rooted English-speaking minority. Its linguistic rights are respected with English-speaking schools (including universities), hospitals in which all services are available in English as well as in French, the right to have a trial in English, to have official services in English, and to use English in the National Assembly. It is also the case that anglophones are taught French in the schools just as francophones are taught English in francophone schools. Quebec realizes it is essential for much of its population – ideally all – to learn English in a North America largely made up of anglophones. The circumstances of the francophone Québécois are, in this respect, closely analogous to that of the Scandinavians, Flemish, Welsh, and Dutch, where it is vital for them to learn English and learn it reasonably well.

Brighouse's example is not Quebec but Wales. But it seems to us, except that their national language is actually threatened, that the situation for the Welsh is essentially the same as it is for the Scandinavians, the Flemish, and the Dutch. Three things are essential in all these places (and in Quebec as well). (1) It is essential to protect the language of the majority and to make it the official language spoken by almost everyone. (2) Where there are national minorities it is essential to preserve their culture while at the same time facilitating the acquisition of the national (official) language of the society in which these minorities, in one way or another, must interact. (We are not claiming that an effort be made to educate them to the level where they have the same proficiency in the language as a native speaker. That is unrealistic and unnecessary, but we are arguing that it is vital for them to come to have a functional acquaintance with the language.) And (3) It is essential to facilitate, for all people living in the society, the learning of the *lingua franca* of the bigger world in which they also have to interact. This now, and for the foreseeable future, means learning English, and it seems to us that the Dutch, Flemish, and Scandinavians have been exemplary in doing this. They have securely maintained their national languages and the sense of nation that goes with it while learning English in a way which offers them at least an equal opportunity in the larger world. Government policy in all such small states or, as the case may be, nations, where they have sufficient resources to do it, should be to ensure (1), (2), and (3). This has been and remains a policy for liberal societies where linguistic problems exist, including liberal societies with a nationalist agenda. Nation-states need a national language to properly function. Where there is no national language but only a myriad of different languages, this inescapably leads to *de facto* inequalities for people who happen to speak the language of the minorities in that society. There will also be *de facto* inequality, even where there is a national language, for people whose first language happens to be a different one. There is no getting around it. The best way of ameliorating it is, as we argued above, by facilitating the acquisition by the national minorities of the national language, while preserving as much as possible, where they want it, their culture and the language which goes with it. The cure of forced assimilation with the destruction of the language and cultures of historical national minorities is worse than the disease, and would make for even more inequalities and loss of autonomy and self-respect.

Here it is crucially important that a liberal nationalism, as Ross Poole in effect shows, should not succumb to the siren song of Bakhtinian multiculturalism. Surely liberal nationalists, like all humane persons, will strongly favour the politics of inclusion. But they will, if they have their wits about them, resist both assimilation and multi-voiced communities, where this comes to the interaction of 'languages of heterogeneity,' and where such interaction is intended to replace the hegemony of the national languages of nations. There can be no society without a Public Reason and there can be no nation without a national language and the comprehensive culture of that nation. Without that there is no full and adequate communication and interaction in the nation and there is no democratic equality for groups not sharing in the dominant language. Moreover, without it, there is no common culture to make a people a people.

There is plenty of historical evidence to support this view. Most of it also shows evidence of violence, domination, and repression of genuine nations whose language should have been recognized, together with their culture in a real multination-state. French was forced on what has become the French people starting just before the French Revolution and coming to be consolidated with the revolution. Where before, as we have previously noticed, there were seventeen languages, now there is one common language and a French nation. The Spanish conquistadors and later revolutionaries forced Spanish on what is now Mexico, English and Afrikaans were forced on the bulk of the population which is now South African, and English was forced on the Irish and the Scots by the British. There was brutality, coercion, and ethnocentric arrogance and sometimes (as in the case of the Highland Scots) ethnic cleansing in the doing of these things. That should never be forgotten. But neither does it need to be repeated in order to create a national and official language. What is different between different peoples in a nation-state should, where it reasonably can, be preserved and respected. This cannot be at the expense of building a nation-wide system of education and common cultural attunement that would give everyone, as far as that is possible, equal access to the national language and the culture that goes with it and the capacity to converse, participate in the public forum, and otherwise interact with each other as equals. If people who are not native speakers of the national language do not develop some reasonable fluency in it, they will be terribly ghettoized, marginalized, and kept from playing an effective role in the society, to say nothing of their being seriously economically disadvantaged. Sometimes this is the effect of multiculturalism. This must be avoided even if it means not *fully* protecting their differences. Ross Poole's discussion of such general issues in this volume is, in our view, very much and perceptively to the point.

In a just society there will be, along with the other more familiar equalities, an equality of being listened to. This is a difficult task to fulfil for those people who are members of the dominant culture. But if we are to have a decent and just society, it must be done. A necessary but not sufficient condition for the doing of this is to have a common encompassing culture in the nation-state, or even (as much as possible) in a genuine multination-state, in which these otherwise diverse people abide. Moreover, it is important that this encompassing culture be ubiquitously present without being oppressive. This is not easy to achieve, but it is essential that it be done. Of course this equality of being listened to – a central element of equality of self-respect – must not stop at the border of the nation-state. There – that is, across these nation-states and multination states – the doing of it is much more difficult because of problems of communication and of the non-existence of a common comprehensive or encompassing culture. We cannot see any way around this except the standard one of having one international or perhaps a very few international languages as Greek once was and then Latin and then French and now English, and as some other language will no doubt be in several hundred years. For an equality of being listened to to become possible, there must be some common communicative idiom across nations that, if cultural autonomy is to be preserved, will still be less than a common comprehensive culture, the latter running along national lines in modern societies. Assimilation to any one comprehensive culture, while probably impossible, is plain ethnocentric arrogance that no cosmopolitan, if she thinks about it carefully, can accept. Still we need a *lingua franca*, but that does not require a common comprehensive or encompassing culture.

Such considerations lead us to Brighouse's theory (conception) of *benign neglect*. We could perhaps shore up national identities and nations in the way suggested above, but, he asks, as does Levine as well, *why do so?* There is, he argues, a better alternative for people living in our conditions of modernity: it is the alternative of *benign neglect toward cultural identities*. Brighouse describes it as "the position that the state should, as far as possible, be neutral among the cultural (and hence national) sentiments of its citizens." That is, to put it unsympathetically, we should have a state that is somehow – mysteriously – above, and neutral towards, all nations. He adds that his position is "implicit in the theoretical work of many contemporary liberals, and also in much socialist theory and some socialist practice." He defends such a conception while we think, *au contraire*, such a conception is a deeply mistaken one for either a liberal or a socialist, and, of course, for a liberal socialist.

However, careful argument is required here, for Brighouse's arguments are powerful and well set against a careful consideration of Will Kymlicka's and David Miller's defences of liberal nationalism and the key importance of cultural (including national) identities. Brighouse argues (*pace* Kymlicka) that we should "design a cultural policy aimed not at protecting any particular cultures, but at a long-term integration of different cultures, so that it is easy to move between them and perhaps even difficult to differentiate between them." Such an aim he identifies, we think mistakenly, with a commitment to cosmopolitanism. And the aim of cosmopolitanism, as Brighouse sees it, is "deliberately ... to erode the significance of national sentiment within civic life." That is, we need in our social policies to engage in a benign neglect toward considerations of nationality.

Part of his argument depends on the soundness of his defence of strict *state neutrality* concerning conceptions of the good life which he takes to include state neutrality concerning considerations of nationality. Rawls has argued plausibly, and Brighouse follows him here, that the state should be neutral concerning conceptions of the good life. Modern societies are irreducibly and inescapably pluralistic. That is to say, within them there is a plurality of ways of life, including religious and secular orientations to the world, with a bewildering variety of conceptions of how best to live. The state should not favour some conceptions at the expense of others.

The state neutrality that Brighouse defends is not the impossible one of neutrality of *effect*, but neutrality of *justification*. "Neutrality of justification," Brighouse puts it, "prohibits that policies be *justified* on the grounds that they favour one conception over another." Neutrality of justification concerns itself with the *reasons* for policies rather than the *effects* of the policy. Neutrality of effect is impossible to achieve. But the state should not seek as a *rationale* – a *justificatory base* – for any of its policies something that is rooted in some particular conception of the good life. It must, in this *justificatory* sense of neutrality, remain strictly neutral on contested terrain concerning the good life and concerning what life-plans the citizens of the state can legitimately have. It has no business intruding in these matters. Indeed it must not do so. In taking that line of neutrality of justification, Brighouse takes the Millian position that among ways of life, anything goes, as long as others are not harmed or their rights violated. As long as they do not violate these constraints individuals may live as they please.

This is the standard liberal position, and (*pace* Brighouse) liberal nationalists and socialists can and should accept it. Brighouse brings out very well why such a conception is so appealing:

> If we accept what Rawls calls the fact of reasonable pluralism – the idea that a free society will inevitably be characterized by reasonable disagreement among its citizens about the good, leading to a multiplicity of competing, conflicting, and sometimes incomparable conceptions of the good – then we should be concerned that the state not presume the falsehood or wickedness of the deepest moral commitments of its reasonable citizens. As the holder of a monopoly on legitimate coercive force, and as a mechanism which is supposed to be accountable to all citizens, the state should pass as little judgment as possible on the content of the ways of life of its own citizens.

We, like Brighouse, think this liberal conception here, coming down to us from Humboldt and Mill, and restated with force in our time by Berlin, Rawls, and Dworkin, is right on target. What we object to is Brighouse's application of it to questions of nationality.

As is well known, Rawls – and many liberals follow him here – does not put matters concerning fundamental principles of justice or constitutional essentials into the pluralistic hopper where anything goes or at least any 'reasonable anything' goes. Unlike for comprehensive conceptions of the good, ways of life, life plans, religious or non-religious orientations, neither the liberal state nor any other state can or should be neutral with respect to constitutional essentials or fundamental principles of justice. (We speak here not only of neutrality of effect but of neutrality of justification as well.) This entails that they cannot and should not be neutral with respect to primary natural and social goods, for these are presupposed in the very choice of principles of justice – indeed in even being able to make such a choice or (even more fundamentally) being able to come to articulate principles of justice. To be acceptable, comprehensive conceptions of the good and the like must be in accordance with the constitutional essentials of a liberal state and its principles of justice. If they are not so acceptable they will not be a part of the reasonable pluralism of such societies. A great motley of quite divergent conceptions of the good are acceptable and must at least be tolerated, and in that sense accepted, in liberal societies. Still, to be acceptable they all must be compatible with the constitutional essentials and the basic principles of justice of the society in which they are held. If, as philosophers such as John Gray believe, there is no consensus here among the citizens of such a society then this whole Rawlsian non-foundationalist rationale collapses. Consensus, of course, isn't sufficient but it is necessary. But this consensus (if it exists), if it is to be reasonable (that is, in accordance with wide reflective equilibrium), requires – and Brighouse does not challenge that – a rough agreement about primary natural and social goods. There can be no state neutrality – justificatory or otherwise – concerning the primary natural and social goods.

It is here that Kymlicka's argument enters and it is of crucial importance for the dispute about nationalism. It is the argument "that membership in a cultural community should count as a primary good in exactly the Rawlsian sense of a good that any rational person should want whatever else she wanted." If Kymlicka's claim is sound, this makes nationality and a sense of national identity – the modern form of membership in a cultural community – not an optional matter of different comprehensive conceptions of the good or of ways of life, but, like other primary goods, something essential for social life itself under modern conditions. Brighouse is at pains to reject Kymlicka's arguments here. Indeed the soundness of this rejection is a linchpin in the consideration in his argument against nationalism.

So we will review Brighouse's argument here and try to make a reflectively critical response to it. Brighouse argues, rightly we believe, that a liberal state cannot pass judgment on the ways of life and comprehensive or, for that matter, non-comprehensive conceptions of the good of any of its citizens so long as these conceptions or ways of life are in accordance with the constitutional essentials and principles of justice of that society. If the state acts here in a non-neutral way it is "an unwarranted sign of disrespect to the person whose views are being disregarded. In treating his conception of the good as inferior to others the state is (and his fellow citizens through the state are) treating that person effectively as worthy of lesser respect." This is standard liberalism, and it seems to us that we have very good reasons to accept it. So far we are with Brighouse.

However, because of these considerations, Brighouse thinks that it is "obvious how neutrality of justification would prohibit special attention to national sentiment." It is here that our disagreement begins. He argues that in "any free society not only can pluralism about ways of life be expected, but so can pluralism about the nation." But, we submit, 'ways of life' and 'nations' are in important ways not parallel. A nation provides the language and the comprehensive culture in which *various* ways of life, life plans, and conceptions of the good get articulated and can flourish. To even exist in modern conditions, they must have these background conditions provided by the nation. That is, the nation or nations within a given society provide the medium or media through which such ways of life get articulated and without which they could not get articulated. They supply the cultural context of choice in which these diverse choices are made. In a non-multination state there is one comprehensive culture and one national language, and that language, in ways we have already delineated, must be privileged by the state for us to have such a society at all. In a state encompassing more than one nation, there will be two or more national languages if the different component nations have different languages, but in such a state these languages will be privileged in the same way a single national language is privileged in a nation-state. *In conditions of modernity no nation, no comprehensive culture; no comprehensive culture, no modern society.* Going further we should recognize that *no common language, no comprehensive culture and thus no society or at least no modern society. And without a society there obviously can be no cultural context of choice at all. A nation-state, or for that matter a multination state, cannot be neutral about such matters, for its very existence depends on their existence.*

The existence of multination states may seem to belie at least some of that, but it does not. With multination states by definition there are several (two or more) nations in a single state. There will not be a *single* comprehensive culture, but a plurality of such cultures in some way politically and culturally linked in some form of common political community. But the state – the multination state – will not be indifferent to the existence of these different nations with their comprehensive cultures and will privilege all of them as being necessary to sustain these various component nations without which that multination state could not function. There is a kind of pluralism here, but not the pluralism of comprehensive conceptions of the good and ways of life of which Rawls speaks. The state cannot and, even if it could, should not remain neutral about the nation or nations that it is the nation-state or multination state of. We need some common language or languages and comprehensive culture or comprehensive cultures to make social life possible, to sustain the nation or nations the state is a state of. Without that, that very state could not exist. To ask for state neutrality in that sense is to ask for the state to put itself out of business or at least to neglect the issue of its own existence. It is, that is, in effect to ask for the demise of that very state.

Nothing even remotely like 'everything goes that does not harm others or violate their rights' is viable *vis-à-vis* nations. It is not a matter of believing that some nations or national sentiments are superior to others, but of recognizing that one or a limited number of them in any territory must be privileged for there to be a society and a state at all. It is analogous to language. It is now generally realized that there are no intrinsically superior or inferior languages. But it is also plain that in any territory some privileged language or a limited number of privileged languages (as in Finland there are Swedish and Finnish) are necessary for there even to be a society at all and for there to be anything recognizable as a human life.

However, we are not quite at the end of the line (if indeed in philosophy we are ever at the end of the line), for Brighouse does not agree that, even in conditions of modernity, membership in a nation is a primary good and he does not accept what Kymlicka says about the cultural context of choice. Presumably (*pace* R. M. Hare and the early

Jean-Paul Sartre) Brighouse would agree with Kymlicka, and almost everyone else, that our ability to form and revise a conception of the good is not just dependent on our own capacities and our being, in some probably illusory individualistic sense, in conditions of freedom, but depends, as well, "on there being background cultural and intellectual institutions which we can realistically draw on in developing our beliefs." We invariably, and inescapably, also critically scrutinize our ideas in a determinate cultural environment which for us moderns is that of the comprehensive culture that is our nation. This is not something that in the first instance we adopt or even can adopt; rather it is a given for us, like our mother tongue.

What Brighouse denies is that a determinate cultural structure – in conditions of modernity the nation – is necessary to provide a context of choice which is essential for our being autonomous agents and thus is essential for our self-respect and flourishing. Here he runs flatly against the arguments of Kymlicka, Tamir, and Miller. He is also, or so it seems to us, running against a more general point which should be of some concern for cosmopolitans. National identity is often linked with politically emancipatory movements. Stateless nations fighting to gain their political sovereignty are also fighting for their recognition and their right to be listened to within the community of nations, or more prosaically, as states among, and equal to, the other states. If cosmopolitanism is committed, as Brighouse believes, to "deliberately trying to erode the significance of national sentiment in the public life," then cosmopolitans will be committed, in many cases, to the erosion of democratic movements and to the perpetuation of domination and repression. We, on the contrary, believe that cosmopolitanism is committed to support struggles for more democracy and more justice wherever we find them.[27] And, in the present world, numerous, and perhaps often the most important, struggles for democracy are fuelled by a sense of national identity.

Brighouse thinks it unclear what it would be like to lack a cultural context of choice. But that seems to us false. We have a clear example

---

27 Jocelyne Couture, 'An Ethical Response to Globalization: Justice or Solidarity?' in Jay Drydyk and Peter Penz, eds., *Global Justice, Global Democracy* (Winnipeg/Halifax: Fernwood 1997), 124–37

of people lacking a cultural context of choice in the case of slaves brought over from Africa by slave traders, people thrown together after their capture who were often from heterogeneous cultures with different languages and who were forced in some way to try to speak their master's language and accept (and first to gain some understanding of what it was to accept) his way of ordering them about and, inasmuch as they had any understanding of it, some of his culture. Even if they (counterfactually) had been allowed to make choices, they lacked, at least in the early period of their enslavement, a cultural context of choice. Any case, though *somewhat* less clearly, of people thrown into an alien culture lacking a command of the language, unable, except in very limited circumstances, to use their own, where the ways of doing and responding to things are foreign and baffling to them, is a case of people lacking a cultural context of choice. The Lithuanian immigrants in Chicago, as they are depicted in the first half of Upton Sinclair's naturalistic novel, *The Jungle*, are vivid and convincing examples of people lacking a cultural context of choice. The interaction of their old culture with the new one uncomprehendingly yields very little meaning and content to their choices. They live in a moral and social wilderness where they lurch with very little understanding or control over their situation, from one horrible circumstance to another – mostly uncomprehendingly – until slowly, and painfully, after a considerable period of time, they partly catch on to how this new society works and impacts on them, though even then their situation is not much better. But for a considerable time, the resources of their old culture fail them in their new situation as they are battered back and forth by their new culture – something which is hardly 'their culture' at all – in ways they do not understand. They are lacking a cultural context of choice, and their autonomy and self-respect are undermined. And they are shown no respect at all, let alone equal respect. There is, as far as we can see, no great puzzle about what it is for people to lack a cultural context of choice in these circumstances. Brighouse, in a manner not unknown to philosophers, is making a problem where there isn't one.

Brighouse next argues that, even assuming that the idea of lacking a cultural context of choice makes sense, Kymlicka's argument is still mistaken that in certain circumstances the state can rightly privilege nations and that the state, for minority nations and national minorities, can sometimes rightly grant them group differentiated rights. Kymlicka's conception, Brighouse points out, is static not dynamic, synchronic not diachronic, and thus it does not attend to the dynamic effects of the reproduction of culture. But it is essential that we attend to this. Consider (counterfactually) what could, and he argues predictably would, have happened in Wales if liberal nationalist ideas had been in place there 150 years ago. At that time, Brighouse remarks, "the vast majority of the inhabitants of Wales were Welsh-speakers, most of them monolingual." Yet they were surrounded by a vast sea of English-speakers. When one considers the whole of the United Kingdom very few people spoke Welsh as compared with English. Now, Brighouse asks us to consider, "two counterfactual histories." Neither involve violations of liberal justice, but in History *A*, the one that would presumably be favoured by liberal nationalists, special language rights are granted to the Welsh to shield them from the recurrent *de facto* pressure of English and to protect the integrity of the Welsh nation with its distinctive culture. In History *B*, by contrast, no special language rights are granted. Given the pressures on Wales from the wider English-speaking society, with History *B* we would in time move from a population which for the most part spoke only Welsh to a population which spoke only English or both English and Welsh. With History *A*, Brighouse has it, we would have continued on with the vast majority of Welsh remaining monolingual Welsh-speakers. But this, he argues, would work against their autonomy and their equality of opportunity because there would for them be "far fewer cultural and material opportunities" than for the people in History *B* who come to a mastery of English. Monolingual Welsh-speakers – what he takes to be the result of History *A* – would, unlike the monolingual English-speakers or the bilingual Welsh/English-speakers of History *B*, have a "realistic access to a much less diverse range of potential life-partners, access to a much less rich body of literature, drama, scholarship, and popular culture in their own language, access to a much less extensive and desirable range of well-paying and rewarding employment opportunities." From this Brighouse concludes that we should not go the route of liberal nationalists which would result in History *A*, but take instead the perhaps somewhat paternalistic 'cosmopolitan' route that would result from History *B*. Social policy, he claims, if it is reasonable, should take the line that would lead to History *B* rather than History *A*.

This assumes, without reason, that Welsh liberal nationalists would be so remarkably stupid and lacking in foresight as to not recognize that a small nation such as Wales would need, in addition to protecting and furthering the use of their own national language and with that indirectly their culture, to see to it that the Welsh *also* learn English. But to see that does not take very great intelligence or foresight. If liberal nationalists were to have come into the environment of a mostly monolingual Welsh-speaking culture of 150 years ago, they would have (if they had their wits about them) argued strenuously for (1) protecting the Welsh language and culture *and* (2) the learning of English. Indeed that is the present position of Welsh nationalists. When there was an earlier national awakening among the Dutch and the Danes, as small nations then threatened with being drowned in a sea of German- and English-speakers, Dutch and Danish nationalists developed policies to protect their own languages and cultures while also insisting on educational policies, including language acquisition, which gave the Danes and the Dutch a window on the world. With two or more languages rather than only one, they came to have even greater equality of opportunity than their English, German, and French counterparts who, given the far greater extent of the use of their languages, tended understandably to be more frequently monolingual than members of small nations with geographically more limited languages. In small nations at least, liberal nationalism and greater equality of opportunity go hand in hand as do (*pace* Brighouse and Levine) liberal nationalism and cosmopolitanism. There is no reason to think Wales would be different from Holland and Denmark (or for that matter all of Scandinavia), and a similar situation obtains for francophones in Quebec. Brighouse seems to assume that nationalism must be inward looking, backward, defensive, and either hostile to or indifferent to ideas from outside. This is unfortunately true of some nationalisms, but, as we have seen, it is not true of others – we speak here of some really existing nationalisms and not just of the very idea of justified nationalism – and, by definition, it cannot be true of liberal nationalism.

It is correct to say, as Brighouse does, that "our ability to revise our practices and question authority depends crucially on what other opportunities are available to us." This, of course, is not the only thing this ability depends on, but it is one crucial feature and having these abilities (*pace* Dostoyevsky) is an unproblematically good thing. This leads us to the conclusion that we should have cultural conditions which make exit from a culture an easy thing. Ready availability of exit will enhance things all around. Autonomous people must have the ability to reconsider and revise their conceptions of the good and of the polities in which they would wish to live. This, Brighouse agrees with liberal nationalists, supports both an interest in cultural membership *and* the standard Rawlsian liberties with their ban on the very idea of an authoritative conception of the good life required of all, or indeed of any *authoritative* conception of the good life, period. If such *authoritative* conception is an essential ingredient of communitarianism then communitarianism is incompatible with liberalism including liberal nationalism.

The crucial moral importance of reconsideration and revisability also supports, as we have seen, having permeable boundaries between nations and cultures. This a liberal nationalist should neither resist nor deplore; indeed he should welcome it. But special language rights do not threaten that, contrary to what Brighouse believes. Special language rights for the Québécois and the Welsh have not inhibited their access to the surrounding English-speaking culture(s) or kept them from becoming reasonably fluent in English. It is also probably true that special language rights, unsupplemented by a thorough English-language instruction, will even more thoroughly ghettoize and marginalize the peoples of the First Nations in Canada, Australia, and the United States than they already are. The injustice of their treatment, rooted in having such unequal resources and unequal material opportunities, will most probably, though no doubt unintentionally, be exacerbated rather than alleviated by their having and exercising such language rights *if* that is not supplemented by a thorough grounding in English or in some circumstances in French. But again we should not attribute such stupidities, without very good evidence, to the nationalist leaders of the First Nations. There is no reason, any more than there was for the Welsh, why they cannot have the protection of their own language and culture *and* access to a wider world. With that both migrating out and remaining in will become real options.

Brighouse thinks – though if our arguments above have been near to the mark it is not evident that he is justified in thinking that – that it would be better for a liberal society – including a socialist society – to "design a cultural policy aimed not at protecting any particular culture, but at the long-term integration of different cultures, so that it is easy to move between them and *perhaps difficult to differentiate between them"* (italics ours). If this 'integration of different cultures' only meant that culture is permeable, then it is something to applaud and support; no *liberal* nationalist, if he is thinking straight, will oppose it. It is a moral truism that we should all be for open societies. But if permeability of cultures and ease of movement led to a world that made it difficult to differentiate between different cultures or societies, then that would be a very great loss indeed. It isn't that diversity is necessarily an *intrinsic* good, but, for at least the reasons that J. S. Mill and Isaiah Berlin have so tirelessly adumbrated, it is a very great instrumental good. For cultures to so collapse or melt (choose your metaphor) into each other would not be, as Brighouse calls it, cosmopolitanism but barbarism. It would be as if we had developed a universal Esperanto or that one language – say, English or French or Chinese – became in time the universal and *sole* language of the world, so that all of world literature would have to be rendered in one language and, from the time of such a linguistic and cultural 'unification,' written in one language and from one cultural point of view. Suppose that English were that language and that culture, and we had to read (as most of us unfortunately do) Sophocles, Dante, Cervantes, Proust, Grass, and Marquez in English and that all the nuances of life that go with these various – sometimes radically various – languages and their associated cultures would be lost to us humans. That would be a horror that would impoverish our lives and deprive individuals of a *cultural* context of choice by so eroding cultural differences. Rather than promoting equality of opportunity, as Brighouse believes it would, and enhancing autonomy, it would limit us by leaving nothing for us to immigrate to or migrate to or transform ourselves into. We would all be much the same with no experiments in living left for us, with whatever difficulty, to try out. The resulting equality would be the equality of *sameness* that anti-egalitarians have tried to foist on egalitarians and that egalitarians, interpreting equality quite differently (say, in a more Rawlsian, Senian, or Barryian way), have rightly resisted as a caricature.

Cultural change, adaptation, and borrowing is very often a good thing – sometimes we gain from having a certain hybrid vigour. The opportunity should always be there and never blocked in an authoritarian way, though sometimes some changes may be argued against

and reasonably resisted, e.g., the 'McDonaldization' of Russia or anywhere else. But *assimilation*, Brighouse's 'cosmopolitanism,' should
generally be resisted strenuously. Such a homogenization of the human race is no genuine cosmopolitanism, even under 'a policy of gentle detachment' from one's culture. Attachment and loyalty to a nation,
or to some smaller group in premodern circumstances, and the ability
to recognize and feel the importance of such local attachments are widespread among us and are, to speak normatively, essential to our very
self-definition – a sense of who we are – which in turn is crucial to our
sense of self-respect and autonomy. Permeable, fluid cultures are also
a good thing, but a deliberate policy of eroding cultures so that they
may be replaced by some 'universal civilization' is not. It misses all the
valuable things about local attachments that such thinkers as in an earlier period Herder and coming to our contemporaries such diverse
philosophers as Isaiah Berlin, Hans Gadamer, David Miller, G. A. Cohen,
Yael Tamir, and Will Kymlicka have brought to our attention.

Brighouse's principle, with which he concludes his essay, is an important one which a liberal nationalist and, we believe, anyone (or at
least anyone touched by the Enlightenment) should accept (as far as
its general thrust goes). It is the principle that we should "aim at making more permeable the boundaries between cultures so as to facilitate
the realization of the values of autonomy and legitimacy over the long
term, as well as equality between individuals across and within cultures." *Perhaps*, as Brighouse believes, this principle is actually compatible with the policy of benign neglect. We have tried here to give
some reasons for doubting that. But it is plainly compatible with liberal nationalism, and we have seen that we have independent grounds
for opting for liberal nationalism rather than for benign neglect.

Brighouse, like Levine and Martha Nussbaum, has taken it that we
have a forced option between nationalism and cosmopolitanism.[28] One
can, they believe, be one or the other but not both, though, of course,
one might be neither. We have argued, on the contrary, that a sound
nationalism must also be a cosmopolitanism and that in certain circumstances (that we have spelled out) a sound cosmopolitanism will
also support nationalist commitments of a distinctive sort.

---

28 Nussbaum, 'Patriotism and Cosmopolitanism,' 2–20, and 'Reply,' 131–44

However, since it is a contentious issue between us and Brighouse and Levine, and indeed more widely, we should say a few more words about what cosmopolitanism is. A cosmopolitan (taken as an ideal type) is a person of wide interests and sympathies, familiar with many ways of viewing things and living; she is a person who is at home in all parts of the world, a person whose view of things is not restricted to that of any one nation or religion or particular cultural orientation and, very crucially, is not fettered by the prejudices of the people of any community, but conversant with and attuned to the ways of viewing things of many cultures. She is also a person who can make a reflective and impartial assessment of these views or, where assessment is not an issue or even much of a possibility or relevant, she can, and does, appreciate a wide variety of these views. In that way she is a person of the world, at home in a wide variety of places and with a mind set that would leave her at home throughout the world. In that sense cosmopolitans are persons of the world free from prejudices. This, of course, is a hyperbolical characterization. No one is literally at home throughout the world. But it is an ideal conception which people who are cosmopolitans aspire to approximate as much as is possible, and it reflects an underlying attitude which is that of the cosmopolitan. Above all, cosmopolitanism is the opposite of ethnocentrism and an inward turning particularism.

Sometimes it is taken that a cosmopolitan will be without national or culturally particular attachments – without any group identity at all – and both Brighouse and Levine make capital out of this sometimes supposed feature of cosmopolitanism in setting cosmopolitanism against nationalism. We do not think, some dictionaries to the contrary notwithstanding, this is a core feature of cosmopolitanism. But if it were, it would make it practically impossible for anyone to be a cosmopolitan, for no one is without particular cultural attachments and identities. And no one can totally free herself from the culture of the society in which she was socialized. Moreover, there seems to be a contradiction in the very requirements of such a cosmopolitanism. To have sympathies for many ways of living, viewing things and for all human beings, one has to know in the first place *what it is to feel sympathy at all*. This is arguably not something that we are born with, but something that we learn very early in a given environment. Whether or not one succeeds in freeing oneself from one's initial attachments, one cannot free oneself from the sense – the particular sense that one has acquired in one's initial environment – of what it is to feel attachments, sympathies, and the like. And if, *per impossible*, one were to succeed in doing so how could it be possible for one to experience sympathy for many ways of living, viewing things and for all human beings? Such cosmopolitans, if there really could be such people, would be cold, indifferent beings more comparable to the international capitalist who claims to be a citizen of the world. No one can *just* be a citizen of the world. The whole idea, if we try to take it with something approaching literalness, is absurd.[29] Nor, for reasons we have adumbrated, is it desirable that anyone should be. *If* we promote cosmopolitanism as Brighouse does, as committed to "deliberately trying to erode the significance of national sentiment within civic life," then we would in effect promote the erosion of any sense of attachment in civic life and with that the very basis of a more reasonable cosmopolitanism. But there is no need to so characterize cosmopolitanism. A cosmopolitan will not be without such attachments though she must, in the ideal case, to be a genuine cosmopolitan, be without cultural prejudices or blinders. In real-life circumstances she must approximate that. She must, as well, be interested in phenomena across the world, be able to see and appreciate the point, purpose, and value of many different views of the world and the attitudes of many people and of diverse ways of living. She will (as we have seen) have local attachments, and prize them, but she must not, if she is a cosmopolitan, regard them as the sole source, as even the most important source, of appropriateness for humankind or let them fetter her understanding and appreciation of other ways of viewing and responding to things or just assume that they are the superior ways. The cosmopolitan's interests and attunements must be, to put it concisely, world-wide.

So construed – and not at all arbitrarily – cosmopolitanism is as perfectly compatible with liberal nationalism as the distinctive particularisms of liberal nationalism are compatible with ethical universalism. Levine and Brighouse wish to see local attachments and national sentiments wither away, leaving us with a stark (or more likely

---

29 Michael Walzer, 'Spheres of Affection,' in Joshua Cohen, ed., *For Love of Country* (Boston: Beacon Press 1997), 125–7

a bland) 'cosmopolitanism.' We, by contrast, think local attachments are part of the very stuff of anything recognizable as a human life and that they should be harmonized with a cosmopolitan view of things. We believe, as well, and have argued the matter, that in certain determinate circumstances – circumstances we have specified – our local attachments should take the form of liberal nationalist attachments and that a cosmopolitan concern about the world requires, in some circumstances, that we give support to the local attachments of different peoples to their cultural identities, something which for them is a condition for their emancipation.

IV

We shall now turn to what in reality, if not in intent, is Allen Buchanan's critique of nationalism and nationalist views on secession. In this section we will contrast something of our particular rendering of liberal nationalism with Buchanan's anti-nationalism (or so we read it). Some forms of liberal nationalism take it as a very central task to articulate a conception of collective rights, and, using this conception, to argue for the collective rights of nations. While for many the very idea of collective rights is conceptually problematic and there are indeed persistent disagreements over how we are to construe them and over whether they are in some significant sense 'mythical,' still they are in a reasonably plain way not *morally* problematic, for it is clear enough (and about this there is a *reasonable* consensus, at least in liberal democracies) that there are rights to equality between all nations, rights to self-determination and to an equal respect of peoples. Those collective rights, however they are to be analyzed, are moral and need not, to have moral force, be legally recognized. We leave aside the question whether these moral rights should be registered in the constitution of nation-states and multination-states, or in the Charter of the United Nations, and thus whether they should become legal rights.

Secession, according to Buchanan, is acceptable only if either of the following two conditions are satisfied: (1) if the group suffers what are plainly recognized to be injustices (if, for instance, human rights are systematically violated within the group by the encompassing state, as in East Timor), or (2) if the group was once a state which was unjustly taken by force by the now encompassing state (as was the case of the Baltic states). If neither of those two conditions is satisfied, then, Buchanan has it, the group is not morally justified in seceding. Buchanan sees secession as something which is essentially meant to repair past injustices: plain unproblematically recognized injustices.

This position already reveals Buchanan's individualist orientation, since he ignores certain problems related to the recognition, promotion, or defence of the collective rights of nations within the encompassing state. Let us suppose, as is often the case, that the encompassing state refuses to recognize its multinational character. This may lead to the ignoring of the diverse cultural, and indeed the multinational, character of the state and, as a result, induce some of the component nations to adopt a nationalist orientation. After all, nationalist movements are not invented out of the blue. Very often, they are brought about by a failure to recognize a minority nation within the state by the majority nation. How should we characterize such a situation according to Buchanan? Clearly it need have nothing to do with a systematic violation of human rights. It also may have nothing to do with recovering a state that was once conquered by force. But can't this nationalist demand for nationhood be justified, in accordance with Buchanan's account, by an appeal to past injustices, if we include among these failures the failure to respect the principles of equality, equal respect, and the self-determination of nations within the encompassing state? A liberal nationalist could accept Buchanan's severe constraints on the justifications of secession, namely that it must be remedial, while still criticizing him for his narrow individualistic account of justice. As long as it is agreed to include among the principles of justice the above collective requirements, then it appears that there are conditions under which secession would be justified even if the two conditions mentioned by Buchanan are not met.

In the Canadian case, for example, Quebec nationalists cannot claim that the human rights of Quebeckers have not been fully respected most of the time, and it is problematic to invoke an event that took place more than two centuries ago in order to justify secession. There is something like a statute of limitations here. If something like that is not invoked the world would be a very chaotic place indeed. As Marx observed, throughout history someone was always conquering and plundering someone else. But, past history aside, it could be argued that Quebeckers have not been recognized as a people, and thus have not been treated as an equal people within Canada. While lip service has been paid to the multinational conception of the two founding nations, it has, some ideological rhetoric aside, never been accepted as a reality. Quebec nationalists would claim, and we believe not unreasonably, that their language has not been properly protected by the federal government (through a policy of bilingualism that was thoroughly applied only in Quebec and New Brunswick), and that their culture has not been adequately protected because the federal government assimilated the culture of one of the two founding peoples within a policy of multiculturalism, in effect treating francophone Quebeckers as an ethnic group rather than as one of the two founding nations. Nationalists would also argue that Quebec's moral self-determination was not respected within Canada (by repatriating the constitution without the consent of the population of Quebec and against the explicit will of the vast majority of members in Quebec's National Assembly). It is not our purpose here to determine whether these arguments are sound and empirically validated. But it is our contention that, *if they are*, then they would lend support to the national aspirations of Quebeckers and provide grounds that could justify the secession of Quebec. That, *if* the above empirical claims *are true*, seems at least to be straightforward enough. Yet, given Buchanan's grounds for a justified secession, secession would not be justified even then. But this, to understate it, seems to put in question his grounds: the underlying rationale of his claim.

The problems that we are raising stem from Quebec – the Quebec nation – being confronted repeatedly by the refusal of the federal government to recognize the multinational character of an encompassing multination state. Or, perhaps what is better called, because of the non-recognition, a pseudo-multination state. The case of Quebec is not unique. Similar situations have emerged repeatedly in recent history. Whenever a nation wants more autonomy and is unable to achieve it within a multination state, there is a *prima facie* case for choosing to become independent if this is the only option left and if it is what its members want after they have shown this by a democratic vote as, for instance, in a referendum.

So it should be admitted that sometimes a nation within a *de facto* multination state may (and perhaps should) choose the course of political independence if it is unable to get sufficient recognition, autonomy, equal opportunity for economic development, and internal self-determination within the encompassing state. But Buchanan seems to be unable to account for that or to accept it. Moreover, he seems to have no counter arguments to show that such a reasonably straightforward claim is mistaken; to show, that is, that a nation, under such conditions should not secede or even consider secession as a very serious option.

Buchanan questions the very legitimacy of accepting a general non-remedial right of self-determination, even if this right does not include a right to secede. In our above responses to him, we accepted for the sake of the discussion that he might be partly right in adopting severe constraints on secession, and we agreed with him as well, again for the sake of that discussion, that secession, to be justified, had to be remedial. But we disagreed with him on the scope of what is to count as 'remedial' in this case. We also rejected Buchanan's narrow – or so it seems to us – scope in this regard. But these constraints, whether they are too narrow or whether they include principles of justice between peoples, apply in the case where a nation wants to exercise its right to self-determination. They constrain the exercise of that very right. This does not, however, mean that the nations have no general right to self-determination. Why should we say, as Buchanan does, that nations do not even have a moral right of self-determination *as such*? His argument is that a liberal must acknowledge what is indeed a social fact, namely, that individuals rank differently their various allegiances. The importance they give to their different affiliations will be different from time to time and will be different from one individual to another. Allowing a general right to self-determination for the nation requires, according to Buchanan, imposing a particular order of priority upon all the individual members of society concerning group affiliations. It seems that it would require overriding the familiar Rawlsian neutrality concerning conceptions of the good and of life-plans articulated by Brighouse which we wholeheartedly accepted in the previous section. To impose such a priority is in reality an insult made against particular choices and sets of values of individuals in our societies, and it thus violates cultural pluralism and the respect for persons. It is in this very important way essentially illiberal. This being so, Buchanan's conclusion is that we must abandon even a general right of *self-determination* for nations, and we must do it even if the right in question does not involve a right to *secede*.

In order to arrive at what seems to us such an astonishing result, Buchanan confuses, or so we think, a number of important but still distinct matters. He must first ignore the fact that it might be sufficient in order to justify nationalist aspirations to found them upon a moral view according to which national communities simply constitute *a* good among others and not *the* good or the highest good. *Pace* Buchanan, it is not necessary to argue that national communities are *the* most important communities or associations. They need not be the most valuable community for each and every individual or indeed even for any individual. Citizens have all sorts of communal attachments, and their belonging to a national community may be just one among many. Even if the majority within a population were to assign less importance to their national affiliation than to their city, family, sexual group or whatever, national affiliation could still count as something that was an important good for them. But that does not entail that they regard it as the highest good, or even that they regard it as a primary good. So *pace* Buchanan, liberal nationalism is compatible with the idea that individuals might have multiple allegiances that give rise to complex self-identifications. It is fully compatible with the idea – an idea that seems to be plainly so – that different people have different priorities *vis-à-vis* their different identifications. Surely there are many individuals in the United States who do not care about their national identity, but no one would even suggest that it would then be illiberal for the United States as a country to exercise a right to self-determination. And how can it be plausibly claimed that simply by doing so, the United States would violate the equal respect principle?

Why should Buchanan claim that nationalists must be committed to ranking national affiliations above all other communal affiliations? Perhaps one reason is this. As an individualist, Buchanan can accept only individualistic justifications to the principle of national self-determination. According to that account groups have rights only if all the individuals within the group give importance to their group membership as a source of self-identification. One of the most powerful arguments to that effect, arguably individualistic, comes from Will Kymlicka who appeals to Rawls's idea of a primary good.

Kymlicka believes that individuals see their own communal attachments to a nation as a primary good. Indeed, they are not only taken by them to be a primary good, the very having of a national identity, Kymlicka argues, is a primary good. We should then protect their cultural affiliation to a national group by protecting and promoting their individual rights to maintain their cultural belonging. A right to national self-determination is thus given an instrumental defence. And so the validity of self-determination depends largely on whether individuals do give a priority, though perhaps only strategically, to their national affiliations.

However, to argue that nationality (a sense of national identity) is a primary good is not to argue that individuals must, do, or even should give priority to their national affiliations over any other affiliations they may happen to have. Probably very few do, but that is not the issue here. The issue is the same as the issue that occurs about any primary good. It is the empirical and causal claim that a national identity or, so as to include some more primitive societies, some form of group identity or cultural membership is necessary (as matter of empirical fact necessary) for people to gain or secure the having of anything else they may want, including, of course, what other identities they prize. Something is a primary good if it is something which is necessary for people to have in order to achieve or realize their ends, no matter what they are. The claim is being made that having a national identity, some group identity, or some cultural membership, is necessary in that way. It has nothing to do with whether people give priority to national affiliation. It rather rests on whether a sense of national identity, no matter what priority they give to it, in conditions of modernity, with the kind of sense of cultural membership that goes with it, is necessary – empirically necessary – to achieve whatever ends people may happen to have. It has nothing to do with how they order their preferences. We sought in section III to counter Brighouse's claims that Kymlicka is mistaken in his belief that cultural membership is a primary good. But if cultural membership and having a sense of national identity are primary goods, then they have a strategic role in our lives. They *may* also be inherently good or intrinsically good (assuming we know what we are talking about here). But whether or not that is so, Kymlicka, if his argument is sound, has provided a secure basis for national self-determination that, whatever his intention, is quite independent of individualistic commitments about the ordering of our affiliations or what we want or philosophically problematic claims about what is or isn't inherently or intrinsically good. Rather, it is an empirical causal claim about what we need to get whatever it is that we want. Again, we are following Rawls's methodological claim about these matters. We travel metaphysically and philosophically light. Buchanan in effect foists controversial metaphysical commitments on liberal nationalists that simply need not be there. Liberal nationalists can be good Rawlsians and travel metaphysically light.

Whenever someone speaks of introducing collective rights and of accepting a reasonable competition between individual and collective rights, individualists tend to interpret that as a claim that there must be an *absolute* priority of collective rights over individual rights. But someone who rejects ethical individualism may do it without endorsing ethical collectivism. We might say, echoing John Austin on another topic, that they take in each other's dirty linen. The claim of liberal nationalists who are not ethical individualists is that individual and collective rights can cohabit side by side and be both accepted without any claim that one has an absolute priority, or even a general presumption of priority, over the other. Sometimes an individual right will trump a collective right and sometimes a collective right will trump an individual right and sometimes we will not know what to say. *The correct account should be neither collectivist nor individualist. One can be an anti-individualist without embracing any form of collectivism.* There might be, and we believe there should be, reasonable limits imposed one on the other by individual and collective rights. And there is no algorithm or general formula specifying what is their appropriate balance. We need to be contextualist and pragmatist about that.

This being so, Buchanan's argument is at the very least problematic. Someone might give more importance to her family than to the city in which she lives, more importance to the city than to her federated state, and more importance to that federated state than to the country (or nation or both). It is quite possible that there are many people like that. But as long as she still gives some importance (perhaps only strategic importance) to the more encompassing group, whether it is the country or nation or both, why not accept the claim that it (the country, nation, or both) has a right to self-determination? It seems simply arbitrary not to do so.

Similar considerations work against Buchanan's suggestion that self-determination is incompatible with the dynamic cultural pluralism which is a characteristic of contemporary liberal societies. *Pace* Buchanan, in accepting self-determination we are not creating barriers to changes in the conception of the good of individuals. On the contrary, if we seriously consider the dynamic character of cultural pluralism within contemporary liberal societies, we should recognize the existence and normative acceptability of multination states and should accept that the component nations within those states have the general right to some form of self-determination.

Buchanan also ignores the fundamental difference raised by Rawls between a political community and an association. One can remove oneself from an association, but one cannot help, to some extent at least, having to integrate, if one remains in a society, within a political community. The argument here is not that we are bound to a political community, even to a genuinely democratic community, in the way we are bound to a linguistic and cultural community, for the links are in this latter case even stronger. We can leave a country or a political community more easily than we can leave a cultural or linguistic affiliation, but there remains still an important difference between a political community and an association. The idea is that in liberal democracies, we shall find political communities, i.e., sets of institutions which govern (in the distinctive way of liberal democracies) society as a whole, wherever we go. There are, of course, many associations which we will never join, and indeed it is in principle possible not to be part of any associations (political parties, trade unions, school associations, etc.), but we can hardly fail to be a member of a political community. We can decide to leave a particular political community and join another, but we can hardly decide to leave, if we want to have any kind of life at all, all political communities. Now, as was argued in the introduction, nations are a particular specie of political community. All political communities in modern societies are the expression of one or many national communities. So, even if we ignore the particular linguistic and cultural attachments involved in these specific political communities that we call nations, there is still a difference in kind between political communities and associations. By blurring the distinction between political communities and associations, Buchanan misses an important difference between nations and other forms of allegiance.

Buchanan also confuses the decision to recognize a particular right to self-determination with the mistaken view, which he attributes to nationalists, according to which it is *only* nations that are good candidates for self-determination. All other groups, in his view, are not such good candidates. The mistake here – or so we believe – is not the previous one that led Buchanan to believe that nations, according to nationalists, had to be the *most important* form of community. It is the more radical mistake of imputing, without grounds, the belief to nationalists that all other affiliations are devoid of any worth whatsoever as possible subjects of self-determination. Nationalists must, according to Buchanan, believe that nations are the *only* communities that can exercise a right of self-determination. Other communities, he alleges that nationalists believe, are not entitled to such a claim. Is this right? If it were right, then it would seem that other groups are devoid of a certain kind of good enjoyed by national communities. But why should this be?

As a matter of fact, nationalists are only committed to the view that nations are in general (in modern societies) the only communities in a position to exercise a right to a *political* self-determination which would involve the right to secession. Linguistic groups, cultural communities, national minorities, groups of immigrants and so on may also enjoy a certain amount of self-determination, but in general not the right of secession. Does that mean that nations should be treated as more important? Different kinds of groups perform different sorts of actions with different rationales. Does that mean that nationalists, and particularly liberal nationalists, must, or even do, implicitly presuppose that some groups are more important than others? The point should be clear. It is not because nations are, in general, the only communities that could legitimately be entitled, under special circumstances, to exercise a full right of self-determination that we must on that basis conclude that they are the most valuable form of communal attachment or the only communities or associations entitled to some form of self-determination. Churches, universities, unions, and corporations have, and should have, and indeed could hardly function if they did not have, some limited forms of self-governance and, in that sense, some forms of self-determination. And the nationalist need not, and should not, say that these collectivities are less important than nations. The whole idea of ranking here, apart from some particular and contextually determined purposes, is absurd. Are universities more or less important than trade unions? Only a blinkered person would think that there is an answer to that question or that we are any worse off without an answer.

It should also be added that liberal nationalists can accept the principle according to which, in a sense, *all* groups that accept liberal principles have a 'right to self-determination.' It is just that their self-determination is secured by a charter of rights and liberties or by the fundamental principles that apply to individuals in the constitutions of liberal democracies. Families, religious groups, trade unions, and political associations all have some kind of self-determination. Why should the nationalist be committed to the absurdity of denying that? If the country of which we are a part adopts fundamental principles such as freedom of speech, freedom of association, and freedom of belief and opinion, then we can confidently claim that all these groups are in a sense entitled within these countries to self-determination. And if a country did not adopt them then it would not be a liberal democracy. But liberal nationalists are defending nationalism and the right, under certain circumstances, to secession within the limits of liberal democracy alone. They need not deny that secession may be justified in other circumstances as well, but that is not their brief.

V

For those of us who happen to be Canadians, as some would put it, or as others would put it, Canadians or Quebeckers – there is no neutral way of putting the matter – questions of nationalism and secession are not merely of theoretical interest. How our society or societies should be ordered turns to some considerable extent on how these questions should be answered. The Quebec sovereignty issue is also one crucial test case concerning the justifiability of liberal nationalism. Of the essays in this volume, Joel Prager's is unique in engaging in a detailed examination bringing to bear many factual considerations concerning the issue of Quebec sovereignty. He wants to see developed a social scientific theory which will tell us what is the relative weight of the various factors involved in the formation of Quebec voters' preferences for or against sovereignty. His contention is that a theory of rational behaviour, as developed in micro-economic theory, will provide the appropriate framework for the development of such a social theory.

Taken in the context of this general contention, it is therefore not surprising to see that for him, the best way to explain Quebeckers' aspirations for sovereignty is that 'Quebeckers seek to maximize their well-being.' But Joel Prager takes this literally; that is, for him well-being comes to economic advantage and his conjecture is, therefore, that the prospect of economic affluence is what best explains Quebeckers' preferences concerning sovereignty. The greater the prospects are, the greater will be their support to the project of sovereignty. We do not want to discuss the empirical plausibility of that conjecture, but it seems to us that Prager is too quick in moving from the premise that fears of economic catastrophe can temper aspirations to sovereignty to the conclusion that the support for sovereignty will increase proportionally to the increasing of the economic gains to be expected. Risk aversion is one thing, and greed is another. While the first one is arguably part of a rational behaviour, the second, as the marginalist economists have shown, is often not.[30] Prager here could have used a bit of that rational-choice theory's wisdom. But his reductionist view goes with a mistake frequently made by those seeking to give explanations in terms of a single causal quantifiable factor.

The grand scientific theory of nationalism Joel Prager wants to see developed has no intention in common with the normative theories that have been articulated in this volume. The intent of such scientific theory is not to say what is right or wrong but to give causal explanations, using game-theoretic models, and to make predictions. Such a theory, if we were to have a sound one, could with predictive reliability ascertain whether Quebec voters are likely to go for the sovereignty option. Such a reliable account would clearly be of great interest both to the Parti Québécois in planning strategy concerning how to win the struggle for secession and to the federalists in trying to defeat it. It could also be useful when the time comes to decide which promises or threats, depending on which side you are on, are likely to be the most effective. Such explanations, we are frequently told by proponents of game-theory as a methodological tool for social science, are normatively neutral. Jocelyne Couture argued that in so believing, social theorists are de-

---

30 See, for instance, Amartya Kumar Sen, 'Equality of What?' in Sterling M. McMurrin (ed.), *The Tanner Lectures on Human Values*, vol. 1 (Cambridge: Cambridge University Press 1980), 195–220.

ceiving themselves.[31] Engaging in what she called 'social Darwinism,' they flatly reason as if they had derived an 'ought' from an 'is,' most of the time without realizing it. Joel Prager's contribution is no exception. Whether his account of Quebeckers' reasons for supporting sovereignty is empirically to the point or not (*we* think it is false), the message Prager's explanatory-predictive account tentatively delivers remains the same: people's preferences are there and they are what should guide the behaviour of the political actors; actual people's preferences, as they just happen to turn out to be, are the ones which should be taken into consideration and the ones that the society should be prepared to adjust to and reinforce. Because they *are* there, they *ought* to be there and of course, with the help of such an explanation, if it is taken seriously by the politicians, these preferences will be reinforced. The naïve belief that game theoretic explanations in social science are normatively neutral is not so different, in its consequences and its general background assumptions, from the reduction, made in this volume by Liah Greenfeld, of *de jure* legitimacy to *de facto* legitimacy.

Joel Prager is not claiming that he has something to say on whether Quebec sovereigntists are *right* or *wrong*. His contribution is not intended either to tell whether, and under which conditions, Quebec secession would be *justified*. It is, however, such questions, though usually posed more generally than just about Quebec, that have been at the centre of interest in this volume, as well as in Miller's *On Nationality*, Tamir's *Liberal Nationalism*, Buchanan's *On Secession*, and in the work, on these and related topics, of G. A. Cohen, David Gauthier, Will Kymlicka, Ross Poole, and Michael Walzer. More sociological accounts, such as Benedict Anderson's, Ernest Gellner's, and E. J. Hobsbawm's, did not attempt to utilize anything like a *wert-frei* sociology (proclaimed by Liah Greenfeld). They neither tried to isolate 'a purely factual side' from 'a purely normative side' nor attempted to treat them separately: sometimes doing the 'purely factual thing' and at other times 'the purely normative thing.' Nor have they for a mo-

---

31 Jocelyne Couture, 'Decision Theory, Individualistic Explanations and Social Darwinism,' in R.S. Cohen and M. Marion, eds., *Quebec Studies in the Philosophy of Science* in *Boston Studies in the Philosophy of Science* 168 (Dordrecht: Kluwer 1995), 229–46.

ment thought that their descriptions can be free of all normative interpretation and conceptualization. Their assumptions, and our contention, is that our language games and forms of life neither are nor can be balkanized like that.[32]

Moreover, as we have seen, an adequate normative political theory or account – we did not say *'purely* normative theory,' for there is no such thing – must consider what *can* be the case in considering what *ought* to be the case. It is surely right, as Carol Prager argued and Joel Prager correctly assumed, that it is silly to take a high *a priori* moralistic road or a 'purist' highly abstract normative ethical theory road and then, proceeding quixotically, to try to ascertain how society should be ordered without a careful consideration of the realistic possibilities of how it can be ordered at a certain historical time and in a certain place. Even *ideal* normative theory, in Rawls's sense of ideal theory, can only operate in a *partial* abstraction from this constraint and then only for very circumscribed purposes, making all kinds of deliberately counterfactual assumptions in seeking to gain a clear conceptualization of some deliberately simplified, for purposes of perspicuous modelling, artificial situations.

One very important point made by Carol Prager is that a theory that reasonably concerns itself with the various possibilities should ask what are the comparative likelihoods of the various possible (feasible) scenarios and what are their advantages and disadvantages when compared to one another. We need to start on the daunting task of trying to figure these things out, by taking very seriously the task of accurately ascertaining what is the case and clearly representing it. That is a necessary prolegomena for ascertaining the possibilities. We can hardly know whether ethnic enmities can be eroded in a given situation without knowing how strong they are in that situation and something of their causes. That is not sufficient for our coming to know whether there is much chance that they can be eroded or even weakened, but it is necessary. To know the possibilities we have to know something about what the social realities actually are.

---

32 Jocelyne Couture and Kai Nielsen, 'Whither Moral Philosophy?' in Jocelyne Couture and Kai Nielsen, eds., *On the Relevance of Metaethics* (Calgary: University of Calgary Press 1995), 273–332

However, not all social realities are equally relevant to our consideration of what we should do in light of the realistic possibilities. Normative reflection has its place here. Normative reflection, for instance, could lead us to realize that it is a terrible thing for a people to lose their language and culture. What is of vital interest, where that possibility is at issue (though that, of course, is not the only thing of interest), is what the best demographic theory tells us about (in the case of Quebec) whether the French language and, with it, francophone culture is threatened in Montreal and not, as Joel Prager at least seems to believe, what polls and surveys reveal about what Montrealers believe about whether French is threatened. Whether French is threatened is a scientific issue, and the opinions of the person-on-the-street or, for that matter, the philosopher in his philosopher's closet, are not very relevant. They are hardly bits of evidence for what is the case or is likely to become the case. And, to say this is not scientism or science worship, but just plain realism about how, in this domain, belief should be fixed.

In debates about Quebec secession, this point needs to be kept firmly in mind. We also need to consider whether in Quebec, and specifically in Montreal, the French language is actually threatened or whether that is francophone paranoia, as some claim, or an understandable, but all the same unjustified, anxiety as some others claim. Here a knowledge of the demographic facts is crucial, including a good understanding of whether we have any sufficiently uncontroversial account of these facts or any sufficiently developed science of demography to draw firm conclusions about what is likely to happen if we just let things run their course as distinct from adopting certain hopefully preventive policies. We very much need to have some reliable demographic predictions here.

Here is a consideration concerning what should be done to ascertain what we critical intellectuals should conclude ourselves and advocate to other people. We need to (1) get the best account that we can get of what the demographic facts are. Depending on what that account says is likely to happen, we should (2) articulate various scenarios about what to do which reflect the various possibilities. We should then (3) try to ascertain which of these various scenarios with their plans of action would most likely best protect the French language from erosion. Critical intellectuals should (4) argue that *ceteris paribus* the plans of action that best protect French language should be adopted.

We say *ceteris paribus* because, as Joel Prager rightly notes, if the costs of protecting their language were to seriously hurt themselves economically or to work (as Brighouse believes) against their autonomy or the autonomy of the non-francophone citizens and landed immigrants of Quebec, then it would not be so obvious what, everything considered, should be done. Here our normative judgments, if they are to be justified, must take into serious consideration what is most reasonable to believe about the economic situation in the case of secession – whether Quebec be (1) fully sovereign, that is, a nation-state of its own, or (2) a sovereign nation in partnership with Canada (and the terms of this must be carefully specified) – as compared with the case if Quebec remained in Canada as it is presently constituted. Case (2), if it is to be more than a phrase, would result in Quebec coming to be a part of a genuine multination state with all the different component nations (including the First Nations) having some very considerable political and legal autonomy. But such a multination state would be (*pace* Joel Prager) very different from the present Canadian state. Each component nation would be fully recognized as a genuine nation. We also need to consider the probability of such a multination state coming into being and being stable. Serious consideration must also be given to the possibilities of enhanced or lessened autonomy for all citizens and landed immigrants of Quebec with or without secession.

We get nowhere in such concrete normative political thinking without close attention to these and similar factual claims and possibilities. But likewise we would not understand what weighting or attention to give to the various factual considerations involved, including the factual possibilities, without attending (*pace* Greenfeld) *to what we think, particularly with adequate knowledge and on due reflection, is right, appropriate, or desirable in such situations and why*. We need, that is, to do some hard specific normative thinking without being fettered by positivist ghosts. We should see here the importance of John Dewey's insistence that we should never consider values in isolation (attempted isolation) from facts or (at least where social and political issues are involved) facts in isolation (attempted isolation) from values.[33]

---

33 Kai Nielsen, *On Transforming Philosophy* (Boulder: Westview Press 1995), 145–253

Here we need to take all of the relevant considerations together: considerations about the attrition of language and culture, about economic security, and about autonomy, equality, rights, and democratic determination. Considering them all we need to see how they best can be made to fit into a coherent whole (a coherent assemblage of beliefs of all sorts, and of desires as well) that rational, reasonable, and informed people accept, or would accept, when they are being reflective concerning how to orient their lives. Doing this is very different from a simple nose-count of the preferences of people as a poll or survey would do.

In arguing about sovereignty – Quebec sovereignty or any other – it is not, as Joel Prager has it, vital to determine what polls tell us about what people actually want, but to ascertain, as well as we can, what people *would* want *if they were well-informed, being reflective, not caught up in ideology, and were being both reasonable and rational.*[34] In the normative thinking in this volume, very often the effort on issues turning around nationalism was to show people what it would be like to arrange their views and feelings into such a coherent pattern, that is, to get them, in the vocabulary of Rawls, Norman Daniels, and Kai Nielsen, into wide reflective equilibrium. (Couture and Nielsen have put it in a distinctive way, taking on board some of Martha Nussbaum's emendations.[35])

Spreading out from this, an effort should be made to give people a narrative and argumentative account, and ask them to reflect on it, and then, taking these matters to heart, to make up their minds what they would opt for, what they would reflectively endorse. Joel Prager's recommended procedure, with its stress on ascertaining what people's preferences actually are, comes in effect – though we do not know whether this was his intention – to giving us to understand that outside of a democratic vote people cannot rightly have a view *authoritatively forced* on them. But accepting this does not mean that acting on their actual preferences is the right thing for them to do. This, as we have seen, is itself plainly a normative contention and not just a bit of realism; it is normativity (sometimes an unwitting normativity) without normative

---

34 John Rawls, *Political Liberalism* (New York: Columbia University Press 1993), 48–54

35 Couture and Nielsen, 'Whither Moral Philosophy?', 326–32

thinking. It is an attempt to sidestep normative thinking, as is Greenfeld's reduction of *de jure* legitimacy to *de facto* legitimacy. Liberal normative thinking does not take it to be *de jure* legitimate to simply force moral views on a people or for that matter on individuals. But such liberal thinking does not simply take *this belief itself* to be just one of their liberal preferences concerning which nothing argumentative can be said. Carol Prager in effect rightly argues that determining *de jure* legitimacy cannot be done without regard for what is taken to have *de facto* legitimacy. But, unlike Greenfeld, she does not think *de jure* legitimacy can be reduced to *de facto* legitimacy or that it just is, if it is a coherent conception, *de facto* legitimacy.[36] Neither social science nor anything else requires that. This central liberal normative notion can be, and has been, argued for, using the method of wide reflective equilibrium or, less pedantically expressed, an extensive coherentist account, taking people's considered judgments as having some initial, but of course defeatable, credibility.[37]

Quebec sovereigntists, in line with liberal nationalism, argue for sovereignty on the grounds that it would best preserve the self-identity of a people – in this instance francophone Quebeckers – by protecting their language and with it their culture. And this, they further argue, is essential to preserve their autonomy, self-respect, and well-being. It would also give all citizens of Quebec more democratic empowerment than they would otherwise have. It points out as well that these two things are not unrelated. But Quebec sovereigntists also argue that, at least after things settle down, citizens of a sovereign Quebec would be economically no worse off than they are now and possibly better off. The central thing to recognize here, they argue, is that no economic disaster would occur with Quebec sovereignty. Sovereigntists also argue that Canada (the rest of Canada, if you will), including Atlantic Canada, need not be harmed with the coming into being of a sovereign Quebec and that this will most plainly be true if Canada will, as Quebec wishes to, enter into a partnership with Quebec. And even if Canada

---

36 Kai Nielsen, 'State Authority and Legitimation,' in Paul Harris, ed., *On Political Obligation* (London: Routledge 1990), 218–51

37 Nielsen, *Naturalism without Foundations*, 12–19, 169–200

does not, the continued economic viability of both countries requires them to cooperate and, as liberal states in interdependency with a cluster of other liberal states, they will cooperate, albeit perhaps grudgingly at first. It is not like being in those parts of the world where barbarous and irrational nationalisms flourish. Moreover, this does not make any strong rationalist claims about people's rationality, though it does, and not unreasonably, assume a rather minimal instrumental rationality, something with which both David Hume and Bertrand Russell would be perfectly content. Quebec sovereigntists also argue that the historically established rights of Quebec's national minority (the anglophones) will continue to be respected, that immigrant groups (the allophones of Quebec) will continue to have full citizenship rights (like anyone else), and that First Nations will be respected as nations with a distinctive, but limited, political autonomy. (For a specification of the distinction between national minorities and nations, see the introduction.)

Quebec sovereigntists not only argue for these things, they argue as well that these things are firm commitments of the Quebec government (commitments which, unfortunately, in the case of First Nations, have not been thoroughly carried out, but here Quebec is no worse off and arguably better off than Canada) and that they are, and always have been, firm commitments (again with the above qualification) of the Parti Québécois. It has been argued by some non-sovereigntists that such protestations by the Quebec government and the Parti Québécois should be taken with a grain of salt: they do not really mean them; they are just trying to soften people up for an acceptance of sovereignty. They are, that is, designed to sucker the gullible. Sovereigntists in turn reply that there is not a shred of evidence that people are being so suckered or even (more moderately) that the firm commitments described above are mere policy matters that might change as circumstances change. They are rather fundamental principles of liberal democracy which are as firm in Quebec as in any other liberal society. (The distinction between matters of policy and matters of principle, and the importance of making that distinction, has been well articulated by Ronald Dworkin.[38])

---

38 Ronald Dworkin, *Taking Rights Seriously* (Cambridge, MA: Harvard University Press, 1977), 22–28 and 90–100

So this, stated succinctly, is something of the argument that Quebec sovereigntists make and it is, in fundamentals, the same as other liberal nationalists make. (The details, of course, will differ with differing situations.) And it is, as well, the narrative that Quebec sovereigntists articulate. Are their arguments sound and is their narrative a 'telling it like it is' and a plausible projection of how things might come to be? And is this something that a reflective, reasonable, and well-informed moral agent should accept, believing that it is not only reasonable to believe that it might come to be the case, but that it *should* come to be the case? Or are their arguments unsound and indeed so fundamentally flawed that no reconstructive retrieval of them is plausible? And are their narratives in reality 'just-so stories' more expressive of sovereigntist mythology and ideology than verisimilitude?

The point here is to note that a response to those questions, if anything determinate can be said, should be and will be determined, if it can be determined at all, and if people are being reasonable, by something like the coherentist way of proceeding (if 'method' is too grand a term) suggested in the last few paragraphs. Being for or against sovereignty is neither an arbitrary existential choice nor simply, positivist style, a matter of what you just happen to want: a matter of 'You pays your money and you takes your choice.'

Bibliography

This bibliography contains a selection of classic studies and very recent work on nationalism.

1) Anthologies

Balakrishnan, Gopal, ed. (1996). *Mapping the Nation* (London: Verso).

Berberoglu, Berch, ed. (1995). *The National Question: Nationalism, Ethnic Conflict, and Self-Determination in the 20th Century* (Philadelphia: Temple University Press).

Berger, Suzanne, and Ronald Dore, eds. (1996). *National Diversity and Global Capitalism* (Ithaca: Cornell University Press).

Bernard, Michel, Nicole Pietri, and Marie-Pierre Rey (1996). *L'Europe, des nationalismes aux nations: Autriche, Hongrie, Russie, Allemagne* (Paris: Sedes).

Birnbaum, Pierre, ed. (1997). *Sociologie des nationalismes* (Paris: Presses Universitaires de France).

Blais, François, Guy Laforest, and Diane Lamoureux, eds. (1995). *Libéralismes et nationalismes. Collection Philosophie et politique* (Laval: Les Presses de l'Université Laval).

Breton, Albert, Gianluigi Galeotti, Pierre Salmon, and Ronald Wintrobe, eds. (1995). *Nationalism and Rationality* (Cambridge: Cambridge University Press).

Burgi, Noëlle, ed. (1994). *Fractures de l'État-nation* (Paris: Editions Kimé).

Cabanel, Patrick, ed. (1995). *Nation, nationalités et nationalismes en Europe, 1850-1920* (Paris: Éditions Ophrys).

Caney, Simon, David George, and Peter Jones, eds. (1996). *National Rights, International Obligations* (Boulder, CO: Westview Press).

Clark, Donald, and Robert Williamson, eds. (1996). *Self-Determination: International Perspectives* (New York: St-Martin's Press).

Cohen, Joshua, ed. (1996). *For Love of Country: Debating the Limits of Patriotism* (Boston: Beacon Press).

Coll. (1995). *Nations et nationalismes* (Paris: La découverte).

Coll. (1996). *Embattled Minorities Around the Globe: Rights, Hopes, Threats.* Summer issue of *Dissent*.

Coll. (1996). Special issue of *Critical Review* on nationalism. **10:2**.

Coll. (1997). *La nation. Philosophie Politique no. 8* (Paris: Presses Universitaires de France).

Dahbour, Omar, and Micheline R. Ishay, eds. (1995). *The Nationalism Reader* (Atlantic Highlands: Humanities Press).

Dahbour, Omar, ed. (1996-97). *Philosophical Perspectives on National Identity, Philosophical Forum* **28:1-2**.

Decaux, Emmanuel, and Alain Pellet, eds. (1996). *Nationalité, minorités et succession d'États en Europe de l'est* (Paris: Montchrestien).

Delannoi, Gil, and Pierre-André Taguieff, eds. (1991). *Théories du nationalisme* (Paris: Éditions Kimé).

Diamond, Larrym and Marc F. Plattner, eds. (1994). *Nationalism, Ethnic Conflict, and Democracy* (Baltimore: Johns Hopkins University Press).

Elbaz, Michael, Andrée Fortin, and Guy Laforest, eds. (1996). *Les frontières de l'identité: modernisme et post-modernisme au Québec* (Ste-Foy: Les Presses de l'Université Laval).

French, Stanley, ed. (1979). *Philosophers look at the Canadian Confederation / La confédération canadienne: qu'en pensent les philosophes* (Montréal: Association canadienne de philosophie).

Giordan, Henri, ed. (1992). *Les minorités en Europe: Droits linguistiques et droits de l'homme* (Paris: Éditions Kimé).

Glazer, Nathan, and Daniel P. Moynihan, eds. (1975). *Ethnicity: Theory and Experience* (Cambridge, MA: Harvard University Press).

Guibernau, Montserrat, and Rex, John, eds. (1997). *The Ethnicity Reader: Nationalism, Multiculturalism and Migration* (Cambridge: Polity Press).

Guillaume, André, Jean-Claude Lescure, and Stéphane Michonneau, eds. (1996). *L'Europe, des nationalismes aux nations: Italie, Espagne, Irlande* (Paris: Sedes).

Gutmann, Amy, ed. (1992). *Multiculturalism* (Princeton, NJ: Princeton University Press).

Hobsbawm, E.J., and Teree Ranger, eds. (1983). *The Invention of Tradition* (Cambridge: Cambridge University Press).

Hutchinson, John, and Anthony D. Smith, eds. (1994). *Nationalism* (Oxford: Oxford University Press).

Hutchinson, John, and Anthony D. Smith, eds. (1997). *Ethnicity* (Oxford: Oxford University Press).

Kupchan, Charles A., ed. (1995). *Nationalism and Nationalities in the New Europe* (Ithaca: Cornell University Press).

Lehning, Percy B., ed. (1998). *Theories of Secession* (London: Routledge).

McMahan, Jeff, and Robert McKim, eds. (1997). *The Morality of Nationalism* (Oxford: Oxford University Press).

Moore, Margaret, ed. (1998). *National Self-Determination and Secession* (Oxford: Oxford University Press).

Periwal, Sukumar, ed. (1995). *Notions of Nationalism* (London: Central European University Press).

Rémi-Giraud, Sylvianne, and Pierre Rétat, eds. (1996). *Les mots de la nation* (Lyon: Presses de l'Université de Lyon).

Rupnik, Jacques, ed. (1993). *Le déchirement des nations* (Paris: Éditions de Seuil).

Saly, Pierre, Alice Gérard, Céline Gervais, and Marie-Pierre Rey, eds. (1996). *Nations et nationalismes en Europe 1848-1914* (Paris: Armand Colin).

Seymour, Michel, ed. (1995). *Une nation peut-elle se donner la constitution de son choix?* (Montreal: Bellarmin).

Shapiro, Ian, and Will Kymlicka, eds. (1997). *Ethnicity and Group Rights* (New York: New York University Press).

Sollors, Werner, ed. (1996). *Theories of Ethnicity: A Classical Reader* (New York: New York University Press).

Twining, W., ed. (1991). *Issues of Self-Determination* (Aberdeen: Aberdeen University Press).

van Willigenburg, Theo, Robert Heeger, and Wilbren van der Burg, eds. (1995). *Nation, State, and the Coexistence of Different Communities* (Kampen: Kok Pharos Publishing).

Walzer, Michael, Edward T. Kantowicz, John Higham, and Mona Harrington, eds. (1982). *The Politics of Ethnicity* (Cambridge, MA: Harvard University Press).

Woolf, Susan, ed. (1996). *Nationalism in Europe. 1815 to the Present* (New York: Routledge).

2) Monographs

Amin, Samir (1994). *L'ethnie à l'assaut des nations: Yougoslavie, Éthiopie* (Paris: L'Harmattan).

Anderson, Benedict (1983). *Imagined Communities: Reflections on the Origin and Spread of Nationalism* (New York: Verso).

Archimbault, Aline, Félix Damette, and Michel Rocard (1995). *La nation, l'Europe, le monde* (Paris: Éditions de l'atelier).

Baggioni, Daniel (1997). *Langues et nations en Europe* (Paris: Payot).

Balibar, Étienne, and Immanuel Wallerstein (1992). *Race, nation, classes: Les identités ambiguës* (Paris: La découverte).

Bauhn, Per (1995). *Nationalism and Morality* (Lund: Lund University Press).

Berlin, Isaiah (1976).*Vico and Herder* (London: Chatto and Windus).

Bernard, Michel (1995). *Nations et nationalismes en Europe centrale XIXe-XXe siècles* (Paris: Aubier).

Bernstein, Serge, and Pierre Milza (1992). *Histoire de l'Europe 4: Nationalisme et concert européen. 1815-1919* (Paris: Hatier).

Bourque, Gilles, and Jules Duchastel (1996). *L'identité fragmentée* (Saint-Laurent: Fides).

Brass, Paul R. (1991). *Ethnicity and Nationalism: Theory and Comparison* (Newbury Park: Sage).

Breton, Albert, Gianluigi Galeotti, and Pierre Salmon (1993). *Nationalism and Xenophobia* (Toronto: Faculty of Law, University of Toronto).

Breuilly, John (1994). *Nationalism and the State*, 2d ed. (Chicago: University of Chicago Press).

Brubacker, William Rogers (1992). *Citizenship and Nationhood in France and Germany* (Cambridge: Harvard University Press).

Brubaker, William Rogers (1996). *Nationalism Reframed* (Cambridge: Cambridge University Press).

Buchanan, Allen (1991). *Secession: The Morality of Political Divorce from Fort Sumter to Lithuania and Quebec* (Boulder, CO: Westview).

Buchheit, L.C. (1978). *Secession: The Legitimacy of Self-Determination* (New Haven: Yale University Press).

Cabanel, Patrick (1997). *La question nationale au XIXe siècle* (Paris: La découverte).

Calhoun, Craig (1997). *Nationalism* (Buckingham: Open University).

Canovan, Margaret (1996). *Nationhood and Political Theory* (Chetelham: Edward Elgar).

Caron, Jean-Claude, and Michel Vernus (1996). *L'Europe au XIXe siècle: Des Nations au nationalisme. 1815-1914* (Paris: Armand Colin).

Cassese, Antonio (1995). *Self-Determination of Peoples: A Legal Reappraisal* (Cambridge: Cambridge University Press).

Chabot, Jean-Luc (1993). *Le Nationalisme* (Paris: Presses Universitaires de France).

Chatterjee, Partha (1995). *The Nation and its Fragments* (Delhi: Oxford University Press).

Coakley, John (1992). *The Socialist Origins of Nationalist Movements: The Contemporary West European Experience* (London: Sage).

Connor, Walker (1984). *The National Question in Marxist-Leninist Theory and Strategy* (Princeton: Princeton University Press).

Connor, Walker (1994). *Ethnonationalism: The Quest for Understanding* (Princeton, NJ: Princeton University Press).

Daniel, Jean (1994). *Voyage au bout de la nation* (Paris: Éditions du Seuil).

David, Marcel (1996). *La souveraineté du peuple* (Paris: Presses Universitaires de France).

Deutsch, Karl (1966). *Nationalism and Social Communication*, 2d ed. (Cambridge, MA: MIT Press).

Deutsch, Karl (1969). *Nationalism and its Alternatives* (New York: Basic Books).

Dieckhoff, Alain (1993). *L'invention d'une nation* (Paris: Gallimard).

Dumont, Fernand (1995). *Raisons communes* (Montréal: Boréal).

Elkins, David J. (1995). *Beyond Sovereignty, Territory and Political Economy in the Twenty-First Century* (Toronto: University of Toronto Press).

Esman, Milton J. (1994). *Ethnic Politics* (Ithaca: Cornell University Press).

Farnen, Russell F. (1994). *Nationalism, Ethnicity, and Identity* (New Brunswick, NU: Transaction Publishers).

Fenet, Alain, Geneviève Koubi, Isabelle Schulte-Tenckhoff, and Tatjana Ansbach (1995). *Le droit et les minorités. Analyses et textes* (Bruxelles: Bruylant).

Finkielkraut, Alain (1987). *La défaite de la pensée* (Paris: Gallimard). English translation (1995): *The Defeat of the Mind* (New York: Columbia University Press).

Finkielkraut, Alain (1992). *Comment peut-on être croate?* (Paris: Gallimard).

Gellner, Ernest (1983). *Nations and Nationalism* (Ithaca: Cornell University Press).

Gellner, Ernest (1987). *Culture, Identity, and Politics* (Cambridge: Cambridge University Press).

Gellner, Ernest (1994). *Encounters with Nationalism* (Oxford: Blackwell).

Gellner, Ernest (1995). *Anthropology and Politics* (Oxford: Blackwell).

Gellner, Ernest (1997). *Nationalism* (London: Weidenfeld & Nicolson).

Girardet, Raoul (1996). *Nationalismes et Nations* (Paris: Éditions Complexe).

Giraud, René (1996). *Peuples et nations d'Europe au XIXe siècle* (Paris: Hachette).

Greenfeld, Liah (1992). *Nationalism: Five Roads to Modernity* (Cambridge, MA: Harvard University Press).

Guéhenno, Jean-Marie (1993). *The End of the Nation State* (Minneapolis: University of Minnesota Press).

Guibernau, Monserrat (1996). *Nationalisms* (Cambridge: Polity Press).

Guiomar, Jean-Yves (1990). *La nation entre l'histoire et la raison* (Paris: La découverte).

Haas, Ernst B. (1997). *Nationalism, Liberalism, and Progress. Vol. 1* (Ithaca: Cornell University Press).

Habermas, Jürgen (1990). *Écrits politiques* (Paris: Cerf).

Habermas, Jürgen (1992). *The New Conservatism, Cultural Criticism and the Historians' Debate* (Cambridge, MA: MIT Press).

Halperin, Morton H. (1992). *Self-determination in the New World Order* (Washington: Carnegie Endowment for International Peace).

Hannaford, Ivan (1996). *Race: The History of an Idea in the West* (Washington, DC: The Woodrow Wilson Center Press).

Hannum, Hurst (1990). *Autonomy, Sovereignty, and Self-determination: The Accomodation of Conflicting Rights* (Philadelphia: University of Pennsylvania Press).

Hannum, Hurst (1993). *Documents on Autonomy and Minority Rights* (Boston: Martinus Nijhoff).

Haupt, Georges, Michael Löwi, and Claudie Weill (1994). *Les marxistes et la question nationale* (Paris: Maspéro).

Hermet, Guy (1996). *Histoire des nations et du nationalisme en Europe* (Paris: Éditions du Seuil).

Hobsbawm, E.J. (1992). *Nations and Nationalism since 1780*, 2d ed. (Cambridge: Cambridge University Press).

Horsman, Matthew, and Andrew Marshall (1995). *After the Nation State* (London: Harper Collins).

Ignatieff, Michael (1993). *Blood and Belonging: Journeys into the New Nationalism* (Toronto: Penguin).

Ishay, Micheline R. (1995). *Internationalism and its Betrayal* (Minneapolis: Minnesota University Press).

Jackson, Robert (1990). *Quasi-States: Sovereignty, International Relations and the Third World* (Cambridge: Cambridge University Press).

Jenkins, Brian, and Spyros A. Sofos (1996). *Nation and Identity in Contemporary Europe* (New York: Routledge).

Jouve, Edmond (1992). *Droit des peuples* (Paris: Presses Universitaires de France).

Juergensmeyer, Mark (1993). *The New Cold War? Religious Nationalism Confronts the Secular State* (Berkeley: University of California Press).

Keating, Michael (1996). *Nations Against the State: The New Politics of Nationalism in Quebec, Catalonia and Scotland* (Basingstoke: Macmillan).

Kedourie, Elie (1994). *Nationalism*, 4th ed. (Oxford: Blackwell).

Kohn, Hans (1944). *The Idea of Nationalism. A Study in its own Origin and Background* (New York: Macmillan).

Kohn, Hans (1945). *The Idea of Nationalism* (New York: Macmillan).

Kohn, Hans (1966). *American Nationalism* (New York: Collier Books).

Kristeva, Julia (1993). *Nations Without Nationalism* (New York: Columbia University Press).

Kymlicka, Will (1989). *Liberalism, Community and Culture* (Oxford: Oxford University Press).

Kymlicka, Will (1995). *Multicultural Citizenship* (Oxford: Clarendon Press).

Kymlicka, Will (1997). *States, Nations and Cultures: Spinoza Lectures* (Amsterdam: Van Gorcum).

Lefebvre, Henri (1988). *Le nationalisme contre les nations* (Paris: Méridiens Klincksieck).

Leliepvre-Botton, Sylvie (1996). *Droit du sol, droit du sang: Patriotisme et sentiment national chez Rousseau* (Paris: Ellipses).

Lellouche, Pierre (1992). *Le Nouveau monde: de l'ordre de Yalta au désordre des nations* (Paris: Grasset).

Matustik, Martin J. (1993). *Postnational Identity: Critical Theory and Existential Philosophy in Habermas, Kierkegaard and Havel* (New York: Guilford).

Mayall, James (1990). *Nationalism and International Society* (Cambridge: Cambridge University Press).

McAll, Christopher (1990). *Class, Ethnicity, and Social Inequality* (Montreal: McGill-Queen's University Press).

Miller, David (1995). *On Nationality* (Oxford: Clarendon Press).

Minc, Alain (1990). *La vengeance des nations* (Paris: Grasset).

Minogue, Kenneth (1967). *Nationalism* (London: Batsford).

Morin, Jacques-Yvan, François Rigaldies, and Daniel Turp (1986). *Droit international public* (Montreal: Themis).

Moynihan, Daniel P. (1994). *Pandæmonium: Ethnicity in International Politics* (Oxford: Oxford University Press).

Musgrave, Thomas (1997). *Self-Determination and National Minorities.* Oxford Monographs in International Law (Oxford: Oxford University Press).

Nairn, Tom (1997). *Faces of Nationalism: Janus Revisited* (London: Verso).

Ohmae, Kenichi (1995). *The End of the Nation State: The Rise of Regional Economics* (New York: The Free Press).

Oomen, T.K. (1997). *Citizenship, Nationality and Ethnicity: Competing Identities* (Oxford: Blackwell).

Pfaff, William (1994). *The Wrath of Nations: Civilization and the Furies of Nationalism* (New York: Simon and Schuster).

Pierré-Caps, Stéphane (1987). *Nations et peuples dans les constitutions modernes* (Nancy: Presses Universitaires de Nancy).

Pierré-Caps, Stéphane (1995). *La Multination* (Paris: Éditions Odile Jacob).

Poole, Ross (1991). *Morality and Modernity* (New York: Routledge).

Poutignat, Philippe, and Jocelyne Streiff-Fenart (1995). *Théories de l'ethnicité* (Paris: Presses Universitaires de France).

Richard, Philippe (1995). *Droits de l'homme, droits des peuples* (Lyon: Chronique sociale).

Rigaux, Francois (1990). *Pour une déclaration universelle des droits des peuples: identité nationale et coopération internationale* (Bruxelles: Chronique sociale).

Rouland, Norbert, Stéphane Pierré-Caps, and Jacques Poumarède (1996). *Droit des minorités et des peuples autochtones* (Paris: Presses Universitaires de France).

Sabourin, Paul (1994). *L'État-nation face aux Europes* (Paris: Presses Universitaires de France).

Sabourin, Paul (1996). *Les nationalismes européens* (Paris: Presses Universitaires de France).

Santamaria, Yves, and Brigitte Waché (1996). *Du Printemps des peuples à la Société des nations: Nations, nationalités et nationalismes en Europe 1850-1920* (Paris: La découverte).

Schnapper, Dominique (1991). *La France de l'intégration: Sociologie de la nation en 1990* (Paris: Gallimard).

Schnapper, Dominique (1994). *La communauté des citoyens: Sur l'idée moderne de nation* (Paris: Gallimard).

Schulze, Hagen (1996). *States, Nations and Nationalism, from the Middle Ages to the Present* (Oxford: Blackwell).

Shafir, Gershon (1995). *Immigrants and Nationalists* (Albany: State University of New York Press).

Sluga, Hans D. (1993). *Heidegger's Crisis: Philosophy and Politics in Nazi Germany* (Cambridge, MA: Harvard University Press).

Smith, Anthony D. (1971). *Theories of Nationalism* (London: Duckworth).

Smith, Anthony D. (1976). *Nationalist Movements* (London: Macmillan).

Smith, Anthony D. (1979). *Nationalism in the Twentieth Century* (Oxford: Martin Robertson).

Smith, Anthony D. (1981). *The Ethnic Revival in the Modern World* (Cambridge: Cambridge University Press).

Smith, Anthony D. (1986). *The Ethnic Origins of Nations* (Oxford: Blackwell).

Smith, Anthony D. (1991). *National Identity* (London: Penguin).

Smith, Anthony D. (1995). *Nations and Nationalism in a Global Era* (Oxford: Polity Press, Blackwell).

Spinner, Jeff (1994). *The Boundaries of Citizenship: Race, Ethnicity, and Nationality in the Liberal State* (Baltimore: Johns Hopkins University Press).

Tamir, Yael (1993). *Liberal Nationalism* (Princeton, NJ: Princeton University Press).

Taylor, Charles (1993). *Reconciling Two Solitudes: Essays on Canadian Federalism and Nationalism* (Montreal: McGill-Queen's University Press).

671

Todorov, Tzvetan (1993). *On Human Diversity: Nationalism, Racism and Exoticism in French Thought* (Cambridge, MA: Harvard University Press).

Tully, James (1995). *Strange Multiplicity: Constitutionalism in an Age of Diversity* (New York: Cambridge University Press).

Viroli, Maurizo (1995). *For Love of Country* (Oxford: Clarendon Press).

Walzer, Michael (1990). *Nation and Universe. The Tanner Lectures on Human Values, Volume XI* (Salt Lake City: University of Utah Press).

Walzer, Michael (1994). *Thick and Thin: Moral Argument at Home and Abroad* (Notre-Dame: University of Notre Dame Press).

Walzer, Michael (1997). *On Toleration* (New Haven: Yale University Press).

Wieviorka, Michel (1993). *La démocratie à l'épreuve: nationalisme, populisme, ethnicité* (Paris: La découverte).

Young, Iris Marion (1990). *Justice and the Politics of Difference* (Princeton, NJ: Princeton University Press).

3) Articles

Appiah, K. Anthony (1997). 'The Multiculturalist Misunderstanding,' *The New York Review of Books* **44:15**, 30-36.

Archard, David (1995). 'Political Philosophy and the Concept of the Nation,' *Journal of Value Inquiry* **29:3**, 379-92.

Bariteau, Claude (1996). 'Pour une conception civique du Québec,' *L'Action nationale* **86:7**, 105-68.

Barry, Brian (1983). 'Self-Government Revisited.' In David Miller and Larry Siedentorp, eds., *The Nature of Political Theory* (Oxford: Clarendon Press), 121-54.

Barry, Brian (1987). 'Nationalism.' In *Blackwell Encyclopedia of Political Thought* (Oxford: Basil Blackweil).

Berlin, Isaiah (1972). 'The Bent Twig: A Note on Nationalism,' *Foreign Affairs* **51**, 11-30.

Berlin, Isaiah (1991). 'Two Concepts of Nationalism,' *The New York Review.* November 21.

Berlin, Isaiah (1991). 'Nationalism: Past Neglect and Present Power.' In Isaiah Berlin, *Against the Current: Essays in the History of Ideas* (Oxford: Clarendon Press), 333-55.

Birnbaum, Pierre (1996). 'From Multiculturalism to Nationalism,' *Political Theory* **24:1**, 33-45.

Brilmayer, L. (1991). 'Secession and Self-Determination: A Territorial Interpretation,' *Yale Journal of International Law*, 16.

Buchanan, Allen (1995). 'Les conditions de la sécession.' In Michel Seymour, ed., *Une nation peut-elle se donner la constitution de son choix?* (Montreal: Bellarmin), 169-79.

Buchanan, Allen (1996). 'Theories of Secession,' *Philosophy and Public Affairs* **26:1**, 31-61.

Carens, Joseph H. (1997). 'Liberalism and Culture,' *Constellations* **4:1**, 35-47.

Cass, Deborah H. (1992). 'Rethinking Self-Determination: A Critical Analysis of Current International Law Theories,' *Syracuse Journal of International Comparative Law* **18**.

Clark, Stephen R.L. (1996). 'Nations and Empires,' *European Journal of Philosophy* **4:1**, 63-80.

Cohen, Mitchell (1995). 'Rooted Cosmopolitanism.' In Michael Walzer, ed., *Toward a Global Civil Society* (Providence, RI: Berghahn Books), 223-34.

Cooper, Wesley (1993). 'Critical Notice of Will Kymlicka's *Liberalism, Community and Culture*,' *Canadian Journal of Philosophy* **23:3**, 433-51.

Copp, David (1979). 'Do Nations Have the Right of Self-Determination?' In Stanley French, ed., *Philosophers Look at the Constitution / La Constitution canadienne: qu'en pensent les philosophes?* (Montreal: Canadian Philosophical Association), 71-96.

Couture, Jocelyne (1992). 'L'art de la séparation.' In *Philosophiques*, **19:2**, 41-55. Reprinted in Michel Seymour ed., *Une nation peut-elle se donner la constitution de son choix?* (Montreal: Bellarmin 1995), 35-51.

Couture, Jocelyne (1993). 'Pluralisme et différences individuelles.' In Daniel Weinstock, ed., *Le défi du pluralisme. Lekton* **3:2**, 171-84.

Couture, Jocelyne (1995). 'Pourquoi devrait-il y avoir un conflit entre le nationalisme et le libéralisme politique?' In François Blais, Guy Laforest, and Diane Lamoureux, eds., *Libéralismes et nationalismes: Collection Philosophie et politique* (Laval: Presses de l'Université Laval), 51-75.

Couture, Jocelyne (1997). 'L'institutionalisation de la Raison Publique: le moral et le politique.' In *Philosophiques*, **24:1**, 43-57.

Couture, Jocelyne (1997). 'Some Ways of Talking,' *Constitutional Forum* **8:4**, 89-94.

Couture, Jocelyne and Kai Nielsen (1995). 'L'ouverture internationale.' In *Manifeste des Intellectuels pour la Souveraineté suivi de Douze essais sur l'avenir du Québec* (Montréal: Fides), 177-200.

Cunningham, Frank (1997). 'The Canada-Quebec Conundrum: A Trinational Perspective,' *Constitutional Forum* **8:4**, 119-29.

Dahbour, Omar (1993). 'Self-Determination in Political Philosophy and International Law,' *History of European Ideas* **16:4-6**, 879-84.

Danley, John R. (1991). 'Liberalism, Aboriginal Rights and Cultural Minorities,' *Philosophy and Public Affairs* **21**, 168-85.

Dumont, Louis (1983). 'Le peuple et la nation chez Herder et Fichte.' In *Essais sur l'individualisme* (Paris: Éditions du Seuil).

Felice, William F. (1996). 'The Case for Collective Human Rights: The Reality of Group Suffering,' *Ethics and International Affairs* **10**, 47-61.

Forst, Rainer (1997). 'Foundations of a Theory of Multicultural Justice,' *Constellations* **4:1**, 63-71.

Freeman, Michael (1994). 'Nation, State and Cosmopolis: A Response to David Miller,' *Journal of Applied Philosophy* **11:1**, 79-87.

Frisch, Morton J. (1993). 'The Emergence of Nationalism as a Political Philosophy,' *History of European Ideas* **16:4-6**, 885-90.

Galston, William (1995). 'Two Concepts of Liberalism.' *Ethics* **105:66**, 516-34.

Gauthier, David (1994). 'Breaking Up: An Essay on Secession,' *Canadian Journal of Philosophy* **24:3**, 357-71.

Geertz, Clifford (1963). 'The Integrative Revolution: Primordial Sentiments and Civil Politics in the New States.' In Clifford Geertz, ed., *Old Societies and New States: The Quest for Modernity in Asia and Africa* (New York: Free Press), 105-57.

Gellner, Ernest (1987). 'Nationalism.' In Vernon Bogdanor, ed., *Blackwell Encyclopedia of Political Institutions* (Oxford: Basil Blackwell), 382-3.

Goldman, Alan H. (1982). 'The Moral Significance of National Boundaries,' *Midwest Studies in Philosophy* **7**, 437-53.

Gomberg, Paul (1990). 'Patriotism Is Like Racism,' *Ethics* **101:1**, 144-50.

Goodin, Robert E. (1988). 'What Is So Special About Our Fellow Countrymen?' *Ethics* **98**, 663-86.

Graff, James A. (1994). 'Human Rights, Peoples, and the Right to Self-Determination.' In Judith Baker, ed., *Group Rights* (Toronto: University of Toronto Press), 186-214.

Green, Michael J. (1996). 'National Identity and Liberal Political Philosophy,' *Ethics and International Affairs* **10**, 191-201.

Greenfeld, Liah (1993). 'Transcending the Nation's Worth,' *Dædalus*, Summer Issue, 47-62.

Greenfeld, Liah (1995). 'The Worth of Nations: Some Economic Implications of Nationalism,' *Critical Review* **9:4**, 555-84.

Habermas, Jürgen (1989). 'Historical Consciousness and Post-traditional Identity: The Federal Republic's Orientation to the West.' In Jürgen Habermas, *The New Conservatism: Cultural Criticism and the Historian's Debate* (Cambridge, MA: MIT Press), 249-67.

Habermas, Jürgen (1989). 'La souveraineté populaire comme procédure: Un concept normatif d'espace public,' *Lignes* **7**, 29-58.

Habermas, Jürgen (1992). 'Citoyenneté et identité nationale.' In J. Lenoble and N. Dewandre, eds., *L'Europe au soir du siècle: identité et démocratie* (Paris: Éditions Esprit).

Habermas, Jürgen (1992). 'Citizenship and National Identity: Some Reflections on the Future of Europe,' *Praxis International* **12:1**, 1-19.

Habermas, Jürgen (1994). 'Human Rights and Popular Sovereignty: The Liberal and Republican Versions,' *Ratio Juris* **7:1**, 1-13.

Habermas, Jürgen (1996). 'The European Nation-state – Its Achievements and Its Limits. On the Past and Future of Sovereignty and Citizenship. In Gopal Balakrishnan, ed., *Mapping the Nation* (London: Verso), 281-94.

Hannum, Hurst (1992). 'Self-Determination as a Human Right.' In B. H. Weston and Richard Pierre Claude, eds., *Human Rights in the World Community: Issues and Action*, 2d ed.

Hobsbawm, E. J. (1995). 'Ethnicity, Migration and the Validity of the Nation-State.' In Michael Walzer, ed., *Toward a Global Civil Society* (Providence, RI: Berghahn Books), 235-40.

Horowitz, Donald L. (1997). 'Self-Determination: Politics, Philosophy and Law.' In Ian Shapiro and Will Kymlicka, eds., *Ethnicity and Group Rights* (New York: New York University Press), 423-63.

Hurka, Thomas (1997). 'The Justification of National Partiality.' In Jeff McMahan and Robert McKim, eds., *The Morality of Nationalism* (Oxford: Oxford University Press), 139-57.

James, Paul (1992). 'Forms of Abstract Community: From Tribe and Kingdom to Nation and State,' *Philosophy of Social Sciences* **22:3**, 313-36.

Judt, Tony (1994). 'The New Old Nationalism,' *The New York Review of Books*, **41:10**, 44-51.

Kamenka, Eugene (1994). 'Nationalism: Ambiguous Legacies and Contingent Futures.' In Alexsandras Shtromas, ed., *The End of Isms?* (Oxford: Blackwell).

Kohn, Hans (1979). 'Nationalism,' *Dictionary of the History of Ideas*, vol. 3, 324-39.

Kukathas, Chandran (1992). 'Are There Any Cultural Rights?' *Political Theory* **20:1**, 105-39.

Kukathas, Chandran (1997). 'Cultural Toleration.' In Ian Shapiro and Will Kymlicka, eds., *Ethnicity and Group Rights* (New York: New York University Press), 69-104.

Kumar, Radha (1997). 'The Troubled History of Partition,' *Foreign Affairs* **76:1**, 22-34.

Kymlicka, Will (1991). 'Liberalism and the Politicization of Ethnicity,' *Canadian Journal of Law and Jurisprudence* **4:2**, 239-55.

Kymlicka, Will (1992). 'The Rights of Minority Cultures: Reply to Kukathas,' *Political Theory* **20:1**, 140-6.

Kymlicka, Will, and Wayne Norman (1994). 'Return of the Citizen,' *Ethics* **104:2**, 352-81.

Kymlicka, Will (1994). 'Individual and Community Rights.' In Judith Baker, ed., *Group Rights* (Toronto: University of Toronto Press), 17-33.

Kymlicka, Will (1995). 'Misunderstanding Nationalism,' *Dissent* (Summer), 130-7.

Kymlicka, Will (1995). 'The Paradox of Liberal Nationalism,' *The Literary Review of Canada* **4:10**, 13-15.

Kymlicka, Will (1996). 'Social Unity in a Liberal State,' *Social Philosophy and Policy* **13:1**, 105-36.

Kymlicka, Will (1997). 'Do We Need a Liberal Theory of Minority Rights? A Reply to Carens, Young, Parikh and Forst,' *Constellations* **4:1**, 72-87.

Laforest, Guy (1992). 'The Liberal Understanding of Nationalism: The Need for a More Prudent Approach,' *History of European Ideas* **15:4-6**, 505-9.

Levinson, Sanford (1995). 'Is Liberal Nationalism an Oxymoron? An Essay for Judith Shklar,' *Ethics* **105:3**, 626-45.

Leydet, Dominique (1995). 'Patriotisme constitutionnel et identité nationale.' In Michel Seymour, ed., *Une nation peut-elle se donner la constitution de son choix?* (Montreal: Bellarmin), 79-91.

MacCormick, Neil (1982). 'Nation and Nationalism.' In Neil MacCormick, *Legal Right and Social Democracy: Essays in Legal and Political Philosophy* (Oxford: Oxford University Press), 247-64.

MacCormick, Neil (1991). 'Is Nationalism Philosophically Credible?' In W. Twining, ed., *Issues of Self-Determination* (Aberdeen: Aberdeen University Press), 8-19.

MacIntyre, Alasdair (1984). 'Is Patriotism a Virtue?' In *The Lindley Lecture* (Lawrence: University of Kansas, Philosophy Department).

Margalit, Avishai, and Joseph Raz (1990). 'National Self-Determination,' *Journal of Philosophy* **87:9**, 439-61.

McRoberts, Kenneth (1997). 'Why We Can't Talk: The Lost Language of Canadian Politics,' *Constitutional Forum* **8:4**, 88-92.

Mill, John Stuart (1975). 'Considerations on Representative Government.' In John Stuart Mill. *Three Essays* (Oxford: Oxford University Press), 144-423.

Miller, David (1988). 'The Ethical Significance of Nationality,' *Ethics* **98**, 647-62.

Miller, David (1989). 'In What Sense Must a Socialism be Communitarian?' *Social Philosophy and Policy* **6**, 51-73.

Miller, David (1993). 'In Defence of Nationality,' *Journal of Applied Philosophy* **10:1**, 3-16.

Nathanson, Stephen (1989). 'In Defense of Moderate Patriotism,' *Ethics* **99**, 535-52.

Nathanson, Stephen (1990). 'On Deciding Whether a Nation Deserves Our Loyalty,' *Public Affairs Quarterly* **4:3**, 287-98.

Nielsen, Kai (1987). 'Cultural Identity and Self-Definition,' *Human Studies* **10**, 383-90.

Nielsen, Kai (1987). 'Undistorted Discourse, Ethnicity and the Problem of Self-Definition.' In Winston A. van Horne, ed., *Ethnicity and Language*, vol. 6 (Milwaukee: University of Wisconsin System), 16-36.

Nielsen, Kai (1991). 'Secession: The Case of Quebec,' *Journal of Applied Philosophy* **10:1**, 29-43.

Nielsen, Kai (1996-1997). 'Cultural Nationalism, Neither Ethnic nor Civic,' *Philosophical Forum* **28:1-2**, 42-52.

Nielsen, Kai (1997). 'Is Global Justice Impossible?' Jay Drydyk and Peter Penz, eds., *Global Justice, Global Democracy* (Winnipeg/Halifax: Fernwood Publishing), 19-54.

Nielsen, Kai (1998). 'Against Partition,' *Dalhousie Review* (forthcoming).

Nielsen, Kai (1998). 'Liberal Nationalism, Liberal Democracies and Secession,' *University of Toronto Law Journal* (forthcoming).

Nielsen, Kai (1998). 'Socialism and Nationalism,' *Imprints* (forthcoming).

Nussbaum, Martha (1996). 'Patriotism and Cosmopolitanism.' In Joshua Cohen, ed., *For Love of Country: Debating the Limits of Patriotism* (Boston: Beacon Press), 3-17.

Nussbaum, Martha C. (1996). 'Reply.' In Joshua Cohen, ed., *For Love of Country* (Boston: Beacon Press).

O'Brien, C.C. (1991). 'Nationalists and Democrats,' *Times Literary Supplement*. August 15.

O'Neill, John (1994). 'Should Communitarians be Nationalists?' *Journal of Applied Philosophy* **11:2**, 135-43.

Parikh, Bhikhu (1997). 'Dilemmas of a Multicultural Theory of Citizenship,' *Constellations* **4:1**, 54-62.

Philpott, D. (1994-95). 'In Defense of Self-Determination,' *Ethics* **105**, 352-85.

Plamenatz, J. (1976). 'Two Types of Nationalism.' In E. Kamenka, ed., *Nationalism: The Nature and Evolution of an Idea* (Canberra: Edward Arnold), 22-36.

Pogge, Thomas (1992). 'Cosmopolitanism and Sovereignty,' *Ethics* **103:1**, 48-75.

Pogge, Thomas (1994). 'An Egalitarian Law of Peoples,' *Philosophy and Public Affairs* **23:3**, 195-224.

Pogge, Thomas (1997). 'Group Rights and Ethnicity.' In Ian Shapiro and Will Kymlicka, eds., *Ethnicity and Group Rights* (New York: New York University Press), 187-221.

Poole, Ross (1992). 'On National Identity: A Response to Jonathan Rée,' *Radical Philosophy* **62**, 14-19.

Poole, Ross (1993). 'Nationalism and the Nation-State in Late Modernity,' *European Studies Journal* **10**, 161-74.

Poole, Ross (1994). 'Nationalism, Ethnicity and Identity,' *Journal of Area Studies* **4**, 30-42.

Poole, Ross (1995). 'Nationalism: The Last Rites?' In Aleksandr Pavkovic, Adam Czarnota, and Halyna Koscharsky, eds., *Nationalism and Postcommunism* (Aldershot: Dartmouth), 203-41.

Poole, Ross (1996-97). 'Freedom, Citizenship, and National Identity,' *Philosophical Forum* **28:1-2**, 125-48.

Rawls, John (1993). 'The Law of Peoples.' In Stephen Shute and Susan Hurley, eds., *On Human Rights. The Oxford Amnesty Lectures 1993* (New York: Basic Books), 41-82.

Rée, Jonathan (1992). 'Internationality,' *Radical Philosophy* **60**, 3-11.

Rée, Jonathan (1993). 'National Passions,' *Common Knowledge* **2:3**, 43-54.

Rée, Jonathan (1996-97). 'Cosmopolitanism and the Experience of Nationality,' *Philosophical Forum* **28:1-2**, 167-79.

Rée, Jonathan (1998). 'Rorty's Nation,' *Radical Philosophy* **87:January/ February**, 18-22.

Renaut, Alain (1991). 'Logique de la nation.' In Gil Delannoi and Pierre-André Taguieff, eds., *Théories du nationalisme* (Paris: Éditions Kimé), 29-46.

Resnick, David (1992). 'John Locke and Liberal Nationalism,' *History of European Ideas* **15:4-6**, 511-17.

Rosenfield, Michel (1996). 'A Pluralist Look at Liberalism, Nationalism and Democracy; Comments on Shapiro and Tamir,' *Constellations* **3:3**, 326-39.

Russell, Peter (1997). 'Aboriginal Nationalism and Quebec Nationalism: Reconciliation through Fourth World Decolonization,' *Constitutional Forum* **8:4**, 110-8.

Schnapper, Dominique (1993). 'Le sens de l'ethnico-religieux,' *Archives des sciences sociales des religions* **81**, 149-63.

Scruton, Roger (1990). 'In Defence of the Nation.' In *The Philosopher on Dover Beach* (Manchester: Carcanet), 299-328.

Seymour, Michel (1994). 'Anti-individualisme, droits collectifs et États multinationaux.' In Daniel Weinstock, ed., *Le défi du pluralisme. Lekton* **4:1**, 41-80.

Seymour, Michel (1995). 'Quelques aspects politiques de l'anti-individualisme.' In Michel Seymour, ed., *Une nation peut-elle se donner la constitution de son choix?* (Montreal: Bellarmin), 59-75.

Seymour, Michel (1998). 'Québécois et autochtones. Une nouvelle alliance.' In Isabelle Schulte-Tenckhoff (dir.), *Altérité et Droit (1)* (Paris: Les papiers du collège international de philosophie), no. 41, 39-50.

Seymour, Michel (1998). 'Une conception sociopolitique de la nation,' *Dialogue* **37:3**.

Shapiro, Ian (1996). 'Group Aspirations and Democratic Politics,' *Constellations* **3:3**, 315-25.

Shklar, Judith N. (1989). 'The Liberalism of Fear.' In Nancy L. Rosenblum, ed., *Liberalism and the Moral Life* (Cambridge, MA: Harvard University Press), 21-38.

Smith, Anthony D. (1987). 'Ethnic Nationalism,' *Blackwell Encyclopedia of Political Institutions* (Oxford: Basil Blackwell).

Smith, Anthony D. (1988). 'The Myth of the "Modern Nation" and the Myths of Nations,' *Ethnic and Racial Studies* **11:1**, 1-26.

Smith, Anthony D. (1989). 'The Origins of Nations,' *Ethnic and Racial Studies* **12:3**, 340-67.

Smith, Anthony D. (1990). 'The Supersession of Nationalism?' *International Journal of Comparative Sociology* **31:1-2**, 1-31.

Smith, Anthony D. (1993). 'Ties that Bind,' *LSE Magazine*, Spring Issue.

Smith, Anthony D. (1994). 'The Problem of National Identity: Ancient, Medieval and Modern?' *Ethnic and Racial Studies* **17:3**, 375-99.

Smith, Anthony D. (1995). 'The Formation of National Identity.' In Henry Harris, ed., *Identity: Essays Based on Herbert Spencer Lectures Given in the University of Oxford* (Oxford: Clarendon Press).

Sunstein, Cass R. (1991). 'Constitutionalism and Secession,' *University of Chicago Law Review* **58:2**, 633-70.

Taguieff, Pierre-André (1995). 'Nationalisme et anti-nationalisme: Le débat sur l'identité française.' In *Nations et nationalismes: Les dossiers de l'état du monde* (Paris: La découverte), 127-35.

Tamas, G. M. (1994). 'Old Enemies and New: A Philosophic Postscript to Nationalism,' *Studies in East European Thought* **46:1-2**, 129-48.

Tamir, Yael (1991). 'The Right to National Self-Determination,' *Social Research* **58**, 565-90.

Tamir, Yael (1991). 'Whose History? What Ideas?' In Edna Margalit, ed., *Isaiah Berlin: A Celebration* (Chicago: University of Chicago Press), 146-59.

Tamir, Yael (1993). 'The Right to National Self-Determination as an Individual Right,' *History of European Ideas* **16:4-6**, 899-905.

Tamir, Yael (1993). 'United We Stand? The Educational Implications of the Politics of Difference,' *Studies in the Philosophy of Education* **12:1**, 57-70.

Tamir, Yael (1996). 'The Land of the Fearful and the Free,' *Constellations* **3:3**, 296-314.

Taylor, Charles (1979). 'Why Do Nations Have to Become States?' In Stanley French, ed., *Philosophers Look at the Canadian Confederation / La confédération canadienne: qu'en pensent les philosophes* (Montreal: Association canadienne de philosophie), 19-35.

Taylor, Charles (1992). 'The Politics of Recognition' In Amy Gutman, ed., *Multiculturalism and 'the Politics of Recognition'* (Princeton, NJ: Princeton University Press), 25-73.

Tomasi, John (1995). 'Kymlicka, Liberalism and Respect for Cultural Minorities,' *Ethics* **105:3**, 580-603.

Van Parijs, Philippe (1993). 'Rawlsians, Christians and Patriots: Maximin Justice and Individual Ethics,' *European Journal of Philosophy* **1:3**, 309-42.

Waldron, Jeremy (1992). 'Minority Cultures and the Cosmopolitan Alternative,' *University of Michigan Journal of Law Reform* **25**, 751-93.

Walker, Brian (1997). 'Plural Cultures, Contested Territories: A Critique of Kymlicka,' *Canadian Journal of Political Science* **30:2**, 211-34.

Walzer, Michael (1996). 'Spheres of Affection.' In Joshua Cohen, ed., *For the Love of Country* (Boston: Beacon Press), 125-7.

Weiler, Gershon (1994). 'What Is the Philosophy of Nationalism?' *Studies in East European Thought* **46:1-2**, 119-28.

Weinstock, Daniel (1995). 'Libéralisme, nationalisme et pluralisme culturel.' In Michel Seymour, ed., *Une nation peut-elle se donner la constitution de son choix?* (Montreal: Bellarmin), 121-52.

Weinstock, Daniel (1996). 'Is There a Case for Nationalism?' *Journal of Applied Philosophy* **13:1**, 87-100.

Wellman, Christopher H. (1995). 'A Defense of Secession and Political Self-Determination,' *Philosophy and Public Affairs* **24:2**, 142-71.

Young, Iris Marion (1986). 'The Ideal of Community and the Politics of Difference,' *Social Theory and Practice* **12**, 1-26.

Young, Iris Marion (1997). 'A Multicultural Continuum: A Critique of Will Kymlicka's Ethnic-Nation Dichotomy,' *Constellations* **4:1**, 48-53.

Notes on Contributors

Harry Brighouse is Assistant Professor of Philosophy at the University of Wisconsin-Madison. He is the author of numerous papers in philosophical journals on ethics and social philosophy.

Allen Buchanan, PhD, is Professor of Philosophy at the University of Arizona at Tucson. He is also the Grainger Professor of Business Ethics and Affiliate Professor of Medical Ethics at University of Wisconsin-Madison. He has published numerous articles in ethics, political philosophy, business ethics, and bioethics. He is the author of *Marx and Justice* (1982), *Ethics, Efficiency and the Market* (1985), and *Secession: The Morality of Political Divorce* (1991).

Jocelyne Couture is a professor in the Department of Philosophy, Université du Québec à Montréal, where she teaches moral and political philosophy. She edited *Ethique et Rationalité* (1992) and co-edited *Ethique sociale et justice distributive* (1981), *Méta-philosophie/Reconstructing Philosophy?* (1993) and *The Relevance of Metaethics* (1996). She is the author of several articles on decision theory, logic, and the methodology of ethics.

Omar Dahbour is Associate Professor of Philosophy at Colorado State University and has previously taught at Hunter College, Colorado College, and Ohio University. He was co-editor of *The Nationalism Reader* (Humanities Press, 1995) and editor of a special issue of *The Philosophical Forum* (Fall-Winter 1996-97) on 'Philosophical Perspectives on National Identity.' In addition, he has published articles or reviews in *Theory and Society, German Politics and Society, History of European Ideas, Constellations,* and *Journal of the History of Philosophy,* and is presently completing a book manuscript on the principle of national self-determination.

Frans De Wachter is Professor of Ethics at the Institute of Philosophy of the Catholic University of Leuven. His recent research concerns the relation of universalism and particularism in ethics. He has published on topics such as human rights, postmodernism, and nationalism.

Liah Greenfeld is a University Professor and Professor of Sociology and Political Science at Boston University. She is the author of *Nationalism: Five Roads to Modernity* and numerous essays on various aspects of nationalism, most recently 'The Worth of Nations: Some Economic Implications of Nationalism,' *Critical Review*, Fall 1995, and 'Nationalism and Modernity,' *Social Research*, Spring 1996.

Andrew Levine is a professor of philosophy at the University of Wisconsin-Madison, and author of *Rethinking Liberal Equality* (Cornell University Press forthcoming), *The General Will* (Cambridge University Press 1993), *The End of the State* (Verso 1987) and other books and articles on social and political philosophy, the philosophy of social science, and Marxism.

David Miller is Official Fellow in Social and Political Theory at Nuffield College, Oxford. His research interests include concepts of social justice, the ethics of markets, and the ideas of nationality and citizenship. Among his books are *Market, State and Community* (Oxford: Clarendon Press 1989), *On Nationality* (Oxford: Clarendon Press 1995), and with Michael Walzer, *Pluralism, Justice and Equality* (Oxford: Oxford University Press 1995).

Barrington Moore Jr. is Senior Research Fellow at the Davis Center for Russian Studies and Lecturer on Sociology, Emeritus of Harvard University. Author of many books and articles, he received the Woodrow Wilson Foundation Award for 1967 for *Social Origins of Dictatorship and Democracy: Lord and Peasant in the Making of the Modern World* (1966), and the Ralph Waldo Emerson Award presented in 1973 by Phi Beta Kappa for his *Reflections on the Causes of Human Misery and upon Certain Proposals to Eliminate Them* (1972). He also gave *The Tanner Lectures* at Brasenose College, Oxford University in 1985, which were published under the title 'Authority and Inequality under Capitalism and Socialism,' *The Tanner Lectures on Human Values*, Vol. VII, 103-224.

Kai Nielsen is Professor Emeritus of Philosophy at the University of Calgary and Adjunct Professor of Philosophy at Concordia University. He is a former editor of the *Canadian Journal of Philosophy*. His most recent book is *Naturalism without Foundations*.

Geneviève Nootens has been a postdoctoral fellow at the Department of Philosophy, University of Ottawa, and at McGill University. She works mainly on issues of reasonableness, impartiality, and public reason in contemporary liberalism. Her most recent publication is 'La nature de la complementairité entre le raisonnable et le rationnel chez Rawls,' *Philosophiques*, XXIV (Printemps 1997).

Thomas Pogge, after studying sociology and philosophy at Hamburg and Harvard universities, is currently teaching and writing mainly on moral and political philosophy and Kant, with a special emphasis on issues in global justice, human rights, and contractualism. His most recent publications include *Realizing Rawls* (Cornell University Press), 'Cosmopolitanism and Sovereignty' in *Ethics*, 'An Egalitarian Law of Peoples' in *Philosophy and Public Affairs*, 'Three Problems with Contractarian-Consequentialist Ways of Assessing Social Institutions' in *Social Philosophy and Policy*, 'Group Rights and Ethnicity' in *NOMOS 39*, and 'Kant on Ends and the Meaning of Life' in *Reclaiming the History of Ethics: Essays for John Rawls*.

Ross Poole teaches at Macquarie University. He published *Morality and Modernity* with Routledge in 1991. In recent years, he has been working on issues related to nationalism, culture and identity. He is currently completing a book entitled *Nation and Identity* for Routledge.

Carol A.L. Prager teaches international relations, normative theories of international relations, and the philosophy of the social sciences in the Political Science department of the University of Calgary. She is the author of numerous essays appearing in journals such as *Canadian Public Policy*, *Political Studies*, and *Queen's Quarterly*, and is presently writing a book on humanitarian intervention.

Joel Prager received his MA and PhD in Politics from Princeton University. He is currently Director of Planning, Tax and Intergovernmental Affairs Division, Saskatchewan Finance. He has taught at Brooklyn College and the University of Calgary, worked as a consultant on the patriation of the Constitution, and was an assistant editorial writer for the *Albertan*.

Dominique Schnapper is Director of Studies at l'École des Hautes Études en Sciences Sociales and President of the Société Française de sociologie. Her principal works are: *l'Italie Rouge et Noire*, Paris, Gallimard, 1971; *Juifs et Israélites*, Paris, Gallimard, 1980; *L'Épreuve du chômage*, Paris, Gallimard, 1981 et 1994; *Six manières d'être européen*, Paris, Gallimard, 1990 (Dir. Coll. Mendras); *La France de l'intégration, Sociologie de la nation en 1990*, Paris, Gallimard, 1991; *L'Europe des immigrés, Essai sur les politiques d'immigration*, Paris, François Bourin, 1992; *Les musulmans en Europe*, Actes Sud, Observatoire du changement social, 1992 (Dir. Coll. Bernard Lewis); *La Communauté des citoyens, Sur l'idée moderne de nation*, Paris, Gallimard, 1994.

Michel Seymour is Associate Professor in the Department of Philosophy at Université de Montréal where he teaches contemporary analytical philosophy. He is the author of *Pensée, langage et communauté: Une perspective anti-individualiste*, published in 1994 at Les Éditions Bellarmin. He also edited *Une nation peut-elle se donner la constitution de son choix?* in 1995, also at Bellarmin. Until now, most of his publications have been on the philosophy of language and the philosophy of mind.

Yael Tamir is Senior Lecturer in Philosophy at Tel Aviv University. She is the author of *Liberal Nationalism* and numerous articles in collections and philosophical journals, one of the latest of which is 'The Land of the Fearful and the Free,' *Constellations* 3:3 (January 1997) 296-314.

André Van de Putte studied philosophy and law at the Catholic University, Leuven and took his PhD with a thesis on L. Althusser. He teaches political and social philosophy and ethics at the Institute of Philosophy and the Faculty of Social Sciences of the Catholic University, Leuven. He has authored publications on E. Weil, C. Lefort, E. Burke, and J. Rawls, as well as on pluralism, nationalism, and citizenship.

Brian Walker is Assistant Professor in the Department of Political Science, UCLA. He is currently at work on a book about attempts to maintain cultural integrity under conditions of advanced modernity.

Robert X. Ware is Professor of Philosophy at the University of Calgary. He has published numerous essays on political philosophy, action theory, and the philosophy of language. He co-edited *Analyzing Marxism* (University of Calgary Press 1989) and *Exploitation* (Humanities Press 1997). He is a former editor of the *Canadian Journal of Philosophy*.

Index

CANADIAN JOURNAL OF PHILOSOPHY
SUPPLEMENTARY VOLUMES

Shipping costs: 1–3 books, $5.00; 4+ books, $8.00; international orders, $9.00.
Unless otherwise indicated, outside Canada, prices are in U.S. dollars.
Canadian orders must include 7% GST. All prices subject to change without notice.

Orders to: UBC Press, University of British Columbia,
6344 Memorial Road, Vancouver, B.C., V6T 1Z2 Canada
Telephone: (604) 822-5959; Fax orders: 1-800-668-0821